Studies of the Max Planck Institute Luxembourg for International, European and Regulatory Procedural Law

edited by
Prof. Dr. Dres. h.c. Burkhard Hess
Prof. Dr. Hélène Ruiz Fabri

Volume 22

Burkhard Hess | Koen Lenaerts (eds.)

The 50th Anniversary of the European Law of Civil Procedure

Co-Editor Vincent Richard

Nomos

HART PUBLISHING

Max Planck Institute LUXEMBOURG for Procedural Law

Coverpicture: © European Union, 1968

Signing of the Brussels Convention on 27 September 1968

Top line, from left to right: Pierre Harmel, Minister for Foreign Affairs, Belgium; Willy Brandt, Vice-Chancellor, Minister for Foreign Affairs, Germany; Michel Debré, Minister for Foreign Affairs, France

Bottom line, from left to right: Giuseppe Medici, Minister for Foreign Affairs, Italy; Pierre Grégoire, Minister for Foreign Affairs, Luxembourg; J.M.A.H. Luns, Minister for Foreign Affairs, Netherlands.

The Deutsche Nationalbibliothek lists this publication in the Deutsche Nationalbibliografie; detailed bibliographic data are available on the Internet at http://dnb.d-nb.de

ISBN: HB (Nomos) 978-3-8487-6944-5
ePDF (Nomos) 978-3-7489-1061-9

British Library Cataloguing-in-Publication Data
A catalogue record for this book is available from the British Library.

ISBN: HB (Hart) 978-1-5099-4592-4

Library of Congress Cataloging-in-Publication Data
Hess, Burkhard / Lenaerts, Koen
The 50th Anniversary of the European Law of Civil Procedure
Burkhard Hess / Koen Lenaerts (eds.)
558 pp.
Includes bibliographic references and index.

ISBN 978-1-5099-4592-4 (hardcover Hart)

Onlineversion
Nomos eLibrary

1st Edition 2020

Foreword

On 27 September 1968, the six foreign ministers of the European Economic Community convened in Brussels to sign the Brussels Convention on Jurisdiction and the Enforcement of Judgments in Civil and Commercial Matters. In what would later prove to be a truly historic moment, they signed one of the most successful instruments of the European Communities to come. Fifty years later, on 27–28 September 2018, an international conference organised by the Court of Justice of the European Union and the Max Planck Institute Luxembourg for Procedural Law took place in the Grande Salle d'Audience of the Court. Prominent academics from different EU Member States and distinguished members of the Court discussed the impact of the case law of the Court of Justice on the development of the "Brussels Regime" during the last decades. The discussions held within the conference demonstrated the impact and acceptance of the Brussels Regime and the case law of the Court in the legal practice of the EU Member States.

However, the conference did not only assess the former and the present state of the Brussels Regime as it transpires from the case law of the Court of Justice. It also took a critical view to the dialogue between the Luxembourg Court and the judges of the EU Member States. Moreover, in a pre-conference colloquium, young scholars met at the Max Planck Institute Luxembourg for Procedural Law to discuss the wider perspective of the current regime, especially in the context of the crises that the European Union is currently facing.

The present volume comprises the presentations delivered during both the conference and the pre-conference colloquium. The joint organisation of this event by the Max Planck Institute Luxembourg for Procedural Law and the Court of Justice of the European Union exemplifies the mutually fruitful exchanges between the Court and the academia in Luxembourg. As this volume demonstrates, this cooperation includes critical debates on the current and future regime on EU judicial cooperation in civil and commercial matters. The editors are grateful to their respective collaborators for their support in the organisation of the conference and the publication of this volume. They also wish to express their gratitude to all the speakers of the conference who submitted their manuscripts for this publication.

Finally, they would like to thank Dr. Vincent Richard, Senior Research Fellow at the MPI Luxembourg, for editing this publication.

Luxembourg, 10 June 2020

Koen Lenaerts — Burkhard Hess

Table of Contents

Seminal Judgments (les Grands Arrêts) in the Case Law of the European Court of Justice

Burkhard Hess[*]

Table of Contents

* Prof. Dr. Dres. h.c. Burkhard Hess is the director of the Department of European and Comparative Civil Procedural Law, MPI Luxembourg.

1. Introduction

When the foreign ministers of the (then) six EEC Member States met on 27 September 1968 in Brussels, they were certainly not aware that they were signing one of the most successful and popular instruments of EU law for the years to come. The Convention they signed was conceived as an international treaty concluded among the EEC Member States in the framework of Article 220 of the Rome Treaty. From the perspective of European Law, the Brussels Convention had only a complementary role, as it should alleviate cross-border debt recovery in the wider framework of the Rome Treaty.[1] However, from a perspective of private international law, the Convention was one of the most modern instruments of its time: it took up experiences of the Hague Conference and provided for a double convention. It addressed not only the recognition of judgments but also established a uniform system of jurisdiction applicable to civil litigation within the European Economic Community.[2]

The most important innovation introduced with the Brussels Convention was the 1971 Protocol on its interpretation by the European Court of Justice. This Protocol made a vast difference to all existing instruments in private international law as it provided for a supranational instance to interpret the Convention in a uniform way. Of course, the ECJ at that time was not familiar with instruments on private international and procedural law. However, there was a positive attitude within the Court to address these issues. Since the mid-1970s, the ECJ decided almost 4 to 5 cases on

1 In its first judgment on the interpretation of the Convention, the ECJ explicitly stressed this relation. "... The Convention was established to implement Article 220 [of the EEC Treaty] and was intended according to the express terms of its preamble to implement the provisions of that article on the simplification of formalities governing the reciprocal recognition and enforcement of judgments of courts or tribunals and to strengthen in the Community the legal protection of persons therein established. In order to eliminate obstacles to legal relations and to settle disputes within the sphere of intra-Community relations in civil and commercial matters the Convention contains, inter alia, rules enabling the jurisdiction in these matters of courts of Member States to be determined and facilitating the recognition and execution of courts' judgments. *Accordingly the Convention must be interpreted having regard both to its principles and objectives and to its relationship with the Treaty*", ECJ, 6.10.1976, case C-12/76, *Tessili*, EU:C:1976:133, para 9 (emphasis added by B.H.).

2 The function of coordinating the autonomous judicial systems of the EU-Member States by uniform rules on jurisdiction, pendency and recognition and enforcement still applies today.

the Brussels Convention per year.[3] Overall, this case law was well received in the EC Member States,[4] and it paved the way for a uniform and more and more expansive competence of the Union in matters of private international law.[5]

The title of this presentation borrows from the French legal culture of "les grands arrêts" insofar as it intends to present the development of EU procedural law by referring to important judgments of the ECJ.[6] Similar to the presentation of "les grands arrêts" I would like to address judgments that marked the development of this area of law or even changed the pre-existing situation.[7] The underlying assumption is that the case law of the Court is as influential as the legal texts of European procedural law.

As this presentation addresses seminal judgments of the ECJ regarding the Brussels system that were rendered in the course of the last 50 years, I will first briefly address different phases of the development of European procedural law (2). These were mainly marked by law-making activities the Union and by the general development of European integration. The following part (3) shall address the case law of the Court on the guiding principles of the Brussels I system (internal view) before I address the wider context, especially the relationship of the Brussels I system with general

---

3 *Kutscher*, Abschied vom Gerichtshof der Europäischen Gemeinschaften, EuR 1981, 1, 4. At present, the Court decides around 30 cases on civil co-operation per year (around 4 % of all incoming cases), *Düsterhaus*, Konstitutionalisiert der EuGH das Internationale Privat- und Vefahrensrecht der EU?, ZEuP 2018, 10, 30.

4 Cf. *Hess/Pfeiffer/Schlosser*, The Heidelberg Report on the Application of the Brussels I Regulation (2008), para 1, fn. 2. According to the statement of a presiding judge of the Landgericht Traunstein, the Brussels I Regulation was "the best piece of legislation we ever got from Brussels."

5 This development ended in a generic competence of the Union: in Art. 65 of the 1998 Treaty of Amsterdam, *Hess*, Europäisches Zivilprozessrecht (2010), § 2, paras 20 *et seq*.

6 *Gonod*, A propos des Grands arrêts de la jurisprudence administrative, Mél. Labetoulle (2007), p. 441 *et seq*. The first "recueil des grands arrêts de la jurisprudence civile" was just published in 1934.

7 According to French authors: "On appelle un arrêt de principe celui dans lequel le juge, à propos d'une question nouvelle, ou à la suite du renouvellement d'une question ancienne, énonce la règle qu'il entend appliquer à cette espèce, et à toutes celles qui poseront le même problème. L'arrêt de principe ne se distingue par aucun signe extérieur, sinon parfois par l'autorité de la formation de jugement dont il émane; c'est sa rédaction, éclairée par les conclusions du commissaire du gouvernement et les commentaires de la doctrine qui le rend reconnaissable", Jean Rivero et Jean Waline, Droit administratif; Précis Dalloz, 15ème édition, 1994, p. 66; *Cossalter*, Les grands arrêts de la jurisprudence administrative (thèse Paris II 1999), p. 6.

Union law (4) with conflict of laws rules, with the procedural laws of the EU Member States and the international dimension. Finally, I will assess the interpretation of the Brussels regime by the Court of Justice (5).

2. *Different Phases of the Legal Evolution*

2.1. *The Brussels Convention (1973–1980)*

After 1973, when the Convention entered into force, its interpretation (and explanation) by the Court of Justice was most important. The Court started in a homogenous environment, as the procedural laws of the six original EEC-Member States were structurally similar (all belonging to continental law).[8] The starting phase was marked by the first decisions of the ECJ where the Court became familiar with the new topic (private international and procedural law): such decisions were instrumental in bringing the Convention in line with general EU law[9]. However, in the starting period, the Convention was mainly regarded as an instrument of private international law and the case law of the ECJ was discussed from this perspective.[10]

2.2. *Cross-border Proceedings in the Internal Market (1980–1998)*

From its very beginning, the Brussels Convention was conceived as an instrument to strengthen the judicial protection in the Common Market.[11] When the concept of the Internal Market was implemented, the ECJ trans-

---

8 However, it must be mentioned that the Court looked from the very beginning at the different solutions in the United Kingdom – and Her Majesty's Government took actively part in the proceedings on the BC before the ECJ. Example: Opinion of AG Capetorti in case C-21/76, *Bier*, EU:C:1976:147, of 10 November 1976, No. 5.

9 ECJ, 6.10.1976, case C-12/76 *Tessili*, EU:C:1976:133.

10 *Schlosser*, Gedächtnisschrift Bruns (1980), p. 45; Report *Droz* summarizing the discussion during the Colloquium on the Brussels Convention at the ECJ, in: EuGH (Hrsg.), Internationale Zuständigkeit und Urteilsanerkennung in Europa (1992), p. 235, 237 *et seq.*

11 *Hess*, Europäisches Zivilprozessrecht (2010), § 1, paras 1 and 2 quoting the Letter of the EC Commission to the EC Member States of 22.10.1959, *Droz*, Compétence judiciaire et effets des jugements dans le marché commun (1972), No. 11.

ferred the approach to procedural law and applied the principle of non-discrimination to the national civil procedures.[12] This case law of the Court considerably affected the national procedures which were mostly based on a model distinguishing between domestic (national) and foreign parties (by discriminating the latter). A second development related to the growing competences of the Union in private international and procedural law under Article K.1 (6) of the Maastricht Treaty.[13] Judicial co-operation in civil matters was the new keyword of this development. At this stage, the close relationship between international procedural law and EU law became evident.[14]

2.3. *Judicial Co-operation under the Treaty of Amsterdam (1999–2009)*

The most important step was the establishment in the Amsterdam Treaty of a full competence of the Union to institute an Area of Freedom, Security and Justice (AFSJ). The Tampere program of 1999 immediately implemented the new competence for judicial co-operation in civil matters.[15] Between 2001 and 2009 eleven new instruments on procedural law were adopted: some of these enlarged the Brussels regime, while others regulated family matters and insolvency.[16] Eventually, secondary law instruments covered the whole range of the competence on civil justice established with the Amsterdam Treaty. This enlargement changed the area of law considerably: The ECJ decides on issues including insolvency, child abduction, divorce, maintenance, succession, payment orders, mediation. In 2002, Regulation No. 44/2001 replaced and reformed the Brussels Convention. From its side, the ECJ made clear that the communitarization of

12 ECJ, 1.7.1993, case C-20/92, *Hubbard./.Hamburger*, EU:C:1993:280. In this judgment, the Court argued that the Brussels Convention had established a framework for cross-border litigation away the EC-Member Status and, therefore, the provision of German law (former Section 917 (2) ZPO) which permitted an arrest order in all situation where enforcement measure would be necessary abroad amounted to an (indirect) discrimination based on nationality.

13 *Hess*, Europäisches Zivilprozessrecht (2010), § 2, para 4.

14 Although it was strongly contested by the legal literature, cf. *Schack*, Rechtsangleichung mit der Brechstange des EuGH, ZZP 108 (1995), 47 ff.

15 *Hess*, Europäisches Zivilprozessrecht (2010), § 2, para 38.

16 The complexity and the legal fragmentation of civil procedural law is criticized by the legal doctrine, see *Frackowiak-Adamska*, CMLR 2015, 191, 193.

the area of law reinforced the (autonomous) interpretation of the Brussels regime and adopted a more comprehensive and systematic approach.[17]

2.4. *Consolidation and Challenges under the Lisbon Treaty (2009 until today)*

The latest developments coincided with the entry into force of the Lisbon Treaty. While, per se, the Lisbon Treaty did not amend the competences of the Union regarding the cross-border co-operation in civil and commercial matters, the Charter of Fundamental Rights (CFR) influences more and more the case law of the CJEU. Article 47 CFR has become important for the interpretation of EU-procedural law.[18] On the other hand, the present crises of the European Union also affect the judicial co-operation.[19] Eventually, the law making processes have slowed down considerably.[20] During the recast of the Brussels I Regulation, the EU Commission had to give up its ambitious endeavour of abolishing the public policy exception.[21] At present, no major law-making project is envisaged; the Commission is mainly working on the consolidation and improvement of the existing instruments.[22] Finally, Brexit confronts European procedural law with a perspective of a Member State leaving the system – a situation which has never been addressed before.[23]

---

17 ECJ, 8.11.2005, case C-443/03 *Leffler*, EU:C:2005:665, paras 43 *et seq.*; *Hess*, Europäisches Zivilprozessrecht (2010), § 4, para 73.

18 See infra at. Current example: ECJ, 9.6.2018, case C-21/17, *Catlin Europe SE*, EU:C:2018:341, para 33, stressing the right of defence in civil proceedings as protected by Article 47 of the CFR.

19 *Hess*, Le droit international privé européen en temps de crise, Travaux du Comité Français du Droit International Privé 2016-2018 (2019), 329 *et seq*.

20 More important law-making activities relate to data protection (Regulation (EU) 2016/679) and to collective redress, cf. COM (2018) 184 final.

21 *Dickinson*, in: Dickinson / Lein (ed.), The Brussels I Regulation Recast (2015), paras 1.23–1.35.

22 Current reforms relate to the amendment of the Service Regulation (Reg. 1393/2007) and of the Evidence Regulation (Reg. 1206/2001), Proposals of the EU Commission of 5/31/2018, COM(2018) 378 and 379 final.

23 *Sonnentag*, Die Konsequenzen des Brexit für das Internationale Privat- und Verfahrensrecht (2017); *Requejo Isidro/Dutta/de Miguel*, The future relationship between the UK and the EU following the UK's withdrawal from the EU in family law (study for the European Parliament, October 2018).

3. *The Systemic Interpretation of the Brussels Regime by the Court of Justice*

If one looks at the most influential, seminal judgments of the ECJ regarding the Brussels Convention and Regulations, a basic distinction must be drawn: firstly, there are judgments which are important for the "inner" understanding of the EU instruments. Secondly, there are judgments which place these instruments in the larger context of European Union law, in the context of the national procedures and, finally, in the international context. The next parts will address both circumstances.

3.1. *Autonomous Interpretation*

According to the constant case law of the ECJ, the terms of the Brussels I^{bis} Regulation are to be interpreted autonomously, according to its system and objectives.[24] This case law was established in the judgment C-29/76 *LTU./.Eurocontrol* of October 14, 1976.[25] In this case, *Eurocontrol*, an International Organization for the air safety navigation in Europe, had obtained a judgment against the air carrier LTU before the Commercial Court in Brussels for unpaid route charges. When *Eurocontrol* sought the enforcement of the judgment, the Court of Appeals of Düsseldorf asked the ECJ whether the interpretation of the term "civil and commercial matters" in Article 1(1) of the Convention should be based on the law of the court of origin or on the law of the court of enforcement. While Advocate General Reischl proposed to apply the law of the court of origin,[26] the ECJ held that Article 1 of the Brussels Convention (BC) defines its scope and that rights and obligations of the parties under the Convention should be equally and uniformly determined and applied. A reference to the internal laws of the Contracting States would not be in line with this objective. The Court stated:

24 *Rösler*, Autonomous Interpretation, in EPIL (2018), p. 1006, 1008 f. stressing the (thin) differences between uniform and autonomous interpretation.

25 ECJ, 14.10.1976, case C-29/76 *LTU./.Eurocontrol*, EU:C:1976:137.

26 Opinion *Reischl*, case C-29/76, EU:C:1976:121, referring to the divergent delineations of public and private law in the EU Member States.

"The concept in question must therefore be regarded as independent and must be interpreted by reference, first, to the objectives and scheme of the Convention and, secondly, to the general principles which stem from the corpus of the national legal systems."[27]

This statement triggered the constant jurisprudence of the Court on the autonomous interpretation of the Brussels' instruments although the term "autonomous" was not yet used in *Eurocontrol*.[28] However, it is interesting to see that the Court did not refer to general Community law but based the judgment mainly on considerations related to the proper functioning of the Convention.[29] The first judgments used the term "independent interpretation", the term autonomous interpretation appeared for the first time in the judgment in case C-125/92, *Mulox*.[30]

Under the Amsterdam Treaty, the scope of application of this concept was further enlarged. In case C-443/03, *Leffler*[31], the Grand Chamber stated that, since the entry of the Treaty of Amsterdam, the autonomous interpretation of the EU instruments generally prevails. The Court held:

"The objective pursued by the Treaty of Amsterdam of creating an area of freedom, security and justice, thereby giving the Community a new dimension, and the transfer from the EU Treaty to the EC Treaty of

27 ECJ, 14.10.1976, case C-29/76, *LTU./.Eurocontrol*, EU:C:1976:137, para 9; ECJ, 14.7.1977, joint cases C-9 and 10/77, *Bavaria Fluggesellschaft u.a../.Eurocontrol*, EU:C:1977:132, para 4 stressing the "independent concept of civil matter" and the need of a uniform application of the Convention providing for legal certainty and equal objects of the parties.

28 According to the elder case-law the convention had to be interpreted "independently, in order to ensure that it is applied uniformly in all Contracting States, cf. ECJ, 21.6.1978, case C-150/77, *Ott*, EU:C:1978:137, ECJ, 19.1.1993, case C-89/91, *Shearson Lehman Hutton./.TVB*, EU:C:1993:15, para 13.

29 In this respect, the argument comes very close to "effet utile", *Lenaerts & Stapper*, RabelsZ 78 (2014), 252, 254, and to the primacy of EU law, *Rösler*, Autonomous Interpretation, in EPIL (2018), p. 1006, 1008.

30 The Court did not make this change explicitly. It simply stated: "It is settled case-law that, as far as possible, the Court of Justice will interpret the terms of the Convention autonomously so as to ensure that it is fully effective having regard to the objectives of Article 220 of the EEC Treaty, for the implementation of which it was adopted." ECJ, 13.7.1993, case C-125/92, *Mulox*, para 10. AG Tesauro used the term in his opinion of 20.11.1991, case C-214/89, *Powell Duffryn*, para 4. It seems that the use of the term in other language versions started earlier, especially in the French language versions.

31 ECJ, 8.11.2005, case C-443/03, *Leffler*, EU:C:2005:665, paras 39 *et seq*. On substance, *Leffler* mainly addressed the interpretation of Article 8 of the Service Regulation (Reg. no 1346/2000).

> the body of rules enabling measures in the field of judicial co-operation in civil matters having cross-border implications to be adopted testify to the will of the Member States to establish such measures firmly in the Community legal order and thus to lay down the principle that they are to be interpreted autonomously".

Consequently, the Court held that a text adopted before 1998 could not overcome the result of an autonomous interpretation by a historic argument.[32] This was a fundamental change: The autonomy and the prevalence of EU law were fully applied to the Brussels regime. Today, the autonomous interpretation permeates European procedural law and permits the implementation of *effet utile* and the integrative function of European procedural law within the Internal Market and in the Area of Security, Freedom and Justice.[33]

3.2. *Jurisdiction: Access to Justice and Legal Certainty*

As a double convention, the Brussels Convention (BC) provided not only for rules on recognition, but also for a set of heads of jurisdiction. In the early case law, the interpretation of Article 5 of the Convention (now Article 7 of the Regulation) was of great importance.[34] The Court developed a jurisprudence according to which predictability and legal certainty were of great importance for the interpretation of the heads of jurisdiction.[35] Therefore, the Court considered the specific heads of jurisdiction as exceptions from the general rule (Article 4 Judgments Regulation (JR)) that the defendant shall be sued at his or her domicile.[36] In *Owusu*, the Court held that national procedural law could not restrict the general jurisdiction

32 ECJ, 8.11.2005, case C-443/03, *Leffler*, EU:C:2005:665, para 45; cf. para 47: "It follows that although the comments in the explanatory report on the Convention, an instrument adopted before the Treaty of Amsterdam entered into force, are useful, they cannot be relied upon to contest an autonomous interpretation of the Regulation".

33 Recently, ECJ, 16.6.2016, case C-511/14, *Pebros Servizi*, EU:C:2016:448, paras 35 *et seq.*: the term "uncontested claim" (Article 3 (b) of Regulation No. 805/2004) must be interpreted autonomously, not by reference to national (Italian) law.

34 One must be aware that the ECJ was the first international body competent to develop its own and self-standing case law in this regard.

35 See *Pontier/Burg*, EU Principles on Jurisdiction and Recognition and Enforcement of Judgments in Civil and Commercial Matters (2004), p. 69 *et seq.*

36 ECJ, 27.9.1988, case C-189/87, *Kalfelis*, EU:C:1988:459, para 19.

under the Convention. Consequently, *forum non conveniens* was not applicable,[37] legal certainty prevailed.[38] Conversely, the Court has stated constantly that the specific heads of jurisdiction should be narrowly construed as they are exceptions from the general rule of (now) article 4 JR.[39]

In practice, however, the ECJ never applied this principle without exceptions as it limits, to some extent, the right of the plaintiff to get effective access to justice.[40] The most pertinent example of a structurally broad interpretation relates to jurisdiction based on tort. Already in 1976, in the seminal case C-21/76, *Bier v. Mines de potasse d'Alsace*, the Court had to the "place where the harmful event occurred".[41] In the case at hand, Dutch nursery gardeners brought an action for damages they had sustained because the French defendants, producers of Kali salt, discharged 10.000 tons of chloride every day into the river Rhine. The river transported the wasted chlorides to the Netherlands where, eventually, the salted water damaged the crops of the gardeners. Seen from the factual background, *Bier* was an easy case as the casual link between the harmful event and the place of damage was clearly established. In *Bier*, the Court construed Article 5 no. 3 BC broadly and held that the place where the harmful event occurred should be considered to cover both: the place of the event giving raise to the damage and the place where the damage occurred. Furthermore, the Court held that the plaintiff could choose between the two heads of jurisdiction. As a result, Article 5 no. 3 BC (today: 7 no. 2 JR) opened up alternative different heads of jurisdiction.[42]

20 years later, *Shevill* enlarged the scope of the provision even further when the ECJ stated that, in the case of infringements of personality rights

---

37 *Owusu* had broad implications on the scope of the Brussels regime: On the one hand, the ECJ clarified that the Convention applied to lawsuits brought by plaintiffs from third states against defendants domiciled within the EU Member States. On the other hand, discretionary powers under national procedural law were discarded from the regime. The English doctrine criticized the judgment harshly.

38 ECJ, 1.3.2005, case C-281/02 *Owusu*, EU:C:2005:120.

39 ECJ, 27.9.1988, case C-189/87, *Kalfelis*, EU:C:1988:459, para 19; ECJ, 15.2.1989, case C-32/88, *Societé Six Constructions./.Humbert*, EU:C:1989:68, para 18 – constant jurisprudence.

40 In cases of tortious liability, the procedural situation of the plaintiff is structurally weak as a contractual designation of the competent court (by a jurisdiction clause) is impossible: according to the case-law of the ECJ, jurisdiction based on tort presupposes that there is no contractual relationship among the parties, ECJ, 13.3.2014, Rs. C-548/12, *Brogsitter*, EU:C:2014:148.

41 ECJ, 30.11.1976, case C-21/76, *Bier*, EU:C:1976:166, paras 20/23.

42 ECJ, 30.11.1976, case C-21/76, *Bier*, EU:C:1976:166, paras 24 and 25. It must be noted that the legal literature largely supported this judgment.

by the press, the affected person can bring an action either at the publisher's domicile (being the place of conduct) or (alternatively) at all places where the article had been distributed. However, aware that this interpretation would entail a multitude of heads of jurisdiction, the court limited jurisdiction at the place of the harm to the partial harm, which occurred at the different places.[43] *Bier* and *Shevill* are interesting in the sense that they demonstrate how the context of a case influences the interpretation of the instrument. When deciding *Bier*, the court was certainly not aware of the possibility of a libel suit brought in many different jurisdictions. The mosaic theory of *Shevill* was a judicial innovation.

However, *Shevill* was not the end of the case law of the Court of Justice. As you all know, in *eDate advertising*[44] and in *Bolagsupplysniggen*[45] the Court expanded this case law further to internet infringements and held that the (potential) victim of a violation of privacy can bring his or her claim either at the place where content was placed on the internet (place of conduct) or at the place where the harm was sustained. In the two later judgments, the Court nevertheless limited the jurisdiction at the place of the harm to the court of the plaintiff's main centre of interest. This place corresponds to the place where his or her reputation is mainly affected.[46] Here, the case law of the Court demonstrates a willingness to balance the interests of the parties and to limit forum shopping.[47] However, *eDate Advertising*[48] and *Bolagsupplysniggen*[49] also demonstrate the Court's reluctance to change its former case law: although both judgments clearly deviate from the mosaic approach, they still refer to *Shevill*. Therefore, it is still

---

43 ECJ, 7.3.1995, case C-68/93, *Fiona Shevill*, EU:C:1995:61, esp. paras 29–31, 33.

44 ECJ, 25.10.2011, joined cases C-509/09 and C-161/10, *eDate Advertising and Martinez*, EU:C:2011:685, commented by *Hess*, in: Hess & Mariottini, Protection of Privacy (2016), p. 81 *et seq*.

45 ECJ, 17.10.2017, case C-194/16, *Bolagsupplysningen*, EU:C:2017:766.

46 ECJ, 25.10.2011, joined cases C-509/09 and C-161/10, *eDate Advertising and Martinez*, EU:C:2011:685, para 52; ECJ, 17.10.2017, Case C-194/16, *Bolagsupplysningen*, EU:C:2017:766, paras 41 *et seq*.

47 *Hau*, Klagemöglichkeiten juristischer Personen nach Persönlichkeitsrechtsverletzungen im Internet, GRUR 2018, 163 *et seq*.

48 ECJ, 25.10.2011, joined cases C-509/09 and C-161/10, *eDate Advertising and Martinez*, EU:C:2011:685, para 52.

49 ECJ, 17.10.2017, case C-194/16, *Bolagsupplysningen*, EU:C:2017:766, para 31. In his Opinion of 13.7.2017, AG Bobek had proposed to discard the mosaic principle, EU:C:2017:554, paras 73–90.

unclear whether the mosaic has been given up or whether it still exists in some instances.[50]

3.3. Protection of the Rights of Defence

The protection of the rights of defence belongs to the most significant principles of European procedural law. The ECJ stated the importance of fair proceedings in case C-125/79, *Denilauler*, where it said:

> "All the provisions of the Convention, both those contained in Title II on jurisdiction and those contained in Title III on recognition and enforcement, express the intention to ensure that, within the scope of the objectives of the Convention, proceedings leading to the delivery of judicial decisions take place in such a way that the rights of the defence are observed. It is because of the guarantees given to the defendant in the original proceedings that the Convention, in Title III, is very liberal in regard to recognition and enforcement."[51]

Denilauler was about the recognition of a French *saisie conservatoire* (an arrest order) rendered without any hearing of the defendant. The ECJ held that the recognition of an *ex parte* order was not possible under the Convention and that the protection of the rights of the defendant had to prevail.[52] Functionally, the Court balanced the need of protecting the defendant against the objective of the Convention to provide for the efficient recognition of judgments.[53] At the same time, it avoided a one-sided interpretation of the instrument permitting the creditor a direct attachment of

50 In both cases, the AG proposed to give up the mosaic principle, Opinion Cruz Villalón, 25.10.2011, case C-509/09, *eDate Advertising*, EU:C:2011:192, paras 49 *et seq.*; Opinion Bobek, 13.07.2017, case C-194/16, *Bolagsupplysningen*, EU:C:2017:554, paras 73 *et seq.*

51 ECJ, 21.5.1980, case C-125/79, *Denilauler*, EU:C:1980:130, para 13 (taking up the foundation of the conclusions). It must be noted that neither the AG nor the Court referred to the fair trial guarantee of Article 6 of the ECHR.

52 Today, this situation has been remedied by Regulation (EU) No. 655/2014 establishing a European Account Preservation Order procedure to facilitate cross-border debt recovery in civil and commercial matters, which permits the direct enforcement of bank accounts in other EU Member States but provides for rules, which protect the defendant's rights.

53 ECJ, 21.5.1980, case C-125/79, *Denilauler*, EU:C:1980:130, para 14.

the debtor's assets in other EU Member States without any prior hearing.[54] In *Denilauler*, the Court set a strict limit to the unilateral enforcement of the creditor's rights without a sufficient protection of the debtor. *Denilauler* also implied that the free movement of judgments requires a set of procedural norms guaranteeing this protection.[55]

The respect of the rights of the defence has become an overarching principle of European cross-border procedural law. The Court invoked it in different instances of cross-border litigation, especially in the context of the service of documents,[56] regarding the translation of documents,[57] necessary information of the defendant about remedies against the decision[58] and the right of the defendant to be represented by a lawyer.[59]

3.4. *Free Movement of Judgments*

The main objective of the Brussels regime is the establishment of a system guaranteeing the free movement of judgments.[60] Already stated in the Preamble of the Brussels Convention, the Court took this objective up in *Hoffmann v. Krieg*[61] and reinforced it in the following case law as "one of

54 Obviously, the Court was concerned by *ex parte* provisional measures of English procedural law, and especially the "Mareva injunction", cf. Opinion AG Mayras of 26.3.1980 (at p. 1580).

55 In 2012, the EU legislator explicitly endorsed this concept in Articles 2 a) and 41 (2) of the Brussels I^{bis} Regulation, *Hess,* in: Schlosser/Hess, Europäisches Zivilprozessrecht (Commentary, 4th ed. 2015), Article 42 EuGVVO, para 5; *Wiedemann*, Vollstreckbarkeit (2017), p. 74–75.

56 In this context, the case law on the Service Regulations completes the case law on the ground of non-recognition regarding the proper information of the defendant in the court of origin, cf. ECJ, 2.3.2017, case C-354/15, *Henderson,* EU:C:2017:157, paras 50 *et seq.*

57 ECJ, 8.5.2008, case C-14/07, *Weiss & Partner*, EU:C:2008:264.

58 ECJ, 14.12.2006, case C-283/05, *ASML*, EU:C:2006:787, paras 26 *et seq.*; ECJ, 16.9.2015, case C-519/13, para 49; ECJ, 2.3.2017, case C-354/15, *Henderson,* EU:C:2017:157, para 55; ECJ, 6.9.2018, Case C-21/17, *Catlin Europe*, EU:C: 2018:675, paras 32 *et seq.*

59 ECJ, 19.12.2012, case C-325/11, *Alder,* EU:C:2012:824; *Mayr,* in: Mayr (ed), Europäisches Zivilverfahrensrecht, paras 14, 34 *et seq.*

60 *Pontier/Burg,* EU Principles (2004), p. 27 *et seq.*; *Dickinson*, in Dickinson / Lein (ed), The Brussels I Regulation Recast (2015), para 1.59.

61 ECJ, 4.2.1988, case C-145/86, *Hoffmann./.Krieg,* EU:C:1988:61, para 10: "In that regard it should be recalled that the Convention 'seeks to facilitate as far as possible the free movement of judgments, and should be interpreted in this spirit'. Recognition must therefore 'have the result of conferring on judgments the

the fundamental principles of the Brussels Convention."[62] Later judgments made the free movement of judgments a cornerstone of the Convention, similar to the other freedoms of the EU Treaty on the free movement of goods, capitals, persons and services.[63] The free movement of judgments was impacted by the development of the Brussels instruments themselves as the EU lawmaker reinforced and streamlined the regime of cross-border enforcement by different reforms.[64]

The Court clarified the regime on several occasions, especially with regard to Courts of new EU Member States. In this regard, *Trade Agency* appears as a seminal decision[65] where the Court summarized the existing regime, explained the different tasks of the court of origin and the requested court in the recognition process[66] and put the Regulation in context with the overarching principles of the free movement of judgments and the protection of the rights of defence. Judging by its results, *Trade Agency* is not innovative but it assesses and explains the state of affairs, including the relationship of the Brussels I Regulation to the Charter of Fundamental Rights.[67] Finally, it reinforced the importance of the free movement of judgments by limiting and fine-tuning the control of the foreign judgment by the requested courts in the Member State of enforcement.[68]

---

authority and effectiveness accorded to them in the State in which they were given'" (referring to the Jenard Report).

62 ECJ, 4.10.1991, case C-183/90, *Van Dalfsen./.Van Loon*, EU:C:1991:379, para 21; ECJ, 2.6.1994, case C-414/92, *Solo Kleinmotoren./.Boch*, EU:C:1994:221, para 20; ECJ, 17.6.1999, *Unibank./.Christensen*, EU:C:1999:312, para 16.

63 *Hess*, Europäisches Zivilprozessrecht (2010), § 3, paras 13 *et seq.*

64 For a short summary of the development, cf. *Wiedemann*, Vollstreckbarkeit (2017), p. 42 *et seq.* and p. 118 *et seq.*; *Frackowiak-Adamska*, CMLR 52 (2015), 191, 194 *et seq.*, distinguishing three different models of recognition and enforcement in the current EU-instruments.

65 ECJ, 6.9.2012, case C-619/10, *Trade Agency*, EU:C:2012:531, cf. *Lenaerts/Stapper*, RabelsZ 78 (2014), 252, 272 *et seq*. This judgment was given in a preliminary reference coming from the Latvian Supreme Court. It concerned the recognition and enforcement of an English default judgment given without grounds.

66 ECJ, 6.9.2012, case C-619/10, *Trade Agency*, EU:C:2012:531, paras 26 *et seq*.

67 ECJ, 6.9.2012, case C-619/10, *Trade Agency*, EU:C:2012:531, paras 49 *et seq*. The judgment is a good example of the dialogue between the ECJ and the national judge about the interpretation of the Brussels regime.

68 *Lenaerts/Stapper*, RabelsZ 78 (2014), 252, 274.

4. *The Wider Context*

The Brussels regime has never operated in a vacuum. Closely embedded in the general law of the Union, developments of the European integration directly influence its expansion. In this respect, two interfaces can be distinguished: On the one hand, vertical impacts coming from superior principles like the principle of mutual trust (4.1) and the Charter of Fundamental Rights (4.2). On the other hand, the Brussels regime has been aligned by several EU-instruments enacted under Article 81 TFEU (4.3). Finally, the interfaces with the autonomous laws of the EU Member States (4.4) need to be addressed.

4.1. *Mutual Trust – a Transversal Principle of the Area of Freedom, Security and Justice*

The embeddedness of EU procedural law in the general law of the Union is best demonstrated by the principle of mutual trust. According to recitals 16 and 17 of the Brussels I Regulation and recital 26 of the Brussels I^{bis} Regulation, the principle is the basis of judicial co-operation.[69] Despite these evocations in the non-operational texts, the ECJ developed mutual trust as a foundational principle of judicial co-operation, not only in civil matters, but in the Area of Freedom, Security and Justice and in general EU law.[70]

The starting point in procedural law was a much-discussed case, C-116/02, *Gasser./.Misat*.[71] An Austrian salesperson had entered into an exclusive jurisdiction clause with his Italian commercial partner, designating the Austrian courts. When the Italian partner failed to pay the price of the goods, the Austrian intended to initiate proceedings in Austria (as agreed) but learned that the other party had already launched proceedings for a negative declaration in Italian courts (in breach of the jurisdiction

---

69 Articles 67 (1) and 81 (1) TFEU only mention mutual recognition (not trust), the same wording is found in Article 82 TFEU regarding the judicial co-operation in criminal matters.

70 *Prechal*, Mutual Trust Before the Court of Justice of the European Union, European Papers 2 (2017), 75 *et seq.*; *Lenaerts*, La vie après l'avis: exploring the principle of mutual but not blind trust, CMLR 54 (2017), 805 *et seq.*

71 ECJ, 9.12.2003, case C-116/02, *Gasser*, EU:C:2003:657, for a summary of the doctrinal debate of *Schmidt*, Rechtssicherheit im europäischen Zivilverfahrensrecht (2015), p. 186–202.

clause). As *Gasser* had filed his claim six months after the start of the Italian proceedings, the Austrian court asked whether, relying on Article 6 ECHR, it could decide the case despite the pendency in Italy. The Court of Justice decided that the rules of pendency literally did not foresee any exception.[72] It noted that the respect of the priority rule should avoid a later non-recognition of the foreign judgment according to Article 27 No. 3 BC/45 I lit c) JR. It stated:

> "...it must be borne in mind that the Brussels Convention is necessarily based on the trust which the Contracting States accord to each other's legal systems and judicial institutions. It is that mutual trust which has enabled a compulsory system of jurisdiction to be established, which all the courts within the purview of the Convention are required to respect, and as a corollary the waiver by those States of the right to apply their internal rules on recognition and enforcement of foreign judgments in favour of a simplified mechanism for the recognition and enforcement of judgments."[73]

The ECJ noted that Article 6 of the ECHR imposed a duty on the national courts to proceed in an efficient way. However, the Convention had established a system of close co-operation, which was based on mutual trust in the proper functioning of the court systems of the Member States. Providing for an exception in case of lengthy proceedings would not be compatible with the system.[74] As a result, the ECJ established a strict principle of mutual trust prevailing over concerns on the efficiency of the court systems not meeting the requirements of Article 6 ECHR. One might argue that the case at hand was not severe enough to raise fundamental concerns regarding an abuse of the system.[75] Eventually, *Gasser* clearly rejected any

72 ECJ, 9.12.2003, case C-116/02, *Gasser,* EU:C:2003:657, paras 41 *et seq*. Since 2015, Article 31 (2) of Regulation No. 1215/2012 provides for an exception from pendency in case of a mandatory jurisdiction clause: The designated court shall decide on the validity of the clause and on its jurisdiction; all other courts must stay the proceedings until the designated court has made its decision.

73 ECJ, 9.12.2003, case C-116/02, *Gasser,* EU:C:2003:657, para 72.

74 ECJ, 9.12.2003, case C-116/02, *Gasser,* EU:C:2003:657, para 72, *Düsterhaus*, ZEuP 2018, 10, 22. The Jenard Report (OJ 1979 C 59/1, 46) has already referred to mutual trust as a reason to reduce the control of foreign decisions at the recognition stage.

75 *Hess*, Europäisches Zivilprozessrecht (2010), § 4, para 4.75.

idea of an exception within the system based on mutual trust.[76] In a similar way, *Turner*[77] and *Allianz (West Tankers)* clearly limited the powers of English courts under national law to issue anti-suit injunctions against parties litigating in the courts of other Member States.[78] Mutual trust implies that courts can expect that the courts of other Member States fully apply EU law.

In the Area of Freedom, Security and Justice, mutual trust has become an overarching ("constitutional") principle of judicial (and administrative) co-operation.[79] Seminal judgments were not only given in civil co-operation, but in criminal matters and in asylum cases.[80] Co-operation has become the genuine concept of Union law of cross-border collaboration. It aims at avoiding parallel controls and proceedings in several Member States. A judicial decision made in one Member State shall be recognized by the others without further control. Consequently, recognition requires trust in the handling of the proceedings in the Member State of origin. Judicial co-operation in the Union is based on the presumption that all EU Member States share the same values and comply, in particular, with fundamental human rights. However, mutual trust is not blind trust and the presumption can be rebutted in extreme cases. As a result, the public policy exception appears as an inherent limitation of mutual trust.

In case C-681/13, *Diageo Brands*,[81] the ECJ clarified the operation of mutual trust in the framework of the Brussels regime. In this case, the Dutch party contested the recognition of a Bulgarian judgment in the Netherlands by asserting that the court of origin had misapplied the EU trademark directive without referring the legal issues to the ECJ under

76 Different opinion *Lenaerts/Stapper*, RabelsZ 78 (2014), 252, 276: The Court decided that Article 21 BC had to be interpreted in a way that it did not provide for an exception when court proceedings in an EU Member State were *generally* ("allgemein") too slow (highlighted by B.H.). Yet, *Gasser* does not make this differentiation.

77 ECJ, 27.4.2004, case C-159/02, *Turner*, EU:C:2004:228; *Fentiman*, International Commercial Litigation (2nd ed 2015), paras 16.131 *et seq*.

78 ECJ, 10.2.2009, case C-185/07, *Allianz*, EU:C:2009:69, paras 29 and 30.

79 *Prechal*, European Papers 2 (2017), 75, 84 *et seq*.; *Lenaerts*, La vie après l'avis: exploring the principle of mutual but not blind trust, CMLR 54 (2017), 805 *et seq*.

80 ECJ, 21.12.2011, joint cases C-411/10 and 493/10, *N.S.*, EU:C:2011:865, and to ECJ, 25.11.2017, joint cases C-404/15 and 659/15 PPU, *Aranyosi and Căldăraru*, EU:C:2016:198 and, especially ECJ, 18.12.2014, Opinion 2/13 *Adhésion de l'Union à la CEDH*, EU:C:2014:2454, paras 163, 192–193.

81 ECJ, 16.7.2015, case C-681/13, *Diageo Brands*, EU:C:2015:471.

Article 267 TFEU. The Dutch party had not lodged an appeal against the Bulgarian judgment that had become final. The Court said:

> "[63] (...) the rules on recognition and enforcement laid down by Regulation No 44/2001 are based on mutual trust in the administration of justice in the European Union. It is that trust which the Member States accord to one another's legal systems and judicial institutions which permits the inference that, in the event of the misapplication of national law or EU law, the system of legal remedies in each Member State, together with the preliminary ruling procedure provided for in Article 267 TFEU, affords a sufficient guarantee to individuals (...). [64] It follows that Regulation No 44/2001 must be interpreted as being based on the fundamental idea that individuals are required, in principle, to use all the legal remedies made available by the law of the Member State of origin."

Under the current Brussels regime, parties cannot simply avoid proceedings in the Member State where the original action was brought and invoke at the enforcement stage severe deficiencies of the process before the court of origin under the public policy exception.[82] To the contrary, they must use the remedies in the Member State of origin in order to prevent a breach of public policy.[83] Otherwise, there is no "manifest" breach of public policy.[84]

The principle of mutual trust does not only impose procedural obligations upon the parties. In addition, the Member States are required to provide for judicial systems protecting effectively the individual rights of litigants.[85] As a result, mutual trust as the overarching principle of the judicial co-operation has reshaped the interplay between the court of origin and

---

82 According to recent judgments, courts in the Member States must thoroughly apply the minimum standards in the Brussels instruments of the 2nd generation in order to protect the right of defence as these instruments do not provide for a review in the Member State of enforcement. ECJ, 28.2.2018, case C-289/17, *Collect Inkasso OÜ*, EU:C:2018:133, paras 36–37; ECJ, 9.3.2017, case C-484/15, *Zulfikarpašić*, EU:C:2017:199, para 48; ECJ, 16.6.2016, *Pebros Servizi*, C-511/14, EU:C:2016:448, para 44.

83 ECJ, 6.9.2012, case C-619/10, *Trade Agency*, EU:C:2012:531, para 64; ECJ, 16.7.2015, case C-681/13, *Diageo Brands*, EU:C:2015:471, para 63. The Court decided that public policy (Article 34 No 1 JR) was not infringed as the applicant had not exhausted the available remedies in Bulgaria.

84 *Prechal*, European Papers 2 (2017), 75, 81 *et seq.*

85 The first judgment was ECJ, 14.12.2006, case C-283/05, *ASML*, EU:C:2006:787, paras 31–32. Article 19 (1)(2) TEU imposes on EU Member States a duty to pro-

the court of enforcement and the role of the parties in cross border disputes.[86] Finally, mutual trust also encourages the dialogue among justices in cross border circumstances.[87] In extreme cases, mutual trust permits exceptions from recognition.[88]

4.2. *The Growing Role of the Charter of Fundamental Rights*

The development of mutual trust already showed the impact of fundamental rights on the Brussels regime. In the early stage of the development, fundamental rights were not explicitly mentioned. They became mostly visible in the context of public policy, especially in cases C-7/98, *Krombach*[89], C-394/07, *Gambazzi*[90], C-420/07, *Apostolides* and C-681/13, *Diageo Brands*.[91] The seminal decision was *Krombach* where the Court explicitly held that the right to a fair trial as enshrined by Article 6 ECHR directly impacted the Brussels regime.[92] By this jurisprudence, the Court of Justice developed a specific concept of public policy (Article 27 no. 1 BC, 34 no. 1/45 I lit. a) JR) consisting of two different layers: At its core, public

---

vide effective legal remedies, *Safjan/Düsterhaus*, A Union of Effective Judicial Protection: Addressing a Multi-level Challenge through the lens of Article 47 CFREU, Yb EuL 33 (2014), 3, 4.

86 *Prechal*, European Papers 2 (2017), 75, 82 *et seq.*; different opinion *Düsterhaus*, ZEuP 2018, 10, 23 (arguing that the protection of legitimate expectation is only of minimal importance within the detailed rules on recognition provided by the Brussels I^{bis} Regulation).

87 *Lenaerts*, CMLR 54 (2017), 805, 836 (referring to judicial co-operation in criminal matters). Article 29 (2) JR requires direct information among different courts seized in the same case.

88 Example: ECJ, 26.4.2018, case C-34/17, *Donnellan*, EU:C:2018:282, see *Hess*, Travaux du Comité Français du Droit International Privé 2016-2018, (2019), p. 329, 345 *et seq.*

89 In case C-7/98, *Krombach*, EU:C:2000:164, paras 24–26, 38–39, 42, the Court stated that public policy could, in exceptional circumstances, cover the fundamental right to a fair hearing, cf. Magnus/Mankowski/*Franq*, Article 45 Brussels I^{bis} Regulation (Commentary 2015), paras 13 and 29.

90 ECJ, 2.4.2009, case C-394/07, *Gambazzi*, EU:C:2009:219.

91 ECJ, 16.7.2015, case C-681/13, *Diageo Brands*, EU:C:2015:471, described *supra* in fn 83.

92 ECJ, 28.3.2000, case C-7/98, *Krombach*, EU:C:2000:164, paras 24–27. In *Krombach*, the Court stressed that the Convention was part of the legal order of the European Community and that human rights were recognized as general principles of EU law. At para 39, the ECJ directly referred to the case law of the ECtHR regarding "contumace" proceedings.

policy refers to the fundamental values of the requested EU Member State – and it is up to the Member States to determine these core values. However, it is up to the Court to review the limits of public policy which, finally, bars the free movement of judgments. In addition, EU law provides for a threshold of human rights protection which is found in the common constitutional values of the EU Member States, the ECHR and – since 2009 – in Article 47 of the CFR. These European standards[93] have expanded continuously as they overlap national standards.[94] As a result, they have limited the "national core" of public policy.[95]

According to the current case law of the Court, Article 47 of the Charter of Fundamental Rights reshapes the Brussels regime in the sense that almost all provisions of the procedural instruments have to be interpreted according to the fundamental right of a fair trial.[96] In case C-112/13 *A v B and others* the Court stated:

> "…the provisions of EU law, such as those of Regulation No. 44/2001, must be interpreted in the light of fundamental rights which, according to settled case-law, form an integral part of the general principles of law whose observance the Court ensures and which are now set out in the Charter (…)[97]. In that respect, it must be borne in mind that all the provisions of Regulation No. 44/2001 express the intention to

93 *Lenaerts*, CMLR 54 (2017), 805, 824 *et seq*. distinguishes national and European public policy.

94 The interplay of the public policy exception of the Brussels regime and the application of the Charter seems to be unsettled: The Brussels regime is an area of full harmonized Union law where the fundamental rights of the Charter are fully applicable according to article 53 CFR, cf. ECJ, 26.2.2013, case C-399/11, *Melloni*, EU:C:2013:107, para 60; Opinion Bobek, 25.7.2018, case C-310/16, *Dzivev*, EU:C:2018:623, paras 85–90. However, the public policy exception in Article 45 (1) (a) of Reg. 1215/2012 refers back to the public policy of the Member States and brings national constitutional law into play again.

95 As a result, it is difficult to find decisions where national courts apply the national public policy exception in a convincing way. A telling example is a decision of the German Federal Court of 7/19/2018, where the 11th Senate refused to recognise a Polish judgment ordering a German television agency to publish the text of a statement on its front website. The Federal Court held that the publication of the pre-formulated text would infringe the freedom of speech under Article 5 of the German Constitution. However, the Court did not consider adapting the foreign decision in a way that would have conformed to German constitutional law.

96 This follows from Article 51 CFR, ECJ, 26.2.2013, case C-617/10, *Åkerberg Fransson*, EU:C:2013:105.

97 The Court referred to *Google Spain and Google*, C-131/12, EU:C:2014:317, para 68 and the case-law cited.

ensure that, within the scope of the objectives of that regulation, proceedings leading to the delivery of judicial decisions take place in such a way that the rights of the defence enshrined in Article 47 of the Charter are observed".[98]

This corresponds to a general development.[99] In this sense, the Court has held that Article 47 CFR is to be engaged when the jurisdiction is based on EU rules[100], service is effected under the Service Regulation[101] and evidence is gathered under the Evidence Regulation.[102] In addition, the Court has decided that the right to effective judicial protection (Article 19 TEU) requires the implication of a judge when a title is certified to be enforced cross-border.[103] Although there are not many judgments addressing Article 47 CFR,[104] there is a growing corpus of jurisprudence that finally entails a constitutionalization as the EU instruments on procedural law are interpreted according to the standards of the Charter.[105] The interplay of the principle of mutual trust and the respect of fundamental rights enshrined in the CFR demonstrates the specific nature of judicial co-operation in the integration process within the AFSJ, which is based on common values shared by the EU Member States.[106]

---

98 ECJ, 11.9.2014, case C-112/13, *A v B and others*, EU:C:2014:2195, para 51; equally ECJ, 25.5.2016, case C-559/14, *Meroni*, EU:C:2016:349, paras 42–45.

99 According to *Lenaerts*, CMLR 54 (2017), 805, 812: "secondary EU legislation that seeks to facilitate the mutual recognition in criminal and civil matters must indeed respect the fundamental rights enshrined in the Charter."

100 ECJ, 11.9.2014, case C-112/13, *A v B and others*, EU:C:2014:2195, paras 51 and 58 *et seq.*; In para 58, the Court referred to ECJ, 17.11.2011, case C-327/10, *Hypoteční banka*, EU:C:2011:745, paras 48–49; ECJ, 15.3.2012, case C-292/10, *G*, EU:C:2012:142, paras 47–48, where Article 47 CFR had not been mentioned.

101 ECJ, 2.3.2017, case C-354/15, *Henderson*, EU:C:2017:157, para 51 – regarding the service of documents the Court has recognized its objective to preserve the right of defence. Cf. ECJ, 16.9.2015, case C-519/13, *Alpha Bank*, EU:C:2015:603, para 49; 28.4.2016, case C-384/14, *Alta Realitat*, EU:C:2016:316; 6.9.2018, case C-21/17, *Catlin Europe*, EU:C:2018:675, para 33.

102 ECJ, 17.12.2015, case C-300/14, *Imtech Marine Belgium*, EU:C:2015:825, para 50.

103 ECJ, 9.3.2017, case C-551/15, *Pula Parking*, EU:C:2017:193, paras 42 *et seq.*; ECJ, 17.12.2015, case C-300/14, *Imtech Marine Belgium*, EU:C:2015:825, para 50.

104 *Düsterhaus*, ZEuP 2018, 10, 19 *et seq.*

105 *Prechal*, European Papers 2 (2017), 75, 81 *et seq.*

106 *Hess*, Europäisches Zivilprozessrecht (2nd ed. 2020, forthcoming), § 4, paras 4.1 *et seq.*; *Lenaerts*, CMLR 54 (2017), 805, 824 *et seq.*

4.3. *The Interplay of the Instruments on Civil Co-operation*

The expansion of the Brussels regime since 2000 has considerably impacted its interpretation. The first area of their interplay relates to the scope of the instruments. Initially, Article 1 (2) BC excluded specific matters which remained subject to the national laws of the Member States.[107] Today, the provisions on the scope of the instruments mainly address the delineation among the different EU-instruments, the delimitation from the laws of EU Member States has become an exception. In *Seagon,*[108] the Court addressed the changed legal scenario: it had been asked whether an action for avoidance falls under the Insolvency Regulation and whether it can be brought before the court of the debtor's main interest (Article 3 Regulation No. 1346/2000).[109] The Court confirmed that jurisdiction for an action to set aside a transaction could be based on Article 3 of the Insolvency Regulation. Referring to its former case-law,[110] the Court held that the purpose of the Insolvency Regulation is to concentrate all insolvency-related proceedings in one Member State and that the proper functioning of the Internal Market (as stated in Recital 4 to the EIR) required to avoid incentives for parties to transfer assets from one Member State to another in order to obtain a more favourable legal protection.[111] In later decisions, the Court stressed the need to align the instruments which implies a uniform interpretation of the criteria defining the scope.[112]

Similar issues of uniform interpretation also arise with regard to the so-called Brussels instruments of the 2nd generation.[113] As these instruments are closely linked to the Brussels I Regulation, a coherent interpretation is needed. In case C-508/12, *Vapenik,*[114] the Court was asked whether the provisions of the EEO-Regulation protecting consumers could be applied to

---

107 Example: Art. 1(2) BC exempted divorce proceedings from the scope of the Convention, national law applied, cf. ECJ, 4.2.1988, case C-145/86, *Hoffmann./.Krieg*, EU:C:1988:61. Since 2001, the Brussels II Regulation applies to divorce.

108 ECJ, 12.2.2009, case C-339/07, *Seagon*, EU:C:2009:83.

109 OJ 2000 L 160/1; in the recast, the issue is addressed by Articles 6–8 of Regulation No. 848/2015.

110 ECJ, 22.2.1979, case C-133/78, *Gourdain./.Nadler*, EU:C:1979:49, para 4.

111 ECJ, 12.2.2009, case C-339/07, *Seagon*, EU:C:2009:83, paras 19, 23 and 24.

112 ECJ, 4.9.2014, Case C-157/13, *Nickel*, EU:C:2014:2145, para 21: Both regulations "must be interpreted in such a way as to avoid any overlap between the rules of law that those texts lay down and any legal vacuum."

113 *Hess*, Europäisches Zivilprozessrecht (2nd ed. 2020, forthcoming), § 10, paras 10.1 *et seq.*

114 ECJ, 5.12.2013, case C-508/12, *Vapenik*, EU:C:2013:790.

proceedings where both private parties had acted for non-professional purposes. If this was the case, each consumer could start proceedings at his or her domicile.[115] The Court referred to the definition of Article 6(1)(d) of Regulation No. 805/2004, requiring a dispute between a consumer and a person acting in the scope of an economic activity (trade, business, craft, liberal profession). It held that the objective of the provision is to protect the consumer as the structurally weaker party in a situation of imbalance. This was not the case when two private parties conclude a contract for the sale of goods or services. The Court compared the enforcement regimes of the Brussels I Regulation and the EEO-Regulation and concluded that the extension of the definition of consumer – as proposed by the referring court – would not only run counter to the objective of protecting a weaker party but would also lead to inconsistencies in the application of the two instruments.[116] As a result, the ECJ refrained from extending the concept of consumer: general provisions of jurisdiction were applicable and the Austrian court was competent to issue the enforcement order.

Similar problems arise with regard to the EU instruments of conflict of laws.[117] The alignment of both areas of law goes back to the 1980 Rome Convention on the law applicable to contractual obligations.[118] Accordingly, recitals 7 of the Rome I and Rome II Regulations state that the scope and the substantive provisions of the Regulation shall be consistently

115 See Articles 17 and 18 (2) Brussels 1[bis] Regulation.

116 See ECJ, 5.12.2013, case C-508/12, *Vapenik*, EU:C:2013:790, para 37: "If, in the context of Regulation No. 805/2004, a definition were to be adopted, which is wider than that in Regulation No. 44/2001, that might lead to inconsistencies in the application of those two regulations. The derogation laid down by Regulation No. 805/2004 might lead to refusal of certification as a European enforcement order of a judgment, whereas it could still be enforced under the general scheme laid down by Regulation No. 44/2001 since the circumstances in which that scheme allows the defendant to challenge the issue of an enforcement order, on the ground that the jurisdiction of the courts for the State in which the consumer is domiciled has not been respected, would not be satisfied."

117 The complementarity is specifically evident in EU instruments addressing both areas like the Succession Regulation. Here, the alignment goes even further since the Regulation establishes a parallelism between the competent forum and the applicable law, cf. Articles 4 and 21.

118 This convention should reduce forum shopping: when the same conflict of laws rules apply throughout the European Union there is no incentive to go to a specific court in order to get a more promising law on the substance applied.

applied with the Brussels regime.[119] As a matter of principle, the Court of Justice strives for a consistent and coherent interpretation of the terms of these instruments[120] but it also regards the specific objectives of the instrument at hand.[121] It interprets the Regulations according to the classical methods,[122] but gives specific consideration to the objectives of each instrument. A prominent case in this regard was case C-45/13 *Kainz./.Pantherwerke* where the Court decided that the interpretation of (now) Article 7 no. 2 of the Brussels I^bis Regulation could not be aligned with the conflict of norms rule in Article 5 of the Rome II Regulation addressing product liability.[123] The Court said:

> "[recital 7] does not mean, however, that the provisions of Regulation No. 44/2001 must for that reason be interpreted in the light of the provisions of Regulation No. 864/2007. The objective of consistency cannot, in any event, lead to the provisions of Regulation No. 44/2001 being interpreted in a manner which is unconnected to the scheme and objectives pursued by that regulation."[124]

---

119 Recital 7 of the Rome II Regulation reads as follows: "The substantive scope and the provisions of this Regulation should be consistent with Council Regulation (EC) No. 44/2001 of 22 December 2000 on jurisdiction and the recognition and enforcement of judgments in civil and commercial matters (Brussels I) and the instruments dealing with the law applicable to contractual obligations."

120 Especially the German doctrine addresses a more comprehensive approach in the context of a so-called "O-Regulation" which shall provide for a "general part" or a set of common rules and principles, see *Leible*, Die Zukunft des Europäischen Zivilprozessrechts, Festschrift Gottwald (2014), p. 381, 390 *et seq.*

121 Examples: ECJ, 19.9.2018, cases C-325/18 PPU and C-375/18 PPU, *C.E. and N.E.*, EU:C:2018:739, para 55 (on the autonomous interpretation of article 1 (2) of the Brussels IIbis Regulation; ECJ, 26.4.2012, case C-92/12 PPU, *Health Service Executive*, EU:C:2012:255, para 59.

122 *Hess*, Europäisches Zivilprozessrecht (2nd ed.2020, forthcoming), para 4.54 *et seq.*

123 ECJ, 16.1.2014, case C-45/13, *Kainz*, EU:C:2014:7. In *Kainz*, the Austrian plaintiff had bought a bicycle in Austria produced by a German manufacturer. The bicycle broke down when the plaintiff made an excursion in Germany. Nevertheless, the plaintiff brought his claim against the manufacturer before the Austrian courts where he had acquired the bike and where it had been marketed, cf. Article 5 (2)(b) of Regulation No. 864/2006. He argued to expand the place of the tort under Article 7 no. 2 JR to the place where the product was acquired and marketed.

124 ECJ, 16.1.2014, case C-45/13 *Kainz*, EU:C:2014:7, para 20, cf. *Requejo Isidro*, Reflection on the Preambles to EU Private International Law Regulations, in: Festschrift Kohler (2018), p. 425, 435 *et seq.*

In order to strengthen predictability, the ECJ interpreted Article 7 no. 2 JR narrowly since it is an exception to Article 4 of the same Regulation.[125] In product liability cases, the Court located the place of the event giving rise to the damage at the place where the product was manufactured.[126] The multitude of different connecting factors of Article 5 (1) Rome II Regulation was not transferred to the Brussels regime.

4.4. EU Procedural Law and National Procedures

Another "neighbouring area" relates to the delineation from and the interfaces with the procedural laws of the Member States. Regarding the interfaces, the point of departure is clear: According to the constant case law of the Court, the Brussels regime does not harmonize national procedures, unless there is a clear provision addressing procedural issues.[127] On the other hand, national procedures cannot impact the self-standing Brussels regime.[128] On balance, the Court has shown self-restraint in favour of the procedural autonomy of the Member States. However, when applying their national procedures in the frame of the Brussels regime, the courts in the EU Member States are bound by the principles of equivalence and effectiveness.[129]

However, the case law of the ECJ sometimes affects indirectly the autonomous laws of the Member States. An important example relates to pendency and to the interpretation of the subject matter of the case. In *Gubisch*,[130] the Court held that the concept of the "same cause of action" (now found in Article 29 of the Recast) was to be determined autonomously according to the "le même objet et cause" (to be broadly defined). According to this case law, an action for payment and an action for the declaration that no obligation of payment exists relate to the same

---

125 Cf. Recital 11 of Regulation No. 44/2001, now Recital 15 of Regulation No. 1215/2012.

126 It still remains to be seen whether this rule also applies in cases of a defectual design.

127 Some authors argue that expanding the scope of the Brussels instruments by analogy is not possible because of the limited competences of the Union. Yet, this argument is not convincing as Article 81 TFEU itself permits the harmonization of procedural law in cross-border cases.

128 ECJ, 1.3.2005, case C-281/02, *Owusu*, EU:C:2005:120.

129 *Hess*, Europäisches Zivilprozessrecht (2nd ed.2020, forthcoming), § 11, paras 4 *et seq.*

130 ECJ, 8.12.1987, case C-144/86, *Gubisch*, EU:C:1987:528, paras 7–8.

cause of action.[131] The same applies between the action to enforce a contract and another for rescission.[132] Legal doctrine criticised this case law: either in Member States where a more limited approach to the scope of pendency (and res judicata) prevails and in others where the action for a negative declaration was unknown. In the long run, it seems that critics are no longer so strongly expressed and that the approach of the ECJ has gained more and more support in the legal doctrine.[133]

However, the courts in the Member States are more reluctant, especially as the equal treatment of the action for a negative declaration and the action for performance encourages a rush to the court.[134] In *Folien Fischer*[135], a competition case, the German Federal Civil Court explicitly asked the ECJ whether (now) Article 7 no. 2 JR applies to an action for a declaration as to the non-existence of civil liability for a tort or delict allegedly committed.[136] This reference gave the ECJ the opportunity to review its case law on the equal treatment of both types of the actions. In his Opinion, AG Jääskinen analysed (now) Article 7 no. 2 JR according to the wording of the provision, its objective and the system of the Regulation. He argued that the objective of the provision was to protect the victim of an (alleged) infringement by establishing jurisdiction at the place where either the infringement was committed or the damage sustained.[137] The AG also argued that the other objectives of the provision – and, notably, proximity to the facts of the dispute, foreseeability and the proximity to the case – favoured a restrictive interpretation of the specific head of jurisdiction. As a result, the AG proposed to change the current case law. In its judgment, the Court did not follow the proposal made by the

131 ECJ, 25.10.2012, case C-133/11, *Folien Fischer,* EU:C:2012:664.

132 ECJ, 8.12.1987, case C-144/86, *Gubisch,* EU:C:1987:528.

133 *Gottwald* in: Münchener Kommentar zur ZPO (5th ed. 2018), Article 29 Brussels Ibis Regulation, paras 13 and 14 with references of the German doctrine. The Working Group on Pendency of the ELI/Unidroit Project on Transnational Rules of Civil Procedure took up the approach of the Brussels regime as developed by the Court as a model for a European approach. However, German courts have not changed their traditional approach to pendency and res judicata in domestic settings.

134 The divergent practice of courts in the Member States is documented in the Opinion AG Jääskinen, 19.4.2012, case C-133/11, *Folien Fischer*, EU:C:2012:226, footnotes 15–17.

135 ECJ, 25.10.2012, case C-133/11, *Folien Fischer*, EU:C:2012:664.

136 Opinion AG Jääskinen, 19.4.2012, case C-133/11, *Folien Fischer*, EU:C:2012:226, para 19.

137 However, the Court had never openly taken up this position which had often been advanced by legal doctrine.

AG. The Court acknowledged that the action for a negative declaration reversed the role of the parties. However, it held that, different to the "protective heads of jurisdiction in chapter II of the Regulation", jurisdiction based on tort was not one-sided and that the wording of the provision does not distinguish the different roles of the parties.[138] Therefore, the Court held that the action for a negative declaration could not be excluded from the scope of (now) Article 7 no. 2 JR.[139] *Folien Fischer* is a decision, which stands for the continuity of the case law of the Court, although the critique of the AG was well founded. The judgment may prompt Member States to introduce (or to reinforce) the action for a negative declaration in their domestic procedural laws in order to preserve the equal treatment of (domestic) parties in international settings.

5. Assessment: European Procedural Law as Interpreted by the ECJ

Where is the Brussels regime standing today, after almost 50 years of practice in the Member States and in the Court of Justice? Any assessment of the practice must be aware of the different perspectives adopted: From the perspective of the Court, the Brussels regime (and private international law in general) only amounts to 4 % of all of its cases.[140] This statistical figure entails that the main perspective of the Court comes from general Union law (and the AFSJ). On the other hand, the perspective of those commenting the case law is different as it usually comes from the specific area in which the commentator is a specialist: private (international) law, civil procedural law or both. However, the different perspectives do not exclude that the ECJ takes into account the specific needs of the instrument it is construing and the academic commentator might take into account the context of EU law. Thus, both approaches can be combined and it appears that a kind of untechnical specialisation regarding the Brussels regime is also present within the ECJ.[141]

---

138 ECJ, 25.10.2012, case C-133/11, *Folien Fischer*, EU:C:2012:664, paras 42 *et seq.*
139 ECJ, 25.10.2012, case C-133/11, *Folien Fischer*, EU:C:2012:664, para 51.
140 *Düsterhaus*, ZEuP 2018, 10, 30.
141 *Schmidt*, Rechtssicherheit (2015), p. 266 *et seq.*

5.1. Interaction between Rules and Principles

The review of the cases demonstrates that the Court closely follows the text of the respective instruments: preliminary references in procedural law usually address the interpretation of specific rules of the regime.[142] The literal text of the instrument is the starting point,[143] but the objective and the scheme of the instrument are equally taken into account.[144] Legal certainty and predictability are important arguments in the textual interpretation of the regime,[145] decisions against the wording of the instruments usually do not take place.[146] Generally, the Court understands the rules of the Brussels regime in a way that they strike a fair balance between the rights of the plaintiff to access the courts in order to effectively enforce the rights claimed and the right of the defendant to bring his defence.[147] This approach equally reinforces the importance of the rules set by the lawmaker: the objective of ensuring a fair balance is primarily found in the provisions of the respective instrument itself.

In addition, general principles of procedural law, Union law and the constitutional guarantees of the Charter play an important (and growing) role in the case law of the Court. Initially, it developed these principles

---

142 *Dickinson*, in: Dickinson/Lein, The Brussels I Regulation Recast (2015), paras 1.45 and 1.49.

143 The different language versions of the instruments may yield to uncertainty about the precise meaning of a provision, cf. *Streinz*, in: Riesenhuber (ed.), European Legal Methodology (2017), p. 151, 159 *et seq.*

144 With regard to the systemic interpretation, it is to note that the Court usually refers to the instrument itself and not so often to parallel instruments.

145 *Dickinson*, in: Dickinson/Lein, para 1.63: "The principle of legal certainty is … anything but certain in its meaning and application."

146 Different opinion *Schmidt*, Rechtssicherheit, p. 249 *et seq.*, who does not distinguish between decisions reducing the scope and wording of the instruments and cases where parties tried to enlarge the system.

147 Example: ECJ, 7.7.2016, case C-70/15, *Lebek*, EU:C:2016:524, para 37: "In that connection, it is apparent from recitals 16 to 18 to the Brussels I Regulation that the system of appeals for which it provides against the recognition or enforcement of a judgment aims to establish a fair balance between, on the one hand, mutual trust in the administration of justice in the Union, which justifies judgments given in a Member State being, as a rule, recognised and declared enforceable automatically in another Member State and, on the other hand, respect for the rights of the defence, which means that the defendant should, where necessary, be able to appeal in an adversarial procedure against the declaration of enforceability if he considers one of the grounds for non-enforcement to be present (judgment of 28.4.2009 in *Apostolides*, C-420/07, EU:C:2009:271, para 73)."

within the text of the Brussels Convention; but the Court always considered the Convention also as an integral part of the EC law.[148] The Amsterdam Treaty fully integrated judicial co-operation into the Treaty and aligned it with other policies of the Union. The replacement of the Brussels Convention by secondary EU law implied an important change as the recitals of the regulations refer to the guiding principles[149] (and, since 2009, to the Charter).[150]

The style of the judgments of the Court[151] reflects this perspective: At present, judgments start by quoting the applicable provisions according to their hierarchy: The introductory part often enounces primary Union law – therefore the Charter is quoted in the first place. Secondary Union law appears in the second place; and again, the judgments place the recitals of the regulations before the operative provisions.[152] This legal context is usually taken up in the operative parts of the judgments: Here, the Court sometimes starts by quoting the overarching principles and objectives of the provisions to be applied.[153] This style of the judgments opens up a perception where the overarching principles and constitutional guarantees support and reinforce the interpretation of the rules.[154]

On the other hand, the practical impacts of the principles remain limited due to their open formulation and their character as values (to be bal-

148 See *supra* text at fn. 24 *et seq*.

149 Example: Recitals 16 and 17 of Regulation No. 44/2001 referred to mutual trust, recital 18 evoked the right of defence. Similarly: Regulation 1215/2012, recital 26 (mutual trust) and 38 (Charter of Fundamental Rights). It must be noted that the recitals of the Brussels I^bis^ Regulation are less explicit than those of its predecessor.

150 Example: Recital 38 of the Brussels I^bis^ Regulation; different opinion *Dickinson*, in *Dickinson/Lein*, The Brussels I Regulation Recast (2015), para 1.117, who regards the evocation of the Charter in the recital as "superfluous".

151 Cf. *Lenaerts/Maselis/Gutman/Nowak*, EU Procedural Law (2014), para 23.88, describing the content and the formal requirements of the judgments of the ECJ.

152 Example: ECJ, 25.6.2016, case C-559/14, *Meroni*, EU:C:2016:349: paras 3 and 4 refer to articles 47 and 51 of the Charter, para 5 quotes recital 16 to 18 of Regulation 44/01, paras 6 *et seq*. quote operative provision of the Regulation.

153 Example: ECJ, 7.7.2016, case C-70/15, *Lebek*, EU:C:2016:524, paras 32 and 33: free movement of judgments, para 34: rights of defence.

154 Example: ECJ, case C-354/15, *Henderson*, EU:C:2017:157, paras 48 *et seq*., addressing Article 8 of the Service Regulation. The right to refuse the acceptance of an (untranslated) document stems from the need to protect the right of defence (Article 47 of the Charter).

anced).[155] They do not impose a specific solution but, rather, reinforce the weight and the objective of specific provisions of the legal instrument at hand.[156] As principles do not impose a specific solution, they do not overcome the text of the instruments. In this respect, *Gasser*[157] was a typical decision when the Court refused to deviate from the wording of (now) Article 29 JR by referring to Article 6 of the ECHR.[158] Similarly, the constitutional principle of mutual trust operates on the basis of the existing instruments. It is interesting to see that, in the context of public policy (Article 34 No. 1 JR), the ECJ (*de facto*) aligned the obligation of the party to first seek redress in the court of origin with the parallel text of the Brussels I Regulation (Article 34 no. 2 JR).[159] Finally, the reference to principles (like mutual trust) permits the Court to place the interpretation of a specific provision in the broader context of Union law – for instance, to relate it to mutual trust as it is applied to judicial co-operation in criminal matters.[160] However, explicit cross-references are rare exceptions in the case law on the Brussels regime.[161]

5.2. Comparative Law in the Brussels Regime

The first decisions on the Brussels Convention were based on a comparative review: This was mainly found in the opinion of the Advocates General and in the arguments of the parties.[162] The situation has progressively

155 *Hess*, Europäisches Zivilprozessrecht (2nd ed 2020, forthcoming) § 4, para 4.81 *et seq.*; *Dickinson*, in: *Dickinson/Lein*, The Brussels I Regulation Recast (2015), para 1.56 (stressing the non-binding nature of recitals).

156 *Mak*, Rights and Remedies, in: Micklitz (ed.), Constitutionalization of European Private Law (2014), p. 236, 239 *et seq.*

157 *Supra* at fn. 69 *et seq.*

158 Article 6 ECHR does not prescribe the length of the proceedings and it was not up to the ECJ to make such a decision.

159 This provision (now Article 45 (1) (b) JR) states: "unless the defendant failed to commence proceeding to challenge the judgement when it was possible for him to do so." The ECJ developed this line of argument in case C-283/05, *ASML*, paras 38 and 39, it was finally (but not explicitly) taken up in case C-681/13, *Diageo Brands*, para 63. However, there is no explicit reference to Art. 34 No. 2 JR in this judgment.

160 ECJ, 26.4.2018, case C-34/17, *Donnellan*, EU:C:2018:282, paras 45 and 50.

161 They are found in the opinions of the Court, see Opinion 2/13 of the Union (*Accession to the ECHR*), EU:C:2014:2454, para 191.

162 At that time, the judgments of the Court briefly summarized the arguments raised in the hearings.

changed and today the autonomous and the systemic interpretation dominate the current practice. In addition, the Court largely refers to its former case law.[163] Legal doctrine has criticized the shift from the comparative approach,[164] but one must acknowledge that comparing 27 different national legal orders is practically more or less impossible.[165] However, this does not exclude that the Court takes note of the different practices in the Member States – often based on comparative notes provided by its scientific service. Still, there are cases where comparative law plays a visible role – in this regard, *Folien Fischer* is a good example.[166] Here, a comparative analysis was not given by the Court in its judgment, but by the Advocate General instead.[167] However, increasing the visibility of the comparative background would certainly improve the acceptance of the Court's judgment in the (other) EU Member States. Thus, it must be regretted that more and more recent AG opinions on the Brussels regime only quote the case law of the Court and do not refer to legal doctrine at all.[168] This

---

163 In this respect, the case law regarding the Service Regulation shows a high degree of consistency, *Hess*, Europäisches Zivilprozessrecht, § 8, paras 8.15 *et seq.*

164 *Rühl*, Rechtsvergleichung und europäisches Kollisionsrecht: Die vergessene Dimension, in: Zimmermann, Zukunft der Rechtsvergleichung (2016), p. 103, 126 *et seq*.

165 The Reports on the Brussels Convention (especially the Jenard Report of 1976 and the Schlosser Report of 1978) provide considerable information on comparative law. This is the reason why the Court refers to those Reports until today; cf. *Schwarze*, Comparative Law, in: Riesenhuber (ed.), European Legal Methodology (2017), p. 61, 70.

166 ECJ, 25.10.2012, case C-133/11, *Folien Fischer*, EU:C:2012:664, *supra* at fn. 135 *et seq*. Another positive example (there are many more) is the Opinion Szpunar, 3.5.2017, case C-231/16, *Merck*, EU:C:2017:330 (quoting case law in the Member States and doctrinal opinions).

167 The ECJ does usually not quote case law of the EU-Member States (a rare exception: ECJ, 2.4.2009, case C-394/07, *Gambazzi*, EU:C:2009:219, paras 35–36). Usually, the ECJ does not even refer to the case law of the Swiss Federal Tribunal despite Protocol No 2 of the Lugano Convention, *Hess*, Das Lugano Übereinkommen und der Brexit, Festschrift Kohler (2018), p. 179, 184.

168 Examples: Conclusion Bot, 26.4.2017, case C-249/16, *Kareda*, EU:C:2016:305; Opinion Wathelet, 29.5.2018, case C-21/17 *Catlin Europe*, EU:C:2018:341 and Opinion 16.11.2017, case C-560/16, *E.O.N. Czech Holding* (quoting as sole doctrinal reference *P. Paschalidis*, a referendaire at the Court); Opinion Tanchev, 10.4.2018, case C-88/17, *Zurich Insurance*, EU:C:2018224; Opinion Øe, 13.7.2017, *Hanssen Beleggingen BV*, EU:C:2017:551. An additional distance between the practice in the Member States and the case law of the Court appears when judgments are given without Opinion of the AG as the Court never quotes the doctrine in the Member States.

enlarges the gap between the jurisprudence in Luxembourg and the legal practice in the EU Member States. However, it must be noted that there are still judgments taking up a genuine comparative approach. In this respect, case C-379/17[169] and the Conclusions of AG Szpunar[170] are a positive example. In his Conclusions, the AG largely referred to the different practices and legal opinions in the EU Member States. Ultimately, however, the ECJ did not follow his Conclusions.

Another aspect where comparative law plays an important role relates to the relationship between the civil and the common law of civil procedure. To some extent, the Brussels regime has operated as a bridge builder.[171] From the very beginning, the different approaches of the common law were openly and largely discussed in the hearings.[172] Again, the judgments of the Court (and the opinion) did not explicitly refer to the specific situation in the United Kingdom[173] unless the reference came directly from English courts.[174] On substance, the Court did not take up the more flexible and discretionary approach of English law regarding jurisdiction and pendency, and stressed the need for a uniform and predictable application of the instruments.[175] Therefore, some of its judgments were harshly criti-

169 ECJ, 4.10.2018, case C-379/17, *Società Immobiliare Al Bosco Srl*, EU:C:2018:806.

170 Conclusions *Szpunar*, 20.6.2018, case C-379/17, EU:C:2018:472, para 48 and footnote 16 addressing the legal situation in Germany, Poland, France and Italy.

171 The Schlosser Report of 1978 (OJ 1979 C 59/71) gives large explanations of procedural specificities of the common law and their impacts on the interpretation of the Brussels Convention.

172 Example: ECJ, 14.10.1976, case C-29/76, *LTU./.Eurocontrol*, EU:C:1976:137, supra at fn. 26 *et seq.*; *Rühl*, in: Zimmermann, Zukunft der Rechtsvergleichung (2016), p. 103, 127–129.

173 In *Denilauler*, different provisional remedies of the civil and the common law were discussed during the hearing. Finally, the Court restricted the free movement of preliminary measures in order to protect the right of defence, see *supra* at fn. 51.

174 ECJ, 2.4.2009, case C-394/07, *Gambazzi*, EU:C:2009:219, paras 29 *et seq.*; Opinion Kokott, 18.12.2008, EU:C:2008:748, paras 20 *et seq.* (debarment, freezing order).

175 ECJ, 1.3.2005, case C-281/02, *Owusu*, EU:C:2005:120, para 41. The EU lawmaker was more receptive, especially in family matters and insolvency law. Furthermore, the idea of direct communication between judges largely borrows from practices of the common law.

cized by the English legal doctrine[176] but the judicial practice in England follows the case law of the Court of Justice.[177]

5.3. *Complementary Roles of the Court and the EU Lawmaker*

Looking at the development of the ECJ's case law during the last 50 years, one must state that the Court has mainly kept its practice within the wording and the scheme of the specific instrument of the Brussels system. This practice has been described as a "black letter approach" of the Court;[178] but it also stands for judicial self-restraint in the field of civil co-operation. Often, the Court hesitated to engage in judicial activism or to transgress the wording of specific provisions. Striking examples are *Gasser* and *Folien Fischer*, where the Court demonstrated a stance to maintain its case law even when it faced strong criticism coming from the referring court and the Advocate General. General consideration as to the uniform application of the regime in all Member States and the implementation of *effet utile* prevented the ECJ from adopting innovative solutions.[179] This caution does not exclude that the solutions adopted by the ECJ do not correspond to the established practices in some of the Member States.[180]

On the other hand, there is an interesting interplay between the ECJ and the European lawmaker. All instruments of the Brussels regime are permanently reviewed and reformed by the EU lawmaker. The Brussels Convention was reformed in 1978, in 1982 and in 1989; the 2001 Regulation was reformed in 2012 – the next report of the Commission is due for 2022.[181] All instruments of European private international and proce-

---

176 Cf. *Hartley*, "The European Union and the Systematic Dismantling of the Common Law of Conflict of Laws", *International and Comparative Law Quarterly*, volume 54 (2005), pp. 813 *et seq.*

177 On 6.6.2018, the Commercial Court confirmed that EU law does not permit English judges to issue anti-suit injunctions in support of arbitration within the Union, *Nori Holdings Ltd v. Bank Financial Corp* [2018] EWHC 1343 (Comm) per Justice *Males*.

178 *Harris*, The Brussels I Regulation, the ECJ and the Rule Book, LQR 124 (2008), 523 commenting very critically the judgment of the ECJ, 22.5.2008, case C-462/06, *Glaxosmithkline und Laboratoires Glaxosmithkline*, EU:C:2008:299.

179 *Lenaerts & Stapper*, RabelsZ 78 (2014), 252, 279 *et seq.*; *Dickinson*, in *Dickinson/Lein*, The Regulation Brussels I Recast (2015), para 1.52.

180 Example: ECJ, 15.11.2012, case C-456/11, *Gothaer Allgemeine Versicherung*, EU:C:2012:719.

181 Article 79 Brussels I^{bis} Regulation.

dural law are subject to permanent review and (hopefully) improvement. Quite often, the EU lawmaker stepped in to fill gaps of the Brussels regime, which the Court had been unwilling (or too cautious) to close. The most prominent examples relate to the autonomous definition of contract in Article 5 no. 1 BC/7 no. 1 JR, the definition of the moment of pendency in Article 32 JR[182] and the new provision on pendency in case of choice of court agreements (Article 31 (2)–(4) JR).[183] Another example is Article 26 (2) of the Brussels I^{bis} Regulation according to which the court must inform the weaker party about the consequences of a submission by appearance.[184] However, one should not overstate these interventions of the EU lawmaker, who eventually maintained the basic structure of the Brussels regime as interpreted by the Court.

From the perspective of this interplay it comes as no surprise that the Court was unwilling to change its case law in areas where political compromise had been difficult to achieve in the law-making process. One example can be found in *Gazprom*[185] where the ECJ declined to change the dividing line between the Regulation and arbitration. Another example is offered by *Schrems II*[186] where the Court followed the opinion of AG Bobek not to extend (now) Articles 17 and 18 JR to assigned claims of consumers. The AG clearly stated that the interpretation of the Regulation as proposed by the plaintiff would amount to the introduction of a new form of collective redress – a decision to be made by the lawmaker.[187] In the judgment, the Court did not refer to the opinion of the AG, and it simply declined to extend Articles 18 and 18 JR to assigned claims.[188]

182 Rectifying ECJ, 7.6.1984, case C-129/83, *Zelger./.Salinitri*, EU:C:1984:215; ECJ, 6.10.1976, case C-12/76, *Tessili*, EU:C:1976:133.

183 Rectifying ECJ, 9.12.2003, case C-116/02, *Gasser*, EU:C:2003:657; *supra* at fn 71 *et seq*.

184 Rectifying ECJ, 20.5.2010, case C-111/09, *Vienna Insurance*, EU:C:2010:290, para 32.

185 ECJ, 13.5.2015, case C-536/13, *Gazprom*, EU:C:2015:316; in his opinion of 4.12.2014, AG Wathelet had proposed to generally permit anti-suit injunctions supporting arbitration, case C-536/13, *Gazprom*, EU:C:2015:2414, paras 124 *et seq*.

186 ECJ, 25.1.2018, case C-498/16, *Schrems II*, EU:C:2018:37.

187 AG Bobek, Conclusion of 14.11.2017, ECJ, 25.1.2018, case C-498/16, *Schrems II*, EU:C:2018:37, paras 119 *et seq*. (123).

188 ECJ, 25.1.2018, case C-498/16, *Schrems II*, EU:C:2018:37, para 48. However, the Court made it clear that the notion of "consumer" includes persons who organize the defence of consumer rights vis-à-vis traders, case C-498/16, paras 39–40.

6. *Conclusion*

Looking back after this *tour d'horizon*, one impression appears to be cogent: The pivotal role of the case law of the Court of Justice for the development of the Brussels regime and for the successful judicial co-operation in civil matters in the European Union cannot be underestimated. The case law of the Court has been criticised, especially for its reluctance with regard to concepts originating in the common law. However, one should not forget that the basic structure of the Brussels regime was elaborated at a time when the United Kingdom was not yet a Member State of the European Union. Nevertheless, the common law solutions have influenced the development of the European procedural law.[189] On the other hand, one must acknowledge that London has become an important judicial centre (maybe even the most important one to date) within Europe. After Brexit is completed, judicial co-operation with the United Kingdom will change dramatically – and this will be a cultural loss for European procedural law.[190]

Finally, one question endures: Can we really speak of seminal judgments of the Court of Justice in the field of civil justice? One shouldn't be hesitant to put judgments like *Eurocontrol*, *Krombach*, *Denilauler* and *Leffler* in the same line as *Costa Enel*, *Simmenthal*, and *Les Verts*. However, there are only few landmark decisions that really changed the scene: most clarified the state of affairs. Landmark decisions are found in the founding phase of the Convention (and after the communitarization: *Leffler*; and, under article 47 CFR: *Diageo Brands*). This is not surprising: The case law of the ECJ endeavours for continuity, predictability, literal interpretation.[191] Innovations are sometimes hidden in quotations of former case law, which might not entirely support the move the Court is making in its current decision.[192] Finally, one only finds a few seminal judgments, but a

---

189 The most prominent examples are found in family and in insolvency law.

190 The Lugano Convention is not a suitable instrument for the post-Brexit period, cf. *Hess*, MPI Working Papers 2/2018, at: https://www.mpi.lu/research/working-paper-series/2018/wp-2018-2/.

191 The "Cartesian Style" of the Court has often been criticized by legal doctrine, see *Weiler*, Epilogue: The Judicial Area Après Nice, in: de Burca and Weiler (eds.), The European Court of Justice (2001), p. 215; contra *Lenaerts*, The Court's Outer and Inner Selves: Exploring the External and Internal Legitimacy of the ECJ, in: Adams et al (eds.), Judging Europe's Judges (2015), p. 1, 45 *et seq*.

192 Example: ECJ, 25.5.2016, case C-559/14, *Meroni*, EU:C:2016:349, para 48, where the Court evokes "the fundamental idea that individuals are required, as a matter of principle, to use all the legal remedies in the Member State of origin" by

line of judgments developing and building up the direction of the jurisprudence. This result might not be wrong for a Court which strives for stability and uniformity in a Union of (still) 28 different Member States.

---

referring to *Diageo Brands*, para 64 (where this requirement was not formulated as a "fundamental idea").

La confiance mutuelle, fondement et témoignage de la valeur de l'Union européenne

Camelia Toader[*]

Table of Contents

1. *Introduction*

L'an de la signature de la Convention de Bruxelles, à laquelle cet ouvrage rend hommage, 1968, fût aussi, du point de vue politico-militaire un tournant de l'humanité du siècle dernier, d'après l'historien britannique Ben Pimlott : c'était la décision de l'Union Soviétique de ne pas attaquer la Roumanie, seul pays du bloc de l'Est à ne pas participer à l'invasion de la Tchécoslovaquie. Cette dernière abstention a ouvert, hélas pour quelques années seulement, une porte de confiance vers mon pays d'origine.

Dans cette contribution, je souhaite réfléchir sur la portée juridique du principe de confiance mutuelle dans le cadre du système Bruxelles et sur son importance dans la jurisprudence de la Cour.

Il me semble intéressant de rappeler que, dans le langage commun, la notion de « confiance » peut être définie comme « le courage qui vient de

* Prof. Dr. Camelia Toader est professeur à l'Université de Bucharest et juge à la Cour de Justice de l'Union européenne

la conscience que l'on a de sa valeur »[1]. De surcroît, le sociologue allemand Niklas Luhmann définit cette notion comme la confiance dans les attentes vis-à-vis du comportement des autres personnes[2].

Dans le processus évolutif de l'Union européenne, une telle confiance doit être « mutuelle », « réciproque », entre les États membres de l'Union. À cet égard, pour citer mon ancien collègue, le regretté avocat général Ruiz-Jarabo Colomer, « la construction d'une Europe sans frontières et le rapprochement des différents ordres juridiques nationaux impliquent que les États concernés s'inspirent des mêmes valeurs »[3].

Le principe de confiance mutuelle témoigne, ainsi qu'il a été rappelé par la Cour en plénière dans l'avis 2/13, du 18 décembre 2014, de la valeur de l'Union européenne en tant que construction juridique reposant sur la prémisse fondamentale selon laquelle chaque État membre partage avec tous les autres États membres, et reconnaît que ceux-ci partagent avec lui, une série de valeurs communes sur lesquelles l'Union est fondée, comme il est précisé à l'article 2 TUE[4]. Cette prémisse implique et justifie l'existence de la confiance mutuelle entre les États membres dans la reconnaissance de ces valeurs et, donc, dans le respect du droit de l'Union qui les met en œuvre.

Dans le domaine du droit procédural et international privé de l'Union européenne, le principe de confiance mutuelle constitue l'une des pierres angulaires de la coopération judiciaire en matière civile et commerciale. Ce principe sous-tend l'application des dispositions concernant la reconnaissance et l'exécution des décisions rendues dans un État membre autre que celui du for dans le système du règlement Bruxelles. Il repose sur l'idée que, quand bien même les États membres ne traitent pas une affaire donnée de manière identique, les décisions adoptées dans un État membre sont à considérer comme équivalentes, puisqu'elles répondent aux mêmes principes et valeurs et, par conséquent, elles peuvent être acceptées en tant que telles par les autorités nationales des autres États membres[5].

---

1 Dictionnaire Larousse.

2 N. Luhmann, *Vertrauen*, 4th ed., 2000, cité par M. Weller, « Mutual Trust: in search of the future of European Union private international law », *Journal of Private International Law*, 2015, p. 68.

3 Conclusions de l'avocat général Ruiz-Jarabo Colomer dans l'affaire *Gözütok et Brügge*, C-187/01, point 55.

4 CJUE, avis 2/13 (Adhésion de l'Union à la CEDH), du 18 décembre 2014, EU:C:2014:2454, point 168.

5 V., en ce sens, B. Nascimbene, « Le traité de Lisbonne et l'espace judiciaire européen : le principe de confiance réciproque et de reconnaissance mutuelle », Intervention auprès du conseil national des avocats, p. 7, disponible sous le lien

2. *Évolution du principe de confiance mutuelle : de sa naissance dans la logique d'un marché commun à sa consolidation avec l'abolition de l'exequatur*

Dans son évolution historique, la libre circulation des décisions de justice a été initialement conçue comme un outil pour la construction du marché intérieur, dont le bon fonctionnement impliquait la circulation transfrontalière des décisions judiciaires tranchant les litiges liés à la libre circulation des marchandises, des capitaux et des services[6]. Par la suite, la libre circulation des décisions a acquis son autonomie en tant qu'élément fondamental pour la création d'un espace de liberté, de sécurité et de justice dans l'Union européenne. Néanmoins, elle a été marquée, dans un premier temps, par une certaine méfiance des États membres quant à la possibilité que les décisions étrangères déploient leurs effets sur leur territoire sans aucun contrôle de leur part[7]. La procédure d'exequatur illustre cette méfiance.

Il y a 50 ans, le 27 septembre 1968, la Convention (inter-gouvernementale) signée à Bruxelles a mis en place un système uniforme de l'exequatur et, à travers le protocole du 3 juin 1971, la Cour de justice a reçu la compétence pour l'interpréter par voie de décisions préjudicielles, ce qui a été l'un des moteurs du développement d'un espace européen de justice[8].

Dans cette évolution, le principe de confiance mutuelle entre les États membres a joué un rôle croissant[9], qui a comporté, dans le passage de la Convention au règlement n° 44/2001, dit Bruxelles I, l'automatisme de la concession de l'exequatur[10] et, ensuite, son abolition lors de la refonte du

---

suivant : http://proxy.siteo.com.s3.amazonaws.com/www.cna-avocats.fr/file/interventionnascimbenecongresdecome.pdf.

6 F. Gascón-Inchausti, « La reconnaissance et l'exécution des décisions dans le règlement Bruxelles I bis », *Le nouveau règlement Bruxelles I bis*, E. Guinchard (ed.), 2014, pp. 206 – 207.

7 M. Weller, « Mutual Trust: in search of the future of European Union private international law », *Journal of Private International Law*, 2015, pp. 69 à 71.

8 Protocole du 3 juin 1971 concernant l'interprétation par la Cour de justice de la convention du 27 septembre 1968 concernant la compétence judiciaire et l'exécution des décisions en matière civile et commerciale.

9 M. Tulibacka, « Europeanization of Civil Procedures: In search of a coherent approach », *Common Market Law Review*, 2009, 46, p. 1540; M. Möstl, « Preconditions and limits of mutual recognition », *Common Market Law Review*, 2010, 47, p. 404.

10 Pour une analyse des changements suite au passage de la Convention de Bruxelles au règlement n° 44/2001 : A. Stadler, « From the Brussels Convention to Regulation 44/2001 : Cornestones of a European Law of Civil Procedure », *Common Market Law Review*, 42, 2005, en particulier pp. 1639 à 1644.

règlement Bruxelles I, avec l'adoption du règlement n° 1215/2012, dit Bruxelles I bis[11].

Il s'agit d'un pas fondamental dans le processus de reconnaissance mutuelle des décisions : celles adoptées dans l'État membre d'origine sont désormais directement exécutées dans l'État membre requis. Conformément au considérant 26 du règlement Bruxelles I bis, les décisions prises dans un autre État membre, sur présentation d'un certificat attestant leur origine et leur teneur, doivent être traitées comme si elles avaient été rendues dans l'État membre requis.

Le principe de confiance mutuelle n'implique toutefois pas, ainsi que M. le professeur Hess l'a rappelé, une confiance « aveugle »[12]. La confiance mutuelle entre les différents États membres suppose l'existence d'une garantie *a priori,* relative au respect des droits fondamentaux dans l'Union, ainsi qu'une vérification *a posteriori*[13]. Ainsi, la suppression de la procédure d'exequatur dans le cadre du règlement Bruxelles I bis a été palliée par l'instauration d'un dispositif permettant de refuser la reconnaissance ou l'exécution transfrontalière d'une décision[14]. En effet, aux termes de l'article 45 du règlement Bruxelles I bis, à la demande de toute partie intéressée, la reconnaissance d'une décision est refusée : a) si elle est manifestement contraire à l'ordre public de l'État membre requis; b) si elle est susceptible de porter atteinte au droit de défense du défendeur; si elle est inconciliable c) avec une décision rendue entre les mêmes parties dans l'État membre requis; ou d) avec une décision rendue antérieurement dans un autre État membre ou dans un État tiers entre les mêmes parties dans un litige ayant le même objet et la même cause, lorsque la décision rendue antérieure-

11 M. Zilinky, « Mutual Trust and Cross-Border Enforcement of Judgments in Civil Matters in the EU: Does the Step-by-Step Approach Work? », *Neth Int Law Rev*, 64, 2017, pp. 119 à 121.

12 B. Hess, Seminal judgments (les grands arrêts) in the case law of the European Court of Justice, dans ce même ouvrage. V. également K. Lenaerts, « La vie après l'avis: exploring the principle of mutual (yet not blind) trust », *Common Market Law Review*, 2017, Vol. 54, 3, pp. 805 à 840.

13 À cet égard, pour une réflexion sur l'interaction entre le principe de confiance mutuelle et le droit à un procès équitable, v. X. Kramer, « Cross-border Enforcement in the EU : Mutual Trust versus Fair Trial? Towards Principles of European Civil Procedure », *International Journal of Procedural Law*, 2011, 2, pp. 202 à 230.

14 En ce sens, M. Mankowski, European Commentaries on Private International Law, Commentary Brussels Ibis Regulation, 2016, p. 877. V. également F. Marchadier, « La suppression de l'exequatur affaiblit-elle la protection des droits fondamentaux dans l'espace judiciaire européen? », Journal européen des droits de l'homme, 2013, 3, pp. 348 à 380.

ment réunit les conditions nécessaires à sa reconnaissance dans l'État membre requis; ou e) dans des cas spécifiques de contrariété avec certaines dispositions du règlement. De même, selon l'article 46, l'exécution d'une telle décision est refusée, à la demande de la personne contre laquelle l'exécution est demandée, en cas d'existence, constatée, de l'un de ces mêmes motifs.

S'agissant du refus de la reconnaissance d'une décision au motif qu'elle est contraire à l'ordre public de l'État membre requis[15], il est intéressant de rappeler deux décisions nationales récentes dont la teneur peut poser quelques signes d'interrogation concernant la (non) confiance mutuelle.

La première décision, rendue par la Cour suprême de Lettonie, le 20 octobre 2015, concerne le refus de reconnaître et exécuter une décision d'une cour de Lituanie. Tout d'abord, il convient de mentionner brièvement les antécédents. Interrogée sur plusieurs questions préjudicielles, posées par la Cour suprême de Lettonie, dans l'affaire *flyLAL Lithuanian Airlines*[16], la Cour de justice de l'Union européenne avait établi, en ce qui concerne la non reconnaissance des décisions étrangères pour des raisons d'ordre public, au sens de l'article 34, point 1, du règlement Bruxelles I, que cette disposition doit être interprétée en ce sens que ni les modalités de détermination du montant des sommes, sur lesquelles portent les mesures provisoires et conservatoires prononcées par une décision dont la reconnaissance et l'exécution sont demandées, lorsqu'il est possible de suivre le cheminement du raisonnement ayant conduit à la détermination du montant desdites sommes, et alors même que des voies de recours étaient ouvertes et ont été exercées pour contester de telles modalités de calcul, ni la simple invocation de conséquences économiques graves ne constituent des motifs établissant la violation de l'ordre public de l'État membre requis permettant de refuser la reconnaissance et l'exécution, dans cet État membre, d'une telle décision rendue dans un autre État membre.

La Cour suprême de Lettonie a, toutefois, jugé que les motifs d'ordre public, aux termes de l'article 34, point 1, du règlement Bruxelles I, justifient le refus de reconnaissance et exécution d'une décision des juridictions de Lituanie[17]. En particulier, la Cour suprême de Lettonie a considéré, en

15 Pour une analyse des motifs d'ordre public pour ne pas reconnaître une décision étrangère, cf. M. Weller, « Mutual Trust : in search of the future of European Union private international law », *Journal of Private International Law*, 2015, pp. 97 et 98; ainsi que E.-A. Oprea, *Droit de l'Union européenne et lois de police*, 2015, pp. 428 à 434.

16 Arrêt du 23 octobre 2014, *flyLAL-Lithuanian Airlines*, C-302/13, EU:C:2014:2319.

17 Affaire n° SKC 5/2015.

premier lieu, que la sécurité de l'État, aux termes de l'article 1 de la Constitution de la République de Lettonie constitue une importante raison pour soulever une exception d'ordre public. En second lieu, cette Cour a reconnu que les droit fondamentaux, proclamés par la Constitution, et notamment ceux établis sur les articles 91 et 105, font partie de l'ordre public letton.

La seconde décision, que j'aimerais mentionner, rendue le 19 juillet 2018, concerne le refus du Bundesgerichtshof de reconnaître une décision de justice polonaise pour violation de l'ordre public, en s'appuyant en particulier sur les droits à la liberté d'expression et à la liberté de la presse[18].

Dans l'affaire au principal, suite à la publication par la chaîne publique d'information allemande, *Zweites Deutsches Fernsehen* (« ZDF »), d'un documentaire concernant les camps d'extermination de Majdanek et Auschwitz, dans lequel ceux-ci étaient définis comme les « camps polonais », la ZDF a été condamnée par la Cour d'appel de Cracovie à s'excuser et corriger une telle affirmation par publication sur son site internet d'un texte prédéterminé. La demande de reconnaissance de la décision de la juridiction polonaise en Allemagne a été, toutefois, rejetée au motif qu'elle violait l'article 5 de la loi fondamentale relatif au droit constitutionnel à la liberté d'expression et à la liberté de la presse ainsi que le principe constitutionnel de proportionnalité.

3. *Le principe de confiance mutuelle illustré dans la jurisprudence de la Cour*

En se rapprochant du fil conducteur de la riche contribution du directeur du Max Planck Institute Luxembourg, M. le professeur Hess, et en ligne avec les remarques de M. le professeur Labayle, dans sa contribution récente à l'honneur de M. l'ancien vice-président de la Cour de justice Tizzano, qui disait que « le principe de confiance mutuelle a acquis ses lettres de noblesse grâce à la jurisprudence de la Cour »[19], force est de constater

18 IX ZB 1O/18, du 19 juillet 2018, disponible sous le lien suivant : http://juris.bundesgerichtshof.de/cgi-bin/rechtsprechung/document.py?Gericht=bgh&Art=en&sid=97febcf2a2b66c60d9b9cbd50b35a6a4&nr=86838&pos=0&anz=2.

19 H. Labayle, « Faut-il faire confiance à la confiance mutuelle? », *Liber amicorum Antonio Tizzano, De la Cour CECA à la Cour de l'Union : le long parcours de la justice européenne*, G. Giappichelli Editore, 2018, p.472.

que la jurisprudence de la Cour de justice a fait, pendant toutes ces années, corps avec les textes législatifs[20].

À cet égard, je souhaite rappeler les arrêts *Prism Investment*[21], *Diageo Brands*[22] ainsi que *Lebek*[23], en ce qui concerne la portée du principe de confiance mutuelle et l'interprétation *stricte* des motifs de refus de reconnaissance des décisions dans le cadre du règlement Bruxelles I, ainsi que les deux arrêts du 9 mars 2017, *Pula Parking*[24] et *Zulfikarpašić*[25], illustrant la mesure dans laquelle le principe de confiance entre les juridictions des États membres a fondé l'interprétation des divers instruments de la coopération judiciaire en matière civile.

3.1. Le principe de confiance mutuelle et la reconnaissance des décisions

D'une part, l'affaire *Prism Investment* offre un exemple intéressant de l'interprétation restrictive que la Cour de justice a donné aux motifs de refus de la reconnaissance des décisions dans le cadre du règlement Bruxelles I. Cela s'inscrit dans la logique du contrôle restreint mis en place par ce règlement, qui repose sur le principe de confiance mutuelle[26].

Le Hoge Raad der Nederlanden avait interrogé la Cour sur le point de savoir si le juge de l'État membre requis pouvait refuser ou révoquer la déclaration constatant la force exécutoire d'une décision adoptée dans l'État membre d'origine (ici, la Belgique) pour des motifs autres que ceux prévus aux articles 34 et 35 du règlement n° 44/2001 (actuellement, 44 et 45 du règlement Bruxelles I bis). La Cour a jugé que le refus d'accorder la reconnaissance des décisions ne peut être fondé que sur les motifs limitativement énumérés aux articles 34 et 35 du règlement Bruxelles I, afin de consentir, sur la base d'une confiance mutuelle dans la justice des États membres, à ce que la décision émise par une juridiction d'un État membre

20 B. Ancel, « Les cinquante ans de la Convention de Bruxelles du 27 septembre 1968 concernant la compétence judiciaire et l'exécution des décisions en matière civile et commerciale », *REDI*, vol. 70, 2018, p. 19.

21 Arrêt du 13 octobre 2011, *Prism Investments*, C-139/10, EU:C:2011:653.

22 Arrêt du 16 juillet 2015, *Diageo Brands*, C-681/13, EU:C:2015:471.

23 Arrêt du 7 juillet 2016, *Lebek*, C-70/15, EU:C:2016:524.

24 Arrêt du 9 mars 2017, *Pula Parking*, C-551/15, EU:C:2017:193.

25 Arrêt du 9 mars 2017, *Zulfikarpašić*, C-484/15, EU:C:2017:199.

26 Cf. L. Idot, « Étendue du contrôle de l'exequatur », *Revue Europe*, n° 12, Décembre 2011, comm. 500; B. Hess, « The Brussels I Regulation : Recent Case Law of the Court of Justice and the Commission Common's Proposed Recast », *Common Market Law Review*, 49, 2012, pp. 1094 et 1095.

autre que l'État membre requis soit exécutée dans ce dernier au moyen de son insertion dans l'ordre juridique de celui-ci[27].

D'autre part, les arrêts *Diageo Brands* et *Lebek*, mentionnés par M. le Professeur Hess, mettent en exergue la nécessité d'assurer un juste équilibre entre le principe de confiance réciproque et le droit à une protection juridictionnelle effective.

Dans *Diageo Brands*, une société néerlandaise invoquait l'article 34, point 1, du règlement n° 44/2001 (contrariété à l'ordre public néerlandais) afin de s'opposer à la reconnaissance au Pays-Bas d'une décision de justice bulgare. Cette société soutenait que la juridiction d'origine avait fait une application manifestement erronée du droit de l'Union, en se fondant sur une décision de la Cour suprême de cassation bulgare qui aurait été adoptée en méconnaissance de l'obligation de poser à la Cour de justice une question préjudicielle. Saisie dans ce contexte, le Hoge Raad a interrogé la Cour sur le point de savoir, en premier lieu, si l'article 34, point 1, du règlement n° 44/2001, qui prévoit l'ordre publique de l'État requis comme motif de refus de la reconnaissance, vise aussi le cas où la décision judiciaire d'origine aurait été manifestement contraire au droit de l'Union et; en second lieu, si le juge de l'État membre requis doit tenir compte du fait que la personne qui s'oppose à cette reconnaissance n'a pas exercé les voies de recours prévues par la législation de l'État membre d'origine.

La Cour a commencé son raisonnement en rappelant que le principe de la confiance mutuelle entre les États membres, qui a, dans le droit de l'Union, une importance fondamentale, impose, notamment en ce qui concerne l'espace de liberté, de sécurité et de justice, à chacun de ces États de considérer, sauf dans des circonstances exceptionnelles, que tous les autres États membres respectent le droit de l'Union et, tout particulièrement, les droits fondamentaux reconnus par ce droit[28].

Elle retient ensuite, en se référant à l'arrêt *flyLAL-Lithuanian Airlines*[29], qu'un recours à la clause de l'ordre public, figurant à l'article 34, point 1, du règlement nº 44/2001, n'est concevable que dans l'hypothèse où la reconnaissance de la décision rendue dans un autre État membre heurterait de manière inacceptable l'ordre juridique de l'État requis, en tant qu'elle porterait atteinte à un principe fondamental. Afin de respecter la prohibition de la révision au fond de la décision rendue dans un autre État membre, l'atteinte devrait constituer une violation manifeste d'une

27 Arrêt du 13 octobre 2011, *Prism Investments*, C-139/10, EU:C:2011:653.
28 Arrêt du 16 juillet 2015, *Diageo Brands*, C-681/13, EU:C:2015:471, point 40.
29 Arrêt du 23 octobre 2014, *flyLAL-Lithuanian Airlines*, C-302/13, EU:C:2014:2319.

règle de droit considérée comme essentielle dans l'ordre juridique de l'État requis ou d'un droit reconnu comme fondamental dans cet ordre juridique[30] ou encore, que « le juge de l'État requis ne saurait, sous peine de remettre en cause la finalité du règlement nº 44/2001, refuser la reconnaissance d'une décision émanant d'un autre État membre au seul motif qu'il estime que, dans cette décision, le droit national ou le droit de l'Union a été mal appliqué. Il importe, au contraire, de considérer que, dans de tels cas, le système des voies de recours mis en place dans chaque État membre, complété par le mécanisme du renvoi préjudiciel prévu à l'article 267 TFUE, fournit aux justiciables une garantie suffisante »[31].

Le bémol nécessaire a été retrouvé dans le litige ayant donné lieu à l'arrêt *Lebek*, où un juste équilibre entre la confiance réciproque dans la justice au sein de l'Union et le respect du droit de la défense a été posé. Ainsi, en renvoyant à l'arrêt *Trade Agency*[32], la Cour a jugé que l'article 34, point 2, du règlement Bruxelles I vise à assurer le respect des droits du défendeur défaillant au cours de la procédure ouverte dans l'État membre d'origine, à travers un système de double contrôle[33]. En vertu de ce système, le juge de l'État membre requis est tenu de refuser ou de révoquer, en cas de recours, l'exécution d'une décision étrangère rendue par défaut, si l'acte introductif d'instance ou un acte équivalent n'a pas été signifié ou notifié au défendeur défaillant en temps utile et de telle manière que celui-ci puisse se défendre, à moins qu'il n'ait pas exercé un recours contre cette décision devant les juridictions de l'État membre d'origine, alors qu'il était en mesure de le faire.

3.2. *Le principe de confiance mutuelle dans l'administration de la justice et la notion de « juridiction »*

Deux arrêts récents, rendus le même jour par la Cour de justice, le 9 mars 2017, *Pula Parking* et *Zulfikarpašić*, illustrent l'importance du principe de confiance mutuelle dans le cadre de la coopération en matière civile et commerciale. Les deux affaires concernent la même procédure croate d'obtention d'un titre exécutoire mais au regard d'instruments juridiques distincts, à savoir le règlement Bruxelles I bis et le règlement nº 805/2004,

30 Arrêt du 16 juillet 2015, *Diageo Brands*, C-681/13, EU:C:2015:471, point 44.

31 *Id.*, point 49 et jurisprudence citée.

32 Arrêt du 6 septembre 2012, *Trade Agency*, C-619/10, EU:C:2012:531, point 32.

33 Arrêt du 7 juillet 2016, *Lebek*, C-70/15, EU:C:2016:524, point 39.

portant création d'un titre exécutoire européen pour les créances incontestées.

La problématique centrale commune dans ces deux affaires concernait la question de savoir si les notaires croates relevaient de la notion de « juridiction ». Les débats sur cette notion étaient nés de l'absence d'une définition de la « juridiction » dans les deux règlements, ainsi que de leur structure qui assimile, dans les procédures concernant les injonctions de payer, d'autres autorités, à savoir les notaires hongrois et les autorités chargées du recouvrement forcé en Suède.

La Cour a décidé que les notaires, en Croatie, agissant dans le cadre des compétences qui leur sont dévolues par le droit national dans les procédures d'exécution forcée sur le fondement d'un « document faisant foi », ne relèvent pas de la notion de « juridiction » au sens desdits règlements.

Son raisonnement a été principalement fondé sur les principes de confiance mutuelle entre les États membres et de reconnaissance mutuelle des décisions judiciaires, qui ont été identifiés comme étant d'une importance fondamentale puisqu'ils permettent la création et le maintien d'un espace sans frontières intérieures[34]. En appliquant ces principes dans le contexte spécifique du règlement Bruxelles I bis, la Cour a indiqué que ceux-ci « se traduisent par le traitement et l'exécution des décisions judiciaires des juridictions d'un État membre comme si celles-ci avaient été rendues dans l'État membre dans lequel l'exécution est demandée »[35]. Elle a jugé que le règlement Bruxelles I bis, « dont la base juridique est l'article 67, paragraphe 4, TFUE visant à faciliter l'accès à la justice, notamment par le principe de reconnaissance mutuelle des décisions judiciaires, tend ainsi [...] à renforcer le système simplifié et efficace des règles de conflit, de reconnaissance et d'exécution des décisions judiciaires [...] afin de faciliter la coopération judiciaire en vue de contribuer à réaliser l'objectif assigné à l'Union de devenir un espace de liberté, de sécurité et de justice, en se fondant sur le degré de confiance élevé qui doit exister entre les États membres »[36].

Le principe de la confiance mutuelle a également fondé l'interprétation de la notion de « juridiction » dans le contexte du règlement n° 805/2004[37].

---

34 Arrêt du 9 mars 2017, *Pula Parking*, C-551/15, EU:C:2017:193, point 51.

35 *Id.*, point 52.

36 *Id.*, point 53.

37 Arrêt du 9 mars 2017, *Zulfikarpašić*, C-484/15, EU:C:2017:199, point 43. Pour un commentaire, v. *inter alia* : F. Mélin, « Notion de juridiction au sens du règlement sur le titre exécutoire européen », *Dalloz actualité* 22 mars 2017.

La Cour a précisé, ainsi qu'il ressort du considérant 3 du règlement n° 805/2004, que le principe de la reconnaissance mutuelle des décisions judiciaires, qui repose notamment sur la confiance mutuelle dans l'administration de la justice dans les États membres, constitue la pierre angulaire de la création d'un véritable espace judiciaire européen[38].

En effet, le principe de confiance mutuelle présuppose que les décisions dont l'exécution est demandée dans un État membre autre que celui d'origine ont été rendues dans une procédure judiciaire offrant des garanties d'indépendance et d'impartialité ainsi que le respect du principe du contradictoire[39]. La reconnaissance en tant que « juridiction » des seules autorités nationales qui respectent ces critères, découlant notamment de l'article 47 de la Charte des droits fondamentaux de l'Union européenne, semble être essentielle pour le maintien de la confiance entre les juridictions nationales dans l'espace de liberté, de sécurité et de justice[40]. Autrement dit, les tribunaux de l'État membre requis reconnaissent une décision étrangère sur la base de la confiance dans le fait que les tribunaux de l'État membre d'origine respectent le droit à une protection juridictionnelle effective.

Si la Cour est arrivée à une définition de la notion de « juridiction » pouvant être qualifiée de restrictive[41], en excluant de son champ d'application les notaires en Croatie, par ces deux arrêts, elle a redonné à la confiance mutuelle son véritable sens.

---

38 *Id.*, point 40.

39 Arrêt du 9 mars 2017, *Zulfikarpašić*, C-484/15, EU:C:2017:199, point 44.

40 V., en ce sens, arrêt du 25 juillet 2018, *Minister for Justice and Equality (Défaillances du système judiciaire)*, C-216/18 PPU, EU:C:2018:586, p. 48.

41 L. Pailler, « "Juridiction" en droit international privé de l'Union européenne », *Revue critique de droit international privé*, 2017, p. 472.

4. Conclusion

Il y a 50 ans, la Convention de Bruxelles a été signée. L'ancienneté des débats sur le principe de confiance mutuelle dans le cadre de la coopération en matière civile et commerciale n'a pas préjugé la contemporanéité des réflexions à ce sujet.

Dans une Union européenne qui doit faire face aux défis actuels[42], le principe de confiance mutuelle acquit une importance croissante, tout en constituant la prémisse de l'unité d'un espace de droit commun, issu de la diversité des systèmes juridiques des États membres.

Luxembourg, the 12th of October 2018

42 Pour une analyse sur les défis dans la coopération judiciaire en matière civile après le Brexit, v. E. Crawford et J. Carruthers, « Brexit : The impact on judicial cooperation in civil matters having cross-border implications – A British perspective », *European Papers*, vol. 3, n° 1, 2018, pp. 183–202.

De l'encadrement de l'ordre public procédural des États membres à l'ordre procédural autonome de l'Union

Marek Safjan[*] et Dominik Düsterhaus[**]

Table of Contents

1. Introduction

Dans cette petite contribution, nous souhaitons exposer comment le régime de reconnaissance et d'exécution sous la convention et le règlement de Bruxelles, tel qu'interprété par la Cour de justice de l'Union européenne (CJUE), s'insère dans une optique plus large qui est la protection juridictionnelle effective au sein de l'Union.

Plus particulièrement, s'agissant du régime commun de reconnaissance et d'exécution, nous allons retracer l'évolution de l'appréciation, au titre de l'ordre public, de la régularité procédurale d'une décision émanant d'un autre État membre. Alors que, dans un premier temps, cette appréciation a été encadrée de manière souple par la CJUE, elle est désormais soumise à des conditions procédurales plus strictes. Fondée sur l'idée de la confiance mutuelle et la compétence primordiale de l'État membre d'origine pour une protection juridictionnelle effective et équitable, cette formalisation du régime de reconnaissance et d'exécution est une belle illustration tant de l'architecture que de la philosophie juridictionnelle dans l'Union européenne. Là où les conceptions nationales divergentes de l'ordre public

---

* Juge[x] à la Cour de justice de l'Union européenne.

** Référendaire à la Cour de justice de l'Union européenne. Les auteurs s'expriment à titre strictement personnel et tiennent à remercier Mme Rachel Bernardi pour son aide précieuse dans l'élaboration du manuscrit.

pourraient freiner la libre circulation des décisions, le droit de l'Union impose une obligation procédurale dont les contours sont sujets à l'interprétation de la CJUE.

L'on pourrait néanmoins considérer, au vu des compétences limitées de l'Union en ce qui concerne l'organisation et la qualité de la justice dans les États membres, que la régularité procédurale d'une décision émanant d'un autre État membre ne devrait jamais être soustraite au regard des juridictions de l'État membre d'exécution, susceptibles de relever d'éventuels défauts procéduraux dans l'État membre d'émission. À cet égard, on soulignera le rôle fondamental que l'article 19 TUE a vocation à jouer pour garantir la qualité de la justice dans tous les États membres, permettant ainsi l'émergence éventuelle d'un ordre procédural autonome de l'Union européenne.

2. *Confiance mutuelle et double contrôle de la régularité procédurale*

Le principe « constitutionnel » de la confiance mutuelle[1] est devenu un leitmotiv de la coopération judiciaire au sein de l'Union européenne. Inscrit dans le considérant 16 du règlement Bruxelles I en 2001, ce principe fut valorisé pour la première fois dans l'arrêt *Gasser*[2] dans lequel la Cour releva que la confiance mutuelle inspirait déjà la convention de Bruxelles.

C'est ce principe de confiance mutuelle qui a permis l'établissement d'un système obligatoire d'attribution de compétence en matière civile et commerciale au sein de l'Union européenne. Corollairement, la confiance mutuelle a facilité la renonciation par les États membres au droit d'appliquer leurs règles internes sur la reconnaissance et l'exécution des jugements étrangers en faveur d'un mécanisme simplifié de reconnaissance et d'exécution des jugements.

Cependant, ni les Traités ni le droit dérivé ne définissent le principe de confiance mutuelle qui imprègne aujourd'hui l'espace européen de liberté, sécurité et justice (ELSJ). Selon l'avis 2/13, la confiance mutuelle requiert que les États membres se considèrent entre eux, à l'exception de circonstances exceptionnelles, comme appliquant le droit de l'Union européenne et en particulier les droits fondamentaux reconnus par ce droit. Ainsi, les

---

1 *D. Düsterhaus*, In the Court(s) We Trust – A Procedural Solution to the Mutual Trust Dilemma [2017] Freedom, Security and Justice: European Legal Studies, 26 – 44.

2 Aff. C-116/02 *Erich Gasser GmbH v MISAT Srl* [EU:C:2010:430] point 72.

États membres peuvent être tenus, en vertu de ce même droit, de présumer le respect des droits fondamentaux par les autres États membres, de sorte qu'il ne leur est pas possible, non seulement d'exiger d'un autre État membre un niveau national de protection des droits fondamentaux plus élevé que celui assuré par le droit de l'Union, mais également, sauf dans des cas exceptionnels, de vérifier si cet autre État membre a effectivement respecté, dans un cas concret, les droits fondamentaux garantis par l'Union[3].

Certes, dans le domaine de la coopération judiciaire en matière civile, la confiance mutuelle est à la base d'une pluralité de régimes de reconnaissance et d'exécution des jugements[4]. Or, pour ce qui nous intéresse à présent, le plus ancien et plus commun de ces régimes, à savoir celui issu de la convention de Bruxelles, permet de refuser la reconnaissance et l'exécution d'une décision judiciaire étrangère dans des cas restreints, lesquels étaient prévus aux articles 34 et 35 du règlement Bruxelles I et le sont toujours à l'article 45 du règlement refondu n° 1215/2012 (Bruxelles Ibis)[5].

S'agissant des motifs de refus tirés d'une violation du droit à un procès équitable, un régime binaire a été instauré. Le premier (article 45(1)(a) de Bruxelles Ibis) soumet les conceptions nationales de l'ordre public, dont l'équité procédurale, à un contrôle restreint de la CJUE. Le second volet (article 45(1)(b) de Bruxelles Ibis) établit un standard autonome, propre au droit de l'Union, pour ce qui concerne les défauts de notification.

2.1. *L'ordre public (procédural)*

La clause d'ordre public de l'article 45(1)(a) de Bruxelles Ibis, qui ne vise pas expressément les irrégularités procédurales, et qui s'efface[6] derrière l'article 45(1)(b) en matière de défaut de notification, permet aux juges de fonder leur refus de reconnaissance ou d'exécution d'un jugement sur la violation manifeste d'un principe fondamental de leur ordre juridique. Il a

---

3 Avis 2/13, EU:C:2014:2454, points 191–192.

4 *D. Düsterhaus*, Judicial Coherence in the AFSJ – Squaring Mutual Trust with Effective Judicial Protection, [2015] Review of European Administrative Law, n. 2, pp. 151 – 182.

5 À noter que la nécessité d'obtenir une déclaration constatant la force exécutoire qui soit attaquable par le débiteur au jugement, a été abandonnée sous Bruxelles Ibis. Le débiteur doit désormais formuler une demande de refus d'exécution.

6 Le contrôle au titre des deux clauses peut cependant occasionnellement converger. Voir aff. C-619/10 *Trade Agency* [EU:C:2012:531].

été constaté que la plupart des rares applications de l'exception d'ordre public dans le cadre des procédures judiciaires sont liées à des aspects procéduraux[7]. Tandis que les États membres sont en principe libres de déterminer selon leurs conceptions nationales les exigences de leur ordre public, les limites imposées par ces exigences sur la reconnaissance ou l'exécution d'une décision peuvent être contrôlées par la CJUE[8].

Dans l'arrêt *Krombach*[9], la CJUE a établi un standard de recours à la clause de l'ordre public selon lequel le recours à cette clause doit être possible lorsque le défendeur n'a pas été protégé d'une violation manifeste du droit à se faire défendre devant la cour d'origine de la décision. Dans l'arrêt *Gambazzi*[10], la CJUE insiste sur le contrôle, au regard des droits de la défense, d'une mesure procédurale d'exclusion ('debarment order') qui résulte en un jugement sur les prétentions du requérant, sans que le défendeur ne soit entendu. Dans la même tendance, la CJUE a relevé dans son arrêt *Trade Agency* que la clause d'ordre public autorise une juridiction à refuser l'exécution d'un jugement par défaut qui ne contient aucune appréciation ni sur l'objet ni sur le fondement du recours et qui est dépourvue de tout argument sur le bien-fondé de celui-ci. Il en est de même lorsqu'il apparait au juge national après une appréciation globale de la procédure et au regard de toutes les circonstances pertinentes, que la décision est une violation manifeste et disproportionnée du droit du défendeur à un procès équitable, du fait de l'impossibilité de former un recours effectif et approprié contre celui-ci[11].

Notons que, dans l'ensemble de ces cas, le droit de l'Union européenne n'avait pas encadré les procédures dans l'État membre d'émission, menées selon les règles procédurales nationales. Or, à l'étape de l'exécution, la clause d'ordre public a pu autoriser, sous le contrôle de la CJUE, le blocage de l'exécution des décisions issues de ces procédures, en raison de garanties procédurales fondamentales reconnues dans l'État membre d'exécution. À ce titre, il est intéressant de s'interroger sur le point de savoir si le droit européen inspire un standard commun en matière d'ordre public procédu-

7 Voir *B. Hess, T. Pfeiffer*, Interprétation of the Public Policy Exception in EU Instruments of Private International and Procedural Law, Commissioned by the European Parliament [2011] PE 453.189, 58.

8 Aff. C-420/07 *Apostolides* [EU:C:2009:271] point 57.

9 Aff. C-7/98 *Krombach* [EU:C:2000:164].

10 Aff. C-394/07 *Gambazzi* [EU:C:2009:219] points 28 – 32 and 48.

11 Aff. C-619/10 *Trade Agency* [EU:C:2012:531].

ral, qui pourrait être la première étape vers un ordre procédural autonome de l'Union.[12]

2.2. *Les défauts de notification*

Selon l'article 45(1)(b) de Bruxelles 1(bis), une décision ne doit pas être reconnue lorsqu'elle a été rendue par défaut, si l'acte introductif d'instance ou un acte équivalent n'a pas été notifié au défendeur en temps utile et de telle manière qu'il puisse se défendre, à moins[13] qu'il n'ait pas exercé de recours à l'encontre de la décision alors qu'il était en mesure de le faire. Ces conditions ont déjà été interprétées par la CJUE, notamment dans l'arrêt *ASML Netherlands*[14], qui concernait la possibilité d'attaquer un jugement dans son État membre d'origine. Le juge de l'État requis doit, selon cet arrêt, déterminer si le défendeur avait pu prendre connaissance du contenu de l'acte introductif d'instance, celui-ci lui ayant été transmis dans un délai suffisant pour lui permettre de préparer sa défense devant les juges nationaux.

La particularité de l'article 45(1)(b) de Bruxelles Ibis est qu'il requiert dans certaines situations une seconde appréciation du standard européen du procès équitable, car l'article 28 du règlement Bruxelles Ibis et le règlement n°1393/2007[15], dans leurs champs d'application respectifs, protègent les défendeurs qui ne sont pas domiciliés dans l'État membre d'origine, d'une décision rendue par défaut à leur encontre sans qu'ils aient été correctement notifiés de la procédure. Précisons néanmoins que, sous l'empire du règlement Bruxelles Ibis, il est tout de même possible de rendre un jugement par défaut, tant que cela apparait proportionnel au regard des droits procéduraux de chacune des parties. C'est la leçon des arrêts *Hypotečni Banka*[16] et *G*[17]. Aux deux étapes d'appréciation du standard du procès équitable ainsi requises, par la juridiction d'émission puis

12 Voir, *J. Basedow*, Die Verselbständigung des europäischen ordre public in M. Coester e.a. (éd.), Privatrecht in Europa. Vielfalt, Kollision, Kooperation; Festschrift Sonnenberger (2004) p. 291.

13 Cette condition distingue le régime en vigueur au titre du règlement Bruxelles I de celui en vigueur au titre de la Convention de Bruxelles de 1968.

14 Aff. C-283/05 *ASML Netherlands BV* [EU:C:2006:787] point 49.

15 Voir sur ce point Aff. C-70/15 *Lebek*, [EU:C:2016:524].

16 Aff. C-327/10 *Hypotečni Banka* [EU:C:2011:745] points 49 – 54.

17 Aff. C-292/10 *G* [EU:C:2012:142].

par celle statuant sur un refus d'exécution, l'article 47 de la Charte constitue la référence[18].

3. Procéduralisation du refus d'exécution sous les auspices de la CJUE

Depuis l'arrêt *Diageo Brands*[19], les conditions de refus dans ces deux hypothèses, de défaut de notification, d'une part, et de considérations d'ordre public, d'autre part, ont convergé. Ainsi, la CJUE requiert à présent également dans le contexte des considérations d'ordre public que les individus concernés usent de toute voie de recours dans le but de prévenir toute violation de l'ordre public, à l'exception des circonstances dans lesquelles il est trop difficile voire impossible d'utiliser les voies de recours de l'État membre d'origine.

Cette avancée de la CJUE peut paraître audacieuse. En effet, peu de temps après le refus du législateur d'abandonner l'exception d'ordre public sous le règlement Bruxelles Ibis[20], la CJUE rapproche davantage le régime d'exécution de ce dernier des régimes spécifiques établis par les règlements relatifs à la création d'un Titre exécutoire européen[21], au règlement des petits litiges[22], à la procédure européenne d'injonction de payer[23] et aux obligations alimentaires[24]. Ceux-ci prévoient des voies de recours exclusivement dans l'État membre d'origine, une idée que la Cour a également sou-

---

18 Voir en détail, *D. Düsterhaus*, Procedural Primacy and Effective Judicial Protection : A Trilogue, Case C-112/13 *A v B and Others* EU:C:2014:2195 [2016] MJECL, 317.

19 Aff. C-681/13 *Diageo Brands* [EU:C:2015:471] point 64.

20 Voir en detail, *X. Kramer*, Cross-Border Enforcement and the Brussels I-Bis Regulation: Towards a New Balance between Mutual Trust and National Control over Fundamental Rights, Netherlands International Law Review 2013, p. 347.

21 Règlement (CE) n° 805/2004 du Parlement européen et du Conseil du 21 avril 2004 portant création d'un titre exécutoire européen pour les créances incontestées (OJ 2004 L 143, p. 15) (ci-après le « règlement TEE »).

22 Règlement (CE) n° 861/2007 du Parlement Européen et du Conseil du 11 juillet 2007 instituant une procédure européenne de règlement des petits litiges (OJ 2007 L 199, p. 1).

23 Règlement (CE) n° 1896/2006 du Parlement européen et du Conseil du 12 décembre 2006 instituant une procédure européenne d'injonction de payer (OJ 2006 L 399, p. 1).

24 Règlement (CE) n° 4/2009 du Conseil du 18 décembre 2008 relatif à la compétence, la loi applicable, la reconnaissance et l'exécution des décisions et la coopération en matière d'obligations alimentaires (OJ 2009 L 7, p. 1).

lignée dans le contexte du règlement Bruxelles IIbis[25,26]. Ainsi, bien qu'ayant auparavant loué les vertus du contrôle par l'État membre requis[27], la Cour semble aujourd'hui évoluer vers une approche plus cohérente de l'exécution transfrontalière parmi les différents instruments de coopération judiciaire, ce qui a été fortement conseillé par la doctrine[28]. Il peut en effet sembler pertinent de laisser l'État membre d'origine assurer le respect de la CEDH et de la Charte par la décision en cause[29].

L'obligation inconditionnelle d'épuiser toutes les voies de recours peut cependant être problématique en ce qu'elle peut, dans certaines circonstances, faire peser une charge trop lourde sur le débiteur. Bien que portant spécifiquement sur l'hypothèse d'un défaut de notification (article 34, paragraphe 2, du règlement Bruxelles I), l'affaire *Lebek*[30] est très instructive à cet égard.

M. Lebek voulait faire exécuter, en Pologne, un jugement français à l'encontre de M. Domino, auquel l'acte introductif d'instance n'avait pas été signifié et qui n'a eu connaissance du jugement à son encontre que plus d'un an après le prononcé. Au vu de l'impossibilité pour M. Domino de se défendre dans la procédure initiale, le tribunal régional de Jelenia Góra (Pologne) n'a pas reconnu la force exécutoire de ce jugement. Ultérieurement, M. Lebek a introduit une seconde requête, en soulevant que la signification du jugement français à M. Domino a entre-temps été effectuée conformément aux dispositions du règlement n° 1393/2007, accompagnée d'une instruction selon laquelle M. Domino pouvait demander le relevé de la forclusion résultant de l'expiration du délai, dans les deux mois suivant la signification du jugement concerné. Le tribunal régional de Jelenia Góra a donc déclaré exécutoire en Pologne le jugement français, en considérant que le respect du droit de se défendre avait été garanti. Saisie de l'affaire, la Cour suprême polonaise a finalement interrogé la CJUE sur le point de savoir si l'article 34, point 2, du règlement Bruxelles I, en tant qu'il mentionne le fait d'être en mesure d'exercer un recours, vise également la situa-

25 Règlement (CE) n° 2201/2003 du Conseil du 27 novembre 2003 relatif à la compétence, la reconnaissance et l'exécution des décisions en matière matrimoniale et en matière de responsabilité parentale abrogeant le règlement (CE) n° 1347/2000 (OJ 2003 L 338, p. 1).

26 Aff. C-491/10 *Aguirre Zarraga* [EU:C:2010:828].

27 Aff. C-327/10 *Hypotečni Banka* [EU:C:2011:745] point 54.

28 Voir A. *Frąnckowiak-Adamska*, Time for a European 'full faith and credit clause' [2015] CMLR 191.

29 Voir en détail, *D. Düsterhaus*, The ECtHR, the CJEU and the AFSJ: A Matter of Mutual Trust, ELRev [2017] 338.

30 Aff. C-70/15 *Lebek*, [EU:C:2016:524].

tion dans laquelle un tel recours présuppose d'obtenir un relevé de la forclusion.

Alors que l'avocat général Kokott avait considéré que la possibilité d'exercer un recours contre un jugement doit être interprétée de façon stricte et notamment ne pas couvrir les situations dans lesquelles, les délais étant dépassés, il est toutefois possible de présenter une demande tendant au relevé de la forclusion, puis, de former un recours une fois cette demande accueillie[31], la Cour s'est montrée plus exigeante en posant l'obligation d'introduire une demande tendant au relevé de la forclusion[32].

Malgré ses mérites incontestables, il semblerait que l'approche de l'épuisement des voies de recours ne fournisse pas de protection effective dans le cas d'un système judiciaire structurellement défaillant dans l'État membre d'émission du jugement[33]. Une partie au litige serait-elle obligée de former un recours contre une décision inéquitable même lorsque son échec est certain, notamment au vu d'un manque d'indépendance et d'impartialité au sein des juridictions civiles?

Qui plus est, la nécessité d'épuiser les voies de recours avant de pouvoir s'opposer à l'exécution d'un jugement pourrait réduire davantage les opportunités pour la CJUE d'exercer son contrôle sur les limites de l'utilisation de la clause d'ordre public. Dès lors que, en raison de cette exigence procédurale, moins de juridictions auront à apprécier le respect du droit au procès équitable dans l'État membre d'émission, une éventuelle divergence des standards parmi les États membres risque de subsister[34].

Ajoutons que ce danger est également présent dans le champ d'application des instruments d'exécution automatique dont il a été fait mention plus haut, qui permettent des voies de recours exclusivement dans l'État membre d'émission. Certes, ces instruments, au contraire de l'article 45(1)(a) du règlement Bruxelles qui illustre parfaitement l'absence d'harmonisation, prévoient des exigences minimales en matière de notification, de garanties procédurales et de voies de recours. Cependant, le respect de ces

---

31 Conclusions du 7 Avril 2016 dans l'affaire C-70/15 [EU:C:2016:226].

32 Voir le point 49 de l'arrêt C-70/15 *Lebek*, [EU:C:2016:524].

33 *D. Düsterhaus*, Effective remedies and fair trial in civil matters: How to Promote Justice within the Confines of EU Powers, in: *S. Iglesias Sánchez* et *M. Pascual*, Fundamental Rights in the AFSJ (à paraître).

34 Voir *D. Düsterhaus*, Constitutionalisation of European Civil Procedure as a Starting Point for Harmonisation? in F. Gascón Inchausti et B. Hess, The Future of the European Law of Civil Procedure, Coordination or Harmonisation (2020) pp. 69 ss.

exigences est contrôlé uniquement par les juges de l'État membre d'origine, qui ne sont pas toujours enclins à impliquer la CJUE[35].

Cela étant, il faut souligner que l'approche visant à limiter le contrôle de la régularité procédurale d'une décision au stade de son exécution est en soi viable et sensée dans une Union composée d'États ayant souscrit à la CEDH, et que la Cour de Strasbourg vient d'avaliser l'exigence d'épuisement des voies de recours dans l'État membre d'origine[36]. Au vu de l'objectif commun de ces États de réaliser un espace de libre circulation non seulement de tous les facteurs économiques mais également des décisions judiciaires, le contrôle desdites décisions au regard de l'ordre public semble quelque peu anachronique et est peu utilisé en pratique[37]. Les clauses d'ordre public ne semblent pas favoriser l'émergence d'un espace judiciaire commun, d'autant moins que le bon fonctionnement du régime originellement mis en place par la Convention de Bruxelles et largement[38] conservé par le règlement Bruxelles I dépend de la supervision par la CJUE des limites à l'imposition par l'État requis de son ordre public à l'État d'origine et aux parties au litige. Or, la plupart des quelques décisions de la CJUE dans lesquelles elle a exercé un tel contrôle n'ont donné que des instructions assez générales[39] au lieu d'élaborer un standard uniforme[40].

À cet égard, l'approche visant à faire de l'épuisement des voies de recours dans l'État membre d'émission une condition nécessaire d'un éventuel refus d'exécution pourrait se révéler bénéfique. En se donnant un droit de regard sur l'organisation et le déroulement des voies de recours, la CJUE pourrait largement contribuer à une protection juridictionnelle effective et équitable dans les États membres. C'est dans ce sens qu'il faut comprendre le rappel que

35 Voir, pour un cas d'exception l'aff. C-300/14 *Imtech Marine Belgium* [EU:C:2015:825].

36 Cour EDH (GC) *Avotiņš* v *Latvia*, Appl. No. 17502/07.

37 Voir *B. Hess / T. Pfeiffer*, Interpretation of the Public Policy Exception in EU Instruments of Private International and Procedural Law, Commissioned by the European Parliament [2011] PE 453.189, 58.

38 Article 34(1) du règlement Bruxelles I a en effet introduit l'exigence selon laquelle un refus pour défaut de notification est soumis à la formation de tous les recours possibles dans l'État membre d'origine.

39 Voir, par exemple, Aff. C-619/10 *Trade Agency* [EU:C:2012:531].

40 Voir cependant M. *Safjan* et *D. Düsterhaus*, A Union of Effective Judicial Protection : Addressing a Multi-level Challenge through the Lens of Article 47 CFREU [2014] Oxford Yearbook of European Law, pp. 3 – 40 pour un exposé de la méthode inductive et transversale d'élaboration d'un standard autonome.

« tout État membre doit assurer que les instances relevant, en tant que "juridiction", au sens défini par le droit de l'Union, de son système de voies de recours dans les domaines couverts par le droit de l'Union satisfont aux exigences d'une protection juridictionnelle effective »[41]?

4. *Vers un contrôle strict des conditions du procès équitable?*

Que le droit procédural des États membres soit loin d'être harmonisé[42] est une chose. Une autre est que, en raison de son champ d'application limité, l'article 47 de la Charte ne permet pas souvent à la CJUE de procéder à un contrôle de la qualité des systèmes judiciaires nationaux en tant que garantie d'une protection juridictionnelle effective et équitable. En effet, en l'absence d'application de règles spécifiques du droit de l'Union[43], une grande partie des procédures civiles devant les juridictions nationales ne se prête pas à une saisine de la CJUE au titre de l'article 267 TFUE[44]. Aussi, comme nous l'avons vu plus haut, le nombre d'occasions pour cette Cour de se pencher, au titre de l'ordre public, sur les exigences du droit au procès équitable dans le cadre du règlement de Bruxelles pourrait encore diminuer.

Par ailleurs, les initiatives législatives de la Commission européenne ainsi que ses activités de supervision ne sont pas non plus, du fait de son manque de compétence et, parfois, de détermination, à même d'entraîner les États membres vers l'élévation de leur standard de protection judiciaire. Or il existe sans nul doute des problèmes dans ce domaine, comme le soulignent de nombreux rapports sur la qualité, l'indépendance et l'impartialité de la justice, notamment dans les États membres de l'Union européenne[45].

---

41 Aff. C-216/18 PPU *LM* (défaillances du système judiciaire) [EU:C:2018:586], point 52.

42 Voir *B. Hess*, Procedural Harmonisation in a European Context, in X. Kramer et C.H. van Rhee (éds.), Civil Litigation in a Globalising World (T.M.C. Asser Press, 2012) pp. 159 – 173.

43 Voir en détail, *M. Safjan, D. Düsterhaus* et *A. Guérin*, « La Charte des droits fondamentaux de l'Union européenne et les ordres juridiques nationaux, de la mise en œuvre à la mise en balance », RTD Eur., 2016, p. 219 à 247.

44 Nombreuses affaires préjudicielles infructueuses témoignent de cette circonstance. Pour ne citer que quelques-unes : aff. C-457/09 *Chartry*, C-483/11 *Boncea*, C-258/13 *Sociedade Agrícola e Imobiliária da Quinta de S. Paio*.

45 Il est possible de se référer à ce titre à la Commission européenne pour l'efficacité de la justice (Conseil de l'Europe), au "Rule of Law Project" (World Justice Pro-

L'on notera spécifiquement, s'agissant de la Pologne, la proposition motivée de la Commission européenne au titre de l'article 7 TUE[46], qui expose certaines défaillances structurelles dans cet État membre, susceptibles d'affecter l'organisation et le déroulement équitables des procédures juridictionnelles. Néanmoins, alors que le manque d'indépendance d'une juridiction semble permettre de refuser, au titre de l'article 45(1)(a) de Bruxelles Ibis, l'exécution dans un autre État membre du jugement qu'elle a prononcé, ce manque d'indépendance reste normalement à l'abri du regard de la CJUE tant qu'il se manifeste exclusivement dans un cadre purement interne au premier État membre.

Cela étant, la Cour vient d'ouvrir une nouvelle voie en matière de contrôle des systèmes judiciaires internes en acceptant de prendre, comme base de l'appréciation de l'indépendance judiciaire, l'article 19(1)(2) TUE. La Cour relève que cette disposition s'applique « dans les domaines couverts par le droit de l'Union européenne[47] », sans qu'il ne soit nécessaire d'établir que l'État membre met en œuvre le droit de l'Union européenne au sens de l'article 5 de la Charte. Selon l'article 2 TUE, l'Union européenne est fondée sur des valeurs, telles que l'état de droit, lesquelles sont communes aux États membres dans une société où, inter alia, la justice prévaut. À ce titre, il convient de souligner que la confiance mutuelle entre les États membres et en particulier entre leurs juridictions est basée sur la présomption fondamentale selon laquelle les États membres partagent un ensemble de valeurs communes sur lequel l'Union européenne est fondée.

Si l'article 2 TUE reconnait l'existence de l'État de droit en tant que valeur, l'article 19 TUE confère une expression concrète à cette notion en donnant à la fois à la CJUE et aux juridictions nationales la responsabilité d'assurer un contrôle juridictionnel dans l'ordre juridique européen. L'existence même d'un contrôle juridictionnel effectif, dont l'objectif est d'assurer le respect du droit de l'Union européenne, est essentielle à l'existence de l'état de droit. Chaque État membre doit assurer que les juridictions, au sens du droit de l'Union européenne, qui font partie de son système judiciaire dans les domaines couverts par ce droit, sont conformes aux exigences de la protection juridictionnelle effective.

ject), au tableau de bord de la justice dans l'Union européenne et au rapport anti-corruption de la Commission européenne (qui exprime des inquiétudes sur les nominations et réformes judiciaires en Bulgarie et en Hongrie en 2014) et, enfin, à l'opinion de la Commission de Venise du Conseil de l'Europe sur les récentes réformes judiciaires en Pologne.

46 Du 20 décembre 2017, COM(2017) 835 final.

47 Aff. C-64/16 *Associação Sindical dos Juízes Portugueses* [EU:C:2018:117].

Lorsqu'elle rappelle ces exigences, la Cour utilise à la fois sa jurisprudence relative à l'article 267 TFUE et à l'article 47 de la Charte, plaçant ainsi l'article 19 TUE en tant que base légale et référence en matière de garantie institutionnelle du caractère indépendant, équitable et effectif de la justice. Dans son arrêt, la Cour souligne que l'indépendance des juridictions nationales est indispensable notamment au bon fonctionnement du système de coopération juridictionnelle mis en place par le mécanisme de recours préjudiciel prévu à l'article 267 TFUE, en ce que ce mécanisme ne peut être utilisé que par un organe compétent pour appliquer le droit de l'Union européenne et satisfaisant, inter alia, le critère d'indépendance. Si la Cour accepte, en fin de compte, une coupe limitée dans les salaires, effectuée au nom de l'intérêt général et n'affectant pas exclusivement les juges, elle signale clairement qu'une mesure spécifiquement dirigée à l'encontre des juges n'aurait pas été tolérée.

Bien que l'article 19 TUE ne porte pas sur les exigences procédurales spécifiques, l'indépendance des juridictions constitue en effet une garantie primordiale du procès équitable dans chaque espèce[48]. Qui plus est, en combinaison avec l'article 47 de la Charte, la voie de l'article 19(1)(2) TUE semble permettre, en fin de compte, un contrôle transversal, par les institutions européennes, des règles et pratiques procédurales dans les États membres. Une telle approche a le mérite de combler les lacunes de protection résultant des limitations tant du champ d'application de la Charte que de la compétence de la Cour pour interpréter celle-ci. Cette voie permet également de passer outre le fait de ne pouvoir garantir le respect du droit à un procès équitable dans l'Union européenne qu'au moyen d'un contrôle concret et individualisé. Enfin, l'article 19(1)(2) TUE permet à la Commission européenne d'introduire des actions en manquement[49] sur une base légale solide.

Nous pouvons donc espérer que, en vertu d'efforts législatifs, exécutifs et judiciaires en faveur d'une justice indépendante, effective et de qualité, la libre circulation de décisions juridictionnelles au sein de l'Union européenne, promue depuis 1968 par les règles issues de la convention de Bruxelles, suscitera de moins en moins de doutes quant au respect de l'ordre public procédural. Une telle perspective peut paraître surprenante aux fidèles du droit international privé. Du point de vue de l'ordre juridique intégré de l'Union européenne, elle est pourtant la seule voie à suivre.

---

48 Aff. C-216/18 PPU *LM* (défaillances du système judiciaire) [EU:C:2018:586], point 53.

49 Voir, à cet égard, les affaires C-192/18 *Commission/Pologne* [EU:C:2019:924] et C-619/18 *Commission/Pologne* [EU:C:2019:531].

EU Private International Law: Consistency of the Scopes of Application and/or of the Solutions

Maciej Szpunar[*]

Table of Contents

1. Introduction

The Rome I[1] and Rome II[2] Regulations as well as the Brussels I Regulation[3], replaced by the Brussels I bis Regulation[4], constitute the core of EU private international law. Several indications seem to point to the fact that, by adapting these regulations, the EU legislature intended to establish a single and generally uniform system of rules addressing the issues that arise in cross-border situations. In particular, recitals 7 of the Rome I and Rome II Regulations provide that the substantive scope and the provisions

---

* First Advocate General at the Court of Justice of the European Union; Professor at the University of Silesia in Katowice (Poland).

1 Regulation (EC) No 593/2008 of the European Parliament and of the Council of 17 June 2008 on the law applicable to contractual obligations (Rome I) (OJ 2008 L 177, p. 6, and corrigendum at OJ 2009 L 309, p. 87; 'Rome I Regulation').

2 Regulation (EC) No 864/2007 of the European Parliament and of the Council of 11 July 2007 on the law applicable to non-contractual obligations ('Rome II') (OJ 2007 L 199, p. 40; 'Rome II Regulation').

3 Council Regulation (EC) No 44/2001 of 22 December 2000 on jurisdiction and the recognition and enforcement of judgments in civil and commercial matters (OJ 2001 L 12, p. 1; 'Brussels I Regulation').

4 Regulation (EU) No 1215/2012 of the European Parliament and of the Council of 12 December 2012 on jurisdiction and the recognition and enforcement of judgments in civil and commercial matters (OJ 2012 L 351, p. 1; 'Brussels I bis Regulation').

of these regulations should be consistent with each other and with the Brussels I Regulation (Brussels I bis).

However, a brief analysis of the literature reveals divergent opinions as to the relevance of the consistency concept set out in these recitals[5]. In fact, the doctrinal debate on the consistency between the instruments of private international law dates back to the beginnings of the Brussels[6] and Rome[7] Conventions.

In my view, the question that recitals 7 of the Rome I and Rome II Regulations are addressing must not be confused with the question of the extent to which the solutions adopted on the basis of those regulations should be consistent with each other. It seems to me that such a distinction is also reflected, at least implicitly, in legal literature to the extent that some authors have argued that 'the goal of consistency between the Brussels I bis and the Rome I / II Regulations' should not be confused with strict parallelism between the determination of the competent court and the designation of the applicable law[8]. Traces of this distinction can also be found in the case-law of the Court of Justice of the European Union (CJEU), in particular the *Kainz* judgment[9]. This judgment gave the Court the opportunity to clarify the scope of the concept set out in recital 7 of the Rome II Regulation in the context of the relationship between that regulation and the Brussels I Regulation.

As a reminder, the facts that led to the *Kainz* judgment concerned a dispute based on liability for defective products brought before an Austrian court. The claim was brought following an accident suffered by the applicant in Germany with a bicycle manufactured in that Member State by the

5 Some authors seem to favour the consistency between these regulation (see T. Azzi, Bruxelles I, Rome I, Rome II : regard sur la qualification en droit international, D. 2009. 1622; E. Lein, The New Rome I / Rome II/ Brussels I Synergy, Yearbook of Private International Law 2008, t. 10, p. 197–198), while others propose a more reserved approach in this regard (see, i.e., B. Haftel, Entre « Rome II » et « Bruxelles I » : l'interprétation communautaire uniforme du règlement « Rome I », *Journal du droit international* n° 3, 2010, p. 763).

6 Convention of 27 September 1968 on jurisdiction and the enforcement of judgments in civil and commercial matters (OJ 1978 L 304, p. 36; 'Brussels Convention').

7 Convention on the law applicable to contractual obligations, opened for signature in Rome on 19 June 1980 (OJ 1980 L 266, p. 1; 'the Rome Convention').

8 See G. Rühl, J. von Hein, Towards a European Code on Private International Law?, vol. 79, n° 4 (2015), p. 720 See also, to that effect, T. Azzi, Bruxelles I, Rome I, Rome II : regard sur la qualification en droit international, *D.* 2009. 1624.

9 Judgment of 16 January 2014, *Kainz* (C-45/13, EU:C:2014:7; '*Kainz* judgment').

defendant – whose head office was also located in Germany – but purchased by the applicant from a retailer in Austria. The applicant relied on Article 5 (3) Brussels I Regulation to justify the jurisdiction of the court seised. That provision concerns jurisdiction in matters relating to tort, delict or quasi-delict of the courts for the place where the harmful event occurred or may occur. The applicant took the view that the place of the event that gave rise to the damage was in Austria because the bicycle had been made available there to the end user.

This reasoning could have been inspired by the wording of Article 5 (1) (a) to (c) Rome II Regulation under which the law applicable to a non-contractual obligation arising from damage caused by a product is, in essence, the law of the country in which the product was marketed. Consequently, in the *Kainz* judgment, the desire to guarantee that consistent solutions be adopted on the basis of the Brussels I and Rome II Regulations could have led to the conclusion that the Member State where the event giving rise to the damage was located is the Member State in which the product was marketed.

However, in paragraph 20 of the *Kainz* judgment, the CJEU considered that although it appears from recital 7 of the Rome II Regulation that the EU legislature sought to ensure consistency between the Brussels I Regulation and the substantive scope and provisions of the Rome II Regulation, it does not follow that the Brussels I Regulation should be interpreted in light of the Rome II Regulation. According to the CJEU, any attempts to achieve consistency cannot, in any event, lead to the provisions of Brussels I Regulation being interpreted in a manner which is unconnected to the scheme and objectives pursued by that Regulation.

2. *The consistency of the scopes of application*

Recitals 7 of the Rome I and Rome II Regulations express the idea that the notions used by the EU legislator to designate the scopes of application of the Rome Regulations, of the Brussels I Regulation (Brussels I bis Regulation) and of their provisions should be interpreted in a consistent manner. This idea ultimately boils down to a postulate of consistency between the scopes of EU private international law regulations and their provisions.

The scopes of these regulations and of their provisions are determined by means of the legal notions used for that specific purpose by the legislator. With that in mind, the postulate that seeks to ascertain that these scopes will be interpreted consistently is closely linked to the issue of 'characterization' ('classification') in the traditional conflict-of-laws sense of this notion[10].

Admittedly, it is true that, unlike, in particular, the Succession Regulation[11] or the Maintenance Regulation[12] accompanied by the Hague Protocol[13], the Rome I and Rome II Regulations as well as the Brussels I Regulation (Brussels I bis Regulation), taken separately, were not conceived as complementary instruments containing conflict-of-laws rules and rules on international jurisdiction. In fact, the Rome I and Rome II Regulations and the Brussels I (Brussels I bis) Regulation have their origins in international conventions, namely the Rome and Brussels Conventions[14], which addressed separately the applicable law and jurisdiction. Against this background, it is important to note that the postulate of consistency between these two conventions was not, at least explicitly, put forward when the Rome Convention was drafted, with the exception of questions related to determination of the scope of application of this Convention[15].

However, I do not consider that the idea set out in recitals 7 of the Rome I and Rome II regulations has been jeopardized by the legacy of original sin dating back to the early development of the Brussels and Rome Conventions. This is not the case. Firstly, I think that autonomous

---

10 M. Szpunar, Wykładnia autonomiczna europejskiego prawa prywatnego, in M. Jagielska, E. Rott-Pietrzyk, M. Szpunar (eds.), Rozprawy z prawa prywatnego. Księga jubileuszowa dedykowana Profesorowi Wojciechowi Popiołkowi, Warsaw, 2017, p. 188.

11 Regulation (EU) No 650/2012 of the European Parliament and of the Council of 4 July 2012 on jurisdiction, applicable law, recognition and enforcement of decisions and acceptance and enforcement of authentic instruments in matters of succession and on the creation of a European Certificate of Succession (OJ 2012 L 201, p. 107, 'Succession Regulation').

12 Council Regulation (EC) No 4/2009 of 18 December 2008 on jurisdiction, applicable law, recognition and enforcement of decisions and cooperation in matters relating to maintenance obligations (OJ 2009 L 7, p. 1, 'Maintenance Regulation').

13 Hague Protocol of 23 November 2007 on the Law Applicable to Maintenance Obligations, approved on behalf of the European Community by Council Decision 2009/941/EC of 30 November 2009 (OJ 2009 L 331, p. 17, 'the Hague Protocol').

14 It is important to note in this context that the Brussels Convention was adopted on the basis of Article 220 of the Treaty establishing the European Economic Community, this provision became Article 220 of the EC Treaty, and now Article 293 EC). This was not the case for the Rome Convention.

15 Report on the Convention on the law applicable to contractual obligations by Mario Giuliano, Professor, University of Milan, and Paul Lagarde, Professor, University of Paris I (OJ 1980 C 282, p. 10–11).

interpretation, which does not necessarily have to follow the lines of interpretation adopted under national law[16] and which, therefore, facilitates the search for concordance between all EU private international law regulations, has in fact been developed by Luxembourg judges in preliminary rulings concerning the interpretation of the provisions of the Brussels Convention. Secondly, notwithstanding that several provisions of the Brussels I (Brussels I bis) and Rome regulations were clearly inspired by the Brussels and Rome Conventions, an analysis of the explanatory memoranda accompanying the proposals for the Rome I and Rome II Regulations shows that the EU legislator wanted to reconcile the scopes of application of some of the provisions contained in these regulations and in the Brussels I Regulation[17].

That said, the fact that the postulate of consistency of the scopes of application and of the provisions is laid down in in the Rome I and II regulations with an explicit reference to the Brussels I (Brussels I bis) Regulation does not imply that this consistency must be attained without any exception in all cases. It is in the nature of the postulates (guiding principles) merely to indicate the directions to be followed in the interpretation of legislative texts. As such, the postulate of consistency of the scopes of application serves as a principle guiding the interpretation of EU private international law instruments.

In that regard, it is necessary to emphasize the fundamental differences between the conflict-of-laws rules and the rules on jurisdiction.

Firstly, the conflict-of-laws rules identify the set of provisions that will govern a specific aspect of a factual situation, while when it comes to the rules on jurisdiction, it is the legal action as a whole that is subject to this rule[18]. Thus, in principle, the number of conflict-of-laws rules being

16 On autonomous interpretation in EU private international law see M. Audit, 'L'interprétation autonome du droit international privé communautaire', *Journal du droit international*, 2004, p. 789–816.

17 A desire to align the Rome I Regulation with the Brussels I Regulation was invoked in the contexts of Article 1 (scope) and of the provision relating to the law applicable to consumer contracts. In addition, other references, concerning the qualification of the pre-contractual obligations and the connecting factor used in order to designate the law applicable to employment contracts, refer to the jurisprudence relating to the Brussels I Regulation. Similar references appear in the explanatory memorandum accompanying the proposal for a Rome II Regulation.

18 See B. Haftel, Entre « Rome II » et « Bruxelles I » : l'interprétation communautaire uniforme du règlement « Rome I », *Journal du droit international* n° 3, 2010, p. 764.

applied (effectively and quite often even potentially) in a particular case is often greater than the number of jurisdiction rules that are being applied to this case.

To illustrate, let us consider a dispute concerning reimbursement of payments transferred to the defendant notwithstanding that, according to the claimant, the contract was void. In such circumstances, several conflict-of-laws rules should be effectively applied in order to designate the laws applicable to the matters related, in particular, to the legal capacity of the parties or to the existence of this contract. However, a single rule on jurisdiction is sufficient to effectively allocate jurisdiction among the national courts for all aspects of this dispute.

Let us now turn to the illustration of the potential application of multiple conflict-of-laws rules. A claim seeks the annulment of company decisions. This claim may be based on a defect of consent, the lack of legal capacity of a body which adopted the contested decision or on a serious breach of the articles of association. From the conflict-of-laws perspective, three laws may be applicable, namely the law applicable to contract, to the personal status of the natural person or the personal status of the legal person.

From the perspective of rules on jurisdiction, such an application will likely fall within the scope of Article 24 (2) Brussels I bis Regulation or – when the validity of the decisions of the organs of a company constitutes a preliminary or secondary question – within the scope of other provisions of this regulation[19].

In the second place, each legal relationship must be subject to an applicable law, even when there is no dispute pending before the national courts. The need to identify competent courts manifests itself when a legal action is brought or at least intended by a plaintiff.

In this context I observe that the striving to maintain consistency between the rules of conflict of laws and the rules on jurisdiction concerns, for example, the articulation between, on the one hand, the fields of application of the Rome I Regulation – which concerns contractual obligations – and the Rome II Regulation – which concerns non-contractual obligations – and, on the other hand, the rules of the Brussels I Regulation (Brussels I bis) designating the courts also competent to settle disputes in contractual matters and in tort or quasi-tort matters.

---

19 See, to that effect, L. de Lima Pinheiro, *in* U. Magnus, P. Mankowski (dirs.), Brussels I *bis* Regulation, Cologne 2016, p. 573. See also order of 26 January 2011 of the Polish Supreme Court, IV CSK 284/10, https://goo.gl/QEgJjk.

The fields of application of the Rome I and Rome II regulations do not overlap. Consequently, as the Court pointed out in *Matoušková*[20] with regard to the interplay between the Succession Regulation and the Brussels IIa Regulation[21], questions falling within the scope of the Rome I Regulation are excluded from the scope of the Rome II Regulation and vice versa.

The same applies to the interplay between Article 7 (1) Brussels I bis Regulation and Article 7 (2) of that Regulation, which establish specific and additional grounds of jurisdiction in relation to, respectively, contractual matters and tort or quasi-tort matters. A single request, relating to an obligation, brought before national courts has either a contractual or a non-contractual qualification, double qualification being, in my view, excluded. Thus, it could be presumed that, in certain cases, the fact of applying the provisions of the Rome I Regulation in order to designate the law applicable to a situation in question indicates that claims linked to this situation could also be brought before the courts competent in contractual matters within the meaning of Article 7 (1) Brussels I bis Regulation.

However, while it is always necessary to identify a conflict-of-laws rule that will designate the law governing an aspect of the factual situation, it is not in all cases necessary to grant an applicant the right to lodge his application before the courts referred to in Article 7 (1) and (2) Brussels I bis Regulation. In any event, the general provision that enshrines the *actor sequitur forum rei* rule remains applicable. It seems to me that those observations are consistent with the position expressed by Advocate General Bobek in his Opinion in the *Feniks* case on the classification of *actio pauliana*, as provided for in Polish law, in the context of the Brussels I bis Regulation[22], even though he was not followed by the Court on that particular point.

20 Judgment of 6 October 2015, *Matoušková* (C-404/14, EU:C:2015:653, point 34).
21 Council Regulation (EC) No 2201/2003 of 27 November 2003 concerning jurisdiction and the recognition and enforcement of judgments in matrimonial matters and the matters of parental responsibility, repealing Regulation (EC) No 1347/2000 (OJ 2003 L 338, p. 1. 'Brussels II Regulation').
22 Opinion of Advocate General Bobek in *Feniks* (C-337/17, EU:C:2018:487, point 98).

3. The consistency of the solutions

It should be at this stage quite clear that the postulate of consistency of scopes of application is not to be confused with the postulate of consistency of solutions. The latter, although also concerning the (autonomous) interpretation of provisions of private international law, cannot intervene in the process of identifying the provisions which should be applied to designate a competent court or applicable law. Indeed, it does not appear, at least explicitly, from recitals 7 that the EU legislature intended to ensure, concerning the results achieved by the application of conflict-of-laws rules and rules on jurisdiction, that what is true for the Rome I and Rome II Regulations is also automatically true for the Brussels I and Brussels I bis regulations.

To illustrate my point[23], I refer to the striving for consistency between the applicable law and the court having jurisdiction to hear the case, expressly referred to by certain acts of the Union in matters of civil cooperation, in particular by the Succession Regulation[24]. To a lesser extent, the same is true in relation to the Maintenance Regulation and the Hague Protocol. The Protocol indeed contains certain provisions which reflect the desire to avoid situations in which the authority ruling on maintenance obligations should (would be required to) apply a foreign law[25].

However, in the first place, even under the Succession Regulation, the consistency of *ius* and forum does not have to be observed in all instances. Furthermore, as I have explained above, the Rome I and Rome II Regulations, as well as the Brussels (Brussels I bis) I Regulation, taken separately,

23 Another example could be drawn from the desire to align the scope of the parties' autonomy as regards the choice of applicable law and of forum as well as from the desire to align the modalities according to which these choices are made. On this issue, see. J.J. Kuipers, "Party Autonomy in the Brussels I Regulation and Rome I Regulation and the European Court of Justice", *German Law Journal* 2009, vol. 10, no. 11, p. 1508–1513. In addition, certain authors seek to fill alleged gaps in the Rome II regulation by having recourse to the solutions adopted within the framework of the Rome I regulation. With regard, for example, to the partial choice of the applicable law, which is not explicitly provided for in Article 14 Rome II Regulation, c. A. Junker in H.J. Sonnenberger (dir.), Münchener Kommentar zum Bürgerlichen Gesetzbuch. Band 10, München 2010, p. 1291. Furthermore, as regards the application of Article 16, § 2, Rome I Regulation in the context of Article 20 Rome II Regulation, c. D. Baetge, Article 20 Rome II, in G.P. Calliess (red.), Rome Regulations. Commentary on the European Rules of the Conflict of Laws, Alphen an den Rijn 2011, p. 598.

24 See my Opinion in Oberle (C-20/17, EU:C:2018:89, points 104 and 112).

25 See my Opinion in Mölk (C-214/17, EU:C:2018:297, point 53).

were not created as a legislative whole containing conflict-of-law rules and rules on jurisdiction.

In the second place, it should be borne in mind that the functions of the conflict-of-laws rules and the functions of the rules on jurisdiction are very different. The rules on jurisdiction are limited to designating the court competent to deal with a dispute. Consequently, they are not intended to guarantee that, on the substantive level, the interests of the parties will be satisfied[26]. In this vein, it follows from the case-law relating to the principles of mutual trust between Member States and mutual recognition[27] that the question of which court has jurisdiction to settle a dispute should not be significant for the parties' substantive interests.

That being said, the rules designating the applicable law address issues that arise due to the cross-border nature of the situation on which a dispute is based. The determination of the law applicable to this situation or some of its aspects should make it possible to resolve these issues in a final and lasting manner, even in the absence of pending litigation before a national court[28]. Differences in the functions of conflict-of-laws rules and rules on jurisdiction may have an impact on the results achieved by their applications. Furthermore, these differences also explain the reasons why rules on jurisdiction lend themselves more to a flexible interpretation[29]. In certain cases, this flexibility is likely to render the results of the interpretation of the conflict of laws rules and the rules on jurisdiction even more divergent, so that certain effects of their applications would not be comparable.

To conclude, the meticulous exercise of achieving balance between, on the one hand, consistency of the scopes of application and of the solutions of the Rome I and Rome II Regulations and of the Brussels I (Brussels I

26 See, to that effect, O. Feraci, Party Autonomy and Conflict of Jurisdiction in the EU Private International Law on Family and Succession Matters, YPIL 2014/2015, vol. 16, p. 108.

27 See judgment of 9 March 2017, *Pula Parking* (C-551/15, EU:C:2017:193, points 51 to 53).

28 See, to that effect, J. von Hein, Protecting victims of Cross-border Torts under Article 7 n°. 2 Brussels I bis : Towards a More Differentiated and Balanced Approach, YPIL 2014/2015, vol. 16, p. 249, qui fait dans ce contexte référence à la position de la Commission présentée dans l'affaire ayant donné lieu à l'arrêt *Bier* (CJCE 30 nov. 1976, 21/76, EU:C:1976:166). E. Lein, The New Rome I / Rome II / Brussels I Synergy, Yearbook of Private International Law 2008, t. 10, p. 196.

29 See C. Marenghi, The Law Applicable to Product Liability in Context: Article 5 of the Rome II Regulation and its Interaction with Other EU Instruments, YPIL 2014/2015, vol. 16, p. 531.

bis) Regulation and, on the other hand, their independence and their specificity is decisive for the functioning of the EU system of private international law. Also, within the framework of its mission aimed at ensuring unity of interpretation of EU law, it is up to the CJEU to ensure that the postulates presented above are respected to the extent of allowing this goal to be achieved. In this respect, the CJEU benefits from a heritage which has its roots in the Brussels Convention, namely the autonomous interpretation of the notions of international law.

Le « régime Bruxelles » dans le droit européen de la procédure civile

Marta Requejo Isidro[*]

Table of Contents

* *Senior Research Fellow*, MPI Luxembourg. Professeur de droit international privé à l'Université de La Laguna (Tenerife).

1. Introduction

Voici quelques réflexions complémentaires à celles de mes collègues, cette fois à propos de l'impact du régime Bruxelles sur le reste des instruments européens du droit procédural[1]: pour rappel, le règlement 2201/2003, Bruxelles IIbis[2]; le règlement 4/2009 sur les obligations alimentaires[3]; le règlement 650/2012 sur les successions[4]; les règlements en matière de régimes matrimoniaux[5] et sur les effets patrimoniaux des partenariats enregistrés[6], les règlements de « deuxième génération »[7], le règlement insolvabi-

1 Par « régime Bruxelles » on entend désigner la Convention de Bruxelles de 1968 concernant la compétence judiciaire et l'exécution des décisions en matière civile et commerciale, JO L 299/32, 31.12.1972, le règlement (CE) n° 44/2001 du 22 décembre 2000 concernant la compétence judiciaire, la reconnaissance et l'exécution des décisions en matière civile et commerciale, JO L 012/1, 16.01.2001, et le règlement (UE) 1215/2012 du Parlement européen et du Conseil du 12 décembre 2012 concernant la compétence judiciaire, la reconnaissance et l'exécution des décisions en matière civile et commerciale, OJ L 351/1, 20.12.2012.

2 Règlement (CE) n° 2201/2003 du Conseil du 27 novembre 2003 relatif à la compétence, la reconnaissance et l'exécution des décisions en matière matrimoniale et en matière de responsabilité parentale abrogeant le règlement (CE) n° 1347/2000, OJ L 338/1, 23.12.2003.

3 Règlement (CE) 4/2009 du Conseil du 18 décembre 2008 relatif à la compétence, la loi applicable, la reconnaissance et l'exécution des décisions et la coopération en matière d'obligations alimentaires, JO, L 7/1, 10.1.2009.

4 Règlement (UE) 650/2012 du Parlement européen et du Conseil du 4 juillet 2012 relatif à la compétence, la loi applicable, la reconnaissance et l'exécution des décisions, et l'acceptation et l'exécution des actes authentiques en matière de successions et à la création d'un certificat successoral européen, JO L 201/107, 27.7.2012.

5 Règlement (UE) 2016/1103 du Conseil du 24 juin 2016 mettant en œuvre une coopération renforcée dans le domaine de la compétence, de la loi applicable, de la reconnaissance et de l'exécution des décisions en matière de régimes matrimoniaux, OJ L/1 183, 8.7.2016.

6 Règlement (UE) 2016/1104 du Conseil du 24 juin 2016 mettant en œuvre une coopération renforcée dans le domaine de la compétence, de la loi applicable, de la reconnaissance et de l'exécution des décisions en matière d'effets patrimoniaux des partenariats enregistrés, JO L 183/30, 8.7.2016.

7 Règlement (CE) 805/2004 du Parlement européen et du Conseil du 21 avril 2004 portant création d'un titre exécutoire européen pour les créances incontestées, JO L 143/15, 30.4.2004, règlement (CE) 1896/2006 du Parlement européen et du Conseil du 12 décembre 2006 instituant une procédure européenne d'injonction de payer, JO L 399/1, 30.12.2006, règlement (CE) 861/2007 du Parlement Européen et du Conseil du 11 juillet 2007 instituant une procédure européenne de règlement des petits litiges, JO L 199/1, 31.7.2007; règlement (UE) 655/2014 du Parlement européen et du Conseil du 15 mai 2014 portant création d'une procédure d'ordonnance européenne de saisie conservatoire des comptes bancaires, destinée à faciliter

lité[8], ainsi que les dispositions relatives à la juridiction, la reconnaissance et l'exécution dans les règlements sur la propriété intellectuelle,[9] ou la protection des données[10]. Les règlements sur la notification et l'obtention de preuves, ainsi que quelques directives, en particulier, mais pas seulement, celle sur l'aide judiciaire dans les affaires transfrontalières, doivent aussi être mentionnés[11].

Cette étude entamée en vue du 50ème anniversaire de la Convention de Bruxelles tient pour acquis que le langage de la Cour, ses énoncés et ses expressions, ne sont pas neutres ; la Cour choisit délibérément ce qu'elle dit, et comment le dire. L'examen ne prétend pas à l'exhaustivité ; le nombre de décisions rendues par la Cour ne le permettrait pas. En outre, pour bien cerner les relations entre le régime Bruxelles et les autres instruments dans toutes leurs nuances, il faudrait séparer ceux qui sont instrumentaux – le règlement sur la notification, par exemple – de ceux qui servent à la distribution de la compétence juridictionnelle entre les États

---

le recouvrement transfrontière de créances en matière civile et commerciale, JO L 189/59., 27.6.2014.

8 Règlement (UE) 2015/848 du Parlement européen et du Conseil du 20 mai 2015 relatif aux procédures d'insolvabilité, JO L 141/19, 5.6.2015.

9 Règlement (CE) 6/2002 du Conseil du 12 décembre 2001 sur les dessins ou modèles communautaires, JO, L 3/1, 5.01.2202, Art. 79. Règlement (UE) 2017/1001 du Parlement Européen et du Conseil du 14 juin 2017 sur la marque de l'Union européenne, JO, L 154/1, 16.06.2017, Préambule para. 32 ; arts. 122, 125, 131. Le règlement Bruxelles Ibis a dû être modifié : voir Règlement (UE) 542/2014 du Parlement européen et du Conseil du 15 mai 2014 ; P.A. de Miguel Asensio, « Tribunal unificado de patentes : competencia judicial y reconocimiento de resoluciones », *Anuario Español de Derecho Internacional Privado*, vol. XIII, 2013, pp. 73–99.

10 Règlement (UE) 2016/679 du Parlement européen et du Conseil du 27 avril 2016 relatif à la protection des personnes physiques à l'égard du traitement des données à caractère personnel et à la libre circulation de ces données, et abrogeant la directive 95/46/CE, JO L 119/1, 4.5.2016.

11 Règlement (CE) 1393/2007 du Parlement européen et du Conseil du 13 novembre 2007 relatif à la signification et à la notification dans les États membres des actes judiciaires et extrajudiciaires en matière civile ou commerciale (signification ou notification des actes), et abrogeant le règlement (CE) 1348/2000 du Conseil, OJ L 324/79, 10.12.2007; règlement (CE) 1206/2001 du Conseil du 28 mai 2001 relatif à la coopération entre les juridictions des États membres dans le domaine de l'obtention des preuves en matière civile ou commerciale, JO L 174/1, 27.6.2001. Directive 2002/8/CE du Conseil du 27 janvier 2003 visant à améliorer l'accès à la justice dans les affaires transfrontalières par l'établissement de règles minimales communes relatives à l'aide judiciaire accordée dans le cadre de telles affaires, JO L 26/41, 31.1.2003.

membres de l'Union Européenne, et à la libre circulation des décisions. Toutefois, la recherche menée soutient suffisamment les conclusions[12]; en même temps, elle soulève de nouvelles questions, en particulier celles des relations entre la Cour et les avocats généraux.

La réserve étant faite, permettez-moi de commencer avec les mots de quelques professeurs célèbres :

> « The Brussels I regulation represents a backbone and a model for all subsequent regulations in Europe »[13].
>
> « Its [of the CJEU] finding may be distinguishable, in that it emphasises (at 40 and 44 in particular) that for the service of documents Regulation, things need to move fast indeed and hence interpretation even of core concepts of the Regulation needs to proceed swiftly (...) However in the remainder of the judgment it does refer to precedent in particular under the Brussels I Regulation, hence presumably making current interpretation de rigueur for European civil procedure generally. »[14]

Ces affirmations reflètent une 'opinion très répandue parmi les universitaires à propos du caractère de « droit commun » du régime Bruxelles ; un état d'esprit qui est par ailleurs confirmé par les plans d'études des universités où le droit international privé est une matière obligatoire : le règlement Bruxelles Ibis (auparavant, la Convention ou le règlement Bruxelles I) est l'instrument clé censé ouvrir les portes du droit judiciaire européen aux étudiants de troisième ou quatrième année.

---

12 Le choix des décisions a été fait sur la base indiquée au point III.1, *in fine*, sans préférence particulière pour aucun des règlements ; si le règlement Bruxelles IIbis est plus souvent mentionné c'est tout simplement parce que les demandes de décision préjudicielle sont plus nombreuses. L'échantillon comprend tant les décisions de la Cour que les conclusions ou les opinions des avocats généraux.

13 B. Hess, V. Richard, « Brussels I (Convention and Regulation) », Encyclopedia of Private International Law, 2017, 226.

14 G. van Calster, "Fahnenbrock: 'Civil and commercial' viz bearers of Greek bonds. ECJ puts forward 'direct and immediate effect', March 2016, at https://gavclaw.com/2015/06/15/fahnenbrock-civil-and-commercial-viz-bearers-of-greek-bonds-ecj-puts-forward-direct-and-immediate-effect/ (dernière visite 24.09.2018).

2. *Le régime Bruxelles et le système : conception et littéralité des instruments.*

À la question du rôle du régime Bruxelles dans la création d'un système, il faut sans aucun doute répondre qu'il a ouvert la voie et préparé le terrain à des développements ultérieurs. Quelques illustrations :

- La Convention de Bruxelles de 1968 est le premier instrument en droit judiciaire concernant les cas transfrontaliers, adopté en vertu du traité instituant la Communauté économique européenne.
- La Convention, puis les règlements Bruxelles I et Ibis, ont créé un modèle de structure de base repris dans les instruments adoptés par la suite (bien qu'ils se démarquent du prototype dans une plus ou moins grande mesure en ce qu'ils introduisent des chapitres sur la coopération administrative et/ou la loi applicable).
- Le régime Bruxelles apporte des solutions paradigmatiques à des problèmes communs, comme par exemple, celui de la litispendance ou de la connexité.
- Les critères de juridiction et/ou les règles sur la reconnaissance et l'exécution du régime Bruxelles ont été adoptés dans les règlements sur des matières civiles et commerciales spécifiques (obligations alimentaires ; marques, dessins, protection de données); ou créant des procédures spécifiques (procédure européenne d'injonction de payer; petits litiges).
- Le régime Bruxelles a été aussi un modèle pour le "outer world", l'exemple classique étant la Convention de Lugano[15]. De plus, certaines de ses solutions caractéristiques furent exportées bien au-delà de l'espace judiciaire européen (voir, par exemple, l'art. 71 règlement Brussels Ibis).

Ceci étant dit, on ne peut pas ignorer que chaque instrument européen présente ses particularités et s'éloigne plus ou moins de ce que nous allons appeler, pour le moment, le « tronc » commun (un tronc commun qui par ailleurs évolue de son côté, à sa façon). Le législateur lui-même souligne les différences et les clivages entre les instruments :

- Au para. 9 du préambule du règlement portant création d'un titre européen pour les créances non-contestées : « Une telle procédure devrait présenter des avantages importants par rapport à la procédure d'exequatur prévue par le règlement (CE) n° 44/2001 ».

---

15 Convention concernant la compétence judiciaire et l'exécution des décisions en matières civile et commerciale – Faite à Lugano le 16 septembre 1988, JO L 319/9, 25.11.1988.

- Au para. 15 du préambule du règlement sur les obligations alimentaires : « Afin de préserver les intérêts des créanciers d'aliments et de favoriser une bonne administration de la justice au sein de l'Union européenne, les règles relatives à la compétence telles qu'elles résultent du règlement (CE) nº 44/2001 devraient être adaptées ».
- Au para. 32 du préambule du règlement sur la marque de l'Union Européenne : « Ce sont les dispositions du règlement (UE) nº 1215/2012 du Parlement européen et du Conseil qui devraient s'appliquer à toutes les actions en justice relatives aux marques de l'Union européenne, sauf si le présent règlement y déroge ». Les arts. 122, 125, 126 fournissent des exemples de dérogation et d'adaptation.
- Au para. 147 du préambule du règlement sur la protection des données : « Lorsque le présent règlement prévoit des règles de compétence spécifiques (...) les règles de compétence générales, telles que celles prévues dans le règlement (UE) no 1215/2012 du Parlement européen et du Conseil, ne devraient pas porter préjudice à l'application de telles règles juridictionnelles spécifiques. »
- Au para. 7 du préambule du règlement sur l'insolvabilité le législateur a établi une relation de complémentarité avec le régime Bruxelles ; aucun des instruments ne prévaut sur l'autre : « L'interprétation du présent règlement devrait, autant que possible, combler les lacunes réglementaires entre les deux instruments. »

Les règlements sur les successions, les régimes matrimoniaux et en matière d'effets patrimoniaux des partenariats enregistrés ne font aucune mention explicite au régime Bruxelles. Au point 59 du préambule du premier, ainsi qu'au para. 56 du préambule des deux autres, on trouve une référence générale aux instruments de l'Union Européenne : « À la lumière de son objectif général, (...) le présent règlement devrait fixer des règles relatives à la reconnaissance (...) qui soient semblables à celles d'autres instruments de l'Union adoptés dans le domaine de la coopération judiciaire en matière civile. »

3. *Le régime Bruxelles dans l'application et l'interprétation du reste des instruments*

3.1. *Absence d'impératif de cohérence?*

Voyons maintenant l'impact du régime Bruxelles sur le reste des instruments du droit européen de la procédure dans une perspective dynamique, c'est-à-dire, du point de vue de l'application et de l'interprétation de ces instruments. En d'autres termes, nous allons aborder le sujet de la cohérence des instruments, en essayant d'y déceler le poids du régime Bruxelles[16].

En vérité, la cohérence n'est pas imposée par la norme au-delà des règlements Rome I et Rome II[17], (et, évidemment, en ce qui concerne les instruments du régime Bruxelles eux-mêmes). Pour le reste, s'il est possible d'identifier quelques renvois ou des références croisées, elles ne sont que ponctuelles. Par exemple :

- Dans le règlement 1896/2006, sur l'injonction de payer, l'art. 3.2 renvoie au règlement 44/2001 pour la détermination du "domicile" des parties ;
- Au règlement 861/2007, « petits litiges », l'art. 3.2 reprend aussi la notion de domicile. En plus, la notion de « demande reconventionnelle est importée expressément du règlement 44/2001 : « La notion de *demande reconventionnelle* devrait s'entendre au sens de l'article 6, paragraphe 3, du règlement (CE) no 44/2001, à savoir une demande dérivant du contrat ou du fait sur lequel est fondée la demande initiale. Il y a lieu d'appliquer les articles 2 et 4, l'article 5, paragraphes 3, 4 et 5, mutatis mutandis aux demandes reconventionnelles. » (para. 16 du préambule);
- Le règlement 655/2014, portant création d'une procédure d'ordonnance européenne de saisie conservatoire des comptes bancaires, renvoie aussi au régime Bruxelles pour la détermination du domicile (art. 4.4.15).

Quelle importance accorder à l'absence d'impératif de cohérence ? À mon avis, elle n'en a aucune. Le principe selon lequel un système juridique doit être interprété de façon à assurer sa cohérence va de soi et il va aussi de soi que la cohérence ne constitue pas le seul critère d'interprétation. Nous ver-

---

16 Il est bien entendu impossible de donner une réponse finale à la question de la cohérence dans cette brève contribution. De plus, elle ne devrait pas être abordée seulement par référence à la CJEU, car si elle a certainement le dernier mot, le gros des affaires est traité par les tribunaux nationaux, qui travaillent quotidiennement avec les instruments européens.

17 Règlement (CE) 593/2008 du Parlement européen et du Conseil du 17 juin 2008 sur la loi applicable aux obligations contractuelles (Rome I), JO L/6 177, 4.7.2008, point 7 du Préambule ; règlement (CE) 864/2007 du Parlement Européen et du Conseil du 11 juillet 2007 sur la loi applicable aux obligations non contractuelles (Rome II), JO L 199/40, 31.7.2007, point 7 du Préambule.

rons dans un instant que le mot « cohérence » ne figure pas souvent dans le discours de la CJUE à propos des instruments de droit procédural[18], mais qu'elle utilise d'autres formules du même sens : « (la jurisprudence) demeure pertinente » ; « voir, par analogie » ; « voir, en ce sens ». De plus, la cohérence globale peut résulter de la continuité dans l'interprétation mais aussi des particularisations ou des distinctions, pour autant qu'elles soient justifiées.

Reprenons alors la question de l'impact du régime Bruxelles sur le reste des instruments européens en examinant trois cas de figure dans lesquels la Cour a été saisie. Dans le premier cas, les termes dont l'interprétation était demandée à la Cour étaient les mêmes dans le règlement en cause et dans le régime Bruxelles. Dans un deuxième ensemble d'affaires, les règles à la base de la demande préjudicielle étaient les mêmes dans le règlement en cause et dans le régime Bruxelles. Dans la troisième situation, des dispositions pour aborder un problème manquaient dans le règlement applicable tandis qu'elles existaient dans le régime Bruxelles. L'examen de la jurisprudence aboutit aux résultats qui suivent.

3.2. Le régime Bruxelles : droit commun, point de repère

3.2.1. Argument décisif (et à suivre)

Le régime Bruxelles est utilisé directement et constitue l'argument central de la solution proposée par la CJUE dans plusieurs cas. L'arrêt C-296/10, *Purrucker*[19], relatif aux notions d' "objet" et de "cause" dans le cadre de l'art. 19.2 du règlement Brussels IIbis, fournit un bon exemple :

> « La Cour a déjà jugé, dans le cadre de la convention de Bruxelles, que l'objet du litige consiste dans le but de la demande (voir arrêt du 6 décembre 1994, *Tatry*, C-406/92, Rec. p. I-5439, point 41). Pour vérifier si deux demandes présentent le même objet, il convient de tenir compte des prétentions respectives des demandeurs dans chacun des litiges (arrêt du 8 mai 2003, Gantner Electronic, C-111/01, Rec. p. I-4207, point 26). Par ailleurs, la Cour a interprété la notion de

18 Voir néanmoins l'arrêt (neuvième chambre) C-508/12, *Vapenik*, 5 décembre 2013, à propos du titre exécutoire européen pour les créances incontestées, ECLI:EU:C:2013:790, para. 25 et 37.

19 Arrêt de la Cour (deuxième chambre) du 9 novembre 2010, ECLI:EU:C:2010:665. Prise de position de l'avocat général M. Niilo Jääskinen, ECLI:EU:C:2010:578.

> « cause » comme comprenant les faits et la règle juridique invoqués comme fondement de la demande (voir arrêt Tatry, précité, point 39) ». (para. 68)

Dans sa décision C-92/12, *Health Service Executive*[20], toujours dans le cadre du règlement Bruxelles IIbis, à propos des effets d'une décision de placement d'un enfant dans un établissement d'un autre État membre, la Cour rappelle au para. 142 que :

> « À cet égard, dans le contexte du règlement (CE) nº 44/2001 du Conseil (...), la Cour a dit pour droit qu'il n'y a aucune raison d'accorder à un jugement, lors de son exécution, des droits qui ne lui appartiennent pas dans l'État membre d'origine ou des effets qu'un jugement du même type rendu directement dans l'État membre requis ne produirait pas (arrêts du 28 avril 2009, Apostolides, C-420/07, Rec. p. I-3571, point 66, et du 13 octobre 2011, Prism Investments, C-139/10, Rec. p. I-9511, point 38) ».

L'arrêt C-215/15, *Gogova*[21], soulevait des questions sur la prorogation de compétence de l'art. 12 du règlement Bruxelles IIbis. La Cour répond, aux para. 42 et 43 :

> « À cet égard, il convient de relever que, d'une part, une telle acceptation suppose a minima que le défendeur ait connaissance de la procédure se déroulant devant ces juridictions. En effet, si cette connaissance ne vaut pas, à elle seule, acceptation de la compétence des juridictions saisies, le défendeur absent auquel la requête introductive d'instance n'a pas été notifiée et qui ignore la procédure entamée ne peut pas, en tout état de cause, être considéré comme acceptant cette compétence (voir, par analogie, s'agissant de l'article 24 du règlement nº 44/2001, arrêt A, C-112/13, EU:C:2014:2195, point 54) ».
> « D'autre part, la volonté du défendeur au principal ne saurait être déduite du comportement d'un mandataire ad litem désigné par lesdites juridictions en l'absence de ce défendeur. Ce mandataire n'ayant pas de contacts avec le défendeur, il ne peut obtenir de ce dernier les informations nécessaires pour accepter ou contester la compétence de

20 Arrêt de la Cour (deuxième chambre) du 26 avril 2012, ECLI:EU:C:2012:255. Prise de position de l'avocat général Julianne Kokott, ECLI:EU:C:2012:177.

21 Arrêt de la Cour (quatrième chambre) 21 octobre 2015, ECLI:EU:C:2015:710. Prise de position de l'avocat général M. Paolo Mengozzi, ECLI:EU:C:2015:725.

ces mêmes juridictions en connaissance de cause (voir, en ce sens, arrêt A, C-112/13, EU:C:2014:2195, point 55) ».

Dans le domaine de la notification à l'étranger, l'arrêt C-14/07, *Weiss und Partner*[22], encore sur le règlement 1348/2000, la Cour raisonne sur la base de la relation particulièrement étroite entre celui-ci et le régime Bruxelles :

> « L'interprétation du règlement n° 1348/2000 ne saurait, cependant, être dissociée du contexte de développement dans le domaine de la coopération judiciaire en matière civile dans lequel ce règlement s'inscrit et, plus particulièrement, du règlement n° 44/2001, qui, à son article 26, paragraphes 3 et 4, fait expressément référence au règlement n° 1348/2000. » (para. 50 ; voir aussi les para. qui suivent)

3.2.2. *Argument décisif (pour en dévier)*

Parfois, le régime Bruxelles est évoqué dans le sens contraire, c'est-à-dire pour justifier une solution différente de celle qui l'aurait emporté en vertu de la Convention de 1968 ou du règlement Bruxelles I ou I bis. Le régime est ici le point de départ et la Cour tire ses conclusions du contraste avec l'instrument en cause. C'est ainsi que la CJEU arrive à sa décision dans l'affaire C-489/14, *A*[23], sur le règlement Bruxelles IIbis, art. 19.1, au para. 33 :

> « Pour déterminer ensuite si une situation de litispendance existe, il ressort des termes de l'article 19, paragraphe 1, du règlement nº 2201/2003 que, contrairement aux règles de l'article 27, paragraphe 1, du règlement nº 44/2001, applicables aux matières civile et commerciale, en matière matrimoniale, une identité de cause et d'objet des demandes formées devant des juridictions d'États membres différents n'est pas requise. (...) s'il importe que les demandes concernent les mêmes parties, celles-ci peuvent avoir un objet distinct, pourvu

22 Arrêt de la Cour (troisième chambre), 8 mai 2008, ECLI:EU:C:2008:264. Conclusions de l'avocat général Mme Verica Trstenjak, ECLI:EU:C:2007:737. À la différence de la Cour, l'avocat général ne fait pas allusion au régime Bruxelles dans son texte, sauf pour deux mentions « cachées » en note de bas de page.

23 Arrêt de la Cour (troisième chambre), 6 octobre 2015, ECLI:EU:C:2015:654. Conclusions de l'avocat général M. Pedro Cruz Villalón, ECLI:EU:C:2015:559.

qu'elles portent sur une séparation de corps, un divorce ou une annulation de mariage (…) »[24].

Dans l'arrêt C-455/15, *P*[25], sur le règlement Bruxelles IIbis et l'ordre public, la Cour commence en disant, au para. 34, que :

> « S'il n'appartient pas à la Cour de définir le contenu de l'ordre public d'un État membre, il lui incombe néanmoins de contrôler les limites dans le cadre desquelles le juge d'un État membre peut avoir recours à cette notion pour ne pas reconnaître une décision émanant d'un autre État membre (voir, par analogie, arrêt Diageo Brands, C-681/13, EU:C:2015:471, point 42) ».

Et continue ensuite, au para 38 :

> « (…) à la différence de la clause d'ordre public figurant à l'article 34, point 1, du règlement (CE) nº 44/2001 du Conseil (…), l'article 23, sous a), du règlement nº 2201/2003 exige que la décision sur un éventuel refus de reconnaissance soit prise eu égard aux intérêts supérieurs de l'enfant ».

Les affaires jointes C-400/13 et C-408/13, *Sanders* et *Huber*[26], à propos du règlement sur les obligations alimentaires donnent un autre exemple : la Cour s'appuie sur le régime Bruxelles au départ, puis s'en distingue et propose une interprétation propre à l'instrument en jeu (para. 23 et para. 27) :

> « À titre liminaire, il convient de préciser que, comme l'a relevé M. l'avocat général au point 33 de ses conclusions, dans la mesure où les dispositions du règlement n° 4/2009 relatives aux règles de compétence ont remplacé celles du règlement nº 44/2001, la jurisprudence de la Cour portant sur les dispositions relatives à la compétence en matière d'obligations alimentaires figurant dans la convention du 27 sep-

24 Tandis qu'au para. 34 la Cour rappelle : « Dans de telles circonstances et en cas d'identité de parties, conformément aux termes de l'article 19, paragraphe 1, dudit règlement, la juridiction saisie en second lieu sursoit d'office à statuer jusqu'à ce que la compétence de la juridiction première saisie soit établie. À cet égard, il y a lieu de considérer que l'interprétation par la Cour de l'article 27 du règlement no 44/2001 vaut également pour l'article 19, paragraphe 1, du règlement no 2201/2003. ».

25 Arrêt de la Cour (quatrième chambre), 19 novembre 2015, ECLI:EU:C:2015:763. Prise de position de l'avocat général Melchior Wathelet présentée le 29 octobre 2015, ECLI:EU:C:2015:770.

26 Arrêt de la Cour (troisième chambre) 18 décembre 2014 : ECLI:EU:C:2014:2461. Conclusions de l'avocat général M. Niilo Jääskinen : ECLI:EU:C:2014:2171.

tembre 1968 ainsi que dans le règlement nº 44/2001, lequel s'inscrit dans le prolongement de la convention de Bruxelles, demeure pertinente pour analyser les dispositions correspondantes du règlement nº 4/2009. »

« (...) le considérant 15 dudit règlement [règlement 4/2009] énonce que les règles relatives à la compétence telles qu'elles résultent du règlement nº 44/2001 doivent être adaptées afin de préserver les intérêts des créanciers d'aliments et de favoriser une bonne administration de la justice au sein de l'Union ».

Dans l'affaire C-144/12, *Goldbet*[27], la Cour, saisie de l'interprétation de l'art. 17 du règlement 1896/2006 et de sa relation avec l'art. 24 du règlement 44/2201, témoigne de la même idée dans le contexte des règlements « de deuxième génération ». Afin de savoir si une opposition à l'injonction de payer européenne, dans laquelle la compétence de la juridiction de l'État membre d'origine n'est pas contestée, vaut comparution, au sens de l'article 24 du règlement nº 44/2001, lorsque cette opposition n'est pas assortie d'un exposé de moyens de fond, la Cour répond en évoquant en premier lieu l'instrumentalité des chefs de compétence du règlement Bruxelles I lors de l'application du règlement 1896/2006. Néanmoins, la Cour ajoute :

> « Or, lorsque le défendeur ne conteste pas, dans son opposition à l'injonction de payer européenne, la compétence de la juridiction de l'État membre d'origine, cette opposition ne saurait produire, à l'égard de ce défendeur, des effets autres que ceux qui ressortent de l'article 17, paragraphe 1, du règlement nº 1896/2006. Ces effets consistent à mettre fin à la procédure européenne d'injonction de payer et à entraîner, sauf si le demandeur a expressément demandé qu'il soit mis un terme à la procédure dans ce cas, le passage automatique du litige à la procédure civile ordinaire. » (para. 31)

Et cela, au regard de la nature non contradictoire de la procédure simplifiée créée par le règlement, des effets de l'opposition d'après le même règlement, et du fait que les formulaires, prévus à l'annexe VI pour former opposition à l'injonction de payer européenne, n'offrent aucune possibilité de contester la compétence des juridictions de l'État membre d'origine.

Pour finir avec les exemples, tournons-nous maintenant vers la notion d'« établissement » dans le règlement 207/2009 sur la marque de l'Union

27 Arrêt de la Cour (troisième chambre), 13 juin 2013, ECLI:EU:C:2013:393. Conclusions de l'avocat général M. Yves Bot, ECLI:EU:C:2013:136.

européenne, qui est définie dans l'affaire C-617/15, *Hummel Holding A/S*[28]. La Cour, après avoir rappelé que :

> « À cet égard, bien que certaines dispositions du règlement n° 44/2001, tels son article 5, paragraphe 5, et son article 18, paragraphe 2, se réfèrent elles aussi à la notion d'« établissement », de telle sorte qu'il n'est pas à exclure que les enseignements découlant de la jurisprudence de la Cour afférente à ces deux dispositions puissent, dans une certaine mesure, être pertinents aux fins d'interpréter la notion d'« établissement » au sens du règlement n° 207/2009, il ne saurait toutefois être considéré que ladite notion devrait nécessairement revêtir la même portée, selon qu'elle est utilisée dans le cadre de l'un ou de l'autre de ces deux règlements ». (para. 25)

conclut avec une définition *ad hoc*, par un raisonnement qui privilégie le contexte et les objectifs propres au règlement 207/2009 sur ceux du régime Bruxelles (voir para. 26–29).

3.3. *Vers l'absence de préférence*

À côté des exemples que nous venons de voir, on constate à plusieurs reprises que la Cour ne montre pas une préférence formelle pour le régime Bruxelles, que ce soit pour produire un continuum dans l'interprétation ou pour s'en séparer. Par ailleurs, le manque de faveur sur la forme indique l'autonomie des raisonnements sur le fond.

3.3.1. *Une « fausse » mention?*

Le régime Bruxelles est un élément du cadre juridique, mais, une fois mentionné en tête du document, il ne réapparaît plus. C'est le cas dans l'arrêt C-300/14, *Imtech Marine Belgium NV*[29], à propos du règlement 805/2004, l'art. 34.2 du règlement Bruxelles I préside le cadre juridique, mais il n'est plus mentionné par la suite. Il en est de même pour l'affaire C-184/14, *A*[30],

---

28 Arrêt de la Cour (deuxième chambre), 18 mai 2017, ECLI:EU:C:2017:390. Conclusions de l'avocat général M. Evgeni Tanchev, ECLI:EU:C:2017:13.

29 Arrêt de la Cour (quatrième chambre), 17 décembre 2015, ECLI:EU:C:2015:825. Conclusions de l'avocat général M. Pedro Cruz Villalón, ECLI:EU:C:2015:557.

30 Arrêt de la Cour (troisième chambre), 16 juillet 2015, ECLI:EU:C:2015:479. Conclusions de l'avocat général M. Yves Bot, ECLI:EU:C:2015:244.

à propos des arts. 3.c et 3.d du règlement 4/2009. La Convention de Bruxelles, ainsi que le règlement 44/2001, sont indiqués au début de l'arrêt, faisant partie du cadre juridique, même avant le règlement sur les obligations alimentaires. Pourtant, aucune mention de l'art. 5.2 de la Convention de Bruxelles ni du règlement 44/2001 n'est faite au sein du raisonnement. Dans la décision C-4/14, *Christophe Bohez*[31], sur le règlement 4/2009, le règlement Bruxelles I est le premier texte mentionné dans le cadre juridique mais, une fois de plus, aucun renvoi n'y ai fait dans la motivation de l'arrêt.

3.3.2. Le régime Bruxelles, un argument parmi d'autres

3.3.2.1. Le cumul d'arguments

Dans ce groupe d'affaires la Cour fait allusion au régime Bruxelles comme un argument parmi d'autres, sans pertinence particulière dans l'ensemble[32]. C'est ainsi que dans son arrêt C-256/09, *Purrucker*[33], sur l'art. 20 du règlement Bruxelles IIbis et en particulier sur la question des effets extraterritoriaux des mesures provisoires ou conservatoires, la Cour revient sur l'origine de l'article 20 (l'article 12 du règlement 1347/2000) et s'en remet au rapport Borrás, qui distingue l'article 12 de la Convention de Bruxelles II et l'article 24 de la Convention de Bruxelles de 1968, para. 85 :

> « Le rapport Borrás souligne à cet égard la différence de rédaction existant entre l'article 12 de la convention de Bruxelles II et l'article 24 de la convention de Bruxelles en ce que "les mesures visées à l'article 24 de cette dernière [...] sont limitées aux matières entrant dans le champ d'application de la convention, et [...] ont en revanche, des effets extraterritoriaux". Il ressort de cette comparaison avec la convention de Bruxelles que les rédacteurs de la convention de Bruxelles II entendaient établir un lien entre les matières sur lesquelles pouvaient porter les mesures provisoires et l'effet territorial de ces mesures ».

---

31 Arrêt de la Cour (première chambre), 9 septembre 2015, ECLI:EU:C:2015:563. Conclusions de l'avocat général M. Maciej Szpunar, ECLI:EU:C:2015:233.

32 Voir M. Requejo Isidro, « El DIPr. y el Derecho Procesal Civil Europeo en la jurisprudencia del TJUE », *Anuario Español de Derecho Internacional Privado*, vol. XV (2015), pp. 55–89.

33 Arrêt de la Cour (deuxième chambre), 15 juillet 2010, ECLI:EU:C:2010:437. Conclusions de l'avocat général Mme Eleanor Sharpston, ECLI:EU:C:2010:296.

La Cour poursuit au para 87 :

> « Le texte du règlement n° 2201/2003 n'atteste en aucune manière d'une volonté de rejeter les explications contenues dans ces travaux préparatoires quant aux effets de mesures relevant de l'article 20 de ce règlement (…) »

Dans l'arrêt C-508/12, *Vapenik*[34], la notion de « consommateur » dans le règlement 805/2004 est interprétée à la lumière du règlement 44/2001, mais aussi par rapport à la Directive 93/13/CEE du Conseil, du 5 avril 1993, et au règlement Rome I :

> « À cet égard, et pour assurer le respect des objectifs poursuivis par le législateur européen dans le domaine des contrats conclus par les consommateurs ainsi que la cohérence du droit de l'Union, il y a lieu, en particulier, de tenir compte de la notion de "consommateur" contenue dans d'autres réglementations du droit de l'Union. Eu égard au caractère complémentaire des règles instaurées par le règlement nº 805/2004 par rapport à celles que comporte le règlement nº 44/2001, les dispositions de ce dernier s'avèrent particulièrement pertinentes ». (para. 25; voir aussi les para. 27 et 28)
> « Ainsi, il y a lieu de rappeler d'emblée que le système de protection des consommateurs mis en œuvre, notamment, par la directive 93/13/CEE du Conseil, du 5 avril 1993, concernant les clauses abusives dans les contrats conclus avec les consommateurs (…) repose sur l'idée que le consommateur se trouve dans une situation d'infériorité à l'égard du professionnel en ce qui concerne tant le pouvoir de négociation que le niveau d'information (voir, notamment, arrêts du 14 juin 2012, Banco Español de Crédito, C-618/10, point 39; du 21 mars 2013, RWE Vertrieb, C-92/11, point 41, ainsi que du 30 mai 2013, Asbeek Brusse et de Man Garabito, C-488/11, point 31) ». (para. 26)
> « Enfin, ainsi que cela ressort des considérants 23 et 24 du règlement nº 593/2008, l'exigence de protection, dans le cadre contractuel, des parties plus faibles, dont les consommateurs, est également reconnue lorsqu'il s'agit de déterminer le droit applicable aux contrats de consommation (…) » (para. 29).

34 Supra note 18.

Dans l'arrêt sur les affaires jointes C-226/13, C-245/13, C-247/13 and C-578/13, *Fahnenbrock*[35], à propos de l'interprétation de "matière civile ou commerciale" dans le cadre du règlement 1393/2007, la Cour utilise comme points de repère tant le régime Bruxelles que le règlement Bruxelles IIbis, pour prendre ses distances par rapport aux deux, aux para. 43 et 44 :

> « (…) la solution à cette question aux fins de l'applicabilité d'autres règlements ou conventions, tels que ceux mentionnés aux points 34 à 36 du présent arrêt [la convention du 27 septembre 1968, le règlement 44/2001, le règlement 2201/2003] n'est normalement décidée qu'après avoir mis toutes les parties au litige en cause en mesure de s'exprimer sur la question afin que la juridiction saisie dispose de tous les éléments nécessaires pour rendre sa décision ».
> « Toutefois, il en va autrement en ce qui concerne la question de savoir si un acte introductif d'instance concerne la matière civile et commerciale au sens du règlement nº 1393/2007 ».

3.3.2.2. Les références « de basse intensité »

Nous regardons ici les situations où les arguments de la Cour lors de l'interprétation d'un instrument se bornent à celui-ci et son contexte, confinant la mention au régime Bruxelles à un point du texte, *ad abundantiam*, précédé par la formule « d'ailleurs » ou similaire. C'est le cas de l'affaire C-384/14, *Alta Realitat SL.*[36], para. 86, à propos du règlement « notification ».

> « Dans un cas tel que celui en cause au principal, où le défendeur ne comparaît pas, le règlement no 1393/2007 exige (…) qu'il soit assuré que l'intéressé a réellement et effectivement reçu l'acte introductif d'instance (voir, en ce sens, arrêt Alder, C-325/11, EU:C:2012:824, points 36 et 41), lui permettant ainsi de prendre connaissance de la procédure judiciaire engagée contre lui ainsi que d'identifier l'objet et la cause de la demande (voir, en ce sens, arrêt Weiss und Partner, C-14/07, EU:C:2008:264, points 73 et 75), et qu'il a disposé de suffi-

35 Arrêt de la Cour (première chambre), 11 juin 2015, ECLI:EU:C:2015:383. Conclusions de l'avocat général M. Yves Bot présentées le 9 décembre 2014, ECLI:EU:C:2014:2424.

36 Ordonnance de la Cour (dixième chambre), 28 avril 2016, ECLI:EU:C:2016:316.

samment de temps pour se défendre (voir, en ce sens, arrêt Leffler, C-443/03, EU:C:2005:665, point 52). Une telle obligation concorde d'ailleurs avec les prescriptions de l'article 34, point 2, du règlement no 44/2001 (voir, en ce sens, arrêts Leffler, C-443/03, EU:C:2005:665, point 68, et Weiss und Partner, C-14/07, EU:C:2008:264, point 51). »

Pareillement, dans l'affaire C-354/15, *Henderson*[37] :

> « Une telle protection des droits du défendeur défaillant, plus particulièrement visée à l'article 19, paragraphe 1, du règlement n° 1393/2007, répond d'ailleurs au but poursuivi par les prescriptions d'autres actes de l'Union relatifs à la coopération judiciaire en matière civile et commerciale, tels que le règlement n° 44/2001, dont l'article 34, point 2, présuppose également que l'acte en cause a été préalablement signifié ou notifié à un tel défendeur (voir, en ce sens, ordonnance du 28 avril 2016, Alta Realitat, C-384/14, EU:C:2016:316, point 86 et jurisprudence citée, ainsi que arrêt du 7 juillet 2016, Lebek, C-70/15, EU:C:2016:524, point 41 et jurisprudence citée) » (para. 91).

3.3.3. Au-delà : le raisonnement (en apparence ?) indépendant

Il arrive aussi que le régime Bruxelles ne soit pas très présent, voire inexistant, dans le raisonnement de la Cour, même s'il était déterminant dans celui de l'avocat général et que la Cour ne s'en écarte pas dans sa décision. La situation est des plus frappantes lorsque la Cour est appelée à se prononcer sur des termes ou des règles communes aux instruments.

---

37 Arrêt de la Cour (dixième chambre), 2 mars 2017, ECLI:EU:C:2017:157. Conclusions de l'avocat général M. Michal Bobek, ECLI:EU:C:2016:650. Dans son arrêt (grande chambre) du 8 novembre 2005, dans l'affaire C-443/03, ECLI:EU:C:2005:665, la Cour établit une relation plus étroite entre les instruments lors qu'elle dit, au para. 68 : « (…) le juge doit surseoir à statuer aussi longtemps qu'il n'est pas établi qu'il a été remédié à l'acte en question par l'envoi d'une traduction et que celui-ci a eu lieu en temps utile pour que le défendeur ait pu se défendre. Une telle obligation résulte également du principe énoncé à l'article 26, paragraphe 2, du règlement n° 44/2001 et le contrôle de son respect est préalable à la reconnaissance d'une décision, conformément à l'article 34, point 2, du même règlement. ».

Dans l'arrêt (Grand Chambre) C-435/06, *C*[38], à propos de la notion de « matières civiles », l'avocat général avait distingué le régime Bruxelles du règlement Bruxelles IIbis (para 38) :

> « Dans ses décisions relatives à la convention de Bruxelles, la Cour a en effet toujours souligné que l'interprétation autonome de la notion de matière civile et commerciale doit tenir compte des objectifs et du système de la convention de Bruxelles ainsi que des principes généraux qui se dégagent de l'ensemble des ordres juridiques nationaux. Les objectifs et le système de cette convention et même – ajouterions-nous – sa genèse ne concordent cependant pas nécessairement avec ceux du règlement nº 2201/2003. D'autre part, les ordres juridiques nationaux peuvent soumettre la responsabilité parentale à des principes généraux du droit différents de ceux qui s'appliquent aux litiges tombant dans le champ d'application de la convention de Bruxelles. La notion de matière civile du règlement nº 2201/2003 doit donc faire l'objet d'une interprétation autonome, dans le contexte de ce règlement même ».

Sur le fond, la Cour arrive à la même conclusion que l'avocat général en ce qui concerne la qualification « civile » de la décision en cause, adoptée dans le cadre des règles de droit public relatives à la protection de l'enfance. Son argumentation comporte une référence explicite à la Convention de Bruxelles 1968 aux para. 40 et 41, mais elle ne sert en fait qu'à rappeler le principe commun d'après lequel « La notion de matière civile et commerciale doit être considérée comme une notion autonome qu'il faut interpréter en se référant, d'une part, aux objectifs et au système de la convention de Bruxelles et, d'autre part, aux principes généraux qui se dégagent de l'ensemble des ordres juridiques nationaux ». Puis, face aux arguments du gouvernement suédois à l'appui de la jurisprudence *Henkel*, la Cour se borne à dire (para. 44) que « [c]ette interprétation de l'article 1er, paragraphe 1, du règlement nº 2201/2003 ne saurait être accueillie », et continue son raisonnement à la lumière, exclusivement, du règlement Bruxelles IIbis[39].

Dans l'arrêt C-215/15, *Gogova*[40], les arguments de l'avocat général dans sa prise de position reposent principalement sur le régime Bruxelles pour

38 Arrêt de la Cour (Grande Chambre), 27 novembre 2007, ECLI:EU:C:2007:714. Conclusions de l'avocat général Mme Juliane Kokott, ECLI:EU:C:2007:543.

39 Voir B. Hess, Seminal judgments (les grands arrêts) in the case law of the European Court of Justice, dans cet ouvrage, sur la tendance de la Cour à raisonner *case-specific, instrument-specific, rule-specific.*

40 Supra, note 21.

délimiter, encore une fois, la notion de matière civile dans le règlement Bruxelles IIbis. On peut lire dans les para. 38, 40 et 48 :

> « En troisième lieu, je souligne que le règlement nº 44/2001 dispose, à l'article 1er, paragraphe 1, qu'"il ne recouvre notamment pas les matières fiscales, douanières ou administratives" (...). Contrairement au règlement no 44/2001, le règlement no 2201/2003 ne prévoit pas, à son article 1er, qu'il ne s'applique pas aux matières administratives. Or, l'adoption du règlement no 2201/2003, le 27 novembre 2003, est postérieure à celle du règlement no 44/2001, le 22 décembre 2000, et surtout à l'introduction, en 1978, de la réserve relative aux matières administratives dans la convention de Bruxelles de 1968. Par conséquent, si l'intention du législateur avait été d'exclure les matières administratives du champ d'application du règlement nº 2201/2003, il me semble qu'il l'aurait prévu expressément ». (para. 38)
> « Or, il me semble que la notion de matières civiles au sens du règlement no 2201/2003 ne saurait être interprétée plus strictement que la notion de matière civile au sens du règlement no 44/2001, dans la mesure où le règlement no 2201/2003, contrairement au règlement no 44/2001, ne prévoit pas expressément l'exclusion des matières administratives (...) ». (para. 40)
> « La jurisprudence relative à la notion de matière civile au sens de l'article 1er, paragraphe 1, du règlement no 44/2001 peut, nous l'avons vu (30), être transposée à la notion de matières civiles au sens de l'article 1er, paragraphe 1, du règlement nº 2201/2003 » (para. 48)

De son côté, la Cour rejoint les conclusions de l'AG sur le fond, mais sans mention du régime Bruxelles sauf pour rappeler le principe commun de l'interprétation autonome au para. 28.

Le régime Bruxelles est absent de l'argumentation de la Cour à propos de l'art. 16.1 Bruxelles IIbis, pourtant identique à l'art. 30.1 du règlement Bruxelles I bis, dans l'ordonnance C-173/16, *M.H.*[41]. Réciproquement, l'ordonnance n'est pas reprise dans l'arrêt C-29/16, *HanseYachts AG*[42] sur l'interprétation de l'art. 30.1 Bruxelles, malgré qu'elle ait été évoquée par l'avocat général.

---

41 Ordonnance de la Cour (sixième chambre), 22 juin 2016, ECLI:EU:C:2016:542.

42 Arrêt de la Cour (deuxième chambre), 4 mai 2017, ECLI:EU:C:2017:343. Conclusions de l'avocat général M. Henrik Saugmandsgaard Øe, ECLI:EU:C:2017:44.

L'arrêt C-484/15, *Zulfikarpašić*[43], où il fallait décider si le terme « juridiction » englobe également les notaires dans le cadre du règlement 805/2004, en fournit un autre exemple. D'une part, l'avocat général propose une définition dont l'origine se trouve dans le régime Bruxelles, bien que complétée par la jurisprudence sur d'autres dispositions ; la Cour partage accepte la solution, mais en ignore les fondements.[44] D'autre part, la décision fût rendue le même jour et par la même chambre que celle dans l'affaire C-551/15, *Pula Parking*[45]. On aurait pu s'attendre à une simple renvoi ; et renvoi il y a, mais seulement pour rappel du texte écrit de la loi :

> « Il y a encore lieu de constater que, à la différence, par exemple, du règlement (UE) n° 650/2012 (…) dont l'article 3, paragraphe 2, précise que le terme « juridiction », au sens dudit règlement, englobe non seulement les autorités judiciaires, mais également toute autre autorité compétente dans cette matière qui exerce des fonctions juridictionnelles et qui satisfait à certaines conditions qu'énumère cette même disposition, le règlement n° 805/2004 ne comporte aucune disposition générale dotée d'un tel effet » (para. 35)
>
> « Cette constatation est confortée par la jurisprudence, relative au règlement (UE) n° 1215/2012 du Parlement européen et du Conseil, du 12 décembre 2012, concernant la compétence judiciaire, la reconnaissance et l'exécution des décisions en matière civile et commerciale (JO 2012, L 351, p. 1), selon laquelle l'article 3 de ce règlement, qui prévoit que le terme « juridiction » englobe le service public suédois de recouvrement forcé et les notaires en Hongrie, ne comprend pas les notaires en Croatie (voir, en ce sens, arrêt de ce jour, Pula Parking, C-551/15, point 46) ». (para. 36)

---

43 Arrêt de la Cour (deuxième chambre), 9 mars 2017, ECLI:EU:C:2017:199. Conclusions de l'avocat général M. Yves Bot, ECLI:EU:C:2016:654.

44 Aux para. 74 ss, l'avocat général cherche à définir le concept « juridiction » à l'appui du régime Bruxelles et la notion de « décision » selon l'art. 25 Convention de Bruxelles : « La notion de « décision », au sens de la convention de Bruxelles, implique, en définitive, l'intervention d'un organe juridictionnel investi d'un pouvoir d'appréciation et statuant dans le respect des droits de la défense ». Face à l'imprécision de la jurisprudence relative au régime Bruxelles sur le contenu de la notion d'organe juridictionnel, il a recours à la jurisprudence qui aborde la question sous l'angle de l'article 267 TFUE.

45 Arrêt de la Cour (deuxième chambre), 9 mars 2017, ECLI:EU:C:2017:193. Conclusions de l'avocat général M. Michal Bobek, ECLI:EU:C:2016:825.

Pour le reste, la Cour, qui conclut dans le même sens dans les deux arrêts, s'explique dans chacun d'entre eux exclusivement par rapport au règlement qui est en cause.

Dans l'affaire C-184/14, *A*[46], à propos des arts. 3.c et 3.d du règlement 4/2009, aucun renvoi n'est fait à l'art. 5.2 de la Convention de Bruxelles, ni du règlement 44/2001, qui règlementait auparavant cette question et qui est pourtant mentionné dans le cadre juridique. L'interprétation reste circonscrite au « cercle intérieur » formé par les instruments de droit de la famille, en l'espèce, les règlements 4/2009 et 2201/2003. En revanche, l'avocat général avait souligné le caractère de *lex specialis* du règlement 4/2009 au para. 9 de ses conclusions.

Voyons maintenant quelques illustrations du manque de réflexion sur le régime Bruxelles dans les questions préjudicielles où l'instrument en cause n'offre pas de solution, tandis qu'elle existe dans la Convention ou les règlements Bruxelles I et Ibis, ou dans la jurisprudence les concernant.

Dans l'affaire C-92/12, *Health Service Executive*[47], relative au placement transfrontalier d'un enfant encadré dans le règlement 2201/2003, la juridiction de renvoi voulait savoir si des mesures d'exécution sont possibles dans certaines circonstances, alors même que la déclaration de force exécutoire n'a pas acquis, en droit national, force de chose jugée. L'avocat général, après avoir rappelé l'inexistence dans le règlement 2201/2003 d'une disposition comparable à l'article 47 du règlement 44/2001, qui prévoit expressément la possibilité d'une exécution à des fins conservatoires avant même l'aboutissement de la procédure d'exequatur, estime qu'une solution semblable pourrait exister pour le règlement 2201/2003 et même être exigée dans l'intérêt supérieur de l'enfant. Le raisonnement de la Cour reprend l'opinion de l'avocat général, mais évite toute mention du règlement Bruxelles.

Dans la demande de décision préjudicielle C-4/14, *Christophe Bohez*[48], le juge national posait à la Cour une question sur le droit de visite imposant une astreinte et l'exécution de l'astreinte dans le cadre du règlement 2201/2003. Face au défaut d'une règle à ce propos, l'avocat général soutient les observations écrites du gouvernement espagnol et de la Commission, qui souhaitent combler l'absence dans le règlement 2201/2003 d'une règle telle que celle figurant à l'article 49 du règlement 44/2001 par une applica-

46 Supra note 30.
47 Supra note 20.
48 Supra note 31.

tion analogue de cette disposition. Les réflexions de la Cour portent exclusivement sur le règlement Bruxelles IIbis.

Finalement, dans l'affaire C-256/09, *Purrucker*[49], la juridiction de renvoi demandait si les dispositions des articles 21 et suivants du règlement Bruxelles IIbis, relatives à la reconnaissance et à l'exécution de décisions d'autres États membres, s'appliquent également à des mesures provisoires exécutoires en matière de droit de garde, au sens de l'article 20 du règlement. Dans ce cadre, la Cour est amenée à réfléchir à la compétence de la juridiction ayant adopté des mesures provisoires. Au para. 76, elle va reprendre sa jurisprudence C-99/96, *Mietz*[50] :

> « Lorsque la compétence au fond, conformément au règlement n° 2201/2003, d'une juridiction ayant adopté des mesures provisoires ne ressort pas, de toute évidence, des éléments de la décision adoptée, ou que cette décision ne contient pas une motivation dépourvue de toute ambiguïté, relative à la compétence au fond de cette juridiction, par référence à l'un des chefs de compétence visés aux articles 8 à 14 de ce règlement, il peut en être conclu que ladite décision n'a pas été adoptée conformément aux règles de compétence prévues par ledit règlement. Cette décision peut cependant être examinée au regard de l'article 20 dudit règlement, afin de vérifier si elle relève de cette disposition ».

Et pourtant, aucune mention expresse n'est faite à cette décision. Encore une fois, la Cour ne suit pas les motifs du raisonnement de l'avocat général.

3.4. Pas de (p)référence, mais prise en compte toute de même?

Bien entendu, même sans référence formelle, il peut arriver qu'il existe une préférence pour le régime Bruxelles. L'analyse doit prendre en considération les précédents cités ou rejetés ; il faut aussi évaluer dans quelle mesure le tribunal résume les arguments de l'avocat général et les approuve.

---

49 Supra, note 33.
50 C-99/96, arrêt du 27 avril 1999, ECLI:EU:C:1999:202.

3.4.1. Les précédents

Dans la question préjudicielle C-484/15, *Zulfikarpašić*[51], à propos du règlement 805/2004, la juridiction de renvoi demandait si les notaires, agissant dans le cadre des compétences qui leur sont dévolues par le droit national dans les procédures d'exécution forcée sur le fondement d'un « document faisant foi », relèvent de la notion de « juridiction » au sens de ce règlement. Dans son raisonnement à propos des droits de la défense la Cour rappelle sa jurisprudence portant sur le régime Bruxelles, para 39 :

> « Selon le considérant 10 dudit règlement, cet objectif ne saurait toutefois être atteint en affaiblissant, de quelque manière que ce soit, les droits de la défense (voir, par analogie, arrêt du 14 décembre 2006, ASML, C-283/05, EU:C:2006:787, point 24 et jurisprudence citée) »

Néanmoins, peu après, d'autres arrêts rendus à propos du règlement créant un titre européen pour les créances incontestées font leur apparition pour appuyer le même argument sur le droit de la défense :

> « L'article 16 dudit règlement, lu à la lumière du considérant 12 de celui-ci, prévoit la délivrance, « en bonne et due forme », d'une information au débiteur afin de lui permettre de préparer sa défense et garantit ainsi le caractère contradictoire de la procédure aboutissant à la délivrance du titre exécutoire susceptible de donner lieu à la délivrance d'un certificat. Ces normes minimales traduisent la volonté du législateur de l'Union de veiller à ce que les procédures menant à l'adoption des décisions relatives à une créance incontestée offrent les garanties suffisantes du respect des droits de la défense (voir, en ce sens, arrêt du 16 juin 2016, Pebros Servizi, C-511/14, EU:C:2016:448, point 44) ». (para. 48)

Cette indifférence à l'origine des décisions citées place les instruments juridiques au même niveau, et empêche de reconnaître à l'un d'eux une position conceptuellement privilégiée sur les autres dans l'argumentation de la Cour. En outre, on constate que la Cour, au fil du temps, préfère citer des cas relatifs au règlement en jeu, s'éloignant ainsi du « tronc commun »[52].

---

51 Supra, note 43.

52 Sauf lorsque la Cour énonce des principes généraux comme celui de l'interprétation autonome ; là, souvent les décisions citées à l'appui n'ont rien à voir avec la matière de la question préjudicielle, et pas non plus avec des sujets proches. De cette façon, la Cour tisse un réseau au-delà des limites de la coopération judiciaire en matière civile.

Certes, le régime Bruxelles peut se trouver à la fin d'une chaîne de citations : la décision nommée s'appuie elle-même sur des précédents excipés du régime Bruxelles ; ou d'abord sur d'autres, et on arrive au régime Bruxelles seulement après avoir descendu quelques « marches ». Pourtant, la tendance à invoquer des jugements sur l'instrument européen à la base de la saisine de la Cour renforce peu à peu l'indépendance de cet instrument par rapport à la Convention et aux règlements Bruxelles I et Ibis. C'est ainsi que dans l'arrêt C-523/07, *A*,[53] puis dans la décision C-215/15[54], à propos de la notion de « matière civile » dans le règlement Bruxelles IIbis, mention est seulement faite à l'arrêt C-435/06[55]. De même dans l'ordonnance C-173/16, *M.H.*[56] sur l'interprétation de l'art. 16 pour les besoins de l'art. 19 du règlement Bruxelles IIbis.

3.4.2. Le régime Bruxelles à travers les avocats généraux

Souvent, les avocats généraux mettent en lumière les relations entre les instruments européens. La Cour, de son côté, fait quelque fois des renvois directs aux opinions ou aux conclusions des avocats généraux (ou les reprend mot par mot), incorporant ainsi des réflexions faites à propos du régime Bruxelles : par exemple à l'arrêt C-404/14, *Marie Matoušková*[57], sur le champ d'application matériel du règlement Bruxelles IIbis, para. 30 :

> « En effet, ainsi que Mme l'avocat général l'a relevé au point 41 de ses conclusions (…) »

Au para. 41, l'avocat général évoquait le règlement Bruxelles I :

> « La Cour a d'ailleurs déjà souligné, dans l'affaire Schneider, que la capacité juridique et les questions de représentation y afférentes doivent être appréciées au regard de critères qui leur sont propres et ne doivent pas être traitées comme des questions préalables dépendantes des actes juridiques y afférents. Ladite affaire portait également sur des problèmes de procédure gracieuse, lesquels toutefois se posaient au

53 Arrêt de la Cour (troisième chambre), 2 avril 2009, ECLI:EU:C:2009:225. Conclusions de l'avocat général Mme Juliane Kokott, ECLI:EU:C:2009:39.

54 Supra, note 21.

55 Supra, note 38.

56 Supra, note 41.

57 Arrêt de la Cour (troisième chambre), 6 octobre 2015, ECLI:EU:C:2015:653. Conclusions de l'avocat général Mme Juliane Kokott, ECLI:EU:C:2009:39.

regard du règlement (CE) no 44/2001 du Conseil, du 22 décembre 2000, concernant la compétence judiciaire, la reconnaissance et l'exécution des décisions en matière civile et commerciale »

Dans d'autres cas, l'avocat général n'apparaît pas dans le discours de la Cour, mais il est cependant facile d'y identifier ses arguments. Néanmoins, les conclusions manquent *per se* de valeur normative ; elles ne peuvent être considérées comme adoptées par la Cour en l'absence d'éléments formels en ce sens. Autrement dit, les décisions de la Cour doivent être comprises comme étant des entités autonomes ; leur *background* peut bien se trouver dans les conclusions mais également dans les arguments fournis par d'autres intervenants, auxquels le grand public n'a pas accès, ou de moins en moins. Une fois intégrées dans les arguments de la Cour, elles deviennent la propriété de cette dernière ; l'absence de mention des conclusions de l'avocat général doit être lue comme une volonté consciente de ne pas les épouser en tant que telles. C'est ainsi que nous comprenons la réponse à la question préjudicielle C-523/07[58], à propos des mesures conservatoires dans le règlement Bruxelles IIbis : l'avocat général fait appel à la Convention de Bruxelles et au règlement 44/2001 ; le discours de la Cour est en concordance avec celui de l'avocat général, mais nulle mention n'est faite à ce dernier. Pareillement, dans l'arrêt C-256/09[59], également à propos des mesures conservatoires et du règlement Brussels IIbis, aucune indication n'apparaît d'un lien avec l'avocat général, et cela, malgré l'inspiration évidente que la Cour a dû trouver dans sa référence au cas *Mietz* au para. 142 de l'opinion.

4. *Conclusions*

Trois conclusions se dégagent, à notre avis, de l'exposé qui précède :

Sans aucun doute, « la Convention, en fin de vie, vaut la peine, est toujours vive, active et actuelle »[60]. Pourtant, la conviction que le régime Bruxelles constitue le droit commun dans le domaine du droit européen de la procédure ou, du moins, le point de repère, est surtout un état d'esprit. À l'appui de cette pensée se trouvent notamment les conclusions et les opinions des avocats généraux, acteurs clés de la construction (ou de la mise en lumière) du réseau de relations entre les instruments juridiques

58 Supra note 53.

59 Supra note 33.

60 B. Ancel, Editorial, *Revista Española de Derecho Internacional*, 2018–1, *in fine.*

de l'Union Européenne. Les références de la Cour à des dispositions du régime Bruxelles, ainsi que la citation de décisions prononcées au sujet de la Convention et/ou des règlements Bruxelles I et I bis, renforcent cette conviction. Et pourtant, la jurisprudence de la Cour ne s'inscrit pas forcément dans ce contexte. Sur une échelle, ses arguments sur le lien entre le régime Bruxelles et les autres règlements procéduraux vont de ce qu'on pourrait appeler la « mention décisive », à la pleine indépendance, tout en passant par la « transposition qualifiée » et la « mention sans objet ». De plus, la Cour aboutit parfois à des solutions différentes de celles en vigueur pour le régime Bruxelles, et d'autres fois aux mêmes résultats, sans pourtant y faire appel en s'appuyant donc sur des considérations portant exclusivement sur l'instrument juridique en jeu.

La relation entre les instruments européens sur le droit de la procédure pour les situations transfrontalières ne peut pas (ou ne peut plus) être décrite en termes de « colonne vertébrale », « tronc » (le régime Bruxelles), et « branches » (le reste). En réalité, elle ne corresponde à aucun plan préconçu ; plutôt, le dessin est aléatoire. Les règlements européens de droit procédural font partie d'un processus organique, évolutif, tout comme un corps ; et, tout comme un corps, ses organes interagissent de manière complexe, et souvent inattendue.

Les notions et les termes des règlements doivent être interprétés de façon autonome. À l'origine et pendant longtemps ce principe a été appliqué « en vertical », pour séparer le droit procédural de l'UE du droit procédural national. À présent il fonctionne également de manière horizontale, faisant du contexte et des objectifs de chacun des instruments les données essentielles de l'interprétation.

The Shift from a Choice of Law-Centred Approach to a Civil Procedure Standpoint

Sabine Corneloup[*]

Table of Contents

It is widely accepted that the Brussels I Regulation holds the function of "a point of reference for other EU private international law regulations". This paper would make the point, more generally, that the Brussels Convention and the Brussels I Regulation triggered a shift from a choice of law-centred approach that has dominated Private International Law in Europe for many decades to a civil procedure standpoint. Indeed, the two main components of the European law of civil procedure – the rules on jurisdiction, and the rules on the recognition and enforcement of judgments – have become the pivot of Private International Law in Europe. Brussels I provides the standpoint from which the legal issues are addressed.[1]

In order to further explain this idea, it is necessary, first of all, to clarify the terminology. Within the French tradition, the name 'Private International Law' covers the whole field, including not only choice of law but also international/European civil procedure (*conflits de lois* and *conflits de*

* Professor at University Paris II Panthéon-Assas.

1 See on this topic the recent article of H. Gaudemet-Tallon, "L'irrésistible ascension des conflits de juridictions", in *Mélanges B. Ancel*, Iprolex-LGDJ, 2018, p. 735.

juridictions). Therefore, for a French lawyer, the title of this book chapter ("The European law of civil procedure and private international law") sounds confusing at first sight, because according to the French understanding, European law of civil procedure is actually part of Private International Law. However, other European countries have different approaches. In Germany, for instance, Private International Law traditionally encompasses only choice of law, whereas international civil procedure is seen as a separate field. In the following reflections, we are referring to the French terminological tradition.

In the 20th century, the dominant approach in Private International Law in continental Europe was based on Savigny's theories. It was therefore a choice of law-centred approach. Cross-border relationships between private persons were addressed through the lens of conflict of laws. For instance, the goal of uniformity of decisions, which is a fundamental objective of Private International Law, has traditionally been achieved through choice of law-techniques. *Renvoi* is a prominent example of it. The main Private International Law literature of the 20th century was dedicated to the study of conflicts of laws, whereas international civil procedure was not a primary object of research. Obviously, the latter was not seen as a potential tool to achieve international harmony of solutions. This has completely changed today, notably under the influence of the EU, and first and foremost of the Brussels Convention.[2] Traditional functions of the rules of choice of law, such as the avoidance of limping situations, are now also implemented, for instance, through the principle of mutual recognition of judgments.

The shift from a choice of law-centred approach to a civil procedure standpoint can be observed, first of all, with respect to the fundamental objectives of the EU in the field of Private International Law. Indeed, the mutual recognition of judgments has become the overall objective (1.). Secondly, the rules on jurisdiction have undergone a profound transformation since the adoption of the Brussels Convention. Fundamental functions of choice of law have been extended to jurisdiction (2.), which has had an impact, in particular, on characterization and interpretation (3.). At present, it is not perfectly clear whether the current policy in favour of non-judicial dispute settlement mechanisms may provoke a rebalancing, in

2 In this paper dedicated to the 50th anniversary of the Brussels Convention, we will be focusing on the role of the Brussels Convention and Regulation. See on other causes more generally: D. Bureau, H. Muir Watt, *Droit international privé*, PUF, 2017, vol. 1, n° 55–1 ff., vol. 2, n° 1123 ff.; H. Gaudemet-Tallon, *op. cit.*, p. 738 ff.

the form of a re-shift from civil procedure to choice of law (4.). Interestingly, in matters of family law and successions, the EU has developed in recent years an integrative approach, uniting all components of Private International Law in one single instrument, which is the most appropriate means to raise awareness of the interplay between the two sets of rules and to achieve a well-balanced coordination of all the tools Private International Law has to offer (5.).

1. Mutual Recognition of Judgments, the Fundamental Objective

The whole legal framework on judicial cooperation in civil matters rests upon the principle of mutual recognition. In other words, one of the components of the law of civil procedure has become the ultimate goal and driving force of EU Private International Law. This approach was already present in Art. 220 of the 1957 Rome Treaty, stating that Member States shall enter into negotiations with each other with a view of securing for the benefit of their nationals "the simplification of formalities governing the reciprocal recognition and enforcement of judgments". The 1999 Tampere meeting of the European Council endorsed the principle of mutual recognition of judgments as the "cornerstone" of judicial cooperation in civil matters,[3] which today is expressed in Art. 81(1) TFEU, providing that the Union shall develop judicial cooperation in civil matters having cross-border implications, "based on the principle of mutual recognition of judgments".

Interestingly, the unification of choice of law rules is conceived by Art. 81(2)c) TFEU as one of the means to achieve the free movement of judgments, which seems to assign them a rather subordinated role. This view is more explicitly stated in recital 4 of the Rome I and Rome II Regulations, identifying measures relating to the harmonization of conflict-of-law rules as those facilitating the mutual recognition of judgments.[4] Indeed, common choice of law rules guarantee that all national courts having concurrent jurisdiction in a given case would apply the same law, which in turn is supposed to lead to the same outcome as to the substance of the dispute, regardless of the court actually hearing the case. Harmo-

---

3 See also, for instance, recital 3 of the Rome I and Rome II Regulations.

4 By reference to the 2000 joint Commission and Council programme of measures for implementation of the principle of mutual recognition of decisions in civil and commercial matters.

nized choice of law rules hence facilitate, as well as legitimize, at a later stage the mutual recognition and enforcement of the judgment without control.

Of course, the harmonization of choice of law rules has several other objectives: it also provides greater predictability of the outcome of litigation – and thus legal certainty -, as well as it prevents *forum shopping,* given the plurality of available *fora* in many situations.[5] However, the ultimate goal of the EU is to achieve the free circulation of judgements.

Moreover, the progressive liberalization of the circulation of judgments, which has led to the complete abolition of the exequatur by Regulation no 1215/2012, has progressively also erased the role choice of law rules had played at the recognition and enforcement stage. Initially, under the Brussels Convention a residual control of the applicable law was maintained by Art. 27(4),[6] whereas today, the law applied by the court of the Member State of origin is not at all controlled anymore in the Member State of recognition. This is another indicator for the decreasing position choice of law has within European Private International Law.

In any case, in areas where the domestic laws of the Member States are harmonized, divergences have become negligible and could hardly be seen as an obstacle to mutual recognition within the EU. Given the substantial equivalence of domestic laws, it does not fundamentally matter whether the law of Member State A or Member State B was applied. However, it is symptomatic that even in non-harmonized areas, such as matters relating to the infringement of personality rights where substantive rules as well as choice of law rules do significantly diverge from one Member State to another, judgments circulate freely under the Brussels I Regulation. The principle of mutual recognition applies without any consideration for choice of law.

5 M. Giuliano / P. Lagarde, Report on the Convention on the law applicable to contractual obligations, JOEC, 31.10.1980, n° C 282/5: "To prevent this 'forum shopping', increase legal certainty, and anticipate more easily the law which will be applied, it would be advisable for the rules of conflict to be unified in fields of particular economic importance so that the same law is applied irrespective of the State in which the decision is given."

6 "A judgment shall not be recognized: [...] if the court of the State in which the judgment was given, in order to arrive at its judgment, has decided a preliminary question concerning the status or legal capacity of natural persons, rights in property arising out of a matrimonial relationship, wills or succession in a way that conflicts with a rule of the private international law of the State in which the recognition is sought, unless the same result would have been reached by the application of the rules of private international law of that State".

The same shift from a choice of law-centred approach to a civil procedure standpoint can also be observed regarding the rules on jurisdiction.

2. *Transformation of the Rules on Jurisdiction*

The rules on jurisdiction have undergone a profound transformation, with the adoption of the Brussels Convention and the development of the case-law of the Court of justice.[7] Most importantly, they have become increasingly specialized. The current rules on jurisdiction are manifold and the trend is still towards further specialization, whereas for instance the French Civil Code of 1804 initially only provided for jurisdiction based on nationality (Art. 14 and 15). The Brussels regime contributed a lot to this specialization and diversification.

In the course of transformation, new functions were assigned to the rules on jurisdiction. Indeed, some of the objectives choice of law rules are serving have been extended to jurisdiction. This holds particularly true for the objective of proximity (1). Moreover, while becoming more sophisticated, jurisdictional rules were also assigned substantive goals, such as the objective of protection of weak parties (2).

2.1. *The Objective of Proximity*

The great number of jurisdictional rules that exist today have in common that they are all based on a close connection either with the parties or with the legal relationship: for instance, the domicile of the defendant, the place where the immovable is situated, or the place where the damage occurred. Thus, like choice of law rules, jurisdictional rules have, among other objectives, an objective of proximity,[8] which is regularly stressed by the Court of justice.[9] Of course, unlike choice of law, jurisdiction does not require to identify *the closest* connection. *A* close connection generally suffices. Never-

7 See on this transformation in particular, D. Bureau, H. Muir Watt, *Droit international privé*, vol. II, PUF, 2017, n° 1123 ff.

8 P. Lagarde, « Le principe de proximité dans le droit international privé contemporain », *RCADI*, vol. 196, 1986, p. 1 ff. (on jurisdiction, see especially p. 128 ff.).

9 For recent illustrations, where the Court referred to the objective of proximity of the rules governing jurisdiction (in addition to the objective of predictability), see for instance CJEU, 5 July 2018, *AB "flyLAL-Lithuanian Airlines"*, case C-27/17, pt 40; CJEU, 12 September 2018, *Löber*, case C-304/17, pt 34.

theless, as jurisdictional rules rely on a close connection, they contribute, in their own way, to locate cross-border relationships. They do not locate the relation's seat, in the sense of Savigny, but it is nonetheless an operation consisting in locating legal relations, and this has important consequences. Indeed, the location of private relationships traditionally is the role of choice of law rules. Hence, a fundamental function of choice of law has shifted, at least partially, to jurisdiction.

2.2. The Objective of Protection

The same shift took place with respect to substantive objectives. Several considerations like the protection of weak parties, which initially have guided only choice of law rules, have been extended to jurisdiction. This can be illustrated with the rules on contracts of employment.

In 1982, when the Court ruled in the *Ivenel* case on the Brussels Convention that for employment contracts, it is the characteristic obligation, which is to be taken into account for jurisdiction, not the obligation in question, the Court referred to the Rome Convention.[10] Hence, the interpretation was not given only in the light of the objectives of the Brussels Convention and the general scheme of its provisions. More precisely, in accordance with the Jenard Report, the decision relied on the idea that the rules on jurisdiction for contracts of employment should coincide with the rules determining the applicable law. According to the Court, the close connection with the case, required by Art. 5 of the Brussels Convention, lies in the law applicable to the contract. Therefore, the connecting factor for jurisdiction was aligned, by the 1989 San Sebastian Convention, with the connecting factor set out in the Rome Convention. In other words, the objective of protection was introduced into the rules on jurisdiction, which resulted in two sets of parallel provisions (i.e. Art. 8 of the Rome I Regulation and Art. 20 – 23 of the Brussels Ibis Regulation), which the Court interprets each of them in the light of the other. For instance, in the *Ryanair* case on jurisdiction, the Court relied on its case law relating to the Rome Convention and Regulation,[11] whereas in the *Koelzsch* case on applicable law, it referred for the purpose of interpreting the Rome Convention

10 ECJ, 28 May 1982, *Ivenel*, case 133/81, pt 12 ff.

11 CJEU, 14 September 2017, *Ryanair*, joined cases C-168/16 et C-169/16, pt 55.

to decisions rendered in application of the Brussels Convention and Regulation.[12]

The above examples show that fundamental functions of choice of law have been extended to the rules on jurisdiction. That is not to say that jurisdiction and applicable law have systematically the same functions; the system and objectives of each regulation remain specific. However, the lines between the two sets of rules are increasingly blurred, which in turn contributes to the fact that cross-border relationships are increasingly addressed from a civil procedure standpoint. Today, decisive choices are made at the jurisdictional stage, when the EU legislator drafts the common rules on jurisdiction, or when the Court of justice interprets these rules. In other words, decisive patterns are set by application of the Brussels I Regulation.

More precisely, with respect to the substance of the rules, the direction of influence seems dominantly be an influence of choice of law on jurisdiction. Solutions generally have their roots in the field of choice of law before being extended to jurisdiction. However, rather than supporting an overall choice of law-oriented approach in Private International Law, this evolution has resulted in conferring a pivotal role to the rules on jurisdiction, which in the end has an impact, in return, on the applicable law. The issues of characterization ("*la qualification*") and interpretation of common notions provide a striking illustration of this interaction.

3. *Impact on Characterization and Interpretation of Common Notions*

Traditionally, qualification has been a component of the methodology of choice of law, and as long as autonomous notions of EU law are not concerned, the principle of the *lex fori* characterization applies. Today, however, as the rules on jurisdiction have become increasingly specialized, it is often necessary to characterize the legal relationship already at the jurisdictional stage.[13] For instance, the application of the Brussels I Regulation requires to assess whether the dispute relates to a civil or commercial matter, to a contract or a tort, to the sale of goods or the provision of services, a consumer or a professional, etc. These are common notions, employed

12 CJEU, 15 March 2011, *Koelzsch*, case C-29/10, pt 33 and 41.

13 S. Lemaire, « La qualification », in Azzi/Boskovic, *Quel avenir pour la théorie générale des conflits de lois?*, Bruylant, 2015, p. 35.

by jurisdictional rules as well as choice of law rules in Regulations Brussels I, Rome I and Rome II.

Consequently, if a dispute arises between the parties, qualification is already required for the purpose of jurisdiction. And since disputes concerning jurisdiction are much more frequent in practice than disputes regarding choice of law, the Court of justice has adopted a rich body of case law under the Brussels Convention and Regulation. Thus, in many instances, decisive orientations were decided in the perspective of jurisdiction. Subsequently, and in accordance with the principle of consistent interpretation, they were transposed to the applicable law under the Rome I and Rome II Regulations. Indeed, recital 7 of the latter regulations provides that the substantive scope and the provisions should be consistent with the other regulations of the trilogy.[14]

Arguably, the fact that several choice of law functions have shifted towards jurisdiction facilitates a uniform interpretation and makes it even natural. An example, among many others, is the qualification of an action brought by a consumer protection association for the purpose of preventing a trader from using unfair terms in consumer contracts. In the 2016 *Verein für Konsumenteninformation* decision, the Court of justice aligned the qualification under Rome I and Rome II with the solution given in the 2002 *Henkel* case[15] on jurisdiction, by deciding that this is a matter relating to tort.[16] According to the Court, "in the light of the aim of consistent application [...], the view that, in matters of consumer protection, non-contractual liability extends also to the undermining of legal stability by the use of unfair terms which it is the task of consumer protection associations to prevent (see, to that effect, judgment of 1 October 2002 in *Henkel*, C-167/00, EU:C:2002:555, paragraph 42) is fully applicable to the interpretation of the Rome I and Rome II Regulations".

Another subject matter governed by highly specialized rules on jurisdiction are infringements of personality rights on the internet. In *eDate Advertising and Martinez*[17] and in *Bolagsupplysningen*,[18] the Court developed a specific interpretation of the notion of the 'place where the damage

14 See on the consistency requirement, M. Szpunar, « Droit international privé de l'Union : cohérence des champs d'application et/ou des solutions? », *Rev. crit. DIP* 2018, p. 573; and the contribution to the present volume, *supra*, p.71.

15 CJEU, 1 October 2002, *Henkel*, case C-167/00.

16 CJEU, 28 July 2016, *Verein für Konsumenteninformation*, case C-191/15, pt 38 and 39.

17 CJEU, 25 October 2011, *eDate Advertising a.o.*, C-509/09 and C-161/10.

18 CJEU, 17 October 2017, *Bolagsupplysningen*, case C-194/16.

occurred', i.e. the place of the victim's centre of interests, which applies only to the violation of personality rights and not to other cyber-torts. In this respect, it is not yet clear in how far decisions on characterization and interpretation for the purpose of jurisdiction may precisely impact the determination of the applicable law, but it is likely that there will be an impact. A court in the State of the victim's centre of interests, which has established its jurisdiction on the ground that the proceedings relate to a violation of personality rights, will presumably transpose that characterization to the conflict of laws. As a result, the proceedings would fall into one of the gaps of the European harmonization and lead to the application of national choice of law rules.[19] On the contrary, if in a dispute similar to the *Bolagsupplysningen* case, a court characterizes the proceedings as relating to an act of unfair competition, since acts of disparagement for instance may fall under that notion, this would not only have consequences on the interpretation of the place where the damage occurred according to Art. 7(2) of the Brussels Ibis Regulation, as the victim's centre of interest would not be available, but would probably also affect the choice of law. By transposing the characterization from jurisdiction to choice of law, the court would make Art. 6 of the Rome II Regulation applicable. And here again, the question of consistent interpretation of common notions would arise, since acts of unfair competition affecting exclusively the interests of a specific competitor fall under Art. 4 and thus are governed by the law of the place where the damage occurred. Arguably, this connecting factor would be understood in the same way as it was for the purpose of jurisdiction.

It should be stressed that, in some cases, consistent interpretation may lead to the application of the law of the forum, but that it does not necessarily result in a general convergence of *forum* and *ius* in all cases.[20] Indeed, as Advocate general M. Szpunar explains, the principle of consistent interpretation according to recital 7 only relates to the substantive scope and the provisions.[21] There is no general requirement of convergence of solutions; in other words, the consistency requirement does not amount to a

19 See Art. 1(2)g of the Rome II Regulation excluding from its scope of application non-contractual obligations arising out of violations of privacy and rights relating to personality, including defamation.

20 For instance, in CJEU, 5 July 2018, *AB "flyLAL-Lithuanian Airlines"*, case C-27/17, pt 41, the Court refers to the consistency requirement of recital 7 as an argument among others in favour of the alignment of the place of damage and the affected market.

21 M. Szpunar, *op. cit.*

general requirement of convergence of jurisdiction and applicable law. Each regulation conserves its own objectives and system and unquestionably jurisdiction and applicable law do not systematically have the same functions. Thus, there may be convergence, if the connecting factors used by the rules on jurisdiction and applicable law are identical, or divergence, if that is not the case.

In any event, even in the absence of such convergence, the above examples show that decisive orientations for the outcome of the proceedings are often set in application of the Brussels I Regulation. To a certain extent, the chronology of judicial proceedings pushes choice of law rules back into the position of followers, whereas Brussels I provides the standpoint from which the legal issues are addressed.

4. *Potential Influence of Policies in Favour of Non-Judicial Dispute Settlement Mechanisms*

Policies in favour of non-judicial dispute settlement mechanisms (conciliation, mediation, collaborative law approaches, etc.) currently exist at national level in most Member States, as well as at EU-level.[22] They are targeting both, family disputes as well as civil and commercial disputes. Alternative dispute resolution mechanisms are generally perceived as appropriate means for the States not only to reduce the workload of national courts, and thus to save costs and time, but also to offer the parties an attractive alternative to court proceedings. They are generally considered to be faster, cheaper and, most importantly, less damaging to ongoing business or family relations.

One may wonder whether the development of such out-of-court mechanisms is going to have an impact on the pivotal role the European law of civil procedure currently plays. It could indeed contribute to a re-shift within Private International Law, from civil procedure to choice of law, since neither the rules on jurisdiction, nor the rules on the recognition and enforcement are applicable to such private, non-judicial settlement agreements. Therefore, if these dispute settlement mechanisms are gaining in

---

22 See in particular Directive 2008/52/EC of 21 May 2008 on certain aspects of mediation in civil and commercial matters; see also the 2017 Report of the JURI Committee of the European Parliament on the implementation of the directive, PE595.445, A8–0238/2017.

importance in the future, the law of civil procedure could correspondingly lose its prominent role.

In order to address this question, it is necessary to distinguish between different types of mechanisms which exist in practice, because they can be more or less closely linked to judicial proceedings. On the one hand, there are types of out-of-court settlements, which indeed involve in no way a State court. They are the kind of settlement agreements the future UNCITRAL convention and model law on the enforcement of international settlement agreements address.[23] In these situations, only choice of law is at stake. More precisely, when the parties are negotiating solutions to their disputes, the applicable law is rarely a decisive factor for them. Generally, the parties follow a more factual than legal approach to settle their disputes. Yet, the underlying legal order serves as a frame of reference for the parties to make credible commitments during the negotiations. Moreover, the applicable law may have an important role at a later stage, if the validity of the settlement agreement is challenged. The development of such ADR could trigger a trend back to a more choice of law-oriented approach, as no forum provides a civil procedure standpoint.

On the other hand, there are also many ADR types, which are closely linked to court proceedings: for instance, where the judge, in the course of judicial proceedings, facilitates a settlement of the dispute, or where a settlement agreement concluded by the parties is subject to subsequent judicial approval in order to become legally binding. The Brussels I Regulation applies to both cases, either for the jurisdiction of the court, or for the enforcement of the court settlement. Therefore, it is rather unlikely that this second type of mechanisms could provoke a re-balancing of the centre of gravity in Private International Law from civil procedure to choice of law, even if they were to gain in importance in the future.

Moreover, the latest legislative evolutions in family matters raise further doubts as to the likelihood of a trend reversal in the near future. A well-known example is the new French divorce by mutual consent.[24] Over the past years, the reform has raised strong concerns regarding the ability of such divorces to develop cross-border effects under EU law since, similarly to out-of-court-settlements, they take place without any court being

23 United Nations draft Convention on International Settlement Agreements Resulting from Mediation, to be adopted in Singapore in 2019 (the future 'Singapore Convention on Mediation'); UNCITRAL Model Law on International Commercial Mediation and International Settlement Agreements Resulting from Mediation, 2018.

24 Art. 229–1 of the French Civil Code.

involved and without being included in an authentic document. Therefore, these divorces rather seemed to fall under the methodology of choice of law. However, during the recast of the Brussels IIbis Regulation, the definition of the notion of 'agreement' for the purpose of recognition and enforcement was broadened, in order to encompass such private divorces, provided that they have been registered by a public authority.[25] This brought the French private divorce by mutual consent under the Brussels regime. In other words, the Brussels IIter Regulation extended the European law of civil procedure to situations, which would normally have fallen under choice of law. In addition, the new Regulation also projects its jurisdictional rules on such private agreements. The certificate necessary for cross-border recognition and enforcement can only be issued if the Member State which empowered the authority to register the agreement had jurisdiction under the Regulation.[26] Hence, the privatization of divorce, rather than operating a re-shift in favour of choice of law, provided another opportunity for the European law of civil procedure to further develop its attractive force and to confirm its pivotal role.

5. Towards an Integrative Approach

In recent years, the EU legislator has increasingly opted for a comprehensive approach, combining in one regulation jurisdiction, choice of law and the recognition and enforcement of decisions. The 2008 Maintenance Regulation[27] (combined with the 2007 Hague Protocol[28]), the 2012 Regulation on Successions[29] and the two 2016 Regulations on the property

---

25 Regulation No 2019/1111 of 24 May 2019 on jurisdiction, the recognition and enforcement of decisions in matrimonial matters and the matters of parental responsibility, and on international child abduction (recast), "Brussels II ter", Art. 2. (2) 3, combined with Art. 64 ff. See e.g. S. Corneloup, T. Kruger, "Le règlement 2019/1111, Bruxelles II : la protection des enfants gagne du ter(rain) ", *Rev. crit. DIP* 2020, vol. 2, forthcoming.

26 Art. 66 (2) a).

27 Regulation No 4/2009 of 18 December 2008 on jurisdiction, applicable law, recognition and enforcement of decisions and cooperation in matters relating to maintenance obligations.

28 Hague Protocol of 23 November 2007 on the law applicable to maintenance obligations.

29 Regulation No 650/2012 of 4 July 2012 on jurisdiction, applicable law, recognition and enforcement of decisions and acceptance and enforcement of authentic

regimes of international couples[30], provide illustrations of this approach.[31] By uniting all components of Private International Law in one single instrument, the legislator has drafted each rule in the light of the others, which made the interplay between them more apparent. Such an integrative perspective inevitably strengthens the consistent characterization and interpretation of common notions, because it seems rather inconceivable to develop divergent interpretations within the same regulation. It also avoids the biases induced by the chronology of judicial proceedings, where jurisdiction comes first, and choice of law second, which inevitably have also an impact on the case law of the Court of justice.

In these matters of family law and successions, it is remarkable that the integrative approach has led to an increasing convergence of jurisdiction and applicable law. The situations where the courts end up applying their own law have become more frequent, be it because the regulations adopt identical connecting factors for jurisdiction and applicable law (common habitual residence of the spouses, last habitual residence of the deceased, habitual residence of the creditor of maintenance, etc.), provide for the application of the law of the forum as subsidiary solution, or make jurisdiction conditional on the applicable law[32]. Various patterns exist, but they all have in common to lead to an increasing convergence of solutions.[33]

Should this model be transposed to civil and commercial matters? From a policy perspective, it would undeniably be advisable to similarly favour an integrative approach, and hence to merge the Rome I, Rome II and Brussels Ibis Regulations into one single instrument. This would first of all lead to a simpler and clearer legal framework for citizens and legal practitioners. Moreover, by raising greater awareness of the interactions between

---

instruments in matters of succession and on the creation of a European Certificate of Succession.

30 Regulation No 2016/1103 of 24 June 2016 implementing enhanced cooperation in the area of jurisdiction, applicable law and the recognition and enforcement of decisions in matters of matrimonial property regimes; Regulation No 2016/1104 of 24 June 2016 implementing enhanced cooperation in the area of jurisdiction, applicable law and the recognition and enforcement of decisions in matters of the property consequences of registered partnerships.

31 The EU is hereby following the Hague Conference on Private International Law, which had implemented a similar integrative approach already in earlier conventions, such as the 1996 Convention on the protection of children.

32 See for instance Art. 5, 6, 7 and 9 of Regulation No 650/2012 on successions.

33 Which may raise interesting questions. See, for instance, in the field of maintenance obligations, CJEU, 20 September 2018, *Mölk*, case C-214/17.

the different components of Private International Law, it would also allow the EU to address the interactions more directly and systematically than today.

In this respect, it is to be stressed that, while strengthening the overall coherence, such a partial codification would not necessarily also result in greater convergence of *forum* and *ius*, which in civil and commercial matters is not an objective *per se*. Indeed, to date, these matters have not been affected to the same extent as family law and successions by the recent trend towards such a convergence. This is not only due to the fact that the rules on civil procedure and the rules on applicable law happened to be harmonized at different moments in time, in separate regulations. The connecting factors are often not the same,[34] and unrestricted party autonomy plays a dominant role, allowing for tailor-made solutions[35]. Notable exceptions are matters subject to exclusive jurisdiction and contracts with weaker parties, where specific considerations explain that the courts normally apply the *lex fori*, but these considerations cannot be generalized.

In summary, after a long period where private international law was dominated by a choice of law-centred approach, a shift towards a more civil procedure-based standpoint took place under the notable influence of the Brussels Convention. However, in family matters and successions, this shift is currently giving way to an all-encompassing perspective, where choice of law and civil procedure are brought more closely together. This appears to be the most suited way forward also in civil and commercial matters.

34 Habitual residence *versus* place of performance, for instance.

35 Even though in practice, parties often opt for the same State, by choosing its courts as well as its law It is indeed not rare that the parties themselves wish to establish such a link, as it has many advantages from a practical point of view.

The Contribution of 'Brussels I' to the Process of EU Integration: a True Trailblazer for the Europeanization and Constitutionalization of Private International Law

Johan Meeusen[*]

Table of Contents

1. *Introduction*

The interaction between the European law of civil procedure and private international law is often examined from the perspective of the consistency and convergences between the Brussels Ibis Regulation[1] (and its predecessors) and the Rome I and II Regulations[2] (and the preceding Rome Con-

---

* Prof. Dr Johan Meeusen LL.M. (UC Berkeley) is Honorary Vice-Rector and Professor of European Union Law and Private International Law at the University of Antwerp, Belgium (www.uantwerpen.be/johan-meeusen). This contribution was concluded on 31 October 2018.

1 Regulation (EU) No 1215/2012 of the European Parliament and of the Council of 12 December 2012 on jurisdiction and the recognition and enforcement of judgments in civil and commercial matters.

2 Regulation (EC) No 593/2008 of the European Parliament and of the Council of 17 June 2008 on the law applicable to contractual obligations (Rome I Regulation);

tracts Convention), and quite understandably so. The respective recitals 7 of the two latter regulations mention that their substantive scope and provisions should be consistent with the Brussels Ibis Regulation, which raises a number of intriguing questions, particularly where the interpretation of these regulations by the Court of Justice of the European Union (CJEU[3]) is concerned[4].

Still, the consistency between the European Union (EU) instruments on private international law, and in particular between 'Brussels I'[5] and the regulations holding choice-of-law rules, can be approached as well from a different perspective. Rather than on their contribution to the development of a generally coherent system of private international law, this alternative perspective could focus on their nature as instruments of EU law. Examined from such point of view, the Brussels I regime has fulfilled a remarkable role as a pioneer, but even more a trailblazer for the Europeanization and constitutionalization of private international law more generally. It is on this particular contribution of Brussels I to the structural embedding of private international law within the EU's legal system that this contribution will focus.

The celebration of the 50th anniversary of the European law of civil procedure, as the Brussels Convention was signed half a century ago, invites us to take stock of the evolutions that have taken place in the past fifty years. This brief contribution examines the relationship between Brussels I and private international law more generally. It develops the thesis that Brussels I overcame primary law deficiencies and has served as a major and dynamic trailblazer for the Europeanization and even constitutionalization of private international law more generally, including choice of law. This process is however still characterized by some important challenges, specifically relating to non-discrimination, which should be taken on when,

---

Regulation (EC) No 864/2007 of the European Parliament and of the Council of 11 July 2007 on the law applicable to non-contractual obligations (Rome II Regulation).

3 In this contribution, the term 'CJEU' is used systematically to refer to the Court of Justice of the European Union, also where its pre-Lisbon judgments are concerned.

4 See also recitals 17 and 24 of the Rome I Regulation.

5 In this contribution, "Brussels I" as well as "the Brussels I regime" are referred to as general terms for the European rules on jurisdiction, recognition and enforcement in civil and commercial matters, as provided respectively by the so-called Brussels Convention of 27 September 1968, the Brussels I Regulation (Regulation 44/2001 of 22 December 2000) and the current Brussels Ibis Regulation (Regulation 1215/2012 of 12 December 2012).

within a few years, a new, further modernized Brussels Iter regulation will be prepared[6].

2. *Brussels I as an Integration Instrument*

Any analysis of Brussels I that focuses solely on its position as an important source of private international law for the EU Member States risks being only one-dimensional and would overlook both the way it serves (or should serve) to achieve the EU's objectives and the way it is determined by the particular principles and characteristics of EU law. Within the EU, private international law is today to a large extent EU law and should be understood and interpreted first and foremost in that sense[7].

Such EU-centred approach of course rests on recognition of the great pertinence of private international law for the process of European integration. Economic integration and, more generally, the development of "an area without internal frontiers", as put forward since the adoption of the Single European Act in 1986, would simply be impossible without adequate European rules on the private law aspects of cross-border acts and facts.

Still, one cannot deny that private international law has not easily found its true place within the European legal order, and this search is probably not even over yet. Most likely, this is due to the uneasiness that has long characterized the EU as regards the position which must be granted within its legal system to private law more generally. Its objective of integration was initially approached through the elimination of all kinds of obstacles stemming from, in particular, public, administrative and economic law, with marginal attention only paid to the impact of private law[8]. This awkwardness as regards private law could actually be detected in the original EEC Treaty, which in Art. 220 (as well as later in Art. 293 EC Treaty, consolidated version after Amsterdam) recognized the pertinence of private international law only in a very limited way, by holding that

> "Member States shall, so far as is necessary, enter into negotiations with each other with a view to securing for the benefit of their nationals: (...)

6 Cf. the task assigned to the Commission by Art. 79 Brussels Ibis.

7 R. Michaels, "The New European Choice-of-Law Revolution", 82 *Tulane L. Rev.*, 2008, (1607), 1642.

8 *Id.*, 1626.

– the simplification of formalities governing the reciprocal recognition and enforcement of judgments of courts or tribunals (…).”

The attention that the drafters of the EEC Treaty devoted to private (international) law was not only minimal, but moreover isolated from the regular integration instruments and made subject to traditional intergovernmental negotiations.

Today, things are very different as the area of freedom, security and justice (AFSJ), which includes private international law, has been granted a prominent place in the process of European integration and its achievement has been recognized as one of the Union's objectives at the same level as the internal market (Art. 3(2) TEU[9]). Nevertheless, the provisions of the TFEU[10] on judicial cooperation in civil matters having cross-border implications still suffer from deficiencies and uncertainties[11]. A more careful and precise phrasing of these Treaty provisions – Articles 67(4) and 81 TFEU – would further strengthen the position of private international law within the EU.

Against that background, it is noteworthy that an essential impulse for the growth and impact of the Brussels I regime can be traced back to the original concept of the Brussels Convention of 1968, which on two important points differed from the approach that characterized (then) Art. 220 EEC Treaty.

While Art. 220 EEC Treaty did not require this, the Brussels Convention from the start has been a '*convention double*', providing rules not only with regard to the recognition and enforcement of foreign judgments, but on international jurisdiction as well. This way, Brussels I has introduced a procedural regime that is essentially built on mutual trust, as this is emphasized in recital 26 of the current Brussels Ibis Regulation. The Member States have been able to build confidence on the basis of the reciprocal application of identical jurisdiction rules, which has also convinced them to abandon exorbitant and protective jurisdiction rules for the so-called intra-European relationships (Art. 5 Brussels Ibis). Equally important is that, in spite of the wording of the original Art. 220 EEC Treaty, Brussels I has fortunately not been limited to the sole benefit of the Member States'

9 Treaty on European Union.

10 Treaty on the Functioning of the European Union.

11 J. Meeusen, "De 'ruimte van vrijheid, veiligheid en recht' en de 'justitiële samenwerking in burgerlijke zaken' in de Europese Unie: pleidooi voor een beter verdragsrechtelijk kader" in *Voor recht, rechtvaardigheid en Camus. Liber Amicorum Bernard Hubeau*, Bruges, Die Keure, 2018, (177), 177–191.

nationals. The adoption of the limited approach that was referred to by Art. 220 EEC Treaty would have strongly increased the importance of the Member States' residual rules, or could have initiated the adoption by the Member States of a full-fledged alternative system with nationality as the decisive criterion. The focus on domicile for the jurisdictional system and the generalization of recognition and enforcement to all Member State judgments have managed to develop Brussels I as the Member States' common regime for the internal market and, even more broadly today, the European area without internal frontiers.

Hence, while Art. 220 EEC Treaty was framed in the typical terms of intergovernmental cooperation, the two elements mentioned demonstrate that the ambitions of Brussels I have from the start been much greater: it has rather been conceived as an instrument serving integration. In that same respect, the introduction, by the Protocol of 3 June 1971[12], of the possibility for (many, though not all) Member State courts to refer preliminary questions to the Court of Justice has been of particular significance as well. It was a first major step, that eventually turned out to have a great impact, to tie the Brussels Convention firmly within the EU's general system of judicial protection and uniform interpretation.

These essential links between Brussels I and the process of European integration have impacted in turn on the leading position that this instrument has acquired within the so-called AFSJ and the effect it has had on the further development – through Europeanization and constitutionalization – of private international law within the EU.

3. *Brussels I as a Trailblazer for the Europeanization of Private International Law*

Through its main characteristics as described above, the Brussels I regime has greatly contributed to embedding private international law, choice of law included, firmly within the EU legal system. Brussels I, which the European Commission has even described as "the matrix of civil judicial cooperation in the European Union"[13], has first triggered and then strengthened the Europeanization of private international law. This also

12 Protocol on the interpretation by the Court of Justice of the Convention of 27 September 1968 on jurisdiction and the enforcement of judgments in civil and commercial matters, signed in Luxembourg on 3 June 1971.

13 European Commission, *Proposal for a Regulation of the European Parliament and of the Council on jurisdiction and the recognition and enforcement of judgments in civil*

affects the position of private law more generally within the EU's legal system.

A first important step in this process of Europeanization of private international law, far beyond the significance of the (current) Brussels Ibis Regulation itself, is that Brussels I has paved the way for a European procedural network. Brussels I has not remained an isolated instrument, but has triggered the integration of other procedural concerns under the broad concept of "access to justice", which is today referred to by Art. 67(4) TFEU. The latter concept has not yet been adequately defined and one can even doubt whether the drafters of this Treaty provision envisaged any precise understanding[14]. Still, it has long[15] served as the common denominator, sometimes jointly with "access to law"[16], for the adoption of a whole set of legislative acts, in particular regulations. Together, and actually in addition to the specific procedural rules which are provided by Brussels I itself, such as those on *lis pendens* and related actions[17], they constitute a network of procedures that has complemented Brussels I[18]. The diverse procedural rules involved must obviously be considered in their own right,

---

and commercial matters (Recast), COM(2010) 748 final, 3 (Explanatory memorandum).

14 J. Meeusen, F. van Overbeeke and L. Verhaert, "The Link Between Access to Justice and European Conflict of Laws After Lisbon. Much Ado About Nothing?", 81 *RabelsZ*, 2017, 858–883.

15 See e.g. the references to access to justice in the early policy documents, such as § 2 of the Commission communication to the Council and the European Parliament – 'Towards greater efficiency in obtaining and enforcing judgments in the European Union', (COM)1997 609 final, and § 15–16 of the Action Plan of the Council and the Commission of 3 December 1998 on how best to implement the provisions of the Treaty of Amsterdam on an area of freedom, security and justice (*O.J.*, 23 January 1999, C 19, 1), followed later by the Presidency conclusions of the European Council's Tampere meeting (1999), § 30 and the Hague and Stockholm Programmes (European Council, "The Hague Programme: strengthening freedom, security and justice in the European Union", Chapter III.3; European Council, "The Stockholm Programme – An open and secure Europe serving and protecting citizens", § 3).

16 Presidency conclusions of the European Council's Tampere meeting (1999), § 38.

17 Articles 29ff Brussels Ibis Regulation.

18 See e.g. Council Regulation n°1206/2001 of 28 May 2001 on cooperation between the courts of the Member States in the taking of evidence in civil or commercial matters; Council Directive 2003/8/EC of 27 January 2003 to improve access to justice in cross-border disputes by establishing minimum common rules relating to legal aid for such disputes; Regulation n°805/2004 of the European Parliament and of the Council of 21 April 2004 creating a European Enforcement Order for uncontested claims; Regulation (EC) n°1896/2006 of the European Parliament

as they each have their own precise objectives. But certainly, the broad ambition shown by the Brussels I regime has laid bare the need and prompted the search for other common procedural regimes which would complete the European law of civil procedure[19] and unite the Member States' systems in a single procedural network that, on the one hand, ensures efficient and accessible cross-border litigation in civil and commercial matters[20] and, on the other hand, even provides specific alternatives for the main regime that Brussels I constitutes[21]. Ultimately, this procedural network has facilitated in its turn the transition from the Brussels I Regulation to the Brussels Ibis Regulation and, in particular, the abolition of exequatur by the latter[22]. Very probably therefore, the European law of civil procedure would today be very different, and in particular have a much less impressive scope and impact, if Brussels I had been approached as a typical intergovernmental instrument holding common rules with a limited scope of application and separate from a solid institutional framework.

The impact of Brussels I has not been limited to procedural issues – it has been at the root of the Europeanization of choice-of-law rules as well. The European unification of private international law started with Brussels I and the focus on what one might call a 'procedural approach'. According to the Presidency conclusions of its Tampere meeting (1999), the European Council famously destined the principle of mutual recognition to become "the cornerstone of judicial co-operation in both civil and criminal matters" (§ 33), and a similar approach was clearly present in, e.g., the European Council's Hague and Stockholm Programmes (of 2004 and 2009

and of the Council of 12 December 2006 creating a European order for payment procedure (as amended by Regulation (EU) 2015/2421 of the European Parliament and of the Council of 16 December 2015); Regulation n°861/2007 of the European Parliament and the Council of 11 July 2007 establishing a European Small Claims Procedure (as amended by Regulation (EU) 2015/2421 of the European Parliament and of the Council of 16 December 2015).

19 See e.g. Art. 6(1) of Regulation 1896/2006 (European order for payment).

20 See e.g. recital 8 of Regulation 1206/2001 (Taking of evidence) and recitals 8–10 of Directive 2003/8 (Legal aid).

21 See recital 20 of Regulation 805/2004 (European Enforcement Order).

22 P. Mankowski, "The impact of the Brussels Ibis Regulation on the 'second generation' of European procedural law" in P. Mankowski (ed.), *Research Handbook on the Brussels Ibis Regulation*, Cheltenham, Edward Elgar Publishing, 2020, 230.

respectively)[23], which both mentioned the harmonization of choice-of-law rules in the context of their emphasis on the mutual recognition of decisions. The easy intra-European recognition and enforcement of judgments, and their free movement, was (and actually still is) considered a goal of prime importance. The harmonization of choice-of-law rules was originally approached as instrumental to that end as the adoption of common choice-of-law rules would increase the confidence granted by each State to other States' judgments[24]. To a certain extent, this also explains why the Europeanization of choice of law has first focused on the unification of the rules on international contracts and torts through the Rome I and Rome II Regulations. But as this is also true in other fields of EU law, the process of Europeanization has eventually turned out to be unstoppable. It has resulted in a broad, European harmonization of private international law, stretching to topics that in 1968 were still unimaginable. The success of Brussels I, with corresponding choice-of-law legislation on contracts and torts, has been extended to other fields where similar approaches, with due attention given to the links between jurisdiction, choice of law and recognition and enforcement, have been introduced. Moreover, the emergence and steadily increasing importance of Union citizenship has prompted renewed attention regarding the free movement of persons and a corresponding move to family law and related areas. While the legislature in the introductory recitals to its regulations still routinely refers to the "general objective" of the mutual recognition of decisions[25], these (more recent) regulations approach choice of law in its own right.

---

23 European Council, "The Hague Programme: strengthening freedom, security and justice in the European Union" (III, § 3.4.2) and "The Stockholm Programme – An open and secure Europe serving and protecting citizens" (§ 3.1.2 and 3.3.2).

24 See for more detailed references and clarification: A. Fillers, "Implications of Article 81(1) TFEU's recognition clause for EU conflict of laws rules", 14 *JPIL*, 2018, (476), 484ff.

25 Recital 59 of Regulation (EU) n°650/2012 of the European Parliament and of the Council of 4 July 2012 on jurisdiction, applicable law, recognition and enforcement of decisions and acceptance and enforcement of authentic instruments in matters of succession and on the creation of a European Certificate of Succession (Successions Regulation), recital 56 of Council Regulation (EU) 2016/1103 of 24 June 2016 implementing enhanced cooperation in the area of jurisdiction, applicable law and the recognition and enforcement of decisions in matters of matrimonial property regimes (Matrimonial property Regulation) and recital 55 of Council Regulation (EU) 2016/1104 of 24 June 2016 implementing enhanced cooperation in the area of jurisdiction, applicable law and the recognition and enforcement of decisions in matters of the property consequences of registered partnerships (Partnership Property Regulation).

Apart from its impact on the adoption of further legislation on private international law, both on procedure and choice of law, it appears that Brussels I has had an even broader influence. It has laid the basis for a joint European approach to the resolution of cross-border private law disputes by national courts that act, through the system of preliminary references, in close cooperation with the Court of Justice. The national courts have, as from the mid-seventies, not hesitated to refer preliminary questions on Brussels I to the Court of Justice. This has resulted in a steady stream of preliminary judgments on a variety of interpretation issues. These preliminary references have not only contributed to, first of all, concrete dispute resolution by the national courts, but have had the further advantage of familiarizing the Court of Justice itself with the interpretation of private law at European level. In view of the scope and substance of the original EEC Treaty, this was at the time a quite new subject of interpretation in Luxembourg. With hindsight, it can be stated that the Court's preliminary judgments on the then Brussels Convention have very much contributed to the recognition of the pertinence of private law for the European integration process and, more particularly, the full integration of private international law as a standard topic of interest for the European legal order as we know it today. In that respect, it must be added that the CJEU's preference for the autonomous interpretation of Brussels I as well as the importance that is attached to the consistency between the various EU regulations on private international law[26] have reinforced its typically European character, away from the divergent Member States' interpretations of identical concepts.

The impact that Brussels I has had on the process of Europeanization of private international law in the previous decades is therefore undeniable. The Brussels Convention has triggered the recognition of its pertinence, which was later confirmed in more general terms in, at first, various policy documents and thereafter through the introduction of an explicit treaty basis (first Art. 65 EC Treaty, today Art. 81 TFEU). This formal treaty basis has meanwhile often served for the adoption of further legislation regarding both procedural issues and choice of law. This way, the application and interpretation of Brussels I, but probably even its mere existence, have strongly contributed to the transformation of private international law

26 See in particular recitals 7 of the Rome I and Rome II Regulations; recital 59 of the Successions Regulation, recital 56 of the Matrimonial Property Regulation, recital 55 of the Partnership Property Regulation. See also recital 7 of Regulation (EU) 2015/848 of the European Parliament and of the Council of 20 May 2015 on insolvency proceedings (recast).

from a very specific set of rules on the margins of European integration to a full-fledged part of the so-called area of freedom, security and justice, which today is considered a key objective for the EU (Art. 3(2) TEU).

4. Brussels I as a Trailblazer for the Constitutionalization of EU Private International Law

Brussels I has not only paved the way for the Europeanization of private international law, but has also strongly contributed to the constitutionalization of private international law within the EU. It has therefore not only been at the root of the progressive extension *ratione materiae* of the field covered by private international law rules of European origin, but it has left its mark on the very substance of this domain. This is particularly noteworthy with regard to the significance of both fundamental rights and the principles of mutual trust and mutual recognition[27].

4.1. Brussels I, Private International Law and Fundamental Rights Protection

Just as the importance of fundamental rights protection has steadily increased in the EU legal system as a whole, it has in the field of our inquiry broadened from Brussels I to civil judicial cooperation in the area of freedom, security and justice more generally. Although the particular pertinence of fundamental rights for the EU's legal system was recognized many years earlier, in particular through the Court's innovative case law[28], the entering into force of the Treaty of Lisbon has given a real boost to fundamental rights protection, also as regards its significance for EU private international law. Of particular importance are the explicit recognition by the Treaty of Lisbon of the legal value of the Charter of Fundamental Rights (Art. 6 (1) TEU) and of the CJEU's consistent case law on the status of fundamental rights as general principles of EU law (Art. 6(3) TEU), as well as its explicit confirmation in Art. 67(1) TFEU that the Union shall constitute an area of freedom, security and justice "with respect for fundamental rights".

---

27 Cf. R. Michaels, "The new European Choice-of-Law Revolution", *l.c.*, 1624ff.

28 See e.g. CJEU, 17 December 1970, case 11/70, *Internationale Handelsgesellschaft*, paragraph 4 and many later judgments in the same sense.

As they constitute general principles of Union law, fundamental rights are obviously pertinent for the whole of EU law, its private international law instruments included. Still, they have been specifically recognized in the latter field through the definition of the public policy exception in Brussels I. In its famous *Krombach* judgment, the CJEU defined the public policy exception as referring to an infringement which constitutes "a manifest breach of a rule of law regarded as essential in the legal order of the State in which enforcement is sought or of a right recognised as being fundamental within that legal order"[29]. The Court gave further substance to this by its reference to the protection of fundamental rights, in that particular case the right to a fair hearing as derived from the common constitutional traditions of the Member States and the European Human Rights Convention[30]. The Court of Justice hence recognized fundamental rights protection as a full part of the Brussels I regime, which even counterbalances the importance that is in principle attached to the free circulation of judgments within the Union. This conforms to the Court's consideration in its more recent judgment in *FlyLAL-Lithuanian Airlines*, that the concept of 'public policy' in Brussels I "seeks to protect legal interests which are expressed through a rule of law, and not purely economic interests"[31]. Hence, the mere invocation of serious economic consequences does not constitute an infringement of the public policy of the Member State in which recognition is sought[32]. In that respect, as has been made clear by the Court's consistent case law since *Krombach*, the free circulation of judgments – in spite of its importance for the proper functioning of the internal market and the economic interests that are at stake – must not be considered an absolute right that could claim priority over respect for fundamental rights.

Krombach dates back to 2000. Although it is still recognized, and rightly so, as one of the CJEU's seminal judgments on the Brussels I regime, the pertinence of fundamental rights for Brussels I and EU private international law has developed further. The new TEU provisions introduced by the Treaty of Lisbon (*supra*) and the CJEU's case law on the impact of the EU Charter of Fundamental Rights, e.g. on the direct effect of its Art. 47 (right to effective judicial protection) in so-called horizontal disputes

---

29 CJEU, 28 March 2000, case C-7/98, *Krombach*, paragraph 37.

30 CJEU, 28 March 2000, case C-7/98, *Krombach*, paragraphs 38–45.

31 CJEU, 23 October 2014, C-302/13, *flyLAL-Lithuanian Airlines AS, in liquidation*, paragraph 56.

32 CJEU, 23 October 2014, C-302/13, *flyLAL-Lithuanian Airlines AS, in liquidation*, paragraph 58.

between private parties[33], quite obviously are pertinent as well for private international law litigation. This evolution in EU law in favour of ensured effectiveness and further expansion of fundamental rights is clearly discernible as well in the current interpretation by the CJEU of Brussels I in light of the Charter, and its Art. 47 in particular. The Court today approaches Brussels I *in toto* as an instrument that embodies the right to a fair trial as laid down in Art. 47 of the Charter. In its recent judgment in *Meroni*, which also related to the interpretation of the public policy exception[34], the CJEU considered that the provisions of EU law, such as those of Brussels I, must be interpreted in the light of fundamental rights which, according to settled case-law, form an integral part of the general principles of law whose observance the Court ensures and which are now set out in the Charter. According to the CJEU, "all the provisions of Regulation No 44/2001 express the intention of ensuring that, within the scope of the objectives of that regulation, proceedings leading to the delivery of judicial decisions are conducted in such a way that the rights of the defence laid down in Article 47 of the Charter are observed"[35]. This way, the CJEU has been able to make use of Art. 47 of the Charter to update and grant a more specific legal basis to its earlier case law. In *Denilauler*, still under the regime of the Brussels Convention, the Court had already considered – though without further explanation nor references – that all its provisions express the intention to ensure that proceedings within the scope of the objectives of the Brussels Convention take place in such a way that the rights of the defence are observed[36]. This interpretation has now been tied to the EU's general system of fundamental rights protection and so has transformed the Brussels Ibis regulation in an instrument which actually implements the Charter's concern for effective judicial protection.

A similar, broad reference to fundamental rights protection, and Art. 47 of the Charter more specifically, has been introduced as well, in contrast to what was the case previously with the Brussels Convention and the Brussels I Regulation, in recital 38 of the Brussels Ibis Regulation, according to

33 CJEU, 17 April 2018, case C-414/16, *Egenberger*, paragraphs 78–82.

34 See also on other issues related to Brussels I: CJEU, 10 March 2016, case C-94/14, *Flight Refund*, paragraph 59; CJEU, 11 September 2014, case C-112/13, *A/B and others*, paragraph 51; CJEU, 15 March 2012, case C-292/10, *G/Cornelius de Visser*, paragraph 47; CJEU, 17 November 2011, case C-327/10, *Hypoteční banka*, paragraph 48.

35 CJEU, 25 May 2016, case C-559/14, *Meroni*, paragraph 45.

36 CJEU, 21 May 1980, case 125/79, *Denilauler*, paragraph 13; CJEU, 2 April 2009, case C-394/07, *Gambazzi*, paragraph 23.

which that Regulation "respects fundamental rights and observes the principles recognised in the Charter of Fundamental Rights of the European Union, in particular the right to an effective remedy and to a fair trial guaranteed in Article 47 of the Charter". Actually, Brussels Ibis here followed the earlier references to the Charter of Fundamental Rights which, soon after it had been proclaimed, have been incorporated, but mostly in recitals only, in the Brussels IIbis Regulation[37] and the Regulations on the Enforcement Order for uncontested claims[38] and the European Small Claims Procedure[39].

References to fundamental rights protection were made as well by the European Council in its conclusions of Tampere (which actually were adopted a few months before the *Krombach* judgment) and the Hague Programme (2004). It is the Stockholm Programme (2009) however, adopted after the Treaty of Lisbon, that holds its strongest confirmation, moreover formulated in the same sense as Art. 67(1) TFEU: "The area of freedom, security and justice must above all be a single area in which fundamental rights are protected"[40].

The significance for the whole area of freedom, security and justice of fundamental rights protection was first confirmed in the regulations on procedural matters, but now logically affects choice of law, as a component of the judicial cooperation in civil matters under that heading, as well. After the Treaty of Lisbon entered into force, references to fundamental rights and to the Charter particularly, have meanwhile become standard as well in the recitals of recent regulations that (*inter alia*) hold choice-of-law rules, also where the determination of the applicable law is concerned[41]. Article 10 of the Rome III Regulation even holds a specific clause of non-discrimination on grounds of sex concerning access to divorce or legal separation and further gives particular attention to non-

37 See recital 33 as well as Art. 23 Brussels IIbis Regulation, which refers to the non-recognition of a judgment relating to parental responsibility if it was given, except in case of urgency, without the child having been given an opportunity to be heard, in violation of fundamental principles of procedure of the Member State in which recognition is sought.

38 Recital 11 of Regulation 805/2204.

39 Recital 9 of Regulation 861/2007.

40 "The Stockholm Programme – An open and secure Europe serving and protecting citizens", § 1.1.

41 See the references to fundamental rights that appear to have become standard by now in recitals 58 and 81 of the Successions Regulation, recitals 54 and 73 of the Matrimonial Property Regulation and recitals 53 and 71 of the Partnership Property Regulation.

violation of the Charter of Fundamental Rights and the prohibition of discrimination in its recitals[42].

Given the enormous evolution that has taken place in EU law in this regard, it is beyond doubt that this pertinence of fundamental rights protection will not remain limited to the application of the Union's legislation on private international law, but will stretch beyond that to cases involving elements of private international law that are referred to the Court of Justice for a preliminary interpretation of the EU's rules, of primary or secondary law, on the internal market or Union citizenship. A first indication thereof can be found in the CJEU's reliance on the respect for private and family life, as guaranteed by Art. 7 of the Charter, in the recent judgment in *Coman*[43]. Although, as the Court emphasized several times[44], its judgment was limited to the recognition of marriage between persons of the same sex for the sole purpose of granting a derived right of residence to a third-country national, it may be expected that the inevitable ties between free movement rights under the TFEU and the private law status of the persons concerned will require it sooner rather than later to further examine the interaction, within the scope of EU law, between private international law and fundamental rights[45].

4.2. *Brussels I, Private International Law and the Principles of Mutual Trust and Mutual Recognition*

Article 67 TFEU not only refers to fundamental rights (Art. 67(1)), but also, in view of facilitating access to justice, to mutual recognition of judicial and extrajudicial decisions in civil matters (Art. 67(4)). Article 81(1) TFEU emphasizes the latter principle as well.

Since the adoption of the Brussels Convention in 1968, hence long before the Court's judgment in *Cassis de Dijon* revolutionized the free movement of goods through the introduction of the principle of mutual recognition[46], this concept of mutual recognition has been central to European judicial cooperation. The original Art. 220 of the EEC Treaty aimed at the "reciprocal recognition and enforcement of judgments". According

42 Recitals 16, 25 and 30 of the Rome III Regulation.

43 CJEU, 5 June 2018, case C-673/16, *Coman*, paragraphs 48–50.

44 See paragraphs 36, 40, 45 and 46 of its judgment.

45 See in particular the recent CJEU judgment, dating from after the conclusion of this contribution, in *SM* (26 March 2019, case C-129/18), paragraphs 64–72.

46 CJEU, 20 February 1978, case 120/78, *Rewe-Zentral* ('*Cassis de Dijon*').

to the Brussels I regime as it is laid down today in the Brussels Ibis Regulation, neither the jurisdiction of the court of origin nor the substance of the judgment may be reviewed in the host State, where refusal grounds as well as intermediate procedures are kept to a minimum.

From Brussels I, mutual recognition has gradually broadened to the whole policy field that is known today as the area of freedom, security and justice. In the so-called "Tampere Milestones" (1999), which followed upon a first indication in that sense at its Cardiff summit of 1998[47], the European Council endorsed the principle of mutual recognition which, in its view, "should become the cornerstone of judicial co-operation in both civil and criminal matters within the Union" (§ 33; *supra*). Today, we see this confirmed in Arts. 67(4) and 81(1) TFEU, which both explicitly recognize the key importance of mutual recognition of judgments and decisions for the area of freedom, security and justice in general and judicial cooperation in civil matters more specifically.

Mutual recognition is not an isolated concept. Brussels I is essentially characterized by mutual trust among the Member States, which constitutes the true basis of the far-reaching obligation to mutually recognize each other's judgments, even in the absence of any procedural or substantive harmonisation[48]. Although it originally appeared hesitant to refer to it explicitly[49], the Court of Justice had already reasoned in that sense where the Brussels Convention was concerned, considering that the Convention was "necessarily based on the trust which the Contracting States accord to each other's legal systems and judicial institutions"[50]. In that same spirit, recital 26 of the Brussels Ibis Regulation today holds, as did recital 16 of the previous Brussels I Regulation 44/2001, that the smooth recognition of judgments is justified by "mutual trust in the administration of justice in

47 "The European Council underlines the importance of effective judicial cooperation in the fight against cross-border crime. It recognises the need to enhance the ability of national legal systems to work closely together and asks the Council to identify the scope for greater mutual recognition of decisions of each others' courts" (§ 39 of the Presidency Conclusions).

48 S. Clavel, "L'harmonisation des règles de compétence et des procédures de règlement des conflits (exception de litispendance)" in F. Jault-Seseke e.a. (dir.), *L'espace judiciaire européen civil et pénal*, Paris, Dalloz, 2009, (45), 58–59.

49 M. Weller, "Mutual trust within judicial cooperation in civil matters: a normative cornerstone – a factual chimera – a constitutional challenge", 35 *NIPR*, 2017, (1), 6–7.

50 CJEU, 9 December 2003, case C-116/02, *Gasser*, paragraph 72. See for more details on the Court's case law development: M. Weller, "Mutual trust: in search of the future of European Union private international law", 11 *JPIL*, 2015, (64), 85–89.

the Union"[51]. This essential link between mutual trust and mutual recognition, with the latter as the former's operational instrument[52], now characterizes other Union instruments adopted within the framework of the AFSJ as well[53], and has been confirmed by the CJEU with regard to judicial cooperation in both civil[54] and criminal matters[55].

As the CJEU has recently held in several judgments[56] which followed upon its famous Opinion 2/13[57], both the principle of mutual trust between the Member States and the principle of mutual recognition, which is itself based on the mutual trust between the Member States, are of fundamental importance for EU law given that they allow an area with-

51 See also recital 17 of the same Brussels I Regulation, as well as recital 21 of the Brussels IIbis Regulation: "The recognition and enforcement of judgments given in a Member State should be based on the principle of mutual trust".

52 K. Lenaerts, "Der Grundsatz der gegenseitigen Vertrauens im internationalen Privatrecht: Über den Dialog der Gerichte" in B. Hess, E. Jayme and H-P. Mansel (eds.), *Europa als Rechts- und Lebensraum. Liber amicorum für Christian Kohler zum 75. Geburtstag am 18. Juni 2018*, Bielefeld, Verlag Ernst und Werner Gieseking, 2018, (287), 290: "das funktionale Instrument". See also D. Düsterhaus, "Judicial Coherence in the Area of Freedom, Security and Justice – Squaring Mutual Trust with Effective Judicial Protection", 8 *Review of European Administrative Law* 2015, (151), 157, considering mutual recognition to entertain a symbiotic relationship with mutual trust and the latter to constitute "the aim, the cause and the consequence" of the former.

53 E.g. recital 18 of Regulation 805/2004 (European Enforcement Order) and recital 27 of Regulation 1896/2006 (European order for payment). See for more details, with regard to judicial cooperation in civil matters in the AFSJ: M. Weller, "Mutual trust: in search of the future of European Union private international law", *l.c.*, 82–85.

54 CJEU, 9 March 2017, case C- 484/15, *Zulfikarpašić*, paragraph 40 (European Enforcement Order); CJEU, 27 October 2016, case C-428/15, Child and Family Agency, paragraph 57 (Brussels IIbis).

55 See e.g., on the European Arrest Warrant, CJEU, 10 August 2017, case C-270/17 PPU, *Tupikas*, paragraph 49; CJEU, 1 June 2016, case C-241/15, *Bob-Dogi*, paragraph 33; CJEU, 5 April 2016, joined cases C-404/15 and C-659/15PPU, *Aranyosi and Căldăraru*, paragraph 77.

56 CJEU, 25 July 2018, case 220/18 PPU, *ML*, paragraph 49; CJEU, 25 July 2018, case C-216/18 PPU, *LM*, paragraph 36; CJEU, 9 March 2017, case 551/15, *Pula Parking*, paragraph 51; CJEU, 10 November 2016, case C-453/16 PPU, *Özçelik*, paragraph 24; CJEU, 10 November 2016, case 477/16 PPU, *Kovalkovas*, paragraph 27; CJEU, 10 November 2016, case C-452/16 PPU, *Poltorak*, paragraph 26; CJEU, 5 April 2016, joined cases C-404/15 and C-659/15PPU, *Aranyosi and Căldăraru*, paragraph 78.

57 CJEU, 18 December 2014, Opinion 2/13 (Accession of the European Union to the European Convention for the Protection of Human Rights and Fundamental Freedoms), paragraph 191.

out internal borders to be created and maintained. This key importance of both principles for the process of European integration is essentially tied to the equality of all Member States (Art. 4(2) TEU)[58] and – as has been explicitly confirmed by the CJEU – their mutual sincere cooperation (Art. 4(3) TEU)[59].

As the CJEU further links mutual trust (and mutual recognition) to the values that the Member States and the EU share according to Art. 2 TEU[60], both principles are of key importance for EU law in general. Still, the CJEU has insisted as well on the particular importance of the principle of mutual trust for the AFSJ specifically, by emphasizing in its Opinion 2/13 (which it has often repeated thereafter[61]) not only that the principle of mutual trust is of fundamental importance in EU law, but also that it requires "particularly with regard to the area of freedom, security and justice, each of those States, save in exceptional circumstances, to consider all the other Member States to be complying with EU law and particularly with the fundamental rights recognised by EU law."[62]. In *Pula Parking*, the CJEU applied that same reasoning specifically to the Brussels Ibis Regulation[63].

Undoubtedly, therefore, the principle of mutual trust which for the past fifty years has constituted a solid basis for the mutual recognition principle that characterizes the Brussels I regime, although not without limita-

---

58 K. Lenaerts, "La vie après l'avis: exploring the principle of mutual (yet not blind) trust", 54 *CMLR*, 2017, (805), 808.

59 CJEU, 6 February 2018, case C-359/16, *Altun*, paragraph 40: "Indeed, the principle of sincere cooperation also implies that of mutual trust". See also CJEU, 6 March 2018, case C-284/16, *Achmea*, paragraph 34. See on the interaction between mutual recognition and sincere cooperation: M. Fartunova, "La coopération loyale vue sous le prisme de la reconnaissance mutuelle: quelques réflexions sur les fondements de la construction européenne", 52 *Cahiers de droit européen*, 2016, 193ff.

60 CJEU, 18 December 2014, Opinion 2/13, paragraph 168; CJEU, 6 March 2018, case C-284/16, *Achmea*, paragraph 34. See already earlier judgments such as CJEU, 21 December 2011, joined cases C-411/10 and C-493/10, *N.S.*, paragraph 83, CJEU, 29 January 2013, case C-396/11, *Radu*, paragraph 34 and CJEU, 26 February 2013, case C-399/11, *Melloni*, paragraph 37.

61 CJEU, 19 September 2018, case C-327/18 PPU, *RO*, paragraph 35; CJEU, 25 July 2018, case 220/18 PPU, *ML*, paragraph 49; CJEU, 25 July 2018, case C-216/18 PPU, *LM*, paragraph 36; CJEU, 26 April 2018, case C-34/17, *Donnellan*, paragraph 40; CJEU, 5 April 2016, joined cases C-404/15 and C-659/15 PPU, *Aranyosi and Căldăraru*, paragraph 78.

62 CJEU, 18 December 2014, Opinion 2/13, paragraph 191.

63 CJEU, 9 March 2017, case C-551/15, *Pula Parking*, paragraphs 51–53.

tions[64], constitutes today "a constitutional principle that pervades the entire AFSJ"[65].

In the field of judicial cooperation, it implies that the recognizing, host State accepts to abandon its own view on how a particular case should be solved, even when there are important links with its citizens or its territory, and even where the choice-of-law rules or substantive law have not been harmonized. That all Member States are supposed to share the same values, including the rule of law and fundamental rights, obviously opens the door to such mutual confidence, and even dispenses them from further procedural harmonization[66].

As regards judicial cooperation in criminal matters, the CJEU considered that a re-examination in the host State of the judicial decisions adopted in the issuing Member State would infringe and render ineffective the principle of mutual recognition, which implies that there is mutual trust as to the fact that each Member State accepts the application of the criminal law in force in the other Member States, even though the implementation of its own national law might produce a different outcome[67]. The executing judicial authority is therefore not allowed to substitute its own assessment[68]. The provisions of the Brussels Ibis Regulation, which provide for the circulation of judgments without review as to their substance in the host State[69], rely on that same approach.

Moreover, a comparable approach – not identical in a strict sense, but inspired by a similar type of reasoning[70] – is discernible today where the impact on private international law, including choice of law, of Union citi-

---

64 As is true for mutual trust in the internal market as well: see C. Janssens, *The Principle of Mutual Recognition in EU Law*, Oxford, Oxford University Press, 2013, 29. See further on the pertinence of limitations and control as essential components of genuine and sincere mutual confidence or trust: T. Wischmeyer, "Generating Trust Through Law? Judicial Cooperation in the European Union and the 'Principle of Mutual Trust'", 17 *German L.J.*, 2016, (339), 368–382.

65 K. Lenaerts, "La vie après l'avis: exploring the principle of mutual (yet not blind) trust", *l.c.*, 813 and 838.

66 D. Düsterhaus, "Judicial Coherence in the Area of Freedom, Security and Justice – Squaring Mutual Trust with Effective Judicial Protection", *l.c.*, 151 and 153–154.

67 See already in that sense the pioneer judgment of 11 February 2003, joined cases C-187/01 and C-385/01, Gözütok and Brügge, paragraph 33 (cf. C. Janssens, *The Principle of Mutual Recognition in EU Law*, *o.c.*, 133).

68 CJEU, 23 January 2018, case C-367/16, *Piotrowski*, paragraph 52.

69 Cf. Art. 52 Brussels Ibis Regulation.

70 Cf. P. Lagarde, "Développements futurs du droit international privé dans une Europe en voie d'unification: quelques conjectures", 68 *RabelsZ*, 2004, (225), 232.

zenship and the internal market is concerned: rejection of the unilateral application of the host State's national choice-of-law system but recognition of the choice-of-law process that has been gone through in the home State[71]. In that sense, mutual recognition, which rests on mutual trust, lies at the basis of the particular identity that the internal market and Union citizenship impose on the non-harmonized private international law rules of the Member States.

In *Grunkin and Paul*, the CJEU interpreted the Treaty rules on Union citizenship to oblige Germany to recognize the outcome of the choice-of-law process in Denmark as to the determination of the surname of a German child, rather than apply its own choice-of-law rules[72]. In other words, the CJEU imposes upon the Member States a similar duty of recognition of the foreign choice-of-law process that they must apply, according to the Brussels I regime, to judgments of the other Member States. Legal situations that have been established abroad are to be given effect[73], whatever the law that was applied in that State of origin[74]. Even in those fields where the choice-of-law rules have not been harmonized, Member States (acting as host States) hence cannot just apply, blindly and from a one-sided perspective, their national choice-of-law rules to all cases brought before their courts but must take the European nature of the dispute into account and grant recognition to the earlier choice-of-law process in the home Member State. This compulsory, reciprocal recognition of the Member States' choice-of-law processes requires the host Member State to add another layer of interests to its approach of cross-border mobility in civil matters and makes EU conflict of laws differ intrinsically from the typical national or intergovernmental conflict of laws approach[75].

Similar principles govern the CJEU's interpretation of the effect of the Treaty rules on freedom of establishment on the Member States' choice-of-law rules regarding companies. As the CJEU's case law since the mid-1980s makes clear, the Court prioritizes mutual recognition by the Member

---

71 See also H. Muir Watt, "European Federalism and the 'New Unilateralism'", 82 *Tulane L. Rev.*, 2008, (1983), 1985–1986.

72 CJEU, 14 October 2006, case C-353/06, *Grunkin and Paul*.

73 In principle, not excluding exceptional justification of non-recognition, see e.g. CJEU, 22 December 2010, case C-208/09, *Sayn-Wittgenstein*, paragraphs 81–95.

74 C. Kohler, "La reconnaissance des situations juridiques dans l'Union européenne: le cas du nom patrynomique" in P. Lagarde (dir.), *La reconnaissance des situations en droit international privé*, Paris, Pedone, 2013, (67), 72.

75 J. Meeusen, "The *Grunkin and Paul* Judgment of the CJEU, or How to Strike a Delicate Balance between Conflict of Laws, Union Citizenship and Freedom of Movement in the EC", 18 *Zeitschrift für Europäisches Privatrecht*, 2010, (186), 198.

States of the choice-of-law process in the home Member State and so obliges the Member States to abandon, within the internal market, the universal claim that is proper to the traditional multilateral choice-of-law rules. In other words, the application of the still non-harmonized choice-of-law rules, which according to the CJEU's steadfast interpretation are intrinsically valid under EU-law[76], must be qualified in light of the duty of mutual recognition in the internal market[77].

It can be concluded from the foregoing that mutual recognition, based upon mutual trust, was first introduced by Art. 220 EEC Treaty and the Brussels Convention, and has gradually extended to what is known today as the area of freedom, security and justice, including judicial cooperation in civil matters. The CJEU's case law on a variety of problems indicates that it even governs the interaction between the internal market, Union citizenship and private international law. The constitutionalization of EU private international law through mutual recognition and mutual trust has far-reaching effects. It has served to grant a particular identity to this field, as it is characterized by principles and interests that are different from those that govern private international from national or intergovernmental (treaty-made) origin.

5. *The Challenge ahead – a Future Brussels Iter Regulation as the Necessary Next Step towards Further Europeanization and Constitutionalization*

Brussels I has strongly contributed to the Europeanization and constitutionalization of private international law within the EU. Pertinent for both these processes is the principle of non-discrimination.

Due to its objective of differentiation, private international law is always vulnerable to potential claims of discrimination[78]. This is especially sensitive where its rules are supposed to contribute to integration within an

---

76 See most recently CJEU, 25 October 2017, case C-106/16, *Polbud*, paragraph 34.

77 See e.g. CJEU, 5 November 2002, case C-208/00, *Überseering*, paragraphs 78–82. See for more details and references: J. Meeusen and M. Myszke-Nowakowska, "International Company Law in the European Internal Market: Three Decades of Judicial Activity" in L. Nemer Caldeira Brant (ed.), *XI Anuário Brasileiro de Direito Internacional – Vol.II*, Belo Horizonte, CEDIN, 2016, (92), 109ff.

78 Cf. B. Currie, "Unconstitutional Discrimination in the Conflict of Laws: Privileges and Immunities", *Yale L.J.*, 1960, 1323, reprinted in B. Currie, *Selected Essays on the Conflict of Laws*, Durham N.C., Duke University Press, 1963, 523: "Problems of discrimination are inherent in conflict-of-laws cases".

area without internal frontiers. It is therefore imperative to stay alert and face the important challenge that is still ahead in this process of Europeanization and constitutionalization and actually concerns Brussels I itself[79].

In spite of the original order to the Member States, as was laid down in Art. 220 EEC Treaty, to enter into negotiations on recognition and enforcement "for the benefit of their nationals", and the phrasing of current Art. 3(2) TEU, according to which the Union shall offer "its citizens" an area of freedom, security and justice, the Brussels I regime rejects nationality privileges as well as any further differentiation along that line. The defendant's domicile, a customary and non-discriminatory jurisdictional factor which the CJEU considers a general principle[80] and which the Jenard Report called equitable and practical[81], is generally decisive for both the applicability of the jurisdiction rules and the determination of jurisdiction itself and is complemented by the explicit non-discrimination rules that are laid down in both Arts. 4(1) and 4(2) of the Brussels Ibis Regulation. Further, nationality and even the domicile of the parties involved are irrelevant where recognition and enforcement are concerned.

By breaking away from a regime aimed at protecting the Member States' nationals, Brussels I has managed to accommodate the needs of the internal market and judicial cooperation in an area without internal frontiers. In that respect, however, the wisdom of two important limitations to the scope of the Brussels I regime is often questioned. On the one hand, the Brussels recognition and enforcement rules are pertinent only for judgments given in a Member State; third State judgments are not within the scope of the Brussels Ibis regulation. On the other hand, the jurisdictional regime of Brussels I typically distinguishes between so-called intra- and extra- EU disputes; apart from some important exceptions, Brussels I has excluded this last category, defined by the defendant's third State domicile, from its scope. For many disputes, Article 6 of the Brussels Ibis Regulation subjects the determination of jurisdiction regarding defendants domiciled

79 See for a more profound analysis of the significance of the non-discrimination principle for the Brussels Ibis Regulation: J. Meeusen, "The Brussels Ibis Regulation and the prohibition of discrimination under EU primary law" in P. Mankowski (ed.), *Research Handbook on the Brussels Ibis Regulation*, Cheltenham, Edward Elgar Publishing, 2020, 285.

80 CJEU, 13 July 2000, case C-412/98, *Group Josi Reinsurance Company*, paragraph 35.

81 Report by Mr P. Jenard on the Convention of 27 September 1968 on jurisdiction and the recognition and enforcement of judgments in civil and commercial matters, *O.J.*, 5 March 1979, C 59, 18–19.

in third States to the residual Member States' rules, including those that are commonly considered excessive or exorbitant.

While both scope limitations are subject to debate, they are explained by different concerns and considerations. As Brussels I essentially rests on the guiding principle of mutual trust among the EU Member States (and their courts), it is easy to understand that not so much the exclusion of third State judgments, but rather the jurisdictional scope limitation of Brussels I continues to stir controversy, as its ratio is dubious but its impact far-reaching.

Certainly, one should not neglect the important political considerations involved, which relate to the lack of reciprocity with third States and the possibility to conclude bilateral conventions to remedy this to the mutual advantage of the EU and pertinent third States[82]. From a legal, and even human rights perspective, however, it is very difficult if not impossible to justify a system that allows one category of defendants, domiciled in third States, to be subject to jurisdiction rules from which EU-domiciled defendants are explicitly shielded, due to their possibly exorbitant or even discriminatory character[83].

Moreover, this distinction between 'intra-EU' and 'extra-EU' disputes has important consequences within the specific framework of Brussels I. It is not only the case that Art. 6(2) of the Brussels Ibis regulation extends the

---

82 H. Gaudemet-Tallon, "Les frontières extérieures de l'espace judiciaire européen: quelques répères" in A. Borrás e.a. (eds.), *E Pluribus Unum. Liber Amicorum Georges A.L. Droz. On the Progressive Unification of Private International Law*, The Hague, Martinus Nijhoff Publishers, 1996, (85), 93–94.

83 See, amongst many other authors criticizing this regime : P. Franzina, "L'universalisation partielle du régime européen de la compétence en matière civile et commerciale dans le règlement Bruxelles I*bis*: une mise en perspective" in E. Guinchard (ed.), *Le nouveau règlement Bruxelles I*bis, Brussels, Bruylant, 2014, (39), 59–60; W. Hau, "Gegenwartsprobleme internationaler Zuständigkeit" in *Grenzen überwinden – Prinzipien bewahren. Festschrift für Bernd van Hoffmann zum 70. Geburtstag om 28. Dezember 2011*, Bielefeld, Verlag Ernst und Werner Gieseking, 2011, (617), 621; E. Pataut, "Qu'est-ce qu'un litige 'intracommunautaire'? Réflexions autour de l'article 4 du Règlement Bruxelles I" in *Justice et droits fondamentaux. Etudes offertes à Jacques Normand*, Paris, Litec, 2003, (366), 380; F. Pocar, "Access to Justice and European Rules on Jurisdiction" in J. Forner Delaygua e.a. (cords.), *Entre Bruselas y La Haya. Estudios sobre la unificación internacional y regional del Derecho internacional privado. Liber Amicorum Alegria Borrás*, Madrid, Marcial Pons, 2013, (743), 744–747; P. Schlosser, "Unzulässige Diskriminierung nach Bestehen oder Fehlen eines EG-Wohnsitzes im europäischem Zivilprozessrecht" in S. Lorenz e.a. (eds.), *Festschrift für Andreas Heldrich zum 70. Geburtstag*, Munich, Verlag C.H. Beck, 2005, (1007), 1008–1011.

right to rely on the national jurisdiction rules to "any person domiciled in a Member State". Equally important is that, due to the Regulation's sweeping recognition and enforcement rules which, apart from some exceptions, consider the parties' domiciles or even the application of the correct jurisdiction rules by the original court irrelevant, a Member State judgment against third-State defendants that is based on that Member State's residual rules, whatever their content, will circulate freely within the Union and enjoy the benefit of the Member States' obligations of mutual trust and mutual recognition. While recourse to exorbitant jurisdiction typically results in other States' refusal to recognize the judgment that is eventually obtained on that basis, Art. 6(2) Brussels Ibis Regulation explicitly follows the opposite path[84].

Although the wisdom of the distinguishing criterion – the defendant's domicile – can be debated[85], the real problem lies with the complete tolerance of the application to so-called extra-EU disputes of all kinds of Member State residual rules whatever their exorbitant, protective or even purely discriminatory character, as explicitly confirmed by Art. 6(2) of the Brussels Ibis regulation[86].

In spite of that reference to the Member States' residual jurisdiction rules, the EU is undoubtedly involved here as well. Firstly, there is the internal ratio of the Brussels I regime. Brussels I has been set up as a double system, as it holds both jurisdiction and recognition and enforcement rules and the system essentially rests on their interaction. Yet, this double system is unbalanced, or even incomplete, as the judgments which the Member State courts render on the basis of their non-unified, residual jurisdiction rules enjoy the benefit of the regime's liberal recognition and enforcement rules as well. Secondly, and most importantly from a legal perspective, the EU cannot be shielded from its own legal responsibilities vis-à-vis defendants domiciled in third States. In its famous "Lugano Opinion", the CJEU, taking into account the adoption by the EU of the Brussels

84 P. Kinsch, "Droits de l'homme, droits fondamentaux et droit international privé", *Rec. Cours*, 2005, vol.318, (9), 78.

85 E. Pataut, "Qu'est-ce qu'un litige 'intracommunautaire'? Réflexions autour de l'article 4 du Règlement Bruxelles I", *l.c.*, 380–382.

86 The continued application of Art. 14 of the French Code civil illustrates this problem well and has often been criticized (see e.g. J.J. Fawcett, M.N. Shúilleabháin and S. Shah, *Human Rights and Private International Law*, Oxford, Oxford University Press, 2016, 467; L. Usunier, "La compatibilité de l'article 14 du Code civil avec les droits fondamentaux, une question dépourvue de caractère sérieux? A propos de l'arrêt Cass. civ. 1er, 29 février 2012", 101 *Rev. crit.*, 2012, (775), 784–788).

I Regulation with its particular scope and content, confirmed that the conclusion of the Lugano Convention on jurisdiction and the recognition and enforcement of judgments in civil and commercial matters fell entirely within the sphere of exclusive competence of the (then) European Community, both regarding its rules on jurisdiction and those on recognition and enforcement[87]. As regards (current) Art. 6 Brussels Ibis Regulation, the Court considered that "given the uniform and coherent nature of the system of rules on conflict of jurisdiction" established by Brussels I, this provision "must be interpreted as meaning that it forms part of the system implemented by that regulation, since it resolves the situation envisaged by reference to the legislation of the Member State before whose court the matter is brought"[88]. In other words, the application of the residual Member State rules must be considered the result of a particular kind of delegation by the EU, as a part of its uniform system, to the Member States of the determination of jurisdiction in these cases, and therefore still affects the responsibility of the EU itself[89].

In 2010, the European Commission had already proposed a new approach, consisting of a combination of worldwide coverage and differentiated jurisdiction rules[90]. Nevertheless, the Commission's ideas on this precise issue were rejected in the further legislative process and eventually did not make it into the new Brussels Ibis Regulation. As the Commission, according to Art. 79 of the Brussel Ibis Regulation, must present by 11 January 2022 a report on the application of the Brussels Ibis Regulation, including an evaluation of the possible need for a further extension of its jurisdiction rules to defendants not domiciled in a Member State, this issue will inevitably become the subject of negotiations again. This indeed

87 CJEU, 7 February 2006, Opinion 1/03, Competence of the Community to conclude the new Lugano Convention on jurisdiction and the recognition and enforcement of judgments in civil and commercial matters, paragraphs 134–173.

88 CJEU, 7 February 2006, Opinion 1/03, Competence of the Community to conclude the new Lugano Convention on jurisdiction and the recognition and enforcement of judgments in civil and commercial matters, paragraph 148.

89 P. Franzina, "L'universalisation partielle du régime européen de la compétence en matière civile et commerciale dans le règlement Bruxelles Ibis: une mise en perspective", *l.c.*, 60–61; F. Pocar, "Access to Justice and European Rules on Jurisdiction", *l.c.*, 745. P. Kinsch ("Droits de l'homme, droits fondamentaux et droit international privé", *l.c.*, 80–81) expresses more reservations in this regard.

90 European Commission, *Proposal for a Regulation of the European Parliament and of the Council on jurisdiction and the recognition and enforcement of judgments in civil and commercial matters (Recast)*, COM(2010) 748 final, 3 and 8 (Explanatory memorandum).

seems, of all outstanding issues, the most prominent and urgent one that, in view of the necessary coherence of Brussels I and also of the many difficult political issues involved, would deserve priority. As to the possible introduction of a unified recognition and enforcement regime for third State judgments, the outcome of the ongoing Hague Judgments Convention process – as a process to establish a global regime – is obviously of the highest importance[91].

Reconsideration of the scope limitation through the elimination of reference to the defendant's domicile for the determination of the applicability of the unified jurisdictional rules would be a logical, even necessary next step in the double process of the Europeanization and constitutionalization of Brussels I, and hence of private international law in the EU. Even more, this process would actually come full circle as a possible future Brussels Iter Regulation along the lines just mentioned could actually seek inspiration in the more recent sources of EU private international law which, *mutatis mutandis*, lack the scope limitations that still characterize the Brussels Ibis Regulation. In that sense, not only the "standard"[92] set by the full Europeanization of the jurisdiction rules in the more recent regulations[93], but also the unified choice-of-law rules in the EU regulations which typically have a universal character[94] can specifically be referred to and could in their turn constitute a valuable source of inspiration for the possible amendment of the current Brussels Ibis Regulation.

---

91 The Hague Judgments Convention has eventually been adopted, after the conclusion of this contribution, on 2 July 2019. See for more details:https://www.hcch.net/en/instruments/conventions/full-text/?cid=137.

92 T. Domej, "Das Verhältnis nach 'aussen'. Europäische v. Drittstaatensachverhalte" in J. von Hein and G. Rühl (eds.), *Kohärenz im Internationalen Privat- und Verfahrensrecht der Europäischen Union*, Tübingen, Mohr Siebeck, 2016, (90), 93.

93 See the replacement of the Member State jurisdiction rules by unified European rules which characterizes the Maintenance Regulation (Council Regulation (EC) n°4/2009 of 18 December 2008 on jurisdiction, applicable law, recognition and enforcement of decisions and cooperation in matters relating to maintenance obligations), as well as the Successions, Matrimonial Property and Partnership Property Regulations.

94 See in particular Art. 2 Rome I Regulation, Art. 3 Rome II Regulation, Art. 4 Rome III Regulation, Art. 20 Successions Regulation, Art. 20 Matrimonial Property Regulation and Art. 20 Partnership Property Regulation.

The Application of the European Law of Civil Procedure in the Dialogue Between the CJEU and the National Judges

Henrik Saugmandsgaard Øe[*]

Table of Contents

Ladies and Gentlemen,

First of all, let me thank you for the opportunity to speak at this conference. In the next thirty minutes I will try to give you a brief overview of the current application of the European law of civil procedure in the dialogue between the Court of Justice of the European Union (Court of Justice) and the national judges.

Due to the size and complexity of the subject, my speech does not imply any claim to be exhaustive. Nevertheless, several Court decisions already illustrate the current development of European law of civil procedure.

---

* Advocate General at the Court of Justice of the European Union.

1. Introduction

The starting point of the European law of civil procedure was the "Convention on jurisdiction and the enforcement of judgments in civil and commercial matters", whose 50th anniversary we are celebrating today.

Based on this so-called Brussels Convention, the European legislator adopted the Brussels I Regulations, namely Regulation No 44/2001 and the recast version of this Regulation, Regulation No 1215/2012 that applies to legal proceedings introduced after January 10th 2015. The Brussels I Regulation became and still represents the core of the European law of civil procedure.[1] That is why I will focus on the application of these Regulations in the dialogue between the Court of Justice and the national judges.

To be clear, today the European law of civil procedure comprises much more than the international civil procedure law as it results from the Brussels I Regulations.[2] The laws of civil procedure of the Member States are, for example, more and more influenced and changed by European Directives such as Directive 2013/11/EU on alternative dispute resolution for consumer disputes[3] or Directive 2014/104/EU[4] on certain rules governing actions for damages under national law for infringements of the competition law provisions of the Member States and of the European Union. Furthermore, autonomous types of proceedings have been created such as the European order for payment procedure[5]. I would also like to mention the growing influence of the jurisprudence of the Court of Justice on national civil procedure law via the application of the non-discrimination rule[6] and Article 47 of the Charter.

---

1 See also Hess, Europäisches Zivilprozessrecht, 2010, § 1 I., point 2.

2 Stadler, JZ 2017, p. 693, 694 f., see also regarding the notion of "European law of civil procedure", Berger, Organisation und Verfahren der ordentlichen Gerichtsbarkeit im Lichte der Rechtsprechung des Gerichtshofs der Europäischen Union, 2013, p. XLV.

3 Directive 2013/11/EU of the European Parliament and of the Council of 21 May 2013 on alternative dispute resolution for consumer disputes and amending Regulation (EC) No 2006/2004 and Directive 2009/22/EC (Directive on consumer ADR).

4 Directive 2014/104/EU of the European Parliament and of the Council of 26 November 2014 on certain rules governing actions for damages under national law for infringements of the competition law provisions of the Member States and of the European Union.

5 Regulation (EC) No 1896/2006 of the European Parliament and of the Council of 12 December 2006 creating a European order for payment procedure.

6 See for example, judgment of 26 September 1996, *Data Delecta and Forsberg* (C-43/95, EU:C:1996:357); judgment of 10 February 1994, *Mund & Fester*

Before we take a closer look at the decisions of the Court of Justice regarding the Brussels I Regulations, I think it is also necessary to bring to mind how the dialogue between the Court of Justice and the national judges is actually taking place, as it is imposed by EU constitutional procedures.

2. *The Preliminary Ruling Procedure as an Instrument of Cooperation between the CJEU and the National Judges*

It is the preliminary ruling procedure according to Article 267 TFEU that enables the national judges to collaborate with the Court of Justice to ensure a uniform interpretation and application of EU law in the Member States. The preliminary ruling procedure establishes a direct cooperation between the Court of Justice and the national jurisdictions via a non-contentious procedure that has the character of a step in the action pending before the national court[7].

The importance of the preliminary ruling procedure is already shown by the statistics. In 2017, for example, over 70 % of the new cases brought before the Court of Justice were requests for a preliminary ruling.[8] Furthermore, inter alia, with regard to the further development of the European law of civil procedure the dialogue between the Court of Justice and the national judges by the means of the preliminary ruling procedure has proved to be a significant key driver. For example, in 2017 the Court issued 12 judgments regarding the interpretation of the Brussels I Regulations.

As you all know the functioning of the preliminary ruling procedure I don't have to explain it any further. However, I would like to emphasize a few aspects that are important for the fruitfulness of this dialogue between courts and judges:

We have to be aware that there is a clear partition of competences between the Court of Justice and the national jurisdictions in the context of the preliminary ruling procedure. The Court of Justice provides the

---

(C-398/92, EU:C:1994:52); judgment of 1 July 1993, *Hubbard* (C-20/92, EU:C:1993:280); see also Hess, Europäisches Zivilprozessrecht, 2010, § 1 III., point 19.

7 Judgment of 6 December 2001, *Clean Car Autoservice* (C-472/99, EU:C:2001:663, paragraph 24).

8 CJEU Annual Report 2017, *Judicial Activity* (https://curia.europa.eu/jcms/upload/docs/application/pdf/2018-04/_ra_2017_en.pdf), p. 102.

national judges with the elements of interpretation of the European law that are needed to solve the litigations that are brought before them on a national level.[9] The task of the Court of Justice is to give the national judges a clear and useful answer to their question[10], which in the end, they have to use in their independent decisions. This requires that the Court of Justice understands the facts of the case, as they are explained by the national judges, and the questions asked. In this context, I would also like to emphasize that in my opinion it is very useful for us members of the Court to receive feedback from academics in conferences like the one today as to whether we understand the questions raised and whether we give clear and useful answers.

As, in my opinion, the Brussels I Regulations are among the texts with the highest quality and practical relevance in the EU, the answers given by the Court of Justice have to be particularly clear and have to provide legal certainty as well, because otherwise a uniform interpretation of EU law is not possible and the aims of the Regulations cannot be met.

3. *Examples from the Jurisprudence of the CJEU Regarding the Further Development of the European Law of Civil Procedure*

The cases that I will present to you now illustrate very well how the Court of Justice and the national judges collaborate in the domain of the Brussels I Regulation and how the European law of civil procedure is evolving through this collaboration. I have picked a small number of recent preliminary rulings with respect to important fields of the Brussels I Regulation as whether an action is contractual or tortious in nature, how situations of *lis pendens* are to be solved and which courts are competent regarding actions of employees against their employer and actions because of infringements committed on the internet.

---

9 Judgment of 5 July 2016, *Ognyanov* (C-614/14, EU:C:2016:514, paragraph 16); judgment of 9 June 2016, *Nutrivet* (C-69/15, EU:C:2016:425, paragraph 58).

10 Judgment of 14 March 2013, Aziz (C-415/11, EU:C:2013:164, paragraph 39); judgment of 19 June 2012, The Chartered Institute of Patent Attorneys (C-307/10, EU:C:2012:361, paragraph 31).

3.1. Granarolo, C-196/15, 14 July 2016

I would like to start with a judgment rendered by the Court in July 2016, in the case of *Granarolo*[11].

The Court had to rule on the determination of the court with jurisdiction in relation to abrupt termination of a long-standing business relationship.

Ambrosi, an undertaking established in France, distributed for approximately 25 years food products in France that were made by an Italian company named Granarolo. The distribution relationship was not the subject of a framework contract. Then suddenly Granarolo informed Ambrosi about its decision to terminate the distribution relationship. Thereupon Ambrosi brought an action for damages against Granarolo before the French courts. Granarolo contested the jurisdiction of the French courts, on the ground that the action in question was a matter relating to a contract.

The Court of Justice was thus in particular[12] asked whether that action was a matter relating to tort or delict or a matter relating to a contract, which was relevant for the determination of the competent court according to Article 5 of the Brussels I Regulation from 2001.

As a first step the Court of Justice brought to mind some general rules regarding the interpretation of the Brussels I Regulation:

The Court pointed out that the Brussels I Regulation pursues an objective of legal certainty which consists in strengthening the legal protection of persons established in the EU, by enabling the applicant to easily identify the court in which he may sue and by enabling the defendant to foresee before which court he may be sued.[13]

Therefore, the terms "matters relating to a contract" and "matters relating to tort, delict or quasi delict" within the meaning of Article 5 of the Brussels I Regulation must only be interpreted autonomously in order to ensure a uniform application in all Member States.[14]

As a second step, on the grounds of these general rules the Court of Justice interpreted Article 5 of the Brussels I Regulation and stated that an action for damages based on an abrupt termination of a long-standing business relationship is not a matter relating to tort or delict if a tacit con-

11 Judgment of 14 July 2016, *Granarolo* (C-196/15, EU:C:2016:559).
12 I will focus in this speech only on the first of the two questions asked by the referring court.
13 Judgment of 14 July 2016, *Granarolo* (C-196/15, EU:C:2016:559, paragraph 16).
14 Judgment of 14 July 2016, *Granarolo* (C-196/15, EU:C:2016:559, paragraph 19).

tractual relationship existed between the parties, which according to the Court is a matter for the national judge to ascertain.[15]

On this basis, in order to give a clear and useful answer to the referring court and to ensure legal certainty in all Member States, the Court of Justice determined the aspects that have to be considered in this examination. The demonstration of the existence of a tacit contractual relationship must be based on a "body of consistent evidence", which may include for example the existence of a long-standing business relationship, the good faith between the parties and the regularity of the transactions.[16]

However, it is irrelevant how the action for damages in relation to the abrupt termination of a long-standing business relationship is classified under national law, because this qualification may differ from Member State to Member State.[17] That means that in the present case it didn't matter that the claim for damages was, under French law, tortious in nature, but the French courts had to examine the existence of a tacit contractual relationship.

3.2. *Austro-Mechana, C-572/14, 21 April 2016*

Another preliminary ruling regarding the applicability of Article 5 of the Brussels I Regulation from 2001 was the judgment *Austro-Mechana*[18], rendered by the Court of Justice in April 2016. The referring court asked the Court of Justice whether the obligation to pay fair compensation for private copying was a matter relating to tort delict or quasi-delict within the meaning of Article 5 (3) of the Regulation. The Court of Justice affirmed this by answering that a claim for payment of compensation that is owed by virtue of a national law that applies a system of fair compensation does indeed fall within the scope of this Article.

15 Judgment of 14 July 2016, *Granarolo* (C-196/15, EU:C:2016:559, paragraphs 25 and 28).

16 Judgment of 14 July 2016, *Granarolo* (C-196/15, EU:C:2016:559, paragraph 26).

17 Judgment of 14 July 2016, *Granarolo* (C-196/15, EU:C:2016:559, paragraphs 19 and 23).

18 Judgment of 21 April 2016, *Austro-Mechana* (C-572/14, EU:C:2016:286).

3.3. *Hanse Yachts AG, C-29/16, 4 May 2017*

Another important part of the Brussels I Regulation is the rules on how to tackle situations of *lis pendens* between two actions before the courts of different Member States. The Court of Justice has clarified these rules in the case of *Hanse Yachts AG*[19] of May 2017.

HanseYachts, a company established in Germany, sold a yacht to the French company, Port D'Hiver Yachting. The yacht was then resold to another French company named SMCA. Subsequently, HanseYachts and Port D'Hiver Yachting concluded a dealer contract which should replace all previous agreements between those parties and contained a clause conferring jurisdiction on German courts. As far as clauses conferring jurisdiction are concerned, Advocate General Wahl concluded in the *Apple Sales International* case recently that it is up to the national courts to determine the scope of such a clause[20].

A short time later, some damage appeared in one of the yacht's engines and SMCA applied to the Commercial Court of Marseilles for proceedings for the preservation of evidence. Both Port D'Hiver Yachting and Hanse Yachts were parties to the proceedings.

After the termination of these proceedings Hanse Yachts brought an action against Port D'Hiver Yachting and SMCA before the Regional Court of Stralsund in Germany seeking in a negative declaration that Port D'Hiver Yachting and SMCA were not in any way its creditors with respect to the yacht in question.

Thereupon, SMCA for its part brought an action against Port D'Hiver Yachting and HanseYachts before the Commercial Court of Toulon seeking compensation.

It is quite clear that there was a situation of *lis pendens* between the different cases pending before the court of Stralsund and before the court of Toulon. But the referring court of Stralsund asked the Court of Justice whether the action brought before the court of Toulon had already started with the proceedings for the taking of evidence brought before the court of Marseille with the result that according to Article 27 of the Brussels I Regulation from 2001 the court of Stralsund would have to stay its proceedings until such time as the jurisdiction of the court of Toulon is established.

19 Judgment of 4 May 2017, *HanseYachts* (C-29/16, EU:C:2017:343).

20 Opinion of Advocate General Wahl in *Apple Sales International and Others* (C-595/17, EU:C:2018:541, paragraph 54).

In its judgment the Court of Justice pointed out first of all that it is solely for the referring Court to determine both the need for a preliminary ruling in order to enable it to deliver judgment as well as the relevance of the questions which it submits to the Court.[21] So in order to stay within the dialogue the Court of Justice did not prejudge the issue whether the German Courts had international jurisdiction because of the choice of forum clause concluded between HanseYachts and Port D'Hiver Yachting.

Furthermore, the Court of Justice stated that Articles 27 to 30 of the Brussels I Regulation from 2001 seek to reduce to the greatest extent possible concurrent proceedings before the courts of the various Member States, to avoid the delivery of irreconcilable decisions[22] and to provide legal certainty[23].

The Court of Justice explained that the mechanism to resolve situations of *lis pendens* according to Articles 27 and 30 is objective and automatic and is based on a purely chronological order.[24]

Therefore, according to the Court, the date on which a procedure for a measure of inquiry prior to any legal proceedings was commenced is not relevant for the determination of the date on which a court called upon substantive application, which was brought in the same Member State following the result of that measure, was "deemed to be seised".[25] The Court based this interpretation on the analysis that in French law the proceedings for the taking of evidence are clearly independent in relation to the substantive proceedings, but also reminded the national judges to assess whether this analysis is correct as it does not fall within the jurisdiction of the Court of Justice to interpret national law.[26]

As a result, the German court was deemed to be seised first. But let me add, as I did in my Opinion in the present case, that the procedural approach taken by *HanseYachts* does not constitute abuse. To be clear, "forum shopping" is not prohibited per se by the Brussels I Regulation from 2001.[27]

---

21 Judgment of 4 May 2017, *HanseYachts* (C-29/16, EU:C:2017:343, paragraph 24).
22 Judgment of 4 May 2017, *HanseYachts* (C-29/16, EU:C:2017:343, paragraph 25).
23 Judgment of 4 May 2017, *HanseYachts* (C-29/16, EU:C:2017:343, paragraph 30).
24 Judgment of 4 May 2017, *HanseYachts* (C-29/16, EU:C:2017:343, paragraph 28).
25 Judgment of 4 May 2017, *HanseYachts* (C-29/16, EU:C:2017:343, paragraph 36).
26 Judgment of 4 May 2017, *HanseYachts* (C-29/16, EU:C:2017:343, paragraphs 33, 34 and 35).
27 Opinion of Advocate General Saugmandsgaard Øe in *HanseYachts* (C-29/16, EU:C:2017:44, paragraph 66).

3.4. *Nogueira and Others, C-168/16 and C-169/16, 14 September 2017*

Another domain with a great practical relevance in the EU is the determination of the court with jurisdiction in matters relating to individual contracts of employment. The preliminary rulings of the Court of Justice have had a great impact on the evolution of this domain as, for example, the judgment of the Court in the case of *Nogueira and Others*[28], rendered in September 2017.

In this case the applicants in the main proceedings were all members of cabin crew of the flight company Ryanair. The applicants brought proceedings against their employer before Belgian courts, because they wanted to obtain various heads of compensation.

The contracts of employment were all drafted in English and specified that the work relationship was subject to Irish law. It was furthermore stipulated that as the planes of Ryanair are registered in Ireland, the work of the employees was also regarded as being carried out in Ireland.

But the contracts of employment also stipulated that Charleroi airport was the home base of those employees and that they had to reside within an one hour journey of the home base. Each of these employees started and ended their working day at this airport.

It was clear that the applicants could have sued their employer before the courts of Ireland but the question was whether they were also able to sue in Belgium.

Article 19 (2) of the Brussels I Regulation from 2001 allows an employee to sue his employer in the courts of the place where the employee habitually carries out his work. Therefore, the Court of Justice was asked by the referring Belgian court whether in the event of legal action by an airline crew the concept of "place where the employee habitually carries out his work" can be equated with that of "home base" within the meaning in Annex II to Regulation No 3922/91 on the harmonization of technical requirements and administrative procedures in the field of civil aviation.[29]

The Court pointed out that it is the objective of Article 19 of the Brussels I Regulation to protect the weaker party, namely the employee, by

---

28 Judgment of 14 September 2017, *Nogueira and Others* (C-168/16 and C-169/16, EU:C:2017:688).

29 Judgment of 14 September 2017, *Nogueira and Others* (C-168/16 and C-169/16, EU:C:2017:688, paragraph 44).

allowing him to sue his employer before the courts that are closest to his interests.[30]

The Court of Justice also recalled its own settled case law according to which the place where the employee habitually carries out his work in the meaning of Article 19 of the Brussels I Regulation must be interpreted as referring to the place where, or from which, the employee performs the essential part of his duties.[31]

In order to determine in the present case the "place from which" members of an air crew principally perform their obligations, the national judges have to refer to a set of indicia, as the place from which the employee carries out his tasks, the place where he returns afterwards and where he receives instructions concerning his tasks.[32] Although, according to the Court, the "place where, or from which the employee habitually performs his work" could not be equated with any concept referred to in another act of EU law, including the concept of "home base" in the Annex III to Regulation No 3922/91,[33] the Court of Justice pointed out that the national judges are able to refer to the concept of "home base" as a significant indicium in determining the "place where the employee habitually carries out his work".[34]

Again, the Court answered the questions asked by a national court with regard to the Brussels I Regulation from 2001 by a preliminary ruling interpreting EU law and by giving guidance with respect to procedural questions to be answered by the national court but without lifting the partition of competences.

In the context of this case, it is also interesting to know that, in its initial version, the Brussels Convention did not include any specific provision relating to contracts of employment. The Court of Justice at that time nonetheless held that disputes arising out of a contract of employment were subject to that convention and came, more particularly, under Article

30 Judgment of 14 September 2017, *Nogueira and Others* (C-168/16 and C-169/16, EU:C:2017:688, paragraphs 49 and 50).

31 Judgment of 14 September 2017, *Nogueira and Others* (C-168/16 and C-169/16, EU:C:2017:688, paragraph 58).

32 Judgment of 14 September 2017, *Nogueira and Others* (C-168/16 and C-169/16, EU:C:2017:688, paragraphs 60, 61 and 63).

33 Judgment of 14 September 2017, *Nogueira and Others* (C-168/16 and C-169/16, EU:C:2017:688, paragraphs 65 and 66).

34 Judgment of 14 September 2017, *Nogueira and Others* (C-168/16 and C-169/16, EU:C:2017:688, paragraph 77).

5(1) of the convention.[35] Finally on the occasion of the San Sebastián Convention of 26 May 1989, Article 5(1) of the Brussels Convention was supplemented by a specific rule relating to contracts of employment that reflected the Court's earlier case-law.[36] That rule has virtually identical terms as the rule later on stated in Article 19 (2) of the Brussels I Regulation from 2001 and is now not only kept under Article 21 (2) of the "new" Brussels I Regulation from 2012 but also supplemented by the terms "from where" the employee habitually carries out his work, which reflects the Courts' newer case-law that I have just illustrated.

So here you can see very clearly how a preliminary ruling contributed to the development of civil procedure law and how the interpretation by the Court has even been codified in the end.

3.5. Bolagsupplysningen and Ilsjan, C-194/16, 17 October 2017

The last domain we will have a look at is the domain of infringements committed on the internet. In October 2017 the Court of Justice, sitting as the Grand Chamber, delivered an important judgment in the case of *Bolagsupplysningen* and *Ilsjan*[37].

This judgment was rendered in the context of litigation between an Estonian company and an employee of that company on the one hand, and a Swedish company on the other hand, regarding the request of the Estonian parties for the rectification of allegedly incorrect information published on the website of the Swedish company, the deletion of related comments on a discussion forum on that website, and compensation for harm allegedly suffered.[38]

The problem was whether the Estonian courts had jurisdiction on the grounds that they were the courts of the place where, in the matters relating to tort, delict or quasi-delict, the harmful event occurred according to

---

35 Opinion of Advocate General Saugmandsgaard Øe in Joined Cases *Nogueira and Others* (C-168/16 and C-169/16, EU:C:2017:312, paragraph 62 with further references).

36 Opinion of Advocate General Saugmandsgaard Øe in Joined Cases *Nogueira and Others* (C-168/16 and C-169/16, EU:C:2017:312, paragraph 67 with further references).

37 Judgment of 17 October 2017, *Bolagsupplysningen and Ilsjan* (C-194/16, EU:C:2017:766).

38 Judgment of 17 October 2017, *Bolagsupplysningen and Ilsjan* (C-194/16, EU:C:2017:766, paragraph 2).

Article 7(2) of the Brussels I Regulation from 2012. In fact, the information and comments at issue had been published in Swedish without a translation, on a Swedish website, but could nevertheless be retrieved in Estonia.

As the wording of Article 7 (2) of the Brussels I Regulation from 2012 is identical to the wording of Article 5 (3) of the Brussels I Regulation from 2001, the Court of Justice clarified first of all that its former interpretation of the rule also applies with regard to the new Regulation from 2012.[39]

It was settled case-law that the term "place where the harmful event occurred or may occur" covers both the place where the damage occurred and the place of the event giving rise to it.[40] As far as competition law is concerned, the Court recently clarified the latter in its *FlyLAL* case as being the place where the anticompetitive agreement was definitely concluded which is up to the national jurisdiction to determine.[41]

In order to determine whether the damage caused via Internet actually occurred in Estonia, the Court of Justice recalled its judgment in the case of *eDate Advertising*, delivered in 2011.[42] The Court of Justice held in that case that in the event of an alleged infringement of personality rights by the means of content placed online on a website, the concerned person must have the possibility to bring an action for damages, in respect of all the harm caused in the Member State in which the centre of its interests is based.[43]

In fact, the infringement in the context of the internet is – as the Court explains – usually felt most keenly in the centre of the interests of the person and this is therefore also the place where the damage caused by online material occurs most significantly.[44] Consequently the courts of the Member State in which the centre of interests of the person is situated are most

---

39 Judgment of 17 October 2017, *Bolagsupplysningen and Ilsjan* (C-194/16, EU:C:2017:766, paragraph 24).

40 Judgment of 17 October 2017, *Bolagsupplysningen and Ilsjan* (C-194/16, EU:C:2017:766, paragraph 29).

41 Judgment of 5 July 2018, *flyLAL-Lithuanian Airlines* (C-27/17, EU:C:2018:533, paragraph 49).

42 Judgment of 25 October 2011, *eDate Advertising and Others* (C-509/09 and C-161/10, EU:C:2011:685).

43 Judgment of 25 October 2011, *eDate Advertising and Others* (C-509/09 and C-161/10, EU:C:2011:685, paragraph 52); judgment of 17 October 2017, *Bolagsupplysningen and Ilsjan* (C-194/16, EU:C:2017:766, paragraph 32).

44 Judgment of 17 October 2017, *Bolagsupplysningen and Ilsjan* (C-194/16, EU:C:2017:766, paragraph 33).

suitable to assess the impacts of such content on the rights of that person.[45] Furthermore, this criterion accords with the aim of predictability pursued by the Brussels I Regulation.[46]

Whereas the judgment *eData Advertising* was rendered only with respect to a natural person, the Court of Justice made it clear in the present judgment that the centre of interests is as well the criterion to determine the court with jurisdiction with respect to a legal person. The Court furthermore pointed out how the national judges have to identify the centre of interests. With regard to a legal person it is the place where it carries out the main part of its economic activities. The location of its registered office however is in itself not a conclusive criterion.[47]

Finally, the Court brought to mind that instead of an action for damages in respect of all the harm caused, the concerned person may also bring his action before the courts of each Member State in whose territory content placed online is or has been accessible. But the courts of these Member States then have jurisdiction only with respect of the harm caused in their territory.[48]

However, an application for the rectification of information and the removal of content placed online on a website can, because of the ubiquitous nature of that information and content, only be made before a court with jurisdiction to rule on the entirety of an application for compensation for damage.[49]

3.6. *Concurrence SARL, C-618/15, 21 December 2016*

In this context, I would also like to draw your attention to the preliminary ruling of the Court of Justice in the case of *Concurrence*[50], rendered in December 2016. This case was about an infringement of the prohibition on resale outside a selective distribution network committed on the inter-

---

45 Judgment of 17 October 2017, *Bolagsupplysningen and Ilsjan* (C-194/16, EU:C:2017:766, paragraph 34).

46 Judgment of 17 October 2017, *Bolagsupplysningen and Ilsjan* (C-194/16, EU:C:2017:766, paragraph 35).

47 Judgment of 17 October 2017, *Bolagsupplysningen and Ilsjan* (C-194/16, EU:C:2017:766, paragraph 41).

48 Judgment of 17 October 2017, *Bolagsupplysningen and Ilsjan* (C-194/16, EU:C:2017:766, paragraph 47).

49 Judgment of 17 October 2017, *Bolagsupplysningen and Ilsjan* (C-194/16, EU:C:2017:766, paragraph 48).

50 Judgment of 21 December 2016, *Concurrence* (C-618/15, EU:C:2016:976).

net. The Court of Justice stated that the fact that the websites, on which the offer of the products covered by the selective distribution right appear, operate in Member States other than that of the court seised is irrelevant, as long as the events which occurred in those Member States resulted in or may result in the alleged damage in the jurisdiction of the court seised, which it is for the national court to ascertain.[51]

4. *Conclusion*

There are a lot more interesting preliminary rulings with respect to the interpretation of the Brussels I Regulation. For example, to mention a last one, the judgement of 5 October 2017 in the case of *Hanssen Beleggingen*[52] where the Court decided that Article 22(4) of the Brussels I Regulation of 2001 must be interpreted as not applying to proceedings to determine whether a person was correctly registered as the proprietor of a trade mark.

However, I hope I was already able to give you a small overview of the issues currently treated by the Court of Justice in the scope of the Brussels I Regulations. In my opinion, the European law of civil procedure has continued to develop in the past years especially due to the increasing number of preliminary ruling procedures before the Court of Justice.

I am now looking forward to the panel discussion with Professor Hau, Professor Oberhammer and Professor Kramer.

Thank you very much for your attention.

51 Judgment of 21 December 2016, *Concurrence* (C-618/15, EU:C:2016:976, paragraph 34).

52 Judgment of 5 October 2017, *Hanssen Beleggingen* (C-341/16, EU:C:2017:738).

The Dialogue on the European Law of Civil Procedure between the Court of Justice and National Courts from a German Perspective

Wolfgang Hau[*]

Table of Contents

1. *The Early Reception of the Brussels Convention in Germany*

The Rome Treaty establishing the European Economic Community of 1957 required the then six Member States in its Article 220, inter alia, to simplify the formalities governing the reciprocal recognition and execution of judicial decisions. A little more than ten years later, in September 1968, the Brussels Convention on jurisdiction and the enforcement of judgments in civil and commercial matters,[1] came into the world: a masterpiece of international law-making, distinguished by its clear language, sublime architecture and wise underlying principles.

Soon after its entry into force in 1973, the Convention has been intensely discussed in German literature[2] and has gained practical impor-

---

* Dr Wolfgang Hau is a professor of private law and German, international and comparative civil procedure, Ludwig-Maximilians-University Munich, and a part-time judge at the Oberlandesgericht (Higher Regional Court) Munich.

1 OJ 1972 L 299, p. 32; Bundesgesetzblatt 1972 II, 774.

2 For early general accounts of the Brussels Convention see *Hans Arnold*, Das EWG-Gerichtsstands- und Vollstreckungsübereinkommen vom 27.9.1968, AWD 1969, 89; *Hellmuth Bauer*, Das EWG-Gerichtsstandsübereinkommen, DB 1973, 2333; *Reinhold Geimer*, Eine neue internationale Zuständigkeitsordnung in Europa, NJW 1976, 441; *Reinhold Geimer*, Anerkennung gerichtlicher Entscheidungen nach dem EWG-Übereinkommen vom 27. September 1968, AWD/RIW 1976, 139; *Wolfgang*

tance before German courts.[3] Since 1976, starting with the famous ruling in *Tessili v Dunlop*,[4] it has been frequently applied by important decisions of the European Court of Justice. In Germany, from the very beginning, such rulings from Luxembourg have not only been noted by a few law professors riding their academic hobbyhorses, but have been published and analysed in major legal periodicals[5] by practitioners and scholars alike. When reading some of the first published German cases dealing with the Brussels Convention, it is remarkable that they show no trace of reservation. It seems as if from the mid-seventies onwards the new instrument was applied as a matter of course without further ado and that parties and courts very soon adapted quite well to the new European rules.

Obviously, it was a very wise move from the Member States to opt for a *convention double*, an approach that went beyond what was required by Article 220 of the EEC-Treaty: The convention included not only rules on recognition and enforcement but also on international jurisdiction, the latter being of greater importance in most cross-border cases. Much of the credit given to the Brussels Convention by German practitioners was surely owed to its very well drafted jurisdictional regime, in particular with regard to the requirements and effects of jurisdiction agreements. Furthermore, this receptiveness might also be due to the insight that the Convention in many respects complied with the German legal tradition. Since

---

Grunsky, Probleme des EWG-Übereinkommens über die gerichtliche Zuständigkeit und die Vollstreckung gerichtlicher Entscheidungen in Zivil- und Handelssachen, JZ 1973, 641; *Bernd von Hoffmann*, Das EWG-Übereinkommen über die gerichtliche Zuständigkeit und die Vollstreckung gerichtlicher Entscheidungen in Zivil- und Handelssachen, AWD/RIW 1973, 57; *Jörg Pirrung*, Zum Gesetz zur Ausführung des EWG-Gerichtsstands- und Vollstreckungsübereinkommens vom 27. September 1968, DGVZ 73, 178; *Manfred Wolf*, Das Ausführungsgesetz zu dem EWG-Gerichtsstands- und Vollstreckungsübereinkommen, NJW 1973, 397. Even authors from the then German Democratic Republic took notice, cf. *Horst Fincke*, Zum westeuropäischen Übereinkommen über Entscheidungen in Zivil- und Handelssachen, DDR-Außenwirtschaft 33/1974, Beilage RiA 8.

3 As far as can be seen, the first published German decision mentioning the Brussels Convention was given by the Bayerisches Oberstes Landesgericht (Highest Regional Court of Bavaria) on 21 December 1973 – Breg 1 Z 99/73, NJW 1974, 421, and the first relevant decision of the Bundesgerichtshof (German Federal Court of Justice) was rendered on 24 September 1975 – VIII ZR 23/74, NJW 1975, 2143.

4 Judgment of 6 October 1976 – Case 12–76 (*Industrie Tessili Italiana Como v Dunlop AG*), ECLI:EU:C:1976:133.

5 See the annotations by *Reinhold Geimer*, NJW 1977, 492, and *Hartmut Linke*, RIW 1977, 40.

procedural law in Germany is mainly determined by statutory law, not by case law, for German lawyers the handling of a convention or regulation is not very different from working with the *Zivilprozessordnung* (Code of Civil Procedure). With regard to content, the Convention is widely compatible with traditional German thinking, as well. For example, both underline the importance of the defendant's domicile as the fundamental rule of international jurisdiction, leave very little room for judicial discretion, and adhere to the first-in-time principle when it comes to parallel proceedings. Furthermore, it was appreciated that the Convention, as proved by the Protocol annexed to it, left some margin for separate national approaches where for once a conventional solution was regarded as irreconcilable with features of national law (or simply as too progressive).[6] For instance, with respect to third party proceedings, Article V of the Protocol allowed Germany to retain its traditional instrument (*Streitverkündung*, cf. Sections 68 et seq. of the Code of Civil Procedure) instead of adopting the Roman concept of actions on a warranty or guarantee (Article 6 (2) Brussels Convention).

It seems remarkable that in Germany the early development of European legislation and case law in the field of cross-border litigation ran parallel to the establishment of the law of international civil procedure as a fully-fledged academic discipline. Formerly this field of law has been rather ambiguously positioned between the law of domestic civil procedure on the one hand and the rules of conflict of laws on the other. At the time of the adoption of the Convention, the German law of international civil procedure was being increasingly understood as emancipated.[7] In this context, the Brussels Convention was welcomed not only as an object of practical interest but also as an expression of this spirit of academic optimism. Law professors and outstanding practitioners wrote ground-breaking articles and books in the field.[8] In due course, the first "Kommentare"

---

6 Protocol of 27 September 1968 annexed to the Convention.

7 One indication of this emancipation was the publication of pioneering monographs, such as *Andreas Heldrich's* "Internationale Zuständigkeit und anwendbares Recht" in 1969, and *Jochen Schröder's* "Internationale Zuständigkeit – Entwurf eines Systems von Zuständigkeitsinteressen im Zwischenstaatlichen Privatverfahrensrecht aufgrund rechtshistorischer, rechtsvergleichender und rechtspolitischer Betrachtungen" in 1971. For a recent discussion of the development of the law of international civil procedure see *Peter Mankowski*, Über den Standort des Internationalen Zivilprozessrechts, RabelsZ 82 (2018) 576.

8 The decision of the *Max-Planck-Institut für Ausländisches und Internationales Privatrecht* in Hamburg to edit a "Handbuch des internationalen Zivilverfahrensrechts"

on the Brussels Convention have been published[9], i.e. volumes providing lengthy article-by-article annotations with plenty of footnotes and cross-references, a very typical genre of German legal literature, and the favoured reading of German judges and lawyers. The availability of such working tools has, in turn, greatly facilitated the reception of the Convention in practice.

Yet, the pioneering years should not be misunderstood as an attempt to nationalise the Brussels Convention, to press it into the trusted patterns of German doctrine and working-routine or to distract attention away from its truly international nature. Quite the contrary, not only have the official Report by *Paul Jenard*[10] and its early sequel by *Peter Schlosser*[11] been intensely analysed in Germany, but also the contributions of foreign authors, such as *Georges Droz*,[12] *Hélène Gaudemet-Tallon*,[13] *Pierre Gothot and*

---

was of particular importance in this respect. The first volume was published in 1982 and already included two comprehensive sections dealing with the Brussels Convention, authored by *Jürgen Basedow* (general matters) and *Jan Kropholler* (international jurisdiction).

9 See *Reinhold Geimer & Rolf A. Schütze*, Internationale Urteilsanerkennung, Band I, Halbband 1: Das EWG-Übereinkommen über die gerichtliche Zuständigkeit und die Vollstreckung gerichtlicher Entscheidungen in Zivil- und Handelssachen, 1983 (meanwhile: *Reinhold Geimer & Rolf A. Schütze*, Europäisches Zivilverfahrensrecht, 4th edition, forthcoming); *Jan Kropholler*, Europäisches Zivilprozessrecht, 1983 (meanwhile: *Jan Kropholler & Jan von Hein*, Europäisches Zivilprozessrecht, 10th edition, forthcoming). Even before such special treatments were available, the Brussels Convention was treated in some of the general commentaries on the German code of civil procedure (such as *Wieczorek/Schütze*, Zivilprozessordnung, 2nd edition 1980, and *Zöller*, Zivilprozessordnung, 13th edition 1981). Its text was already published in *Stein/Jonas*, Kommentar zur Zivilprozessordnung, 19th edition 1969 (Anhang A.III zu § 328 ZPO).

10 *Paul Jenard*, Report on the Convention on jurisdiction and the enforcement of judgments in civil and commercial matters (Signed at Brussels, 27 September 1968), OJ 1979 C 59, p. 1.

11 *Peter Schlosser*, Report on the Convention of 9 October 1978 on the Association of the Kingdom of Denmark, Ireland and the United Kingdom of Great Britain and Northern Ireland to the Convention on jurisdiction and the enforcement of judgments in civil and commercial matters and to the Protocol on its interpretation by the Court of Justice, OJ 1979 C 59, p. 71.

12 *Georges Droz*, Compétence judiciaire et effets des jugements dans le Marché Commun (Étude de la convention de Bruxelles du 27 septembre 1968), Paris 1972; *Georges Droz*, Pratique de la Convention de Bruxelles du 27 septembre 1968: le nouveau régime de la compétence judiciaire et des effets des jugements dans l'Europe des six, Paris 1973.

13 *Hélène Gaudemet-Tallon*, Les Conventions de Bruxelles et de Lugano: Compétence internationale, reconnaissance et exécution des jugements en Europe, Paris 1993.

Dominique Holleaux,[14] *Fausto Pocar*[15] and *Peter Kaye*.[16] Some of their works have repeatedly been cited by the Federal Court of Justice and even by the lower courts. Last but not least, it seems noteworthy that even the German legislator took inspiration from the Brussels Convention: The reform of 1974 on the requirements of jurisdiction agreements was expressly modelled on Article 17 of the Convention.[17]

2. *The Halting Dialogue between the Court of Justice and German Courts*

Against the backdrop of the friendly reception, as sketched so far, it is not surprising that German courts asked for preliminary rulings on many occasions when the interpretation of the Brussels Convention seemed doubtful. During the first five years of rulings by the Court of Justice on the Convention, i.e. between 1976 and 1980, twelve out of a total of twenty references came from German courts – eight from the Federal Court of Justice[18] and four from various Courts of Appeal.[19] Indeed, when trying to

14 *Pierre Gothot & Dominique Holleaux*, La Convention de Bruxelles: compétence judiciaire et effets des jugements dans la CEE, Paris 1985.

15 *Fausto Pocar*, Codice delle convenzioni sulla giurisdizione e l'esecuzione delle sentenze straniere nella C.E.E. con la giurisprudenza sulla Convenzione di Bruxelles del 1968 e sulle convenzioni bilaterali concluse dall'Italia, Milan 1980; *Fausto Pocar*, La convenzione di Bruxelles sulla giurisdizione e l'esecuzione delle sentenze, Milan 1995.

16 *Peter Kaye*, Civil Jurisdiction and Enforcement of Foreign Judgments: The application in England and Wales of the Brussels Convention of 1968 on jurisdiction and the enforcement of judgments in civil and commercial matters under the Civil Jurisdiction and Judgments Act 1982, Abingdon 1987.

17 Cf. Bundestags-Drucksache (parliamentary documents) 7/1384, p. 4.

18 Judgment of 14 December 1976 – Case 24–76 (*Estasis Salotti di Colzani Aimo e Gianmario Colzani s.n.c. v Rüwa Polstereimaschinen GmbH*), ECLI:EU:C:1976:177; Judgment of 14 December 1976 – Case 25–76 (*Galeries Segoura SPRL v Société Rahim Bonakdarian*), ECLI:EU:C:1976:178; Judgment of 14 July 1977 – Joined cases 9–77 and 10–77 (*Bavaria Fluggesellschaft Schwabe & Co. KG and Germanair Bedarfsluftfahrt GmbH & Co. KG v Eurocontrol*), ECLI:EU:C:1977:132; Judgment of 9 November 1978 – Case 23/78 (*Nikolaus Meeth v Glacetal*), ECLI:EU:C:1978:198; Judgment of 22 February 1979 – Case 133/78 (*Henri Gourdain v Franz Nadler*), ECLI:EU:C:1979:49; Judgment of 27 March 1979 – Case 143/78 (*Jacques de Cavel v Louise de Cavel*), ECLI:EU:C:1979:83; Judgment of 17 January 1980 – Case 56/79 (*Siegfried Zelger v Sebastiano Salinitri*), ECLI:EU:C:1980:15; Judgment of 6 March 1980 – Case 120/79 (*Louise de Cavel v Jacques de Cavel*), ECLI:EU:C:1980:70.

understand the success story of the Brussels Convention, one can hardly overestimate the relevance of the fact that the Member States very soon realised that it would be wise to confer jurisdiction on the Court of Justice to interpret the Convention.[20]

By absolute numbers, Germany might still be the all-times European champion when it comes to referring questions to the Court of Justice, currently done under Article 267 TFEU. Nevertheless, one should not ignore the fact that things have changed since the early years of the Brussels Convention.[21] Thirty years later, between 2006 and 2010, the Court of Justice has rendered 21 judgments. These judgements gave guidance on the then new Brussels I Regulation of 2001[22] which replaced the Convention after the coming into force of the Treaty of Amsterdam[23] and brought important alterations to the Brussels regime. It seems astonishing that only three of these cases came from Germany.[24] This observation can only partly be explained by the unwise decision of the Amsterdam Treaty to

---

19 Judgment of 6 October 1976 – Case 12–76 (*Industrie Tessili Italiana Como v Dunlop AG*), ECLI:EU:C:1976:133 (submitted by the Oberlandesgericht Frankfurt am Main); Judgment of 14 October 1976 – Case 29–76 (*LTU Lufttransportunternehmen GmbH & Co. KG v Eurocontrol*), ECLI:EU:C:1976:137 (submitted by the Oberlandesgericht Düsseldorf); Judgment of 22 November 1978 – Case 33/78 (*Somafer SA v Saar-Ferngas AG*), ECLI:EU:C:1978:205 (submitted by the Oberlandesgericht Saarbrücken); Judgment of 21 May 1980 – Case 125/79 (*Bernard Denilauler v SNC Couchet Frères*), ECLI:EU:C:1980:130 (submitted by the Oberlandesgericht Frankfurt am Main).

20 Protocol of 3 June 1971 on the interpretation by the Court of Justice of the Convention of 27 September 1968 on jurisdiction and the enforcement of judgments in civil and commercial matters. For early German discussions of the Protocol cf. *Hans Arnold*, Das Protokoll über die Auslegung des EWG-Gerichtsstands- und Vollstreckungsübereinkommens durch den Gerichtshof in Luxemburg, NJW 1972, 977, and *Peter Schlosser*, Neue Zuständigkeiten des Gerichtshofs der Europäischen Gemeinschaften, AWD/RIW 1975, 534.

21 In the following, such cases are left out of consideration in which, for whatever reason, the request did not lead to a judgment of the Court of Justice.

22 Regulation (EC) No 44/2001 of 22 December 2000 on jurisdiction and the recognition and enforcement of judgments in civil and commercial matters, OJ 2001 L 12, p. 1.

23 OJ 1997 C 340, p. 173.

24 Judgment of 13 December 2007 – Case C-463/06 (*FBTO Schadeverzekeringen NV v Jack Odenbreit*), ECLI:EU:C:2007:792 (submitted by the Bundesgerichtshof); Judgment of 9 July 2009 – Case C-204/08 (*Peter Rehder v Air Baltic Corporation*), ECLI:EU:C:2009:439 (submitted by the Bundesgerichtshof); Judgment of 25 February 2010 – Case C-381/08 (*Car Trim GmbH v KeySafety Systems Srl.*), ECLI:EU:C:2010:90 (submitted by the Bundesgerichtshof).

allow only courts of last instance to ask the Court of Justice for preliminary rulings in the field of judicial cooperation in civil matters.[25] Although the Treaty on the Functioning of the European Union has thankfully abolished this unreasonable restriction, it seems that the general trend is still towards less incoming communication from German courts. Between 2016 and 2018, the Court of Justice has rendered 37 judgments dealing in their operative parts with the Brussels I Regulation and/or the most recent Brussels I *bis* Regulation.[26] Only five of these cases came from Germany.[27]

When this paper was completed in late 2018, similar findings emerged with regard to the other regulations in the field of judicial cooperation in civil and commercial matters. In matrimonial matters and matters of parental responsibility, only three of the then 31 preliminary rulings regarding the Brussels II *bis* Regulation[28] were initiated by German courts,[29] the last one dating back to 2010. Moreover, the situation was not

---

25 Article 68 (1) EC Treaty (Amsterdam consolidated version), OJ 1997 C 340, p. 173.

26 Regulation (EU) No 1215/2012 of 12 December 2012 on jurisdiction and the recognition and enforcement of judgments in civil and commercial matters, OJ 2012 L 351, p. 1.

27 Judgment of 4 May 2017 – Case C-29/16 (*HanseYachts AG v Port D'Hiver Yachting SARL and Others*), ECLI:EU:C:2017:343 (submitted by the Landgericht Stralsund); Judgment of 27 September 2017 – Joined Cases C-24/16 and C-25/16 (*Nintendo Co. Ltd v BigBen Interactive GmbH and BigBen Interactive SA*), ECLI:EU:C:2017:724 (submitted by the Oberlandesgericht Düsseldorf); Judgment of 5 October 2017 – Case C-341/16 (*Hanssen Beleggingen BV v Tanja Prast-Knipping*), ECLI:EU:C:2017:738 (submitted by the Oberlandesgericht Düsseldorf); Judgment of 7 March 2018 – Joined Cases C-274/16, C-447/16 and C-448/16 (*flightright GmbH v Air Nostrum, Líneas Aéreas del Mediterráneo SA, Roland Becker v Hainan Airlines Co. Ltd and Mohamed Barkan and Others v Air Nostrum, Líneas Aéreas del Mediterráneo SA*), ECLI:EU:C:2018:160 (submitted by the Amtsgericht Düsseldorf and the Bundesgerichtshof); Judgment of 4 October 2018 – Case C-379/17 (*Proceedings brought by Società Immobiliare Al Bosco Srl*), ECLI:EU:C:2018:806 (submitted by the Bundesgerichtshof).

28 Regulation (EC) No 2201/2003 of 27 November 2003 concerning jurisdiction and the recognition and enforcement of judgments in matrimonial matters and the matters of parental responsibility, OJ 2003 L 338, p. 1.

29 Judgment of 15 July 2010 – Case C-256/09 (*Bianca Purrucker v Guillermo Vallés Pérez*), ECLI:EU:C:2010:437 (submitted by the Bundesgerichtshof); Judgment of 9 November 2010 – Case C-296/10 (*Bianca Purrucker v Guillermo Vallés Pérez*), ECLI:EU:C:2010:665 (submitted by the Amtsgericht Stuttgart); Judgment of 22 December 2010 – Case C-491/10 PPU (*Joseba Andoni Aguirre Zarraga v Simone Pelz*), ECLI:EU:C:2010:828 (submitted by the Oberlandesgericht Celle).

much different with regard to the Maintenance Regulation[30] (one out of six[31]), the European Enforcement Order Regulation[32] (one out of seven[33]), the Service Regulation[34] (one out of eight[35]) and the Evidence Regulation[36] (none out of three). At least the German figures with regard to the Insolvency Regulations[37] were significantly better (seven out of 24[38]).

The obviously increasing reluctance is remarkable in several respects. Germany is a Member State of more than 82 million citizens and by far the

30 Regulation (EC) No 4/2009 of 18 December 2008 on jurisdiction, applicable law, recognition and enforcement of decisions and cooperation in matters relating to maintenance obligations, OJ 2009 L 7, p. 1.

31 Judgment of 18 December 2014 – Joined Cases C-400/13 and C-408/13 (*Sophia Marie Nicole Sanders v David Verhaegen and Barbara Huber v Manfred Huber*), ECLI:EU:C:2014:2461 (submitted by the Amtsgericht Düsseldorf and the Amtsgericht Karlsruhe).

32 Regulation (EC) No 805/2004 of 21 April 2004 creating a European Enforcement Order for uncontested claims, OJ 2004 L 143, p. 15.

33 Judgment of 15 March 2012 – Case C-292/10 (*G v Cornelius de Visser*), ECLI:EU:C:2012:142 (submitted by the Landgericht Regensburg).

34 Regulation (EC) No 1393/2007 of 13 November 2007 on the service in the Member States of judicial and extrajudicial documents in civil or commercial matters (service of documents), OJ 2007 L 324, p. 79.

35 Judgment of 11 June 2015 – Case C-226/13 (*Stefan Fahnenbrock and Others v Hellenische Republik*), ECLI:EU:C:2015:383 (submitted by the Landgericht Wiesbaden).

36 Regulation (EC) No 1206/2001 of 28 May 2001 on cooperation between the courts of the Member States in the taking of evidence in civil or commercial matters, OJ 2001 L 174, p. 1.

37 Regulation (EC) No 1346/2000 of 29 May 2000 on insolvency proceedings, OJ 2000 L 160, p. 1; Regulation (EU) 2015/848 of 20 May 2015 on insolvency proceedings, OJ 2015 L 141, p. 19.

38 Judgment of 17 January 2006 – Case C-1/04 (*Susanne Staubitz-Schreiber*), ECLI:EU:C:2006:39 (submitted by the Bundesgerichtshof); Judgment of 12 February 2009 – Case C-339/07 (*Christopher Seagon v Deko Marty Belgium NV*), ECLI:EU:C:2009:83 (submitted by the Bundesgerichtshof); Judgment of 16 January 2014 – Case C-328/12 (*Ralph Schmid v Lilly Hertel*), ECLI:EU:C:2014:6 (submitted by the Bundesgerichtshof); Judgment of 4 December 2014 – Case C-295/13 (*H v H.K.*), ECLI:EU:C:2014:2410 (submitted by the Landgericht Darmstadt); Judgment of 16 April 2015 – Case C-557/13 (*Hermann Lutz v Elke Bäuerle*), ECLI:EU:C:2015:227 (submitted by the Bundesgerichtshof); Judgment of 10 December 2015 – Case C-594/14 (*Simona Kornhaas v Thomas Dithmar als Insolvenzverwalter über das Vermögen der Kornhaas Montage und Dienstleistung Ltd*), ECLI:EU:C:2015:806 (submitted by the Bundesgerichtshof); Judgment of 26 October 2016 – Case C-195/15 (*SCI Senior Home v Gemeinde Wedemark and Hannoversche Volksbank eG*), ECLI:EU:C:2016:804 (submitted by the Bundesgerichtshof).

biggest economy within the European Union. When talking to German judges, one does not get the impression that they play coy when it comes to considering a reference for a preliminary ruling. On the contrary, they are well aware of this instrument and, of course, where applicable, of their obligation under Article 267 (3) TFEU to bring a matter before the Court of Justice. Furthermore, European Civil Procedure really matters in German legal practice. In 2018, in almost 11,000 civil or commercial lawsuits before German regional courts (*Landgerichte*) at least one of the parties was domiciled in another Member State of the European Union.[39] In September 2018, a research in the most common German legal data base (*juris*) revealed 230 decisions by the Federal Court of Justice and 360 decisions of higher regional courts applying the Brussels I and/or the Brussels I *bis* Regulation. Such data oddly contrasts with the low number of recent requests for preliminary rulings.

Of course, one could ask whether this development is disturbing at all. Does it not simply indicate that the national courts get along very well? Is it not much the same as grown-up children who have left home and now are living their own lives, rarely call and finally even stop sending their laundry home? Why should the parents care instead of enjoying their quiet house, convinced that their children would stop by and ask for advice when they face something bothering? Unfortunately, this analogy does not work: the preliminary ruling procedure is not merely an emergency line that national judges can call when a case has already gone in the wrong direction. Rather, it is a key instrument to ensure that EU law is interpreted and applied in the same way in all EU Member State.[40]

---

39 Statistisches Bundesamt (Federal Statistical Office), Zivilgerichte – Fachserie 10 Reihe 2.1 2018 (published 2019), p. 60: In 1.8 % of the 304,000 cases the plaintiff and in 1.8 % of the cases the defendant is resident in another EU Member State (not stated is the presumably rather low number of cases in which both parties come from another EU Member State).

40 There is a broad discussion in Germany on the relevance of the preliminary ruling procedure in the field of European civil justice. Cf. *Jürgen Basedow*, Der Europäische Gerichtshof und das Privatrecht – Über Unsicherheiten, Allgemeine Grundsätze und die europäische Justizarchitektur, AcP 210 (2010), 157; *Thomas von Danwitz*, Die Aufgabe des Gerichtshofs bei der Entfaltung des europäischen Zivil- und Zivilverfahrensrechts, ZEuP 2010, 463; *Beate Gsell & Wolfgang Hau*, Zivilgerichtsbarkeit und Europäisches Justizsystem, 2012; *Burkhard Hess*, Der europäische Gerichtsverbund, 2017; *Andreas Piekenbrock*, Vorlagen an den EuGH nach Art. 267 AEUV im Privatrecht, EuR 2011, 317; *Hannes Rösler*, Das Rechtsgespräch zwischen dem EuGH und den verschiedenen zivilgerichtlichen Instanzen über das Vertrags- und Deliktsrecht, EuZW 2014, 606. For Austrian perspectives

In fact, there are two different problematic constellations. On the one hand, when reading rulings from Luxembourg or opinions of the Advocates General, one sometimes wonders why so many cases with very particular facts and of very limited general interest reach the Court of Justice. What seems more troublesome is that, on the other hand, every expert can tell stories about cases in which a reference would have been highly advisable to give the Court of Justice an opportunity to clarify an important point of European wide interest, but this chance was missed for whatever reason.[41]

It is not suggested that national courts prefer to insist entirely on their own perspective, thereby intentionally leaving the Court of Justice out. In the field of judicial cooperation in civil matters, there is no indication of an inappropriately selective perception of the case law from Luxembourg.[42] A much more likely explanation is that judges are sometimes tempted to resort over-optimistically to the doctrine of *acte clair* (or *acte éclairé*, respectively). A rather extreme example is the long-standing but hardly sustainable position of the Federal Court of Justice as regards the admissible grounds for refusal of recognition under Article 45 of the Brussels I Regulation,[43] which was only overcome when eventually the *Hoge Raad der Nederlanden* gave the Court of Justice an opportunity to correct the German approach.[44] Occasionally, judges simply assume that it is in the best interest of the parties to get a prompt decision on the merits,

---

see *Selena Clavora/Thomas Garber*, Das Vorabentscheidungsverfahren in der Zivilgerichtsbarkeit, 2014.

41 Cf. *Hannes Rösler*, Das Rechtsgespräch zwischen dem EuGH und den verschiedenen zivilgerichtlichen Instanzen über das Vertrags- und Deliktsrecht, EuZW 2014, 606, 610: "dunkle Masse der Nichtvorlagen" ("dark mass of missed references").

42 For a much more pessimistic view (although without paying special attention to matters of judicial cooperation), see *Fabian Michl*, Zur selektiven Rezeption europäischer Rechtsprechung, EuR 2018, 456.

43 Cf., for example, Bundesgerichtshof, order of 14 March 2007 – IX ZB 174/04, NJW 2007, 3432. On this, see *Burkhard Hess*, Die Unzulässigkeit materiellrechtlicher Einwendungen im Beschwerdeverfahren nach Art. 43 ff. EuGVVO, IPRax 2008, 25, rightly criticising that the Federal Court was in breach of its duty to refer the question to the Court of Justice.

44 Judgment of 13 October 2011 – Case C-139/10 (*Prism Investments BV v Jaap Anne van der Meer*), ECLI:EU:C:2011:653. This, in turn, did not only lead to adjusted decisions of the German courts (see Bundesgerichtshof, order of 12 July 2012 – IX ZB 267/11, NJW 2012, 2663) but also triggered a reform of the German act implementing the Brussels I Regulation (Bundesgesetzblatt 2013 I, 273; cf. Bundestags-Drucksache 17/10492, p. 12).

accepting that a mere procedural issue may not be settled right down to the last detail of European law. Hand in hand with this problematic position might go an over-pessimistic estimation of the duration and effort of preliminary ruling proceedings.

One may, however, not completely rule out that there are also quality considerations involved. It seems obvious that German courts have considered some rulings from the Court of Justice, irrespectively of whether or not they sympathised with the result in substance, as less helpful than hoped for, in particular when not matters of principle but rather technical procedural problems were concerned. This might be illustrated by the irritation that followed after the ruling on the practically important question whether a set-off requires the judge to have international jurisdiction over the defendant's claim: in the *Danværn Production v Schuhfabriken Otterbeck* case, the Court of Justice underlined the obvious (i.e. that a set-off is not a counterclaim in the strict sense of Article 6 (3) Brussels Convention, now Article 8 (3) Brussels I *bis* Regulation), but did not get to the heart of the problem and eventually pointed to the applicability of the national law.[45] In a subsequent case, the Federal Court made no secret of its difficulties understanding what the Court of Justice actually meant, but avoided another reference.[46] To give a more recent example: with all due respect, it seems rather questionable whether the long-awaited answer of the Court of Justice in the *Società Immobiliare Al Bosco* case,[47] dealing with the applicability of time limits for enforcement in the *lex fori executionis*, sufficiently reflects the complexity of the problem (and further implications for cases of cross-border enforcement) which was judiciously discussed both in the foregoing reference of the Federal Court of Justice[48] and the opinion of the Advocate General.[49]

Maybe more often than not, the Court of Justice, when finally asked, only confirms what has already been practised for years without going through the bother of initiating a preliminary ruling procedure. And in cases in which the Court of Justice gets to a conclusion that departs from

45 Judgment of 13 July 1995 – Case C-341/93 (*Danværn Production A/S v Schuhfabriken Otterbeck GmbH & Co.*), ECLI:EU:C:1995:239.

46 Bundesgerichtshof, judgment of 7 November 2001 – VIII ZR 263/00, NJW 2002, 2182.

47 Judgment of 4 October 2018 – Case C-379/17 (*Proceedings brought by Società Immobiliare Al Bosco Srl*), ECLI:EU:C:2018:806.

48 Bundesgerichtshof, order of 11 May September 2017 – V ZB 175/15, RIW 2017, 305.

49 Opinion of Advocate General *Spunar* of 20 June 2018, ECLI:EU:C:2018:472.

national case law, it does not necessarily mean that the new position serves the principle of mutual recognition of judgments better than the earlier practice. To give just one example: under the Polish rules of civil procedure, it was assumed that judicial documents addressed to a defendant domiciled abroad could simply be placed in the case file and deemed to have been effectively served, if the defendant has failed to appoint a Polish representative who is authorised to accept service. On a number of occasions, the German Federal Court held that a Polish decision has to be recognised and enforced even when the Polish court had applied this rule.[50] This liberal approach only ended when the Court of Justice, in the *Alder v Orlowski* case, clarified in 2012 that the Polish rule was not in line with the standards of European law.[51] In other words, there was more mutual trust before than after the intervention by the Court of Justice. By the same token, mutual trust is not the only principle at stake, and it is clear that there is also more protection of defendant's rights since than before this intervention.

3. *The Dialogue and the Promotion of European Civil Procedure*

The preliminary ruling procedure is not only a dialogue between the Court of Justice and a single national court, but it is a public and well-documented course of events, from the reference to the preliminary ruling to the final decision of the case. Interested practitioners and academics throughout the European Union observe this process, irrespectively of where the original case comes from. Of course, rulings by the Court of Justice are important because (more precisely: as far as) they clarify certain legal issues. However, at the same time, they draw a lot of attention to European instruments, thereby giving national courts an opportunity to reconsider their own practice and making lawyers start thinking about whether such instruments could be useful tools that serve the needs of their clients.

In other words, preliminary rulings are extremely helpful in promoting the standards and instruments of European Civil Procedure, the backbone

---

50 Cf., for example, Bundesgerichtshof, order of 14 June 2012 – IX ZB 183/09, NJW-RR 2012, 1013.

51 Judgment of 19 December 2012 – Case C-325/11 (*Krystyna Alder and Ewald Alder v Sabina Orlowska and Czeslaw Orlowski*), ECLI:EU:C:2012:824. Referring to that and thus refusing the recognition of a Polish decision: Bundesgerichtshof, order of 10 September 2015 – IX ZB 39/13, NJW 2010, 160.

of judicial cooperation in the area of freedom, security and justice. This is why it seems crucial to get more decisions dealing with the many open questions for example as regards the Regulation establishing a European Small Claims Procedure[52] or the more recent Regulation establishing a European Account Preservation Order Procedure.[53] More guidance from Luxembourg could enhance the general awareness for these instruments just as early landmark-decisions such as *Tessili*,[54] *De Bloos*,[55] *Eurocontrol*[56] or *Mines Potasse d'Alsace*[57] once helped promoting the Brussels Convention in the seventies of the last century. It seems obvious that there are still more than enough cases brought before the Member States' courts raising open questions of European-wide interest that are well worth being referred to Luxembourg. But this requires national judges who give the Court of Justice the opportunity to accomplish its important mission.

52 Regulation (EC) No 861/2007 of 11 July 2007 establishing a European Small Claims Procedure, OJ 2007 L 199, p. 1; amended by Regulation (EU) 2015/2421 of 16 December 2015, OJ 2015 L 341, p. 1.

53 Regulation (EU) No 655/2014 of 15 May 2014 establishing a European Account Preservation Order procedure to facilitate cross-border debt recovery in civil and commercial matters, OJ 2014 L 189, p. 59.

54 Judgment of 6 October 1976 – Case 12–76 (*Industrie Tessili Italiana Como v Dunlop AG*), ECLI:EU:C:1976:133.

55 Judgment of 6 October 1976 – Case 14–76 (*A. De Bloos, SPRL v Société en commandite par actions Bouyer*), ECLI:EU:C:1976:134.

56 Judgment of 14 October 1976 – Case 29–76 (*LTU Lufttransportunternehmen GmbH & Co. KG v Eurocontrol*), ECLI:EU:C:1976:137.

57 Judgment of 30 November 1976 – Case 21–76 (*Handelskwekerij G. J. Bier BV v Mines de potasse d'Alsace SA*), ECLI:EU:C:1976:166.

European Civil Procedure and the Dialogue between National Courts and the European Court of Justice

*Xandra Kramer & Jos Hoevenaars**

Table of Contents

* Xandra Kramer is Professor of Private Law, Erasmus University Rotterdam, and Professor of Private International Law, Utrecht University (The Netherlands). Jos Hoevenaars is Postdoc Researcher at Erasmus University Rotterdam. This research has received funding from the European Research Council (ERC) under the European Union's Horizon 2020 research and innovation programme (grant agreement No 726032), ERC consolidator project 'Building EU Civil Justice: challenges of procedural innovations – bridging access to justice'; see <www.euciviljustice.eu>.

1. Introduction

Celebrating the 50th anniversary of what has become known as the 'Brussels Regime' – starting with the 1968 Brussels Convention, currently the Brussels I-bis Regulation[1] – it is no overstatement to say that civil justice in Europe has changed fundamentally. While civil procedures, rules, and judicial systems continue to be dominantly national and are firmly rooted in their respective national traditions, EU legislation increasingly Europeanizes our legal systems. The Brussels I-bis and its predecessors not only mark the starting point of the gradual Europeanization; it is still the most used and considered to be the most successful instrument to facilitate cross-border litigation in Europe. This is also clear from the preliminary rulings of the Court of Justice; the vast majority of rulings in the area of judicial cooperation in civil matters are on the application of the Brussels I-bis Regulation and its predecessors.

While the core of civil procedure in the Member States is still regulated by national law, the growing number of European instruments on civil justice has resulted in the gradual harmonization of civil procedure. Through a process known as 'functional spill over'[2] in one academic discipline or 'competence creep'[3] in another, the EU increasingly encroached on national civil laws by pointing to the necessity of completion of the internal market, the elimination of distorted competition, the removal of obstacles to cross-border trade, the strengthening of consumer protection, and more recently, the establishment of a genuine area of justice. The dialogue between national courts and the CJEU plays an unmistakable role in this dynamic.

At present some twenty civil justice instruments are in place relying on different legislative bases, having different scopes of application and relying on different approaches. While many of the instruments are directly binding regulation and are self-standing regimes, the rules operate within the national context and rely on a proper implementation and application.

---

1 Regulation (EU) No 1215/2012 of 12 December 2012 on jurisdiction and the recognition and enforcement of judgments in civil and commercial matters [2012] OJ L289.

2 In International Relations literature, see L. N. Lindberg, 'The Political Dynamics of European Economic Integration' in M. Eilstrup-Sangiovanni (ed), *Debates on European Integration: A Reader* (Palgrave Macmillan 2005) 123.

3 In legal analysis, see S. Vogenauer and S. Weatherill, 'The European Community's Competence for a Comprehensive Harmonisation of Contract law-An Empirical Analysis' (2005) 30 European Law Review 821.

Considering the legislative diversity at both the European and national level and the diverging legal practices in the Member States, the uniform application of the European rules is challenging. At the grass-roots level the application of rules of European civil procedure lies with the national courts. The role of the European Court of Justice as the European upper judge in the interpretation and harmonization of European civil procedure cannot be underestimated. At the same time, the preliminary reference procedure institutionalizes the dialogue between the national courts and the European Court of Justice.[4]

This paper focuses on the dialogue between the European Court of Justice (CJEU) and the national courts in the application and development of European civil procedure. It questions the role of the preliminary reference procedure in the discourse with the national courts. It will consider to what extent the reference procedure may fill the European legislative deficit and bridge the divergences of national civil justice systems and practice, and how the dialogue between the CJEU and the national courts can be improved. First, the paper discusses the legislative disparities in the area of European civil procedure and the impact on court practice. Next, it zooms in on the dialogue between the national courts and the CJEU and on measures to improve the dialogue. Finally, the discussion is placed into the broader challenges for European civil procedure.

2. *The Complex Harmonization of Civil Procedure in Europe*

The harmonization of civil procedure has traditionally been regarded as one of the most intricate issues considering the great variety in procedural laws and the embeddedness into and intertwinement with local legal culture, institutions, and traditions. At the global level, the conventions on private international law and judicial cooperation of the Hague Conference on Private International Law are the most significant. At the European level, substantial progress has been made since the introduction of the competence on judicial cooperation in the Treaty on the Functioning of the European Union (TFEU) two decades ago. European civil procedure is one of the most vital areas of European law.[5] This section focuses on the

4 See Consolidated version of the Treaty on the Functioning of the European Union [2012] OJ C326/47 (TFEU), art. 267.

5 See inter alia X. E. Kramer, 'Strengthening Civil Justice Cooperation: The Quest for Model Rules and Common Minimum Standards of Civil Procedure in Europe' in M. A. Rodrigues and H. Zaneti Jr. (eds), *Coleção Grandes Temas do Novo CPC –*

development of European civil procedure. It serves to illustrate how the patchy legislative approach creates challenges for legal practice, increasing the need for a true dialogue between the national courts and the European Court of Justice.

2.1. *Europeanization of Civil Procedure: Goals and State of Affairs*

The gradual harmonization of civil procedure in Europe should be viewed in the broader context of Europeanization of laws and of civil law more in particular. National legal systems have become progressively Europeanized with a view to further the various goals of the European Union, including securing peace, freedom, security and justice, and economic sustainability.[6] However, the EU's encroachment on the realm of civil law has been an issue of great sensitivity and debate, since civil law remains, as such, squarely within the domain of national competence. In the past twenty years the extended competence in the area of civil justice has spurred harmonization tremendously. However, the principles of subsidiarity and proportionality,[7] the limitations imposed by the relevant treaty rules as well as the compromises resulting from the sometimes difficult tripartite negotiations between the Commission, the European Parliament and the Council, have also resulted in a fragmented legislative framework.[8]

The EU legislation in the area of civil procedure aims to support judicial cooperation in civil matters between the Member States, as is clear from Article 81 TFEU. The overriding objective is to invigorate judicial coopera-

---

v.13 – Cooperação Internacional (Editora Juspodivm 2019) 593–598; B. Hess and X. E. Kramer (eds), *From Common Rules to Best Practices in European Civil Procedure* (Nomos/Hart Publishing 2017); B. Hess, M. Bergström and E. Storskrubb (eds), *EU Civil Justice: Current Issues and Future Outlook* (Hart Publishing 2016); X. E. Kramer, 'Procedure Matters: Construction and Deconstructivism in European Civil Procedure' (Inaugural Lecture, Erasmus Law Lectures 33, Eleven International Publishing 2013); Z. Vernadaki, 'Civil Procedure Harmonization in the EU: Unravelling the Policy Considerations' (2013) 9 *Journal of Contemporary European Research* 298–312; M. Tulibacka, 'Europeanisation of Civil Procedures: In Search of a Coherent Approach' (2009) 46 *Common Market Law Review* 1527.

6 Consolidated Version of the Treaty on European Union [2012] OJ C326/13 (TEU), art. 3.

7 Art 5 TEU.

8 See for an overview and discussion X. E. Kramer, 'Judicial Cooperation in Civil Matters' in P. J. Kuijper and others (eds), *The Law of the European Union* (Kluwer Law International 2018) 721–740.

tion, based on the principle of mutual trust, with the aim of enhancing access to justice for EU citizens.[9] An important limitation imposed by this provision is that it only provides competence for rules addressing cases "having cross-border implications". These are generally defined as cases in which at least one of the parties is domiciled or habitually resident in a Member State other than the Member State of the court or tribunal seized for the dispute.[10] Several attempts of the European Commission to stretch the competence to instruments on civil justice cooperation that also apply to domestic cases were not acceptable for the Member States.

On the basis of this competence, twenty regulations and a directive have been adopted over the past twenty years. Many of the regulations based on this provision concern traditional private international law issues, including international jurisdiction, recognition and enforcement of judgments, and the applicable law. The best known is the Brussels I-bis Regulation, while in more recent years another strand of instruments based on this provision are those introducing uniform procedures or harmonising specific aspects of civil procedure. These include the Regulations on a European Order for Payment Procedure, a Small Claims Procedure, and an Account Preservation Order[11] as well as the Mediation Directive.[12]

Another pillar for harmonisation is Article 114 TFEU, which gives competence to enact sector-specific legislation that introduces harmonised rules for a specific substantive EU law area, including consumer law and competition law. In the civil justice area these notably include two instruments on Consumer ADR and Consumer ODR,[13] and a non-binding Rec-

9 European Commission, 'The EU Justice Agenda for 2020 – Strengthening Trust, Mobility and Growth within the Union' COM (2014) 144 final, point 3; European Commission, 'Proposal for a directive on representative actions for the protection of the collective interests of consumers, and repealing Directive 2009/22/EC' COM (2018) 184 final.

10 See *e.g.* Council Regulation (EC) 1896/2006 of 12 December 2006 on creating a European Order for Payment Procedure [2006] OJ L399 (EOP), art. 3.

11 Regulation (EU) 2015/2421 of 16 December 2015 amending Regulation (EC) No. 861/2007 establishing a European Small Claims Procedure and Regulation (EC) No. 1896/2006 creating a European order for payment procedure [2015] OJ L341/1; Regulation (EU) 655/2014 of 15 May 2014 establishing a European Account Preservation Order to facilitate cross-border debt recovery in civil and commercial matters [2014] OJ L189/59 (EAPO).

12 Council Directive 2008/52/EC of 21 May 2008 on certain aspects of mediation in civil and commercial matters [2008] OJ L136/3 (Mediation Directive).

13 Directive 2013/11/EU of 21 May 2013 on alternative dispute resolution for consumer disputes and amending Regulation (EC) No. 2006/2004 and Directive

ommendation on Collective Redress.[14] A Commission proposal for representative actions for the protection of the collective interests of consumers was put forward in 2018.[15] In addition, a number of other sectorial instruments that primarily regulate substantive law issues, in particular intellectual property and competition law, also contain rules on civil procedure.[16]

Last but not least, the influence of primary EU law and human rights law on the development and interpretation of European civil justice is considerable. This includes notably the fair trial principle laid down in Art. 6 European Convention on Human Rights and Art. 47 of the EU Charter on Fundamental Rights.[17]

2.2. *The European Civil Justice Patchwork: Legislative Disparities and the Role of the Courts*

The specifics of the EU supranational order, the limited competence of the EU legislator, and the reluctance of the Member States to harmonize civil procedure have resulted in a scattered legislative framework. While national legal orders generally rely on an encompassing view on the justice system, and civil procedural rules are designed to enforce rights in the

---

2009/22/EC [2013] OJ L165/63 (Directive on consumer ADR); Regulation (EU) 524/2013 of 21 May 2013 on online dispute resolution for consumer disputes and amending Regulation (EC) No. 2006/2004 and Directive 2009/22/EC [2013] OJ L165/1 (Regulation on consumer ODR).

14 Commission Recommendation 2013/396/EU of 11 June 2013 on common principles for injunctive and compensatory collective redress mechanisms in the Member States concerning violations of rights granted under Union Law [2013] OJ L201 (Recommendation on collective redress).

15 European Commission, 'Proposal for a directive on representative actions for the protection of the collective interests of consumers, and repealing Directive 2009/22/EC' COM (2018) 184 final. See also A. Biard and X. E. Kramer, 'The EU directive on representative actions for consumers: a milestone or another missed opportunity?' (2019) *Zeitschrift für Europäisches Privatrecht* 249–259.

16 See most notably Council Directive 2004/48/EC of 29 April 2004 on the enforcement of intellectual property rights [2004] OJ 2004 L195/16 ((IPR) Enforcement Directive); Directive 2014/104/EU of 26 November 2014 on certain rules governing actions for damages under national law for infringements of the competition law provisions of the Member States and of the European Union [2014] OJ L349/1 (Actions for Damages under Competition Law Directive).

17 C. Mak, 'Rights and Remedies. Article 47 EUCFR and Effective Judicial Protection in European Private Law Matters' in H.W. Micklitz (ed), *Constitutionalization of European Private Law* (Oxford University Press 2014) 236–258.

domestic context, the European civil justice system is piecemeal legislation that is put into existence on a seemingly somewhat ad hoc basis, relying on political priorities and feasibility to reach an agreement on a proposed instrument at a given time.

Resulting from the different heads of competence and the negotiating character of the legislative process, both legislative technique and scope differ greatly between the instruments. Many instruments are direct binding regulations, but some are directives – either relying on minimum or maximum harmonisation – that require national implementation, or are non-binding instruments. Some are horizontal instruments applying to civil and commercial matters with only few exceptions (including the Brussels I-bis Regulation), while others are sectorial instruments that apply to specific types of cases or subject-matters only (for instance the European Small Claims Regulation). Some instruments apply to both domestic and cross-border cases, while many others – those based on Article 81 TFEU – are limited to the latter. Most instruments are of a mandatory nature, however the uniform European procedures[18] are optional for the claimant and thus co-exist with domestic civil procedures. In addition, owing to their special position in relation to judicial cooperation instruments under the Treaty, Denmark has a general opt out,[19] while the United Kingdom and Ireland have opted in on many, but not all civil procedure instruments under Article 81. It goes without saying that the United Kingdom is no longer bound by any instrument following its departure from the EU after the transition period expires. This legislative patchwork can be characterised as unintended deconstructivism.[20] Not only does European civil procedure add a layer to the national legal order and the international conventions on civil justice cooperation, its multi-regulation and multi-methodology are a problem in itself.[21]

The incoherence of the European civil justice framework and the confrontation with the diverging domestic legal orders in the application of the rules increase the need for progressive and assertive courts. The prelim-

18 The European Order for Payment, the European Small Claims Procedure and the Account Preservation Order (n. 10, 11).

19 Denmark does take part in the Brussels I-bis Regulation and the Service Regulation pursuant to a parallel agreement.

20 X. E. Kramer, *Procedure Matters: Construction and Deconstructivism in European Civil Procedure* (Eleven International Publishing 2013) 23–26.

21 A staff member of the CJEU who participated in the conference from which this paper results commented that the huge number of diverging instruments makes their work difficult.

inary reference procedure is crucial not only for a harmonized interpretation and application; it also gives body to underlying principles and goals of judicial cooperation, ties the European instruments together, and connects the national legal orders.

3. *National Courts and CJEU in Dialogue*

This section zooms in on the dialogue between the national courts and the CJEU through the preliminary reference procedure against the background of the development of European civil procedure.

3.1. *Cooperation at the Centre of the EU Legal System*

A common way to judge the state of European harmonization in the legal realm is to look at the cooperation between national courts and the CJEU through the use of Article 267 TFEU. The preliminary ruling procedure gives every national court the power – and even imposes an obligation on some courts – to refer preliminary questions concerning the interpretation of European law and the validity of the acts of EU institutions to the Court of Justice of the European Union (CJEU). Historically Art. 267 has proven itself to be the most successful provision in the European Treaties. In the words of the institution itself, the preliminary ruling procedure is the 'keystone' of the EU judicial system,[22] as it guarantees the uniformity of EU law and it is crucial to its development. Moreover, the preliminary procedure contributes to the legal protection of individual citizens within the EU by ensuring a uniform application of EU rules in the different Member States.

Since many major concepts of European law as well as many ground breaking judgments have followed from a request for a preliminary ruling by a national court, a vast corpus of academic literature in the political sciences has designated the CJEU as the motor of European integration and the preliminary reference procedure as the fuel.[23] Founding doctrinal prin-

---

22 See, for instance, Opinion 2/13 of 18 December 2014 on Accession of the European Union to the European Convention for the Protection of Human Rights and Fundamental Freedoms [2014] ECLI:EU:C:2014:2454, para 176.

23 For a comprehensive literature review see L. Conant, 'Review Article: The Politics of Legal Integration' (2007) 45 *Journal of Common Market Studies* 45.

ciples such as the primacy and direct effect of EU law, as well as the principle of mutual trust, among others, found their expression in preliminary rulings. Beyond its role in the development of such fundamental doctrinal principles, the preliminary reference procedure provides national judges with a tool in fulfilling their task of applying EU law in national cases and functions to ensure uniform interpretation and validity of EU law across all Member States. Today the procedure is the most frequently used channel of access to the Court in Luxembourg.

The preliminary reference procedure takes the somewhat unusual form of a dialogue between courts. As the CJEU itself reaffirms on a regular basis in its judgments, a 'spirit of cooperation' between national judges and the CJEU characterizes the procedure. Apart from the collaborative connotations of a dialogue this cooperation is reinforced by a mutual dependence. National courts that refer a case to the CJEU are dependent on the Court's response in settling the domestic dispute. In turn, without the procedure, the CJEU cannot fulfil its role as the highest European court with final jurisdiction over the interpretation of EU law. This is why national courts and the CJEU have a shared interest and responsibility in making this dialogue a successful one. The Court itself likes to stress the success of the procedure, as well as the spirit of cooperation between the CJEU and national courts. However, viewed from both a macro standpoint – the diversity in its use among different Member States – and the micro perspective – the day-to-day practice of referrals – the procedure does not function without its drawbacks and challenges.[24]

3.2. *Europeanization of National Judicial Practice*

The developing area of European civil procedure raises important and unique questions as many instruments have only been established in recent years. Apart from the Brussels Convention and a number of Hague Conventions focusing on cooperation in international cases, twenty years ago civil procedure was an exclusively national matter. Civil procedure rules have always been closely interwoven with legal culture, state organization and judicial infrastructure. The present multi-layered nature of civil justice and the national divergences creates unique challenges for national

---

24 See R. van Gestel and J. de Poorter, *In the Court We Trust: Cooperation, Coordination and Collaboration between the ECJ and Supreme Administrative Courts* (Cambridge University Press 2019).

judges. Not only are they responsible for ensuring the enforcement of national law and the correct application of European civil procedure rules, they are also faced with the sometimes complex interaction between the domestic legal order and the European rules.[25] In some Member States, the legislator ensured that the European rules are embedded into the domestic legal order through the Code of Civil Procedure (*e.g.*, in Germany). In other Member States, implementation acts are put into place which at least consider how the European civil procedure rules interact with domestic procedures (*e.g.*, in the Netherlands). In a number of Member States hardly any implementation rules are enacted, disconnecting the European rules and procedures from the domestic legal order and making the application more difficult (*e.g.*, in Belgium).

National judges are tasked with finding their way through the collection of rules in judging civil disputes. With ever-progressing internationalization of commercial activity and personal mobility, maintaining coherence and unity in judging is an increasingly daunting task. The highest civil law courts have traditionally had the responsibility for monitoring the uniformity of law and legal certainty in their Member States. Now this monitoring has to be fulfilled against the backdrop of a growing body of European civil procedural rules that are not always sufficiently clear or are not aligned with national rules and procedures. These challenges increase the number of cases in which uncertainty arises about the interpretation or application of these rules. This is reflected by the number of preliminary references cases that reach the CJEU each year regarding civil matters, as shown in Figure 1.

25 See for a some of the European uniform procedure, based on an EU wide evaluation, X. E. Kramer, 'Specific Instruments' in B. Hess and P. Ortolani (eds), *Impediments of National Procedural Law to the Free Movement of Judgments* (Luxembourg Report on European Procedural Law: Volume I, Beck/Hart/Nomos 2019) 213, 214, 216, 220, 229.

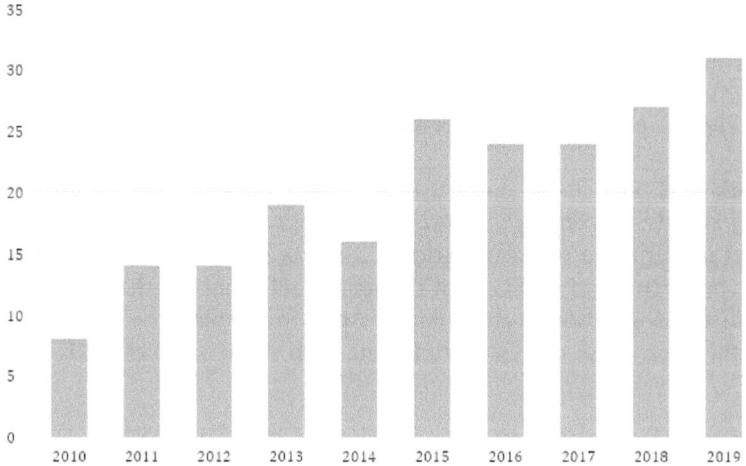

Figure 1: Total number of references for a preliminary ruling (judgments only) in 'civil matters'

Source: EUR-Lex (selection 'Judicial Cooperation in Civil Matters', per year)

Although the numbers fluctuate per year it is clear that there has been a steady increase in references for a preliminary ruling in this area over the past ten years. This can also be explained by the increase in the number of instruments on civil justice, as discussed in Section 2 above. They make up approximately 7 % of all references to the CJEU, and though the percentage fluctuates per year it seems to largely keep pace with the total growth of the caseload.[26] Looking at the preliminarily rulings on content, it is no surprise that most cases are on the Brussels I-bis Regulation and its predecessors, the Regulation being the oldest instrument in this area, and key in cross-border litigation.[27] A substantial number of the other rulings con-

26 The total number of judgments in this period on civil justice cooperation was 203, with 8 judgments in 2010, 14 in 2011, 14 in 2012, 19 in 2013, 16 in 2014, 26 in 2015, 24 in 2016 and 2017, 27 in 2018 and 31 in 2019. In this period, the number of times the topic of civil justice was included in all questions to the CJEU amounted to 7 %, ranging between 3 % and 9 %, with fluctuations per year and no obvious increase over the years.

27 This is also an indication that it still raises questions despite its improvement and clarification in the different versions over the past fifty years.

cern in particular the Insolvency Regulation and the Brussels II-bis Regulation, the latter being the key instrument in the area of family law.

3.3. Variable Use of the Reference Procedure in the Civil Justice Area

A stark difference in the number of references coming from the Member States signals the variance in use of the option for referral by national judges operating in different national contexts. Figure 2 shows the differences between Member States in number of references in the area of area of judicial cooperation in civil matters. Apart from Poland being in the top 5 in this area, these numbers are in line with those in other fields of EU law.[28]

28 From these numbers, one might be tempted to draw conclusions as to the importance the Member State national courts attach to questions of private international law. Most 'top scorers' in the area of judicial cooperation in civil matters in the reference period – Germany, Austria, the Netherlands, Italy and France – do not differ significantly from those that refer most references for a preliminary ruling in general. However, unlike in other areas of EU law, Poland one of the 'top scorers' in the area of judicial cooperation in civil matters in the reference period. The opposite applies to Belgium and the UK, that refer most references for a preliminary ruling in general, but not in the area of judicial cooperation in civil matters.

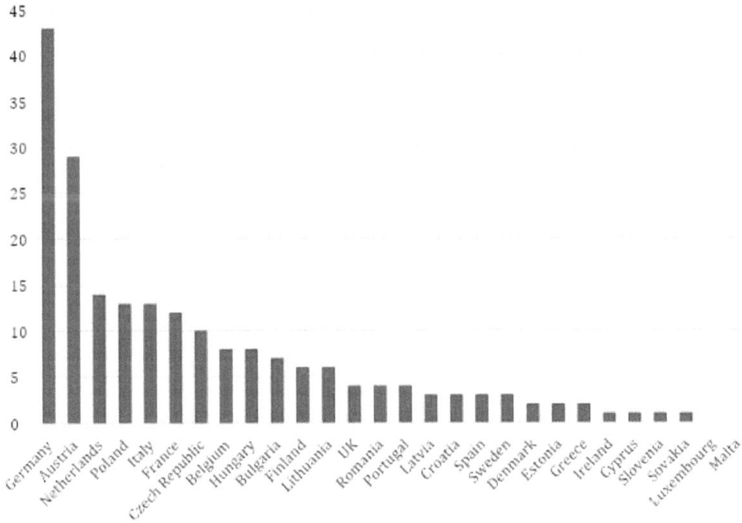

Figure 2: References for a preliminary ruling (judgments only) regarding 'judicial cooperation in civil matters' per Member State over the period 2010–2019

Source: EUR-Lex (selection 'Judicial Cooperation in Civil Matters', per year and per Member State)

Over the past decades, attempts have been made to understand these disparities between Member States in terms of aggregate national trends. Econometric approaches to the conundrum of the variable use of Art. 267 have attempted to correlate references with indicators such as public support for integration, the presence of a monist or dualist legal tradition, judicial review, population size, and intra-EU trade activity.[29] These analyses have been somewhat unsatisfactory in their ability to tie these variations to distinguishable macro factors. However, they do point to the different features of the legal and judicial systems of Member States as well as specific characteristics of the national legal culture that may create obstacles to the effective fulfilment of expectations stemming from EU law.

In an attempt to get more grip on the practical inner workings of the procedure, research focus has recently shifted from the question why

29 See Conant (n. 23).

national judges refer towards focusing more on what keeps judges from sending cases to the CJEU. Bottom-up approaches have inquired into what moves a national judge to refer a case and, more importantly, what considerations play a role in refraining from using the reference procedure.[30] That research has revealed a number of factors that make the use of the procedure less than straightforward.

3.4. National Civil Judges as European Judges

Nominally, national courts serve as the 'guardians of EU law' based on Article 19(1) TEU, which stipulates that 'Member States shall provide remedies sufficient to ensure effective legal protection in the fields covered by Union law'.[31] In practice, national judges are tasked with applying relevant EU rules in cases brought before their courts. In order for judges to effectively fulfil this task, EU law provides them with various tools in applying EU law in national cases. These include inter alia the fundamental principles of EU law such as primacy, direct effect, indirect effect, and *effet utile* as well as their ability to use the preliminary ruling procedure when they are in doubt about the application or interpretation of EU law in a particular case. In the civil justice area, the principle of mutual trust and the need for legal certainty have been dominant in providing guidance, along with specific aims set out in the recitals of the different regulations. The need for a uniform and equal application led the CJEU to adopt a predominantly autonomous interpretation of legal terms, meaning interpretation in line with the objectives and general schemes of the regulation.[32]

In practice, being an effective European judge has proven to require a considerable dose of willingness and engagement on the part of national

---

30 A. Dyevre and others, 'Who refers most? Institutional incentives and judicial participation in the preliminary ruling system' (2019) *Journal of European Public Policy*; U. Jaremba and J.A. Mayoral, 'The Europeanization of national judiciaries: definitions, indicators and mechanisms' (2019) *Journal of European Public Policy* 386; J. Krommendijk, 'The highest Dutch courts and the preliminary ruling procedure: critically obedient interlocutors of the Court of Justice' (2019) *European Law Journal* 394; T. Nowak and others, *National judges as European Union judges: Knowledge, experiences and attitudes of lower court judges in Germany and the Netherlands* (Eleven Publishers 2011).

31 See TEU, art. 19(1).

32 Case 29/76 *LTU* v. *Eurocontrol* [1976] ECR 1541.

judges.[33] Despite the fact that the national judge has been given a powerful role in the process of European rights enforcement, research among national judges suggests that a proper and uniform use of these new tools in practice is challenging. Empirical studies among national judges suggest that national judges lack adequate knowledge of EU law, are not familiar with the specific methods of legal interpretation as practiced by the CJEU, lack the foreign language skills to study what goes on in other jurisdictions or they simply have no access to EU law sources.[34] Consequently, the uniform fulfilment of the expectations stemming from EU law by national judges cannot be taken for granted. Sacha Prechal, the current judge from the Netherlands at the CJEU, concluded earlier in this respect that 'These quality and capacity of the national courts to apply [EU] law and to do so correctly is a matter for serious concern. [...] National judges, even the 'younger' generation, are rather still struggling with [EU] law than smoothly applying it.'[35]

When national judges run into the limits of their knowledge in applying EU law in national proceedings, the preliminary reference procedure can provide a valuable tool in resolving issues of interpretation. However, the limited number of cases that reach the CJEU on an annual basis, as well as the difference in the number of references per Member State, point to the fact that the use of Art. 267 is not self-evident. Empirical studies show that national judges' decisions (not) to refer are based predominantly on pragmatic and practical considerations, such as the consequences of referring in terms of delays or the importance of the issue at stake. In fact, through extensive fieldwork in Italian (and in later work French and German) courts, Pavone has pointed to the fact that rather than being driven by a strategic quest for power, judges are constrained very much by the demands of everyday labour, and as a result develop a 'diffuse discipline' that 'everyday practice that resists encounters with "lesser" known courts and fields of law.'[36] As a result, referring to the CJEU becomes something that is avoided rather than pursued.

33 See Nowak (n. 30).

34 Ibid.

35 S. Prechal, 'National Courts in EU Judicial Structures' (2006) 25 YEL 429, 432–433.

36 T. Pavone, 'Revisiting judicial empowerment in the European Union: Limits of empowerment, logics of resistance' (2018) *Journal of Law and Courts* 303.

As was also commented by an English expert on European civil justice at the conference from which this paper results,[37] in the past decade the number of references from English courts on the Brussels I-bis Regulation has decreased. This may have been triggered by English procedural law being outlawed by the CJEU on a number of occasions. Well-known and illustrative are the rulings in *Turner*,[38] *Owusu*,[39] and *West Tankers*.[40] In the *Turner* case, the CJEU considered an English anti-suit injunction – prohibiting a party from litigating in a Spanish court in view of a pending procedure in England – as being contrary to the Brussels regime. While this was based on the principle of mutual trust that underpins civil justice cooperation – requiring full independence for the courts of the Member States to decide on their respective jurisdiction – the result was that a national procedural mechanism intended to prohibit abusive litigation was banned from the European civil justice area. This has been criticized both by English and other commentators, but in the *West Tankers* case this ruling was nevertheless confirmed and extended by the CJEU to vexatious litigation interfering with an arbitration clause between parties. An equally rigid approach was taken in the heavily debated *Owusu* case, in which the CJEU prohibited Member States to apply the *forum non conveniens* doctrine in any situation where the Brussels I Regulation affords jurisdiction.

3.5. (Re)formulating the Questions

A seminal part of the dialogue between national judges and the CJEU, and one that can be cause for some hesitation is the formulation of the preliminary questions themselves. The questions asked by national courts, and in particular their formulation, are an essential element in the interaction between the institutions, because they determine to a great extent the types of answers given by the CJEU.

One important problem that occurs in the dialogue is the information asymmetry between the institutions. On the one hand, the national judge knows the details of the case and the national legal context, while on the other hand the CJEU has superior knowledge of the EU law context as

37 Alexander Layton QC, 'Future perspectives on the European law of civil procedure' (Conference The 50th Anniversary of the European Law of Civil Procedure, Luxembourg, 28 September 2018).

38 C-159/02 *Turner* [2004] ECR I-03565.

39 C-281/02 *Owusu* [2005] ECR I-1445.

40 C-185/07 *West Tankers* [2009] ECR I-00663.

well as the scope of the questions it can actually answer. This asymmetry can result in the CJEU choosing to reformulate the questions and, by doing so, either broadening or limiting the scope of the answers it provides. The examples under the Brussels Regulation are numerous.

Voss has identified three different situations in which the Court chooses to reformulate questions.[41] Firstly, the relatively uncontroversial situations where there is some type of 'mistake' in the formulation of the question. Secondly, reformulations also occur where the national court has apparently not understood EU law or the jurisdiction of the CJEU correctly. In these cases, the court has to adjust the questions to avoid declaring the question inadmissible. Thirdly, there are cases where the Court appears to want to avoid answering the question as it is posed by the national court, particularly where the question is politically sensitive.

Additionally, Langer identifies situations where the Court does this because it is more practical to group certain questions together, or in order to make its response more suitable for application in all Member States.[42] While such broader framing can make for a more effective dialogue in terms of uniform application of its judgments across the board, it can cause difficulties applying the ruling to the specific case.

3.6. Applying CJEU Judgments in National Cases

The framing of the matter at hand in preliminary references gives national courts a large hand in the issue to be decided upon, but it is also important for the remainder of the procedure before the national court. Even if the CJEU occasionally reformulates the questions asked, the Court will always be bound by the facts and the way in which these are presented by the national court, and it depends in large part on the representation of the relevant national law as provided by the national judge in its application.

In its request for a preliminary ruling the national court is required to supply the history and legal context of the case in which the questions arise. Once the national court submits its request, it generally loses contact with the case as well as the Court of Justice itself. Unless the Court asks for clarification with respect to the questions or the relevant national legal

41 Katharina Voss, 'But That's Not What I Asked! The Reformulation of Questions Asked in Preliminary Rulings' (2016) 18 *Europarättslig tidskrift* 939.

42 J. Langer, 'The Preliminary Ruling Procedure: Old Problems or New Challenges?' (Inaugural Lecture, Rijksuniversiteit Groningen 2016), <https://ssrn.com/abstract=2885256> last accessed 28 January 2020.

context at a later stage, the national judge has no further voice in the proceedings. In that sense, the procedure appears to be less of dialogue. This can result in some friction in both directions.[43]

For the CJEU, the absence of the national judge in the proceedings means that there is little opportunity to seek clarification once issues of interpretation arise during proceedings. Once proceedings have started, the CJEU is limited in its ability to request clarification to the parties present during the oral stage. On the other hand, for the national court this can mean that the resulting CJEU judgment may lack national specificity resulting in national courts having a hard time in actually applying the CJEU's findings to the case at hand and more broadly in their national jurisdiction. While in general the CJEU judgements are loyally implemented, it can be argued that merely looking at implementation rates obscures the fact that national court judges are not always satisfied with all judgments.[44]

Though there are differences per Member State, also considering the style and length of judgments, it seems that the CJEU case law in the area of civil justice is frequently referenced and generally followed. For instance, in the Netherlands, it is common to refer to CJEU case law and in particular the case law on Brussels I-bis is widely referenced both by lower instance courts and the Supreme Court.[45]

---

43 J. Hoevenaars & J. Krommendijk, 'Black box on the Kirchberg: the bewildering experience of national court judges and lawyers with the ECJ' (forthcoming) *European Law Review*.

44 J. Krommendijk, 'The highest Dutch courts and the preliminary ruling procedure: critically obedient interlocutors of the Court of Justice' (2019) 25(4) *European Law Journal* 394–415.

45 See inter alia in these recent Dutch decisions: Supreme Court 21 December 2018, ECLI:NL:HR:2018:2361; Supreme Court 14 June 2019, ECLI:NL:HR:2019:925; Supreme Court 20 September 2019, ECLI:NL:HR:2019:1400; Supreme Court 22 February 2019, ECLI:NL:HR:2019:292; District Court Oost-Brabant 15 May 2019, ECLI:NL:RBOBR:2019:2869; Court of Appeal 's-Hertogenbosch 23 July 2019, ECLI:NL:GHSHE:2019:2794; Court of Appeal The Hague 10 December 2019, ECLI:NL:GHDHA:2019:3316; District Court Overijssel 16 April 2019, ECLI:NL:RBOVE:2019:1605; District Court Oost-Brabant 29 November 2017, ECLI:NL:RBOBR:2017:6333.

3.7. Resistance to CJEU Authority

Despite general trends of increasing interaction between national courts and the EU legal system, as evidenced by an ever-rising number of references reaching the CJEU, a growing body of research demonstrates that national judges may also contest EU legal developments.[46] Doctrinal analyses have demonstrated that historically many national courts did not accept the CJEU's rulings on direct effect and supremacy and some constitutional courts have moved to justify EU law's primacy according to their own terms in order to reaffirm national constitutional norms, as well as their own prominence.[47] Such resistance to the acceptance of EU law can lead national judges to refrain from sending references and interpret EU law independently in order to shield domestic practices from unwelcome CJEU rulings. An accurate view of the prevalence of such practices is hard to establish since, in general, the overwhelming majority of all national court decisions on EU law are independent decisions that do not involve references to the CJEU. As such, references for preliminary rulings represent only a fraction of national court interpretation of EU law.

A remarkably clear recent example of refusal to comply with a CJEU ruling is the *Ajos*[48] case, in which the Danish Supreme Court decided to disregard a judgment from the CJEU, handed down as a result of a preliminary reference it had itself sent to Luxembourg. The case, over labour dispute, turned into a case in which the Danish court redefined the boundaries of the applicability of the CJEU's rulings in Denmark. Rather than an orderly judicial dialogue resolving the matter and fostering legal certainty, the process gradually enhanced frictions and ended in disagreement and collision.

Holdgaard et al. have concluded that, while the judgments of both the CJEU and the Danish Supreme Court were legally sound and understandable when read from each courts' legal perspective, both courts failed in carrying out a judicial dialogue in the spirit of good faith. Instead, they

46 See A. Torres Pérez, '*Melloni* in Three Acts: From Dialogue to Monologue' (2014) 10 *European Constitutional Law Review* 2, 308; T. de la Mare and C. Donnelly, 'Preliminary Rulings and EU Legal Integration: Evolution and Stasis' in P. Craig and G. de Búrca (eds), *The Evolution of EU Law* (OUP 2011) 363, 390–391.

47 A. M. Slaughter, A. S. Sweet and J. Weiler (eds), *The European Court and National Courts: Doctrine & Jurisprudence: Legal Change in its Social Context* (Hart Publishing 1998).

48 C-15/2014 *Dansk Industri (DI) acting for Ajos A/S vs. The estate left by A* [2016] ECLI:EU:C:2015:776.

conclude, "the preliminary reference procedure was used in a way that gradually built up tensions and ended in a clear clash."[49] The clash was a result of tensions between the different legal cultures of, in this case, the EU and Denmark. While the preliminary reference procedures, and the interjudicial dialogue made possible by it, is ostensibly the key instrument for avoiding deadlocks and fostering fruitful cross-fertilization, *Ajos* reveals how the procedure does not function well without a clear commitment by courts on both levels to the spirit of collaboration in good faith.

Also, in the area of civil justice cooperation there have been several instances where the boundaries of the rules were explored or challenged. These include the cases *Turner*, *Owusu*, and *West Tankers* referred by the English court, as discussed above.[50] A German Court of Appeal explored and may have challenged the mutual trust principle underlying the abolition of exequatur under Brussels II-bis Regulation in *Zarraga v. Pelz*.[51] In the *Diageo* case the Dutch Supreme Court challenged the limits of the public policy exception under the Brussels I Regulation.[52] A striking example of resistance to the CJEU authority is offered by a Dutch lower court decision regarding flight compensation case under the European Small Claims Procedure.[53] The sub-district court dismissed the *Sturgeon* ruling of the CJEU,[54] granting compensation in the case of flight delays, stating that Regulation 261/2004 does not give such right to compensation and that the CJEU cannot change the law. Luckily, this clearly wrong judgment was not followed in later case law by the same court.

4. *Improving the Dialogue*

With a view to furthering the harmonization of European civil procedure, the dialogue between national judges and the CJEU plays an unmistakable role in the interpretation and uniform application of the rules, and developing underlying principles. With the increasing body of rules there is little doubt that the use of the reference procedure by national courts in this

---

49 G. K. Holdgaard, D. Elkan and G. Krohn Schaldemose 'From cooperation to collision: The ECJ's Ajos ruling and the Danish Supreme Court's refusal to comply' (2018) *55 CMLR* 17, 53.

50 Section 3.4.

51 C-491/10 PPU *Zarraga v. Pelz* [2010] ECR I-14247.

52 C-681/13 *Diageo Brands BV v Simiramida-04 EOOD* [2015] ECLI:EU:C:2015:471.

53 District Court 's-Hertogenbosch 19 January 2012, ECLI:NL:RBSHE:2012:BV1931.

54 Joined cases C-402/07 and C-432/07 *Sturgeon and others* [2009] ECR I-10291.

area will continue the upward trend that has been set in over the past decade. With that in mind, the proper functioning of the preliminary reference procedure is of paramount importance. The previous sections have identified a number of stumbling blocks that also indicate where possible measures for improvement may be appropriate.

4.1. Measures at the National Level

Effective dialogue depends to a significant degree on the cooperation of the national courts in activating the procedure and on national judges and parties to the proceedings in providing the CJEU with the necessary information to effectively judge on matters of European civil procedure. However, even assuming there is a general willingness among national judges to send references (as we have seen, an overoptimistic view), a lot hinges on the national judges' awareness of relevant EU legislation and the necessary expertise to effectively use the instruments. There is thus a dire need for increased EU law awareness and expertise among judges as well as parties. Almost a decade ago, Nowak et al. already suggested, among other things, training courses for judges on increased awareness of areas in which EU law may become important in their daily work.[55] The increase in the number of European private international law and civil procedure instruments and their practical relevance necessitates including these in EU law training as well.[56] National judicial networks, additional training and the sharing of best practices are therefore important in further improving the expertise among national judges.

Expertise is, however, not only needed from the referring courts, in drafting up sufficiently detailed orders for reference, but also plays an important role later on in the procedure. Langer discusses the information asymmetry and the need for the court to be informed about the national context that is specific to the Member State where a reference originated: "*The Court regularly invites the parties to the national proceedings and the Member States to answer written questions in the run-up to a hearing. During the hearing, it also routinely asks them to give further details about specific*

55 Nowak (n. 30).

56 See for existing structures in several Member States X. E. Kramer, 'A Common Discourse in European Private International Law? A View from the Court system' in J. Von Hein, E.-M. Kieninger and G. Rühl (eds), *How European is European Private International Law? Sources, Court Practice, Academic Discourse* (Intersentia 2019) 226–230.

aspects of the case. What is striking is that these requests frequently concern the facts or the applicable national law."[57] The Court with some regularity feels the need to ask for additional information or considerations, which it cannot deduce from the national courts' reference order itself.

As a rule, there is no judge from the referring legal system on the court's panel, as is the case in the ECtHR. Therefore, written questions, as well as the hearing, can serve to provide and clarify 'pure facts or aspects of national law'.[58] This places a responsibility on the parties and their representatives.[59] Hoevenaars has warned about the resulting asymmetry in expertise and effective advocacy between Member State representatives and parties to the proceedings that may occur after referral, with Member State agents being able to frame matters of national law to their benefit.[60] This information asymmetry has stirred the debate about whether or not to allow for a greater role for the referring judge during the proceedings.[61] As of today that debate is still ongoing.

Some degree of court specialization can contribute to better equipping national courts to deal with matters of European civil procedure and to effectively communicate with the CJEU. Within national courts this can be done by allocating court cases involving important private international law questions to judges with the required knowledge and experience, and/or involving court assistants with such expertise.[62] Centralized expertise on (aspects of) European private international law and civil procedure could contribute to expanding the required knowledge and skills for referring the preliminary questions to the CJEU, thereby fostering a more effective and efficient dialogue as well as possibly curtailing some of the

---

57 Langer (n. 42).

58 D. Edward, 'How the Court of Justice Works' (1995) 20(1) *European Law Review* 545. See also D. Vaughan and M. Gray, 'Litigating in Luxembourg' (2007) 11 *Jersey & Guernsey Law Review* 1–14.

59 J. Hoevenaars & J. Krommendijk, 'Black box on the Kirchberg: the bewildering experience of national court judges and lawyers with the ECJ' (forthcoming) *European Law Review*.

60 J. Hoevenaars, 'Advocaten in Europa: Vertegenwoordiging op het Hoogste Niveau?' (2019) 40(3) *Recht der Werkelijkheid* 7.

61 M. Bobek, 'Of Feasibility and Silent Elephants: The Legitimacy of the Court of Justice Through the Eyes of National Courts' in Maurice Adams and others (eds), *Judging Europe's Judges: The Legitimacy of Case Law of the European Court of Justice Examined* (Hart 2013) 197–234.

62 X. E. Kramer (n 56); P. A. de Miguel Asensio, 'National Court Systems and Uniform Application of European Private International Law' in J. Von Hein, E.-M. Kieninger and G. Rühl (eds), *How European is European Private International Law? Sources, Court Practice, Academic Discourse* (Intersentia 2019) 243–245.

existing resistance to cooperation with the CJEU. For instance, in the Netherlands the *Eurinfra* project was initiated in 2000, and courts have a coordinator for European Law that ensures access to EU law, publishes case law, and enables the exchange of information.[63]

A more far-reaching solution is to create special courts or units (chambers) within courts for matters involving European civil procedure and private international law.[64] As regards uniform European procedures, the concentration of specific procedures in certain courts within a country can be useful. For instance, the handling of the European Order for Payment Procedure has been concentrated in one court in Austria, Croatia, Finland, Germany, Malta, Sweden, the Netherlands, Portugal, and Hungary.[65] Interesting in this regard is also the recent establishment of international commercial courts in Europe and beyond, including in France, the Netherlands, and Germany.[66] Their establishment is also triggered by other aspects than the desire to bundle expertise, notably attracting high value cases to the jurisdiction.[67] Their aim to provide effective dispute resolution for business parties may even be at odds with the time consuming referral of questions to the CJEU. Nevertheless, these specialized courts can play a role in singling out relevant issues of international litigation and increasing the quality of the application of European civil procedure.

---

63 M. Claes, M. de Visser and M. de Werd, 'Operationalizing the European mandate of national courts: Insights from the Netherlands' in B. de Witte et al (eds), *National Courts and EU Law. New Issues, Theories and Methods* (Edward Elgar 2016) 105–126.

64 X. E. Kramer (n 56) 226–233; P. A. De Miguel Asensio (n. 61) 239–243.

65 See X. E. Kramer, 'Specific Instruments' in B. Hess and P. Ortolani (eds), *Impediments of National Procedural Law to the Free Movement of Judgments* (Luxembourg Report on European Procedural Law: Volume I, Beck/Hart/Nomos 2019) 217.

66 See X. E. Kramer (n. 56), 230–233 in respect to European private international law. See for an extensive analysis of courts in different jurisdictions X. E. Kramer and J. Sorabji (eds), *International Business Courts: A European and Global Perspective* (Eleven International Publishing 2019); X. E. Kramer and J. Sorabji, 'International Business Courts in Europe and Beyond: A Global Competition for Justice?' (2019) 1 *Erasmus Law Review* 1–9.

67 See in particular J. Sorabji and X. E. Kramer, 'Introduction – The International Business of Courts' in X. E. Kramer and J. Sorabji (n. 65) 9–12.

4.2. Measures at the EU level

While the national judicial infrastructure, training and information flow are essential, also at the EU level measures to improve the application of European civil procedure and the court dialogue is crucial. In recent years, efforts have been made to increase awareness and to provide information and training for practitioners. Access to information has been improved greatly through the e-Justice portal, which serves at the 'electronic one-stop-shop in the area of justice'.[68] It is a rich source of information on EU and national legislation, procedures, and case law for practitioners, citizens, and businesses. While the information is not always up to date and the website is not in all respects easy to navigate, it is a huge step forward. The European Network in Civil and Commercial Matters (EJN) and the national contact points through which information is exchanged promote understanding, facilitate access to European civil procedure and national implementation.[69] The European Commission has also invested in training programmes, among others by co-financing the European Judicial Training Network (EJTN).[70] The EJTN is an independent organization that also coordinates judicial exchanges and the exchange of information. The training programmes of the European Law Academy (ERA), including extensive training programmes on cross-border civil procedures, key issues of EU law as well as language courses, are another important source in educating judges and judicial staff. These activities are of great importance for the correct application of EU instruments on civil procedure, the strengthening judicial cooperation in the EU, and furthering best practices.

It is not likely that the above measures will be able to stave off future clashes between the CJEU and national (supreme) courts, like we have seen in the *Ajos* case. However, such relatively overt conflicts that threaten to undermine the legitimacy of the EU legal order, are rare, and the

---

68 See <http://e-justice.europa.eu/home.do>.

69 See <https://e-justice.europa.eu/content_ejn_in_civil_and_commercial_matters-21-en.do>.

70 See http://www.ejtn.eu/. The support for judicial training is also laid down in Article 81(2)(g) TFEU. See also European Union [2012] OJ C326/47; European Commission, 'Communication on judicial training in the European Union' COM (2006) 356; European Commission, 'Building trust in EU-wide justice – a new dimension to European Judicial training' COM (2011) 551 final. Annual reports on the progress are available through the e-Justice Portal, see page on 'European judicial training'.

arguably most valuable function of the preliminary reference procedure is and remains the release of tensions before they build into a clash of such magnitude. As for European civil justice we can expect much more of a role for the dialogue between the courts in line with the 'spirit of cooperation' as envisioned by the CJEU itself. To improve the dialogue specific training and gaining experience in how to formulate preliminary questions to the CJEU is required at the national level.

At the EU level, the CJEU should ensure that it has a proper understanding of national civil procedure in order to be able to assess the context in which the question arises. To further the development of a truly European civil justice system that finds its roots in the European traditions and connects with the national systems, the CJEU should also engage in comparative civil procedure. A real dialogue between national courts and the CJEU also requires a well-functioning communication system through which the European and national court can exchange the necessary additional information required to assure that the appropriate answers are given to the appropriate questions.

5. *Concluding Remarks and Outlook*

European civil justice consists of a plethora of European instruments, having different legislative bases, different scopes of application and relying on different approaches and, in part, different concepts. These European rules, even if they are laid down in directly applicable Regulations, interact with the national procedural rules, need embedding in the domestic legal environment, and in any case, they are to be applied by the Member States' national courts. The preliminary reference procedure, and more specifically the dialogue between national courts and the CJEU it institutionalizes, plays an important role in reducing uncertainty resulting from the patchy legislative framework, furthering implementation at the national level and harmonizing the application of the rules.

While the influence of the case law of the CJEU cannot be underestimated, the preliminary reference procedure is also plagued with a number of practical issues which impede its consistent use by national courts. The required expertise and willingness of national courts to refer matters to Luxembourg make the use of this mechanism less than self-evident. The number of references in the field of civil justice cooperation and the great differences per country in this regard mirrors the numbers with regard to preliminary reference procedure in general. In view of the lack of familiarity of many national judges with this limited, yet growing, field of European civil justice there are quite a few obstacles to be overcome before the procedure can fulfil its role in providing the necessary clarity and legal development.

Along with improvements at the legislative level, practical measures to support the proper application of European civil procedure include continuous court training as well as securing access to information at both national and European level. The exchange of information, a comparative approach of laws by the European Court of Justice and improving the direct communication between the requesting national court and European Court of Justice are essential. While it is for the European Court to take the initiative when it requires more information about the facts or the national legal context, it goes without saying this is a two-way street. It has been commented by European judges that requests for more information are not always followed up by the requesting court, whereas the European Court does not always understand the national legal context in which the questions arise.

In recent years the changing dynamics in the EU, increased Euroscepticism and the departure of the United Kingdom have rightfully received attention. Understandably, many of the discussions in European private international law and civil procedure focused on the legal and practical implications of Brexit, the position of London as the centre of international litigation, and the resulting increase of civil justice competition.[71] But the influence on the process of legal integration and judicial cooperation is of course much bigger. Specifically for European civil procedure and the operation of the Brussels I-bis Regulation and related instruments, the loss of the English common law culture, the cross-fertilization and the checks and balances created by the UK contributions to the negotiations – not seldom aligned and allied with the Dutch – are beyond comprehension.[72] This, and along with global challenges of environmental pollution,

71 See for the latter E. Themeli, *Civil justice system competition in the European Union: The great race of courts* (PhD dissertation, Erasmus University Rotterdam 2018, Eleven International Publishing 2018) 1–6,135–146, 250–257; X. E. Kramer and J. Sorabji, 'Introduction: The International Business of Courts' in X. E. Kramer and J. Sorabji (eds), *International Business Courts: A European and Global Perspective* (Eleven International Publishing 2019) 9–12; X. E. Kramer and J. Sorabji, 'International Business Courts in Europe and Beyond: A Global Competition for Justice?' (2019) 1 *Erasmus Law Review* 1, 2–4, 8.

72 B. Hess and X. E. Kramer, 'From Common Rules to Best Practices in European Civil Procedure: An Introduction' in X. E. Kramer and B. Hess (n. 5), 27–29; B. Hess, 'Back to the Past: BREXIT und das europäische internationale Privat- und Verfahrensrecht' (2016) 36 *IPRax* 409.

immigration, financial stability, corporate governance and security call for civil justice cooperation with third countries in Europe and globally.[73]

Important challenges of European civil procedure continue to be the lack of coherence and the interaction with national law and practice. The lack of a comprehensive approach to, and vision on, the civil justice area hampers the maturing of this field of law. The more recent shift in focus from launching new instruments to the proper implementation at the national level is of great importance. This should be strengthened by paying attention to the interaction between national procedural law and institutions and the exchange of best practices. This shift to implementation, however, should not withhold the European legislature to pursue measures to increase coherence with the aim of strengthening a genuine European judicial cooperation. A more horizontal approach or at least ensuring alignment and interconnectedness of sectorial instruments is needed.

More coherence can also be achieved by establishing an overarching framework focusing on general rules of civil procedure and by implementing existing or new rules for designated areas. Two important developments in this regard are the 2017 European Parliament's resolution for a Directive on common minimum standards[74] and the ELI-UNIDROIT European Rules of Civil Procedure (ERCP).[75] The latter are scheduled for adoption as a model law by the two respective institutes in 2020. Thus far the European Commission has not followed up on the European Parliament's initiative and both the proposed Directive and the ERCP have their limitations and flaws.[76] Nevertheless, they are instrumental to contributing to a common framework, increasing coherence in European civil procedure, and eventually a true civil justice dialogue in Europe.

73 X. E. Kramer (n. 56) 233–234.

74 Committee on Legal Affairs (European Parliament), 'Report with recommendations to the Commission on common minimum standards of civil procedure in the EU' 2015/2084(INL)).

75 See the project websites of ELI: < https://www.europeanlawinstitute.eu/projects-publications/current-projects-feasibility-studies-and-other-activities/current-projects/civil-procedure/> and of UNIDROIT: <>.

76 X. E. Kramer, 'Strengthening Civil Justice Cooperation: The Quest for Model Rules and Common Minimum Standards of Civil Procedure in Europe' (n 5) 598–606.

L'autonomie procédurale dans la jurisprudence de la Cour de justice de l'Union européenne – Réflexions naïves d'un Huron au Palais du Kirchberg[1]

Loïc Cadiet[*]

Table of Contents

Il m'appartient de vous parler de l'autonomie procédurale dans la jurisprudence de la Cour de justice européenne; il était initialement prévu que je traitasse du développement d'un droit procédural autonome dans la jurisprudence de la Cour de justice européenne, ce qui n'est pas tout à fait la même chose. L'intitulé du sujet a donc été élargi afin d'englober les différents aspects de l'autonomie procédurale qui doit être considérée, à la fois, du point de vue du droit de l'Union européenne et du point de vue du droit des Etats membres car, si la référence à l'autonomie procédurale des Etats membres est une référence récurrente dans la jurisprudence de la Cour de justice de l'Union européenne, depuis les années 1970, cette référence est tout aussi régulièrement flanquée de la référence au principe

---

1 Hommage à Jean Rivéro, « Le Huron au Palais Royal ou réflexions naïves sur le recours pour excès de pouvoir », *D.* 1962, pp. 37–40.

* Professeur à l'Université Paris 1 Panthéon-Sorbonne (Ecole de droit de la Sorbonne) Président de l'Association internationale de droit processuel

d'équivalence et d'effectivité des règles nationales de procédure au regard du droit de l'Union européenne.

J'ignorais à quoi je m'engageais lorsque l'invitation de la Cour et du Max Planck Institute de Luxembourg, que je remercie, m'a été présentée par mon ami Burkhard Hess. L'amitié vous fait parfois faire des bêtises. Je ne suis qu'un simple juriste de droit privé français, largement ignorant, comme la majorité des juristes internistes français, du droit de l'Union européenne. Bien sûr, comme processualiste, je n'ignore pas tout à fait les développements importants de la coopération judiciaire au sein de l'Union européenne, qui intéressent aussi bien la procédure civile que la procédure pénale; ces développements ont d'ailleurs suscité une littérature abondante[2] au point de faire bouger certaines frontières disciplinaires, comme celle de la procédure civile et du droit international privé dont relève, dans la conception française, le droit des conflits de juridictions[3].

Mais ce n'est pas de procédure civile internationale qu'il s'agit ici; c'est de procédure civile interne et de l'effet qu'exerce sur elle la jurisprudence de la Cour de justice de l'Union européenne au fil des renvois préjudiciels qui lui sont soumis. Disons-le d'emblée, cette question est à peu près inconnue des juristes nationaux[4], pour lesquels, ainsi que l'ont écrit Rostane Mehdi et Estelle Brosset, « *le droit de l'Union continue à être appréhendé invariablement comme un droit second* »[5]. Cette question n'apparaît quasiment pas dans les manuels de droit judiciaire privé, sauf quelques vagues références en introduction[6] ou en note de bas de page à l'office dérogatoire

2 Outre les manuels de droit judiciaire privé (ou procédure civile), et ceux de droit international privé, V. p. ex. J.-S. Bergé, D. Porcheron et G. Vieira da Costa Cerqueira, *V°* « Droit international privé et droit de l'Union européenne », *Rép. eur. Dalloz*, 2017. *Adde* L. Cadiet, E. Jeuland et S. Amrani Mekki (dir.), *Droit processuel civil de l'Union européenne*, Paris, LexisNexis, 2011.

3 V. not. S. Bollée, L. Cadiet, E. Jeuland et E. Pataut (dir.), *Les nouvelles formes de coordination des justices étatiques*, Paris, IRJS Editions, 2013.

4 V. en revanche C. Franklin (ed.), *The Effectiveness and Application of EU and EEA Law in National Courts,* Cambridge, Intersentia, 2018. – K. Riesenhuber (ed.), *European Legal Methodology*, Cambridge, Intersentia, 2017. *Adde* A. Beka, *The Active Role of Courts in Consumer Litigation – Applying EU Law of the National Court's Motion,* Cambridge, Intersentia, 2018. *V.*, en dernier lieu, B. Krans, A. Nylund (eds*), Procedural Autonomy across Europe,* Cambridge, Intersentia, 2020.

5 R. Mehdi et E. Brosset, « De quoi le droit de l'Union est-il le nom? A propos du droit de l'Union en tant que droit commun des Etats membres », *in* J.-B. Bonnet, *op. cit.*, p. 669 et s., spéc. p. 685.

6 V. p. ex. J. Héron et T. Le Bars, *Droit judiciaire privé*, Montchrestien, 6ème éd. 2015, n° 20. – L. Cadiet et E. Jeuland, *Droit judiciaire privé*, LexisNexis, 10ème éd. 2017, n°

du juge en matière de clauses abusives[7] et, c'est un comble, l'article consacré à l'Union européenne et la procédure civile dans le *Répertoire de procédure civile* de l'*Encyclopédie Dalloz*, qui est l'une des deux grandes références de la littérature procédurale, a été rédigé par un spécialiste de droit européen[8].

C'est dire l'innocence de mon regard sur l'autonomie procédurale dans la jurisprudence de la Cour de justice de l'Union européenne. J'avais bien sûr vu passer, de temps en temps, la référence faite par la Cour au principe d'autonomie procédurale des Etats membres, mais je dois confesser, à ma grande honte, que je ne m'y étais pas spécialement arrêté. C'est donc quasiment une *terra incognita* qu'il m'a été donné de découvrir et ce sont mes impressions de voyage en cette terre qui m'était inconnue que je voudrais vous livrer, avec modestie, ne doutant pas que mes observations profanes paraîtront banales, voire naïves, peut-être erronées, aux oreilles des éminents spécialistes que vous êtes[9]. J'ai cependant tâché de jouer le jeu de la sincérité et, au terme de ce périple, périlleux mais stimulant, mes principales impressions sont que la notion de l'autonomie procédurale qui se dégage de la jurisprudence de la Cour de justice de l'Union européenne (1) m'apparaît aussi mystérieuse que sa portée, telle qu'elle peut se révéler à partir de la jurisprudence de la Cour, me semble incertaine (2). Ce sont ces deux impressions que je développerai tour à tour.

29, le plus complet étant C. Chainais, F. Ferrand et S. Guinchard, *Procédure civile – Droit interne et européen du procès civile*, Dalloz, 33ème éd. 2016, n° 79–87.

7 L. Cadiet et E. Jeuland, *Droit judiciaire privé*, préc., n°533, note 304. V. cep. C. Chainais, F. Ferrand et S. Guinchard, *Procédure civile – Droit interne et européen du procès civil*, préc., n° 155–156, à propos du droit d'agir en justice.

8 T. Debard, *V°* « Droit de l'Union européenne et procédure civile », *Rép. proc. civ.*, Dalloz, 2018.

9 Dans ce voyage, j'ai eu le bonheur et le plaisir de pouvoir compter sur les conseils d'un précieux guide en la personne de Janek T. Nowak, chercheur au Max Planck Institute de Luxembourg et à l'Institut de droit européen de l'université catholique de Leuven, fin connaisseur du droit processuel de l'Union européenne. Je lui exprime ma plus vive gratitude.

1. La mystérieuse notion de l'autonomie procédurale à travers la jurisprudence de la Cour de justice de l'Union européenne

La notion d'autonomie procédurale des Etats membres, qui semble aujourd'hui monnaie courante, est nimbée d'un certain mystère aux yeux du profane que je suis : mystère d'abord de ses origines (1.1), mystère surtout de ses limites (1.2).

1.1. Origine de l'autonomie procédurale des Etats membres

La chose semble avoir existé avant l'expression, dont l'apparition est tardive.

L'autonomie des Etats membres est traditionnellement associée à deux arrêts *Rewe* et *Comet* rendus par la Cour de justice des Communautés européennes en décembre 1976[10] dans lesquels la Cour déclarait que « *en l'absence de règlementation communautaire (…), il appartient à l'ordre juridique interne de chaque Etat membre de désigner les juridictions compétentes* [c'est l'autonomie institutionnelle] *et de régler les modalités procédurales des recours en justice destinés à assurer la sauvegarde des droits que les justiciables tirent de l'effet direct du droit communautaire* [c'est l'autonomie procédurale] ». En vérité, cette affirmation était incomplète autant qu'elle n'était pas tout à fait inédite[11].

Dès avril 1968, dans une affaire *Gebrüder Lück*, la Cour de justice avait déjà indiqué, à propos d'une disposition du traité CEE qu'elle ne limitait pas « *le pouvoir des juridictions nationales compétentes d'appliquer, parmi les divers procédés de l'ordre juridique interne, ceux qui sont appropriés pour sauvegarder les droits substantiels conférés par le droit communautaire* »[12]. Puis, quelques mois plus tard, dans une affaire *Société par actions SALGOIL*, elle ajoutait que « *il appartient à l'ordre juridique national de déterminer la juridic-*

---

10 CJCE, 16 déc. 1976, aff. 33/76, *Rewe-Zentralfinanz eG et Rewe-Zentral AG c. Landwirtschaftskammer für das Saarland.* – CJCE, 16 déc. 1976, aff. 45/76, *Comet BV c. Produktschap voor Siergewassen.*

11 Comp. J. T. Nowak, « Chapter 1. Considerations on the Impact of EU Law on National Civil Procedure : Recent Examples from Belgium », *in* V. Lazić and S. Stuij (eds), *International Dispute Resolution – Selected Issues in International Litigation and Arbitration*, T.M.C. Asser Press, 2018, pp. 1–41, spéc. 1.2.1.1.

12 CJUE, 4 avr. 1968, aff. 34/67, *Firma Gebrüder Lück c. Hauptzollamt Köln-Rheinau.*

tion compétente pour assurer cette protection »[13]. D'autres arrêts suivront, dans le même ordre d'idée, comme l'arrêt *International Fruit Company*[14] et l'arrêt *Fleischkontor* en 1971[15].

C'est d'ailleurs à partir de là, dès 1972, que la doctrine forgera l'expression et théorisera la notion d'autonomie institutionnelle et procédurale des Etats membres[16]. Mais il faudra attendre les années 1990 pour que quelques avocats généraux à la Cour de justice en proposent l'emploi avant que celle-ci, à partir des années 2000, finisse par se référer, « *conformément à une jurisprudence constante* »[17], mais de manière variable, à l'autonomie procédurale des Etats membres[18], au principe d'autonomie procédurale des Etats membres ou au principe de l'autonomie procédurale des Etats membres[19]. La référence explicite à l'autonomie procédurale est loin d'être systématique et encore moins la référence au principe d'autonomie procédurale ou de l'autonomie procédurale, outre que la formulation précise a évolué au fil du temps avec les évolutions institutionnelles de l'Europe elle-même. C'est ainsi que, dans un arrêt du mois de mai 2018, la Cour rappelle que, « *en l'absence de réglementation du droit de l'Union en la matière, les modalités des procédures destinées à assurer la sauvegarde des droits que les justiciables tirent dudit droit de l'Union relèvent de l'ordre juridique interne des États membres, en vertu du principe de l'autonomie procédurale de ces derniers* »[20]. Le droit de l'Union a remplacé le droit communautaire et il n'est plus fait référence à l'effet direct. Cette suppression, qui manifeste un élargissement du champ de la protection des citoyens au-delà du seul effet direct des normes européennes[21], rappelle que l'autonomie procédurale des Etats membres a partie liée avec les principes mêmes de la construction européenne, qui en constituent ainsi le fondement.

---

13 CJCE, 19 déc. 1968, aff. 13/68, *Société Salgoil c. Ministère du commerce extérieur de la République italienne*.

14 CJCE 15 déc. 1971, aff. C-51/71 à 54/71, *International Fruit Company.*

15 CJCE 11 février 1971, aff. C-39/70, *Fleischkontor*.

16 Point de départ : J. Rideau, « Le rôle des Etats membres dans l'application du droit communautaire », *AFDI* 1972, p. 864 et s.

17 Ex. CJUE, 21 avr. 2016, aff. C-377/14, *Ernst Georg Radlinger et Helena Radlingerová c. Finway a.s.*

18 Ex. CJUE, 27 juin 2018, aff. C-246–17, *Ibrahim Diallo c. Etat belge*.

19 Ex. CJUE, 22 févr. 2018, aff. C-572/16, *INEOS Köln GmbH c. Bundesrepublik Deutschland*.

20 Ex. CJUE, 17 mai 2018, aff. C-147/16, *Karel de Grote – Hogeschool Katholieke Hogeschool Antwerpen VZW c. Susan Romy Jozef Kuijpers.*

21 V. K. Lenaerts, I. Maselis and K. Gutman, *EU Procedural Law*, edited by Janek Tomasz Nowak, Oxford, Oxford University Press, 2015, 4.02, note 4.

Dès 1960, la Cour de justice a rappelé que les traités instituant les Communautés européennes reposent sur le « *principe d'une séparation rigoureuse des compétences des institutions communautaires et de celles des Etats membres* »[22], aujourd'hui consacré et organisé par les articles 4 et 5 du traité du l'Union européenne. Le projet européen ne pouvait réussir que dans le respect des souverainetés nationales de sorte que, par réalisme politique[23], une fédéralisation des structures d'application du droit, telle qu'elle existe aux Etats-Unis, en Allemagne, en Suisse ou au Canada, a été exclue[24]. Le Traité de Rome s'est abstenu de créer des juridictions spécialement chargées de l'application du droit communautaire aussi bien que des voies de droit spécifiques pour y procéder[25], à la seule exception du renvoi préjudiciel devant la Cour de justice (ex. art. 177 CEE, devenu art. 234 TCE, puis art. 267 TFUE). Aux institutions européennes, la production du droit, c'est-à-dire la compétence législative; aux Etats membres, la mise en œuvre du droit, c'est-à-dire la compétence d'exécution[26], de sorte que le système communautaire, construit sur une logique d'intégration à laquelle Pierre Pescatore a donné ses lettres de noblesse, est centralisé sur le plan législatif mais décentralisé sur le plan exécutif[27]. Cette compétence nationale d'exécution est une nécessité. Comme il a été souligné, « *sans les droits nationaux, leur organisation juridictionnelle et l'ensemble des règles de procédures, le droit européen serait un droit figé, incapable de se mettre en mouvement en dehors des procédures proprement européennes* »[28]. C'est ainsi, par exemple,

---

22 CJCE 16 éd. 1960, aff. C-6/60, *J.-E. Humblet c. Etat belge.*

23 G. Isaac et M. Blanquet, *Droit général de l'Union européenne*, Sirey, 10ème éd., 2012, p. 205, devenu M. Blanquet, *Droit général de l'Union européenne*, Sirey, 11ème éd. 2018, n° 1021, p. 594. – R. Mehdi et E. Brosset, « De quoi le droit de l'Union est-il le nom? A propos du droit de l'Union en tant que droit commun des Etats membres », préc., spéc. p. 686.

24 L. Azoulai et E. Dubout, « Repenser la primauté – L'intégration européenne et la montée de la question identitaire », *in* J.-B. Bonnet, p. 567 et s., spéc. p. 576.

25 CJCE, 7 juill. 1981, *Rewe II*, aff. C-155/80.

26 V. aussi K. Lenaerts, « National remedies for private parties in the light of the EU principles of equivalence and effectiveness", *Irish Jurist* (2011) 46, pp. 13–37, spéc. p. 13 : « *There is effectively a division of functions between the EU and the national legal systems, with the former providing the rights and the latter the remedies* ».

27 P. Pescatore, *Le droit de l'intégration – Emergence d'un phénomène nouveau dans les relations internationales selon l'expérience des Communautés européennes*, Leiden, A. W. Sijtoff, 1972, réimp. Bruylant, 2005. L'image est devenue habituelle sous la plume des auteurs : V. p. ex. M. Blanquet, *op. cit.*, n° 1017, p. 592. – K. Lenaerts, *op. cit.*, p. 13. – J. T. Nowak, *op. cit. et loc. cit.*, and note 7.

28 J.-S. Bergé, « Enrichir les rapports entre ordres juridiques par les rapports de mise en œuvre », *in* J.-B. Bonnet, *op. cit.*, p. 593 et s., spéc. n° 4, p. 594.

que relèvent en principe du droit national la compétence juridictionnelle, les délais de procédure, les règles de preuve, l'office du juge ou l'étendue et l'autorité de la chose jugée.

L'autonomie procédurale des Etats membres est une manifestation de leur autonomie plus générale dans l'exécution du droit de l'Union[29] au même titre que leur autonomie institutionnelle[30], à laquelle se rattache l'autonomie d'organisation juridictionnelle[31] aussi bien que l'autonomie d'organisation administrative[32], encore qu'une distinction soit faite entre les deux, le caractère complet ou absolue de l'autonomie institutionnelle étant opposé au caractère partiel ou relatif de l'autonomie procédurale[33], ce qui nous conduit à la question, également mystérieuse à mes yeux, des limites de l'autonomie procédurale des Etats membres.

1.2. Limites de l'autonomie procédurale des Etats membres

Ces limites, au nombre deux, sont généralement présentées ensemble comme bornant, dès l'origine, l'autonomie procédurale des Etats membres[34]. La première limite est référée au principe d'équivalence, la seconde au principe d'effectivité.

Sans doute, en même temps que les arrêts *Rewe I* et *Comet* affirmaient, sans l'exprimer ainsi, l'autonomie procédurale des Etats membres, ils assortissaient cette autonomie de deux limites : d'une part, que les modalités procédurales du droit national ne soient pas « *moins favorables que celles concernant des recours similaires de nature interne* »[35] et que, d'autre part, qu'elles n'aboutissent pas « *à rendre, en pratique, impossible l'exercice de droits*

29 M. Roccati, « Quelle place pour l'autonomie juridictionnelle des Etats membres? », *RIDE*, 2015/4, p. 152 et s.

30 Ou que leur autonomie juridique quant aux règles de fond applicables dans l'hypothèse, par exemple, de la transposition d'une directive : T. Debard, « Droit de l'Union européenne et procédure civile », préc., n° 21.

31 Selon l'expression de Thierry Debard, *op. cit.*, n° 23.

32 V. T. Debard, *op. cit.*, 21. – M. Blanquet, *op. cit.*, n° 1022, p. 594. – M. Roccati, art. préc., p. 152.

33 V. en ce sens M. Blanquet, *op. cit.*, n° 1023, p. 595.

34 V. en ce sens T. Debard, *op. cit.*, n° 25. – M. Roccati, *op. cit.*, 1.1.

35 CJCE, 16 déc. 1976, aff. C-33/76, *Rewe*, n° 5, et aff. C-45/76, *Comet*, préc., n° 13 : « *en l 'absence de règlementation communautaire en la matière, il appartient à l 'ordre juridique interne de chaque Etat membre de désigner les juridictions compétentes et de régler les modalités procédurales des recours en justice destinés à assurer la sauvegarde des droits que les justiciables tirent de l'effet direct du droit communautaire étant*

que les juridictions nationales ont l'obligation de sauvegarder »[36]. Il s'agit de permettre la mise en œuvre du droit européen dans toute la plénitude de son champ d'application de manière égale dans l'ensemble des Etats membres.

Le propos demande cependant à être précisé. D'abord, des arrêts ultérieurs réuniront ces deux limites dans une même phrase, ce qui n'était pas le cas originairement[37], en même temps qu'ils élargiront la deuxième limite, l'impossibilité pratique s'étendant à la difficulté excessive[38]. C'est à cette époque également que ces limites de l'autonomie procédurale seront explicitement référées, dans les arrêts de la Cour de justice, « *consacrant les dénominations que la doctrine leur avait données* »[39], aux « *principes* » d'équi-

---

entendu que ces modalités ne peuvent être moins favorables que celles concernant des recours similaires de nature interne ».

36 CJCE, 16 déc. 1976, aff. C-33/76, *Rewe*, n° 5, et aff. C-45/76, *Comet*, préc., n° 15–16 : « *A défaut de (…) mesures d'harmonisation, les droits conférés par le droit communautaire doivent être exercés devant les juridictions nationales selon les modalités déterminées par la règle nationale; (…) qu'il n'en serait autrement que si ces modalités et délais aboutissaient à rendre, en pratique, impossible l'exercice de droits que les juridictions nationales ont l'obligation de sauvegarder* ».

37 CJCE, 9 nov. 1983, aff. C- 199/82, *Administration des finances de l'État italien c. SpA San Giorgio*, n° 12 : « *s'il est vrai que le remboursement ne peut être poursuivi que dans le cadre des conditions, de fond et de forme, fixées par les diverses législations nationales en la matière, il n'en reste pas moins, ainsi qu'il résulte d'une jurisprudence constante de la cour, que ces conditions ne sauraient être moins favorables que celles qui concernent des réclamations semblables de nature interne et qu'elles ne sauraient être aménagées de manière à rendre pratiquement impossible l'exercice des droits conférés par l'ordre juridique communautaire* ».

38 V. CJCE, 25 févr. 1988, aff. C-331, 376 et 378/85, *Les Fils de Jules Bianco SA et J. Girard Fils SA c. Directeur général des douanes et droits indirects*, n° 12 : « *Il convient de rappeler à ce sujet, ainsi que la Cour l'a jugé dans l'arrêt du 9 novembre 1983 (San Giorgio, 199/82, Rec. p. 3595), que sont incompatibles avec le droit communautaire toutes modalités de preuve dont l'effet est de rendre pratiquement impossible ou excessivement difficile l'obtention du remboursement de taxes perçues en violation du droit communautaire* ». – CJCE, 3 févr. 2000, aff. C-228/98, *Charalampos Dounias et Ypourgou Oikonomikon*, n° 69 : « *Dans la mise en œuvre de cette exigence, les États membres doivent s'assurer que les modalités de preuve applicables aux recours portant sur des litiges relatifs à une violation du droit communautaire, en premier lieu, ne sont pas moins favorables que celles concernant des recours similaires de nature interne et, en second lieu, ne rendent pas en pratique impossible ou excessivement difficile l'exercice par le justiciable des droits conférés par l'ordre juridique communautaire* ».

39 T. Debard, *op. cit. et loc. cit.*

valence (ou de l'équivalence) et d'effectivité[40], avant d'être qualifiées par elle de « *principes généraux de droit communautaire* »[41]. La formulation s'est par la suite stabilisée, ainsi qu'en témoigne encore une série d'arrêts rendus au cours de cette année 2018[42], jusque très récemment comme l'indiquent deux arrêts du 20 septembre 2018[43].

---

40 V. not. CJCE, 10 juill. 1997, aff. C-271/95, *Rosalba Palmisani c. Istituto nazionale della previdenza sociale (INPS)*, n° 27 : "*il résulte d'une jurisprudence constante depuis l'arrêt Francovich e.a., précité, points 41 à 43, que, sous réserve de ce qui précède, c'est dans le cadre du droit national de la responsabilité qu'il incombe à l'État de réparer les conséquences du préjudice causé, étant entendu que les conditions, notamment de délai, fixées par les législations nationales en matière de réparation des dommages ne sauraient être moins favorables que celles qui concernent des réclamations semblables de nature interne (principe de l'équivalence) et ne sauraient être aménagées de manière à rendre en pratique impossible ou excessivement difficile l'obtention de la réparation (principe d'effectivité)* ».

41 CJCE, 18 sept. 2003, aff. C-125/1, *Peter Flücke c. Bundesansalt für Arbeit*, n° 33–34 : « *(33) Dans ces conditions, les États membres sont en principe libres de prévoir dans leur droit national des dispositions fixant un délai de forclusion pour l'introduction de la demande d'un travailleur salarié visant à obtenir, selon les modalités de la directive 80/987, le paiement d'une indemnité d'insolvabilité, pour autant, toutefois, que ces dispositions respectent les principes généraux du droit communautaire. (34). S'agissant de ces principes, il est de jurisprudence constante que de tels délais de forclusion prévus en droit national ne peuvent être moins favorables que ceux concernant des demandes semblables de nature interne (principe d'équivalence) et ne peuvent être aménagés de manière à rendre en pratique impossible l'exercice des droits reconnus par l'ordre juridique communautaire (principe d'effectivité)* ».

42 CJUE, 17 mai 2018, aff. C-147/16, *Karel de Grote – Hogeschool Katholieke Hogeschool Antwerpen VZW c. Susan Romy Jozef Kuijpers*, n° 33 : : « *il convient de rappeler que, en l'absence de réglementation du droit de l'Union en la matière, les modalités des procédures destinées à assurer la sauvegarde des droits que les justiciables tirent dudit droit de l'Union relèvent de l'ordre juridique interne des États membres, en vertu du principe de l'autonomie procédurale de ces derniers. Cependant, ces modalités ne doivent pas être moins favorables que celles régissant des situations similaires soumises au droit interne (principe d'équivalence) ni être aménagées de manière à rendre en pratique impossible ou excessivement difficile l'exercice des droits conférés aux consommateurs par l'ordre juridique de l'Union (principe d'effectivité)* ». – *Adde* CJUE, 27 juin 2018, aff. C-246/17, *Ibrahim Diallo c. Etat Belge*, n° 45 : « *il convient de relever que la directive 2004/38 ne contient aucune disposition régissant les conséquences qui découlent du dépassement du délai visé à l'article 10, paragraphe 1, de la directive 2004/38, cette question relevant, en principe, de l'autonomie procédurale des États membres sous réserve du respect des principes d'effectivité et d'équivalence (voir, en ce sens, arrêt du 17 mars 2016, Bensada Benallal, C-161/15, EU:C:2016:175, point 24)* ».

43 CJUE, 20 sept. 2018, aff. C-518/17, *Stefan Rudigier c. Salzburger Verkehrsverbund GmbH*, n° 61 : « *En l'absence de précision d'ordre procédural prévu par le droit de l'Union pour sanctionner un droit, et conformément à une jurisprudence constante de la*

Le refrain serait-il cependant en train de changer?

Il faut en effet avoir égard à deux arrêts prononcés par la 2ème chambre de la Cour en matière de protection des consommateurs le 31 mai et le 13 septembre 2018[44]. Dans ces arrêts, la Cour, après avoir rappelé le principe du renvoi à l'ordre juridique interne des Etats membres, en l'absence d'harmonisation par le droit de l'Union des procédures applicables à l'examen du caractère prétendument abusif d'une clause contractuelle, conditionne ce renvoi à ce que ces procédures nationales « *ne soient pas moins favorables que celles régissant des situations similaires soumises au droit interne (principe d'équivalence) et qu'elles prévoient un droit à un recours effectif, tel que prévu à l'article 47 de la charte des droits fondamentaux de l'Union européenne* »[45].

Cour, il appartient à l'ordre juridique interne de chaque État membre de régler les modalités procédurales destinées à assurer la sauvegarde des droits que les justiciables tirent du droit de l'Union. Ces modalités ne doivent, toutefois, pas être moins favorables que les voies similaires de nature interne (principe d'équivalence) et ne doivent pas rendre pratiquement impossible ou excessivement difficile l'exercice des droits conférés par l'ordre juridique de l'Union (principe d'effectivité) (voir, en ce sens, arrêt du 5 avril 2017, Marina del Mediterráneo e.a., C-391/15, EU:C:2017:268, point 32 et jurisprudence citée). » – CJUE, 20 sept. 2018, aff. C-448/17, *EOS KSI Slovensko c. Ján Danko, Margita Danková*, n° 36 : « *En l'absence de réglementation de l'Union en ce qui concerne le droit des associations de protection des consommateurs d'intervenir dans des litiges individuels impliquant des consommateurs, il appartient à l'ordre juridique interne de chaque État membre d'établir de telles règles, en vertu du principe de l'autonomie procédurale, à condition toutefois qu'elles ne soient pas moins favorables que celles régissant des situations similaires soumises au droit interne (principe d'équivalence) et qu'elles ne rendent pas impossible en pratique ou excessivement difficile l'exercice des droits conférés par le droit de l'Union (principe d'effectivité) (voir, en ce sens, arrêt du 27 février 2014, Pohotovosť, C-470/12, EU:C:2014:101, point 46).* ».

44 CJUE, 31 mai 2018, aff. C-483/16, *Zsolt Sziber c. ERSTE Bank Hungary Zrt.*, n° 35 et CJUE, 13 sept. 2018, aff. C-176/17, *Profi Credit Polska S.A. w Bielsku Białej c. Mariusz Wawrzosek*, n° 57 : « *Si la Cour a ainsi déjà encadré, à plusieurs égards et en tenant compte des exigences de l'article 6, paragraphe 1, et de l'article 7, paragraphe 1, de la directive 93/13, la manière selon laquelle le juge national doit assurer la protection des droits que les consommateurs tirent de cette directive, il n'en reste pas moins que, en principe, le droit de l'Union n'harmonise pas les procédures applicables à l'examen du caractère prétendument abusif d'une clause contractuelle, et que celles-ci relèvent, dès lors, de l'ordre juridique interne des États membres, à condition, toutefois, qu'elles ne soient pas moins favorables que celles régissant des situations similaires soumises au droit interne (principe d'équivalence) et qu'elles prévoient une protection juridictionnelle effective, telle que prévue à l'article 47 de la Charte* ».

45 V. déjà, dans une formulation antérieure associant explicitement principe d'effectivité et protection juridictionnelle effective, CJUE 14 sept. 2017, aff. C-628/15, *The Trustees of the BT Pension Scheme c. Commissioners for Her Majesty's Revenue and*

Cette évolution, sur laquelle les discutants de ce rapport nous fourniront leurs lumières[46], invite à prendre la mesure des raisons, des manifestations des limites ainsi posées à l'autonomie procédurale des Etats membres. Le champ est immense; je l'ai découvert en préparant cet exposé; il a d'ailleurs donné lieu à une littérature abondante qui me dispense de trop longs développements

Les raisons de ces limites sont de plusieurs sortes et relèvent de plusieurs niveaux.

Dès 1972, dans un arrêt *Schlüter*, la Cour de justice avait précisé que l'application de leur droit national par les Etats membres devait se concilier avec la nécessité d'une application uniforme du droit communautaire, destiné à éviter un traitement inégal, ou discriminatoire, des opérateurs économiques[47], ce que rappellera l'arrêt *Deutsche Milchkontor* en 1983[48]. Voilà pour le principe d'équivalence. Quant au principe d'effectivité, les auteurs l'expliquent généralement par la nécessité d'assurer l'effet utile du droit de l'Union[49]. Mais ces principes d'équivalence et d'effectivité sont eux-mêmes, ainsi qu'ils ont été qualifiés en doctrine, l'expression pratique, « *practical expression* », des principes de primauté et d'effet direct du droit

---

Customs, n° 59 : « *En outre, en application du principe d'effectivité, les États membres ont la responsabilité d'assurer, dans chaque cas, une protection effective des droits conférés par le droit de l'Union et, en particulier, de garantir le respect du droit à un recours effectif et à accéder à un tribunal impartial, consacré à l'article 47, paragraphe 1, de la charte des droits fondamentaux de l'Union européenne* ». Mais comp. CJCE, 15 avr. 2008, aff. C-268/06, *Impact*, préc., n° 45–47 et CJUE, 18 mars 2010, aff. C-317/08, C-318/08, C-319/08 et C-320/08, *Rosalba Alassini*, n° 46, visant « *les principes d'équivalence et d'effectivité ainsi que le principe de protection juridictionnelle* », et qui considère que « *ces exigences d'équivalence et d'effectivité (…° expriment l'obligation générale pour les Etats membres d'assurer la protection juridictionnelle des droits que les justiciables tirent du droit de l'Union* ».

46 V. *infra* l'intervention de M. Vilaras proposant notamment de distinguer selon l'objectif poursuivi (assurer la primauté du droit de l'Union : principe d'effectivité, ou protéger les droits fondamentaux : art. 19.1 TUE, puis art. 47 CDFUE) et l'effet recherché (mise à l'écart de la règle nationale ou édiction d'obligations positives à l'endroit du juge national).

47 CJCE, 6 juin 1972, aff. 94–71, *Schlüter & Maack c. Hauptzollamt Hamburg-Jonas*.

48 CJCE, 21 sept. 1983, aff. C-205 à 215/82, *Deutsche Milchkontor GmbH et autres c. République fédérale d'Allemagne*, n° 17.

49 V. p. ex. T. Debard, *op. cit.*, n° 27.

de l'Union[50]. Un auteur a également parlé de « *déclinaisons* »[51]. Nous touchons là au cœur de la construction européenne[52], conçue comme une intégration juridique en faveur des droits individuels plutôt qu'en faveur des souverainetés nationales. Les principes de primauté et d'effet direct ne sont en effet eux-mêmes que l'expression instrumentale de la nature de la construction européenne[53] définie par la Cour de justice, dans les arrêts fondateurs *Van Gend en Loos*[54] et *Costa*[55], comme « *un ordre juridique propre intégré au système juridique des Etats membres (…) et qui s'impose à leurs juridictions* ». Or, comme l'a souligné Jean-Victor Louis dans ses conclusions générales des actes du colloque sur le 50ème anniversaire de l'arrêt *Van Gend en Loos*, la notion d'autonomie de l'ordre juridique communautaire formait « *l'épine dorsale du raisonnement de la Cour* »[56], sans que le mot lui-même ne soit jamais prononcé[57].

C'est cette association intime des principes d'équivalence et d'effectivité à l'essence même de la construction européenne qui explique sans doute que ces principes se soient renforcés en même temps que la construction européenne et, singulièrement, le principe d'effectivité, fer de lance de l'effet direct, qui a pu favoriser une intervention accrue de la Cour de justice sur le terrain des règles nationales de procédure là où le seul principe

---

50 K. Lenaerts, I. Maselis and K. Gutman, *op. cit.*, 4.04. – K. Lenaerts, *op. cit.*, p. 13. – J. Rideau, « Ordre juridique de l'Union européenne – Sources non écrites », *Juris-Classeur Europe*, fasc. 191, (2014), n° 26, pour lequel le principe d'autonomie « *est cependant loin d'être absolu et de nombreuses limitations y ont été apportées par la Cour. Il ne peut, en toute hypothèses, contrarier le jeu de la primauté et de l'effet direct* ».

51 M. Roccati, *op. cit.*, 1.1. : « *Equivalence et effectivité sont ainsi les déclinaisons de l'objectif initial, tourné vers la sauvegarde des droits issus des normes européennes* ».

52 Rappr. M. Roccati, *op. cit. et loc. cit.* : « *De là dépend la raison d'être du système juridique européen* ».

53 Ses « *murs porteurs* » selon l'expression de R. Mehdi, « Ordre juridique de l'Union européenne – Effet direct », *JurisClasseur Europe*, fasc. 195, (2018), n° 1.

54 CJCE, 5 févr. 1963, aff. 26/62, *Van Gend en Loos*.

55 CJCE, 15 juill. 1964, aff. 6/64, *Costa*.

56 R. Mehdi, *op. cit.*, n° 17. Conf. F. Picod, "La Cour de justice de l'Union européenne et les rapports entre les ordres juridiques de l'Union européenne et des Etats membres", *in* J.-B. Bonnet (dir.), *op. cit.*, p. 995 et s.

57 J.-V. Louis, « Conclusions générales », *in* Cour de justice de l'Union européenne, *50ème anniversaire de l'arrêt Van Gend en Loos 1963–2013*, Office des publications de l'Union européenne, 2013, p. 205 et s., spéc. p. 213 et s. V. également D. Simon, « Les fondements de l'autonomie du droit communautaire », *in* SFDI, *Droit international et droit communautaire : perspectives actuelles*, Pedone, 2000, p. 222 et s. *Adde* M. Klamert, « The autonomy of the EU (and of EU law) : through the kaleidoscope », *European Law Review* 2017, 42(6), pp. 815–830.

d'équivalence pouvait justifier une attitude plus passive[58]. Il ne s'agit plus seulement pour le juge national de laisser au besoin inappliquée, de sa propre autorité, l'application de la règle nationale, même postérieure à une disposition du droit de l'Union[59]; il s'agit de mettre à la charge des juridictions nationales des obligations positives à peine de responsabilité de l'Etat membre[60]. Je ne m'arrêterai pas sur les manifestations de ce renforcement des principes d'équivalence et d'effectivité, largement documenté[61], dès lors que la règle nationale de procédure porte atteinte à la réalisation des objectifs essentiels du droit de l'Union et met en cause la protection effective que les citoyens tirent de l'ordre juridique de l'Union européenne[62] : chacun a notamment en tête les solutions adoptées par la Cour de justice en ce qui concerne le droit à une protection juridictionnelle provisoire[63], l'application d'office par le juge national d'un moyen tiré du droit de

---

58 V. en ce sens K. Lenaerts, *op. cit.*, p. 13.

59 CJUE, 9 févr. 2017, aff. C-283/16, *M. S. c. P. S.*, n° 50.

60 Selon une jurisprudence constante, le principe de la responsabilité de l'État pour des dommages causés aux particuliers par des violations du droit de l'Union qui lui sont imputables est inhérent au système des traités sur lesquels cette dernière est fondée. Les particuliers lésés ont un droit à réparation dès lors que trois conditions sont réunies, à savoir que la règle de droit de l'Union violée a pour objet de leur conférer des droits, que la violation de cette règle est suffisamment caractérisée et qu'il existe un lien de causalité direct entre cette violation et le préjudice subi par les particuliers : V. CJCE, 19 nov. 1991, aff. 6/90 et 9/90, *Francovich e.a.*, n ° 35. – CJCE, 5 mars 1996, aff. 46/93 et 48/93, *Brasserie du pêcheur et Factortame*, n° 31. V. K. Lenaerts, I. Maselis and K. Gutman, *op. cit.*, 4.42 – 4.57. Ce principe est valable quel que soit l'auteur public à l'origine de la violation, y compris, à certaines conditions, lorsque la violation découle d'une décision d'une juridiction nationale statuant en dernier ressort : CJCE, 30 sept. 2003, aff. C-224/01, *Köbler*, n ° 32–36 et 59. – CJUE, 9 sept. 2015, aff. C-160/14, *João Filipe Ferreira da Silva e Brito, e. a.*, n° 46–60. – CJUE, 28 juill. 2016, aff. C-168/15, *Milena Tomášová*, n° 20. V. T. Debard, op. cit., n° 54–57, spéc. n° 56–57 à propos du « *manquement judiciaire* ».

61 V. not. K. Lenaerts, *op. cit.*, 12, p. 37. – K. Lenaerts, I. Maselis and K. Gutman, *op. cit.*, chap. 4.

62 V. p. ex. CJCE, 15 avr. 2008, aff. C-268/06, *Impact*, n° n° 47. – CJUE, 18 mars 2010, aff. C-317/08, C-318/08, C-319/08 et C-320/08, *Rosalba Alassini*, préc., n° 49 : « *Ces exigences d'équivalence et d'effectivité expriment l'obligation générale pour les Etats membres d'assurer la protection juridictionnelle des droits que les justiciables tirent du droit communautaire/de l'Union* ».

63 V. not. K. Lenaerts, *op. cit.*, 7, p. 27 et s. et, p. ex., CJCE, 19 juin 1990, aff. C-213/89, *Factortame*. – CJCE, 21 févr. 1991, aff. C-143/88 et C-92/89, *Zuckerfabrik Süderdithmarschen AG* et *Zuckerfabrik Soest*. – CJCE, 13 mars 2007, aff. C-432/05, *Unibet*.

l'Union[64] ou, plus spécifiquement, l'éviction de l'autorité de la chose jugée en matière d'aides d'Etat lorsque les compétences de la Commission sont en jeu[65].

Il est notable que la référence aux principes d'équivalence et d'effectivité s'est élargie en même temps que ces principes se sont renforcés. Initialement limitée à l'hypothèse d' « *absence de règlementation communautaire* », la référence a évolué vers l'absence, dans le droit de l'Union, de disposition spécifique[66], y compris dans le domaine de la coopération judiciaire intraeuropéenne[67] où elle remplit, *mutadis mutandis,* un rôle comparable à celui des notions autonomes[68]. La législation européenne y fait du reste elle-même référence[69].

---

64 Voir A. Beka, *The Active Role of Courts in Consumer Litigation – Applying EU Law of the National Court's Motion,* préc. – *Adde*, dans une vue à la fois plus large et plus étroite, au regard du droit français, E. Bazin, « Le juge et le droit de la consommation », *Droit et procédures* 2018, p. 142 et s.

65 CJCE, 18 juill. 2007, aff. C-119/05, *Lucchini.*

66 V. p. ex. CJUE, 20 sept. 2018, aff. 518/17, *Stefan Rudigier*, n° 60. – CJUE, 20 déc. 2017, aff. C-102/16, *Vaditrans BVBA*, n° 55.

67 V. p. ex. CJUE, 8 juin 2017, aff. C-54/16, *Vinyls Italia SpA*, n° 26; *JCP* G 2017, 711, obs. Berlin : "il est de jurisprudence constante que, en l'absence, dans le droit de l'Union, d'une harmonisation de ces règles, il appartient à l'ordre juridique interne de chaque État membre de les établir, en vertu du principe d'autonomie procédurale, à condition toutefois qu'elles ne soient pas moins favorables que celles régissant des situations similaires soumises au droit interne (principe d'équivalence) et qu'elles ne rendent pas impossible en pratique ou excessivement difficile l'exercice des droits conférés par le droit de l'Union (principe d'effectivité) », à propos du Règl. (CE) n° 1346/2000 du 29 mai 2000 relatif aux procédures d'insolvabilité, art. 13, qui contient une disposition relative à la charge de la preuve mais précise pas ses aspects procéduraux spécifiques (modes d'administration, moyens de preuve, principes régissant l'appréciation de la force probante, etc.).

68 V. en ce sens, L. Charbonneau, « Notions autonomes et intégration européenne », *Cahiers de droit européen*, 2013, p. 21 et s., spéc. n° 76, pp. 50–51, qui observe que « *le développement de notions autonomes permet d'abord une limitation de l'autonomie procédurale et institutionnelle des Etats en restraignant le pouvoir d'interprétation des juges internes* ». Il est tout à fait notable que les notions autonomes apparaissent, dans la jurisprudence de la Cour de justice, en même temps que s'affirme le principe de l'autonomie procédurale des Etats membres sous réserve du respect des principes d'équivalence et d'effectivité : V. p. ex. CJCE, 1er févr. 1972, aff. 49/71, *Hagen*, n° 6 : "*Sauf renvoi, explicite ou implicite, au droit national, les notions juridiques utilisées par le droit communautaire doivent être interprétées et appliquées de façon uniforme dans l'ensemble de la communauté* ». – Puis CJCE 14 oct. 1976, aff. 29/76, *Eurocontrol*, n° 3. Sur la participation des notions autonomes à l'autonomie de l'ordre juridique du droit de l'Union européenne, V. également J.-CL. Gautron

Cette évolution a quelque chose de troublant dans la mesure où, en définitive, à travers les principes d'équivalence et d'effectivité, c'est à l'autonomie du droit de l'Union européenne que l'autonomie procédurale des Etats membres se heurte. En vérité, il est bien étrange de présenter comme des limites à un principe, celui de l'autonomie procédurale des Etats

et S. Platon, « La naissance d'une singularité doctrinale : les européanistes », *in* J.-B. Bonnet (dir.), *op. cit.*, p. 109 et s., spéc. p. 116. Pour une vue plus générale, V. D. Simon, « Les 'notions autonomes' en droit de l'Union », *in Mélanges Henri Oberdorf*, LGDJ, 2015, p. 93 et s. Et, pour les applications privilégiées qui en sont faites en droit international privé, conf. M. Audit, « L'interprétation autonome du droit international privé communautaire », *Journal du droit international* 2004, p. 789 et s. – F. Mailhé, « Entre Icare et Minotaure. Les notions autonomes de droit international privé de l'Union », *Mélanges Bertrand Ancel*, Paris, Dalloz, 2018, p. 1137 et s.

69 V. p. ex. Directive 2014/104/UE du Parlement européen et du Conseil du 26 novembre 2014 relative à certaines règles régissant les actions en dommages et intérêts en droit national pour les infractions aux dispositions du droit de la concurrence des États membres et de l'Union européenne, art. 4 : « *Principes d'effectivité et d'équivalence. Conformément au principe d'effectivité, les États membres veillent à ce que toutes les règles et procédures nationales ayant trait à l'exercice du droit de demander des dommages et intérêts soient conçues et appliquées de manière à ne pas rendre pratiquement impossible ou excessivement difficile l'exercice du droit, conféré par l'Union, à réparation intégrale du préjudice causé par une infraction au droit de la concurrence. Conformément au principe d'équivalence, les règles et procédures nationales relatives aux actions en dommages et intérêts découlant d'infractions à l'article 101 ou 102 du traité sur le fonctionnement de l'Union européenne ne sont pas moins favorables aux parties prétendument lésées que celles régissant les actions similaires en dommages et intérêts découlant d'infractions au droit national.* ». – Règlement (UE) 2017/1939 du Conseil du 12 octobre 2017 mettant en œuvre une coopération renforcée concernant la création du Parquet européen, consid. n° 88 : « *La légalité des actes de procédure du Parquet européen qui sont destinés à produire des effets juridiques à l'égard de tiers devrait être soumise au contrôle juridictionnel des juridictions nationales. À cet égard, il convient de garantir des voies de recours effectives, conformément à l'article 19, paragraphe 1, deuxième alinéa, du TUE. Par ailleurs, comme la Cour de justice l'a souligné dans sa jurisprudence, les règles de procédure nationales régissant les recours relatifs à la protection des droits individuels octroyés par le droit de l'Union ne doivent pas être moins favorables que les règles régissant des recours similaires au niveau national (principe d'équivalence) et ne doivent pas rendre pratiquement impossible ou excessivement difficile l'exercice des droits conférés par le droit de l'Union (principe d'effectivité).* » V. également, *de lege ferenda*, le projet de règles procédurales minimum proposé par la Commission des affaires juridiques du Parlement européen, *infra* note 146.

membres, d'autres principes, les principes d'effectivité et d'équivalence[70]. Il y a, dans cette terminologie, quelque chose qui heurte l'entendement : où est le principe, où est la limite? Et l'on comprend, en revanche, que l'existence, non seulement d'un *principe* d'autonomie procédurale, mais de l'existence même d'une autonomie procédurale des Etats soit très vigoureusement contestée[71], et pas seulement parce que le prétendu principe de l'autonomie procédurale des Etats membres aurait fini par être anéanti en raison de l'expansion continu des exigences imposées par la jurisprudence « *audacieuse mais logique* » de la Cour de justice[72]. La proposition est d'ailleurs faite d'abandonner l'expression « *autonomie procédurale* » pour lui préférer celle de « *compétence procédurale fonctionnelle* »[73], ce qui conduit à s'interroger sur la portée de l'autonomie procédurale des Etats membres, qui m'apparaît aussi incertaine que sa notion me semble mystérieuse.

70 *Conditions* conviendrait mieux que *limites*. V. d'ailleurs CJUE, 17 mars 2016, aff. C-161/15, *Bensada Benallal*, n° 25 : « *Il s'ensuit que deux conditions limitatives, à savoir le respect des principes d'équivalence et d'effectivité, doivent être réunies pour qu'un Etat membre puisse faire valoir le principe de l'autonomie procédurale dans des situations qui sont régies par le droit de l'Union* », qui emploie ici *limitatives* au sens de *exclusives*.

71 V. p. ex. M. Bobek, "Why there is no principle of 'procedural autonomy' of the Member States', *in* H. Micklitz et B. De Witte (eds), *The European Court of Justice and the autonomy of the Member States,* Antwerp/Cambridge, Intersentia, 2012, pp. 305–323. – D. U. Galetta, *Procedural Autonomy of EU Member States: Paradise Lost?,* Berlin, Springer-Verlag, 2011. – C. Kakoukis, "Do the Member States Possess Judicial Procedural 'Autonomy'?", *Common Market Law Review,* 1997, vol. 34, Issue 6, Issue 6, pp. 1389–1412. – J. Nowak, *op. cit.,* 1.2.1.1. Comp. P. Girerd, "Les principes d'équivalence et d'effectivité: encadrement ou désencadrement de l'autonomie procédurale des Etats membres?", *RTD. eur.*, 2002, p. 75 et s.

72 En ce sens T. Debard, *op. cit.*, n° 51.

73 V. D. U. Galetta, *Procedural Autonomy of EU Member States : Paradise Lost?,* Berlin, Springer-Verlag, 2011, p. 123. – En ce sens également M. Roccati, *op. cit.,* 2.2., *in fine.*

2. *L'incertaine portée de l'autonomie procédurale à partir de la jurisprudence de la Cour de justice de l'Union européenne*

Nous changeons ici de registre en quittant celui du droit positif pour celui de l'épistémologie juridique en raison des effets perturbateurs, voire « *mutagènes* »[74] du droit de l'Union européenne sur les droits des Etats membres. Il est plus précisément permis de se demander si le traitement de l'autonomie procédurale des Etats membres dans la jurisprudence de la Cour de justice n'invite pas à penser de manière nouvelle, à la fois, l'articulation des ordres juridiques de l'Union européenne et des Etats membres, ainsi que les catégories structurantes du droit des Etats membres. C'est au regard du droit français que j'aborderai ainsi, tour à tour, brièvement, l'autonomie procédurale et les rapports de systèmes (2.1), puis l'autonomie procédurale et les structures du droit (2.2), par où se dessine peut-être une nouvelle *épistémê* de la procédure en Europe.

2.1. *Autonomie procédurale et rapports de systèmes*

La réflexion en termes de rapports de systèmes part de l'impasse théorique à laquelle conduit l'analyse de l'autonomie procédurale des Etats membres en termes de principe que limiteraient les principes d'équivalence et d'effectivité qui sont l'expression de l'autonomie de l'ordre juridique constitué par le droit de l'Union européenne. Depuis que le terme est attesté, l'autonomie (emprunté au grec α ὐ τ ο ν ο μ ί α) est le droit de se régir par ses propres lois; on ne peut donc rationnellement combiner deux autonomies, l'une excluant l'autre et *vice versa*. En quelque sorte, autonomie sur autonomie ne vaut. Laissant de côté les tentatives d'explication historique[75] ou psychologique[76] de l'aporie, c'est plutôt vers l'idée d'interdé-

74 R. Mehdi et F. Brosset, « De quoi le droit de l'Union est-il le nom? A propos du droit de l'Union en tant que droit commun des Etats membres », préc., p. 669 et s., p. 687.

75 Qui décrirait une évolution allant historiquement d'une autonomie à l'autre, soit de l'autonomie de l'Union européenne (des Communautés européennes) à celle des Etats membres, soit de l'autonomie des Etats membres à celle de l'Union européenne.

76 De l'ordre du verre à moitié plein ou à moitié vide, selon que l'on adopte le point de vue du droit de l'Union ou celui du droit national.

pendance qu'il convient de se tourner[77]. L'autonomie, entendue comme la capacité à se gouverner soi-même, a été au cœur du projet de la modernité tel qu'il a été élaboré par les philosophes des Lumières et tel qu'il a été, ensuite, repris par le projet démocratique, à la fois dans sa dimension individuelle et collective. C'est une notion qui fait sens dans une conception kelsénienne du droit, mais cette conception ne peut plus rendre compte de la réalité complexe[78] du monde juridique dit post-moderne[79] caractérisé, notamment, par la globalisation des échanges, l'émergence des droits fondamentaux, la fragmentation des sources du droit, la contractualisation de la régulation sociale, l'horizontalisation de la production normative. Le phénomène est particulièrement sensible dans un pays comme la France où, au début du 19ème siècle, le droit avait été réduit à la loi et la loi enfermée dans des codes, en un légicentrisme exacerbé.

L'Europe qui se construit depuis soixante ans est au rebours de ce modèle; elle révèle une réalité composite et dynamique, transcendant la distinction des sources du droit autant que la division du droit en systèmes nationaux[80]. « *Entre ordre et désordre* », selon l'expression de François Ost et Michel van de Kerchove[81], ce n'est plus d'autonomie qu'il s'agit, mais d'interdépendance, ou d'indépendance dans l'interdépendance si l'on veut être rassurant. Le passage de l'ordre juridique traditionnel, centré sur la loi et identifié à l'Etat-Nation, à un ordre juridique régional conduit à articuler entre eux des processus normatifs et juridictionnels de niveaux différents afin d'harmoniser les solutions juridiques dans un espace normatif

---

77 Rappr. L. Azoulai et E. Dubout, « Repenser la primauté – L'intégration européenne et la montée de la question identitaire », *in* J.-B. Bonnet (dir.), *op. cit.*, p. 567 et s., spéc. p. 571 : « *Dans la Communauté, le droit communautaire et les droits nationaux se rejoignent. Non qu'ils se confondent. Suivant la doctrine de la Cour, il s'agit de deux espèces de droit également autonomes qui sont de facto en situation de proximité mais, de jure, en relation d'interdépendance. La primauté est précisément ce qui distingue ces deux espèces en les maintenant dans une relation de dépendance* ».

78 V. en ce sens J.-P. Jacqué, « Quelques considérations sur les rapports de système entre ordres juridiques en Europe », *in* J.-B. Bonnet (dir.), *op. cit.*, p. 1108 et s., spéc. p. 1109.

79 Voir not. J. Chevallier, *L'Etat post-moderne*, LGDJ, 2ème éd. 2004; « Vers un droit post-moderne? », *in* J. Clam et G. Martin, *Les transformations de la régulation juridique*, LGDJ, 1998, p. 21 et s.

80 Elle est à l'image de ce que Mireille Delmas-Marty appelle « *la grande complexité juridique du monde* » : M. Delmas-Marty, « La grande complexité juridique du monde », *in Mélanges Gérard Timsit*, Bruylant, 2005, p. 89 et s.

81 F. Ost et M. van de Kerchove, « *Le juge entre ordre et désordre* », *in Mélanges Jacques van Compernolle*, Bruylant, 2004, p. 470 et s.

commun[82]; les institutions, les règles et les juridictions ne se substituent pas les unes aux autres, elles interagissent « *en raison de leur aptitude à produire ensemble un effet juridique propre qu'aucune d'elles ne permettrait d'atteindre seule* »[83]. A la rassurante métaphore kelsénienne de la pyramide se substituent les métaphores, perturbantes, du réseau[84] ou des nuages ordonnés[85], dans le cadre de ce que Mireille Delmas-Marty appelle un « *pluralisme ordonné* »[86], qui est juridictionnel autant que juridique[87]. La hiérarchie fait place à la complémentarité, la suprématie à la primauté[88]. Les rapports de systèmes deviennent des rapports de mise en œuvre coopérative s'inscrivant dans une logique d'exécution[89].

Cette réalité-là appelle au développement de procédures de coopération, de dialogue, d'échanges, destinées à trouver des équilibres normatifs[90]. Le

82 Sur la notion d'espace, comme révélateur de la nouvelle organisation juridique qui se met en place au niveau régional : V. M. Delmas-Marty, « Vers une cinétique juridique : D'une approche statique à une approche dynamique de l'ordre juridique », *in* J.-B. Bonnet (dir.), *op. cit.*, p. 145. V. également, sur les notions d'ordre et de système « *pour désigner la réalité juridique de l'intégration* », L. Azoulai et E. Dubout, « Repenser la primauté – L'intégration européenne et la montée de la question identitaire », *in* J.-B. Bonnet (dir.), *op. cit.*, p. 567 et s., spéc. p. 574 et s., qui voit dans le choix du mot ordre le choix de l'institutionnalisme d'Hauriou contre le normativisme kelsénien. Conf. F. Picod, "La Cour de justice de l'Union européenne et les rapports entre les ordres juridiques de l'Union européenne et des Etats membres", préc., pp. 995–996.

83 J.-S. Bergé, « Enrichir les rapports entre ordres juridiques par les rapports de mise en œuvre », *in* J.-B. Bonnet (dir.), *op. cit.*, p. 593 et s., spéc. p. 593.

84 F. Ost et M. van de Kerchove, *De la pyramide au réseau? Pour une théorie dialectique du droit*, Bruxelles, Presses universitaires Saint-Louis, 2002, ainsi que « Repenser la coexistence des ordres – repenser leurs relations », *in* J.-B. Bonnet (dir.), *op. cit.*, p. 151 et s.

85 M. Delmas-Marty, « Au pays des nuages ordonnés », postface de *Pour un droit commun*, Seuil, 1994, p. 283 et s.

86 M. Delmas-Marty, *Les forces imaginantes du droit – Le relatif et l'universel*, Seuil, 2004, pp. 19–20 et 412–414.

87 Rappr. M. Guyomar, « La recherche de l'harmonie entre normes internes et européennes : repenser l'équivalence », *in* J.-B. Bonnet (dir.), *op. cit.*, p. 585 et s., spéc. p. 585.

88 Comp. L. Azoulai et E. Dubout, « Repenser la primauté – L'intégration européenne et la montée de la question identitaire », préc., spéc. p. 569.

89 J.-S. Bergé, « Enrichir les rapports entre ordres juridiques par les rapports de mise en œuvre », préc., *loc. cit.*, qui y voit plus précisément des rapports de mise en œuvre « *institutionnels* », à distinguer des rapports de mise en œuvre « *matériels* », intéressant les droits plus que les institutions.

90 Rappr. G. Canivet, « Les influences croisées entre juridictions nationales et internationales », *RSC* 2005, p. 799 et s.

processus d'intégration est un processus d'interaction[91]. Là où la conception traditionnelle des hiérarchies normatives « *conduit à une détermination prioritairement conflictuelle des relations entre normes juridiques et décisions juridictionnelles* »[92], l'interdépendance postule nécessairement la coopération, loyale, des institutions, ce qui ne signifie pas que l'entreprise soit aisée car une coopération loyale n'est pas une coopération spontanément harmonieuse[93]; c'est une affaire de dosage subtil[94], d'ajustement permanent et, partant, incertain[95], entre les intérêts nationaux et l'intérêt commun[96], si l'on veut bien admettre que le droit de l'Union européenne est le droit commun des Etats membres, « *entendu comme droit de la mitoyenneté* » selon l'expression proposée par Rostane Mehdi et Estelle Brosset, le droit de l'Union étant « *comme le mur mitoyen, un droit tout à la fois intermédiaire, partagé, mais propre à chacun* », ne pouvant se maintenir que « *grâce à une harmonie acceptable entre intérêt commun et intérêt singulier* »[97].

---

91 Rappr. M. Delmas-Marty, « Vers une cinétique juridique : D'une approche statique à une approche dynamique de l'ordre juridique », préc., p. 141 et s. – J.-S. Bergé, « Enrichir les rapports entre ordres juridiques par les rapports de mise en œuvre », préc.

92 D. Simon, « Repenser le raisonnement interprétatif : autonomie ou circulation des principes, des méthodes et des techniques, dans les rapports de systèmes », *in* J.-B. Bonnet (dir.), *op. cit.*, p. 605 et s., spéc. p. 605.

93 V. p. ex. R. Mehdi et E. Brosset, « De quoi le droit de l'Union est-il le nom? A propos du droit de l'Union en tant que droit commun des Etats membres », *in* J.-B. Bonnet (dir.), *op. cit.*, p. 669 et s., spéc. p. 686–687. – F. Ost et M. van de Kerchove, « Repenser la coexistence des ordres – repenser leurs relations », préc., p. 167 : « *Si l'articulation de ces différents ordres juridiques suscite l'apparition de nombreux mécanismes de coopération, elle n'exclut pas la subsistance de différents phénomènes partiels de dissonance* ».

94 « *Balancing emerges as the only viable solution* » : K. Lenaerts, *op. cit.*, p. 14.

95 Rappr. L. Azoulai et E. Dubout, « Repenser la primauté – L'intégration européenne et la montée de la question identitaire », préc., spéc. p. 577 : « *Il y a un excès propre à la manière dont la Cour de justice a développé les caractères de la primauté du droit de l'Union. Cela résulte de la manière idéale dont elle a été conçue et de la volonté qui s'ensuit de donner toutes les preuves de son existence concrète. Cela vient aussi sans doute de la position incertaine dans laquelle se trouve la Cour de justice elle-même, qui cherche dans les caractères de la primauté qu'elle a forgée le miroir de son identité* ».

96 V. déjà P. Pescatore, *Le droit de l'intégration*, préc., p. 85, selon lequel droit communautaire et droits nationaux sont dans un « *rapport entre le tout et la partie, entre l'intérêt commun et l'intérêt particulier* ».

97 V. R. Mehdi et E. Brosset, « De quoi le droit de l'Union est-il le nom? A propos du droit de l'Union en tant que droit commun des Etats membres », préc., p. 672.

Cette coopération loyale est inscrite de manière déclaratoire au fronton du pacte communautaire, à l'article 4 du traité sur l'Union européenne[98]. Elle s'incarne, techniquement, dans le mécanisme de coopération juridictionnelle que constitue la procédure de renvoi préjudiciel dans laquelle Pierre Pescatore voyait un « *lien de communication organique créé entre la Cour communautaire et les juridictions nationales de tout ordre et de tout degré* »[99] et, de fait, la Cour de justice y fait régulièrement référence lorsqu'elle se réfère à l'autonomie procédurale des Etats membres au regard des exigences d'équivalence et d'effectivité[100]. Ce dialogue des juges[101], destiné à faciliter la résolution des conflits de normes en favorisant « *la définition du réglage optimal entre les offices des différents juges* »[102], est concrètement mis en œuvre lorsque la Cour de justice, pour aider les juridictions nationales[103] à satisfaire aux principes d'équivalence et d'effec-

98 Art. 4, 2° TUE : « *En vertu du principe de coopération loyale, l'Union et les États membres se respectent et s'assistent mutuellement dans l'accomplissement des missions découlant des traités.* ». Le principe de coopération innerve plus largement l'Union européenne, sans se limiter aux processus verticaux de coopération entre la Cour de justice et les juridictions nationales : V. A. Rosas, "The European Court of Justice in context: forms and patterns of judicial dialogue", *European Journal of Legal Studies,* 2007, Vol. 1, No. 2, pp. 13–14; il infuse de plus les relations horizontales des juridictions nationales entre elles dans le domaine de la coopération judiciaire : V. L. Cadiet, "The Emergence of a Model of Cooperative Justice in Europe: Horizontal Dimensions", Florence, *European University Institute*, 5 December 2013, *Working Paper Series*, 2014, http://cadmus.eui.eu/handle/1814/32632.

99 P. Pescatore, *op. cit.*, p. 89. Selon L. Azoulai et E. Dubout, *op. cit.*, p. 571, « *l'analyse de Pescatore anticipe mot pour mot l'approche de la Cour dans son arrêt Simmenthal* » (CJCE, 9 mars 1978, aff. C-106/77, *Administration des finances de l'Etat c. SA Simmenthal* », et. P. 577, c'est la procédure du renvoi préjudiciel qui « *a rendu possible l'affirmation de la primauté* » en faisant « *surgir le droit de l'Union et son juge dans le cours d'une procédure judiciaire nationale* ».

100 V. K. Lenaerts, *op. cit. et loc. cit.* : "*Moreover, in accordance with the principle of sincere cooperation laid down in art. 4(3) TEU, national courts are required, so far as possible, to interpret and apply national procedural rules governing the exercise of rights of action in a way that achieves that result. It should be stress that the relationship between EU institutions and national courts is not hierarchical, but co-operative*".

101 Selon l'expression consacrée depuis les conclusions de B. Genevois sur CE, ass., 22 déc. 1978, n° 11604, *Cohn-Bendit,* Rec. Lebon 524.

102 M. Guyomar, « La recherche de l'harmonie entre normes internes et européennes : repenser l'équivalence », *in* J.-B. Bonnet (dir.), *op. cit.*, p. 586 et s., spéc. p. 586.

103 Rappr. CJUE, 9 nov. 2017, aff. C-217/6, *Commission européenne c. Dimos Zagoriou,* n° 43 : « *assister la juridiction de renvoi dans la solution du litige concret pendant devant* elle ».

tivité, définit des directives qui sont une sorte de guide méthodologique[104] destiné à permettre l'unité d'interprétation dans la mise en œuvre de ces principes[105]. C'est ainsi que, s'agissant du *principe d'équivalence*, elle invite le juge national à vérifier l'équivalence des modalités procédurales « *sous l'angle de leur objet, de leur cause et de leurs éléments essentiels* »[106]. En ce qui concerne le *principe d'effectivité*, afin de déterminer si une disposition procédurale nationale rend impossible ou excessivement difficile l'application du droit de l'Union, la Cour appelle les juges nationaux à tenir compte « *de la place de cette disposition dans l'ensemble de la procédure, de son déroulement et de ses particularités devant les diverses instances nationales* »[107] et, dans cette perspective, à « *prendre en considération, le cas échéant, les principes qui sont à la base du système juridictionnel national, tels que la protection de droits de la défense, le principe de sécurité juridique et le bon déroulement de la procédure* »[108].

Jusqu'à présent, l'avis des observateurs réguliers de la jurisprudence de la Cour de justice est que cette coopération s'est avérée fructueuse grâce à « *la modération réciproque des acteurs* »[109], jusqu'à considérer que les rapports entre la Cour de justice et les juridictions nationales sont même entrés, « *au cours des dernières années, dans une ère de rassurante clarté* » et qu'ils paraissent aujourd'hui « *empreints de la sagesse que l'on prête souvent aux connivences qui se sont imposées après de longues périodes de défiance* »[110].

---

104 Rappr. 14 sept. 2016, aff. C-184/15 et C-197/15, *Florentina Martínez Andrés c. Servicio Vasco de Salud et Juan Carlos Castrejana López*, n° 44 : "*La Cour, statuant sur renvoi préjudiciel, peu, néanmoins, apporter des précisions visant à guider ladite juridiction dans son appréciation*".

105 V. T. Debard, *op. cit.*, n° 26–27.

106 V. p. ex. CJCE, 16 mai 2000, aff. C-78/98, *Preston*. – CJUE, 26 janv. 2101, aff. C-118/08, *Transportes urbanos*. – CJUE, 17 mars 2016, aff. C-161/15, *Bensada Benallal*. – CJUE, 9 nov. 2017, aff. C-217/6, préc., n° 20. V. K. Lenaerts, *op. cit.*, 2, pp. 16–19.

107 V. p. ex. CJUE, 3 oct. 2013, aff. C-32/12, *Soledad Duarte Hueros c. Autociba SA. et Automóviles Citroën España SA*, n° 34. – CJUE, 9 nov. 2017, aff. C-217/6, préc.

108 V. p. ex. CJCE, 14 déc. 1995, aff. C-312/93, *Petebroeck*, n° 14. – CJUE, 8 juill. 2010, *Bulicke*, C-246/09, n° 35. – CJUE, 8 sept. 2011, aff. C-177/10, *Rosaldo Santana*, n° 92. – CJUE, 14 sept. 2016, aff. C-184/15 et C-197/15, préc., n° 61. – CJUE, 7 mars 2018, aff. 494/16, *Giuseppa Santoro*.

109 J.-P. Jacqué, *op. cit.*, p. 1121, se référant, en matière de protection des droits fondamentaux, à A. Tizzano, « La protection des droits fondamentaux en Europe et les juridictions constitutionnelles nationales », *Rev. dr. UE* 2006, p. 9 et s.

110 R. Mehdi et E. Brosset, *op. cit.* p. 686. Rappr. J.-P. Jacqué, *op. cit.*, p. 1108 : « *Les différentes juridictions nationales ou internationales, déploient, à travers un dialogue constructif, de louables efforts pour tenter de démêler l'écheveau des contradictions*

Le jugement appelle cependant deux observations. D'abord, la Cour de justice, si elle n'est pas une autorité politique, ne peut cependant pas faire abstraction de la dimension politique des arrêts qu'elle rend et, sans doute, sa jurisprudence révèle-t-elle, ici et là, les signes d'ajustements que nécessite, par exemple, l'émergence du respect revendiqué de l'identité nationale des Etats membres à travers, notamment, certaines de leurs spécificités constitutionnelles[111]. A cet égard, il ne faut pas négliger l'incidence que pourrait avoir à l'avenir, sur le fonctionnement des institutions européennes et, par ricochet, sur la jurisprudence de la Cour de justice, y compris dans le domaine qui nous intéresse ici, ce que Loïc Azoulai et Edouard Dubout appellent « *la montée de la question identitaire* », corrélée au développement du populisme et invitant, selon eux, à « *repenser la primauté* »[112]. Il y a là un élément d'incertitude auquel il faut ajouter, en outre, la nature même de « *ce pouvoir judiciaire européen* » dont Pierre Pescatore avait fait, avec prescience, une des caractéristiques majeures du droit de l'intégration européenne[113]. C'est alors sur les structures du droit national que la jurisprudence de la Cour de justice relative à l'autonomie procédurale des Etats membres exerce son effet perturbateur.

2.2. *Autonomie procédurale et structures du droit*

Cette dernière question est complexe et mériterait une étude à elle seule. Je me bornerai donc ici à quelques observations lapidaires relatives à l'effet perturbateur de la jurisprudence de la Cour de justice sur les sources du droit et les divisions du droit, au regard du moins du droit français.

---

inhérentes aux rapports de système », p. 1110 : « *La survie du système doit beaucoup à la tolérance et à l'ouverture réciproque des juridictions nationales et européennes* » et p. 1141 : « *la sagesse a prévalu jusqu'à présent grâce à l'attitude coopérative des juridictions suprêmes* ».

111 Sur la théorie des « *contre-limites* » développée par certaines juridictions constitutionnelles nationales, V. J.-P. Jacqué, « Quelques considérations sur les rapports de système entre ordres juridiques en Europe », *in* J.-B. Bonnet (dir.), *op. cit.*, p. 1108 et s., spéc. p. 1120 et s. Rappr. D. Simon, « Repenser le raisonnement interprétatif : autonomie ou circulation des principes, des méthodes et des techniques, dans les rapports de systèmes », préc., spéc. p. 627 et s., à propos de la place que prend, au sein du raisonnement interprétatif, la référence à l'identité propre du système, notamment à l'identité constitutionnelle.

112 L. Azoulai et E. Dubout, « Repenser la primauté – L'intégration européenne et la montée de la question identitaire », *in* J.-B. Bonnet (dir.), *op. cit.*, p. 567 et s.

113 P. Pescatore, *op. cit.*, p. 73 et s.

Il apparaît, en premier lieu, que la mise en œuvre coopérative du droit de l'Union européenne par le juge national suppose une exacte et claire connaissance, par celui-ci, des sources du droit de l'Union. Or cette connaissance est problématique en ce qui concerne la jurisprudence de la Cour de justice. La question n'est pas tant celle de savoir si la jurisprudence de la Cour de justice est une source de droit, ce qui peut être discuté[114] comme pour toute jurisprudence[115], que celle de son intelligibilité et de sa prévisibilité, non seulement par les juridictions suprêmes des Etats membres, mais aussi par les juridictions du fond, qui devraient participer pleinement au dialogue de juges, et, plus largement, par les avocats des parties, sans parler des citoyens eux-mêmes qui sont les premiers destinataires de l'effet direct des normes européennes. Les acteurs de la justice nationale sont aussi les acteurs de la justice européenne; ils doivent pouvoir s'en emparer dès la première instance. A défaut de s'imposer par raison d'autorité, comme la loi générale et abstraite, la jurisprudence, particulière et concrète, ne peut s'imposer que par l'autorité de ses raisons, *auctoritate rationis sed non ratione auctoritatis*.

La difficulté est que ces raisons, même si elles sont exposées amplement et précisément, ne le sont, inévitablement, qu'à l'occasion de chaque affaire dont la Cour de justice est saisie sur renvoi préjudiciel et cette casuistique, aléatoire[116], complique considérablement une connaissance systématique de la jurisprudence de la Cour de justice, malgré le soin apporté aux renvois auxquels elle procède à ses arrêts antérieurs et leur contribution à la définition, jugée insuffisante, de « *lignes de jurisprudence* »[117]. Un auteur s'interroge ainsi : « *Par exemple, la Cour de justice a très largement investi le champ des litiges de consommation en ce qui concerne le*

---

114 La jurisprudence de la Cour de justice de l'Union européenne n'apparaît pas toujours comme une source du droit de l'Union européenne : V. cep. M. Blanquet, *op. cit.*, p. 428 et s. – J. Rideau, « Ordre juridique de l'Union européenne – Sources non écrites », préc.

115 Source ou autorité? Source de droit ou source du droit? Le débat est classique : V. not. J. Carbonnier, *Droit civil*, vol. I, Paris, PUF, Quadrige, 2004, pp. p. 190 et s. – L. Cadiet, « Quelques observations, en demi-teinte, sur la prévisibilité du jugement et la jurisprudence concrète », *in La justice du 21ème siècle – Le citoyen au cœur du service public de la justice, Les actes du débat national*, Paris, Ministère de la justice, 2014, pp. 156–159. Ce débat se modernise avec le développement des nouvelles technologies, de l'*open data* des décisions de justice et de l'intelligence artificielle : V. p. ex. P. Deumier, "La jurisprudence d'aujourd'hui et de demain", *RTD civ.* 2017, p. 600 et s. spéc. pp. 604–606.

116 V. p. ex. M. Roccati, *op. cit.*, 1.2.

117 M. Roccati, *op. cit. et loc. cit.*

relevé d'office des clauses abusives, mais quid de ce relevé d'office dans les autres domaines du droit de l'Union? Peut-on transposer à un cas de discrimination fondée sur le sexe ou à toute autre disposition européenne? »[118]. A l'intérieur d'un même domaine, comme celui des clauses abusives, qui donne lieu à une jurisprudence abondante, les distinctions auxquelles se livre la Cour de justice peuvent apparaître « *relativement subtiles* »[119], ce qui peut nuire à la compréhension, par les acteurs nationaux, du fondement et de la portée des solutions adoptées par la Cour de justice et, par voie de conséquence, à l'efficacité de sa jurisprudence même. L'incertitude quant au fondement a déjà été mentionnée en ce qui concerne le principe d'effectivité des arrêts *Rewe* et *Comet* dans sa relation avec la protection juridictionnelle effective de l'article 19,1 TUE et le droit à un recours effectif de l'article 47 CDFUE[120]; l'incertitude quant à la portée tient à la fois à la variabilité du comportement attendu du juge national par la Cour de justice afin d'assurer le respect des principes d'équivalence et d'effectivité[121] et à l' « exportabilité » d'une solution retenue pour un droit national vers d'autres droits nationaux[122], surtout lorsqu'est en cause la conformité « *d'une pratique des juridictions nationales* »[123] avec les exigences du droit de l'Union européenne.

---

118 M. Roccati, *ibidem*.

119 M. Roccati, *ibidem*, qui illustre son propos en confrontant CJUE, 14 juin 2012, aff. C-618/10, *Banco Español de Crédito SA c. Joaquin Calderón Camino*, et CJUE, 12 févr. 2015, aff. C-567/13, *Nóra Baczó*.

120 V. *supra* 1.1. En ce sens, également, J. Nowak, *op. cit.*, 1.2.1.3. – M. Roccati, *op. cit.*, 2.2.

121 Dans certaines affaires, la Cour de justice demeure très générale, requérant simplement du juge national qu'il veille au respect des principes d'équivalence et d'effectivité : ex. CJUE, 9 nov. 2017, aff. C-217/6, *Commission européenne c. Dimos Zagoriou*, préc., n° 12–26; CJUE 13 déc. 2017, aff. C-403/16, *El Hassani*, *D.* 2018, p. 313, obs. Jault-Seseke. Dans d'autres cas, elle attend du juge national qu'il prenne des mesures particulières, préjugeant de l'issue de l'affaire : ex. CJUE, 14 sept. 2016, aff. C-184/15 et C.197/15, *Florentina Martínez Andrés*, préc., n° 34–54, spéc. n° 43 : « *il incombe donc à la juridiction de renvoi…* », n° 52 : « *Plus particulièrement, la juridiction nationale doit s'assurer…* ».

122 V. p. ex. CJUE, 3 oct. 2013, aff. C-32/12, *Soledad Duarte Hueros*, préc., à propos des obstacles procéduraux résultant des règles du code de procédure civile espagnole et contrariant le succès d'une demande en résolution d'un contrat de vente d'un véhicule pour défaut de conformité de celui-ci à un contrat au regard de la directive 1999/44/CE du 25 mai 1999 sur certains aspects de la vente et des garanties de biens de consommation.

123 C'est l'expression retenue par la Cour de justice : V. p. ex. CJUE, 14 sept. 2016, aff. C-184/15 et C.197/15, *Florentina Martínez Andrés*, préc., n° 28.

Ces difficultés sont aggravées par le fait que l'accès aux solutions procédurales définies par la Cour de justice ne se fait pas par la procédure (mesures provisoires, charge de la preuve, autorité de chose jugée, délais de procédure, relevé d'office), mais par la substance du droit en cause (clauses abusives, aides d'Etat, droits de propriété intellectuelle, garantie des biens de consommation, contrats de travail à durée déterminée successifs, etc.), ce qui provoque une connaissance morcelée des solutions procédurales de la Cour de justice et nous amène à la question, finale, de l'effet perturbateur de la jurisprudence de la Cour de justice sur les divisions du droit.

En second et dernier lieu, en effet, le droit de l'Union européenne en général, la jurisprudence de la Cour de justice en particulier, se jouent des divisions qui structurent les droits nationaux.

Les travaux ne manquent pas sur l'ébranlement de la distinction du droit interne et du droit international sous l'effet du droit de l'Union européenne[124], mais aussi entre ce qui relève du droit de l'Union et ce qui n'en relève pas, pas seulement en raison du développement des instruments de coopération judiciaire en matière civile et pénale[125]. Un arrêt rendu par la Cour de justice au début de l'année 2018 dans une affaire *Associação Sindical dos Juízes Portugueses*, en fournit une remarquable illustration, cette affaire opposant le syndicat des juges portugais à la Cour des comptes du Portugal au sujet de la réduction temporaire du montant des rémunérations versées aux membres de cette juridiction dans le cadre des orientations de politique budgétaire de l'Etat portugais. Certes, la politique budgétaire du Portugal était sous contrainte européenne; sans doute était invoquée l'espèce l'atteinte portée par cette mesure de réduction salariale au principe de l'indépendance des juges consacré par l'article 19, 1, al. 2 TUE et par l'article 47 de la Charte des droits fondamentaux de l'Union européenne. Il n'en reste pas moins, comme l'écrivent Rostane Mehdi et Estelle Brosset, que « *la notion de situation purement interne est (…) en voie de démonétisation* »[126]. L'apparition d'une doctrine européaniste a joué un rôle certain dans cette évolution[127]. J'évoque cet aspect pour mémoire car,

124 V. p. ex. Société française pour le droit international, *Droit international, droit communautaire : perspectives actuelles*, Paris, Pedone, 2000. – L. Dubouis, « Introduction », *Droit communautaire, droits nationaux, influences croisées, en hommage à Louis Dubouis*, coll. Monde européen et international, La Documentation française-CERIC, 2000, p. 11.

125 V. *supra* notes 2 et 3.

126 R. Mehdi et E. Brosset, *op. cit.*, p. 685.

127 V. J.-C. Gautron et S. Platon, *op. cit.*

aujourd'hui, ce sont même, et surtout, les distinctions structurant le droit interne qui se trouvent bousculées.

Il en va d'abord ainsi de la distinction du droit privé et du droit public, étrangère au droit européen[128], qui les enveloppe dans un même mouvement. Non seulement, le droit privé s'est européanisé dans sa totalité, y compris en ce qui concerne les relations familiales[129], mais le droit de l'Union européenne a provoqué un déplacement, sinon un dépassement des clivages structurant traditionnellement l'ordre français[130] : clivages *matériels* séparant la sphère publique et la sphère privée[131]; clivages *institutionnels* résultant par exemple du dualisme juridictionnel, permettant ainsi à la Cour de cassation, juridiction suprême de l'ordre judiciaire de ne pas poser une question préjudicielle au Conseil d'Etat, juridiction suprême de l'ordre administratif, lorsque est en cause devant elle, à titre incident, la conformité d'un acte administratif au droit de l'UE[132]. Même si la question ne relève pas à proprement parler de la problématique de l'autonomie procédurale, la manière dont la Cour de justice a été invitée, si ce n'est instrumentalisée, dans le débat français sur la question prioritaire de constitutionnalité, fournit une autre illustration de l'effet perturbateur des normes européennes sur l'architecture juridictionnelle des Etats membres, de la France en l'espèce[133].

---

128 R. Mehdi et E. Brosset, *op. cit.*, p. 687 : « *Le droit de l'UE n'est pas sensible à la distinction 'droit public – droit privé' car elle ne présente, le concernant, aucune véritable valeur heuristique* ».

129 R. Mehdi et E. Brosset, *op. cit.*, pp. 683–684, selon lesquels cette européanisation du droit privé a été rendue possible par la combinaison des libertés fondamentales garanties par les traités tels qu'interprétés par la Cour de justice, du principe de non-discrimination fondée sur la nationalité et du principe de reconnaissance mutuelle.

130 R. Mehdi et E. Brosset, *op. cit.*, pp. 687–688.

131 R. Mehdi et E. Brosset, *op. cit.*, p. 688. – J.-B. Auby, « La distinction du droit public et du droit privé », *in* J.-B. Auby (dir.), *L'influence du droit européen sur les catégories du droit public*, Paris, Dalloz, 2010, p. 300, selon lequel « *le droit de l'UE peut, en fonction de ses seuls impératifs, placer la frontière entre ce qui est propre à la puissance publique, à l'ordre public, ailleurs que là où elle est située par les droits nationaux* ».

132 T. confl.., 17 oct. 2011, n° 3828, *SCEA du Cheneau*, dérogeant ainsi, partiellement, au principe traditionnel issu d'une jurisprudence quasiment séculaire du Tribunal des conflits : T. confl., 16 juin 1923, *Septfonds*. V. M. Gautier, *op. cit.*, pp. 946–948.

133 M. Gautier, *op.cit.*, pp. 948–951, à propos des affaires *Melki* et *Abdeli* : V. C. cass., QPC,16 avr. 2019, n° 10–40.002; CJUE, 22 juin 2010, aff. C-188/10 et 189/10. Conf. Cons. const. 12 mai 2010, n° 210–605 DC, *Loi relative à l'ouverture à la concurrence des jeux d'argent*, et CE 14 mai 2010, n° 312305, *Rujovic*.

En vérité, au-delà de cette incidence sur les relations des juridictions nationales entre elles, y compris sur les relations entre les juridictions suprêmes et les juridictions qui leur sont subordonnées, c'est la séparation des pouvoirs qui est affectée par la jurisprudence de la Cour de justice de l'Union européenne, comme elle l'est aussi d'ailleurs par celle de la Cour européenne des droits de l'homme. Appelé à œuvrer de conserve avec la Cour de justice à la réalisation des objectifs du droit de l'Union et à la protection juridictionnelle effective des citoyens européens, le juge national, juge européen de droit commun, est appelé à s'émanciper de la loi nationale en laissant au besoin inappliquée toute disposition contraire aux principes d'équivalence et d'effectivité. Si certaines dispositions des droits nationaux sont de nature à légitimer cette émancipation, comme l'article 55 de la Constitution française, l'évolution récente de la jurisprudence de la Cour de justice conduit à se demander si cette émancipation n'est pas appelée à trouver dans l'article 47 de la charte des droits fondamentaux de l'Union européenne, relatif au droit à une protection juridictionnelle effective, un fondement renforcé, autonome, quasiment constitutionnel, par rapport au droit national[134], susceptible d'habiliter le juge national, en l'absence de toute législation, à déterminer lui-même de nouveaux types de recours juridictionnel propres à assurer l'effectivité de la protection juridictionnelle des particuliers, ce qui pourrait porter encore plus loin que les solutions consacrées en matière de mesures provisoires ou de responsabilité de l'Etat. La perspective est audacieuse, sans doute politiquement discutable, et elle se heurte d'ores et déjà à certaines limites plus techniques tenant à la forme de ce droit procédural prétorien.

C'est ici la distinction du droit matériel, ou substantiel, et du droit procédural, ou processuel, qui est affectée par le droit de l'Union européenne, qu'il soit issu de la jurisprudence de la Cour de justice ou des instruments de droit dérivé. M. Janek Nowak en a remarquablement traité dans une communication présentée à Maastricht en novembre 2016 lors du congrès *Ius Commune*[135]. En substance, il y oppose deux approches de la procédure civile, l'approche sectorielle et fonctionnelle de l'Union européenne à l'approche horizontale et autonome des Etats membres. Dans l'approche des Etats membres, les règles de procédure civile, contenues dans des codes

---

134 V. p. ex. CJUE, 17 avr. 2018, aff. C-414/16, *Egenberger*, spéc. n° 78 : « *l'article 47 de celle-ci, relatif au droit à une protection juridictionnelle effective, se suffit à lui-même et ne doit pas être précisé par des dispositions du droit de l'Union ou du droit national pour conférer aux particuliers un droit invocable en tant que tel* ».

135 J. T. Nowak, *op. cit.*, spéc. 1.4 : « Different Approaches to Civil Procedure », p. 29 et s.

ou des lois dédiées, couvrent l'ensemble du procès civil, jusques y compris, parfois, l'arbitrage, les modes alternatifs de règlement des conflits, les procédures d'exécution; elles s'appliquent en toute matière et devant l'ensemble des juridictions, sous réserve ici et là de dispositions particulières à certaines juridictions ou à certaine matières[136], qui n'affectent cependant pas l'unité de la législation et de son application jurisprudentielle. Au contraire, dans l'approche européenne, la procédure civile n'est pas considérée dans sa neutralité et sa globalité; elle n'est qu'un instrument au service de droits matériels qui en plient les règles à leur convenance de sorte que, par exemple, les pouvoirs d'office du juge, les règles de preuve ou de prescription, ne seront pas réglés de la même manière selon le contentieux dans lequel ils sont appelés à s'exercer[137]. Les solutions procédurales sont donc dispersées dans une multitude d'instruments ou d'arrêts sans cohérence d'ensemble. M. Nowak ne pense pas que cette distorsion puisse perdurer sur le long terme; la contamination des droits nationaux par l'approche européenne est à craindre, conduisant à une fragmentation des codes nationaux de procédure dont le contenu se disperserait dans des codes ou des lois de droit matériel, à moins que la règle européenne, spécifique au regard de sa fonction au service d'une règle matérielle du droit de l'Union, fasse l'objet, de la part du législateur national, d'une généralisation de nature à préserver l'unité du droit procédural de l'Etat membre[138]. Mais, en définitive, dans les deux cas, le pouvoir du législateur de l'Etat

136 V. exemplairement, dans le code de procédure civile français, les livres 2 (« Dispositions particulières à chaque juridiction » et 3 (« Dispositions particulières à certaines matières »).

137 Une ambigüité doit être ici levée. Sans doute, le droit processuel est traditionnellement un droit sanctionnateur au service du droit matériel (L. Cadiet et E. Jeuland, *op. cit.*, n° 9). Usant d'une judicieuse métaphore, Gérard Cornu et Jean Foyer ont écrit du droit judiciaire qu'il était la « *servante des autres lois* » et, qu'à ce titre, il était « *moins une espèce particulière de loi que la sanction de toutes les autres* » (G. Cornu et J. Foyer, *Procédure civile*, Paris, PUF, 3ème éd. 1996, p. 67). Mais il n'en demeure pas moins, dans cette conception, global et neutre : la finalité matérielle qu'il poursuit est la réalisation des droits substantiels. C'est autre chose de le concevoir de telle manière qu'il serve un certain nombre d'objectifs spécifiques du droit matériel comme, par exemple, la protection du consommateur, du travailleur, de l'assuré, de la victime (V. p. ex. L. Raschel, *Le droit processuel de la responsabilité civile*, préf. L. Cadiet, IRJS éd., 2010).

138 Rappr. M. Campos Sanchez-Bordona, concl. sur CJUE, 5 avr. 2016, C-57/15, *United Video Properties*, n° 3 : « *L'objectif d'harmonisation de certaines règles procédurales des États membres est perceptible dans quelques directives, notamment dans la directive qui habilite la Cour à se prononcer dans une affaire qui, autrement, relèverait exclusivement des États membres. Le champ d'application de ces directives est, logiquement,*

membre d'édicter les règles de procédure civile s'en trouverait affecté, directement ou indirectement.

L'issue est incertaine car l'évolution peut se faire du côté des droits nationaux comme du côté du droit de l'Union.

D'ores et déjà, les droits nationaux, ce qui est le cas du droit français, laissent se développer, en dehors du code de procédure civile, dans des codes de droit matériel, comme le code du commerce, le code de la consommation, le code de l'environnement, le code de la propriété intellectuelle, des pans entiers de règles procédurales provenant du droit de l'Union européenne[139], l'office du juge en matière de clauses abusives[140], la communication et la production des pièces en matière d'actions en dom-

limité à un ou plusieurs secteurs particuliers (la propriété intellectuelle, la protection de la concurrence, l'environnement, la protection des consommateurs, notamment). La multiplication des règles procédurales « sectorielles » – qui ne sont pas toujours cohérentes entre elles – qui doivent être transposées dans les ordres juridiques nationaux peut provoquer comme conséquence indésirable la fragmentation du droit procédural dans les pays qui sont parvenus, après de nombreuses années et un effort codificateur méritoire, à promulguer des lois de procédure civile générales destinées à se substituer précisément à la multiplicité des procédures préalables et à les ramener à une procédure commune. ».

139 Ou non : ainsi, pour l'action de groupe dont les règles, selon la matière litigieuse, sont dispersées dans différents codes de droit matériel, code de la consommation (art. L. et R. 623–1 et s.), code de l'environnement (art. L. 142–3–1), code de la santé publique (art. L. et R. 1143–1), code du travail (art. L. 1134–6 et s.) ou loi spéciale comme la Loi n° 78–17 du 6 janvier 1978 relative à l'informatique, aux fichiers et aux libertés, art. 43 ter. L'édiction de quelques règles générales dans une loi par ailleurs quasiment vidée de son contenu (art. 60–83, L. n° 2016–1547 du 18 novembre 2016 de modernisation de la justice du XXIe siècle), dont est d'ailleurs exclue l'action de groupe en matière de consommation, est loin de remédier aux inconvénients de cette méthode. C'est cependant dans le code de procédure civile qu'ont été accueillies les dispositions règlementaires d'application de ces règles générales d'origine législative : art. 848 à 849–1, réd. D. n° 2019–1133, 11 déc. 2019. Il en résulte un redoutable, et détestable, *patchwork* normatif.

140 Art. R. 632–1 C. consom. : "*Le juge peut relever d'office toutes les dispositions du présent code dans les litiges nés de son application.* (al. 1) *Il écarte d'office, après avoir recueilli les observations des parties, l'application d'une clause dont le caractère abusif ressort des éléments du débat.* (al. 2). La Cour de justice de l'Union européenne ne requiert pas du juge national, tenu par le principe dispositif, qu'il examine d'office chacune des clauses contractuelles qui n'ont pas été attaquées par le consommateur afin de vérifier *proprio motu* si elles peuvent être considérées comme abusives : CJUE 11 mars 2020, aff. C-511/17, *Dalloz.actualité* 31 mars 2020, obs. Pellier.

mages et intérêts du fait des pratiques anticoncurrentielles[141], la protection du secret des affaires devant les juridictions civiles et commerciales[142] ou la protection juridictionnelle contre la contrefaçon[143]; en revanche, et paradoxalement, c'est dans le code de procédure civile (livre 5, art. 1528–1567) qu'a été accueilli le décret n° 2012–66 du 20 janvier 2012 relatif à la résolution amiable des différends, pris pour l'application de l'ordonnance n° 2011–1540 du 16 novembre 2011 portant transposition de la directive 2008/52/CE du 21 mai 2008 sur certains aspects de la médiation en matière civile et commerciale.

Quant au droit de l'Union, il a développé des instruments sectoriels de droit dérivé contenant des dispositions d'ordre procédural[144], qui sont autant d'outils d'encadrement législatif de l'autonomie procédurale des Etats membres[145] complétant l'encadrement jurisprudentiel de la Cour de justice. La méthode a ses vertus, notamment pour garantir, mieux que ne peut le faire la jurisprudence, une protection équivalente dans toute l'Union; mais elle a aussi ses limites en ce qu'elle ne remédie pas à la fragmentation de la procédure civile, pas plus que ne peut y remédier la consécration des solutions de la Cour dans les instruments législatifs pertinents[146]. Le droit de l'Union pourrait aussi s'orienter vers une approche

---

141 V. C. com., art. L. 483–1 et s., réd. Ord. n° 2017–303, 9 mars 2017, compl. D. n° 2017–305, 9 mars 2017, transposant la directive 2014/104/UE du 26 novembre 2014 relative à certaines règles régissant les actions en dommages et intérêts en droit national pour les infractions aux dispositions du droit de la concurrence des Etats membres et de l'Union européenne.

142 Art. L. 153–1 et L. 153–2 C. com., L. réd. n° 2018–670, 30 juill. 2018 relative à la protection du secret des affaires, transposant la directive 2016/943/UE du 8 juin 2016 sur la protection des savoir-faire et des informations commerciales non divulguées.

143 C. propr. intell., art. L. 521–1 et s., L. 615–3 et s., L. 623–7 et s., L. 716–3 et s., réd. L. n° 2007–1544, 29 oct. 2007 de lutte contre la contrefaçon, compl. D. n° 2008–624, 27 juin 2008 pris pour l'application de la loi n° 2007–1544 du 29 octobre 2007, transposant la directive 2004/48/CE du Parlement européen et du Conseil du 29 avril 2004 relative au respect des droits de propriété intellectuelle.

144 V. p. ex. *supra* notes 134–137.

145 V. M. Roccati, *op. cit.*, 2.

146 V. d'ailleurs le jugement porté par la Commission des affaires juridiques du Parlement européen, dans son Projet de rapport contenant des recommandations à la Commission relatives à des normes minimales communes pour les procédures civiles dans l'Union européenne, Parlement européen – Commission des affaires juridiques, 2015/2084(INL), 10 févr. 2017, point H : « *la nature fragmentaire de l'harmonisation des procédures au niveau de l'Union a été maintes fois critiquée et que l'émergence d'un droit de l'Union de type sectoriel dans les procédures civiles ne favorise guère la cohérence des systèmes nationaux de procédure civile ni des divers instruments*

globale et horizontale ainsi que le projet en a été envisagé au sein du parlement européen avec la proposition de recommandations à la Commission relatives à des normes minimales communes pour les procédures civiles dans l'Union européenne. Faisant référence aux travaux actuellement menés par l'Institut européen du droit (*European law institute*), conjointement avec UNIDROIT, sur l'élaboration d'un *corpus* de *Règles européennes de procédure civile*[147]. Ce rapport mentionne, dans ses visas, la jurisprudence de la Cour de justice de l'Union européenne (CJUE) sur les principes de l'autonomie procédurale nationale et de la protection juridictionnelle effective, spécialement de l'arrêt Comet[148] et de l'arrêt UNIBET[149]. Mais, s'il rend hommage au « *rôle capital que joue la Cour de justice dans la mise en place des fondements de la procédure civile dans l'Union, puisqu'elle a défini le sens de cette procédure dans l'ordre juridique de l'Union* » et « *même si la jurisprudence de la Cour a fixé des normes procédurales qui font aujourd'hui partie intégrante du régime procédural de l'Union* », ce rapport souligne cependant que « *le rôle de la Cour devrait essentiellement être considéré comme un rôle d'interprétation plutôt que de définition des normes* ». Il serait présomptueux d'affirmer que la messe est dite. La question est en tout cas posée de savoir si, vingt ans après le projet Storme, les résistances des Etats membres seront définitivement toujours aussi fortes pour faire obstacle à ce que le législateur de l'Union investisse davantage le champ de la procédure[150].

C'est mon souhait personnel, mais ce n'est que le souhait d'un Huron au palais du Kirchberg.

---

de l'Union », Au demeurant, ainsi que l'observe M. Roccati, *op. cit. et loc. cit.*, le législateur européen s'est montré très discret dans sa proposition de directive « *alors même que la Cour de justice avait déjà bien affirmé sa jurisprudence relative au relevé d'office des clauses abusives* » : Proposition de directive relative aux droits des consommateurs COM(2008) 614 final, 8 oct. 2008, art. 38 : « *Les États membres habilitent les tribunaux ou les autorités administratives à mettre en œuvre des moyens adéquats et efficaces pour empêcher que les professionnels continuent d'utiliser des clauses jugées abusives* ».

147 Projet de rapport contenant des recommandations à la Commission relatives à des normes minimales communes pour les procédures civiles dans l'Union européenne, préc.

148 V. *supra* notes 10 et 35.

149 CJCE, 13 mars 2007, C-432/05, *Unibet (London) Ltd c. Justitiekanslern :* en l'absence de dispositions de l'Union harmonisant les modalités procédurales, la primauté des États membres pour fixer des modalités procédurales pour l'application des droits conférés par l'Union ne s'étend pas à l'ouverture de nouvelles voies de recours dans les ordres juridiques nationaux pour garantir l'applicabilité du droit de l'Union.

150 Conf. M. Roccati, *op. cit. et loc. cit.*

La Charte des droits fondamentaux et les nouvelles frontières de l'autonomie procédurale des États membres L'exemple du droit européen de la procédure civile

Michail Vilaras[*]

Table of Contents

---

[*] Juge à la Cour de justice de l'Union européenne.

Merci Monsieur le Président,
Mesdames et Messieurs,

Dans le peu de temps qui m'est imparti, je m'efforcerai, sinon de définir, à tout le moins d'esquisser les paramètres de la problématique relative à ce que l'on pourrait qualifier de « nouvelles frontières » de l'autonomie procédurale des États membres dessinées par la Charte des droits fondamentaux de l'Union européenne.

À cette fin, l'une des première questions qui se pose, est celle de savoir si la Cour a, peut, ou encore doit, substituer au contrôle classique du respect des principes d'équivalence et d'effectivité qu'elle utilise pour encadrer l'autonomie institutionnelle et procédurale dont jouissent les États membres, en dehors du domaine harmonisé par le législateur de l'Union, un contrôle de non-discrimination, au titre de l'article 18 TFUE, et de proportionnalité au titre de l'article 47 de la Charte des droits fondamentaux?

Il n'est, je crois, pas nécessaire de rappeler ici ce qu'est le principe d'autonomie procédurale et ce que recouvre le contrôle du respect des principes d'équivalence et d'effectivité, ni de longuement décrire ce que ces principes entretiennent de commun avec le principe de protection juridictionnelle effective.

Je me bornerai à rappeler que, comme la Cour a pu le relever, les « exigences d'équivalence et d'effectivité expriment l'obligation générale pour les États membres d'assurer la protection juridictionnelle des droits que les justiciables tirent du droit de l'Union »[1].

Il n'est, en revanche, pas inutile de souligner que la pertinence du questionnement trouve un fondement sérieux dans l'évolution récente de la jurisprudence de la Cour, à tout le moins dans certains domaines.

Ainsi, dans le domaine des marchés publics, qui se caractérise par l'existence de directives procédant à l'harmonisation à la fois des dispositions matérielles et des dispositions procédurales des États membres [je vise par là la directive 89/665[2] et la directive 92/13[3], concernant le procédures de recours en matière de passation des marchés publics], la Cour est passée

1 Voir arrêts du 15 avril 2008, *Impact* (C-268/06, EU:C:2008:223, point 47); du 29 octobre 2009, *Pontin* (C-63/08, EU:C:2009:666, point 44); du 18 mars 2010, *Alassini e.a.* (C-317/08 à C-320/08, EU:C:2010:146, point 49).

2 Directive 89/665/CEE du Conseil, du 21 décembre 1989, portant coordination des dispositions législatives, réglementaires et administratives relatives à l'application des procédures de recours en matière de passation des marchés publics de fournitures et de travaux, JO 1989, L 395, p. 33.

3 Directive 92/13/CEE du Conseil, du 25 février 1992, portant coordination des dispositions législatives, réglementaires et administratives relatives à l'application des

d'un contrôle du respect des principes d'équivalence et d'effectivité à un contrôle du respect de l'effet utile des directives, telles qu'interprétées à la lumière des exigences de l'article 47 de la Charte.

Je me permets, à cet égard, de vous renvoyer à l'arrêt du 15 septembre 2016, *Star Storage e.a.*[4], qui constitue la première manifestation de ce mouvement jurisprudentiel.

D'autres arrêts s'inscrivent dans ce mouvement de substitution. L'arrêt rendu par la Grande chambre, le 8 novembre 2016, *Lesoochranárske zoskupenie VLK*[5], concernant la convention d'Aarhus du 25 juin 1998, sur l'accès à l'information, la participation du public au processus décisionnel et l'accès à la justice en matière d'environnement, en constitue un autre exemple topique.

C'est également à la lumière de l'article 47 de la Charte que la Cour a, dans certaines affaires, examiné la définition par les États membres des modalités procédurales de recours en justice dans le domaine du droit d'asile et de l'immigration[6].

Les trois domaines ainsi répertoriés, marchés publics, protection de l'environnement et asile et immigration constituent autant de branches de ce que l'on peut considérer comme relevant du « droit administratif de l'Union ».

Dans ces domaines, le droit de l'Union se caractérise par l'existence de dispositions explicites garantissant le droit à une protection juridictionnelle effective. Certes, ces normes sont souvent minimales, en ce sens qu'elles se bornent à définir l'objectif, garantir une protection juridictionnelle effective, en imposant en termes plus ou moins généraux l'obligation de prévoir des voies de recours appropriées, pour laisser aux États membres le soin de régler les détails institutionnels et procéduraux.

Toutefois, quand bien même les compétences résiduelles ainsi conservées par les États membres dans la mise en œuvre de l'objectif de protection juridictionnelle effective s'apparentent, ni plus ni moins, à l'ancienne autonomie procédurale, il demeure que la Cour tend à contrôler leur compatibilité avec le droit de l'Union non plus à l'aune des principes d'équiva-

---

règles communautaires sur les procédures de passation des marchés des entités opérant dans les secteurs de l'eau, de l'énergie, des transports et des télécommunications, JO 1992, L 76, p. 14.

4 C-439/14 et C-488/14, EU:C:2016:688.

5 C-243/15, EU:C:2016:838.

6 Voir arrêt du 19 juin 2018, *Gnandi* (C-181/16, EU:C:2018:465), points 52 et suivants.

lence et d'effectivité, mais bien à la lumière des exigences découlant de l'article 47 de la Charte.

Ce mouvement n'est cependant pas totalement univoque, à tout le moins pas encore.

En effet, la jurisprudence de la Cour opérant un contrôle d'équivalence et d'effectivité continue à se développer, dans les autres domaines du droit de l'Union, mais parfois aussi dans ces mêmes domaines.

Il peut ainsi être observé que c'est dans le cadre d'un contrôle plus classique du respect des principes d'effectivité et d'équivalence que la Cour analyse le respect par les États membres des exigences des droits de la défense dans le cadre des procédures administratives en matière d'asile et d'immigration[7].

De même, interrogée dans l'affaire *El Hassani*[8] sur la question de savoir si l'article 32, paragraphe 3, du code des visas[9], lu à la lumière de l'article 47 de la Charte, doit être interprété en ce sens qu'il impose aux États membres l'obligation de prévoir un recours juridictionnel, ce n'est pas sur le fondement de l'article 47 de la Charte que la Cour a construit sa réponse, mais sur une analyse classique en termes de respect des principes d'effectivité et d'équivalence.

Nombreux, à vrai dire, sont les arrêts qui, avant mais aussi après le prononcé des arrêts *Star Storage e.a.* et *Lesoochranárske zoskupenie VLK*, opèrent un contrôle « classique » de l'autonomie procédurale, en intégrant, le cas échéant, un contrôle au titre de l'article 47 de la Charte dans le cadre du contrôle du respect du principe d'effectivité. Dans une telle perspective, l'analyse de la réglementation nationale à la lumière de l'article 47 de la Charte permet à la Cour d'intensifier le contrôle usuel du respect du principe d'effectivité.

Or, il se trouve que la jurisprudence de la Cour intéressant le droit de la procédure civile a ceci de particulier qu'elle illustre parfaitement ces différentes tendances.

En effet, et tout d'abord, la jurisprudence de la Cour relative à l'interprétation de la directive 93/13/CEE du Conseil, du 5 avril 1993, concernant

---

7 Sur les droits de la défense, au plan administratif : arrêts du 10 septembre 2013, *G. et R.* (C-383/13 PPU, EU:C:2013:533); du 5 novembre 2014, *Mukarubega* (C-166/13, EU:C:2014:2336); arrêt du 11 décembre 2014, *Boudjlida* (C-249/13, EU:C:2014:2431).

8 Arrêt du 13 décembre 2017, *El Hassani* (C-403/16, EU:C:2017:960).

9 Règlement (CE) n° 810/2009 du Parlement européen et du Conseil, du 13 juillet 2009, établissant un code communautaire des visas, JO 2009, L 243, p. 1.

les clauses abusives dans les contrats conclus avec les consommateurs[10] fournit plusieurs exemples d'arrêts intégrant l'article 47 de la Charte dans le contrôle classique du principe d'effectivité.

Mais c'est également dans le domaine de la procédure civile que l'on trouve sans doute les exemples les plus significatifs d'une substitution d'un contrôle au regard de la Charte au contrôle du respect des principes d'effectivité et d'équivalence.

Le domaine de la procédure civile constitue, ainsi, un très bon observatoire des nouvelles frontières de l'autonomie institutionnelle et procédurale nationale. Il pourrait même apparaître comme l'un des principaux laboratoires où se forgent les outils appelés à encadrer l'exercice par les États membres des compétences qui sont les leurs dans le domaine de leur organisation juridictionnelle et procédurale au sens large.

1. *Le renforcement du contrôle de l'effectivité du droit de l'Union à travers l'intégration de la Charte dans le contrôle (l'exemple de la jurisprudence sur les clauses abusives)*

Je rappelle pour mémoire que, afin de garantir la protection effective de consommateurs poursuivie par la directive 93/13 concernant les clauses abusives dans les contrats, la Cour a posé le principe que les juridictions nationales devaient pouvoir apprécier d'office le caractère abusif d'une clause contractuelle relevant du champ d'application de la directive 93/13[11].

Rapidement, la Cour a été confrontée à des réglementations venant limiter la portée de cette faculté. C'est à l'aune des principes d'équivalence et d'effectivité qu'elle a tout naturellement examiné, dans un premier temps, la compatibilité des réglementations de cette nature, avant, dans un second temps, d'intégrer dans son contrôle les exigences découlant de l'article 47 de la Charte.

Encore faut-il préciser que cette intégration s'opère de manière variable : il est des cas dans lesquels la Cour intègre la Charte dans le contrôle du respect du principe d'effectivité, et d'autres où elle substitue le contrôle du respect de la charte au contrôle du principe d'effectivité[12].

---

10 JO 1993, L 95, p. 29.

11 Arrêt du 27 juin 2000, *Océano Grupo Editorial et Salvat Editores* (C-240/98 à C-244/98, EU:C:2000:346, points 26 à 29).

12 Voir arrêt du 31 mai 2018, *Sziber* (C-483/16, EU:C:2018:367, points 29 et 35).

1.1. *La définition initiale des limites à l'autonomie procédurale nationale : la jurisprudence classique opérant un double contrôle d'équivalence et d'effectivité*

Dans une première étape du développement de sa jurisprudence « Clauses abusives », c'est suivant une logique d'autonomie procédurale que la Cour s'est employée à encadrer les compétences des États membres, mais en s'écartant, à tout le moins formellement, de la formulation traditionnelle du principe.

Ainsi, par exemple, dans l'affaire ayant donné lieu à l'arrêt du 21 novembre 2002, *Cofidis*[13], elle s'est opposée à une règle portant fixation, dans les procédures ayant pour objet l'exécution de clauses abusives, d'une limite temporelle au pouvoir du juge d'écarter, d'office ou à la suite d'une exception soulevée par le consommateur, une telle clause. Une telle règle de forclusion est, en effet, de nature à porter atteinte à l'effectivité de la protection voulue par les articles 6 et 7 de la directive 93/13. Bien que la Cour se soit abstenue, dans son arrêt, de rappeler les termes de sa jurisprudence classique concernant l'autonomie procédurale des États membres, c'est bien à un contrôle du respect du principe d'effectivité auquel elle se livre. Elle conclut, ainsi :

> « *une disposition procédurale qui interdit au juge national, à l'expiration d'un délai de forclusion, de relever, d'office ou à la suite d'une exception soulevée par un consommateur, le caractère abusif d'une clause dont l'exécution est demandée par le professionnel,* est de nature à rendre excessivement difficile, *dans les litiges auxquels les consommateurs sont défendeurs, l'application de la protection que la directive entend leur conférer.* »

Cette approche sera confirmée dès l'arrêt suivant, à savoir l'arrêt du 26 octobre 2006, *Mostaza Claro*[14].

Je pourrais citer nombre d'autres exemples, mais il ne me semble pas nécessaire de consacrer de trop longs développements à cet égard.

Ce qu'il convient de retenir, c'est que, quel que soit le contexte procédural dans lequel la question de l'obligation éventuelle pour les juges nationaux de soulever d'office le caractère abusif des clauses contractuelles se pose, c'est dans le cadre des limites à l'autonomie procédurale nationale qu'il y est répondu. Les juges doivent ainsi examiner d'office le caractère

---

13 C-473/00, EU:C:2002:705, points 35 et 36.

14 C-168/05, EU:C:2006:675.

abusif des clauses contractuelles, **dès lors qu'ils disposent des éléments de droit et de fait nécessaires à cet effet.**

1.2. *L'évolution du contrôle des limites à l'autonomie procédurale induite par l'entrée en vigueur de la Charte*

Cette ligne classique d'analyse des restrictions apportées aux pouvoirs des juridictions nationales dans le domaine d'application de la directive 93/13 va cependant progressivement s'enrichir avec l'entrée en vigueur de la Charte. Deux tendances principales peuvent être distinguées.

La première, la plus importante en nombre, consiste à étoffer le contrôle du respect du principe d'effectivité avec les exigences découlant de l'article 47 de la Charte.

La seconde, constituée pour l'instant d'une seule affaire, consiste à substituer le contrôle au titre de l'article 47 de la Charte au contrôle du respect du principe d'effectivité.

À vrai dire, comme on le verra, la jurisprudence fournit des exemples d'une troisième tendance, consistant à juxtaposer et à cumuler les deux types de contrôle.

1.2.1. *L'intégration du contrôle au titre de la Charte au contrôle du respect du principe d'effectivité : la jurisprudence opérant un double contrôle d'équivalence et d'effectivité renforcé par la Charte*

C'est dans son arrêt du 21 février 2013, *Banif Plus Bank* (C-472/11, EU:C:2013:88) que la Cour a, pour la première fois, intégré l'article 47 de la Charte dans le cadre de son examen du contrôle du respect du principe d'effectivité. La Cour était, en l'occurrence, saisie d'une demande visant à déterminer les conséquences à tirer de la constatation du caractère abusif d'une clause, étant précisé que l'article 6, paragraphe 1, de la directive 93/13 exige que les États membres prévoient qu'une telle clause ne lie pas les consommateurs « *dans les conditions fixées dans leurs droits nationaux* ».

C'est sur le terrain de l'autonomie procédurale que la Cour va s'employer à donner réponse à la question, en se livrant à un contrôle du respect du principe d'effectivité. Elle va, toutefois, pour la première fois, intégrer l'article 47 de la Charte à son contrôle :

> « 27 *S'agissant de l'obligation d'assurer l'effectivité de la protection prévue par la directive en ce qui concerne la sanction d'une clause abusive, la Cour*

a déjà précisé que le juge national doit tirer toutes les conséquences qui, selon le droit national, découlent de la constatation du caractère abusif de la clause en cause afin de s'assurer que le consommateur n'est pas lié par celle-ci (arrêt Asturcom Telecomunicaciones, précité, point 59). La Cour a toutefois précisé que le juge national n'est pas tenu, en vertu de la directive, d'écarter l'application de la clause en cause si le consommateur, après avoir été avisé par ledit juge, entend ne pas en faire valoir le caractère abusif et non contraignant (voir arrêt Pannon GSM, précité, points 33 et 35).
28 Il découle de cette jurisprudence que la pleine efficacité de la protection prévue par la directive requiert que le juge national qui a constaté d'office le caractère abusif d'une clause puisse tirer toutes les conséquences de cette constatation, sans attendre que le consommateur, informé de ses droits, présente une déclaration demandant que ladite clause soit annulée.
29 Toutefois, en mettant en œuvre le droit de l'Union, le juge national doit également respecter les exigences d'une protection juridictionnelle effective des droits que les justiciables tirent du droit de l'Union, telle qu'elle est garantie par l'article 47 de la charte des droits fondamentaux de l'Union européenne. Parmi ces exigences figure le principe du contradictoire, *qui fait partie des droits de la défense et qui s'impose au juge notamment lorsqu'il tranche un litige sur la base d'un motif retenu d'office (voir, en ce sens, arrêt du 2 décembre 2009, Commission/Irlande e.a., C-89/08 P, Rec. p. I-11245, points 50 ainsi que 54). »*

En l'occurrence, la Cour jugera que la règle nationale en cause dans le litige au principal, selon laquelle le juge qui a relevé d'office une cause de nullité doit en avertir les parties et leur donner la possibilité de faire une déclaration sur l'éventuelle constatation de l'absence de validité du rapport de droit concerné, répond à cette exigence.

Ce premier arrêt sera suivi de plusieurs autres reproduisant globalement la même ligne de raisonnement :

- arrêt du 27 février 2014, *Pohotovosť* (C-470/12, EU:C:2014:101)
- arrêt du 17 juillet 2014, *Sánchez Morcillo et Abril García* (C-169/14, EU:C:2014:2099)
- arrêt du 10 septembre 2014, *Kušionová* (C-34/13, EU:C:2014:2189)

Ce qui ressort nettement de cette jurisprudence, sans qu'il soit besoin d'en faire revue dans le détail, c'est que le principe d'effectivité, dans son acception traditionnelle, ne permet pas d'appréhender les réglementations nationales restrictives qui affectent les différentes composantes du droit à une protection juridictionnelle effective et/ou droit à un recours effectif et à accéder à un tribunal impartial : le principe du contradictoire dans l'affaire *Banif Plus Bank*, le principe d'égalité des armes dans l'affaire *Sánchez Morcillo et Abril García*, le droit à l'aide juridictionnelle dans l'affaire *Pohotovosť* sont les chevaux de Troie de la Charte dans la logique traditionnelle de l'autonomie procédurale nationale.

Cette ligne de jurisprudence, il faut le souligner, n'a cependant pas totalement remplacé la ligne de jurisprudence traditionnelle : les deux lignes cohabitent donc et se développent en parallèle, avec une troisième, plus récente, que je vais maintenant présenter.

1.2.2. *La substitution du contrôle au titre de la Charte au contrôle du respect du principe d'effectivité : la jurisprudence opérant un double contrôle d'équivalence et au titre de la Charte*

La jurisprudence offre, en effet, un autre exemple de mixité du contrôle opéré par la Cour, mêlant un contrôle du respect du principe d'équivalence et un contrôle au titre de l'article 47 de la Charte, mais totalement détaché du contrôle du respect du principe d'effectivité.

Dans l'affaire *Sziber*[15], la Cour était interrogée sur le point de savoir si l'article 7 de la directive 93/13 devait être interprété en ce sens qu'il s'oppose à une réglementation nationale qui prévoit des exigences procédurales spécifiques pour des recours formés par des consommateurs ayant conclu des contrats de prêt libellés en devise étrangère contenant une clause relative à l'écart du taux de change et/ou une clause concernant l'option de modification unilatérale.

D'emblée la Cour a considéré que, eu égard à l'objet du litige au principal, il convenait de procéder à l'interprétation de la directive 93/13, lue à la lumière des dispositions pertinentes de la Charte, notamment de son l'article 47, consacrant le droit à une protection juridictionnelle effective. C'est toutefois bien à un contrôle mixte auquel la Cour va finalement procéder, en se plaçant sur le terrain de l'autonomie procédurale et en se livrant, d'une part, à un contrôle du respect du principe d'équivalence et, d'autre part, à un contrôle du respect du droit à une protection juridictionnelle effective :

> « *Si la Cour a ainsi déjà encadré, à plusieurs égards et en tenant compte des exigences de l'article 6, paragraphe 1, et de l'article 7, paragraphe 1, de la directive 93/13, la manière selon laquelle le juge national doit assurer la*

15 Arrêt du 31 mai 2018, *Sziber* (C-483/16, EU:C:2018:367, points 29).

protection des droits que les consommateurs tirent de cette directive, il n'en reste pas moins que, en principe, le droit de l'Union n'harmonise pas les procédures applicables à l'examen du caractère prétendument abusif d'une clause contractuelle, et que celles-ci relèvent, dès lors, de l'ordre juridique interne des États membres, à condition, toutefois, qu'elles ne soient pas moins favorables que celles régissant des situations similaires soumises au droit interne (principe d'équivalence) et qu'elles prévoient une protection juridictionnelle effective, telle que prévue à l'article 47 de la Charte *(voir, en ce sens, arrêt du 14 avril 2016, Sales Sinués et Drame Ba, C-381/14 et C-385/14,* EU:C:2016:252, *point 32 ainsi que jurisprudence citée).* »

Il est à noter que, dans ce point, la Cour se réfère expressément au point 32 de l'arrêt du 14 avril 2016, *Sales Sinués et Drame Ba*[16], alors même que ce dernier se référait de manière traditionnelle aux deux principes d'effectivité et d'équivalence, sans même mentionner la Charte, pas plus, du reste, que l'arrêt du 5 décembre 2013, *Asociación de Consumidores Independientes de Castilla y León* qu'il citait[17].

Cet arrêt est, à ma connaissance, unique.

Il importe cependant de préciser que les deux tendances évoquées ci-dessus, répertoriées dans le domaine d'application de la directive 93/13, ne sont nullement exclusives d'autres modalités du contrôle opéré par la Cour.

1.2.3. *La juxtaposition du contrôle au titre de la Charte et du contrôle du respect des principes d'équivalence et d'effectivité : la jurisprudence opérant un triple contrôle d'équivalence, d'effectivité et au titre de la Charte*

La Cour, en effet, avait déjà expérimenté, avant l'adoption de son arrêt du 21 février 2013, *Banif Plus Bank*[18], une autre modalité de contrôle, en examinant une réglementation nationale, en premier lieu, au titre du contrôle du respect des principes d'équivalence et d'effectivité puis, en second lieu, au titre de l'article 47 la Charte, en l'occurrence dans l'arrêt du 18 mars 2010, *Alassini e.a.*[19].

---

16 C-381/14 et C-385/14, EU:C:2016:252.
17 C-413/12, EU:C:2013:800, point 30.
18 C-472/11, EU:C:2013:88.
19 C-317/08 à C-320/08, EU:C:2010:146.

Dans cette affaire, la question qui se posait était de savoir si la directive 2002/22/CE du Parlement européen et du Conseil, du 7 mars 2002, concernant le service universel et les droits des utilisateurs au regard des réseaux et services de communications électroniques (directive « service universel »)[20] et le principe de protection juridictionnelle effective s'opposait à une réglementation nationale, italienne en l'occurrence, en vertu de laquelle les litiges en matière de services de communications électroniques entre utilisateurs finals et fournisseurs de ces services doivent faire l'objet d'une tentative de conciliation extrajudiciaire obligatoire comme condition de recevabilité des recours juridictionnels.

La Cour juge, en l'occurrence qu'une telle réglementation n'est incompatible ni avec les principes d'effectivité et d'équivalence, ni avec l'article 47 de la Charte.

2. *La substitution du contrôle au titre de la Charte au contrôle traditionnel de l'effectivité : une approche exceptionnelle pour des cas particuliers? la jurisprudence supprimant le contrôle d'équivalence et d'effectivité*

Le mouvement d'intensification du contrôle de l'effectivité du droit de l'Union lié à l'intégration du contrôle au titre de la Charte examiné ci-dessus, à travers l'exemple de la jurisprudence sur les clauses abusives, n'est pas exclusif d'autres tendances de la jurisprudence.

La jurisprudence de la Cour intéressant le droit de la procédure civile des États membres au sens large fournit en effet des exemples dans lesquels la Cour s'est livrée à un contrôle direct au titre de la Charte, sans se référer aux principes d'équivalence et d'effectivité, alors même que l'affaire s'y prêtait assurément parfaitement.

L'arrêt du 22 décembre 2010, *DEB*[21], dans lequel la Cour consacre l'existence d'un droit à l'aide juridictionnelle des personnes morales, sur le fondement de l'article 47 de la Charte, en constitue un exemple particulièrement parlant.

Dans cette affaire, la juridiction de renvoi demandait si les principes d'équivalence et d'effectivité devaient être interprétés en ce sens qu'ils s'opposaient à une réglementation nationale qui subordonnait l'exercice d'une action en réparation au paiement d'une avance sur frais et prévoyait

20 JO 2002, L 108, p. 5.
21 C-279/09, EU:C:2010:811.

que l'aide judiciaire ne pouvait être accordée à une personne morale qui n'est pas en mesure de faire cette avance.

La Cour a choisi de reformuler la question, et d'examiner la réglementation nationale au regard de l'article 47 de la Charte seulement (point 33). Se livrant notamment à un examen minutieux de la jurisprudence pertinente de la Cour européennes droits de l'homme, la Cour a jugé que « *le principe de protection juridictionnelle effective, tel que consacré à l'article 47 de la charte, doit être interprété en ce sens qu'il n'est pas exclu qu'il soit invoqué par des personnes morales et que l'aide octroyée en application de ce principe peut couvrir, notamment, la dispense du paiement de l'avance des frais de procédure et/ou l'assistance d'un avocat* ».

Ce qu'il est remarquable de noter dans cette affaire, c'est que la Cour ne tranche pas elle-même définitivement la question : elle renvoie au juge national le soin de « *vérifier si les conditions d'octroi de l'aide judiciaire constituent une limitation du droit d'accès aux tribunaux qui porte atteinte à ce droit dans sa substance même, si elles tendent à un but légitime et s'il existe un rapport raisonnable de proportionnalité entre les moyens employés et le but visé* ».

Certes, les exemples de ce type de raisonnements et d'analyses sont plus nombreux dans le domaine du droit administratif.

Mais la Cour l'a également récemment utilisé dans son arrêt du 14 juin 2017, *Menini et Rampanelli*[22], qui posait une question proche de celle qui se posait dans l'arrêt du 18 mars 2010, *Alassini e.a.*[23].

La question qui se posait était en effet celle de savoir si le droit de l'Union s'opposait à une réglementation nationale, qui prévoyait, notamment, comme dans l'affaire *Alassini e.a.*, le recours obligatoire à une procédure de médiation, dans les litiges visés à l'article 2, paragraphe 1, de la directive 2013/11/UE du Parlement européen et du Conseil, du 21 mai 2013, relative au règlement extrajudiciaire des litiges de consommation et modifiant le règlement (CE) n° 2006/2004 et la directive 2009/22/CE (directive relative au RELC)[24], comme condition de recevabilité de la demande en justice relative à ces mêmes litiges.

À la différence de l'arrêt dans l'affaire *Alassini e.a.*, c'est sur le seul fondement du principe de protection juridictionnelle effective que la Cour examine la question, concluant en l'occurrence à la compatibilité de la réglementation nationale.

---

22 C-75/16, EU:C:2017:457.

23 C-317/08 à C-320/08, EU:C:2010:146.

24 JO 2013, L 165, p. 6.

3. *Propos conclusifs*

Que peut-on tirer de cette analyse?

D'aucuns pourraient voir dans cette coexistence de lignes de jurisprudence diverses une certaine cacophonie, la marque d'un certain manque de rigueur dans les analyses, voire, plus grave, le témoignage de divergences de vues, de dissensions, entre les différentes formations de jugement de la Cour.

Je considère, pour ma part, qu'il suffit de prendre un peu de hauteur pour comprendre ce qui est à l'œuvre.

L'analyse de l'incidence du droit européen sur le droit de la procédure civile des États membres est, en réalité, très illustrative de l'évolution des outils utilisés par la Cour pour garantir l'effectivité des droits que les justiciables tirent du droit de l'Union et le cas échéant, quand cela s'avère nécessaire, assurer la primauté du droit de l'Union.

Ce qui est à l'œuvre, c'est un processus de normalisation des procédures administratives, civiles, commerciales ou encore pénales des États membres, opéré au cas par cas par la Cour de justice, qui utilise à ces effets les outils à sa disposition pour résoudre les problèmes qui lui sont posés.

La technique de l'autonomie procédurale suffit dans nombre de cas à garantir l'effectivité du droit de l'Union, des droits garantis aux justiciables par le droit de l'Union, par application non discriminatoire de l'arsenal national disponible.

La Charte peut être mobilisée le cas échéant pour imposer des obligations positives, sur la base d'une interprétation utile, voire optimale, des dispositions du droit de l'Union créant des droits pour les justiciables.

La primauté du droit de l'Union constitue bien entendu l'arme ultime de résolution des conflits de normes, qui demeurent finalement assez rares.

Il apparaît ainsi assez clairement que, bien que casuistique, la jurisprudence de la Cour n'en présente pas moins de solides éléments de cohérence.

La variété des configurations procédurales auxquelles la Cour est confrontée, décuplée par la variété des ordres juridiques qui les génèrent, est la principale raison de la complexité de la jurisprudence de la Cour, de son raffinement devrait-on plutôt dire.

La Cour règle les problèmes qui lui sont soumis sur la base des informations dont elle dispose en utilisant tous les moyens disponibles.

Il peut être utile de rappeler ici, pour conclure, que d'autres dispositions du droit de l'Union ont été exploitées dans une même perspective.

Je pense tout d'abord à l'article 19, paragraphe 1, alinéa 2, TUE, que la Cour a mobilisé pour rappeler aux États membres les devoirs qui leur incombe au titre de la garantie de l'indépendance de la justice : arrêt du 27 février 2018, *Associação Sindical dos Juízes Portugueses*[25].

Mais je pourrais aussi évoquer le rôle du principe d'autonomie du droit de l'Union, qui a également récemment été utilisé dans un objectif proche, dans l'affaire ayant donné lieu à l'arrêt du 6 mars 2018, *Achmea*[26], pour trancher la question de la compatibilité avec le droit de l'Union des mécanismes de règlements des différends entre investisseurs privés et États généralement prévus par les accords bilatéraux d'investissement des États membres.

Je vous remercie de votre attention.

25 C-64/16, EU:C:2018:117.
26 C-284/16, EU:C:2018:158.

The Brussels Convention: 50 Years of Contribution to European Integration[1]

Fausto Pocar[*]

The Convention on jurisdiction and the enforcement of judgments in civil and commercial matters, concluded in Brussels on 27 September 1968,[2] is celebrating today its 50th anniversary. It is a significant date and a long way off from its conclusion, marked by many important and successful events, some of which are also celebrating their anniversary this year. Indeed, the sister of the Brussels Convention, the Lugano Convention,[3] is 30 years old. Her son, the Brussels I Regulation,[4] is 18 years old and has just come of age. It is the anniversary year of a whole family, not to mention the growing of the family through accession agreements, which has brought its membership from the initial 6 to 28 members. Among them, it is worth mentioning here the accession convention concerning the United Kingdom,[5] which is now 40 years old, and might soon be repealed should a hard Brexit occur, as reflected in a recent document[6] issued by the British Government on handling civil cases if there is a no Brexit deal between the EU and the UK. Will it be the first, and hopefully the last, divorce in the family?

The above is an unparalleled series of events in the life of an international legal instrument, which confirm that the Brussels Convention has

---

* Professor emeritus, University of Milan; Dr. h. c. Antwerpen and Buenos Aires.

1 Dinner speech held at the Max-Planck-Institute, Luxembourg, on 27 September 2018.

2 The Convention entered into force between the original 6 Member States of the EEC on 1st February 1973, was given the n. 72/455/CEE, and published in *OJEC*, 1972, L 229.

3 Convention on jurisdiction and the enforcement of judgments in civil and commercial matters done at Lugano on 16 September 1988, *OJEC*, L 319, 25 November 1988.

4 Council Regulation (CE) No. 44/2001, 22 December 2000, *OJEC*, L 12, 16 January 2001.

5 Convention on the Accession of the Kingdom of Denmark, of Ireland and of the United Kingdom of Great Britain and Northern Ireland, concluded in Luxembourg on 9 October 1978, *OJEC*, L 304, 1978.

6 *Handling civil legal cases that involve EU countries if there's no Brexit deal*, doc. gov.uk, 13 September 2018.

been the starting point of a prodigious development of European civil procedural law and legal cooperation through half a century, and more in general of European private international law. The Convention, indeed, permeated and continues to permeate many other EU instruments, until the most recent regulation which refers to the Brussels I Regulation as the governing procedural law for the settlement of disputes before the European Patent Court.[7]

But it is also the starting point of a cooperation on international civil procedure in a wider context, in particular if one considers that the Convention was the inspiring document of the initiative in 1993 – 25 years ago, another anniversary! – to draft a worldwide double convention on jurisdiction and the recognition and enforcement of decisions in civil and commercial matters within the Hague Conference on Private International Law.[8] That initiative faced a setback in 1999 and 2002, but later resurged with the adoption in 2005 of a more limited Convention on choice of court agreements, and recently with a more general, though restricted in scope, draft Judgment Convention which will be adopted by the Hague Conference in 2019, thus missing by only one year the fiftieth anniversary we are celebrating today.

The just mentioned series of events marks a fascinating story, which would deserve much more attention that it can receive in a short speech, where it is impossible to go through all the many lights and the few shadows that accompanied the life of the Brussels Convention and its achievements as a central international and European legal instrument. Thus, this speech will try to address briefly only one main question: why is the Brussels Convention and are its developments so important for Europe and its citizens? and it will point only to a few features which appear particularly notable for the progress of the European integration.

In this perspective it may be worth quoting an eminent French scholar, Berthold Goldman, who already in 1971 – before the entry into force of

7 Regulation (EU) No. 542/2014, 15 May 2014, *OJEU*, L 163, 29 May 2014 and Art. 31 of the Agreement on a Unified Patent Court, *OJEU*, C 175, 20 June 2013.

8 The Special Commission, which was established in 1996, submitted in 1999 a "Preliminary Draft Convention on Jurisdiction and Foreign Judgments in Civil and Commercial Matters", as well as a "Report of the Special Commission" drawn up by Peter Nygh and Fausto Pocar, but the following discussion at the first part of the 19th session of the Diplomatic Conference held in June 1999 did not lead to the adoption of a convention and its outcome is reflected in a Summary that took note of the proposals endorsed by Member States' delegations. All these documents are published in Hague Conference on Private International Law, *Proceedings of the Twentieth Session 14 to 30 June 2005, tome II, Judgments*, 197, 207 (2013).

the Brussels Convention[9] but, importantly, just the year of the adoption of the Protocol establishing the competence of the EC Court of Justice to interpret its provisions[10] – wrote an essay where the Convention was characterized as a "*traité fédérateur*", a federating treaty.[11] While the article is more a description of the Convention than a discussion about why it is a federating treaty, the definition is hitting the mark.

Why does the Convention deserve to be referred to as a federating treaty? This question may beg other questions and multifaceted answers, some of which I will try to address hereafter.

Firstly, it must be recalled that the Convention was concluded in September 1968, at a time when the transitional period of the common market came to an end, due to the so called "acceleration decision", adopted by the EEC Commission on 1st July 1968, eighteen months ahead of schedule, to introduce the common customs tariff and to eliminate all customs duties on trade between Member States. This temporal coincidence with the achievement of the common market may be fortuitus, especially in light of the several years of negotiations, starting in 1960, that were necessary for agreeing on a text and arriving at the conclusion of the Convention.[12]

However, the adoption of a treaty providing for the simplification of the formalities governing the reciprocal recognition and enforcement of judgments envisaged in Article 220 of the EEC Treaty was a timely and appropriate measure to complement the free circulation of goods and services. It added a significant instrument of judicial cooperation aimed at supporting that circulation and making the settlement of disputes linked to the common market more uniform, speedy and effective. As the EEC Commission pointed out in a note inviting the Member States to commence the negotiations that led to the adoption of the Convention, a true internal market between them would be achieved only if adequate legal protection and, hence, legal security could be secured by providing for the recognition and

9 See *supra*, ftn 2.

10 The Protocol was adopted in Luxembourg on 3 June 1971 and entered into force on 1st September 1975, *OJEC*, L 204, 1975; see also an amended version of the Protocol in *OJEC*, C 97, 11 April 1983.

11 Berthold Goldman, "Un traité fédérateur : La Convention entre Etats membres de la CEE sur la reconnaissance et l'exécution des décisions en matière civile et commerciale", 7 *Revue trimestrielle de droit européen*, 1–39 (1971).

12 See Paul Jenard, "Report on the Convention on jurisdiction and the enforcement of judgments in civil and commercial matters", *OJEC*, C 59/3, 5 March 1979.

enforcement of judicial decisions beyond the boundaries of each national territory.[13]

Secondly, and even more importantly, the adoption of the Convention contributed substantially to enhance, within its scope of application, the respect for human rights in the international civil procedural domain at a time in which their respect in this area of law was not felt so urgent and important as it is nowadays. On one hand, the suppression of exorbitant fora based on nationality that characterized the rules governing jurisdiction in civil matters in some contracting States and conflicted with human rights, as legal literature recognised much later, represented a significant step in that direction.[14] On the other hand, a simplified procedure for the enforcement of foreign judgments, based on an injunction according to the model provided in the Hague Conventions on civil procedure concluded in 1905 and 1954 with respect to the decisions on costs, went in the same direction.[15]

There is no doubt that making justice more equal and efficient meant enhancing the protection of a basic human right as is the right to access to justice. And there is also no doubt that an equal protection of that right, as well as of all human rights, represented an essential federative pillar in a group of States as was the European Community, as is now the European Union. It is not by mere accident that when the Communities moved towards forming a closer union, the need was felt for the adoption of a common bill of rights, the Charter of fundamental rights of the European Union,[16] which was subsequently made formally binding for the European institutions in relation to their legislative and administrative activity, as

13 Paul Jenard, *supra* ftn 12, *ibidem*.

14 See Fausto Pocar, "Etude comparative des règles de conflit de juridictions dans les Etats membres de la C.E.E.", in *The Influence of the European Communities upon Private International Law of the Member States* (François Rigaux ed.), 77–96 (1981); Patrick Kinsch, Human Rightrs and Private International Law, in *Encyclopedia of Private International Law* (Jürgen Basedow et al. ed), 880–886 (2017), and, more specifically, the interesting analysis of Laurence Usunier, "La compatibilité de l'article 14 du Code civil avec les droits fondamentaux, une question dépourvue de caractère sérieux?, 102 *Revue critique de droit international privé*, 775–788 (2013).

15 Fausto Pocar, "Alcune osservazioni in merito al procedimento per il riconoscimento e l'esecuzione delle sentenze straniere previsto nelle convenzioni dell'Aja e della C.E.E.", in 5 *Rivista di diritto internazionale privato e processuale*, 132–138 (1969).

16 The Charter was solemnly proclaimed at Nice on 7 December 2000 (*OJEC*, C364/1, 18 December 2000), and was made formally binding only much later, with the Lisbon Treaty (see the adapted wording of the text, replacing the original one, in *OJEU*, C326/391, 26 October 2012). However, most of its content was sub-

well as for the Member States with respect to the implementation of Union law.[17]

A third additional factor should not be neglected. The exclusive competence for the interpretation of the Convention, granted to the Court of Justice with the Protocol of 3 June 1971,[18] aligned the provisions of the Convention to those of the founding Treaties and the secondary community legislation for the purposes of their exclusive judicial interpretation, and recognised their equal role in contributing to the European integration and in providing for an additional guarantee in this respect. The importance of the Protocol as a powerful tool in the hands of the Court should by no means be underestimated in the perspective of the European integration. After a few years from the entry into force of the Protocol the jurisprudence became so rich in this new field of European law that its impact on the harmonization of the legal systems of the Member States was substantial.

In this context, it cannot be denied that the determination of autonomous legal notions independent of national law for the interpretation of the Convention contributed to the unification of the law and performed a federative task. However, even when the Court chose the option not to interpret a notion autonomously, and rather preferred to refer to the national systems for its interpretation, such referral frequently meant that the national legislators were indicated to proceed themselves to unify the law. An example lies in the well-known question of the definition of the place of performance of contractual obligations. The Court's reference to national private international law[19] was regarded as a confirmation of the importance of the initiative whereby the States parties of the Convention were going to adopt common legislation with a view to unifying their private international law on the matter of contractual and non-contractual obligations.[20] The Court's decision not only confirmed the link between the Brussels Convention and the future Rome Convention of 19 June 1980

---

stantially applicable as of its proclamation, because it dealt with rights that were either present in the European Convention on Human Rights or in EU legislative acts, as well as affirmed in the case law of the European Court of Justice: see Fausto Pocar, in F. Pocar and M. Baruffi, *Commentario breve ai trattati sull'Unione europea,* 2nd ed., 1793–1795 (2014).

17 See Art. 51 of the Charter.

18 *Supra*, ftn 10.

19 *Industria Tessili Italiana Como v. Dunlop* (12/76), Court of Justice, October 6, 1976, *Report,* 1976, 1473 concl. Mayras.

20 See the Draft Convention on the law applicable to contractual and non-contractual obligations, Commission doc. XIV/398/72-E, Rev. 1 (1972), and the "Report"

on the law applicable to contractual obligations.[21] It also served the purpose of contributing to identify a legal basis for that Convention, which could be indirectly be brought back to Article 220 of the EC Treaty as being ancillary to the Brussels Convention.[22] In the same perspective, the Brussels Convention had also opened the door for the development of a more general "communitarisation" of private international law in Europe.

But perhaps the main contribution to the recognition of a federative role of the Brussels Convention was provided by the Court of Justice with the Opinion rendered on 7 February 2006 on the competence of the European Community to conclude the new Lugano Convention on jurisdiction and the recognition and enforcement of judgments in civil and commercial matters.[23] On that occasion the Court expressed the view that the conclusion of the revised Lugano Convention falls entirely within the sphere of the exclusive competence of the European Community, rather than within a shared competence with the member States.

In rendering such an opinion, the Court settled the scholarly dispute about the value of the reference made in Article 4(1) of the Brussels Convention to national rules of competence in order to establish jurisdiction over defendants non domiciled in a Member State. In particular, it had to decide whether that reference was a mere recognition of an original member States' competence, as suggested by a part of legal literature, or marked the attribution to Member States of a competence of the Community, as suggested by another part of legal doctrine. By stating that Regulation Brussels I "contains a set of rules forming a unified system which apply not only to relations between different Member States, ...but also to relations between a Member State and a non-member country",[24] the Court concluded in favour of the second alternative option.[25]

---

of Mario Giuliano, Paul Lagarde and Th. Van Sasse van Ysselt, doc. XIV/408/72-E, Rev. 1 (1972). See also these documents, in French, in 9 *Rivista di diritto internazionale privato e processuale*, 159–260 (1973).

21 *OJEC*, L 266, 9 October 1980. As it is well known, the initial project which comprised contractual and non-contractual obligations was later restricted to the domain of contractual obligations: see Mario Giuliano and Paul Lagarde, "Report on the Convention on the law applicable to contractual obligations", *OJEC*, No C 282, 31.10.80, at 4 f.

22 Fausto Pocar, "Jurisdiction and the Enforcement of Judgments under the EC Convention of 1968. A Review of Court Decisions", 42 *Rabels Zeitschrift für ausländisches und internationales Privatrecht*, 405–430 (1978), at 418.

23 Opinion of the Court (Full Court), 1/03, *European Court Reports*, 2006, I-01145.

24 Opinion, *supra* ftn 23, at 144.

25 Opinion, *supra* ftn 23, at 148.

It also drew from such a conclusion that there was a need to unify the national rules of jurisdiction over defendants domiciled in third countries, as it was subsequently proposed by the Commission in its Green Paper on the review of Brussels I Regulation.[26] By offering a basis to the Commission's proposal the Court substantially contributed to the establishment of an external competence of the European Union, which represents of itself a federative factor.

An additional contribution in this perspective lies in the statement of the Court that a lack of uniformity of the rules of competence over defendants domiciled in third countries may constitute an obstacle to the good functioning of the internal market. It could determine a forum shopping in favour of the most convenient jurisdiction, whose decision will have effect in all the Member States as a consequence of the liberalisation of the circulation of judgments. Furthermore, conflicts between different rules of jurisdiction drawn up by various legal systems "could give rise to the concurrent jurisdiction of several courts to resolve the same dispute, but also to a complete lack of judicial protection, since no court may have jurisdiction to decide such a dispute".[27]

By advocating the Union's competence, the Court's opinion thus not only underlined the importance of the unification of the external jurisdiction for the proper functioning of the internal market. It also stressed its importance for the establishment of a market where stakeholders receive equal and full protection of their right to access to justice, thus completing the scope of the agreement reached at the conclusion of the Convention with the deletion of the national exorbitant fora. In this respect the position taken by the Court contains a significant federative element.

It is highly unfortunate that the competent EU institutions – the Parliament and the Council – as well as the Member States disregarded the opinion of the Court of Justice and did not implement it but to a limited extent in the revision of the Brussels I Regulation carried out some years later, in contrast with the proposal submitted by the Commission.[28] This attitude of the legislative institutions is the more regrettable if one considers that

26 Green Paper on the review of Council Regulation (EC) No 44/2001 on jurisdiction and the recognition and enforcement of judgments in civil and commercial matters, COM(2009) 175 final, 21 April 2009.

27 Opinion *supra* ftn 23, at 141.

28 See European Commission, "Proposal for a Regulation of the European Parliament and of the Council on jurisdiction and the recognition of judgments in civil and commercial matters (Recast)", 14 December 2010, doc COM(2010) 748 final. The new Regulation Brussels I (*supra* ftn 4) accepts the Commission's proposal

the Court's arguments – which rely on the proper functioning of the internal market and on the respect for a fundamental right like the access to justice – show that its opinion was not expressing a mere option but a binding obligation on the European legislator and the Member States. By failing to enhance the equal access to justice of its citizens, the EU institutions did not comply with Article 47 of the Charter of fundamental rights that they are obliged to respect within the powers conferred to them by the Treaties.[29] It is highly desirable that this attitude changes in the near future with a view to putting the European legislation in line with the jurisprudence of the Court.

These last developments show that, notwithstanding the many significant results achieved by the Brussels Convention and its related instruments during half a century, significant gaps still exist and need to be filled in order to enable the Convention to fully perform its federative role and reach the finish line pre-determined by its founding fathers. Harmonized rules on jurisdiction over defendants domiciled in third countries, as well as common rules concerning the recognition and enforcement of judgments rendered outside of the EU, are still missing and need to be adopted.

Will the Convention succeed in achieving this goal in the next future? Or will the EU abandon this target with the hope that the lacunae will be filled in a worldwide convention concerned with the relations with third countries within the framework of the Hague Conference on private international law?

While this perspective may be desirable, it does not seem to be realistic, at least in a short term, at the present stage of the harmonization of international law of civil procedure. As mentioned earlier, after 25 years of negotiations there are still serious difficulties of States to reach consensus on a double convention dealing both with direct jurisdiction and the recognition and enforcement of judgments. The current draft Judgment Convention is limited to the recognition and enforcement of foreign judgments and an addition of rules on direct jurisdiction is not at hand; furthermore, the scope of application of the draft is far more restricted than the scope of the Brussels I Regulation. As a consequence, a Hague conven-

only as far as some protective jurisdiction is involved, in particular over consumer contracts and contracts of employment, but disregards the arguments, convincingly made by the Court of Justice and endorsed by the Commission, in favour of a general harmonisation of jurisdiction over defendants domiciled outside of the territory of any Member State.

29 Art. 51 of the Charter.

tion will govern the relations of the EU Member States with third countries only to some extent, leaving out many areas of those relations, which will continue to be governed either by national laws or by a European uniform legislation.

Therefore, while a full success of the future Hague Judgement Convention may help to resolve a number of problems in the relations of the EU Member States with third countries, its worldwide dimension will not be suitable to ensure the coherence of a regional system as far as the equality of access to justice for all the persons residing in the Union is concerned. A legislative initiative of the Union will still be necessary to achieve this goal, and its importance needs to be pointed out on the occasion of this anniversary. A celebration is not only a time for expressing satisfaction with past accomplishments, but rather an opportunity to look at the way ahead.

Delendum est Forum Delicti[1]? Towards the Jurisdictional Protection of the Alleged Victim in Cross-Border Torts

Etienne Farnoux[*]

Table of Contents

---

* Professor at University of Strasbourg

1 In 1997, Georges A. L. Droz authored an article in French published in the *Recueil Dalloz* titled "*Delendum est forum contractus?* (vingt ans après les arrêts De Bloos et Tessili interprétant l'article 5.1 de la Convention de Bruxelles du 27 septembre 1968)" (*Recueil Dalloz*, 1997, p. 351) in which he expressed frustration at what was then article 5.1 of the Brussels Convention, the *forum contractus*. The title of the present article is intended as a reference to this seminal contribution, which itself was a reference to the Latin sentence "Carthago delenda est" ("Carthage must be destroyed"). The present paper outlines some of the conclusions of a PhD dissertation entitled *Les considérations substantielles dans le règlement de la compétence internationale des juridictions – Réflexion autour de la matière délictuelle*, defended in October 2017 at the Sorbonne Law School. The author wishes to thank MPI Luxembourg and the participants of the pre-seminar to "The 50th Anniversary of the European Law of Civil Procedure" conference for the thorough discussion and comments.

At first glance, the European rules of international jurisdiction are based on two fundamental principles.

First, according to Recital 15 of the Regulation Brussels 1 Recast ("RB1R"), "the principle that jurisdiction is generally based on the defendant's domicile" (the *forum rei*). The *forum rei* is not just one among several jurisdiction rules: it is a principle rule. This is expressed in the Latin maxim "*actor sequitur forum rei*" which means that the claimant should bring proceedings against the defendant at his/her domicile. This principle is expressed by the letter of article 4.1 Brussels Regulation (recast) ("... persons domiciled in a Member State shall ... be sued in the courts of the Member State") as well as by Recital 15 ("The rules of jurisdiction should be highly predictable and founded on the principle that jurisdiction is generally based on the defendant's domicile"). There is a fairness justification for this: when the claimant and the defendant are not domiciled within the same State, it is the claimant who should bear the burden of litigating abroad because, in the absence of evidence to the contrary, the defendant does not owe anything to the claimant. In other words, the Brussels system adheres, like many jurisdictional systems, to the principle of jurisdictional protection of the defendant[2].

Second, according to Recital 16 RB1R, "there should be alternative grounds of jurisdiction based on a close connection between the court and the action or in order to facilitate the sound administration of justice".

One such alternative ground of jurisdiction is found in article 7§ 2 RB1R which "in matters relating to tort, delict or quasi-delict" provides for the jurisdiction of "the courts for the place where the harmful event occurred or may occur".

This connecting factor exemplifies the research for a close connection between the court whose jurisdiction is envisaged and the subject-matter of the dispute. The general idea behind such a *forum delicti* is that it is the geographical localization of the dispute (or rather of the material elements of the dispute) that should determine the jurisdiction of a given domestic court. Apart from the generally accepted notion in private international law that localization is a relevant way of organizing state jurisdiction (both prescriptive and adjudicative), it is expected that the jurisdiction of a court with a close geographical connection with the dispute will offer both pre-

2 P. Jenard, Report on the Convention on jurisdiction and the enforcement of judgements in civil and commercial matters, Official Journal of the European Communities, N° C 59, p. 1, (hereinafter Jenard Report) spec. p. 18.

dictability and sound administration of justice (especially concerning evidentiary issues)[3].

As a result, from the beginning, a significant part of the case-law, both by the domestic courts of the Member States and by the European Court of Justice ("ECJ"), under article 5.3/7.2 of the European jurisdiction system (the Brussels Convention and its progeny), dealt with issues concerning the localization of the material elements of the dispute (the "harmful event", that is both the event causing the loss and the loss itself[4]). At first sight, it frames the jurisdictional debate as a debate on the localization of the material elements of the dispute.

Yet, this program is faced with dire difficulties, namely the growing virtualization of entire swathes of human activities and the rise in cross-border private relations. In recent years, the ECJ, as well as the courts of the Member States, have been grappling with complex issues pertaining to the localization of the elements of a tort. It proves difficult, and in many cases artificial, to find the localization of an element "taking place" on the Internet and, thus, deprived of any materiality.

Simultaneously, it becomes evident that the other founding principle of the European jurisdictional system faces difficulties. It becomes increasingly common that, in a given case, the result of the interpretation of the *forum delicti* allows the plaintiff to sue at home and not at the defendant's home, opening a *de facto forum actoris*, contrary to the principle *forum rei*.

This is problematic because, as stated above, *forum rei* is not just one among several jurisdiction rules: it is a principle rule. The question is whether this principle still holds or whether it has effectively been overturned.

One way to look at it, one that finds resonance in the case law of the ECJ, is that this phenomenon is only the result of the attempt to localize the elements of the tort. As such, this proposition might not be found entirely sufficient. The creation of such accidental *fora actorum* through special heads of jurisdiction has indeed been the subject of intense criticism. Admittedly, the usual suspect had been for a long time the *forum contractus* of article 5.1 of the Brussels Convention. In 1997, in an insightful article published in French and entitled "*Delendum est forum contractus?*" (in the interrogative form), Georges Droz demonstrated that the *forum con-*

3 This idea was present from the very start, see *Jenard Report*, p. 25.

4 ECJ, *Bier v. Mines de Potasse d'Alsace*, 30 November 1976, 21/76.

tractus, as it was construed under *De Bloos* and *Tessili* judgments[5], often led to a *forum actoris*. In Droz's mind, this result had to be avoided because it was contrary to the inspiration of the Brussels Convention. He concluded with this last plea: if this unfortunate result could not be remedied either through a modification in the Court's case-law or through an amendment to the provision itself, the *forum contractus* should be deleted ("*Delendum est forum contractus!*", in the exclamative form). Maybe the same should be said of article 5.3/7.2 of the European jurisdiction system: *Delendum est forum delicti*?

However, another way to look at it is that the *forum delicti* actually plays an undercover role of jurisdictional protection of the alleged victim, outside of the scope of the provisions offering a more traditional protection to the weaker party (Section 3, 4 and 5 RB1R). From this perspective, the creation of a *forum actoris* through a special head of jurisdiction should no longer be regarded as accidental but as the true function of the *forum delicti*.

In this case, the reason brought forward by Droz to advocate for the deletion of a special jurisdiction would be turned upside down: the exception to the principle *actor sequitur forum rei* would no longer be the anomaly but the goal. However, it might still be necessary to put an end to the *forum delicti* as we know it, but only to reveal it to its true function, that of protecting the alleged victim by allowing him or her to initiate litigation at home. To the question *Delendum est forum delicti*?, the answer would then be yes, but not only…

It is this paper's ambition to review the case-law relating to cross-border tort disputes and to determine whether there is a possibility and a need to transform the current *forum delicti* into a *forum actoris* of the victim.

The scope of this paper is disputes with subject matter pertaining to tort, as defined by the ECJ[6].

A phenomenon that is striking is the rise of a *forum actoris* in European private international law concerning torts (1). This phenomenon argues in favour of replacing the current *forum delicti* by a *forum actoris* of the victim (2).

---

5 ECJ, *De Bloos v. Bouyer*, 6 October 1976, 14/76 and ECJ, *Tessili*, 6 October 1976, 12/76.

6 See for instance ECJ judgment in *Kolassa*, 28 January 2015, C-375/13, paragraph 44 : "the concept of 'matters relating to tort, delict or quasi-delict' within the meaning of Article 5(3) of Regulation No 44/2001 covers all actions which seek to establish the liability of a defendant and do not concern 'matters relating to a contract' within the meaning of Article 5(1)(a) of that regulation".

1. *The Rise of* Fora Actorum *in Tort Litigations*

First, as the rise of *fora actorum* in cross-border tort litigation appears somewhat counter-intuitive under the Brussels jurisdictional system, the exact magnitude of the phenomenon should be evaluated. Once its scale has been established, this phenomenon calls for an inquiry into its causes or justifications.

Accordingly, an overview of the rise of *fora actorum* is provided (1.1.) as well as an explanation (1.2.).

1.1. *An Overview*

The European system of international jurisdiction holds the view that *as a matter of principle* the defendant should be sued at his domicile. In contrast, it is clear that the *forum actoris* should be avoided because it is unfair to the defendant: it is legitimate only when the claimant is identified as a weaker party (insurance taker, consumer, employee). As a consequence, the European Court of Justice has repeatedly ruled that the exceptions to the *forum rei* (art 2/4) should be interpreted narrowly or restrictively both with regards to the material scope of the rule and with regards to the interpretation of the connecting factor. However, the application of the *forum delicti* often results in a *forum actoris* (1.1.1.). Nevertheless, the *forum delicti* is by no means the only channel through which a *forum actoris* is eventually offered to the alleged victim; derived jurisdictions also play a key role (1.1.2.). The rules of jurisdiction are not the only ones that come into play: the low standard of proof at the jurisdictional stage is crucial too (1.1.3.). Outside of the scope of the Brussels jurisdictional system, this tendency towards *forum actoris* is exemplified in the realm of data protection (1.1.4.).

1.1.1. Forum actoris *through forum delicti (art. 5.3/7.2)*

In many recent cases, the application of the *forum delicti* rule led to opening a *forum actoris*. The origin of this phenomenon lies with the *Mines de Potasse* judgment and the principle of ubiquity[7]: the place where the harmful event occurred (in art. 7§2 BIR recast) covers both the place of the event causing the loss (*Handlungsort*) and the place where the loss occurred

7 ECJ, *Bier v. Mines de Potasse d'Alsace, op. cit.*, paragraph 24.

(*Erfolgsort*). The principle of ubiquity allowed for a doubling of the plaintiff's opportunity to sue away from the defendant's home forum.

Following the rule set in *Fiona Shevill*[8], a distinction should be drawn, at least in the abstract, between instances where the damage is plurilocalized and instances where the damage is localized in one Member State only.

In several cases this allowed de facto the plaintiff to sue at home for the whole loss, usually by locating the loss (through the second "leg" of the *forum delicti* under *Mines de Potasse*) within the victim's home State. This occurred in the *Wintersteiger* case[9], which involved online infringement of a trademark in which the court ruled that the loss was located at the place where the trademark is registered, oftentimes where the alleged victim is domiciled (here, Austria). Similarly in the *Kolassa* case[10] which dealt with a prospectus liability litigation and in which the Court ruled that the loss occurred in the applicant's bank account. The same outcome was later reached in the *Löber* case[11]. In the *CDC* case, the Court ruled that "for loss consisting in additional costs incurred because of artificially high prices, the place where the alleged damage ... is located, in general, at that victim's registered office"[12]. In *Concurrence SARL*[13], in the context of an action to establish liability for infringement of the prohibition on resale

8 ECJ, *Shevill and Others*, 7 March 1995, C-68/93.

9 ECJ, *Wintersteiger*, 19 April 2012, C-523/10, paragraph 29.

10 *Loc. cit.*

11 ECJ, *Löber*, 12 September 2018, C-304/17.

12 ECJ, *CDC*, 21 May 2015, C-352/13, paragraph 56. In later cases, the solution seemed to have evolved. In the *flyLAL* case (ECJ, 5 July 2018, C-27/17), the Court ruled, in the context of an action seeking compensation for damage caused by anticompetitive conduct, that the 'place where the harmful event occurred' covers the place where the loss of income consisting in loss of sales occurred, that is to say, the place of the market which is affected by that conduct and on which the victim claims to have suffered those losses. This market approach was confirmed in the *Tibor-Trans* case (ECJ, 29 July 2019, C-451/18), in which the court ruled that, in an action for compensation for damage caused by collusive arrangements on pricing, 'the place where the harmful event occurred' covers the place where the market which is affected by that infringement is located, that is to say, the place where the market prices were distorted and in which the victim claims to have suffered that damage, even where the action is directed against a participant in the cartel at issue with whom that victim had not established contractual relations. It seems that the Court is moving away from the direct *forum actoris* determination illustrated in the *CDC* case, as far as damage caused by anticompetitive conduct is concerned. In all these cases, however, the claimants were allowed to bring action at their home forum.

13 ECJ, *Concurrences SARL*, 21 December 2016, C-618/15, paragraph 35.

outside a selective distribution network, the Court ruled that the place where the damage occurred was to be regarded as the territory of the Member State which protects the prohibition on resale by means of the action at issue, a territory on which the appellant alleges to have suffered a reduction in its sales. In the *Zuid Chemie* case[14], a product liability litigation, the Court ruled that the loss occurred at the place where the initial damage occurred as a result of the normal use of the product for the purpose for which it was intended. In all these cases, the reasoning effectively allowed the claimant to sue at home for the whole of the loss.

The European Court of Justice did make clear that, following *Fiona Shevill*, the jurisdiction of the court based at the place where the loss occurred is limited to the damage that was felt locally, in the case where the damage might be felt in several Member States. In this case, the *forum actoris* created by the localization of the loss is limited by the mosaic principle. The Court did so, famously, in the *eDate* case[15], in *Pinckney*[16], in *Hi Hotel*[17], in *Hejduk*[18], and in *Bolagsupplysningen*[19].

The distinction between jurisdiction for the entirety of the loss and jurisdiction limited to the damage felt locally is fundamental in the ECJ's case law, in order to rein in the alleged victim's opportunities to sue at home for the whole of the loss. However, in many cases, this functional limitation of the jurisdiction was made void because it seemed that the damage was only or predominantly local (it was not actually a case of plurilocalized damage, in the sense of *Fiona Shevill*)[20].

---

14 ECJ, *Zuid Chemie*,16 July 2009, C-189/08, paragraph 32.

15 ECJ, *eDate Advertising and Others*, 22 October 2011, C-509/09 and C-161/10, paragraph 51 "Moreover, instead of an action for liability in respect of all of the damage, the criterion of the place where the damage occurred, derived from *Shevill and Others*, confers jurisdiction on courts in each Member State in the territory of which content placed online is or has been accessible. Those courts have jurisdiction only in respect of the damage caused in the territory of the Member State of the court seised".

16 ECJ, *Pinckney*, 3 October 2013, C-170/12, paragraph 45.

17 ECJ, *Hi Hotel*, 4 April 2014, C-387/12, paragraph 38.

18 ECJ, *Hejduk*, 22 January 2015, C-441/13, paragraph 37.

19 ECJ, *Bolagsupplysningen*, 17 October 2017, C-194/16, paragraph 44.

20 See for instance ECJ, *CDC*, 21 May 2015, C-352/13, paragraph 55 : "However, given that the jurisdiction of the court seized of the matter by virtue of the place where the loss occurred is limited to the loss suffered by the undertaking whose registered office is located in its jurisdiction, an applicant such as CDC, who has consolidated several undertakings' potential claims for damages, would therefore, in accordance with the case-law set out in paragraph 35 above, need to bring sepa-

Granted, it might be argued, with reason, that it is only accidentally that in these particular cases the tribunal of the claimant has jurisdiction over the case: on the face of it, the connecting factor is still the "place where the loss occurred" and the loss might have occurred elsewhere. This objection is only relevant in the abstract, where it is indeed very different to use the place where the loss occurred or the domicile of the claimant (or the victim) as connecting factors. However, it is significant that, in the particular factual cases that gave rise to the rulings, the claimant was allowed to sue "at home" for two reasons. First, it is not a wild guess that the rationale expressed in the above-mentioned cases will statistically lead to the same outcome more often than not. While analyzing the elements that constitute the tort (namely, the event giving rise to the damage and the damage), it appears that the damage is the element that is closer to the alleged victim (while the event giving rise to the damage is closer to the alleged tortfeasor, and indeed often located at the tortfeasor's domicile by the Court[21]). Second, and more importantly, it is reasonable to assume that in most tort cases the claimant will try and sue at home. The relevant question is not whether *forum delicti* allows the alleged victim to sue somewhere else than at their domicile, but whether or not it allows them to sue at their domicile: it seems that *forum delicti* does allow them to do so.

Finally, and more strikingly, in the *eDate/Martinez* cases, the Court of Justice ruled that the alleged victim could sue the author of an infringement of a personality right on the internet at the centre of the victim's interest, opening an explicit *forum actoris* of the victim[22]. This solution was furthered by the *Bolagsupplysningen* case in which the Court extended the principle to legal persons[23]. The exact reasoning behind this solution is somewhat elusive. On the one hand, in *eDate/Martinez*, the Court stated

rate actions for the loss suffered by each of those undertakings before the courts with jurisdiction for their respective registered offices".

21 See for instance *eDate*, *op. cit.*, paragraph 42.

22 The court ruled (paragraph 49) that the place where a person has the centre of his interests corresponds in general to his habitual residence. However, a person may also have the centre of his interests in a Member State in which he does not habitually reside, in so far as other factors, such as the pursuit of a professional activity, may establish the existence of a particularly close link with that State.

23 The court ruled (paragraph 41) that, as regards a legal person pursuing an economic activity, "the centre of interests of such a person must reflect the place where its commercial reputation is most firmly established and must, therefore, be determined by reference to the place where it carries out the main part of its economic activities". The Court further noted that "while the centre of interests of a legal person may coincide with the place of its registered office when it carries out

explicitly that the solution found its justification in the contrast between "the difficulties of giving effect, within the context of internet, to the criterion relating to the occurrence of the damage which is derived from Shevill" and "the serious nature of the harm which may be suffered by the holder of a personality right who establishes that information injurious to that right is available on a world-wide basis"[24]. On the other hand, in *Bolagsupplysningen*, the Court presented the solution as closely connected to the localization of the loss[25].

To mark the full extent of the phenomenon, it should also be noted that the place where the loss occurs may be used against several defendants, even though they play different roles in the causation chain, as illustrated in *Pinckney*[26] and *Hi Hotel*[27]. The fact that the localization of the damage

---

all or the main part of its activities in the Member State in which that office is situated and the reputation that it enjoys there is consequently greater than in any other Member State, the location of that office is, not, however, in itself, a conclusive criterion for the purposes of such an analysis".

24 *eDate*, *op. cit.*, paragraph 47.

25 Clearly in this sense *Bolagsupplysningen*, *op. cit.*, paragraph 33.

26 In *Pinckney*, the question was whether Article 5(3) allowed "where there is an alleged infringement of a copyright which is protected by the Member State of the court seised, that court (...) to hear an action to establish liability brought by the author of a work against a company established in another Member State, which has in the latter State reproduced that work on a material support which is subsequently marketed by companies established in a third Member State through an internet site which is also accessible in the Member State of the court seised". The Court ruled that the court seised had jurisdiction ("only to determine the damage caused in the Member State within which it is situated"). Hence, the place where alleged damage occurred offers a base for jurisdiction exercised over a defendant whose role in the tort is not immediate (here the company that reproduced the copyrighted work as opposed to the company that marketed them through a website accessible in the Member State whose courts are seised).

27 In *Hi Hotel* (*op. cit.*), the question was whether, where there are several supposed perpetrators of the damage allegedly caused to rights of copyright protected in the Member State of the court seised, article 5§ 3 allows jurisdiction to be established with respect to one of those perpetrators who did not act within the jurisdiction of that court. The Court ruled that although "that provision does not allow jurisdiction to be established, on the basis of the causal event of the damage, of a court within whose jurisdiction the supposed perpetrator who is being sued did not act, [it] does allow the jurisdiction of that court to be established on the basis of the place where the alleged damage occurs, provided that the damage may occur within the jurisdiction of the court seised" (in which case, the court has jurisdiction only to rule on the damage caused in the territory of the Member State to which it belongs).

allows the plaintiff to litigate at his/her own domicile is all the more striking.

However, the *forum delicti* is not the only channel through which the alleged victim is allowed to sue at home.

1.1.2. Forum actoris *through derived jurisdiction*

The derived jurisdiction of articles 8.1 (in the case of multiple defendants) and 8.2 (in the case of third-party proceedings) also plays a key role in allowing a claimant to initiate proceedings against out-of-forum defendants.

The general idea, to turn these bases of jurisdiction into *forum actoris*, is to establish jurisdiction in the claimant's home forum against a defendant (a forum anchor-defendant in the case of article 8.1) and to use this base as a stepping stone to reach other out-of-forum defendants.

The feasibility of this depends of course on the preconditions that have to be met in order for the claimant to invoke a derived jurisdiction against an out-of-State defendant. The first precondition as far as article 8.1 is concerned, is that the claimant be able to identify a credible local defendant, the anchor defendant. The case law is however favourable to a certain extent. Particularly in the *Reisch Montage*[28] and *CDC*[29] judgments, the Court held that the inadmissibility of the first claim, was not an obstacle to the extension of jurisdiction to the derived claim. Admittedly, in these two cases, the derived jurisdiction did not open a *forum actoris* but, in general, this loosening of the requirement regarding the anchor defendant undeniably makes it easier for the claimant to litigate at home against other out-of-forum defendants[30].

The second precondition would be that the claims are "so closely connected it is expedient to hear and determine them together to avoid the risk of irreconcilable judgements resulting from separate proceedings"[31].

---

28 ECJ, *Reisch Montage*, 13 July 2006, C-103/05.

29 *Loc. cit.*

30 See for instance French *Cour de cassation*, *3e Chambre Civile*, 19 dec. 2007, n° 06–18.811.

31 In that regard, the Court of Justice ruled in *Freeport* that "in order for judgments to be regarded as irreconcilable, it is not sufficient that there be a divergence in the outcome of the dispute, but that divergence must also arise in the context of the same situation of fact and law" (ECJ, *Freeport*, 11 October 2007, C-98/06, paragraph 40).

On the closeness of the connection (or the connectedness) required under article 8.1, the Court held in recent cases that "a difference in legal basis between the actions brought against the various defendants, does not, in itself, preclude the application of Article 6(1) of Regulation No 44/2001"[32] which loosens the threshold for connectedness[33] and again made it easier for a plaintiff to sue at home against out-of-forum defendants.

1.1.3. Low standard of proof at the jurisdictional stage

One other point that should be raised with respect to tort victims under the Brussels regime is that claimants seeking the jurisdiction of their home tribunals in tort litigations will typically be favoured by the low standard of proof required to establish the facts relevant at the jurisdictional stage. This question boils down to the obligations of the national court in the course of determining their international jurisdiction. It was raised in the *Kolassa* case. The question was whether it was necessary "in the context of the determination of international jurisdiction under Regulation n 44/2001, to conduct a comprehensive taking of evidence in relation to disputed facts that are of relevance both for the question of jurisdiction and for the existence of the claim or whether it is, instead, to be considered that the allegations of the applicant in the main proceedings alone are correct for the purposes of the decision on jurisdiction". The Court ruled that "it is not necessary to conduct a comprehensive taking of evidence in relation to disputed facts that are relevant both to the question of jurisdiction and to the existence of the claim. It is, however, permissible for the court seised to examine its international jurisdiction in the light of all the information available to it, including, where appropriate, the allegations made by the defendant"[34].

32 ECJ, *Painer*, 7 March 2013, C-145/10, paragraph 84 and *CDC*, *op. cit.*, paragraph 23.

33 Even though the Court did add the requirement that "it was foreseeable by the defendant that they might be sued in the Member State where at least one of them is domiciled", which is some ways only restates the connectedness requirement from another perspective.

34 *Kolassa*, *op. cit.*, paragraph 66.

1.1.4. Forum actoris *in the specific realm of personal data protection*

It should be noted that in the specific case of data protection, when Regulation 2016/679 (*Personal data*) is applicable, a specific jurisdiction rule is available to the person who considers that their rights under the Regulation have been infringed as a result of the processing of their personal data in non-compliance with the Regulation.

Article 79.2 of the Regulation reads that "proceedings against a controller or a processor shall be brought before the courts of the Member State where the controller or processor has an establishment. Alternatively, such proceedings may be brought before the courts of the Member State where the data subject has his or her habitual residence ...". This clearly allows for a *forum actoris*.

Even though this rule is found outside of the realm of the Brussels I (recast) Regulation it offers an interesting comparison, which shows that, apart from the more classical hypothesis where weaker parties are offered jurisdictional protection (consumers, workers, insurance takers), there are instances, conceptually close (if not included within) the category of tort litigation, where a *forum actoris* is granted up front to the claimant.

The conclusion to be drawn from this is that, even though the *forum rei* is held to be the principle within the European jurisdictional system, this system allows in many instances for the alleged victim to litigate at home, for the whole or part of the alleged damage. This begs the question of whether it is only a coincidence or if it is the result of some deeper tendency within the jurisdictional system.

1.2. An Explanation

There are essentially two opposite ways to look at this phenomenon (the rise of *forum actoris*). The first one, in line with the history and traditionally held beliefs and creeds about the jurisdictional system, refuses to acknowledge this rise, or rather pictures it as the mere result of the localization process which, only by coincidence, leads to the designation of the tribunal at the claimant's domicile (1.2.1.). However, one may harbour doubts as to how absolutely convincing this explanation is, if only because of the magnitude of the phenomenon. In this case, one should envisage another, less popular explanation: what if the opening of *forum actoris* was deliberate as a way to favour the alleged victim? (1.2.2).

1.2.1. The traditional explanation: localization

The most obvious and simple (and reassuring!) explanation to this avalanche of *fora actorum* can be found in the idea that it is only by coincidence that the *forum delicti* allows the jurisdiction of the court of domicile[35]. The *forum delicti* relies on the localization of the factual elements of a situation, and it so happens that these factual elements point towards the territory of the Member State of the alleged victim domicile[36]. This finds massive support from as far back as the *Mines de Potasse* and *Fiona Shevill* judgements, that have been instrumental in enabling the multiplication of available tribunals, leading in turn to *de facto forum actoris*. Indeed, in these two seminal cases, as well as in the rest of the case law, the reasoning always follows the original localizing approach: the doubling of the claimant's option and the limitation of the jurisdiction to the damage caused in the territory are presented as merely the result of geographical localization of the elements of the case (damage and event giving rise to it).

This justification is not entirely satisfactory. First, even if it is indeed true, it still means that the *forum rei* is not actually the principle, the "jurisdictional protection of the defendant" principle no longer holds true. Another element of doubt is that the *forum delicti* is not the only rule at stake; as explained above, the derived jurisdictions of article 8 also play a role. This means that it is not only a question of localization but that there seems to be a broader, more complex, configuration of rules allowing the alleged victim to sue at home.

More importantly, in many of the cases mentioned above the localization itself is not very convincing: for financial loss, for cybertorts, for infringements of personality rights or even of intellectual property rights, it is difficult to think that the localization offers indications strong enough

---

35 See for instance the *flyLAL* case and the *Tibor-Trans* case (*op. cit.*). In the earlier *CDC* case (*op. cit.*), the Court had located the place where the damage occurred directly at the victim's registered office, for an anticompetitive conduct. In those later cases, the Court located the place where the damage occurred by reference to the market affected by the conduct, admittedly a stricter localizing approach.

36 See for eg. the *Löber* case (*op. cit.*) in which the Court of Justice ruled that « the courts of the investor's domicile, as the courts for the place where the harmful event occurred within the meaning of that provision, have jurisdiction to hear and determine that action, *where the damage the investor claims to have suffered consists in financial loss which occurred directly in that investor's bank account with a bank established within the jurisdiction of those courts and the other specific circumstances of that situation also contribute to attributing jurisdiction to those courts* » (emphasis added), paragraph 36.

to effectively dictate the establishment of jurisdiction in one place or the other.

If one takes the example of the infringement of personality rights on the internet, the Court ruled in *eDate/Martinez* that "the criterion of the place where the damage occurred, derived from *Shevill and Others*, confers jurisdiction on courts in each Member State in the territory of which content placed online is or has been accessible". In so deciding, the Court subscribed to the so-called "accessibility theory", holding that everywhere where a website is accessible there is a potential damage. Another approach was available, under the so-called "focalization theory" that requires the tribunal to check if the website was actually directed at a given population (through several factual elements such as language) in order to find a potential damage. Both approaches are framed in terms of localization and localization itself does not justify choosing one approach or the other, precisely because the localization of online activities is always artificial.

To be perfectly thorough, it should be noted that the matter is complicated further by the notion, alluded to in *Bolagsupplysningen*, that the extra forum opened in the *eDate/Martinez* case at the victim's centre of interest was actually related to the localization of the loss[37]. In this sense, AG Bobek opined in this case that the *Fiona Shevill* 'mosaic approach' should be discarded for infringements of personality rights on the internet[38]. The Court did not follow him on that particular issue, but it still gives a sense that the way the loss is located remains open for debates.

---

37 *Bolagsupplysningen*, *op. cit.*, paragraph 33 : "As regards such content, the alleged infringement is usually felt most keenly at the centre of interests of the relevant person, given the reputation enjoyed by him in that place. Thus, the criterion of the 'victim's centre of interests' reflects the place where, in principle, the damage caused by online material occurs most significantly, for the purpose of Article 7(2) of Regulation n°1215/2012".

38 AG Bobek opinion in *Bolagsupplysningen* "95. The *second* possibility concerns the place where *the harm occurred*. The present case concerns harm allegedly caused to the reputation of a legal person. That harm is likely to be suffered in the place where that person does business or is otherwise professionally active. 96. If the *Shevill* 'mosaic' approach were to be discarded, the place where the harm occurred would be limited to one jurisdiction. As what is protected is the reputation of the claimant, that place should be where that protected reputation was most strongly hit. That is in turn likely to be in the place where that person, whether natural or legal, has his or its centre of interests. Such a place would then represent the place of the true centre of the dispute, to which a special ground of jurisdiction, based on the closest link, should properly lead".

This discussion is not complete without recalling, more broadly, the debate that was ongoing before the *Fiona Shevill* case about the localization of offline personality rights infringements: it was rather convincingly argued that this damage could be localized at the victim's domicile. Instead, the court located it at the place of distribution of the publication, a criterion that was usually linked to the event giving rise to the damage rather than to the loss itself.

This shows that from the very start, and well before the rise of cyber-torts, the localization of the elements of the tort is unable to dictate the organization of the international jurisdiction of domestic tribunals.

This is not only the case with the place of loss, but also with the place where the event giving rise to the harm occurs. Even in this case, localization is usually very artificial. In *Fiona Shevill*, the court ruled that in the case of defamation by means of a newspaper article distributed in several Member States, the victim may bring action for damages against the publisher, under the event giving rise to the damage, before the courts of the Member State of the place where the publisher of the defamatory publication is established, even though other factual elements might have been considered (such as the place of distribution). The localization of the event giving rise to the damage at the alleged tortfeasor domicile has become widespread in the case law[39] but it remains artificial.

To some extent, it might be argued that these difficulties are inherent to the localization of immaterial elements, and it is true that the difficulties are particularly acute in this case. However, even for "material" torts where both the damage and the event giving rise to it are material (that is they have a physical existence in the world, that makes it easy to locate them on the surface of the earth), the localization approach is facing difficulties. For instance, the 'complex tort' figure with the geographical dissociation of the causal event and the damage could in many cases be re-analyzed as territorial local torts (with local causal events and local damages).

The mosaic principle can hardly be said to be dictated by localization either: it is not very convincing to slice the loss in territorial subsections, especially for infringement in the private life and defamation.

In other words, it seems hard to believe that localization dictates any of these orientations within the jurisdictional system. Undeniably, there are choices that are made, choices that are not limited to taking into account the localization of the elements of the tort.

39 Especially for cyber counterfeits, see for instance *Wintersteiger* (*op. cit.*) and *Hejduk* (*op. cit.*).

But then, what explains these choices? What justifies the way the international jurisdiction of tribunals is organized?

To a certain extent, this critical stance on the role of localization calls for a renewal of the approach to international jurisdiction. The starting point lies with the realization that, essentially, the question of international jurisdiction boils down to the opposition between the claimant and the defendant, and the allocation of the costs and inconvenience of litigating abroad between them. The question of the international jurisdiction is not that of the localization of the elements of the tort, but whether the plaintiff is allowed (or not) to attract the out-of-forum defendant into their home forum. It is not the localization, often artificial, of the factual elements of the case that provides the answer to this question but a political choice that either favours the claimant or favours the defendant. This proposition resonates, again, with AG Bobek's opinion in *Bolagsupplysningen* in which he asked the Court to discard the *Fiona Shevill* construction and to offer a simple option between the domicile of the defendant and the centre of the interests of the victim[40]. At first glance this proposal seems to stop midstream: it does away with the localization approach and presents the question for what it is, an opposition between the *forum rei* and the *forum actoris*, but it stops short of choosing between them. In fact, in this case, leaving an option to the claimant amounts to allowing the claimant to litigate at home (which will happen in virtually all cases).

The paradox is that, once the question of the international jurisdiction is framed as an opposition between the *forum rei* and the *forum actoris*, the Brussels I system readily offers an answer: *actor sequitur forum rei*; as a principle a person domiciled in a Member State shall be sued in the courts of that Member State. However, the study conducted above informs us otherwise thus provoking the question: has the principle of jurisdictional protection of the defendant been overturned? Was *forum delicti* granted as means of favouring the alleged victim?

40 AG Bobek opinion in *Bolagsupplysningen* "97. There would thus be two possible fora open to the claimant. The first one would be the domicile of the defendant as the general rule under Article 4(1) of Regulation No 1215/2012, which also corresponds to the place of the origin of the harm. The second would be the centre of interests of the claimant which corresponds to the place where the harm occurred. Both fora would confer upon the competent court *full* jurisdiction to adjudicate on the totality of the damages claimed and all the remedies available under the respective national laws, including the issue of a possible injunction if so requested".

1.2.2. *Favouring the plaintiff?*

Looking at the rise in *fora actorum* in tort litigation, one may legitimately ask if the "jurisdictional protection of the plaintiff" has not replaced "the jurisdictional protection of the defendant".

This idea, that the *forum delicti* is actually a favour granted to the alleged victim, is an old idea. It has been present ever since the *Mines de Potasse* to justify the doubling of the claimant's options.

The Court of Justice seems to be reluctant, to say the least, towards that analysis. In the *Folien Fischer* case[41], the Court of Justice held that an action for a negative declaration is not excluded from the scope of article 5.3/7.2 which undermines considerably the thesis of a *forum actoris* of the victim, since the alleged tortfeasor will be able to benefit from it. More specifically, the Court held that "The objectives, pursued by that provision and repeatedly stressed in case-law of ensuring that the court with jurisdiction is foreseeable and of preserving legal certainty are not connected either to the allocation of the respective roles of claimant and defendant or to the protection of either"[42].

The question here is whether when organizing the international jurisdiction of the courts, the legislator and the Court of Justice only have in mind the alleged victim as claimant. In many instances, it seems that the Court uses the term 'defendant' and 'alleged tortfeasor' indifferently. The most striking one is the *eDate* case. This would indicate that the current architecture of the international jurisdiction system is intended, at least primarily, to benefit the alleged victim taken as claimant.

With this in mind, the ruling in *Folien Fischer* seems particularly unfortunate. The outcome is that very often in actions for a negative declaration of liability, the plaintiff (the alleged tortfeasor) will be able to benefit from a *forum actoris* against the alleged victim, whereas there are reasons to believe that this option was intended for the alleged victim only. It is not impossible to argue that actions for a negative declaration should be limited to the court of domicile of the defendant (the alleged non-victim).

However, in *Bolagsupplysningen*, the Court doubled down on the idea that the jurisdictional system did not aim at protecting the alleged victim. Indeed, in order to allow legal persons to benefit from the additional forum at the centre of interests of the alleged victim, the Court ruled that "given that the option of a person who considers that his rights have been

41 ECJ, *Folien Fischer and Fofitec*, 25 October 2012, C-133/11.

42 ECJ, *Folien Fischer*, *op. cit.*, paragraph 45.

infringed to bring an action before the courts of the Member State in which his centre of interests is located for all the alleged damage is justified in the interests of the sound administration of justice and not specifically for the purposes of protecting the applicant, the matter of whether the person is a natural or legal person is also not conclusive". The Court added that "In that regard, the Court has pointed out that the rule of special jurisdiction in matters relating to tort, delict or quasi-delict does not pursue the same objective as the rules on jurisdiction laid down in Sections 3 to 5 of Chapter II of Regulation No 1215/2012, which are designed to offer the weaker party stronger protection (see, to that effect, judgment of 25 October 2012, *Folien Fischer and Fofitec* ...)". It concluded that "The criterion of the centre of interests is intended to determine the place in which damage caused by online content occurs and, consequently, the Member State whose courts are best able to hear and to rule upon the dispute".

This is not particularly convincing, if only because of the great uncertainty and, further, artificiality, concerning the localization of non-material loss: it is not clear at all what is in the "interests of the sound administration of justice". Furthermore, it cannot be ignored that the reasoning has somewhat evolved between *eDate/Martinez* and *Bolagsupplysningen*. In *eDate*, the Court did mention that the reason behind the opening of a new option at the centre of interests of the alleged victim was the contrast between the reduced usefulness of the criterion relating to distribution in the context of internet and the serious nature of the harm thus inflicted. This, implicitly, amounts to an acknowledgement that the alleged victim needs to be protected, or at least that this solution has more to do with fairness than localization.

It is therefore possible not to take the reasoning in *Bolagsupplysningen* at face value.

If there is indeed a movement of favouring the plaintiff[43], it would be legitimate to ask why. There are reasons of course to think that the plaintiff would be unfairly treated if the jurisdictional system strictly applied

---

43 To be fair, it should be noted that this phenomenon is not unequivocal. For instance, in cases dealing with financial loss, the *Universal Music* case (ECJ, *Universal Music*, 16 June 2016, C-12/15) on the localization of financial loss is closer to the logic of the *Kronhofer* case (ECJ, *Kronhofer*, 10 June 2004, C-168/02), in which the Court ruled that domestic courts should not take into account the consequential loss for localization purposes, effectively barring the way for a *forum actoris*. However, it could be argued that the judgement in the *Kolassa* case departed from the reasoning in *Kronhofer*.

the *actor sequitur forum rei*, or even that the plaintiff is often weaker than the defendant, but it might not be sufficient to overcome the principle of protection of the defendant. Maybe the tendency to favour the claimant comes from the substance of the disputes, that is of the torts and tort law.

2. *The Replacement of the* Forum Delicti *by a* Forum Victimae

It has been shown that the Brussels I jurisdictional system showed a tendency to favour the plaintiff, notably through the *forum delicti*, undercover of localization of the factual elements of the case. If this is the case, then why not go ahead and envisage a *forum actoris* of the victim, a *forum victimae*.

This proposal needs to state clearly the reasons why *forum delicti* should be turned into a *forum actoris* for the victim (2.1.) and how can it be done (2.2.).

2.1. *Reasons to Replace the* Forum Delicti *by a* Forum Victimae

The main reason to replace the *forum delicti* by a *forum victimae* is that the Court's interpretation of the *forum delicti* often turns it into a *forum actoris* for the victim. However, one may wonder why the Court reaches such a result, why there seems to be an unescapable, irresistible push in favour of the alleged victim, in spite of the principle of jurisdictional protection of the defendant.

At this point, there can only be hypotheticals because this discussion delves into the deeper aspects of the legal world, beyond recitals and judicial opinions.

One hypothetical could be that it is the substantive tendencies at the core of tort liability that favour the victims and this creates an incentive both for the legislator and the court system to allow the plaintiff to litigate at home. These tendencies stem from the two functions of tort liability: the reparation/compensation function and the normative/regulatory function.

The reparation/compensation function of tort law influences the jurisdictional rule to favour the plaintiff and allow him to recover his loss whereas the normative/regulatory function of tort law emphasizes that the claim for damages by the plaintiff is in the general interest of the community by deterring harmful conduct. This mechanism borrows traits from the concept of private enforcement.

These functions of tort law are inseparable from one another. They can be studied in substantive tort law, but also in private international law in the rules of conflict of laws. It is beyond the scope of this article to discuss at length the influence of the reparation and normative functions of tort law on the rules of private international law. It should be noted however, that these functions do not dictate any connecting factor in particular. Take for instance the general rule in the Rome II Regulation that the law applicable to a non-contractual obligation arising out of a tort/delict shall be the law of the country in which the damage occurs. It is difficult to argue that such a choice of connecting factor derives exclusively from the reparation function of tort liability, if only because the law thus designated might not be the most favourable to the alleged victim. However, at the normative level, it clearly indicates the legitimacy of the law of the victim to regulate the conduct causing damage, even when that conduct takes place on the territory of another State.

It could be argued that the substance of tort law influences the rules of international jurisdiction so that the alleged victim may sue at home the alleged tortfeasor. In this respect, the influence of the functions of tort liability on the jurisdictional rules is more straightforward than on the rules of conflict of laws. Conflict of laws rules are typically indirect and abstract, in the sense that the substantive content of the law that will eventually be applicable is not known when the connecting factor is chosen. As a result, the choice of a connecting factor, such as the law of the country in which the damage occurs, is not *per se* favourable to the alleged victim (except in the sense that it is the law that is best known to him). The only conflict of laws rules that directly favour the alleged victim are rules that offer him/her a discretionary choice between laws, such as article 7 in Rome II Regulation. These rules allow the plaintiff to compare the laws potentially applicable and to choose the law that is most favourable to his position. Jurisdiction rules, however, have a much more direct effect for several reasons. First, the Brussels I jurisdictional system usually offers the plaintiff a choice between jurisdictions. Any option open to the claimant is in itself a favour. Second, contrary to a conflict of laws rule, a jurisdiction rule that allows the plaintiff to litigate at home is always favourable to the plaintiff because of the practical advantages that it entails. It derives from that that a jurisdictional rule that allows the plaintiff to litigate at home is always favourable to both functions of tort liability: it enables the plaintiff to easily claim compensation (reparation function) which has a deterrent effect on potential tortfeasors (normative function).

It may be argued that it is the reparatory and normative functions of tort law that incite the legislator and the courts to favour the plaintiff. It is this substantive element that overturns the principle of jurisdictional protection of the defendant.

In the abstract, it should be noted that the influence of both functions at the jurisdictional stage is not beyond criticism. It has been argued that at this stage there is only an alleged victim and an alleged tortfeasor. There seems to be no reason at this early stage to favour the plaintiff at the expense of the defendant. This argument is precisely the base of the *actor sequitur forum rei* principle: since the alleged defendant does not owe anything to the claimant (until proven to the contrary), it is the latter that should bear the cost of litigating abroad, not the former. However, this criticism does not have the same clout against both functions of tort liability. It might be relevant when directed at the reparation function, because there is indeed no reason to believe that the defendant is liable at this point. It is therefore a question of fairness to determine who should bear the initial cost, and it is legitimate to argue that it should be the claimant. As far as the normative function is concerned, however, the perspective is no longer interpersonal or purely commutative; the interests at stake are not limited to those of a particular defendant against a particular claimant. The question here is whether it is in the general interest that, for the greater good, the claimant should bear the cost of litigating abroad, or the defendant. And here, it might be argued that even though there is no proof as of yet that the defendant is liable, the alleged tortfeasor should bear the cost nonetheless. The reason being that if it is the claimant who bears the costs, chances are that he/she will not claim compensation, failing to give to the deterrence effect its full power.

It would be all the easier to replace the *forum delicti* by a *forum victimae* given that there are also good reasons to get rid of the *forum delicti* in any case.

Firstly, the way it is interpreted makes it unforeseeable, and this even once the harmful event actually took place. This risk exists concerning cybertorts where the localization is artificial, as has been demonstrated above. Unfortunately, it is not only the case in that category of torts. For instance, if one looks at the *Kronhofer-Kolassa* stream of cases, it is not always easy to localize the factual elements of financial torts. In *Kronhofer*, the Court ruled that "the expression 'place where the harmful event occurred' does not refer to the place where the claimant is domiciled or where 'his assets are concentrated' by reason only of the fact that he has suffered financial damage there resulting from the loss of part of his assets which arose and was incurred in another Contracting State"[44]. In line with this case, the French *Cour de Cassation* decided in the *Luxalpha* case that "the place where the harmful event took place should not be confused with the domicile of the victim where his assets are located"[45]. In the *Kolassa* case, the Court of Justice ruled that "Under Article 5(3) of Regulation No 44/2001, the courts where the applicant is domiciled have jurisdiction, on the basis of the place where the loss occurred, to hear and determine such an action, particularly when the damage alleged occurred directly in the applicant's bank account held with a bank established within the area of jurisdiction of those courts"[46]. It proves quite difficult to reconcile these three cases: there were of course factual differences between them, but they were still quite close and the fact that they were decided differently exposes the risk of unforeseeability.

Secondly, the *forum delicti* allows for forum shopping in ways a *forum actoris* does not. To be perfectly honest, even if one is convinced that forum shopping is harmful and offers an unjust advantage to the claimant, it is undeniable that offering an option to the claimant, especially one that multiplies into sub-options (that can be further manipulated because of the artificiality of localization in many cases), not only allows the claimant to shop, but quite literally forces him to do so. And the fact that actions for a negative declaration were brought within the *forum delicti* only makes it even between the alleged victim and the alleged tortfeasor by doubling forum shopping. Conversely, a *forum victimae* offers no opportunity for forum shopping (except of course if it comes as an alternative to a *forum rei*).

Thirdly, a *forum delicti* is open to actions for a negative declaration which overturns the jurisdictional alternative intended to favour the victim whereas a *forum victimae* is not, being reserved to the victim. In any case, a plain *forum actoris*, open to both parties should be avoided.

At the end of the day, one should come to the conclusion that it is for the legislator, and not for the Court, to replace the *forum delicti* by a *forum victimae*. Indeed, this evolution (or rather revolution) is not without thorny issues that have been validly touched upon by AG Bobek in his opinion in the *Bolagsupplysningen* case. AG Bobek sought to rebut the argument that the *eDate* solution only aimed at protecting weaker natural

---

44 ECJ, *Kronhofer*, *op. cit.*, paragraph 21.

45 Cass. Com. 7 janvier 2014, *Luxalpha*, n° 11–24.157, "le lieu où s'est produit le fait dommageable ne saurait se confondre avec le lieu du domicile où est localisé le patrimoine de la demanderesse".

46 ECJ, *Kolassa*, *op. cit.*, paragraph 57.

persons and should not be applied to stronger legal persons. AG Bobek disagreed for four reasons. The first aside[47], they all relate to the practical difficulties that the protection of the weaker party would entail in tort litigations.

Generally, AG Bobek wondered about the consequences of a systematic application of "the weaker party rationale" in the silence of Regulation No 1215/2012. Should natural persons be considered "by definition always weak and legal persons always strong, independently of the concrete 'rapport des forces' in a given dispute?" It is indeed easy to imagine counterexamples and borderline cases. The problem is that, in the cyberworld as well as in the real world (and even more so) there is a sheer diversity "on the side of the claimant, but also on the side of the potential defendant". If "one were to embrace the logic of an individual assessment of mutual rapport de forces in concrete cases" this would have catastrophic consequences on the objective of the 'high predictability' of jurisdictional rules that Brussels I jurisdictional system pursues. Whatever the criteria, it is likely that a case by case approach would lead to a "laborious examination with an uncertain result (that) is perhaps not the best approach for deciding on international jurisdiction, which ought to be as swift and easy as possible".

Those are valid concerns that need to be addressed. A proposal to transform the *forum delicti* into a *forum victimae* shall not stop short of giving a few elements of its regime.

2.2. Regime of the Forum Victimae

It should be very clear that the *forum victimae* is a *forum actoris* for the victim and for the victim only. This is so because the main argument in favour of turning the *forum delicti* into a *forum actoris* is so that the alleged victim (not the alleged tortfeasor!) claims compensation more easily as part as a deterrence system. The alleged tortfeasor should only be allowed to initiate an action for a negative declaration at the domicile of the victim

47 The first one is of dogmatic nature and, as such, is not entirely convincing for the reasons already stated above. AG Bobek noted that "the jurisdictional rule under Article 7(2) of Regulation No 1215/2012 does not aim at protection of the weaker party (…). (T)he 'weaker party' rationale is clearly not present within the special jurisdictional rule for tortious matters. That type of jurisdiction relies instead on the *close connection* between the claim and the court competent to adjudicate upon it" (§ 64).

(here the *forum rei* and the *forum victimae* coincide because the victim is the defendant).

The second point, or rather question, is whether the *forum victimae* will be the only forum available to the victim. It is quite clear that the *forum delicti* should be eliminated, the last thing we need right now is yet another alternative *forum*. It cannot be ignored that in *Bolagsupplysningen* the Court refused to follow its Advocate General who was proposing a system along these lines. However, there would be no benefit, quite the contrary, in keeping the *forum delicti* if a *forum victimae* is opened. The thorniest issue remains that of the *forum rei*. Should it stay or should it go? It is a well-established rule and there is no reason to eliminate it since, if the claimant wishes so, it is in favour of the defendant. The only drawback is that it opens an alternative, and hence, forum shopping. At the end of the day, the claimant will only make use of it if he finds an advantage so powerful that it overcomes the advantage of litigating at home (for instance, enforcement of the decision, but within the Brussels system this concern might play a lesser role because cross-border enforcement is made considerably easier).

The question that begs to be asked is whether the *forum delicti* should give way to a general *forum victimae* or a *forum victimae* only for the weaker party.

It is tempting to envisage a general *forum victimae* for all alleged victims (weaker or not), notably in order to get rid of the *forum delicti* altogether. However, the risk of abuse should not be overlooked. One possibility would be to put in place a procedural control, maybe of the type that exists under English law for service out of the jurisdiction. The claimant could be required to establish, at a preliminary procedural stage (one that would not have to be contradictory, at first) that his claim has a reasonable prospect of success, that his domicile is not fraudulent (it is the basis of the jurisdiction). However, this should not lead to a *forum non conveniens*, a path barred by the Court of Justice, with good reasons, arguably.

Another possibility would be to restrict the *forum victimae* to the weaker party only. This would have the serious advantage (to some at least) of not completely overturning the principle of jurisdictional protection of the defendant. It would only put it aside when it is feared that the alleged victim is too weak to bear the cost of litigating abroad. The situation would be very close to the classical hypothesis of jurisdictional protection of weaker parties. In this case, it would be possible to replicate the protection of the consumer where there is no contract: when the loss occurs outside the profession of the victim and the alleged tortfeasor is a professional.

An argument in favour of this path is that in many of the cases where the Court seemed inclined to envisage a *forum actoris*, the alleged victim was in a weak position (*Kolassa*, *eDate*). However, the judgement in the *Bolagsupplysningen* case changes direction a bit.

Nor is this path without drawbacks: it would leave professionals and small businesses without protection, and it might well be argued that they deserve it as well.

The last issue to be settled is whether this *forum victimae* would be open only for individual actions, or if it would also be available for class actions. At the general level, one element to consider is that, if the reason to open a *forum victimae* in the first place is to protect a weaker party, there might not be any need for it when the weaker parties are made stronger by collective action. Another argument in favour of restricting class actions to the *forum rei* is that this would allow for broader EU-wide class actions whereas a class action initiated at the domicile of the victims would by definition be limited to forum victims. Ultimately, it is a policy question to determine if victims receive a protection that is sufficient through the collective redress or if it is necessary also to allow them to litigate at home. One difficulty is that not all Member States have collective redress mechanisms, and those collective redress mechanisms that exist have very different features. Allowing class actions only at the domicile of the defendant would encourage corporations to move their domicile to Member States that do not have a collective redress mechanism whereas allowing class actions at the victims' domicile could put pressure on the national legislator to adopt an efficient collective redress mechanism.

In conclusion, the rise in *Fora Actorum* seems hard to resist in cross-border tort litigations (with notable exceptions, such as *Universal Music*[48]). This paper argues that this can be explained by an incentive at the substantive level to favour the plaintiff. At the same time, there are reasons to eliminate the *forum delicti*, a jurisdiction rule that relies on a localization that often proves illusive and deceptive. However, if the true function of the *forum delicti* is to offer protection to the alleged victim, it should be possible to eliminate the *forum delicti* and replace it with a *forum victimae*. From this perspective, a *forum victimae* limited to the weaker party would not only realise this protection function but also allow for some protection of the defendant, when the alleged victim is not in a weak position.

48 ECJ, *Universal Music*, loc. cit.

CJEU Case-Law and *Forum Connexitatis*: an Analysis of the Close Connection Criterion

Lucilla Galanti[*]

Table of Contents

1. *Introduction*

Art 8(1) of Brussels Regulation (EU) No 1215/2012 (BR *Ibis*)[1] provides for a rule of special jurisdiction that applies to multiparty proceedings. In particular, it allows the claimant to sue the defendants before the court of the Member State in which one of them is domiciled, thus derogating the natural forum based on the domicile of the others, when the claims are so closely connected that there is a risk of irreconcilable judgements if not determined together.[2]

---

* Researcher in civil procedural law at the University of Florence, School of Law.

1 Regulation (EU) No 1215/2012 of the European Parliament and of the Council of 12 December 2012 on jurisdiction and the recognition and enforcement of judgments in civil and commercial matters (2012) 55 OJ L 351, 1.

2 Art 8(1) BR *Ibis* states that a person domiciled in a Member State may be sued, when there are multiple defendants 'in the courts for the place where any one of them is domiciled, provided the claims are so closely connected that it is expedient

Under this rule of jurisdiction, the anchor claim retains an attractive *vis*,[3] addressing the purpose of consolidating connected actions, with the objective of assuring procedural economy and compatible judgments.[4] The principle of *forum connexitatis* in fact meets 'the wish to facilitate the sound administration of justice, to minimise the possibility of concurrent proceedings and thus to avoid irreconcilable outcomes if cases are decided separately'.[5]

The relevance of the provision has progressively increased.[6] While the Regulation was grounded in the paradigm of traditional two-party litiga-

---

to hear and determine them together to avoid the risk of irreconcilable judgments resulting from separate proceedings'.

3 As the claims against a number of defendants may be brought before a court of a Member State in whose jurisdiction at least one of them is domiciled, i.e. the 'anchor defendant', the provision establishes a kind of derived jurisdiction, based on the connection between the proceedings. See Trevor Hartley, Civil jurisdiction and judgments in Europe (Oxford University Press 2017) 9.06; Francesco Salerno, *Giurisdizione ed efficacia delle decisioni straniere nel Regolamento (UE) n. 1215/2012* (Cedam 2015) 181 ff; Christoph Althammer, 'Die Anforderungen an die «Ankerklage» am forum connexitatis' [2006] Praxis des Internationalen Privat- und Verfahrensrechts, 558.

4 See Michele Angelo Lupoi, 'Il regolamento UE n. 1215 del 12 dicembre 2012', in Paolo Biavati and Michele Angelo Lupoi (eds), *Regole europee e giustizia civile* (3rd edn, Bononia University Press 2017) 41; Elena D'Alessandro, La connessione tra controversie transnazionali (2nd edn, Giappichelli 2009) 44 ff; Sergio Maria Carbone, Il nuovo spazio giudiziario europeo: dalla Convenzione di Bruxelles al Regolamento CE 44/2001 (4th edn, Giappichelli 2002) 100 ff; Sergio Maria Carbone, 'Giurisdizione ed efficacia delle decisioni in materia civile e commerciale nello spazio giudiziario europeo: dalla Convenzione di Bruxelles al Regolamento (CE) n. 44/2001', in Sergio Maria Carbone, Manlio Frigo, Luigi Fumagalli (eds), *Diritto processuale civile e commerciale comunitario*, (Giuffrè 2004) 27 ff; Paolo Vittoria, La competenza giurisdizionale e l'esecuzione delle decisioni in materia civile e commerciale nella giurisprudenza della Corte di Giustizia (Giuffrè 2005) 159 ff; Fabrizio Ravidà, 'Il Regolamento n. 44/2001 sulla Competenza Giurisdizionale, il Riconoscimento e l'Esecuzione delle Decisioni in Materia Civile e Commerciale', in Stefano Scarafoni (ed), *Il processo civile e la normativa comunitaria* (Utet 2012) 113, 218 ff.

5 Judgment of 20 April 2016, Case C-366/13, *Profit Investment Sim SpA, in liquidation v Stefano Ossi and Others*, ECLI:EU:C:2016:282, para 61; see also judgment of 21 May 2015, Case C-352/13, *Cartel Damage Claims (CDC) Hydrogen Peroxide SA v Akzo Nobel NV and Others*, ECLI:EU:C:2015:335, para 19; judgment of 12 July 2012, Case C-616/10, *Solvay SA v Honeywell Fluorine Products Europe BV and Others*, ECLI:EU:C:2012:445, para 19; judgment of 1 December 2011, Case C-145/10, *Eva-Maria Painer v Standard VerlagsGmbH and Others*, [2011] ECR I-12533, para 77.

6 See Burkhard Hess, 'The Brussel I Regulation: Recent Case Law of the Court of Justice and the Commission's Proposed Recast', (2012) 49 Common Market Law

tions, its implementation has gradually faced the proliferation of multi-party proceedings.[7]

The actual wording of the provision is the result of the CJEU's case-law. Under the Brussels Convention (BC), the consolidation of claims was based on the mere presence of a plurality of defendants: the 'so close connection' was not part of the original version of the rule.[8] This requirement was set out in the judgment in *Kalfelis*,[9] confirmed by the subsequent case-

Review, 1075, 1090, where it is stressed that '[s]ince the millennium, Article 6(1) Reg. 44/2001 has become one of the most important heads of jurisdiction'.

7 As the disposition applies by exception to the general rule laid down in art 4, it must be strictly interpreted; in fact, as the domicile of the defendant is involved as the general grounds of jurisdiction, it is only by way of derogation from it that BR *Ibis* provides for different (special) rules. See judgment in *CDC* (n 5), para 8; judgment in *Profit Investment* (n 5) para 63; judgment of 11 April 2013, Case C-645/11, *Land Berlin v Ellen Mirjam Sapir and Others*, ECLI:EU:C:2013:228, para 41; judgment in *Solvay* (n 5) paras 19–21; judgment in *Painer* (n 5) para 74; judgment of 11 October 2007, Case C-98/06, *Freeport plc v Olle Arnoldsson* [2007] ECR I-08319, paras 34–35; judgment of 13 July 2006, Case C-103/05, *Reisch Montage AG v Kiesel Baumaschinen Handels GmbH* [2006] ECR I-06827, paras 22–23; in relation to the Brussels Convention see also Judgment of 27 September 988, Case C-189/87, *Athanasios Kalfelis v Bankhaus Schröder and Others* [1988] ECR 5565, para 8; Judgment of 27 October 1998, Case C-51/97, *Réunion européenne SA and Others v Spliethoff's Bevrachtingskantoor BV and the Master of the vessel Alblasgracht V002* [1998] ECR I-06511, para 16.

8 Art 6(1) of the Brussels Convention on jurisdiction and the enforcement of judgments in civil and commercial matters [1972] OJ L 299, 32 ff, stated that a person domiciled in a Contracting State 'may also be sued', 'where he is one of a number of defendants, in the courts for the place where any one of them is domiciled'. See Antonietta Di Blase, Connessione e litispendenza nella Convenzione di Bruxelles (Cedam 1993) 39; Ana Quiñones Escámez, El foro de la pluralidad de demandados en los litigios internacionales (Eurolex 1996); Heredia Cervantes, *Proceso* internacional y pluralidad de partes (Comares 2002); Pierre Gothot and Dominique Holleaux, La Convention de Bruxelles du 27 septembre 1968 (Jupiter 1985) 62 ff.

9 In *Kalfelis* (n 7) para 13 the CJEU stated that between various actions brought by the same plaintiff against different defendants there must exist 'a connection of such a kind that it is expedient to determine those actions together in order to avoid the risk of irreconcilable judgments resulting from separate proceedings'. See also Paul Jenard, 'Report on the Convention on jurisdiction and the enforcement of judgments in civil and commercial matters' (1979) 591 OJ, 26, where it is underlined that '[i]n order for this rule to be applicable there must be a connection between the claims made against each of the defendants'.

law,[10] and then expressly introduced by law in art 6(1) of Regulation(EC) No 44/2001 (BR I),[11] as actually replaced by art 8(1) BR I*bis*.[12]

However, the scope of the rule has proven to be problematic, since the content of the 'close connection' remains undefined in concrete terms.

As the provision does not supply a definition, the close connection has been progressively identified through a case-by-case approach, which will be analysed in section 2.

Section 3 will conversely examine if, beyond the close connection, further requirements are involved in order to implement the rule.

Lastly, section 4 will draw some conclusions.

2. *Connected Claims and Irreconcilability between Judgments*

In the wording of art 8(1) the close connection between the claims is related to the risk of irreconcilable judgments.

The provision does not expressly outline the notion of irreconcilability. In particular, it does not clarify when different judgments between linked claims could be regarded as incompatible,[13] nor specify if the meaning of

---

10 See Judgment in *Réunion européenne* (n 7) para 48.

11 Art 6(1) of the Council Regulation (EC) No 44/2001 of 22 December 2000 on jurisdiction and the recognition and enforcement of judgments in civil and commercial matters [2001] OJ L 12, 1 ff, stated that a person domiciled in a Member State could also be sued 'where he is one of a number of defendants, in the courts for the place where any one of them is domiciled, provided the claims are so closely connected that it is expedient to hear and determine them together to avoid the risk of irreconcilable judgments resulting from separate proceedings'.

12 In the analysis of art 8(1), CJEU case-law referring to the previous dispositions of the rule has to be taken into consideration. See recital (34), which affirms the continuity between the 1968 Brussels Convention (BC), the Regulation No 44/2001 and the BR I*bis* and their CJEU interpretation. It should be noted that the provision also matches the rule comprised in the Lugano Convention (Convention on jurisdiction and the recognition and enforcement of judgments in civil and commercial matters of 30 October [2007] OJ L 339, 3), which at art 6(1) states that a person domiciled in a State bound by the Convention may also be sued 'where he is one of a number of defendants, in the courts for the place where any one of them is domiciled, provided the claims are so closely connected that it is expedient to hear and determine them together to avoid the risk of irreconcilable judgments resulting from separate proceedings'.

13 At the same time the disposition must be interpreted independently, in accordance with the purpose of the Regulation, and without deriving its interpretation from the domestic law. See Judgment in *CDC* (n 5), para 16; CJEU Judgment in *Reisch Montage* (n 7) paras 29–30. On the theme of the inter-relationships between

the provision has an equivalent in other provisions of the Regulation, where the concept of irreconcilability is considered also in the context of related actions and non-recognition.[14]

On the one hand, irreconcilability between judgments is considered as a ground for non-recognition under art 45(1), lett c.[15] This rule is not perfectly comparable to art 8(1), since they have different objectives:[16] while art 8(1) seeks to avoid the risk of irreconcilable judgments before they occur, non-recognition refers to already existing judgments.[17]

As a consequence, non-recognition, as an exceptional case, has to be narrowly interpreted, in relation to judgments entailing mutually exclusive legal consequences.[18] Art 8(1) instead refers to judgments between the claimant and different defendants, which could not involve, by definition,

---

European and national law under a procedural perspective, see Remo Caponi, 'Addio ai controlimiti? (Per una tutela della identità nazionale degli Stati Membri dell'Unione Europea)', in Elena Falletti and Valeria Piccone (eds), *Il nodo gordiano tra diritto nazionale e diritto europeo* (Cacucci 2012) 43, 44 ff.

14 For the purpose of the stay of connected actions under art 30(3), 'actions are deemed to be related where they are so closely connected that it is expedient to hear and determine them together to avoid the risk of irreconcilable judgments resulting from separate proceedings' (as, before, the related actions, under art 28(3) BR I, and, analogously, art 22 BC). Art 45, instead, in relation to the refusal of recognition, states that the recognition of a judgement shall be refused when characterized by irreconcilability with other judgments (similarly, art 34 BR I and, before, art 27 BC). On the concept of 'irreconcilable judgments' see Trevor Hartley (n 3) para 9.08; Michele Angelo Lupoi (n 4) 41–42.

15 According to art 45(1), lett c, on the application of any interested party, the recognition of a judgment shall be refused also 'if the judgment is irreconcilable with a judgment given between the same parties in the Member State addressed'. This provision is equivalent to art 34(3) of BRI and 27(3) of BC.

16 See the opinion of AG Trstenjak in *Painer*, 12 April 2011, ECLI:EU:C:2011:239, para 61, in which it is affirmed that 'Article 34(3) of the regulation and Article 6(1) concern different situations and therefore have a different objective'.

17 *Ibid*, para 63.

18 *Ibid*, para 62, where it is underlined that non-recognition is 'an exceptional case, where a derogation from the principle of the virtually automatic recognition of judgments (…) is exceptionally justified. For that reason, that provision must be given a narrow interpretation and be restricted to judgments entailing legal consequences that are mutually exclusive'. In this perspective, in order to ascertain whether different judgments are irreconcilable 'it should be examined whether they entail legal consequences that are mutually exclusive': Judgment of 4 February 1988, *Horst Ludwig Martin Hoffmann v Adelheid Krieg* (*Hoffman*), C 145/86 [1988] ECR 645, para 22; Judgment of 6 June 2002, *Italian Leather SpA v WECO Polstermöbel GmbH & Co.*, C-80/00 [2002] ECR I-4995, para 40. Since the rule 'constitutes an obstacle to the achievement of one of the fundamental objectives

mutually exclusive consequences, only existing where the two judgments are given between the same parties.[19]

On the other hand, art 30(3) BR I*bis* provides for the stay of proceedings referring to the risk of irreconcilable judgments.[20] This provision also does not perfectly correspond to art 8(1).[21] In fact, it does not have the effect of systematically removing the defendants from their 'natural' jurisdiction (i.e. the one of their domicile, according to art 4 BR I*bis*): the court can decline jurisdiction only if the law of that court permits the consolidation of related actions, on the application of one of the parties. However, art

---

of the Convention, which is to facilitate, to the greatest extent possible, the free movement of judgments by providing for a simple and rapid enforcement procedure', it must be interpreted strictly: Judgment of the Court of 2 June 1994, *Solo Kleinmotoren GmbH v Emilio Boch*, C-414/92 [1994] ECR I-2237, para 20.

19 Referring to the previous version of art 8(1), see opinion AG Trstenjak in *Painer* (n 16) para 16: 'A case where the legal consequences of two judgments are mutually exclusive will, as a rule, exist only where the two judgments are given between the same parties. Because Article 6(1) of the regulation does not apply to this case, however, but a case where the two judgments are given, first, between the applicant and the defendant in the anchor claim and, secondly, between the applicant and another defendant, there will not, as a rule, be legal consequences that are mutually exclusive within the meaning of Article 34(3) of the regulation. Even if the judgments were irreconcilable, they could nevertheless both generally be enforced'.

20 To the extent of art 30, which provides for the staying of proceedings where related actions are pending before the courts of different Member States, any court other than the court first seised may stay its proceedings where related actions are pending in the courts of different Member States. As the provision states, 'actions are deemed to be related where they are so closely connected that it is expedient to hear and determine them together to avoid the risk of irreconcilable judgments resulting from separate proceedings'. The article is the same as art 28(3) BRI and 22(3) BC.

21 The original provision outlined in art 6(1) BC did not contain any reference to irreconcilability, introduced by the judgment in *Kalfelis* referring to the connection between the actions as considered under art 22 BC. On this point, see opinion AG Trstenjak in *Painer* (n 16) para 67: 'the wording of Article 6(1) of the regulation stems from the Court's case-law on Article 6(1) of the Brussels Convention and the Court took the predecessor provision to Article 28(3) of the regulation, the third paragraph of Article 22 of the Brussels Convention, as its reference point'. See also the opinion of AG Léger of 8 December 2005 in *Roche Nederland*, ECLI:EU:C:2005:749, para 73. Even if art 8(1) has been modelled on art 22 BC, which represents the original version of art 30 BR I*bis*, the content of the dispositions is not equivalent.

8(1) automatically leads to the result of derogating the general rule of jurisdiction.[22]

Furthermore, under art 30(3) the reasons for the proceedings to be consolidated are established by the court – and, thus, they should be inspired by considerations regarding the proper administration of justice – while the option rests with the claimant under art 8(1).[23]

Therefore, even if the Court broadly interprets the irreconcilability for the purpose of the stay of proceedings,[24] as a notion which does not necessarily involve the risk of mutually exclusive legal consequences, the more invasive effects of art 8(1) on the scope of art 4 justifies a narrower interpretation of the rule.[25]

Accordingly, the notion of irreconcilability under art 8(1) cannot be defined by comparison to art 30(3), nor to art 45(3), since it is narrower than the former and broader than the latter. Even if the rule excludes that

---

22 *Ibid*, paras 81–82: '[t]he end result of such a mechanism for extending jurisdiction' is 'systematically' to deprive the defendants 'of their natural jurisdiction', while 'the effect of the mechanism' provided for in the rule related to stay of proceeding on the general rule of jurisdiction 'is not systematic'.

23 In fact, while 'the option for the second court seised to decline jurisdiction pursuant to Article 22 of the Brussels Convention rests entirely with that court, and not with the applicant, who may only make application to that effect', the decision 'to apply Article 6(1) of the said Convention rests solely with the applicant, and not with the court': *Ibid*, paras 92 and 95. The 'national court will take the decisions (...) having regard to the need for the harmonious administration of justice'; on the contrary, the applicant will not 'be guided by the need for the harmonious administration of justice, but according to the jurisdiction which is more favourable to him': opinion AG Trstenjak in *Painer* (n 16) paras 70–71.

24 In *Tatry* (judgment of 6 December 1994, The owners of the cargo lately laden on board the ship 'Tatry' v the owners of the ship 'Maciej Rataj', C-406/92 [1994] ECR I-5439, paras 51–52 and 57), referring to art 22 BC, the Court held that '[t]he purpose of that provision is to avoid the risk of conflicting judgments and thus to facilitate the proper administration of justice in the Community'; '[i]n order to achieve proper administration of justice, that interpretation must be broad and cover all cases where there is a risk of conflicting decisions, even if the judgments can be separately enforced and their legal consequences are not mutually exclusive'.

25 In this perspective, the difference between the provisions regarding their effect on the general rule of jurisdiction justifies 'the different conditions of connectedness required for their respective application'; a broad interpretation of art 8(1) 'would inevitably lead to a significant reduction' of the situations in which the general rule of jurisdiction would be applied: opinion AG Léger in *Roche Nederland* (n 21) paras 88–89 and 91, where it is considered 'preferable not to transpose [...] the broad interpretation of the concept' of related actions.

proceedings could be consolidated solely for reasons of expediency and proper administration of justice[26], it 'may be interpreted in many ways'.[27]

---

26 The 'possibility for the national court to extend its jurisdiction to co-defendants domiciled abroad solely for reasons of expediency, however legitimate they may be, based on the needs of the proper administration of justice' is excluded: opinion AG Bot of 23 April 2015 in *Profit Investment* ECLI:EU:C:2015:274, para 95. As stated also by CJEU in *Profit Investment* (n 5) paras 66–67, the mere fact that the result of one of the procedures may have an effect on the result of the other 'does not suffice to characterise the judgments to be delivered in the two procedures as "irreconcilable"'. On the case, see Luca Penasa, 'Corte di giustizia: decisioni in materia di giurisdizione' [2016], Il Corriere giuridico, 117; Sabine Corneloup, 'Investor Issuer Disputes under the Brussels I Regulation. The CJEU Profit Investment Sim Ruling on Enforceability of Jurisdiction Clauses', (2016) 3 Revue Internationale des Services Financiers 24.

27 As explained by AG Maduro in the opinion of 17 January 2008 in *GlaxoSmithKline, Laboratoires GlaxoSmithKline v Jean-Pierre Rouard*, ECLI:EU:C:2009:40, paras 29 ff, on a 'strict' interpretation, the application of the rule depends on a risk that separate judgments might give rise to mutually exclusive legal consequences, while, under a 'broad' interpretation, the notion would involve the risk of conflicting decisions. The strict approach seems to be adopted by AG Léger in *Roche Nederland*, where it is affirmed that there could be a consolidation of claims where it is 'expedient to hear and determine them together in order to avoid the risk of irreconcilable judgments' (in the perspective attributed to *Kalfelis*) and not just 'conflicting ones' (within the meaning of the judgment in *Tatry*). In the perspective of the AG there is no irreconcilability where the defendants concerned by the judgments are different, as the decisions 'may be enforced separately and simultaneously for each of them'. At the same time, there is no mutual exclusion between the judgments when their legal consequences cover a different territory, as happens where the court rules only on the alleged infringements of the rights of the patent holder in each of the States over which these courts have jurisdiction: opinion AG Léger in *Roche Nederland* (n 21) paras 101 and 109. On the contrary, in the opinion of AG Trstenjak in *Painer* (n 16) para 68, the rule is considered to be interpreted 'to the effect that it is sufficient for the existence of a connection between two questions that separate judgment would involve the risk of conflicting decisions', without necessarily involving the possibility of giving rise to mutually exclusive legal consequences. Yet in *Kalfelis*, the opinion of AG Darmon of 15 June 1988 [1988] ECR 5565, para 15 emphasized that the expression 'contradictory decisions' stresses 'unequivocally, that the choice made favours a solution of sufficient breadth' instead of requiring the impossibility of enforcing two decisions simultaneously. The same broad approach seems (incidentally) to emerge also in other cases, where the irreconcilability seems to be linked to a mere divergence between the judgments. See judgment in *CDC* (n 5) para 20; judgment in *Sapir* (n 7) para 43; judgment in *Painer* (n 5) para 79; judgment in *Freeport* (n 7) para 40; judgment of 13 July 2006, Case C-539/03, *Roche Nederland BV and Others v Frederick Primus and Milton Goldenbergin* [2006] ECR I-6535, para 26.

On these bases, an analysis focused only on the notion of irreconcilability could not lead to a clear individuation of connected claims.[28]

As indicated by case law, irreconcilability represents a part of a more comprehensive examination. From this perspective, a divergence in the outcome of the disputes does not suffice for judgments to be regarded as irreconcilable 'but that divergence must also arise in the context of the same situation of fact and law'.[29]

This requirement – the same situation of law and fact – seems to represent the very core issue in defining the close connection and to individuate the scope of the rule.[30]

2.1. *The Same Situation of Fact and Law: An Early "Rigorous" Approach*

The interpretation of this requirement has sensibly changed in CJEU case law.

At first, the CJEU adopted a rigorous approach in assessing the existence of a same situation of fact and law, requiring a strict identity: there was not a same situation of law when the provisions of different national laws were applicable, and a same situation of fact was to be excluded in the existence of different misconducts. This approach emerges from the judgements in *Réunion européenne* as well as in *Roche Nederland.*

---

28 In fact, the 'general guidelines' established by the Court 'do not provide a very clear indication of the scope of the condition as to the irreconcilability of judgments'; this also because 'the assessment of the connecting link depends in large measure on the factual circumstances of each case, which makes it difficult to establish a clear criterion': See the opinion AG Bot of 23 April 2015 in *Profit Investment* (n 26) para 94.

29 Judgment in *CDC* (n 5) para 20; judgement in *Sapir* (n 7) paras 42–43; judgement in *Solvay* (n 5) para 24; judgement in *Painer* (n 5) para79; judgement in *Freeport* (n 7) para 40; judgment in *Roche Nederland* (n 27) para 26; most recently see also judgement in *Profit Investment* (n 5) para 65 and judgement of 27 September 2017, Joined Cases C-24/16 and C-25/16, *Nintendo Co. Ltd v BigBen Interactive GmbH and BigBen Interactive SA*, ECLI:EU:C:2017:724, para 45.

30 Individuating the requirement of close connection 'is no doubt the most difficult issue of interpretation in respect of the text of Art 8 (1)': See Horatia Muir Watt, 'Art 8', in Ulrich Magnus, Peter Mankowski (eds), *Brussels Ibis Regulation* (Otto Schmidt 2016) para 25.

In *Réunion européenne*[31] the existence of a same situation of law was denied regarding claims based on contractual lability and liability in tort or delict.[32]

Both sides of the notion were considered in *Roche Nederland*, where the Court equally excluded the application of what is now art 8(1),[33] showing a similar strict approach.[34]

---

31 The case was related to proceedings brought by nine insurance companies (and, as lead insurer, *Réunion Européenne*), which, after paying compensation for the damages suffered by a company, were subrogated to its rights; the insurers claimed that the dispute was indivisible since the proceedings involved the same transport operation. In such a context, the Court excluded the so close connection; in fact, it held that various claims 'directed against different defendants and based in one instance on contractual liability and in the other on liability in tort or delict cannot be regarded as connected': CJEU judgement in *Réunion européenne* (n 7) para 50. However, as should be noted, in that case the applicability of what is now art 8(1) was to be excluded in advance as the proceedings were not brought before the courts of the defendant's domicile, while the *forum connexitatis* relies only on that grounds for jurisdiction. As the Court underlines (paras 44–45), it is clear from the very wording of the provision that it applies 'only if the proceedings in question are brought before the courts for the place where one of the defendants is domiciled', which was not in that case, where the jurisdiction was founded on art 5(3).

32 The Court's ruling in *Réunion européenne* has been criticized for its strict interpretation of the 'same situation of law'. See Horatia Muir Watt, 'Art 6', in Ulrich Magnus, Peter Mankowski (eds), *Brussels I Regulation on Jurisdiction and Recognition in Civil and Commercial Matters* (2nd edn, Sellier 2012) para 13, who underlines the 'practically undesirable results' deriving from this interpretation. On this case, see Trevor Hartley, 'Carriage of goods and the Brussels Jurisdiction and Judgments Convention' [2000] European Law Review, 89–93; Marco Lopez De Gonzalo 'Questioni di giurisdizione in tema di concorso di azione contrattuale ed extracontrattuale' [1999] Diritto del commercio internazionale, 517; Ana Crespo Hernández, 'Delimitación entre materia contractual y extracontractual en el Convenio de Bruselas: Implicaciones en orden a la determinación de la competencia judicial internacional' (1998) 4681, La ley – Unión Europea 1998, 1 ff.

33 The case was related to proceedings brought against *Roche Nederland BV* and other companies of the Roche group in respect of an alleged infringement of an European patent. On this case, see Annette Kur, 'A Farewell to Cross-Border Injunctions? The CJEU Decisions GAT v Luk and Roche Nederland v Primus and Goldenberg' [2006] International Review of Intellectual Property and Competition Law, 844; E. Bodson, 'Le brevet européen est-il différent?: L'arrêt Roche Nederland de la Cour de justice: vers une révision du réglement de Bruxelles en ce qui concerne la concentration de litiges transfrontaliers en matière de contrefaçon de brevets européens?' (2007) 84 Revue de droit international et de droit comparé, 447; Michael Wilderspin, 'La compétence juridictionnelle en matière de

In that case, related to an alleged infringement of European patent law, the Court excluded the existence of the same situation of law. Since under the Munich Convention a European patent continues to be governed by the national law of each of the Contracting States for which it has been granted, even if some common rules are laid down, any action for infringement must be examined in light of the relevant national law in force in each of these States.[35] Thus, where infringement proceedings are brought against defendants domiciled in various Contracting States in respect of acts allegedly committed in each of those States in which the patent is granted, 'any divergences between the decisions given by the courts concerned would not arise in the context of the same legal situation'.[36]

At the same time, the Court also excluded the existence of the same situation of fact. This requirement could not be inferred in the case of European patent infringement proceedings involving a number of companies established in various States with respect to acts committed in various territories, as, in the adopted perspective, 'the defendants are different and the infringements they are accused of (…) are not the same'.[37]

It should be noted that in that case the defendants were companies belonging to the same group. Notwithstanding, the conclusion does not change even if the defendant companies have acted in an identical or similar manner in accordance with a common policy elaborated by one of

litiges concernant la violation des droits de propriété intellectuelle', [2006] Revue critique de droit international privé, 777.

34 The Court in fact stated that the rule 'does not apply in European patent infringement proceedings involving a number of companies established in various Contracting States in respect of acts committed in one or more of those States even where those companies, which belong to the same group, may have acted in an identical or similar manner in accordance with a common policy elaborated by one of them': judgment in *Roche Nederland*, (n 27) para 41.

35 *Ibid*, paras 29–30.

36 The context of a same situation of fact and law is excluded since 'any action for infringement of a European patent must be examined in the light of the relevant national law in force in each of the States for which it has been granted': Judgment in *Roche Nederland* (n 27) paras 30–31. As referred also by AG Léger (n 21) paras 114 and 117, 'outside the scope of the common rules laid down in the Munich Convention (…), such a patent continues to be governed by the national legislation', and, one granted, it becomes 'a bundle of national patents'.

37 Judgment in *Roche Nederland* (n 27) para 27, where it is specified that the same situation of fact cannot be inferred where 'the defendants are different and the infringements they are accused of, committed in different Contracting States, are not the same'.

them: even assuming that in this perspective 'the factual situation would be the same', nevertheless 'the legal situation would not be the same'.[38]

In that conclusion, the predictability of the consolidation between the claims also has a role.[39]

Since art 8(1) derogates the natural forum of the defendant's domicile and represents an exception to the general rule provided for in art 4,[40] it is expedient that the defendants are able to foresee they may be sued in a different (and presumably more cumbersome) forum.[41]

According to the early strict perspective, the consolidation of the claims was not considered foreseeable if different legal bases were involved: pre-

38 *Ibid*, paras 34–35.

39 Within the wording of BC no reference to the notion of predictability is made; notwithstanding, the CJEU used to link this concept to the provisions on legal certainty. In this perspective, in the judgment in *Roche Nederland* (n 27) para 37 the potential undermining of the predictability of the rules of jurisdiction laid down by the Convention is associated to the undermining of the principle of legal certainty. An express indication on predictability is firstly introduced in BR I, at recital(11), where it is stated that '[t]he rules of jurisdiction must be highly predictable and founded on the principle that jurisdiction is generally based on the defendant's domicile'. That principle, enhanced by case-law – see judgment in *Painer* (n 5) para 75; judgment in *Freeport* (n 7) para 36; judgment in *Solvay* (n 5) paras 19–20; judgment in *Profit Investment* (n 5) para 62 – is considerably implemented by BR I*bis*. In this context, in addition to recital (15) BR I*bis* – replacing the previous version of recital (11) – recital (16) affirms that, in relation to the alternative grounds of jurisdiction based on close connection between the court and the action or in order to facilitate the sound administration of justice, legal certainty should be ensured avoiding 'the possibility of the defendant being sued in a court of a Member State which he could not reasonably have foreseen'.

40 It is underlined that the lack of predictability 'is still a problem' under the rule: see Thomas Pfeiffer 'Jurisdiction', in Burkhard Hess, Thomas Pfeiffer and Peter Schlosser (eds), *Report on the Application of Regulation Brussels I in the Member States* (Study JLS/C4/2005/03, Institut für ausländisches und internationales Privat- und Wirtschaftsrecht 2007, para 223.

41 In this perspective, predictability seems to have an equivalent value – when not even greater – with respect to procedural economy and to the avoidance of legal inconsistencies, objectives to be pursued without prejudice to the former. See opinion in *Painer* (n 16) paras 96 and 98, where AG Trstenjak notes that the avoidance of legal inconsistencies can justify a transfer of jurisdiction 'only where this is predictable for the defendant', and also considerations of procedural economy can be taken into account but 'strict regard must be had to the defendant's interest in the predictability of jurisdiction'. See Paul Torremans, 'Jurisdiction for Cross-Border Intellectual Property Infringement Cases in Europe' (2016) 53 Common Market Law Review 1625, 1641, where the predictability is considered 'one of the foundations' of the regulation.

dictability was automatically excluded if the laws applicable to the claims were not identical. In *Roche Nederland*, the CJEU stated that a rule of jurisdiction based solely on factual criteria, which are concretely set out by the national courts, would be liable to undermine the predictability of the Brussels system.[42] The same perspective emerges from the opinion of AG Léger. To ensure predictability, it is the view of the AG that the same situation of fact will not suffice, nor in a context where the defendant companies belong to a same group and committed identical or similar infringements.[43]

2.2. *The Evolution of the Concept of "Same Situation of Fact and Law"*

This interpretation was not completely satisfying as it could lead to the undesirable result of determining separately claims presenting a connection[44]. Thus, at a later stage, CJEU case-law came to a less formalistic approach in relation to both the requirements.

When it could be said that the same situation of law exists, this means that a legal framework, even if not fully harmonized, would suffice for the application of the rule.

This perspective emerges from the judgement in *Freeport*.[45] The Court, notwithstanding that it referred to its precedent case-law where it pointed out that the divergence in the outcome of the dispute must arise in the context of same law and fact,[46] stated that the rule applies not only when a

42 Judgment in *Roche Nederland* (n 27) paras 37–38.

43 Opinion of AG Léger in *Roche Nederland* (n 21) paras 127–129; thus, expressly rejecting 'the spider in the web' theory. The AG also underlines the importance of interpreting the rules of the BC 'in such a way as to enable a normally well-informed defendant reasonably to foresee before which courts, other than those of the State in which he is domiciled, he may be sued': *Ibid*, para 126.

44 Horatia Muir Watt (n 30) para 27, where it is underlined that the previous approach was 'overly dogmatic'.

45 The case was related to an action brought seeking an order against two linked companies for the payment of a sum that only one of them had expressly agreed on: see Judgment in *Freeport* (n 7) paras 12–13. On this case, see Andrew Scott, 'Réunion Revised? Freeport v. Arnoldsson' [2008] Lloyd's Maritime and Commercial Law Quarterly, 113.

46 As held in *Roche Nederland* (n 27) para 26.

single law is involved, but also when different legal bases are involved in the claims brought against a number of defendants.[47]

In the subsequent case-law this interpretation has been confirmed[48], particularly from the judgements in *Painer* and in *Sapir.*

In the latter, the Court further specifies that even if the claims do not have a single legal basis, they could have an origin in a single situation of law and fact and an identical nature when directed at the same interest. In that case, the common origin and interest was represented by the repayment of an erroneously transferred surplus amount.[49]

In *Painer*, where the case was related to proceedings for copyright infringements[50] and the actions brought against the defendants were based on differing national legal grounds, the 'enlarged' notion of identical legal basis has been confirmed. The Court also recognized the existence of a same situation of law, since the essential elements were the same in their substance.[51]

---

47 Judgment in *Freeport* (n 7). As held by the Court para 38 and 47, it is not apparent from the wording of the article 'that the conditions laid down for application of that provision include a requirement that the actions brought against different defendants should have identical legal bases', thus the rule 'is to be interpreted as meaning that the fact that claims brought against a number of defendants have different legal bases does not preclude application of that provision'.

48 Interpretation which has been appreciated also by legal literature; see Michele Angelo Lupoi (n 4) 42; Francesco Salerno (n 3) 186.

49 *Ibid*, paras 45 and 47–48. In that case, related to a request concerning the repayment of an amount overpaid in error following an administrative procedure, the claims were based on the recovery of the sum unduly paid and, regarding one of the defendants, on a tortious act. The Court, restating that the same legal basis is not a necessary requirement for the application of the article, affirmed that the rule 'must be interpreted as meaning that there is a close connection […] in circumstances such as those at issue in the main proceedings, rely on rights to additional compensation which it is necessary to determine on a uniform basis'.

50 The case was related to proceedings between a freelance photographer, Ms Painer, as applicant, and five newspaper publishers, as defendants, concerning some photographs produced and sold by the former without conferring on third parties any rights nor providing consent to their publication.

51 In fact, as the Court notes, 'a difference in legal basis between the actions brought against the various defendants, does not, in itself, preclude the application', reasoning which is even stronger if 'the national laws on which the actions against the various defendants are based are (…) substantially identical; thus, the article 'must be interpreted as not precluding its application solely because actions against several defendants for substantially identical copyright infringements are brought on national legal grounds which vary according to the Member States concerned': judgment in *Painer* (n 5) paras 81–82 and 84. In fact, in cases governed by a law which is the same in substance even if not fully harmonized, a 'suf-

A similar trend characterizes the factual situation. The formalistic perspective, in which differences between the plurality of infringements committed in various States could exclude the existence of a same situation of fact, appears dismissed in favour of a "substantial" appraisement of the fact. From this perspective, it seems that different misconducts could be deemed as a same situation of fact when concerted.

If in *Roche Nederland* the Court had already incidentally considered if the defendants acted 'in accordance with a common policy',[52] in *Painer* it expressly holds that 'the fact that defendants against whom a copyright holder alleges substantially identical infringements of his copyright did or did not act independently may be relevant'. Thus, in determining whether there is a connection between different claims, the evaluation has to be carried out in the light of all the elements of the case, also considering the presence of independent or concerted actions.[53]

The more extensive approach in the evaluation of the same situation of fact and law has some consequences also on predictability. The Court explained that a difference in the legal basis does not in itself preclude the consolidation of proceedings if foreseeable by the defendants, meaning that predictability is no longer exclusively connected to the existence of the same law.[54] Thus, when claims are not based on the same legal basis, predictability involves consideration of the fact: in these cases, the existence of concerted actions seems to become the crucial factor in the evaluation of predictability. If the defendants have previously coordinated their actions,

---

ficient legal connection' may equally exist: opinion AG Trstenjak in *Painer* (n 16) para 80 and 105.

52 Judgment in *Roche Nederland* (n 27) para 34.

53 Judgment in *Painer* (n 5) para 83. The importance of an agreement between the defendants emerges, *a contrario*, also from the opinion of AG Trstenjak (n 16) para 104, where it is affirmed that a single factual situation 'cannot be taken to exist where the contested conduct of the anchor defendant and of the other defendant appears to be unconcerted parallel conduct'. See Paul Torremans (n 41) 1642, where it is underlined that 'after *Painer*, neither the first nor the second condition established in *Roche Nederland* remains intact.' See also Beatriz Campuzano Diaz, 'The CJEU Again with the Forum of the Plurality of Defendants', (2012) 4 Cuadernos Derecho Transnacional 245, 255.

54 Judgement in *Painer* (n 5) para 81. In fact, 'a difference in legal basis between the actions brought against the various defendants, does not, in itself, preclude the application' of the article, 'provided however that it was foreseeable by the defendants that they might be sued in the Member State where at least one of them is domiciled'.

they have to be considered as being reasonably able to foresee the consolidation of the proceedings.[55]

2.3. *The Confirmation of the Extensive Approach in Patent and Design Cases*

The more extensive approach has been recently confirmed in *Solvay*, a case related to proceedings regarding alleged infringements of a European patent – i.e. the very same field where the judgment in *Roche Nederland* took a strict approach – where the Court, even without overruling its precedent,[56] adopted a less formalistic perspective.[57]

---

55 While in *Roche Nederland* predictability of consolidation between proceedings was exclusively related to law, excluding the possibility to foresee the consolidation of claims when the legal basis was not identical, this element is no longer necessary. As emerges from the judgment in *Painer*, a difference in legal basis between the actions brought against various defendants does not preclude the application of what is now art 8(1), recognizing that such a difference does not, in itself, preclude predictability. When not related to the same law, predictability seems to be related to the fact, and, in particular, to the existence of concerted actions. On these bases, the Court states that what is now art. 8(1) 'must be interpreted as not precluding its application solely because actions against several defendants for substantially identical copyright infringements are brought on national legal grounds which vary according to the Member States concerned' (para 84).

56 The judgment in *Solvay* (n 5) para 25 in fact recalls the principle ruled in *Roche Nederland* that the existence of the same situation of fact 'cannot be inferred where the defendants are different and the infringements they are accused of [...] are not the same'. Notwithstanding, the Court distinguished the conclusion to be reached on the case in relation to its 'specific features', since the case was related to the 'same national part' of the patent. For this reason, the two cases could be distinguished: see Trevor Hartley (n 3) para 9.19.

57 In this perspective, the Court stated that '[i]t follows from the specific features of a case such as that in the main proceedings that potential divergences in the outcome of the proceedings are likely to arise in the same situation of fact and law' and that connection between the different claims has to be established also taking into account 'the dual fact that, first, the defendants in the main proceeding are each separately accused of committing the same infringements with respect to the same products and, secondly, such infringements were committed in the same Member States, so that they adversely affect the same national parts of the European patent at issue': judgment in *Solvay* (n 5) paras 27 and 29. On these bases, the CJEU held that what is now art 8(1) applies where two or more companies from different Member States are accused of committing an infringement 'of the same national part of a European patent which is in force in yet another Member State by virtue of their performance of reserved actions with regard to the same

In this particular matter, there could not be in existence, by definition, an identical legal basis, if strictly considered since under the Munich Convention a European patent appears as a bundle of national patents. On the contrary, as the alleged infringements were related to the 'same national part' of a patent, if the *forum connexitatis* were not applicable the infringements would have been examined by the courts in the light of the different national legislations governing the various national parts of the patent.

This perspective seems to be (even more) suitable to the new Unitary Patent.[58] In light of the rules laid down by the Agreement on a Unified Patent Court, the coordination between art 8(1) and the rule of exclusive jurisdiction in this matter, i.e. art 24(4) BR I*bis*, could also be (re)examined:[59] contrary to the previous interpretation, the question of validity of

---

product': *Ibid*, para 30. As AG Villalón said in the opinion in *Solvay*, 29 March 2012, ECLI:EU:C:2012:193, para 23, this interpretation could be confirmed also because it is possible to adopt a more 'nuanced' approach, carefully circumscribing the scope of the ruling in *Roche Nederland*.

58 See the EU regulations providing the legal framework for the Unitary Patent system (patent package): Regulation (EU) No 1257/2012 of the European Parliament and of the Council of 17 December 2012 implementing enhanced cooperation in the area of the creation of unitary patent protection [2012] OJ L 361, 1 ff, creating the European patent with unitary effect, and Council Regulation (EU) No 1260/2012 of 17 December 2012 implementing enhanced cooperation in the area of the creation of unitary patent protection with regard to the applicable translation arrangements [2012] OJ L 361, 89 ff. It has to be emphasized that the Agreement on a Unified Patent Court [2013] OJ C 175, 1 ff also established a Unified Patent Court. Subsequently to its establishment the BR I*bis* has been amended: see the Regulation (EU) No 542/2014 of the European Parliament and of the Council of 15 May 2014 amending Regulation (EU) No 1215/2012 regarding the rules to be applied with respect to the Unified Patent Court and the Benelux Court of Justice [2014] OJ L 163, 1 ff. On the developments related to this point, see Peter Schlosser, 'Intellectual Property Rights' in Burkhard Hess, Thomas Pfeiffer and Peter Schlosser (n 40) paras 828–832.

59 Art 24(4) BR I *bis* (as well as its previous version in BR I, art 22(4) 4 and 16(4) BC) provides for a rule of exclusive jurisdiction in relation to proceedings concerned with the registration or validity of patents, trademarks, designs, or other similar rights, irrespective of whether the issue is raised by way of an action or as a defence. On the basis of this rule, there could be a fragmentation of the consolidated proceedings when the issue of validity of patent is raised, also determining problems of 'torpedo' and 'super torpedo' cases: Peter Schlosser, 'Intellectual Property Rights' in Burkhard Hess, Thomas Pfeiffer and Peter Schlosser (n 40) paras 804 ff. See also Marketa Trimble, *Global Patents: Limits of Transnational Enforcement* (Oxford university press 2012) 47 ff; Benedetta Ubertazzi, *Exclusive Jurisdiction in Intellectual Property* (Mohr Siebeck 2012) 45. The problem of 'tor-

the patent must be expressly raised in order to fall within the scope of the rule.[60]

The Court also confirmed the same principle in the judgment in *Nintendo*, where the proceedings were related to an infringement of a Community design.[61] In that case, the prerequisite of a same situation of law would not have been recognized according to the previous 'strict'

---

pedo' was intensified since the Court gave a wide interpretation of the rule in GAT (Judgment of 3 July 2006, *Gesellschaft für Antriebstechnik mbH & Co. KG v Lamellen und Kupplungsbau Beteiligungs KG*, Case C-4/03 [2006] ECR 2006 I-6509), para 25, where stated that the exclusive jurisdiction provided for by that provision should apply when the issue of a patent's validity is raised by way of an action or a plea in objection. The principle was restated in *Roche Nederland* (n 27), para 40. The problem has been again faced in judgment in *Solvay* (n 5) paras 34, 36 and 40, where the Court seems to partially mitigate its previous interpretation, stating that the rule of exclusive jurisdiction must be interpreted as not precluding the request for provisional measures even if the courts of another Member State have exclusive jurisdiction as to the substance of the matter. To this conclusion the Court also considers that there is no risk of conflicting decisions since the provisional decision taken by the court before which the interim proceedings have been brought will not in any way prejudice the decision to be taken on the substance by the court having jurisdiction: *ibid*, paras 49–50. This interpretation has to be verified under the new Agreement on a Unified Patent Court: according to art 32 lett c, in fact, the Court has exclusive competence on interim measures.

60 See Paul Torremans (n 41) 1644: '*de facto* the Gat v. LuK approach will not be followed. Inside the common Unitary Patent Court, the division before which the validity is raised during infringement proceedings will have the option to continue with the infringement case and rule on validity too. The question does, then, need to be raised whether it makes sense to keep the strict Article 24(4) rule for national patents and other registered intellectual property rights. It should be noted also that art 32(1) of the Agreement on a Unified Patent Court, which provides for the exclusive competence of the Court, deals with claims and counterclaims for revocation of patents and declaration of invalidity, without any express references to what emerges from defences as plea in objection. Art 33, instead, provides for a rule of connection very similar to art 8(1), stating that an action may be brought against multiple defendants only where the defendants have a commercial relationship and where the action relates to the same alleged infringement.

61 These proceedings referred to claims brought against two linked companies for infringement of the rights conferred by the Community designs, which were presented as connected because of a supply chain of the allegedly infringing goods. On this case see Annette Kur, 'Unionsweite Zuständigkeit in Gemeinschaftsgeschmacksmustersachen' [2017] Gewerblicher Rechtsschutz und Urheberrecht, 1127; Dominique Berlin, 'La protection européenne de Super Mario' (2017) 42 La Semaine Juridique, 1897; Sebastian Kubis, 'Die Verletzung unionsweiter Schutzrechte in grenzüberschreitenden "Lieferketten"' [2017] Zeitschrift für

approach', as the infringement proceedings involved different national laws. Notwithstanding this, since by bringing the claims 'the holder seeks to protect his exclusive right to use the Community design', which has the same effect throughout the EU, the Court recognized the existence of the same situation of law.[62]

In *Nintendo* the appraisement of the fact also comes into consideration. The CJEU – endorsing the view of the referring court, which considered that such a requirement was met – confirmed the importance of concertation. Where the defendants are a parent company and its subsidiary, and they are accused 'of similar, if not identical, acts that infringe the same protected designs and relate to identical allegedly infringing goods', there exists a same situation of fact.[63]

As particularly emerges from the judgments in *Painer*, *Solvay* and *Nintendo*, the more extensive approach is undoubtedly useful in relation to cases where the plurality of parts and infringements are involved in a substantially similar situation, as when Intellectual Property (IP) rights violation cases occur. In this field of law, where both the exploitation of property rights as well as the infringements normally extend beyond national boundaries, a further improvement of the 'close connection' rule would be

geistiges Eigentum, 471; Laurence Idot, 'Contrefaçon de dessins ou modèles' (2017) 11 Europe, 54.

62 In fact, even if 'it follows from the Court's case-law on patents that, where infringement proceedings are brought before a number of courts in various Member States in respect of a European patent granted in each of those States, against defendants domiciled in those States in respect of acts allegedly committed in their territory, any divergences between the decisions given by the courts concerned would not arise in the context of the same situation of law'. Since that right 'has the same effect throughout the European Union, the fact that some of the orders that may be adopted by the court having jurisdiction with a view to ensuring that that right is respected depend on provisions of national law is irrelevant to the existence of the same situation of law': Judgment in *Nintendo* (n 29) paras 46, 48–49.

63 In relation to the same situation of fact, 'it is apparent from the orders for reference that the referring court starts from the premise (…) that requirement is met'. The existence of a same fact 'must in such circumstances — if proven, which is for the referring court to verify, and where an application is made to that effect — cover all the activities of the various defendants, including the supplies made by the parent company on its own account, and not be limited to certain aspects or elements of them': *Ibid*, paras 50–52.

convenient.[64] In this perspective, in relation to IP cases, it has been proposed to amend the rule taking into consideration if the defendants have acted in an identical or similar manner in accordance with a common policy.[65] What is more, it has been suggested to enhance the role of the management epicentre of the group in the individuation of the grounds of jurisdiction according to the 'spider in the web' theory.[66] Thus, if one defendant has coordinated the relevant activities or is otherwise more closely connected with the dispute in its entirety, jurisdiction would be only conferred on the courts in the State where that defendant is habitually domiciled.[67]

2.4. *The Position of the CJEU on Cartels*

The implementation of the rule could also be developed in relation to competition law.

In this field of law, since the infringements are normally put in place under a coordinated policy involving several jurisdictions, the *forum connexitatis* is also particularly useful even if not considerably enhanced by the

64 Paul Torremans (n 41) 1637. It is in fact 'easily intelligible that it would be particularly cumbersome and costly to institute proceedings for infringement of patents in several jurisdictions': Peter Schlosser, 'Intellectual Property Rights' in Burkhard Hess, Thomas Pfeiffer and Peter Schlosser (n 40) para 729.

65 See the Principles on Conflict of Laws in Intellectual Property Prepared by the European Max Planck Group on Conflict of Laws in Intellectual Property [2011] www.ip.mpg.de/fileadmin/ipmpg/content/clip/Final_Text_1_December_2011.pdf, art 2:206. With respect to the shortcomings in the system of patent litigation also the Green Paper in the Review of Council Regulation (EC) No44/2001 on Jurisdiction and the Recognition and Enforcement of Judgments in Civil and Commercial Matters, Brussels, 21.4.2009, COM(2009) 175 final, proposed an extension of the rule contained in art 6(1).

66 On this point see Cristina Gonzalez Beilfuss, 'Is there any Web for the Spider? Jurisdiction over Co-defendants after Roche Nederland', in Arnaud Nuyts (ed), *International Litigation in Intellectual Property and Information Technology*, (Kluwer Law International 2008) 79, 83; Paul Torremans (n 41) 1637–1639; Thomas Jaeger, 'The EU Patent: Cui bono et quo vadit?' (2010) 47 Common Market Law Review EU, 63, 92; Stefan Luginbuehl, *European Patent Law: Towards a Uniform Interpretation*, (Edward Elgar Publishing 2011) 96.

67 Principles on Conflict of Laws (n 65) art 2:206.

legislator.[68] With respect to the *CDC* case – the first in which the CJEU has adjudicated concerning the interaction between competition law and jurisdictional aspects in regard to damages actions against cartel members – it has been affirmed that the Brussels system 'is not fully geared towards ensuring effective private implementation of the Union's competition law'.[69]

---

68 On this matter, see David Ashton, Competition Damages Actions in the EU (2nd edn, Elgar Competition Law and Practice, 2018) para 12.10; Mihail Danov, Jurisdiction and Judgments in Relation to EU Competition Law Claims (Hart Publishing 2011) 53; Michael Wilderspin, 'Jurisdiction Issues: Brussels I Regulation Articles 6(1), 23, 27 and 28' in Jürgen Basedow, Stéphanie Francq and Laurence Idot (eds), *International Antitrust Litigation* (Hart Publishing 2012) 51 ff. The plurality of defendants is not considered in the White Paper on Damages actions for breach of the EC antitrust rules, Brussels, 2.4.2008 COM(2008) 165 final, nor in the Directive 2014/104/EU on certain rules governing actions for damages under national law for infringements of the competition law provisions of the Member States and of the European Union. Art 15 instead expressly refers to the hypothesis of actions for damages brought by various claimants. On the applicability of art 8(1) see Marco De Cristofaro, Il private enforcement antitrust ed il ruolo centrale della disciplina processuale, di nuovo conio legislativo o di nuova concezione giurisprudenziale, [2015] Int'l lis, 123, 125.

69 Opinion AG Jääskinen in *CDC*, ECLI:EU:C:2014:2443, para 7–8 and 10. The suggestion drawn by the AG is that, *de lege ferenda*, it would be advisable to incorporate in the Regulation a rule of jurisdiction that is apt to cover cross-border anticompetitive practices; in fact, the AG proposes to take into consideration the lines of the conflict-of-laws provision which applies to obligations deriving from acts restrictive of competition under the Rome II Regulation, art 6(3). In cases related to cartel agreements it has also been suggested to take into consideration the unity of various misconducts, even if concerning a different spatial and temporal context, when they are coordinated by one of the firm's companies, even accepting the domicile of the parent company as the sole ground for jurisdiction. Michael Wilderspin (n 68) 51–52; Wolfgang Wurmnest, 'International Jurisdiction in Competition Damages Cases Under the Brussels I Regulation: CDC Hydrogen Peroxide' (2016) 53 Common Market Law Review 225, 233, where it is considered the 'more controversial (…) question whether also a subsidiary of a firm that has participated in a cartel – and which has distributed the cartelized product in a Member State without being aware of the cartel agreement concluded by its parent company – may serve as an anchor defendant'. On these matters, see also Mihail Danov, 'Jurisdiction in Cross-Border EU Competition Law Cases: Some Specific Issues Requiring Specific Solutions', in Mihail Danov, Florian Becker, Paul Beaumont (eds), *Cross-Border EU Competition Law Actions* (Hart Publishing 2013) 170–173; Mihail Danov, Florian Becker, 'Conclusion: Proposing Specific Solutions To Promote Regulatory Competition And Address The Enforcement Gap', *ibidem*, 287; Richard Whish, David Bailey, *Competition law* (8th edn, Oxford University Press 2015) 330; Jürgen Basedow, 'Jurisdiction and

The case was related to proceedings concerning actions for damages – which were directly or indirectly transferred to *CDC* by 71 damaged subjects – linked to an infringement of art 101 TFEU and art 53 of the Agreement on the European Economic Area. Before the introduction of the proceedings, a decision of the Commission had already established the existence of a singular infringement of EU law and found the participation of several undertakings in a single and continuous cartel.[70]

The Court stated that the requirement of the same situation of fact and law was satisfied.

On the one side, since different misconducts were involved in the proceedings, the presence of the decision of the Commission finding a singular infringement seems sufficient to recognize the same situation of fact.[71]At the same time, the Court considered that predictability is also satisfied in the case of a decision of the Commission finding the existence of a single infringement of EU law and holding each participant liable for the consequent loss resulting from the infringement. In fact, in such circumstances, the participants could have expected to be sued in the courts of a Member State in which one of them is domiciled.[72]

---

choice of law in the private enforcement of EC Competition Law', in Jürgen Basedow (ed), *Private enforcement of EC Competition Law* (Kluwer Law International 2007) 229 ff; Jonathan Fitchen, 'Allocating jurisdiction in private competition law claims within the EU' [2006] Maastricht Journal of European and Comparative Law, 381 ff; Christopher Withers, 'Jurisdiction and applicable law in antitrust tort claims' [2002] Journal of Business Law, 250 ff.

70 On this case, see Thomas Thiede, Gerhard Klumpe, 'A Christmas Carol – strongly inspired by Charles Dickens and CDC Hydrogen Peroxide' [2017] Neue Zeitschrift für Kartellrecht 643; Nicole Boyle, Gurpreet Chhokar, Stella Gartagani, 'Jurisdiction in follow-on damages claims: update on the judgment of the European Court of Justice in the hydrogen peroxide cartel claim' (2015) 8 Global Competition Litigation Review 58 ff; Oliver Geiss, Horst Daniel, 'Cartel Damage Claims (CDC) Hydrogen Peroxide SA v Akzo Nobel NV and Others: A summary and critique of the judgment of the European Court of Justice of May, 21 2015', [2015] European Competition Law Review, 430.

71 As the Court states, '[t]he requirement that the same situation of fact and law must arise is satisfied in circumstances such as those of the case in the main proceedings. Despite the fact that the defendants in the main proceedings participated in the implementation of the cartel at issue by concluding and performing contracts under it, in different places and at different times', according to the decision of the Commission 'upon which the claims in the main proceedings are based, the cartel agreement amounted to a single and continuous infringement': Judgment in *CDC* (n 5) para 21.

72 In this case, predictability is directly linked to the decision of the Commission. In fact, the condition 'is fulfilled in the case of a binding decision of the Commis-

On the other side, regarding the same situation of law, the Commission's decision did not specify the requirements for holding the defendants liable in tort, which were to be determined by national law. Notwithstanding, the Court confirmed the principle that the same situation of law is not excluded by the presence of different legal bases. In fact, 'even in the case where various laws are, by virtue of the rules of private international law of the court seised, applicable to the actions for damages brought by CDC against the defendants in the main proceedings', such a different legal basis does not, in itself, preclude the application of what is now art 8(1).[73]

The Court's thinking seems to go even further. Since the requirements for determining the liability for cartel infringement may differ between the various national laws, there would be a risk of irreconcilable judgments if the actions were not determined together. Thus, from the previous standpoint where the difference in the legal bases would necessarily exclude the application of the rule, that divergence becomes an element that may be relevant for the consolidation of the claims, when it could lead to irreconcilable judgments.[74]

---

sion finding there to have been a single infringement of EU law and, on the basis of that finding, holding each participant liable for the loss resulting from the tortious actions of those participating in the infringement': see judgment in *CDC* (n 5) para 24. In fact, 'they could reasonably expect subsequently to be sued together for compensation': opinion AG Jääskinen (n 69) para 67. See Wolfgang Wurmnest (n 69) 231 and 236 where it is underlined that CJEU '"upgraded" the criterion of foreseeability', even if the recourse to the Commission's decision 'is not very convincing'.

73 Even if the decision of the Commission did not determine the requirements for holding the defendants liable in tort, 'such a difference in legal basis does not, in itself, preclude the application' of the rule: *ibid*, para 23.

74 Judgment in *CDC* (n 5) para 22. On this basis, the Court held that the article in comment must be interpreted as the rule on centralisation of jurisdiction in the case of several defendants 'can apply in the case of an action for damages (…) brought jointly against undertakings which have participated in different places and at different times in a single and continuous infringement, which has been established by a decision of the Commission': *ibid*, para 33. See Wolfgang Wurmnest (n 69) 235, underlying the 'CJEU's victim-friendly interpretation' which 'opens ample possibilities for persons harmed by horizontal cartels to shop for the best forum'. See also Marcella Negri, 'Una Pronuncia a Tutto Campo sui Criteri di Allocazione della Competenza Giurisdizionale nel Private Antitrust Enforcement Transfrontaliero: il Caso Esemplare delle Azioni Risarcitorie c.d. Follow-on Rispetto a Decisioni Sanzionatorie di Cartelli pan-europei [2015] Int'l lis 78, 80.

2.5. An Interim Conclusion

The foregoing considerations lead to some interim conclusions.

Firstly, the 'so close connection' represents an objective element of connection,[75] existing when the claims lie on a same substantial situation of fact and law.[76] Thus, irreconcilability between the judgments emerges from a comprehensive evaluation that has to be related to the same situation of fact and law, as defined by case law in a non-formalistic but substantial approach.

There is a same situation of fact also in the presence of different misconducts, when concerted, and concertation could also occur when the defendants are companies of the same group that have acted in a similar manner in compliance with a common policy, as is particularly shown by *Nintendo*. What is more, when the unity of fact had already been found before the introduction of the proceedings, as happened in *CDC* in relation to the decision of the Commission, the same situation of fact can be assumed as unitary without requiring further investigations by the referring court.

At the same time, a legal framework could be relevant even if not fully harmonized.

There could be a unitary consideration of the matter, also having regard to the interest pursued by the defendants, as stated in *Sapir*. Furthermore, there are identical facts justifying a consolidation between the claims without the necessity of a sole legal basis. Independently from the applicable law, there are differences between the judgments on linked cases that can be attributed exclusively to a different appraisement of a fact; with respect

---

75 In the view of AG Trstenjak in *Painer* (n 16) para 97, a close connection 'first and foremost' emerges in 'cases where the outcome of one claim is dependent on the outcome of the other claim' as where there is a 'contingent liability (alternative liability)' or 'the defendants are jointly and severally liable, co-owners or a community of rights'. The relevance of joint liability is also underlined in the opinion AG Jääskinen (n 69), para 68.

76 On these bases, the disposition regulates the jurisdiction referring to an element of objective connection that excludes a joinder of parties in merely cumulative proceedings: see Caterina Silvestri, 'Il regolamento (CE) n. 44/2001 del Consiglio, del 22 dicembre 2000, concernente la competenza giurisdizionale, Il riconoscimento e l'esecuzione delle decisioni in materia civile e commerciale. La competenza giurisdizionale', in Michele Taruffo and Vincenzo Varano (eds), *Manuale di diritto processuale europeo* (Giappichelli 2011) 28.

to them the difference of the law does not retain any significance.[77] Thus, as underlined in *Painer*, the identical legal basis, which in the previous ruling represented an essential element, becomes only one of the relevant factors, thus relegated to a possible one.[78] There are cases in which the connection between claims hardly depends on whether the same law is applicable.[79]

The rule can not be applied when the defendants are not able to reasonably foresee the consolidation of the claims. So far as concerns predictability, from a starting point where this condition was to be excluded if different laws were applicable, the consolidation between the claims is foreseeable even when a single law is not involved.[80] In such cases, the concertation seems to represent the crucial factor, compensating for the lack of the same legal basis.[81]Thus, predictability may depend on concerted actions, which could also be supposed as existent when the defendants belong to a same group of companies or when the unity of the misconducts had already been found.

---

77 As underlined by AG Trstenjak, opinion in *Painer* (n 16) para 79; thus, even if different courts apply essentially comparable laws, they can reach different conclusions because they differently appraise the facts.

78 See judgment in *Painer* (n 5) para 80; in *Freeport* (n 7) para 41; in *Sapir* (n 7) para 44. The CJEU in fact underlines that the identical legal basis between the actions brought against different defendants is not included among the conditions laid down for application of the provision in the wording of art 6(1): Judgment in *Painer* (n 5) para 76 and in *Freeport* (n 7) para 38.

79 AG Trstenjak, opinion in *Painer* (n 16) para 78, considers the requirement of the same legal situation as based on the incorrect 'mental assumption' that no irreconcilable judgments 'can exist where different laws are applicable to the actions and those laws are not fully harmonised'. This assumption would be correct only where all inconsistencies between the judgments could be attributed solely (which is not) 'to the differences between the two applicable laws'. In cases 'of contingent liability (alternative liability) in which one of the defendants is liable only where the other defendant is not liable, there is (…) a clear interest that the case is decided by the same court in order to avoid the risk of irreconcilable judgments. In such a case, the legal connection between both claims is not dependent on whether the same law is applicable to both claims': *Ibid*, para 83.

80 See Paul Torremans (n 41) 1641 where it is noted that the Court links the predictability 'specifically to a discretional appreciation of the legal situation and to the absence of the requirement of an identical legal basis'.

81 As emerges *a contrario* also from the opinion of AG Trstenjak in *Painer* (n 16) paras 91–92, in the case of 'unconcerted parallel conduct' this condition is not fulfilled since for the other defendants it is not sufficiently predictable that they can also be sued 'at a court in the place where the anchor defendant is domiciled'.

The risk of irreconcilable judgements has to be assessed in concrete by the referring court according to the indications given by the CJEU: where the conditions defined by case law for the existence of a same situation of fact and law are met, the outcomes of the proceedings could be irreconcilable if separately determined.[82]

3. *The Relevance of the Abuse in Excluding the Close Connection*

The analysis would not be complete without considering if the consolidation of the claims is based solely on the objective element of connection outlined above or if the application of the rule further requires any subjective condition.

Art 8(1) does not specify what happens if the choice of forum amounts to an abuse.[83] While to the extent of art 8(2) BR I*bis* the proceedings could not be consolidated if they were instituted solely with the purpose of unlawfully removing the defendants from their natural forum,[84] art 8(1) does not contain any express wording on this point.[85]

---

82 In order for art 8(1) to apply, such a risk of irreconcilable judgments has to be established in concrete by the national court: judgment in *CDC* (n 5) para 20; judgment in *Solvay* (n 5) para 23; judgment in *Profit Investment* (n 5) para 66; judgment in *Sapir* (n 7) para 42; judgment in *Freeport* (n 7) para 39; judgment in *Painer* (n 5) para 84, where it is affirmed that it is for the referring court to assess, 'in the light of all the elements of the case, whether there is a risk of irreconcilable judgments if those actions were determined separately'. The judgment in *Kalfelis* (n 7) para 12 also stated that it is for the national court 'to verify in each individual case whether that condition is satisfied'.

83 On this matter, see Thomas Pfeiffer 'Jurisdiction', in Burkhard Hess, Thomas Pfeiffer and Peter Schlosser (n 40) para 222; Trevor Hartley (n 3) para 9.22 ff; Laurence Usunier, 'Le règlement Bruxelles I bis et la théorie de l'abus de droit', in Emmanuel Guinchard (ed), *Le nouveau règlement Bruxelles I bis, Règlement no 1215/2012 du 12 décembre 2012 concernant la compétence judiciaire, la reconnaissance et l'exécution des décisions en matière civile et commerciale* (Bruylant, 2014) 449 ff; Laurence Idot, 'Pluralité de défendeurs et fraude à la compétence juridictionnelle' (2007) 12 Europe 2007, 35; Arnaud Nuyts L'exception de forum non conveniens: étude de droit international privé comparé (Bruylant, 2003) 527 ff.

84 As well as the previous versions contained in art 6(2) BR I and BC.

85 The opportunity to extend the provision contained in the wording of what is now art 8(2), by analogy, to art 8(1) has also been affirmed, thus precluding its application 'to situations which do not fall within its natural scope as well as to prevent the basis for jurisdiction which it lays down being relied on if that is designed to serve interests which do not merit protection': see opinion AG Mengozzi in *Freeport* [2009] ECR I-03327, paras 64–65. In fact, the AG sees 'no reason – linked

Notwithstanding this, the Jenard Report stated that the actions cannot be brought with the sole object of ousting the general rule of jurisdiction.[86] The same principle was upheld in *Kalfelis*[87] and then restated in the subsequent case-law.[88]

Even if the relevance of an abuse is stated in terms of principles, the Court shows some hesitation in concretely implementing the proposition that an abusive misconduct in the introduction of the proceedings against a plurality of defendants could preclude the applicability of art 8(1).

In this perspective, the judgment in *Reisch Montage* considered the special rule of jurisdiction to also be applicable when one of the linked claims has to be regarded as inadmissible from the time it is brought against the defendant under a national provision.[89] Notwithstanding, in this way it would be very easy to oust the general rule of jurisdiction by bringing inadmissible claims, which would create the appearance of a connection with the purpose of choosing the forum. Where under national law a claim must be ruled inadmissible at the outset, the plurality of defendants is based on artificial reasons: 'there are not a number of defendants in the

---

in particular to the need for a uniform application and independent interpretation of the regulation's provisions – that would prevent it from applying to the cases regulated by Article 6(1)', and, thus, by actual art 8(1).

86 Paul Jenard (n 9) 26.

87 In that case the CJEU excludes the possibility for the plaintiff to make a claim against a number of defendants, before the court of the anchor defendant, with the sole object of ousting the jurisdiction of the courts of the States where the others are domiciled: see judgment in *Kalfelis* (n 7) para 8.

88 In fact, the Court held that the exceptional rule of jurisdiction provided for in what is now art 8(1) 'must be construed in such a way that there is no possibility of the very existence of that principle being called in question, in particular by allowing a plaintiff to make a claim against a number of defendants with the sole purpose of ousting the jurisdiction of the courts of the State where one of those defendants is domiciled': see judgment in *Réunion européenne* (n 7) para 47. In the same perspective, see the judgment in *Painer* (n 5) para 78 and in *Solvay* (n 5) para 22.

89 In this case, concerning the repayment of a debt, the action brought against one of the defendants was dismissed as inadmissible by the time the claim was brought because of the commencement of bankruptcy proceedings. The CJEU stated that the rule must be interpreted as meaning that it 'may be relied on in the context of an action brought in a Member State against a defendant domiciled in that State and a co-defendant domiciled in another Member State even when that action is regarded under a national provision as inadmissible from the time it is brought in relation to the first defendant': judgment in *Reisch Montage* (n 7) para 33.

true sense and, therefore, the prerequisite for the choice of jurisdiction is not satisfied'.[90]

In *Freeport* the relevance of abuse is put into discussion also as a matter of principles, since the Court excluded the consideration of abusive misconducts. The judgment states that what is now art 8(1) applies where the claims brought against different defendants are connected 'without there being any further need to establish separately that the claims were not brought with the sole object of ousting the jurisdiction of the courts of the Member State where one of the defendants is domiciled'.[91] As an argument, it also considered the different wording between art 8(1) and art 8(2).

This approach has been reconsidered in *CDC*, where the Court for the first time finds a precise misconduct that is deemed to reveal, if proved, a circumvention of the rule.[92]

In that particular case, some of the parties alleged that, before bringing the action in the main proceedings, the applicant and the anchor defendant had reached an out-of-court settlement, but the formal conclusion of the agreement was 'purposefully delayed' until the institution of the proceedings to the extent of securing the jurisdiction of the court. Then, after the introduction of the proceedings, the claimant withdrew the anchor claim.

---

90 See the opinion AG Colomer in *Reisch Montage* of 14 March 2006 [2006] ECR I-06827, paras 42–45. In the same manner, the consolidation of proceedings does not fulfil its function: the possibility of conflicting decisions is excluded by the same fact that there will be no decision from the court of the disqualified defendant's domicile. On these bases, the AG concludes that it is not possible to rely on the article when the claim against the anchor defendant 'must be ruled inadmissible at the outset of the proceedings': *ibid*, para 52. See Horatia Muir Watt (n 30) para 35.

91 Judgment in *Freeport* (n 7) para 54.

92 The possibility of a circumvention of the rule is found after recalling its previous ruling on the matter: Judgment in *CDC* (n 5) paras 27–28. On the one side, the Court affirms that the provision cannot be interpreted as allowing an applicant to make a claim against a number of defendants for the sole purpose of removing one of them from the jurisdiction of the courts related to the domicile. On the other side, if claims brought against various defendants are connected within the meaning of the article 'when the proceedings are instituted, the rule of jurisdiction laid down in that provision is applicable without there being any further need to establish separately that the claims were not brought with the sole object of ousting the jurisdiction of the courts of the Member State where one of the defendants is domiciled'.

Even if it is certain that a transaction where intentionally postponed with the aim of obtaining a prolongation of the applicability of the rule may be regarded as abusive, the Court denied the concrete relevance of that specific agreement in order to exclude the applicability of the special rule of jurisdiction.[93] In fact, allegations concerning an abusive behaviour of the claimant must be supported by 'firm evidence' of collusion: the defendants have to demonstrate that 'at the time that proceedings were instituted, the parties concerned had colluded to artificially fulfil, or prolong the fulfilment of, that provision's applicability'.[94] Notwithstanding, 'simply holding negotiations with a view to concluding an out-of-court settlement' does not in itself prove a collusion.[95]

3.1. Abuse and Real Claims: How to Apportion the Burden of Proof?

The judgment in *CDC* shows that cases involving abuse raise a problem regarding the allocation of the burden of proof.

On the one side, it seems very tough to prove collusion in the introduction of the proceedings if the burden of proof lying on the defendants requires a 'firm evidence' related to such a collusive intent: the possibility that the defendants could ever realistically supply such evidence could be questionable.[96]

---

93 Wolfgang Wurmnest (n 69) 238–239 considers that '[f]or good reasons, the CJEU set the hurdles very high for showing such a circumvention' as '[a]ny rule that weakens the willingness of the parties to settle would have a negative impact on the sound administration of justice'.

94 Judgment in *CDC* (n 5) paras 29–31.

95 *Ibid*, para 32. Thus, the Court held that there is no concrete circumvention of the rule where the applicant withdraws its action 'against the sole co-defendant domiciled in the same State as the court seised, unless it is found that, at the time the proceedings were instituted, the applicant and that defendant had colluded to artificially fulfil, or prolong the fulfilment of, that provision's applicability': Judgment in *CDC* (n 5) para 33. As also expressed by AG Jääskinen, opinion in *CDC* (n 69) paras 78 ff, the applicant's withdrawal of its action against the anchor defendant does not in itself have the effect of terminating the jurisdiction established under what is now art 8(1). That withdrawal does not retain any relevance when it is subsequent to the date on which the court was validly seised and a connecting link between the claims against several defendants had been established at the time the action was brought.

96 Horatia Muir Watt (n 30) para 49 underlines that the burden of proving by the defendant represents 'a very demanding task'.

On the other hand, if an abusive misconduct is alleged by the defendants, it appears equally hard for the claimant to demonstrate the absence of the abuse.

In this perspective, it could be asked whether, when an abusive misconduct is alleged, and proved in its objective content, the burden of proof could be shifted to the claimant, who should demonstrate that the claim is 'real'.[97]

For a 'real claim' to exist, there must be an effective interest at the time of institution of proceedings, which is not the case when the action against the anchor defendant appears to be 'manifestly unfounded in all respects [...] or devoid of any real interest for the claimant'.[98]It is self-evident that when there is no real claim, there is neither a plurality of claims and consequently there could not be a connection between them.

In this perspective the existence of a 'real claim' could represent a limit to the scope of art 8(1), whose application has to be excluded when the close connection between the claims is the result of an abuse.[99] In fact, if the plurality of claims and their connection is the result of an abusive mis-

---

97 See Mihail Danov (n 68) 103, where it is underlined that to rely on the article 'a plaintiff has to show that there is a "real issue"'. See also Thomas Pfeiffer 'Jurisdiction', in Burkhard Hess, Thomas Pfeiffer and Peter Schlosser (n 40) para 221, where it is underlined that '[t]here must be a "real claim" against the anchor defendant', even if without 'need to show a good arguable case on the merits against the anchor defendant'. In that perspective, it has been proposed to add 'a requirement that the claim against the anchor defendant should not be manifestly inadmissible or unfounded': Michael Wilderspin (n 68) 53. On evidence and burden of proof see Paolo Biavati, *Diritto processuale dell'Unione Europea* (5th edn, Giuffrè 2015) 217 ff; Paolo Biavati, 'Il diritto delle prove nel quadro normativo dell'Unione europea' [2006] Rivista trimestrale di diritto e procedura civile 483.

98 Opinion AG Mengozzi in *Freeport* (n 85) para 66. If considered solely from an objective view, the element of connection between the claims does not prevent the claimant from bringing an action against a fictitious co-defendant, with the exclusive purpose of removing the other defendants from the courts of their domicile. The risk of a fraud or abuse could emerge from the institution of proceedings which, even if objectively connected, are 'manifestly unfounded' or of 'no real interest' for the claimant: *Ibid*, paras 61 and 54, where the AG underlines that 'there must *be a real and current interest in the disputes being heard together*'.

99 AG Mengozzi (n 85) paras 62 and 65, suggests the consideration of a general limit to the applicability of the uniform rules on conflict laid down in the Brussel system, whose implementation has to be excluded by 'fraud relating to the jurisdiction of the courts'; this fraud also occurs in the presence of 'manipulation on the part of the claimant' with the effect of ousting the rules of jurisdiction. Thus, the interpretation of art 8(1) would require an additional element, avoiding its application 'to situations which do not fall within its natural scope as well as to pre-

conduct, the application of the rule would be based on artificial reasons since the requirement for the choice of forum under art 8(1) does not concretely exist.

4. Some Final Remarks

The irreconcilability between judgments arising in the context of a same situation of fact and law, if properly considered according to CJEU interpretation, also seems a suitable concept for those fields where a plurality of parties and infringements are naturally involved.[100] Accepting the notion of close connection with respect to the requirement of the same situation of fact and law, as it emerges from the abovementioned case-law, would ensure greater certainty in the concrete application of the rule. To deal with the increasing occurrence of multi-party proceedings, an improvement of the rule also may be convenient, even enhancing the relationship between the defendants, as where they are companies belonging to the same group and acting in accordance with a common policy.

Concerning the relevance of the abuse, a clarification of the applicability of the rule would be advisable, specifying if the existence of abusive misconducts in the introduction of the proceedings has the effect of excluding the close connection between claims and, thus, the special rule of jurisdiction.[101]

---

vent the basis for jurisdiction which it lays down being relied on if that is designed to serve interests which do not merit protection'.

100 A clarification on the scope of art 8(1), according to the abovementioned case-law, would pursue the aim of preventing national courts from applying the rule in accordance to their procedural concepts; which seems remarkable even considering that the concept of derived jurisdiction in cases of connected claims 'is not familiar to all national systems' and that 'connexity as a procedural concept does not necessarily coincide with categories of substantive law': Horatia Muir Watt (n 30) para 26.

101 In this perspective, according to the rules laid down by the Brussels system, it is necessary to avoid the exercise of that choice 'in a fraudulent or wrongful manner': see the opinion AG Mengozzi in *Freeport* (n 85) paras 52–53 and 72.

Cross-border Collective Redress and the Jurisdictional Regime: Horizontal vs Sectoral Approach

Cinzia Peraro[*]

Table of Contents

1. Introduction

The issue of collective redress in cross-border contexts is topical given the political debates, legislative developments and the controversial (scant) case law of the Court of Justice, mainly concerned with the consumer protection, where it assessed the existence of collective proceedings under national law and the applicability of the Brussels I or I *bis* Regulation[1] over such collective proceedings.

Member States' procedural laws present divergences on collective mechanisms and the absence of European rules on collective redress in general or in specific sectors requires solutions, also under a private international law perspective, whenever transnational elements characterise the dispute.

* Ph.D., Post-doc research fellow in European Union Law, University of Verona, Italy.

1 Council Regulation (EC) No 44/2001 of 22 December 2000 on jurisdiction and the recognition and enforcement of judgments in civil and commercial matters, now Regulation (EU) No 1215/2012 of the European Parliament and of the Council of 12 December 2012 on jurisdiction and the recognition and enforcement of judgments in civil and commercial matters [2012] OJ L351/1.

At European Union level, the Commission attempted to provide a horizontal framework by establishing common principles on collective redress contained in the 2013 Recommendation[2], aimed at ensuring that collective redress and minimum procedural requirements are granted in all Member States in mass harm situations[3] occurring in various sectors specifically but not exclusively dealing with the infringement of consumer rights[4].

Collective mechanisms have been introduced in certain fields, such as competition and consumer protection, where private means of enforcement to protect collective interests are regulated[5]. The sector-specific approach may however be implemented also in other fields taking into account the respective specificities and with a view to offering effective means of protection to weaker parties. This could be the case for employees. Indeed, forms of collective action should be ensured in national legal orders given the recognition of the fundamental right to collective action (Article 28 of the Charter), implemented in general provisions in the relevant legislation on the protection of workers. Trade union action may be qualified as a collective redress mechanism according to the definition adopted by the Commission that determines it as a representative action.

The arising necessity to establish a European framework on collective redress as a means for an effective and efficient enforcement of rights granted under Union law stems from the mass harm situations that occurred in recent decades and that are increasing in transnational context due to different factors, such as use of internet and free movement that facilitates trade across Europe. Consumers are mainly involved, for instance in the case of car emissions, passenger rights, and financial services. However, mass cases may also occur around environmental issues, antidiscrimination law, or employment matters.

The practical relevance of collective mechanisms meets the need to enhance effective protection for low value claims which are seldom brought before the courts, and to reduce the costs, length and complexity of cross-border litigation. Judicial collective redress also ensures legal certainty for claimants, defendants and the judicial system alike by avoiding parallel litigation of similar claims.

---

2 Commission Recommendation on common principles for injunctive and compensatory collective redress mechanisms concerning violations of rights granted under EU law (2013/396/EU) [2013] OJ L201 (from now onwards: 'Recommendation on common principles').

3 *Ibid*, para. 1.

4 *Ibid*, Recitals 4 and 7.

5 See *infra* paragraph 3.

Differences among national collective procedural mechanisms that are mostly made available to consumers[6] have a negative impact on cross-border litigation because of the divergent criteria to admissibility, legal standing, funding, and fees.

A European Union action in the procedural field is thus welcome whenever it may better pursue the objectives of justice efficiency and effectiveness in order to protect rights granted under EU law across Member States. In compliance with the principle of subsidiarity, any such action must respect national legal traditions and procedural autonomy[7]. In this context, two perspectives may be identified: on the one side, the protection of national prerogatives and legal orders and, on the other side, the protection of individual rights granted under Union law.

The Commission's activities related to collective redress matters started early in the 1990s and aimed at understanding and assessing the national systems and the opportunity for an EU action. The documents and proposals adopted in this field can be considered in two categories based on a horizontal and sectoral approach. The two-fold approach may reflect uncertainty in the determination of a European procedural framework, which as a result is inconsistent, as observed by stakeholders during the 2011 public consultation on a coherent European framework for collective

---

6 See the outcomes of the 'An evaluation study of national procedural laws and practices in terms of their impact on the free circulation of judgments and on the equivalence and effectiveness of the procedural protection of consumers under EU consumer law – Report prepared by a Consortium of European universities led by the MPI Luxembourg for Procedural Law as commissioned by the European Commission, JUST/2014/RCON/PR/CIVI/0082, National Reports – Consumer Protection Strand and Strand 2 – Procedural Protection of Consumers', June 2017 and May 2018, all available at *http://ec.europa.eu/newsroom/just/item-detail.cfm?item_id=612847.*

7 On national procedural autonomy, see Maria Caterina Baruffi, 'Art. 4 TUE', in Fausto Pocar, Maria Caterina Baruffi (eds), *Commentario breve ai Trattati dell'Unione europea* (CEDAM 2014), 13–24; Chiara Favilli, 'I ricorsi collettivi nell'Unione europea e la tutela antidiscriminatoria: verso un autentico approccio orizzontale' (2014) 3 Il Diritto dell'Unione europea 439, 440 f.; Burkhard Hess, 'A coherent approach to European collective redress', in Duncan Fairgrieve, Eva Lein (eds), *Extraterritoriality and collective redress* (Oxford University Press 2012) 107, 110; Giuseppe Tesauro, *Diritto dell'Unione europea* (CEDAM 2012), 112; Diana Urania Galetta, *L'autonomia procedurale degli Stati membri dell'Unione Europea: «Paradise Lost?»* (Giappichelli 2009).

redress[8]. In the 2013 Communication, the Commission admitted that 'it adopted a balanced approach by issuing in 2013 a horizontal Recommendation and a proposal for antitrust damages actions[9] and, on the other, committed itself to take a horizontal approach on collective redress that is necessary to increase policy coherence'. In this last regard, it recognised the need to shape a European framework on a collective procedural mechanism based on a horizontal approach 'in order to avoid the risk of uncoordinated sectorial EU initiatives and to ensure the smoothest interface with national procedural rules, in the interest of the functioning of the internal market'[10].

The scope of the present paper is thus to evaluate the horizontal and sectoral approaches on collective redress procedures, and the private international law issues, in particular with regard to the jurisdictional regime.

2. *The Horizontal Approach: Common Principles for Collective Redress*

Collective redress, as a procedural mechanism that facilitates access to justice, improves justice efficiency and strengthens the power to act, has been addressed in certain legislative acts related to antitrust and consumer law and, lately, as a general procedural means of private enforcement in non-legislative initiatives to be applied in any areas where collective claims for violations of the rights granted under Union law would be relevant[11]. These initiatives rely on the horizontal approach adopted by the Commission with a view to establishing a coherent framework applicable in various sectors.

Based on the Information Note of 2010 on the need for a coherent European approach to collective redress[12], the Commission promoted a series of initiatives aimed at assessing the opportunity to submit a legislative proposal on collective redress in the EU.

8 Communication from the Commission to the European Parliament, the Council, the European Economic and Social Committee and the Committee of the Regions, Towards a European Horizontal Framework for Collective Redress, COM(2013)401 final of 11 June 2013 (from now onwards: 'Commission Communication'), 5.

9 *Ibid*, 4, fn. 10.

10 *Ibid*, 16, para. 4.

11 Recommendation on common principles cit., Recital 7.

12 Towards a Coherent European Approach to Collective Redress: Next Steps, Joint information note by Vice-President Viviane Reding, Vice-President Joaquín Almunia and Commissioner John Dalli, SEC(2010)1192 of 5 October 2010.

In 2011 the Commission carried out a public consultation 'Towards a coherent European approach to collective redress' with the purpose of identifying common legal principles on collective redress and evaluating the fields in which the different forms of collective redress could have an added value for better protecting the rights of EU citizens and businesses, and for improving the enforcement of EU law.

The European Parliament contributed to the debate by adopting the 2012 Resolution based on a comprehensive own-initiative report on collective redress[13]. It determined various aspects of collective redress and specified that such 'legally binding horizontal framework must cover the core aspects of obtaining damages collectively', and that 'procedural and international private law issues must apply to collective actions in general irrespective of the sector concerned'[14]. It clearly recognised that 'in the European area of justice, citizens and companies must not only enjoy rights, but must also be able to enforce those rights effectively and efficiently'[15].

Effectiveness was then emphasised in the 2013 Communication of the Commission, which reported the main findings of the public consultation launched in 2011 and addressed some central issues regarding collective redress[16].

Taking into account common features of national collective systems, it first defined collective redress as 'a procedural mechanism that allows, for reasons of procedural economy and/or efficiency of enforcement, many similar legal claims to be bundled into a single court action. Collective redress facilitates access to justice in particular in cases where the individual damage is so low that potential claimants would not think it worth pursuing an individual claim. It also strengthens the negotiating power of

13 European Parliament resolution of 2 February 2012 on 'Towards a Coherent European Approach to Collective Redress', 2011/2089(INI) (from now onwards: 'European Parliament resolution'). It called on the Commission to propose legislation on a harmonised system of collective redress for EU consumers also in the Recommendation of 4 April 2017 to the Council and the Commission following the inquiry into emission measurements in the automotive sector (2016/2908(RSP), P8_TA(2017)0100).

14 *Ibid*, point 17, where it added that 'while a limited number of rules relevant to consumer protection or competition law, dealing with matters such as the potential binding effect of decisions adopted by national competition authorities, could be laid down, for instance, in separate articles or chapters of the horizontal instrument itself or in separate legal instruments in parallel or subsequent to the adoption of the horizontal instrument'.

15 *Ibid*, letter A.

16 Commission Communication (n 8).

potential claimants and contributes to the efficient administration of justice, by avoiding numerous proceedings concerning claims resulting from the same infringement of law'[17].

The Commission called upon the Member States to follow its 2013 Recommendation on common principles for injunctive and compensatory collective redress mechanisms concerning violations of rights granted under EU law[18]. This was based on the consideration that collective redress is intended 'to facilitate access to justice in relation to violations of rights under Union law and to that end to recommend that all Member States should have collective redress systems at national level that follow the same basic principles throughout the Union, taking into account the legal traditions of the Member States and safeguarding against abuse'[19]. Indeed, thanks to a horizontal approach the alignment of national systems on some central issues regarding collective redress may be better achieved. Such principles should be common across the EU to 'ensure that fundamental procedural rights of the parties are preserved and to prevent abuse through appropriate safeguards'[20].

Briefly, the Recommendation lays down principles common to injunctive and compensatory collective redress, followed by more principles specifically applicable to each individual category[21]. These principles are

---

17 *Ibid*, 4, para. 1.2.

18 Recommendation on common principles cit. In the present analysis attention is paid only to the concept of collective redress as a procedural means for the protection of rights in court proceedings, therefore no reference is made to collective out-of-court settlements, that are also covered by the Recommendation. On the policy process that led to the Recommendation, see Alexandre Biard, 'Collective redress in the EU: a rainbow behind the clouds?' (2018) ERA Forum; Christopher Hodges, Stefan Voet, *Delivering Collective Redress. New Technologies* (Hart Publishing 2018) 20 ff.

19 Recommendation on common principles cit., Recital 10.

20 *Ibid*, Recital 13.

21 The first set of common principles applicable to injunctive and compensatory collective redress deals with issues such as standing, the admissibility of actions, adequate information for potential claimants, funding of collective actions, and the application of the 'loser pays' principle to the costs of lawsuits (paragraphs 4 to 18). In relation to the injunctive procedure, it is recommended that the Member States ensure expedient procedures and appropriate sanctions (paragraphs 19–20). For compensatory redress, other features are proposed, such as the constitution of the claimant party on the basis of express consent (opt-in principle), the recourse to alternative dispute resolution and settlements, limits on lawyers' fees, the prohibition of overcompensation and punitive damages, and the coordination with public enforcement proceedings (paragraphs 21 to 34).

supposed to represent the 'minimum standards' that Member States are encouraged to apply in the national legislation governing collective procedures. In the Commission's opinion, compliance with these standards would improve the judicial protection offered to group rights by means of procedures that are 'fair, equitable, timely, and not prohibitively expensive'[22].

In the Recommendation, under paragraph 3, collective redress is defined as '(i) a legal mechanism that ensures a possibility to claim cessation of illegal behaviour collectively by two or more natural or legal persons or by an entity entitled to bring a representative action (injunctive collective redress); (ii) a legal mechanism that ensures a possibility to claim compensation collectively by two or more natural or legal persons claiming to have been harmed in a mass harm situation or by an entity entitled to bring a representative action (compensatory collective redress)'. Then, in paragraph 4, collective redress is conceived of as a representative action, because standing to sue is granted only to the representative entities identified in advance by Member States or to the public authorities: both shall act on behalf of a group of individuals (or legal persons) equally affected by unlawful acts performed by the same defendant.

Collective redress is thus considered as an instrumental means of furthering economic and social objectives[23]. It constitutes a procedural tool that encourages injured individuals to act so that their rights are respected and ensures that courts will be able to manage mass actions effectively and in a reasonable timeframe. Among national systems, the terminology[24] may vary and the definition offered by the Commission clarifies the nature and the aims of this procedural mechanism to be commonly accepted.

Focusing on the Recommendation, the fact that it is a non-binding act based on Article 292 TFEU, containing common principles and guidelines for injunctive and compensatory collective mechanisms, has been criti-

22 Recommendation on common principles cit., paragraph 2.

23 Rebecca Money-Kyrle, 'Legal Standing in Collective Redress Actions for Breach of EU Rights: Facilitating or Frustrating Common Standards and Access to Justice?', in Burkhard Hess, Maria Bergström, Eva Storskrubb (eds), *EU Civil Justice. Current issues and Future Outlook* (Hart Publishing 2016) 223, 231.

24 For comments on the terminology, see Favilli (n 7) 448 f.; Rebecca Money-Kyrle, Christopher Hodges, 'European Collective Action: Towards Coherence?' (2012) 19, 4 Maastricht Journal of European and Comparative Law 477, 479 ff.

cised[25] due to its limited practical influence in improving effectiveness[26] and thus concretely interfering with national justice systems. The Commission clearly affirmed and repeated throughout the Recommendation that the legal systems and traditions of the Member States must be respected[27] and that the common principles should be integrated in the existing national legal systems. In any case, the flexibility of the principles and the discretion given Member States to provide exceptions may increase heterogeneity across national mechanisms[28]. Even if the Recommendation is not legislative, on the one hand, it is a first (welcome) initiative suggesting a horizontal harmonisation of a selected area of civil procedure, i.e. collective mechanisms, for private enforcement in various EU fields. On the other hand, however, if Member States do not provide for effective remedies, they may violate other duties enshrined in the Treaties, such as under Article 19 TEU and Article 47 of the Charter, which require them to provide access to justice[29].

Collective procedures are deemed to be a viable means of protection favouring (mostly) weaker parties, although no express reference (to categories of weaker parties, except for consumers) is made in the Communication or in the Recommendation of the Commission. The scope of application of the common principles enshrined in the Recommendation is determined in its Recital 7, according to which 'amongst [the] areas where the supplementary private enforcement of rights granted under Union law in the form of collective redress is of value, are consumer protection, competition, environment protection, protection of personal data, financial services legislation and investor protection'. Nonetheless, the horizontal application of the common principles may cover 'any other areas where collective claims for injunctions or damages in respect of violations of the

25 See Burkhard Hess, 'The Role of Procedural Law in the Governance of Enforcement in Europe', in Hans-Wolfgang Micklitz, Andrea Wechsler (eds), *The Transformation of Enforcement. European Economic Law in Global Perspective* (Hart Publishing 2016) 343, 350, where the author commented: 'Neither minimum procedural standards of collective actions, nor a maximum harmonisation have been proposed. The Recommendation and the Communication of the Commission appear as a kind of 'position paper' in an on-going political discussion'.

26 Iris Benöhr, 'Collective Redress in the Field of European Consumer Law' (2014) 41, 3 Legal Issues of Economic Integration 243, 252 ff.

27 Cf. Recommendation on common principles cit., Recitals 10 and 13, para. 2, as already claimed by the European Parliament Resolution cit. (point 16).

28 Biard (n 18) para. 1.1.

29 Favilli (n 7) 453 f.

rights granted under Union law would be relevant'[30]. Cases involving differences between the victims and the actor, such as a violation of human rights[31] or employment terms and conditions may thus be governed. Such finding also follows from paragraph 1, that refers generally to 'mass harm situations caused by violations of rights granted under Union law'. This formula reflects the commitment of the Commission to rely on a horizontal approach in establishing a common European framework for collective redress with a broad scope.

Two paragraphs (17 and 18) of the Recommendation concern cross-border situations by proposing the mutual recognition of representative entities officially designated in the Member States, i.e. the *lex fori* may not limit the power conferred to the representative entity under its *lex causae*. This principle is meant to assure the possibility for the representative entity to act across borders; however, the Recommendation does not provide sufficient clarifications on private international law issues to solve transnational cases[32].

Overall, the principles do not attempt to affect national procedural autonomy and pursue the objective of offering a (first) solution to the divergences among Member States' systems. The reason for inviting Member States to adopt common principles governing collective mechanisms is the need to align their procedural systems so that thanks to similar requirements access to justice and enforcement of EU law would be improved.

As envisaged under paragraph 41 of the Recommendation, the Commission published on 25 January 2018 the Report on its implementation[33].

---

30 See also Xandra E. Kramer, 'Cross-border Enforcement in the EU: Mutual Trust versus Fair Trial? Towards Principles of European Civil Procedure' (2011) 2 International Journal of Procedural Law 202, 228, where the author noted that 'The recent legislative action in the area of collective redress may also offer a valuable contribution to a uniform recovery of (probably both domestic and cross-border) claims'.

31 Favilli (n 7) 446. On business-related human rights abuse, see EU Agency for Fundamental Rights, *Improving access to remedy in the area of business and human rights at the EU level*, Opinion of 10 April 2017, available at *http://fra.europa.eu/en/opinion/2017/business-human-rights*.

32 Biard (n 18) para. 1.1. See *infra*, paragraph 4.

33 Report from the Commission to the European Parliament, the Council and the European Economic and Social Committee on the implementation of the Commission Recommendation of 11 June 2013 on common principles for injunctive and compensatory collective redress mechanisms in the Member States concerning violations of rights granted under Union law (2013/396/EU), COM(2018)40 final of 25 January 2018 (from now onwards: 'Report on the implementation of the common principles').

According to the outcomes of the questionnaire and the assessment studies[34], the impact of the Recommendation has been limited and the legislative activities promoted in just a few Member States mostly related only to consumer matters. Divergences still remain in terms of the availability of collective redress procedures and of their nature (injunctive or compensatory) and, where such means exist, difficulties are linked to the complexity and length of the proceedings and the restrictive criteria on admissibility[35]. Certainly, national political realities and policy-making have influenced the legislative development.

The adoption of common principles may indeed facilitate the alignment of national systems governing collective procedures, and thus have positive outcomes, while respecting national procedural autonomy. The EU may intervene in the civil procedure field whenever a European action may better pursue the objectives of justice efficiency and effectiveness in order to protect rights granted under EU law. Similar to the legal basis of the existing sector-specific acts, the adoption of a legislative framework providing for a horizontal approach may be based on Article 114 TFEU aimed at approximating the national provisions on collective procedures, which allows, on the one hand, the safeguarding of national priorities and sovereignty and, on the other, the harmonising of the different legal systems[36].

However, another remark on the Recommendation concerns its doubtful applicability to transnational disputes. In other words, the Commission invited Member States to implement these principles in their legal order; whereas no reference is made to cross-border-related issues, apart from the two paragraphs on the mutual recognition of foreign representative entities. Even if uniformity will be achieved with the implementation of common procedural principles, private international law issues still remain in the absence of European rules.

In the optimistic scenario where all Member States did fully implement the Recommendation, it could have been asserted that by having similar

---

34 State of Collective Redress in the EU in the Context of the Implementation of the Commission Recommendation, JUST/2016/JCOO/FW/CIVI/0099, prepared by The British Institute of International and Comparative Law, November 2017, available at *http://ec.europa.eu/newsroom/just/item-detail.cfm?item_id=612847*; and 'An evaluation study' (n 6).

35 Report on the implementation of the common principles cit., 3–4.

36 See Hess (n 7) 111; Gerhard Wagner, 'Harmonisation of Civil Procedure: Policy Perspectives', in Xandra E. Kramer, C.H. van Rhee (eds), *Civil Litigation in a Globalising World* (T.M.C. Asser Press 2012) 93, 107.

conditions on collective mechanisms, their harmonisation would have been facilitated, especially the circulation of decisions. However, in the negative reality, according to the 2018 Report on the implementation of the 2013 Recommendation, not very many legislative developments have been enacted and only little progress has been realised. This demonstrates that the harmonisation has not yet been achieved.

All these findings may be considered by the Commission with a view to developing further initiatives. On the one side, difficulties and the inactivity of some Member States may not be basically justified because the proposed principles summarised the existing national legal traditions by identifying common minimum procedural guarantees. Therefore, such principles could result in an added value to the national systems, promoting similar standards across all EU Member States and facilitating litigation when moving across borders. On the other side, the Recommendation was a first step towards the adoption of legislative proposals and thus a motion for raising awareness at national level about the need to comply with certain standards in collective proceedings.

The horizontal approach adopted by the Commission with the abovementioned initiatives is certainly welcome because it pursued the objective of effectively providing common requirements for collective mechanisms as a transversal instrument irrespective of the sector concerned. It is nevertheless true that having regard to the majority of the national legal orders such collective systems are (at the moment) made available for specific fields, such as consumer protection and antitrust law, also because the respective legislation transposes EU directives. This is linked to the fact that it is more likely in these sectors that mass harm situations occur and individuals are able to act collectively, mainly through representative actions.

In light of the above, the adoption of a horizontal European framework on collective redress may meet the need to provide similar minimum requirements and avoid procedural difficulties in collective litigation. However, the peculiarities that characterise certain sectors may be undermined, and specific rules should be introduced in the respective legislation.

3. The Sectoral Approach: Specific Rules for Collective Redress in Specific Policies

Provisions on collective redress as a private enforcement means are included in certain legislative acts concerning antitrust law and consumer protection, whose adoption was promoted by the Commission with the aim of ensuring access to justice to protect collective interests.

A series of initiatives by the Commission has addressed the need to provide consumers with effective remedies since 1993 with the publication of the Green Paper on access of consumers to justice, in which national systems for the protection of collective interests and the related difficulties were assessed[37]. After the entry into force of the Treaty of Amsterdam, binding measures to promote access to justice were enacted, including the first Injunctions Directive of 1998[38], which was aimed at the approximation of national laws by establishing a common procedure to allow qualified entities to bring injunctive actions in order to stop unlawful practices that harm collective interests of consumers anywhere in the EU. The debate on effective protection and collective redress mechanisms has intensified since the adoption of the Consumer Policy Strategy for 2007–2013[39]. In November 2008, the Commission published the Green Paper on Consumer Collective Redress[40], in which it proposed possible future actions on collective procedures to be undertaken with a view to providing concrete and effective solution at EU level for the protection of collective interests, including injunctive as well as compensatory measures. The proposal was welcomed by the European Parliament[41], which deemed that collective redress, as a means to facilitate access to justice, is also an important deter-

---

37 Green Paper Access of consumers to justice and the settlement of consumer disputes in the Single Market, COM(93)576 final of 16 November 1993.

38 Directive 98/27/EC of the European Parliament and of the Council of 19 May 1998 on injunctions for the protection of consumers' interests, in *OJ* L 166 of 11 June 1998, 51–55. See Benöhr (n 26) 248 ff.

39 Communication from the Commission to the Council, the European Parliament and the European Economic and Social Committee, *EU Consumer Policy Strategy 2007–2013, Empowering consumers, enhancing their welfare, effectively protecting them*, COM(2007)99 final of 13 March 2007.

40 Green Paper on Consumer Collective Redress, COM(2008)794 final of 27 November 2008.

41 European Parliament resolution of 26 March 2009 on the White Paper on damages actions for breach of the EC antitrust rules (2008/2154(INI)), P6_TA(2009)0187, spec. point 4.

rent to unlawful practices[42]. Still, the Directive on injunctions adopted in 2009, replacing the 1998 Directive, does not allow collective redress for damages, which would compensate consumers for the harm or loss they have suffered[43].

The institutions have engaged in many reflections about the legal context of collective actions in the EU, where the need of claimants to access to justice and the risk of litigation abuse must be balanced[44]. The common starting point is the need to protect the fundamental rights, which is an objective that EU law must pursue.

Similarly, remedies in antitrust law were addressed by the Commission starting with the Green Paper of 2005, in which it identified the obstacles to a more efficient system for bringing claims and proposed options for problem solving to benefit consumers, as well as to improve the enforcement of antitrust law[45]. The Commission indeed recognised that it was unlikely that small claims by consumers or purchasers would be initiated, and that collective actions consolidating a large number of smaller claims into one action, thereby saving time and money, could better protect their interests[46]. As a follow up[47], the European Parliament, assuming private actions to be complementary to and compatible with public enforcement[48], stressed that 'in the interests of justice and for reasons of economy, speed and consistency, victims should be able voluntarily to bring collec-

42 *Ibid.*

43 Directive 2009/22/EC of the European Parliament and of the Council of 23 April 2009 on injunctions for the protection of consumers' interests (Codified version) [2009] OJ L110/30.

44 On the relevant developments see, *inter alia*, Thijs Bosters, *Collective Redress and Private International Law in the EU* (T.M.C. Asser Press 2017), 241 ff.; Favilli (n 7) 443 ff.; Lukasz Gorywoda, 'The Emerging EU Legal Regime for Collective Redress: Institutional Dimension and its Main Features', in Arnaud Nuyts, Nikitas E. Hatzimihail (eds), *Cross-border Class Actions: the European Way* (Sellier European Law Publishers 2014) 59; Christopher Hodges, *The Reform of Class and Representative Actions in European Legal Systems. A new Framework for Collective Redress in Europe* (Hart Publishing 2008) 102; and Commission Communication cit., spec. para. 1.3 ff.

45 Green Paper Damages actions for breach of the EC antitrust rules, COM(2005)672 final of 19 December 2005, accompanied by SEC(2005)1732.

46 *Ibid*, para. 2.5.

47 European Parliament resolution of 25 April 2007 on the Green Paper on Damages actions for breach of the EC antitrust rules (2006/2207(INI)), P6_TA(2007)0152.

48 *Ibid*, point 6.

tive actions, either directly or via organisations whose statutes have this as their object'[49].

The findings in the 2005 Green Paper demonstrated that the obstacles to enforcement arose from the various legal and procedural rules of the Member States governing actions for antitrust damages before the national courts. The main problem was legal uncertainty. Thus, in the following White Paper of 2008 on damages actions for breach of the EU antitrust rules, the Commission went further[50]. It proposed two collective redress mechanisms that shall be complementary, which are (i) representative actions brought by qualified entities, such as consumer associations, state bodies or trade associations, on behalf of identified or, in rather restricted cases, identifiable victims; and (ii) opt-in collective actions, in which the victims expressly decide to combine their individual claims for the harm they suffered into one single action[51]. The outcomes of the consultation launched with this White Paper were considered for the development of the proposal on remedies for violations of antitrust law.

The following Directive 2014/104 on antitrust damages actions[52] provides that any natural or legal person who has suffered harm caused by an infringement of competition law can effectively exercise the right to claim full compensation for that harm[53] through individual or collective (representative) actions[54]. However, it does not regulate procedural conditions concerning the admissibility of collective redress. Moreover, this Directive does not require Member States to introduce collective redress mechanisms for the enforcement of Articles 101 and 102 TFEU[55].

---

49 *Ibid*, point 21.

50 White Paper on damages actions for breach of the EC antitrust rules, COM(2008)165 final of 2 April 2008, accompanied by SEC(2008)404, SEC(2008)405, SEC(2008)406. See also the impact assessment of group litigation in Final Report, Making antitrust damages actions more effective in the EU: welfare impact and potential scenarios, 21 December 2007, 268 ff., available at *https://ec.europa.eu/competition/antitrust/actionsdamages/documents.html*; Tiffany Chieu, 'Class Actions in the European Union?: Importing Lessons Learned from The United States' experience into European Community Competition Law' (2010) 18 Cardozo Journal of International & Comparative Law 123, 143 ff.

51 White Paper cit., section 'Standing: indirect purchasers and collective redress'.

52 Directive 2014/104/EU of the European Parliament and of the Council of 26 November 2014 on certain rules governing actions for damages under national law for infringements of the competition law provisions of the Member States and of the European Union [2014] OJ L349/1.

53 *Ibid*, Article 1.

54 *Ibid*, Article 2(4).

55 *Ibid*, Recital 13.

In relation to EU competence in the field of procedural law, it must be noted that the sector-specific legislation was adopted on the basis of Article 114 TFEU, with the aim of achieving the approximation of national laws and a high level of protection of rights granted under Union law to contribute to the proper functioning of the internal market.

Against this context, the Commission has promoted studies and initiatives concerning in general the procedural means of collective redress, as the Communication and the Recommendation of 2013 described above under the horizontal approach analysis[56]. It appears that the Commission tried, in those fields where legislation on collective actions already exist, to further develop the procedural mechanisms, also in light of the evolving scenario of the internal market due to increasing transnational commercial activities, and, at the same time, to propose general principles on procedural requirements for collective redress that would facilitate and improve access to justice in different sectors.

On the basis of the outcomes of the 2018 Report on the implementation of the said Recommendation and as a follow-up to the REFIT Fitness Check of EU consumer and marketing law[57], in April 2018 the Commission submitted the Proposal for a Directive on representative actions for the protection of the collective interests of consumers[58] in the context of its 'New deal for consumers'[59]. This Proposal is aimed at defining at Union level a common framework for representative actions to ensure effective and efficient treatment of infringements of Union law arising from domestic or cross-border transactions in a variety of sectors, such as data protection, financial services, energy, telecommunications, health and the envi-

56 See *supra* paragraph 2.

57 See the Report SWD(2017)209 final of 25 May 2017.

58 Proposal for a Directive of the European Parliament and of the Council on representative actions for the protection of the collective interests of consumers, and repealing Directive 2009/22/EC, COM(2018)184 final of 11 April 2018 (from now onwards: 'Proposal on representative actions').

59 Communication from the Commission to the European Parliament, the Council and the European Economic and Social Committee, *A New Deal for Consumers*, COM(2018)183 final of 11 April 2018, which also includes the Proposal for a Directive of the European Parliament and of the Council amending Council Directive 93/13/EEC of 5 April 1993, Directive 98/6/EC of the European Parliament and of the Council, Directive 2005/29/EC of the European Parliament and of the Council and Directive 2011/83/EU of the European Parliament and of the Council as regards better enforcement and modernisation of EU consumer protection rules, COM(2018)185 final.

ronment[60]. Contrary to the common principles set forth in the 2013 Recommendation, this Proposal only regulates certain procedural aspects of mechanisms for the protection of consumers interests[61]. Moreover, the proposed framework is not meant to replace the national systems for collective redress, but Member States are required to design the representative action set out by the Proposal as an alternative procedure or to integrate their national provisions[62].

The described legislation on procedural means aimed at ensuring effective consumer protection relies on a sectoral approach, which takes into account the peculiarities of the category and the existing legal traditions of the Member States, whose majority already provides for collective procedures in this field. Focusing on the specificities of certain policies may better pursue the assessment of the opportunity to establish collective procedures, rather than applying horizontal principles with a broad scope. Nevertheless, if this sector-specific approach is to be welcomed, on the basis of the developments in the legislative and jurisprudential context related to consumer protection, a European collective redress procedure would prove to be useful in other sensitive policy fields, as mentioned above, which could be the case of human rights violations or employment law. In respect of the latter, similar to consumer actions, collective proceedings involving workers usually take the form of representative actions, promoted by trade unions acting on their behalf. It is thus significant to evaluate in the context of the protection of workers' rights the application of common principles or the inclusion of specific provisions on collective redress systems.

As a preliminary consideration, it must be noted that in the relevant legislation on workers there are no clear provisions on procedural means of private enforcement, but Member States are required to provide for effective remedies to ensure respect for the rights granted under Union or national law, among which collective procedures may be included.

A second issue concerns the fact that workers' rights are connected to the freedom of movement of persons and the free provision of services across the EU. This connection entails a twofold consideration: on the one side, workers enjoy rights under Union law because of their freedom to move and work across borders, they are entitled to claim the protection of such rights and thus, according to the relevant legislation, to bring actions,

60 Proposal on representative actions cit., Recital 6.
61 *Ibid*, section 'Consistency with existing policy provisions in the policy area', 4.
62 *Ibid*, Recital 24.

also collectively, as granted under Article 28 of the Charter; on the other side, the protection of workers' rights and their exercise may be subject to the balancing test with the economic freedoms, and as such to the primary principles governing the European integration process, where for instance the exercise of the right to collective action has been undermined vis-à-vis the freedom of establishment or to provide service[63]. Thus, in the law-making process, attention shall be paid to the need to protect the weaker parties, on the one side, and businesses' interests, on the other side.

In EU legislation on the protection of workers, the right to collective action is included in Directive 2014/54[64], which was adopted in the framework of the free movement for workers[65] and requires national authorities to ensure that judicial procedures are available for all EU workers in cases of discrimination or violations of EU or national law, provided that collective actions comply with national laws and practice[66]. In addition, organisations, associations, trade unions or other entities may represent or support EU workers and their families[67]. No specific procedural requirements are established, but only a generic clause on respecting the right to take action is included. It is worth noting that under Recital 15 of Directive 2014/54 Member States are invited 'to examine the implementation of common principles for injunctive and compensatory collective redress mechanisms, with a view of ensuring effective legal protection, and without prejudice to the existing collective defence mechanisms available to the social partners and to national law or practice'. Such a statement is not

63 Cf. Court of Justice (Grand Chamber), judgment of 18 December 2007, Case C-341/05, *Laval un Partneri Ltd* v *Svenska Byggnadsarbetareförbundet, Svenska Byggnad-sarbetareförbundets avdelning 1, Byggettan and Svenska Elektrikerförbundet*, EU:C:2007:809; Court of Justice (Grand Chamber), judgment of 11 December 2007, Case C-438/05, *International Transport Workers' Federation and Finnish Seamen's Union* v *Viking Line ABP and OÜ Viking Line Eesti*, EU:C:2007:772.

64 Directive 2014/54/EU of the European Parliament and of the Council of 16 April 2014 on measures facilitating the exercise of rights conferred on workers in the context of freedom of movement for workers [2014] OJ L128/8.

65 The relevant rules are contained in Regulation (EU) No 492/2011 of the European Parliament and of the Council of 5 April 2011 on freedom of movement for workers within the Union [2011] OJ L141/1, that updates (and codifies) earlier legislation on the freedom to move and work of EU citizens in another EU country.

66 Directive 2014/54/EU, Article 3, paras. 2–4.

67 See Directive 2014/54/EU, Recitals 15 and 29 that ensure the possibility for entities to represent workers and the respect for the right to collective action; and in general Article 3 on the defence of rights.

mentioned in the Directive on antitrust damages actions, of nearly the same period, nor in the consumer legislation cited above.

The latter consideration is significant in so far as it highlights the different approaches (horizontal or sectoral) adopted by the European legislator when dealing with collective means of protection. A clear reference to the common principles set out by the 2013 Recommendation is added only in Directive 2014/54 on employment matters. For the purpose of the present analysis, it is indeed relevant that even if the employment field was not mentioned in the said Recommendation, the reference to common principles included in the respective legislation assumes that workers' collective actions may be covered by the future European collective redress framework.

Provisions on the right to collective action can then be found in the legislation concerning posted workers that includes Directive 96/71 (amended by Directive 2018/957)[68] and the Enforcement Directive 2014/67 which complements the former with control mechanisms[69]. Collective actions are envisaged as remedies for workers that may be undertaken in judicial or extra-judicial proceedings by trade unions acting on behalf of them. In any case, except for the obligation upon Member States to ensure effective remedies, collective redress is not outlined with procedural requirements that are accordingly governed by national legislation.

In conclusion, if the sectoral approach is further developed, the opportunity to establish a collective redress procedure for workers should also be evaluated taking into account the peculiarities of the employment field, especially those related to increasing labour mobility and the phenomenon

---

68 Directive 96/71/EC of the European Parliament and of the Council of 16 December 1996 concerning the posting of workers in the framework of the provision of services [1997] OJ L18, cf. Recital 22 and Article 1a, introduced by Directive 2018/957/EU [2018] OJ L173/16.

69 Directive 2014/67/EU of the European Parliament and of the Council of 15 May 2014 on the enforcement of Directive 96/71/EC concerning the posting of workers in the framework of the provision of services and amending Regulation (EU) No 1024/2012 on administrative cooperation through the Internal Market Information System ('the IMI Regulation') [2014] OJ L159/11, cf. Article 11: 'Member States shall ensure that trade unions and other third parties, such as associations, organisations and other legal entities which have, in accordance with the criteria laid down under national law, a legitimate interest in ensuring that this Directive and Directive 96/71/EC are complied with, may engage, on behalf or in support of the posted workers or their employer, and with their approval, in any judicial or administrative proceedings with the objective of implementing this Directive and Directive 96/71/EC and/or enforcing the obligations under this Directive and Directive 96/71/EC'.

of posting, and specific provisions should be included in the relevant legislation.

4. *The Jurisdictional Regime for Cross-Border Collective Redress*

Collective redress mechanisms in the transnational context are not sufficiently or completely addressed in both the horizontal approach, including the 2013 Recommendation on common principles and the existing private international law Regulations, as well as in the sectoral legislation.

As for the Regulations, it can be noted that the collective dimension of the disputes was not new and subject to discussion within the review process of the Brussels I Regulation. According to the Explanatory Statement accompanying the Proposal for the recast of the Brussels I Regulation[70], the Commission acknowledged that within the preliminary public consultation specific concerns were expressed with respect to the abolition of *exequatur*, not only in defamation cases but also in collective redress proceedings[71]. It then clarified that the Proposal abolishes the *exequatur* procedure for all judgments covered by the Regulation with the exception of judgments in defamation and compensatory collective redress cases[72]. In particular, the *exequatur* procedure is maintained for judgments issued in collective 'proceedings brought by a group of claimants, a representative entity or a body acting in the public interest and which concern the compensation of harm caused by unlawful business practices to a multitude of claimants'[73]. Having ascertained the differences among Member States as to the collective mechanisms established in various areas with diverse requirements, the Commission asserted that 'the required level of trust cannot be presumed at this stage' and reported that the issue of collective redress was under discussion[74]. Finally, in the present text of the Brussels I Recast Regulation there are no provisions on the recognition and enforce-

70 Proposal for a Regulation on jurisdiction and the recognition and enforcement of judgments in civil and commercial matters (recast), COM(2010)748 final of 14 December 2010.

71 *Ibid*, para. 2.

72 *Ibid*, para. 3.1.

73 *Ibid*, para. 3.1.1.

74 *Ibid*, where it recalled the initiative on a European approach to collective redress to identify which forms of collective redress could fit into the EU legal system and into the legal orders of the EU Member States.

ment of collective judgments, that are thus subject to the general principles, including the public policy exception.

As reported by the Commission in its 2013 Communication, within the 2011 public consultation on a coherent approach to collective redress in the EU, stakeholders highlighted the need for European provisions tackling cross-border issues with regard to the jurisdictional rules. They suggested different solutions: the introduction of specific connecting criteria, being the domicile of the majority of parties who claim to have been injured or the domicile of the defendant because it is easy to identify; the extension of jurisdiction for consumer contracts to representative entities; the creation of a special panel for cross-border collective actions with the Court of Justice[75]. Such proposals however have not been included in the initiatives of the Commission.

The crucial issues about jurisdiction and applicable law were pointed out by the European Parliament in its 2012 Resolution[76]. As to jurisdiction, it stressed that the horizontal framework should have laid down rules to prevent a rush to the courts (*forum* shopping) and that rules for determining jurisdiction should have taken into account the provisions of the Brussels I Regulation in order to assure a coherent European approach[77]. Ultimately, no response was found in the Commission's text.

In the 2013 Recommendation on common principles, paragraphs 17 and 18 concern cross-border cases by proposing the mutual recognition of representative entities officially designated in the Member States by affirming the principle of non-discrimination in the context of civil proceedings. However, the application of this (common) principle in all national legal orders does not seem to sufficiently ensure coherence and certainty in transnational litigation, because it only relates to admissibility and legal standing of the entities. There may be the case of a conflict of laws applicable to the constitution of the collective redress and to the merits, given that the competent court should assess different laws, whether on contractual or extra-contractual obligations, or the issue of *forum* shopping may be faced, which is more relevant for the purposes of the present analysis. *Forum* shopping means that representative entities may look for the most suitable court to promote a collective redress, because of procedural requirements, other than the ones implementing the 2013 European com-

75 Commission Communication cit., 13.

76 European Parliament resolution cit. (n 13).

77 *Ibid*, para. 26. It then suggested the application of the law of the place where the majority of the victims are domiciled, without prejudice to individual claims (para. 27).

mon principles, that may be more favourable. Such rush to the courts however will not comply with the respect for procedural guarantees recognised at European and national levels as general principles, including the right to defence, and in contrast with the principle of legal certainty.

In particular, the mutual recognition of foreign groups and representative entities is outlined in paragraph 17, where the Commission called upon the Member States to ensure that foreign claimants are not excluded by the national rules on admissibility or standing[78]. These cases may occur when claimants are from several Member States, or foreign groups of claimants or representative entities originate from other national legal systems. In other words, the courts shall recognise procedural standing of foreign groups or entities granted them by the law of their State of origin. This rule is consistent with the fact that, otherwise, due to restrictive criteria provided by the legislation on *locus standi* in the State where the claim is initiated, representative organisations may be prevented from bringing actions[79]. When a diversity of requirements occurs, the public policy exception may also be invoked against the recognition of decisions issued within a collective procedure.

Under the following paragraph 18, the Commission required that any officially designated representative entity shall be permitted to seise the court in the Member State having jurisdiction to consider the mass harm situation. This complements the principle under paragraph 17 stating that the procedural requirements set forth in the *lex fori* cannot limit the power of a foreign representative entity to act before the courts of a different Member State.

In general, the principles at stake do not sufficiently address the implications under the private international law perspective because they merely relate to admissibility and legal standing of representative entities. With regard to the jurisdictional regime, the Commission affirmed that the (then) existing Brussels I Regulation 'should be fully exploited' (even though it covers individual disputes) and thus postponed the assessment of the need to introduce specific rules in light of the further experience involving cross-border cases[80].

78 On this issue see Bosters (n 44) 244 ff.; Astrid Stadler, 'The Commission's Recommendation on Common Principles of Collective Redress and Private International Law Issues', in Eva Lein, Duncan Fairgrieve, Marta Otero Crespo, Vincent Smith (eds), *Collective Redress in Europe: Why and How?* (The British Institute of International and Comparative Law 2015) 235.

79 Money-Kyrle (n 23) 240.

80 Commission Communication cit., 13.

According to the 2018 Report on the implementation of the common principles, Member States do not have general obstacles to or limitations on the participation of foreign persons in group actions before their courts[81], even if the principle of the mutual recognition of the *status* of foreign representative entities is not expressly included in some legal orders, except for the provisions implementing the Injunctions Directive[82]. As marginally noted, two respondents criticised the lack of any provision regarding the applicability of the protective consumer jurisdiction rule to representative entities[83]. Such consideration is now (apparently) overcome by the 2018 proposal on representative actions for consumers.

The lack of any specific provisions included in the 2013 Recommendation on jurisdiction on collective disputes with cross-border implications raises difficulties, because the mutual recognition of foreign entities as a common principle does not solve the question of which is the competent court to hear the case. In addition, the existing uniform private international law rules of the relevant Regulations are not suitable for collective redress procedures. The general principles of private international law aimed at ensuring proper coordination of national systems shall be fulfilled by introducing (in the Regulations or in a European comprehensive framework) provisions that take into account the peculiarities of transnational collective proceedings.

As to the sectoral legislative framework analysed with regard to antitrust law, consumer protection, and workers, no precise provisions on jurisdiction, either on the law applicable to the merits or on the recognition and enforcement of collective judgments are included.

The Court of Justice has rarely addressed the issue of collective redress, the jurisdictional regime and the applicability of the Brussels I Regulation with regard to consumers. In its judgment delivered in the *Schrems* case[84], the Court preliminarily assessed whether the proceedings were to be defined as a collective redress according to the national law or if they consisted of other forms such as an assignment of claims or joined claims[85]. It then analysed the applicability of the protective rules on jurisdiction under the (then) Brussels I Regulation. Indeed, this Regulation (as well as Brussels I *bis*) does not contain specific rules concerning jurisdiction over cross-

81 Report on the implementation of the common principles cit., 10.

82 *Ibid*, 11.

83 *Ibid*, 11, fn. 31.

84 Court of Justice, judgment of 25 January 2018, Case C-498/16, *Maximilian Schrems v Facebook Ireland Limited*, EU:C:2018:37.

85 See also Report on the implementation of the common principles cit., 2.

border collective redress in general[86] or for specific matters. This absence may thus require (i) the extension of the application of the existing grounds where similar claims should be treated in the same way as the actions falling within the scope of the Regulation, or (ii) the introduction of specific connecting factors considering the peculiar features characterising collective proceedings[87].

Among the case law, already in the *Henkel* judgment of 2002[88], the Court clarified, in relation to the assignment of claims, that 'a legal person which acts as assignee of the rights of a private final consumer, without itself being party to a contract between a professional and a private individual, cannot be regarded as a consumer within the meaning of the Brussels Convention and therefore cannot invoke Articles 13 to 15 of that Convention'. It also added that 'that interpretation must also apply in respect of a consumer protection organisation (…) which has brought an action as an association on behalf of consumers'[89]. An action to fall within the scope of application of the Brussels system must be of contractual nature, therefore a contractual relationship must exist between the parties of a dispute[90], and if a consumer protection organisation acts on behalf of individuals this contractual link does not exist. It follows that consumers' special rules of jurisdiction may not be invoked by the representative organisation, or the

---

86 Peter Mankowski, Peter Arnt Nielsen, 'Introduction to Articles 17–19', in Ulrich Magnus, Peter Mankowski (eds), *European Commentaries on Private International Law. Brussels Ibis Regulation* (Sellier European Law Publishers, Ottoschmidt 2016) 450; on private international law issues, mainly with regard to consumers' protection, see Stefania Bariatti, 'Le azioni collettive dell'art. 140-bis del codice del consumo: aspetti di diritto internazionale privato e processuale' (2011) 1 Rivista di diritto internazionale privato e processuale 19; Laura Carballo Piñeiro, *Las acciones colectivas y su eficacia extraterritorial. Problemas de recepción y transplante de las class actions en Europa* (Universidad de Santiago de Compostela 2009) 105 ff. European Parliament resolution of 7 September 2010 on the implementation and review of Council Regulation (EC) No 44/2001 on jurisdiction and the recognition and enforcement of judgments in civil and commercial matters (2009/2140(INI)), P7_TA(2010)0304, point 32, stressed that 'the Commission's forthcoming work on collective redress instruments may need to contemplate special jurisdiction rules for collective actions'. Collective redress proceedings were taken into account within the Proposal for a Regulation, COM(2010)748 final, cit., mainly with regard to recognition and enforcement aspects.

87 Mihail Danov, 'The Brussels I Regulation: cross-border collective redress proceedings and judgments' (2010) 6, 2 Journal of Private International Law 359, 364 ff.

88 Court of Justice, judgment of 1 October 2002, Case C-167/00, *Verein für Konsumenteninformation* v *Karl Heinz Henkel*, EU:C:2002:555.

89 *Ibid*, para. 33.

90 *Ibid*, para. 38.

assignee. However, the specific case concerned a non-contractual situation. The Court ruled that the preventive action submitted by the organisation in the main proceedings was covered by Article 5(3) of the Brussels Convention on jurisdiction over tort disputes because that action was aimed at preventing a trader from using terms considered unfair meaning it was a matter related to torts and according to a broad interpretation of that Article not only damages in individual situations are included, but also 'the undermining of legal stability by the use of unfair terms which it is the task of associations (...) to prevent'[91].

The finding on the extension of the scope of the Brussels I Regulation was upheld by Advocate General Bobek in the *Schrems* case[92]. In his opinion, he addressed the question of whether the *forum actoris* of the consumer under Article 16 of the Brussels I Regulation is applicable to assignees of consumer claims that are not themselves parties to a contract[93]. First, he defined the main proceedings not to be a collective redress as alleged by the claimant, but as an assignment of claims according to the *lex fori* (Austrian law). The exclusion of the applicability of the Brussels jurisdictional rules is based on the following arguments. The wording of Articles 15 and 16 thereof clearly refers to the other party to a contract, and thus the special *forum* is always limited to the concrete and specific parties to the contract[94]. Interpreting Article 16 as including claims made by a consumer-assignee on the basis of consumer contracts concluded by other consumers would weaken the link between the consumer *status* and a given contract, thus producing a paradoxical result[95], and enlarge the scope of the special head of jurisdiction beyond the cases explicitly provided for by those Articles[96]. The aim of the jurisdictional rules relating to consumers is to protect a person in his capacity as a consumer to a given contract. Then, since Articles 15 and 16 are derogations from the general rule and the special rules for contracts, their interpretation must be narrow and should not be extended to include other situations[97].

---

91 Case C-167/00, *Henkel*, para. 42.

92 Opinion of Advocate General Bobek delivered on 14 November 2017, Case C-498/16, *Maximilian Schrems* v *Facebook Ireland Limited*, EU:C:2017:863.

93 *Ibid*, para. 77 ff.

94 *Ibid*, para. 82.

95 *Ibid*, para. 86.

96 *Ibid*, para. 85.

97 *Ibid*, para. 88.

The Advocate General recalled the abovementioned *Henkel* judgment and the earlier *Shearson Lehman Hutton* judgment[98] on the non-applicability of the special consumer jurisdiction to legal persons acting as assignees of the rights of a consumer because those legal persons (a private company and a consumers' association) were not weaker parties and were not themselves parties to the contract[99]. Furthermore, he referred to the ruling in the *CDC Hydrogen Peroxide* case of 2015[100], according to which the Court declared that in relation to Article 5, point 3 of Regulation No. 44/2001 'the transfer of claims by the initial creditor cannot, by itself, have an impact on the determination of the court having jurisdiction. As a consequence, (...) the requirement for the application of that head of jurisdiction (the location of the harmful event) must be assessed for each claim for damages independently of any subsequent assignment or consolidation'[101]. With regard to the *Schrems* case, he then argued that in the absence of any contractual relationship between the assignee and the other party to the original contract, the special consumer *fora* could not be invoked, nor could the creation of a new *forum* for the assignee-consumer be sought[102]. Contrary to what the Commission argued in its opinion with a view to protecting consumers residing within the same State, the Advocate General held that the local (internal) jurisdiction under Regulation No. 44/2001 (the competent courts are those of the place where the consumer is domiciled) may not be disregarded[103] and that it even excludes the consolidation of claims of other consumers domiciled in the same country. Notwithstanding, a new special jurisdiction may be internally provided for by the national law[104]. It was then recognised that the Brussels I Regulation does not provide for specific provisions on the assignment of claims or collective redress procedures[105].

98 Court of Justice, judgment of 19 January 1993, Case C-89/91, *Shearson Lehmann Hutton Inc.* v *TVB Treuhandgesellschaft für Vermögensverwaltung und Beteiligungen mbH*, EU:C:1993:15. See also Biard (n 18) para. 1.2.

99 Opinion of Advocate General Bobek, *Schrems* (n 92), para. 96.

100 Court of Justice, judgment of 21 May 2015, Case C-352/13, *Cartel Damage Claims (CDC) Hydrogen Peroxide SA* v *Evonik Degussa GmbH and Others*, EU:C:2015:335.

101 Opinion of Advocate General Bobek, *Schrems* (n 92), para. 109.

102 *Ibid*, para. 110.

103 *Ibid*, paras. 115–116.

104 *Ibid*, para. 117.

105 *Ibid*, para. 119, where the Advocate General affirmed that 'judicial legislation would be inappropriate' and, in para. 123, 'the issue is too delicate and complex. It is in need of comprehensive legislation, not an isolated judicial intervention

The Court delivered its judgment on 25 January 2018[106] and upheld the findings of the Advocate General. First, it agreed with the interpretation given to the notion of consumer for the purposes of social media platforms[107]. Consequently, it acknowledged the derogative nature of the special provisions related to individual contracts of employment, that must be interpreted narrowly[108] and that the necessary existence of a contractual link between the parties in the disputes serves to ensure the predictability of the *forum actoris*[109]. Second, as to the assignment of claims, in line with its previous case law, the Court held that the consumer cannot bring the assigned claims within the jurisdiction of the courts of the place of his domicile. Situations other than those provided for by the Regulation cannot be included in its scope of application. Thus, 'an assignment of claims cannot provide the basis for a new specific *forum* for a consumer to whom those claims have been assigned'[110], regardless of whether the other consumers are domiciled in the same Member State, in another EU Member State or in a third country[111]. Finally, the Court did not refer to any possible *forum* for assigned claims that may be established under national law and that may nevertheless be in compliance with the objectives of the Regulation. It might have assumed that it is for the national procedural law of the courts having jurisdiction on the basis of a general (defendant's domicile) or special (consumer's domicile) ground to allow the consolidation of claims or the establishment of a collective redress procedure. From a first appraisal, the European judges seem to have limited their ruling to the referred questions by strictly interpreting the Brussels provisions, without addressing the issue of collective litigation, in particular the cross-border collective redress procedure and the related jurisdictional aspects. This presumably relies on the fact that, in accordance with the *lex fori*, the case in the main proceedings was not regarded as a collective redress, but as an assignment of claims, which has already been defined by the Court.

---

within a related but somewhat remote legislative instrument that is clearly unfit for that purpose'.

106 Court of Justice, judgment of 25 January 2018, Case C-498/16, *Maximilian Schrems* v *Facebook Ireland Limited*, EU:C:2018:37.

107 *Ibid*, paras. 25–41.

108 *Ibid*, para. 43.

109 *Ibid*, paras. 44–46.

110 *Ibid*, para. 48.

111 *Ibid*, para. 49.

In conclusion, according to the case law, the Brussels system is not applicable to collective disputes, whether in the form of collective redress or assignment of claims, because the instrument is not fit for purpose.

Against this background, in the recent legislative developments related to consumers, the objective of establishing mechanisms for the protection of collective interests, and related provisions aimed at handling transnational litigation, appears to have been achieved by introducing other forms of collective proceedings, such as a collective action based on a mandate.

The case of a party acting on behalf of a number of individuals on the basis of a mandate is considered in Regulation No. 2016/679 on consumer data protection, which provides for the right to bring an action of organisations or other similar entities (not-for-profit) on behalf of other members when it is based on the data subject's mandate[112]. The wording of Article 80 may lead to the mandate-based action being treated like a representative action, thus being qualified as a collective redress, even if the determination of such an action is left to national law (without recognising it as a European collective action)[113]. In particular, pursuant to said Article the representative organisation may exercise the actions set forth in Articles 77 to 79, where specific *fora* are also established. These grounds for jurisdiction prevail over the general rules contained in the Brussels Regulation pursuant to Recital 147. Accordingly, the application of the specific grounds for jurisdiction available to data subjects (individually) is

---

112 Regulation (EU) 2016/679 of the European Parliament and of the Council of 27 April 2016 on the protection of natural persons with regard to the processing of personal data and on the free movement of such data, and repealing Directive 95/46/EC (General Data Protection Regulation) [2016] OJ L119/1, in particular see Recital No. 142 and Article 80. Heads of jurisdiction are provided for in Articles 77–79. See Biard (n 18) para. 2.3. The question of whether Article 22 on the right of every person to a judicial remedy for any breach of the rights guaranteed him by the national law applicable to the processing in question (jointly with Articles 23 and 24) of Directive 95/46/EC of the European Parliament and of the Council of 24 October 1995 on the protection of individuals with regard to the processing of personal data and on the free movement of such data, allows public-service associations to take action against the infringer in the event of an infringement in order to safeguard the interests of consumers has been referred to the Court of Justice: see Request for a preliminary ruling from the Oberlandesgericht Düsseldorf (Germany) lodged on 26 January 2017, Case C-40/17, *Fashion ID GmbH & Co.KG* v *Verbraucherzentrale NRW eV*.

113 Rafael Amaro, Maria José Azar-Baud, Sabine Corneloup, Bénédicte Fauvarque-Cosson, Fabienne Jault-Seseke, *Collective Redress in the Member States of the European Union*, Study PE 608.829, 2018, 44, available at *www.europarl.europa.eu/supporting-analyses*.

extended to the actions of the representative organisation, thus resulting in a collective redress procedure as conceived of in the earlier initiatives of the Commission, where only designated entities should have the right to act on behalf of a group of consumers.

As a concrete progress in the field of collective redress, the 2018 Proposal for a Directive on consumer representative actions represents a step forward. According to this, qualified entities are empowered to act in defence of the collective interests of consumers. This Directive introduces procedural requirements for such actions. As to cross-border cases, Article 16 affirms the mutual recognition of the *status* of the foreign representative entities, as originally proposed in the 2013 Recommendation, and, what is more significant, it clearly states the application of the existing private international law rules (on jurisdiction, recognition and enforcement of judgments and applicable law) to such representative actions, although this statement is contained in Recital 9 and not in a binding article. However, at the interpretative level, it follows that representative entities may enjoy the protective criteria established in favour of consumers.

Finally, from a practical and individual's perspective, it appears that a general clause on the extension of the application of the existing private international law rules to representative entities does not do enough to satisfy the need for legal certainty as it still leaves unsolved the questions on jurisdiction, as well as recognition and enforcement of judgments and applicable law.

As far as the jurisdictional regime is concerned, the extension of the scope of application of the Brussels Regulation to cover collective redress is allowed when the collective disputes in the form of representative actions regard matters that fall within its scope of application. At the moment, this finding is only applicable to consumers; nevertheless, it is arguable whether such a principle may be also applied analogically to other matters covered by the Regulation, relying on the fact that similar provisions thereof pursue the protection of the weaker parties, such as those on employment. Indeed, in this context, it is common to some Member States' legal orders that trade unions as representative entities acting on behalf of or in support of workers are empowered to bring judicial actions[114].

---

114 See Report on the implementation of the common principles cit. On trade union functions in national context see Rebecca Zahn, *New Labour Laws in Old Member States. Trade Union Responses to European Enlargement* (Cambridge University Press 2017) 17 ff.; D. Schiek, L. Oliver, C. Forde, G. Alberti, *EU Social and Labour Rights and EU Internal Market Law*, PE 563.457, September 2015, spec.

Few cases involving trade unions have been addressed by the Court of Justice, mainly those concerning the exercise of the right to collective action vis-à-vis the economic freedoms or the protection of posted workers' rights. In these decisions, no question concerned the problems related to cross-border collective redress involving workers, except for the *Sähköalojen ammattiliitto* (a Finnish trade union) case of 2015[115], where the Court was requested to determine the law applicable to the constitution and admissibility of the trade union's action in so far as it included also posted workers. The case concerned a Polish undertaking that was sued before a Finnish court by the Finnish trade union, which claimed the minimum pay in accordance with the Finnish collective agreement and with Directive 96/71 on the posting of workers, because that collective agreement provided for more favourable conditions than those under Polish law. The dispute focused on the legal standing of the Finnish trade union and its power to represent posted (Polish) workers. In this regard, the Polish undertaking claimed the application of the law of the State of origin of the posting undertaking (Polish law), which required different conditions for the trade unions' legal standing (in particular, it prohibits the assignment of claims arising from an employment relationship), and asked for the dismissal of the action. The Court did not uphold this argument and applied the *lex fori* (Finnish law), as it was a matter for the national legislation of the court seised. Indeed, in light of Directive 96/71 and Article 47 of the Charter, the law of the State of the posting undertaking must not prevent a trade union of a different State from bringing an action before the courts of its State of origin, in which the workers are posted, in order to recover pay claims that relate to the minimum wage and have been assigned to the trade union in accordance with the law of that second State[116].

---

30 ff., available at *www.europarl.europa.eu/supporting-analyses*, noted that 'effective collective industrial action is a precondition of a functioning system of collective bargaining. However, generally wage levels and levels of employment protection are more favourable for workers where trade union representation is effective, which again depends on the scope for collective industrial action'; Jan Cremers, Martin Bulla, *Collective redress and workers' rights in the EU*, AIAS Working Paper 118, March 2012, 19 f., available at *www.uva-aias.net.*

115 Court of Justice, judgment of 12 February 2015, Case C-396/13, *Sähköalojen ammattiliitto ry* v *Elektrobudowa Spolka Akcyjna*, EU:C:2015:86.

116 *Ibid*, para. 26. See Massimo Roccella, Tiziano Treu, *Diritto del lavoro dell'Unione europea* (Wolters Kluwer CEDAM 2016) 448 f.; Alberto Mattei, 'La Direttiva Enforcement n. 2014/67/UE e il recepimento nell'ordinamento italiano' (2017) 1 Rivista giuridica del lavoro e della previdenza sociale 147, 156 f.

In this case the Court did not address the issue of jurisdiction because, according to the Directive on posting of workers (Article 6) and the Enforcement Directive (Article 11), the courts of the State where the workers are posted shall be competent. In particular, Article 11, paragraph 3 states the right of trade unions to lodge complaints on behalf of posted workers and, even if it is not clearly expressed, the ground of jurisdiction laid down in paragraph 1 shall also be applied to the collective proceedings on the basis of a systematic interpretation of the provisions thereof.

According to the sector-specific legislative framework and the case law of the Court of Justice, the differences in the national laws on collective redress procedures may cause difficulties in initiating proceedings, and in general in granting access to justice and effective remedies in situations with cross-border implications. The determination of the courts having jurisdiction may thus be solved by introducing provisions that (i) affirm the extension of the application of the existing rules of private international law or (ii) establish tailored connecting criteria for collective procedure. A clear rule is thus needed, whether stating a general principle or specific criteria. In comparison with the horizontal approach analysis, new provisions shall be identified according to the specific sector, and not *in abstracto* having regard to the collective dimension of the dispute.

In respect of the latter option (rules applicable in general to collective redress irrespective of the subject matter), as registered within the 2011 public consultation, a new (general) factor has been proposed by stakeholders that could be suitable for the determination of the competent court to hear the case, which is the domicile of the majority of the claimants. This may be valid whenever no representative entities act before the courts and a group of individuals wish to bring an action that does not constitute a representative action. Nevertheless, problems may be faced relating to the right to defence of the residual part of the group or to the possibility of having the decision recognised and enforced in their own Member States. However, in line with the Commission's arguments, in the European context representative actions may better pursue the objective of improving access to justice and offering guarantees in collective redress procedures, thus avoiding the risk of abusive litigation.

5. Concluding Remarks

The path towards the creation of a European framework on collective redress demonstrates that harmonisation among national legal orders as far as procedural remedies are concerned requires efforts from both the European legislator and the Member States to combine principles of procedural law and national legal traditions. Although a consensus on the need to grant effective remedies and to protect individuals' rights can be identified, difficulties in developing and implementing minimum (and common) procedural requirements still remain.

The inconsistency of the approaches adopted by the Commission in providing a horizontal framework or solutions in specific sectors can be justified by the fact that the EU does not retain exclusive competence in the procedural field and the approximation of laws shall respect national legal traditions, whose divergencies represent an obstacle to achieve a high-level of uniformity.

A positive outcome in this evolving scenario on collective redress is that, as a benchmark in the relevant legislation and in the two different approaches, this procedural remedy has been conceived of as a representative action, being the form that most complies with the procedural guarantees needed in judicial litigation and is present both in the 2013 Recommendation on common principles and in the recent 2018 Proposal.

On the one hand, the horizontal approach seems to be too far reaching because of the limited implementation in the national legal orders, whose divergences may still hamper an effective judicial protection. On the other hand, the sectoral approach seems to be the most feasible solution in practice that may be adopted in specific legislation and thus shaped accordingly as in the majority of Member States mechanisms of collective redress already exist in the field of consumer protection and to whose development European directives have contributed. However, as demonstrated above, collective redress should be made available in other sectors, such as in the employment context where collective litigation is not new because of the right of trade unions or other representative organisations to take collective action recognised under Union law.

As to the jurisdictional regime, in the legislation and other soft-law initiatives, no provisions tackle the issue of which court shall be competent for cross-border collective redress procedures. The application of the existing private international law rules to representative actions at the moment introduced with the 2018 Proposal implies an extension of the scope of application of the Regulations concerned. In the absence of specific provisions, such principle may also be applied analogically to collective redress relating to other fields where weaker parties are involved and may be a viable means for the protection of collective interests and enforcement of rights EU-wide.

Moreover, it can be noted that the proposed extension of the application of the existing private international law rules somehow differs from the findings in the abovementioned case law concerning consumers and assignment of claims allegedly qualified as collective action. This extension included in the 2018 Proposal could be considered as a follow-up to the few judicial interventions that have dealt with issues related to collective redress. In those cases, a restrictive interpretation of the Brussels rules has been implemented due to their derogative nature from the general rule of jurisdiction. As observed by Advocate General Bobek, the issue of collective redress is 'too delicate and complex', and it calls for a comprehensive legislation, moreover an 'isolated judicial intervention' that interprets a 'remote legislative instrument that is clearly unfit for that purpose' would be inappropriate[117].

These considerations may be regarded as a motion for legislative intervention, even more needed because of the unfit existing instruments and the increasing mass situations across Europe. Future developments are then expected in relation to the legislative process regarding the 2018 Proposal on consumers representative actions as well as, at jurisdictional level, with regard to the *Fashion ID* case on data protection[118].

In conclusion, the issue of collective redress appears to be at the crossroads between a horizontal and sectoral approach, where, regardless of the adopted form, clear provisions on private international law issues to avoid risk of different and incoherent interpretations should be included.

117 Opinion of Advocate General Bobek, *Schrems* (n 92), para. 119 ff., spec. 123.
118 Case C-40/17, *Fashion ID* (n 112).

Your Place? Mine? Or Theirs? A Legal and Policy-orientated Analysis of Jurisdiction in Cross-Border Collective Redress

Stephanie Law[*]

Table of Contents

---

* Lecturer in Law, University of Southampton. All errors remain mine. I would however like to thank Professors Burkhard Hess and Marta Requejo Isidro, as well as Dr Vincent Richard and Janek Nowak for considerable discussions on the topic over a number of years. Indeed, this chapter is intended to be read in line with that of Janek Nowak. Thanks also to the organisers of the conference. The content of the chapter is up-to-date as of July 2018. It is worth noting that the 2018 Proposal of the European Commission for a Directive on Representative Actions was due to be subject to interinstitutional trilogue negotiations in March 2020.

1. *Introduction*

The relationship between collective redress and the Brussels I bis regime has been highlighted as problematic in academic and political discourses since the mid-2000s; at this time, the European Commission began to contemplate collective consumer redress as a viable means to bolster its consumer law policy but still identified a 'justice gap' in the protection of EU law via collective redress, arising from the piecemeal nature of national collective redress mechanisms and absence of an EU-wide regime.[1] While the EU policymaker has engaged in extensive discussions on mass harms and on the different mechanisms that might ensure redress is available for consumers, it has devoted comparably little attention to cross-border collective redress and the interaction of national mechanisms with private international law (PIL) rules. Indeed, the Commission's Green Paper on Collective Redress,[2] the 2013 Communication and Recommendation[3] as well as the European Commission's 2018 Proposal for a Directive on Representative Actions[4] only briefly touch upon these issues. One can ask whether there is a lack of understanding of these concerns, or a deliberate choice on the part of the institutions not to identify a European solution. Regardless, it appears that the lack of a proper PIL framework for collec-

1 European Commission, 'Green Paper on Consumer Collective Redress' COM(2008) 794 final, p.3. The Commission first broached the issue of collective redress with the completion of a 2004 study concerning damages claims for the infringement of EU competition rules; Ashurst, 'Study on the Conditions of Claims for Damages in Case of Infringement of EC Competition Rules' (August 2004).

2 European Commission, 'Green Paper on Consumer Collective Redress' COM(2008) 794 final.

3 European Commission, 'Recommendation 2013/396/EU on Common Principles for Injunctive and Compensatory Collective Redress Mechanisms in the Member States Concerning Violations of Rights Granted under Union Law' (http://eur-lex.europa.eu/legal-content/EN/TXT/?uri=OJ:JOL_2013_201_R_NS0013) and European Commission, 'Communication – Towards a European Horizontal Framework for Collective Redress' COM(2013) 401 final (http://eur-lex.europa.eu/legal-content/EN/TXT/?uri=celex:52013DC0401).

4 European Commission, 'Proposal for a Directive on Representative Actions for the Protection of the Collective Interests of Consumers and Repealing the Injunctions Directive 2009/22/EC' COM(2018) 184 final (hereinafter 2018 Proposal for a Directive on Representative Actions).

tive redress thwarts the development of collective redress as a means to enforce rights and obligations deriving from EU law across the Member States. From this perspective, the *Schrems II*[5] case is no more than the latest manifestation of the problematic relationship between collective redress and PIL.

This chapter aims to set out the key problem of the *modus operandi* of the EU in regulating civil procedure, and indeed the rapport between substance and procedure; what is identified is a patchwork of uncoordinated measures lacking an overarching approach to collective redress. Delving deeper, the problematic situation reflects the lack of a comprehensive competence on the part of the EU to regulate civil procedure in both national and cross-border cases. This results in different dynamics with conflicting outcomes, with instruments in one area potentially depriving instruments in another of their effectiveness.

The relationship between EU initiatives concerning collective redress and their integration into the Brussels I bis regime is a prime example in this regard. The situation is further complicated when we also bring national mechanisms of collective redress into the equation; the existence, scope and form of such mechanisms diverge across the Member States. The issues that have been highlighted in EU policy documents concerning the relationship between the national and cross-border dimensions of collective redress only scratch the surface of the problem. That is to say, it is not only a question of the recognition and standing of the class representative, or of jurisdiction, but also of the interpretation of connecting factors, *lis pendens*, the notion of related actions, and the recognition and enforcement of decisions rendered in other Member States. The potential for the refusal of recognition and enforcement on public policy grounds is considerable (on the basis of the type of national collective redress mechanism, on the determination of notification, and of the protection of procedural rights).[6] Moreover, even these considerations do not extend to the thorny issues of third-state elements, or the problems posed by rules on applicable law. One must ask whether the Brussels I bis regime is really ready to accommodate the policy move at both the EU and the Member State level to establish cross-border and potentially horizontal collective redress mechanisms. It appears not to be.

In responding to this question, this chapter will examine firstly the correlation between the European Commission's 2018 Proposal for a Direc-

5 Case C-498/16 *Schrems* EU:C:2017:863.

6 On these latter issues, see the chapter of Janek Nowak.

tive on Representative Actions and the Brussels I bis Regulation. Thereafter, the difficulties of integrating the proposal into the Brussels regime are identified; key preliminary conclusions on the options available to resolve these problems of jurisdiction are then set out. The chapter concludes with a proposal for non-action on the part of the Union legislature until such a time as a culture of collective redress has been established and can be identified across the Member States.

2. *The Development of Mechanisms to Redress Mass Harms*

2.1. *The Legal and Political Framework of Collective Redress and its PIL Dimensions*

Collective redress mechanisms constitute legal procedures that aim to allow consumers to stop or deter a violation of EU consumer law or to obtain compensation where they have suffered the same harm as a result of an action or omission of the same trader. These procedures purport to facilitate the enforcement of EU consumer law by ensuring that individual consumers are not precluded by the typical constraints that they might face in individual litigation – discussed below – from obtaining redress for the harm they have suffered. Collective redress mechanisms aim to deal with mass infringements of consumer law by the same trader; recent examples of such mass harms include the Volkswagen Dieselgate scandal, Ryanair mass cancellations, and the Fipronil egg scandal, to name only a few.[7]

In this paper, the discussion is largely focused on compensatory collective redress. Currently, there is no harmonised regime for compensatory collective redress at the EU level; however, the EU institutions have entertained considerable political, policy-orientated and legal discussions on the matter. Nevertheless, the measures adopted are limited in their scope (in terms of the substantive law covered, and their cross-border application)

7 See for example, BEUC, 'A New Deal for Consumers – Revision of the Injunctions Directive' (January 2018). See also, Chris Hodges and Stefan Voet, 'Response to the European Commission's Inception Impact Assessment, 'A New Deal for Consumers – Revision of the Injunctions Directive', Ares(2017) 5324969, who suggest a model of collective redress for mass harms based not only private enforcement via courts but who highlight the need for the integration of public enforcement via public authorities and non-for-profit ombudsmen.

and as regards their binding nature; these measures amount to sector-specific rules and non-binding recommendations.[8]

Collective redress can be said to have two goals, namely deterrence and compensation.[9] As to the satisfaction of the former, the EU has legislated for injunctive collective relief[10] for infringements of consumer rights. As to the satisfaction of the latter goal, namely compensation, the European Commission introduced in 2013 a non-binding Recommendation setting out minimum standards to guide Member States in their adoption of compensatory collective redress mechanisms.[11] While some individual Member States have adopted their own unique approaches to compensatory collective redress, not all have done so, generating further diversity across the EU, particularly as regards the model of collective redress adopted. Some Member States have established a test case model, some a representative

8 For example, the Injunctions Directive 2009/22/EC obliges Member States to provide mechanisms for injunctive relief for violations of EU consumer law. Further examples of sector-specific measures include the Late Payment Directive 2011/7/EU, in the field of commercial transactions and the General Data Protection Regulation 2016/679 for data protection. While it was initially anticipated that collective redress might be included in Directive 2014/104/EU on antitrust damages, ultimately this directive harmonises procedural law issues concerning private enforcement other than collective redress. In 2017, in discussions on the emissions scandal in the automotive sector, the European Parliament specifically urged the Commission to introduce a harmonised system of collective redress for consumers (European Parliament, 'Recommendation of 4 April 2017 to the Council and the Commission following the Inquiry into Emission Measurements in the Automotive Sector', 2016/2908(RSP), paras 58–67) and encouraged it to examine the possibility of introducing collective redress mechanisms for breaches of EU environmental rules (European Parliament, 'Resolution of 26 October 2017 on the Application of Directive 2004/35/EC on Environmental Liability with regard to the Prevention and Remedying of Environmental Damage (the 'ELD')', 2016/2251(INI), para 48).

9 On the need for a balance between the protection of the interests of individual claimants and the regulatory interests in avoiding future violations of rights, see Brigitte Haar, 'Regulation Through Litigation — Collective Redress in Need of a New Balance Between Individual Rights and Regulatory Objectives' (2018) 19 *Theoretical Inquiries in Law* 203. Relatedly, collective redress may play a market correction role, fundamental to the development of the EU's internal market.

10 All Member States now provide for mechanisms for injunctive relief to prevent the continued violation of EU consumer rights (per the Injunctions Directive 2009/22/EC); notwithstanding that each Member State is now obliged to ensure that injunctive relief is available, the Member States nevertheless continue to provide for different mechanisms for such relief.

11 European Commission, 'Communication – Towards a European Horizontal Framework for Collective Redress' COM(2013) 401 final.

action-based model and others still, a group action model. Moreover, certain Member States have chosen to adopt a combination of these models.[12] As a result, the operation of compensatory collective redress mechanisms in respect of cross-border mass harms is particularly problematic. The challenges arising between the operation of national and European collective redress mechanisms and Brussels I bis have thus long been at the forefront of academic debate; the same is true of discussions surrounding on the one hand, the introduction of collective redress mechanisms at the EU level (whether horizontal or sector-specific) and on the other, the review and revision of EU PIL instruments, most notably, those of the Brussels regime.

The discussions at the EU level – including for example, the 2010 Resolution of the European Parliament, in which the need for rules of jurisdiction for cross-border collective redress was recognised[13] – have not come to fruition as regards the implementation of a coherent legal and policy framework for cross-border compensatory collective redress.[14] That is to say, neither the measures promoting the implementation of collective redress mechanisms within the Member States[15] nor the Brussels I bis Regulation provides for specific rules concerning jurisdiction for cross-border collective redress. These two sets of instruments can be examined briefly. The Brussels Convention as introduced in 1968 was predicated on the existence of two-party (individual, legal or natural persons) proceedings; the same is true of the Regulations. The Brussels I bis Regulation does not include specific rules for jurisdiction for cross-border collective redress. Indeed while the significance of collective redress, and the different forms that it might take, was recognised in the 2010 Proposal for the

12 See Section 2.2.

13 European Parliament, 'Resolution on Delivering a Single Market to Consumers and Citizens' (2010/2011(INI)).

14 See Alexandre Biard, 'Collective Redress in the EU: A Rainbow Behind the Clouds?' (2018) 19 *ERA Forum* 189.

15 European Commission, 'Green Paper on Consumer Collective Redress' COM(2008) 794 final (http://eur-lex.europa.eu/LexUriServ/LexUriServ.do?uri=COM:2008:0794:FIN:EN:PDF); European Commission, 'Recommendation 2013/396/EU on Common Principles for Injunctive and Compensatory Collective Redress Mechanisms in the Member States Concerning Violations of Rights Granted under Union Law' (http://eur-lex.europa.eu/legal-content/EN/TXT/?uri=OJ:JOL_2013_201_R_NS0013) and European Commission, 'Communication – Towards a European Horizontal Framework for Collective Redress' COM(2013) 401 final (http://eur-lex.europa.eu/legal-content/EN/TXT/?uri=celex:52013DC0401).

revision of the Brussels I Regulation,[16] this was limited to an ultimately unsuccessful proposal to exclude judgments from collective proceedings from the proposed abolition of exequatur. This exclusion of collective redress proceedings from the abolition of exequatur was made on the basis that the existence (indeed, if at all) of different approaches and procedural requirements for collective redress in the Member States were still considered to be sufficiently significant so as to undermine the possibility for mutual trust, and generate public policy concerns when it comes to recognition and enforcement. This is a matter to which the paper returns in Section 4 below.

While the 2008 Green Paper on Collective Redress made a recommendation – without referring to classification or characterisation – on cross-border collective redress and its integration into the Brussels I bis regime, neither the 2013 Recommendations nor the 2018 Proposal introduce concrete rules on cross-border collective redress, either as regards characterisation, jurisdiction or issues of recognition and enforcement. Instead, in each instrument, there are limited rules on the mutual recognition and standing of the class representative in cross-border cases.[17] For example, the 2018 Proposal is deemed to apply 'without prejudice to the Union rules on private international law'.[18] A number of key PIL issues, concerning standing and admissibility, determination of jurisdiction, the constitution of the class (whether opt-in or opt-out), costs and funding and the determination of the law applicable, therefore remain unclear. The determination at the level of the EU policymaker not to introduce rules that regulate the relationship between collective redress and PIL suggests that certain political choices have been made.[19] These choices are reflective of the limitations of the Union's limited legislative competences in the field of civil procedure; as a result of its limited competence, the approach of

16 European Commission, 'Proposal for a Regulation on Jurisdiction and the Recognition and Enforcement of Judgments in Civil and Commercial Matters' COM(2010) 748 final, 14 December 2010, Art 37(3)(b).

17 2013 Recommendations, paras 17–18 and 2018 Proposal, Art 16.

18 2018 Proposal, Art 2(3).

19 The way in which the Union legislature deals with such issues is fundamentally important for several reasons; against this background, it must be recognised that the legal and policy research and review on all options must be undertaken in light of the EU's commitment to Better Regulation; European Commission, 'Communication on Better Regulation for Better Results: An EU Agenda' COM(2015) 215 final and European Commission, 'Communication on Better Regulation: Delivering Better Results for a Stronger Union' COM(2016) 615 final.

the Union legislature often ends up being piecemeal, leading to fragmentation within the national systems, as well as at the EU level.

The absence of EU legislative measures on cross-border compensatory collective redress has not only been at the fore of policy and academic discussions but has recently been subject to litigation before the ECJ, in the case of *Schrems II*, a reference for a preliminary ruling from the Austrian Supreme Court. Following the Opinion of AG Bobek, the Court ruled that an assignee may not bundle claims assigned to him in the protective forum established under Art 18 of the Brussels I bis Regulation (previously, Art 16 Brussels I Regulation). While both the AG and the Court acknowledged that the current European, cross-border legal framework is not adequately adapted to collective redress, it is nevertheless clear from both the Opinion of the AG and the judgment of the Court that the steps that would be necessary to remedy this lack of collective redress in consumer matters can only be taken by the EU lawmaker. Reference can be made to the words of AG Bobek who wrote of 'the dangers of judicial legislation' and highlighted that the need for an EU-wide instrument 'belong[s] to the *de lege ferenda* sphere'; moreover, AG Bobek recognised that a judicial decision providing for jurisdiction to facilitate cross-border collective redress would go against the wording and logic of the Brussels I regime, and undermine the complexity of the issue. The AG further acknowledged the need for 'comprehensive legislation, not an isolated judicial intervention',[20] recognising that at the time that the Opinion and judgment in *Schrems II* were rendered, the EU lawmaker was already engaged in deliberations which led to the Commission's 2018 Proposal, a process that the AG considered should not be pre-empted or undermined by the judiciary. It is worth noting that the *Schrems II* decision is indeed a reflection of only some of the issues that arise from the lack of a coherent PIL framework for collective redress, accentuated in light of the absence of a coherent framework of collective redress at the level of and across the Member States. Before examining the fruits of discussions of the EU lawmaker in Section 2.3, the paper will firstly provide a brief overview of the different models of collective redress that have been adopted in the national legal systems.

20 Case C-498/16 *Schrems* EU:C:2017:863, paras 119–123.

2.2. *A Short Comparative Overview: The Procedural Design of Collective Redress Mechanisms*[21]

Here, the intention is to provide a brief overview of the divergent procedural designs adopted within a limited number of national legal systems, namely Austria, Belgium, the Netherlands, and England and Wales. The aim of this section is not to provide a comprehensive comparative analysis of the models adopted but to highlight the existence of different models across Europe in light of the Commission's 2013 Recommendations.[22] It is important to note that this diversity is of particular significance given that the 2018 Proposal of the Commission for a binding directive is intended to provide for a system of cross-border collective redress, based on a particular political determination of the institutions, reflective of a representative action-based procedural design model. However, this model is not intended to replace entirely existing national models of collective redress but to operate alongside such mechanisms. The considerations encountered in this respect will be touched upon again later in this paper when it comes to examining the recognition and enforcement of judgments rendered in different Member States, particularly in light of the issue of public policy.

2.2.1. *The Austrian system*

In Austria, collective redress takes the form of representative actions by consumer organisations[23] and is currently available only for injunctions and declaratory actions[24]. A specific mechanism, e.g. a representative action, does not exist for compensatory collective redress. In lieu of such a mechanism, consumers can pursue their claims by aggregating and assigning them to the aforementioned consumer organisations, pursuant to Art

21 I owe my thanks to the Research Fellows at the MPI Luxembourg for their assistance on this section.

22 Moreover, it is also possible to identify the different mechanisms pre-existing the Commission's non-binding initiative.

23 Such as the Verein für Konsumenteninformation (VKI) or the Austrian Federal Chamber of Labour.

24 It is regulated in the Austrian Consumer Protection Act (Konsumentenschutzgesetz) and Austrian Unfair Competition Act (Gesetz gegen den Unlauteren Wettbewerb).

227 of the Austrian Code of Civil Procedure (öZPO).[25] Third-party funding is common. A legislative proposal introduced in 2007 (Zivilverfahrens-Novelle 2007) which aimed at implementing both 'real' group actions and model case proceedings in the Austrian Code of Civil Procedure, has not yet been passed. Beyond the domestic scope, Austria's model of assignment has had an impact at the European level in two cases. In *VKI vs. Amazon EU Sarl;*[26] the ECJ held that the contractual standard terms were unfair and therefore void both regarding the governing law and data protection. The second case is *Schrems II,* discussed above.

2.2.2. *The Belgium system*

Belgian law[27] has provided for a representative compensatory collective redress action for consumers since 2014,[28] which it extended to Small and Medium-sized Enterprises (SMEs) in 2018.[29] The status of group representative is open to a number of recognised entities, such as consumer protection associations or business associations, and consists of four phases. In a first phase, the admissibility of the collective redress procedure is assessed by the competent court, which is a court in the Brussels judicial district. It will verify whether the claim pertains to a violation of one of the 33 instruments listed in Article XVII.37 of the Economic Law Code (ELC), whether the group representative is a recognised entity, whether the group representative is an appropriate representative in light of the claim, and whether the bringing of a collective redress procedure is more effective than proceedings brought by individual consumers. In its admissibility decision,

25 On the domestic level, such a collective action brought by the VKI against a major bank in 2003/2004, claiming damages for 2300 investors, ended as a settlement. While this case illustrates the possibility and actual use of the procedure, in light of its provisional nature, it is still considered to be tedious and time-consuming.

26 Case C-191/15 *VKI v Amazon* EU:C:2016:612.

27 Like in many other systems, some mechanisms in civil procedure allowed for the bringing of multiple claims or by/against multiple parties (joinder, intervention, assignment). Moreover, consumer associations had the power to file for injunctive relief sinds the 1970s. True collective redress was, however, absent.

28 Law of 28 March 2014 concerning an action for collective redress, *Belgian State Gazette* 2014, 35201.

29 Law of 30 March 2018 modifying the Economic Law Code by extending the scope of application of the action for collective redress to SMEs, *Belgian State Gazette* 2018, 41950.

the court will also determine the appropriate group selection mechanism, i.e. whether an opt-in or an opt-out procedure should be followed. Only in collective redress proceedings that concern moral or bodily harm or for persons whose habitual residence is outside of Belgium is the opt-in procedure mandatory. Upon declaring the action admissible, a mandatory settlement phase of minimum three months and maximum six months begins. If a settlement is reached in that period, the judge will homologate the settlement agreement provided that it contains all the mandatory entries and is not unreasonable for the beneficiaries. In absence of a settlement agreement or when the court refuses to homologate the settlement agreement, the proceedings continue to the merits phase. In that phase, the court will decide on whether the claim for collective redress is founded. The final phase is the execution phase, in which an independent claims administrator will take care of the execution of the settlement agreement or the judgment. Its main tasks are drawing up the final list of beneficiaries and overseeing the actual execution of the agreement or judgment, either by supervising the compensation in kind provided by the defendant to the group members or by distributing amongst the group members the monetary compensation transferred to her or him by the defendant.[30]

2.2.3. The Dutch system

Dutch law currently has two legal proceedings designed specifically for collective redress: the collective action and the Collective Settlement of Mass Damages Act (WCAM). Since 1994, Section 3:305a DCC has granted representative organisations the authority to bring a collective action to court. The action may concern any type of civil case, in which similar interests are at stake. Collective actions can provide for injunctive and declaratory relief. The judgment has limited *res judicata* effect.[31] The representative organisation cannot claim for damages. A bill introducing an

30 See further, Janek Tomasz Nowak, 'The New Belgian Law on Consumer Collective Redress and Compliance with EU Law Requirements' in Eva Lein *et al* (eds), *Collective Redress in Europe – Why and How?* (BIICL 2015), 169–201.

31 It only binds the representative organisation and the defendant, not those whose interests are represented. Nevertheless, the verdict can provide a basis for settlement negotiations – possibly followed by a WCAM settlement – or for an individual proceeding to seek monetary compensation.

opt-out compensatory collective action is currently before parliament.[32] The second measure – the WCAM – was established in 2005. It essentially provides for one or more representative organisations on the one hand, and the alleged liable party on the other, to submit a joint application to the Amsterdam Court of Appeal for a settlement, which sets out compensatory rights for class members, to be deemed legally binding.[33] The Court assesses whether the class members' interests are sufficiently guaranteed, and the reasonableness of compensation. During the proceedings, other representative organisations and individual interested parties are entitled to object to the settlement. If the Court declares the settlement to be binding, all individuals affected by the mass damage event are bound, unless they opt out within a certain period following the announcement of the order. Business and consumer organisations can also bring actions for the (abstract) assessment of general conditions. Alternatives also exist, namely joinder, consolidation, test case, and the bundling of assigned claims. Since July 2012, collective redress might also be facilitated by the possibility for a district or an appellate court judge to refer a preliminary question to the Dutch Supreme Court. It can do so if the answer is necessary to render a decision and if it is of direct importance to either a mass dispute or to the resolution of a number of other factually similar civil disputes. Furthermore, in July 2013, the collective action and WCAM regulations were amended to provide for the introduction of the possibility to apply for a pre-trial hearing (*preprocessuele comparitie*).[34]

2.2.4. *The system adopted in England and Wales*

The English system combines different models of collective redress: there are two general procedures with horizontal scope and one mechanism specifically applicable to violations of competition law. The first general

32 It includes stricter adequacy requirements for representative parties, and – in the case of competing representative organisations – the possibility for the court to appoint the one deemed most suitable as the 'exclusive representative'.

33 A WCAM settlement may follow a previous test case or collective action, or may have arisen fully out of court.

34 At such hearing, the court has a facilitative and guiding role – it cannot judge on (a) point(s) of dispute. It may assist parties in formulating the most important matters in dispute, discuss further case management, such as the desirability of bringing collective action, and/or stimulate parties to enter into a settlement, for instance with the aid of a mediator.

mechanism is the representative action, which can be brought by an individual[35] on behalf of other parties without their consent, where the represented parties share the 'same interest'.[36] The judgment will bind such represented non-parties.[37] The model has some disadvantages relevant to the study; in particular, as to scope, 'common interest' is strictly understood and a result, it is not used often in consumer claims. The second procedure is the Group Litigation Order (GLO).[38] It is an opt-in mechanism.[39] The GLO is constituted and managed on the basis of a judicial order, made when the judge is satisfied that all members' claims share 'common or related issues of fact or law'.[40] The judgment is binding on all claimants in the GLO register.[41] The 'loser pays rule' applies; however, arrangements for funding and costs are complex, which poses considerable problems for consumers.[42] Following the 2013 Recommendation, the Consumer Rights Act 2015 introduced a class action mechanism for damages arising from competition law violations.[43] These claims (either 'follow-on' or standalone) are brought in the Competition and Appeals Tribunal (CAT); standing is limited and claims can only be brought by certain bodies or by a party who is authorised by the CAT.[44] The CAT decides whether the pro-

35 Civil Procedure Rules 1998 (as amended) (hereinafter CPR), Part 19.6.

36 The Rules of the Court of Judicature (NI) Rule 12 (1); CPR, Part 19.6 (1). The 'same interest' requirement has been interpreted narrowly by the courts, requiring the individuals represented to share a 'common interest and a common grievance' and 'the relief sought was in its nature beneficial to all whom the plaintiff proposed to represent' (*Duke of Bedford v Ellis* [1901] AC 1, 8.).

37 *Markt & Co Ltd v Knight Steamship Co Ltd* [1910] 2 KB 1021; *Prudential Assurance Co Ltd v Newman Industries Ltd* [1981] Ch 229.

38 Introduced under the reformed Civil Procedure Rules of 1998; CPR, Part 19 III.

39 CPR, Practice Direction 19B-Group Litigation para 1.

40 CPR, Part 19.10. A 'group register' is established and a particular court will manage all claims falling within the Order. The court has significant case management powers to stay cases, or select test cases or generic issues to be resolved.

41 Generally, at the time of the judgment and when the GLO was issued; the court may make exceptions, per CPR, Part 19.12.

42 The general position is that all parties in the register are responsible for generic costs, and they typically are required to enter into cost-sharing agreements amongst themselves.

43 This replaced an earlier procedure that was more restricted, widely criticised, and only gave rise to a single and unsatisfactory case: *JJB Sports v Office of Fair Trading* [2004] CAT 17.

44 The individual must 'fairly and adequately act in the interests of class members'.

ceedings are to be opt-in or opt-out.[45] It makes an award of damages for the entirety of the claim; consequently, the allocation of compensation can be difficult. A 'loser pays' rule also applies. Damages-based agreements and exemplary damages are prohibited. An order similar to the Dutch WCAM procedure may also be made, irrespective of whether collective proceedings exist. It should be noted that other mechanisms of redress are particularly strong in the UK, including criminal[46] or regulatory law. The latter is particularly important for consumers.[47]

2.3. *Three Models of Collective Redress*

This paper will focus on how the different types of collective redress models might be integrated into the Brussels I bis regime; as the Commission's 2018 Proposal advocates an approach based on representative actions, there will be a particular focus on this choice of procedural design. However, it is worth providing a brief outline of representative actions, group claims and test cases before examining the rules applicable to establish jurisdiction. A representative action for collective redress is understood as follows: multiple claimants (who may be domiciled in different Member States), share the same cause of action against the same defendant; litigation is conducted by a representative entity. There may or may not be an assignment of claims from the consumers to the qualified entity. Where the relationship is 'purely' representative, which is to say, there is no assignment, no contractual relationship exists between the litigating parties (i.e. between the qualified entity and the trader). Where there is an assignment of claims between the injured consumer party and the qualified entity bringing the action for collective address, this may attribute a contractual character to the relationship between the litigating parties.

---

45 Under the opt-in procedure, class members notify the class representative of inclusion of their claim. Under the opt-out procedure, claimants domiciled in the UK who fall within the class automatically participate unless they expressly opt out, while claimants not domiciled in the UK must opt in.

46 Compensation orders in respect of personal injury, loss or damage arising under Powers of Criminal Courts (Sentencing) Act 2000, ss 130–133, which since 2012 are mandatory for courts to consider.

47 In financial services, for example, the Financial Conduct Authority can make a Consumer Redress Scheme (FSMA s 404, and ss 404A–G); the Financial Ombudsman Service can aggregate procedures, while complaints can also be made to the Financial Services Compensation Scheme). Similar powers exist for other regulatory authorities in other sectors.

Another model of collective redress is the group action. Typically, the group is composed of a number of individual claims; however, the action may also be initiated by one member of the group on behalf of the individual claims of others. As set out above, a group action may be modelled differently in different Member States. Usually, individuals have to opt in, which dictates that there is a clearly defined group. For example, in England and Wales, a group litigation order is based on an opt-in approach; each claim is an individual one and the GLO is merely the mechanism by which the court manages those individual claims where they give rise to common or related issues of fact or law. In other Member States, for example, in Poland, group actions can only be brought by groups of more than 10 consumers who must self-organise, on an opt-in basis; such actions cannot be brought by associations or organisations. In Portugal, a group action can be brought by individuals, consumer organisations or other associations, on an opt-out basis. The exact model of a group model of collective redress thus diverges considerably across the Member States. The third model of collective redress discussed here is the test case approach; here, there is usually one action – the test case – the judgment rendered in which constitutes a precedent for other cases.[48] The test case is therefore decided first; thereafter, the individual lawsuits continue and the parties to these other lawsuits are bound by the test case judgment.[49]

3. *Towards a Harmonised Approach? The 2018 Proposal of the European Commission*

In April 2018, the Juncker Commission released its Proposal for a Directive on Representative Actions[50], as part of its New Deal for Consumers.[51] The New Deal comprises a set of reforms to substantive and procedural consumer rights, intending to strengthen those rights and the possibilities for their enforcement, both public and private.[52] Recognising the difficul-

---

48 It aims to allow a number of legal questions relevant to a number of claims to be decided upon by a single court at the one time, and thus reduce costs.

49 For example, in Germany, a test case proceeding exists for actions concerning capital investments – the KapMuG.

50 2018 Proposal for a Directive on Representative Actions.

51 European Commission, 'Communication on a New Deal for Consumers' COM(2018) 183 final.

52 On the relationship between judicial enforcement, administrative enforcement and alternative dispute resolution (hereinafter ADR) in the context of collective

ties that arise in a decentralised system,[53] the New Deal aims to provide for 'better enforcement of the rules, effective tools for redress and better consumer knowledge of their rights…[to] enhance consumer trust and confidence'.[54] To this end, the Commission proposed to introduce an EU-wide regime of collective redress, revising and repealing the Injunctions Directive; the 2018 Proposal has been made in light of the Commission's 2013 Recommendations[55] and the Commission's Report on the Implementation of the Recommendation on Collective Redress.[56] While one might question whether this proposal will ultimately be adopted, in light of the timing of its release (nearing the end of the Juncker Commission's mandate in 2019), it is evidently a reflection of the Commission's preferred model of compensatory collective redress. Moreover, even if the proposal is not adopted, it may constitute a blueprint for action at the national level. The section will briefly set out the characteristics of the representative action model advanced by the Commission,[57] highlighting the political choice on the part of the Commission not to choose a model based on a group action, an assignment or a test case.

redress, see Fabrizio Cafaggi, 'Towards Collaborative Governance of European Remedial and Procedural Law?' (2018) 19 *Theoretical Inquiries in Law* 235.

53 The Commission has undertaken a Fitness Check of EU consumer law (European Commission, 'Staff Working Document – Report on the Fitness Check of EU Consumer and Marketing Law', SWD(2017)209, carried out in the framework of the Commission's Regulatory Fitness and Performance (REFIT) programme), as well as a number of impact assessments for the New Deal (Available at: https://ec.europa.eu/info/publications/new-deal-consumers-impact-assessments_en). See also, H Muir Watt, 'Brussels I and Aggregate Litigation or the Case for Redesigning the Common Judicial Area in Order to Respond to Changing Dynamics, Functions and Structures in Contemporary Adjudication and Litigation' (2010) 30 *IPrax* 111.

54 European Commission, 'Communication on the New Deal for Consumers' COM(2018) 183 final, 3.

55 The directive, if adopted, will repeal and replace the Injunctions Directive.

56 European Commission, 'State of Collective Redress in the EU in the Context of the Implementation of the Commission Recommendation' JUST/2016/JCOO/FC/CIVI/0099 (Available at: http://ec.europa.eu/newsroom/just/document.cfm?action=display&doc_id=50236).

57 This choice of model seems to be in line with the broader trends at the EU level, including the 2013 Recommendation, which reflected a preference in III.4 for a representative action model of collective address.

4. *The Characteristics of the Representative Action Model Advanced by the Commission*

The Commission's Proposal aims to create a balanced framework for collective redress that ensures access to justice for groups of individuals while avoiding potential abuses of the US class action system. On the one hand, the Proposal purports to avoid the possibility that individual consumers will abandon well-founded claims due to various resource-based burdens.

These may be related to a lack of resources as regards costs and fees relating to litigation, knowledge, time or representation, and may be exaggerated due to power imbalances between the party harmed and the entity perpetrating the harm. The difficulties faced by consumers may be further accentuated in cross-border cases, where issues concerning a lack of knowledge of a foreign language and the intricacies of the foreign legal system arise. On the other hand, the Proposal introduces various procedural safeguards, with the aim of avoiding the apparent abusive litigation that arises from the US model.[58]

As regards the relationship between the 2018 Proposal and PIL rules, this section will firstly examine how the model advanced in the proposal can be 'integrated' into the existing Brussels I bis regime. This analysis is undertaken in light of the apparent intention that 'the existing Union law instruments should apply to the representative actions set out by this Directive' (proposed Recital 9[59]). Indeed, the explanatory note to the 2018 Proposal further provides that 'The proposal is also without prejudice to the existing EU private international law instruments, in particular the rules related to court jurisdiction and applicable laws'.[60] As a result of this 'without prejudice' approach, only one provision of the Proposal pertains to the relationship between cross-border collective redress and PIL issues. Proposed Art 16 anticipates firstly the need for the mutual recognition of designated qualified entities across the Member States,[61] established in a

58 Fears of excesses or possibilities for abuse have been highlighted in relation to the US system – see US Chamber, Institute for Legal Reform, 'The Growth of Collective Redress in the EU' (March 2017); the political interests underpinning the report should be borne in mind.

59 Proposed Recital 9, 2018 Proposal provides: 'This Directive should not establish rules of private international law regarding jurisdiction, the recognition and enforcement of judgments or applicable law. The existing Union law instruments apply to the representative actions set out by this Directive'.

60 Explanatory Memorandum to the 2018 Proposal, 6.

61 Also included at Recommendation 17, 2013 Recommendations.

publicly-available list (with information about the name and purpose of the representative entity and constituting proof of legal standing) and communicated to the European Commission. The Proposal provides for no special rules on jurisdiction. Art 16 concerns the standing of the qualified entity, which must be distinguished from the issue of jurisdiction, examined in Section 3 below. Proposed Art 16 rather seems to dictate that foreign qualified entities should not be precluded from bringing a claim by national rules of admissibility or standing; the intention is that 'where the infringement affects or is likely to affect consumers from different Member States the representative action may be brought to the competent court or administrative authority of a Member State by several qualified entities from different Member States, acting jointly or represented by a single qualified entity'.[62] Here two questions of procedural design arise: 1) the standing of a qualified entity of one Member State to bring an action in another Member State and 2) whether consumers domiciled or resident in one Member State can join a representative action brought by a qualified entity registered in another Member State.

As the Commission's 2018 Proposal is based on the notion of the mutual recognition of the standing of qualified entities in the EU per Art 16(1), there would appear to be no issue with the first question; a qualified entity registered in Belgium should have standing to bring a representative action in France.[63] This follows not only the principle of mutual recognition[64] but also the principle of non-discrimination (or in the context of the implementation and enforcement of EU consumer law, the principle of equivalence[65]). Similarly, the principle of non-discrimination would oper-

62 Proposed Art 16(2), 2018 Proposal.

63 This is already provided in the laws of certain Member States, for example in Belgium, per Art XVII.39 Code du droit économique belge and the decision of the Belgian Constitutional Court as regards the Service Directive: Arrêt no 41/2016 du mars 2016.

64 This follows the approach in Recital 12 of the Injunctions Directive, which provides for the application of the principle of mutual recognition. Recital 12, Directive 2009/22/EC on injunctions for the protection of consumers' interests, provides: 'For the purposes of intra-Community infringements the principle of mutual recognition should apply to these bodies and/or organisations. The Member States should, at the request of their national entities, communicate to the Commission the name and purpose of their national entities which are qualified to bring an action in their own country according to the provisions of this Directive'. Beyond the Injunctions Directive however, the application of the principle of mutual recognition to different EU legislation is unclear.

65 Usually understood alongside the principle of effectiveness; Case C-33/76 *Rewe* EU:C:1976:188.

ate as regards the second question posed above to suggest that consumers residing in one country, e.g. Belgium, should not be precluded from joining the representative action of a qualified entity of that state. Indeed, Art 4(3) of the 2018 Proposal establishes that 'Member States may designate as qualified entities consumer organisations that represent members from more than one Member State', suggesting that consumers are not tied to qualified entity of the state in which they are domiciled or resident. The 2018 Proposal lacks clarity as regards representative actions brought on behalf of a class of consumers who have their domicile or residence in a number of different Member States. That is to say, the Proposal sets out that for cross-border actions, qualified entities that represent consumers from different Member States will be able to come together and bring a single representative action against the same trader on behalf of all consumers. On the one hand, this suggests that the claims of consumers from different Member States could be consolidated in a single action, avoiding a multiplicity of collective actions before the courts or administrative authorities of different Member States. However, on the other, this provision undermines the clarity as to the response offered to the second question because it suggests that a qualified entity will only represent consumers from the Member State in which it is established and will not represent consumers from other Member States.[66]

5. The Intended Means of Operation of the Representative Action Mechanism

It is necessary to briefly outline how the representative action advanced in the Proposal is intended to operate, beyond the issue of the standing of qualified entities. The directive, if adopted, will introduce representative actions for violations of EU law that affect the collective interests of consumers.[67] The intention is to allow qualified entities to bring an action before national courts or authorities on behalf of a group of consumers for an injunction or compensation; it therefore has the purpose of deterring

66 Eg as seems to be the approach followed by entities for the purposes of Art 80 representative actions under the General Data Protection Regulation (EU) 2016/679 (GDPR). The website of https://www.mydataismine.com for example, suggests that data subjects should register with the entity of their Member State.

67 Per proposed Art 2(1). The relevant EU legislation is set out in Annex 1 of the Proposal. The Proposal does not anticipate a collective redress mechanism that is entirely horizontal but rather one which applies to those areas in which consumers have collective interests to be protected.

violations of consumer law and promoting redress for consumers. Proposed Art 4 provides only three criteria for the designation by Member States of qualified entities. This criterion requires that: '(a) it is properly constituted according to the law of a Member State; (b) it has a legitimate interest in ensuring that provisions of Union law covered by this Directive are complied with; (c) it has a non-profit making character'.[68]

Under proposed Art 5, Member States shall ensure that qualified entities can bring representative actions before national courts or administrative authorities. Qualified entities should be able to bring actions for an injunction as an interim measure to stop or prohibit a practice that constitutes or would constitute a breach of EU law.[69] Per Art 5(3), qualified entities should also be able to bring a representative action 'seeking measures eliminating the continuing effects of the infringement'. Such 'measures should be sought on the basis of any final decision establishing that a practice constitutes an infringement of Union law' (per Annex I), including a final injunctive order per Art 5(2)(b).[70] Art 5(3) is elaborated upon in Art 6, which provides that 'Member States shall ensure that qualified entities are entitled to bring representative actions seeking a redress order, which obligates the trader to provide for, inter alia, compensation, repair, replacement, price reduction, contract termination or reimbursement of the price paid, as appropriate'. It is also anticipated that qualified entities will be able to negotiate a settlement for redress with the trader; this settlement will have to be approved by a court or administrative authority.[71]

One of the most significant matters concerning the procedural design of the collective redress model adopted relates to the constitution of the class in an action for collective redress, that is to say, whether consumers must opt in or opt out. It is particularly important as regards the recognition and enforcement of a judgment in a Member State court other than that in which the judgment was rendered. An opt-in procedure requires all claimants to actively join the claim while an opt-out procedure will encompass all concerned consumers unless they opt out. The Commission's Proposal suggests that the representative action might be constituted

---

68 Qualified entities will be designated by the Member States; the Member States should ensure on a regular basis whether these conditions continue to be satisfied, such that the status of qualified entity may be lost.

69 Proposed Art 5(1)(a) and (b), 2018 Proposal.

70 Proposed Art 5(3), 2018 Proposal.

71 Proposed Art 8, 2018 Proposal.

on either an opt-in or an opt-out basis;[72] however, there is a considerable lack of clarity as regards the constitution of the class. It is also related to the procedure anticipated in the Proposal, which again lacks clarity. It seems to provide for a two-step action; firstly, an action must be brought for a final decision of a court or authority by which it is declared that there has been a violation of EU law. This might constitution a final injunction or final decision of a court or enforcement authority. In the second stage, an action can then be brought for redress (including for compensation, repair, replacement, price reduction, reimbursement or contract termination). Proposed Art 5(2) provides that 'to seek injunction orders, qualified entities shall not have to obtain the mandate of the individual consumers concerned', suggesting an opt-in procedure. However, proposed Art 6(1) establishes that for actions for redress 'a Member State may require the mandate of the individual consumers concerned before a declaratory decision is made or a redress order is issued. The qualified entity shall provide sufficient information as required under national law to support the action, including a description of the consumers concerned by the action and the questions of fact and law to be resolved'.

Special rules apply to cases where the calculation of redress is particularly complex. By derogation from Art 6(1), proposed Art 6(2) provides that the Member State may empower a court or authority to issue a decision by which the liability of the trader towards the consumers harmed is declared, where as a result of the nature of the individual harm suffered, the quantification of that individual redress is difficult.[73] This proposed provision should not apply where the consumers are 'identifiable and suffered comparable harm caused by the same practice in relation to a period of time or a purchase'.[74] In this situation, where the consumers are identifiable, it is not necessary to have the mandate of the individual consumers in order to initiate the action; 'redress shall be directed to the consumers concerned' per proposed Art 6(3)(a). Per proposed Art 6(3)(b), where the amount of loss suffered is small 'and it would be disproportionate to distribute the redress to them', the derogation in proposed Art 6(2) will not apply; in this situation, the 'Member States shall ensure that the mandate of the individual consumers concerned is not required'. That redress will not go to the consumers but to a 'public purpose serving the collective

72 This diverges from the 2013 Recommendation, which advocates an opt-in model (2013 Recommendations, Recommendation 21).

73 Proposed Art 6(2), 2018 Proposal.

74 Proposed Art 6(3)(a), 2018 Proposal.

interests of consumers'.[75] It is submitted that the opt-in and opt-out bases for initiating an action are extremely unclear.

The Proposal also provides for a number of information obligations to ensure consumers are clearly informed about their rights and the ways in which they can bring a follow-on action for redress, following a representative action. The trader who has been found to have breached consumer law will have to inform consumers about the breach and about the final judicial or administrative decision.[76] The trader will then have to inform the consumer about what steps he or she will have to take to obtain compensatory redress. Consumers might be able to go to the trader directly for redress or will be entitled bring a follow up legal action, if necessary. As noted above, the Proposal also introduces a number of protections for defendants, with the aim of avoiding the apparent abuse that arises from the US model.[77] That is to say, the aim is to ensure a balance between access to justice and avoidance of abuse via a variety of rules. As regards funding, the Proposal establishes rules relating to the transparency of funds used by qualified entities. Third-party funding is allowed, however, qualified entities must make clear from where the funds they are using derive.[78] A national court or authority will be able to assess whether there is a conflict of interest between the third-party funder and the qualified entity.[79] Moreover, it should be noted that there is no possibility for punitive damages to be sought.[80] Furthermore, as set out at proposed recital 18, the Member States should require that the court or administrative authority must verify at the earliest stage that the case is apt to be brought as a representative action. The Proposal is not intended to entirely replace national mechanisms; it is for the Member State to decide how to integrate this EU mechanism in its system. This dictates that the diversity of the national regimes, as indicated above at Section 2.2, will retain their significance. Against the background of this brief outline of the Commission's Proposal and the characteristics of the representative action advanced, the

---

75 Proposed Art 6(3), 2018 Proposal.

76 Proposed Art 9, 2018 Proposal.

77 Fears of excesses or possibilities for abuse have been highlighted in relation to the US system – see US Chamber Institute for Legal Reform, 'The Growth of Collective Redress in the EU' (March 2017); the political interests underpinning the report should be borne in mind.

78 Proposed Art 7, 2018 Proposal.

79 Proposed Art 7(3), 2018 Proposal.

80 Per proposed Recital 17, 2018 Proposal.

next section of this paper will examine how this model – and others – might be integrated into the Brussels I bis regime.

6. Founding Jurisdiction in Cross-Border Collective Redress

The short overview of the discussions surrounding the development of cross-border collective redress mechanisms, the brief comparative summary and the outline of the Commission's 2018 Proposal illustrate that different models of collective redress might be adopted at the national and European levels. It is worth providing a brief outline of each of these models, with a focus on consumer redress, in order to examine how each may be integrated into the Brussels I bis regime and in particular the challenges as regards jurisdiction that arise from each of these models, whether representative actions (as advanced by the Commission in its 2018 Proposal), test cases or group claims.

The Regulation provides for different heads of jurisdiction: a general rule of jurisdiction, heads of special jurisdiction and heads of protective jurisdiction. The possibility to engage each of these heads of jurisdiction in line with each model of collective redress will be examined below. Two general points should be made as regards the characteristics of the Brussels I bis Regulation, in so far as they clash with the idea of collective redress. The first is that the Regulation is predicated on cross-border litigation arising between two parties and between two jurisdictions; the second is that the connecting factors used to establish jurisdiction are based on the notion that the litigating party who brings the action does so in his or her own interest. These characteristics give rise to challenges as regards the founding of jurisdiction for actions of collective redress, where there are either multiple litigating parties, or multiple interested parties, represented by an entity that has no real personal interest in the claim.[81] One must generally ask whether any model of collective redress can be integrated into Brussels I bis; a more specific question concerns whether it is possible to concentrate jurisdiction in one forum for all cross-border claims based on the same harm by the same trader.

81 Except perhaps a 'public' interest of a regulatory nature, depending on the nature of the entity (e.g. in dissuading infringements of Union and national law for various – social/market-orientated – purposes).

7. *The Default Approach of Brussels I bis – To the Courts of the Defendant's Domicile*

It is necessary to begin – and as will become clear, perhaps end[82] – with the general rule of jurisdiction in Brussels I bis. Art 4(1) establishes a general rule of jurisdiction and provides that subject to the Regulation it must always be possible for a defendant to be sued in the courts of the Member State in which he or she is domiciled, regardless of the defendant's nationality and regardless of the existence of a specific connection between the claim and the Member State of those courts. The general rule is the default from which all other rules are derogations.[83] It is largely anticipated that the Member State in which the defendant is domiciled should be clear and easily identifiable; in line with the objectives of Brussels I bis, Art 4(1) aims to ensure that the rules of jurisdiction are highly predictable[84] to the extent that they provide certainty and predictability for all parties.[85] While the Art 4 forum will have jurisdiction to hear all claims brought against the same defendant, regardless of the model of collective redress, it nevertheless generates certain difficulties.

Firstly, as regards the power balance between the litigating parties, Art 4(1) gives rise to certain complexities. In a consumer claim, the defendant trader as a market player is typically in a stronger position than the consumer claimant. This position of power is augmented when the defendant is sued in his own Member State.[86] The consumer as a class member may be deemed to lose a certain degree of procedural protection by having to sue in a foreign Member States, losing a degree of proximity either to

82 See Catherine Kessedjian, 'Le droit entre concurrence et coopération' in J-P Ancel *et al* (eds), *Vers de nouveaux équilibres entre les ordres juridiques : Liber amicorum H Gaudemet-Tallon* (Dalloz 2005), 119–131.

83 Case C-412/98 *Group Josi* EU:C:2000:399.

84 Recital 15, Brussels I bis: rules should be highly predictable, legal certainty, proximity (but might also be undermined where consumers are obliged in practice to sue in the courts of the Member State in which the defendant is domiciled) – avoiding conflicting decisions; Paul Jenard, Report on the Convention on Jurisdiction and the Enforcement of Judgments in Civil and Commercial Matters, 27 September 1968, OJ C 59, 5 March 1979, 15.

85 Case C-116/02 *Gasser v Misat* EU:C:2003:657, para 72.

86 Of course, on the other hand, the defendant trader may be a small or medium enterprise (SME) and in fact be in a less strong position than a class of consumer claimants. Indeed, this might be the typical understanding outside of a consumer collective redress situation: Andrew Dickinson and Eva Lein, *The Brussels I Regulation Recast* (OUP 2015), 116.

where performance contracted for was made, where the action or omission giving rise to the harm arose or where the injury was incurred. Typical problems for consumers in litigating concern a lack of resources (knowledge, time and financial), raising the question of whether there exists effective access to justice and efficient administration of justice.[87] These concerns are accentuated when the consumer is required to litigate abroad.[88] These concerns all reflect important goals underlying the Brussels I bis regime.

Issues might arise where there are co-defendants – a situation anticipated in Art 8(1) Brussels I bis – domiciled in different Member States. Art 8(1) allows a claimant to bring an action against a number of defendants in the courts for the place of the domicile of one, providing that the claims are so closely connected (in the same situation of law and fact) that it is expedient to determine them together in order to avoid irreconcilable judgments.[89] This principle should be strictly interpreted,[90] is limited in operation and also in scope; indeed, it is limited to multiple defendants and would not apply in the situation of multiple claimants.[91] A further issue may arise as regards the concentration of jurisdiction in certain Member States in which a number of (especially large) defendants might be domiciled (for example, Facebook in Ireland or Amazon in Luxembourg). If collective redress claims are consistently brought in those particular Member States, concerns as regards resources (for example the courts and qualified entities registered in those Member States) might arise; moreover, it might be the case that there are policy-orientated (and indeed clearly political) efforts to restrict jurisdiction as regards the types of claims that can be initiated and the parties who can join representative actions in those particular states. As noted above, issues concerning the principle of non-discrimination may arise were certain individual consumers or quali-

87 Per Recital 16, Brussels I bis, an objective that has to be balanced with the need for predictability per Recital 15.

88 Moreover, there is a lack of proximity between the harm suffered by the individual consumer and the claim being litigated in the courts of the Member State of the defendant's domicile. See J Sorabji et al (eds), *Improving Access to Justice Through Collective Actions – Developing a More Effective and Efficient Procedure for Collective Actions – Final Report* (Civil Justice Council 2008), 98–99.

89 Case C-189/87 *Kalfelis* EU:C:1988:459; Case C-352/13 *CDC Hydrogen Peroxide* EU:C:2015:335.

90 Case C-145/10 *Painer* EU:C:20111:798, para 74.

91 See Burkhard Hess, 'A Coherent Approach to European Collective Redress' in Duncan Fairgrieve and Eva Lein (eds), *Extraterritoriality and Collective Redress* (OUP 2012), 113–114.

fied entities to be restricted as regards the Member States' courts in which they can join or bring a representative action.

Taking these considerations into account, the consolidation of jurisdiction in the courts of the Member State in which the defendant is domiciled generates a number of policy concerns. The application of the Brussels I bis rules requires us to consider on the one hand whether the rules of jurisdiction should be limited so as to provide sufficient predictability to the defendant; on the other hand, it is necessary to consider whether consumers should not rather be ensured the possibility to rely on a head of jurisdiction sufficiently proximate to them. One must ask which set of policy objectives should be sacrificed in order to facilitate compensatory collective redress. As such, it is appropriate to turn to examine the alternative heads of jurisdiction, each of which have to be interpreted autonomously and independently with a Union approach, with regard to the general scheme and objectives of the Regulation, in order to ensure their uniform application across the Member States.[92]

8. A (First) Rule of Special Jurisdiction for Contracts

The rules of special jurisdiction derogate from the general rule in Art 4(1) and allow a claimant to bring an action in a forum other than the courts of the Member State of the defendant's domicile. The invocation of special jurisdiction is justified on the existence of a close connection or link, within a specific set of circumstances, between the dispute and the court in which jurisdiction is to be founded. These rules offer the claimant a choice of where to sue, which may come, as will be seen below, with certain procedural advantages.[93] The follows section will examine the provisions for special jurisdiction in Art 7(1) (concerning litigation arising from a contractual relationship), turn then to examined the provision for protective jurisdiction in Art 18(1) (concerning litigation arising from a consumer contract), and return to the second head of special jurisdiction in Art 7(2) (relating to litigation that stems from a non-contractual or delictual relationship).

---

92 That is to say, without reference to the classification under the relevant national law of the legal relationship in question before the national court; Case C-167/00 *Henkel* EU:C:2002:555, para 35.

93 Moreover, it should be noted that for the operation of the special jurisdiction rules under Art 7, the defendant has to be domiciled in a Member State.

Art 7(1) Brussels I bis provides that 'a person domiciled in a Member State may be sued in another Member State: (1)(a) in matters relating to a contract, in the courts for the place of performance of the obligation in question'. The determination of place of performance depends on the nature of the relevant obligation. For the sale of goods, this is the place in a Member State where, under the contract, the goods were delivered or should have been delivered. For the provision of services, this is the place in a Member State where, under the contract, the services were provided or should have been provided. Two key issues pertain to the relationship between Art 7(1) and collective redress. The first concerns the notion of 'matters relating to a contract' and the nature of the relationship that exists between the litigating parties in an action for collective redress. The second concerns the identification of the place of performance where there are multiple consumers, who have contracted for performance with the same trader in different places within and across different Member States.

As regards the notion of 'matters relating to a contract', here, from the perspective of collective redress, the status of the party bringing the action will constitute a key challenge in the determination of whether Art 7(1) can be invoked. While Art 7(1) does not explicitly state that this notion must concern the litigating parties, the ECJ case law on the issue is strict; it has confirmed that the notion of 'matters relating to a contract' requires the existence of 'an obligation freely assumed by one party to another'.[94] It is therefore necessary to examine the nature of the relationship between the party bringing the action and the defendant. In collective redress models based on test cases and group actions, there should be no problem in identifying a contractual relationship between the litigating parties; if a contract between the individual trader and trader existed, in either model, the claimant will have entered into a contractual relationship with the defendant.[95]

The situation is different with a representative action. As noted, representative actions are brought by the qualified entity on behalf of and in the

94 C-26/91 *Handte*, para 15; Case C-77/04 *Réunion européenne and Others* EU:C:2005:327, para 17, and Case C-334/00 *Tacconi* EU:C:2002:499, para 23.

95 In the test case, one of the litigating parties will be the consumer; the same is true of the group model, made up of individual claims.

name of two or more consumers[96] against a defendant.[97] Per the 2018 Proposal, a representative action is 'an action for the protection of the collective interests of consumers to which the consumers concerned are not parties'.[98] It is necessary to examine the nature of the relationship that exists between the litigating parties.[99] Firstly, it seems that public authorities (which might also constitute qualified entities) that bring representative actions on behalf of consumers are not necessarily excluded from the scope of Brussels I bis, which determines jurisdiction in civil and commercial matters. In *Frahuil*, the ECJ held that where a public authority seeks a 'legal remedy which is open to it through a legal subrogation provided for in a civil law provision', that action can be understood as one by which private rights are exercised, and thus, to fall within the concept of 'civil and commercial matters'[100]. The same understanding is found in the European Commission's 2008 Green Paper[101] as regards actions brought by public authorities, including for example, an ombudsman.

Nevertheless, as regards the invocation of Art 7(1) Brussels I bis, the key issue concerns whether there is a contractual relationship between the litigating parties. While there may be a contractual relationship between the consumer and the defendant trader[102] and an arrangement (depending on the national system) between the consumer and the representative entity, in a 'purely' representative action, there is no contractual relationship. That is to say, where there is no assignment from the consumer to the

---

96 Defined by the 2018 Proposal in the 'usual' form as 'any natural person who is acting for purposes which are outside their trade, business, craft or profession'. Albeit we can refer to the considerable case law of the ECJ on the consumer status and the need – see eg Max Planck Institute Luxembourg, *An Evaluation Study of National Procedural Laws and Practices in Terms of the Equivalence and Effectiveness of the Procedural Protection of Consumers under EU Consumer Law* (MPI Luxembourg 2017) – for a more coherent definition across the Member States.

97 Art 3(1) and (2) 2018 Proposal. A trader for the purposes of the Proposal is defined as any 'natural person or any legal person, irrespective of whether privately or publicly owned, who is acting, including through any other person acting in their name or on their behalf, for purposes relating to their trade, business, craft or profession'.

98 Art 3(4) 2018 Proposal.

99 Case C-265/02 *Frahuil* EU:C:2004:77, para 20.

100 Case C-265/02 *Frahuil* EU:C:2004:77, paras 20–21.

101 European Commission, 'Green Paper on Consumer Collective Redress' COM(2008) 794 final, para 58.

102 Notwithstanding that the nature of these contracts may change, i.e. payment made be made in data, as is the case, for example, with Facebook and other social media networks.

qualified entity, there is no 'obligation freely assumed by one party to another' between the qualified entity and the defendant. In *Henkel*, concerning an action for an injunction brought in the public interest, the ECJ held that there was no contractual relationship that could be used to engage Art 7(1) as a head of jurisdiction. The reason was that the action had been brought by VKI, an Austrian consumer protection association, which was deemed not to be a real contracting party.[103] That is to say, to use the words of Dickinson, VKI, the representative entity and litigating party could not be said to be 'in the shoes'[104] of the initial party to the contract, i.e. the consumer.[105] The finding might be different of course if the contractual claim is assigned to the representative entity as the claimant. As Dickinson notes, it is not necessary that the litigating parties are the initial parties to the contract: 'it suffices that they have succeeded ex post to the position of one of the contractual parties'.[106] However, even if it could be found that a contractual relationship exists between the representative entity and the defendant, difficulties with connecting factors and the identification of the place of performance nevertheless arise. The same difficulties with connecting factors pertain to test cases and group claims.

The second set of problems concerns the identification of a concentrated place of performance with regards to collective redress. Art 7(1) is based on the notion of proximity and the existence of a territorial connection between the founding of jurisdiction in a particular national court and the place where the goods or services contracted for have been delivered or provided (or should have been delivered or provided).[107] Where

---

103 Case 167/00 *Henkel* EU:C:2002:555, paras 38–39 and Case C-265/02 *Frahuil* EU:C:2004:77.

104 Andrew Dickinson and Eva Lein, *The Brussels I Regulation Recast* (OUP 2015), 145.

105 Here again, it should be highlighted that the focus is on representative actions; the situation will be different with group actions and test cases, where the existence of a contractual relationship may not be as problematic.

106 Andrew Dickinson and Eva Lein, *The Brussels I Regulation Recast* (OUP 2015), 145. See however, Case C-77/04 *Réunion européenne and Others* EU:C:2005:327. The case of *Réunion européenne and Others* concerned an action for damages that had been brought by insurers, who had been subrogated the right of the party whose goods had been damaged; the insurers relied on the bill of lading and sought damages from the parties who had carried the goods by sea. The ECJ considered the action could not be considered to constitute a matter relating to contract as the defendant was not a direct party to the bill of lading; the ECJ avoided responding to the question of whether a contractual relationship arises from the assignment of rights however.

107 Art 7(1)(a) and (b) Brussels I bis.

the action is between two litigating parties, i.e. a consumer and a trader, it is usually not difficult to identify the place of delivery or provision of services; in this situation, the consumer will (usually) have contracted for performance in the place where he or she is resident.[108] It is however more difficult to determine the place of performance in a collective action, if the aim is to concentrate jurisdiction in one court. A collective redress action will encompass multiple contracts between multiple consumers and the same trader; each contract will usually provide for performance in a different place. The connecting factor in a single collective redress action would then be linked to different Member States. This renders it difficult to assert that the courts of one particular Member State are competent to hear the claims of all individual consumers; this problem arises regardless of the model adopted. A further complication arises as 'place of performance' for Art 7(1) purposes will provide a basis for the founding of jurisdiction within Member States; that is to say, for example, if multiple French consumers have contracted for performance in different places in France, the courts of those different places will have jurisdiction.

It is therefore clear that Art 7(1) does not allow for the consolidation of jurisdiction in a single fora, where the claims are based on the same infringements brought against the same defendant, but where there are multiple contracts each providing for different places of performance.[109] Instead, we might try to determine how this issue could be solved where there are multiple places of performance, i.e. how could jurisdiction be extended to deal with collective actions? Three alternative interpretations of Art 7(1) might be relevant. A 'principal delivery or provision' could be adopted, determined by economic data per the ECJ's findings in *Color Drack.*[110] This would suggest, for example, that the principal place of performance is identified as the Member State (or the place within a Member

---

108 Sophia Tang, 'Consumer Collective Redress in European Private International Law' (2011) 7 *J.Priv.Int.Law* 101, 140. Certain difficulties may arise, for example, where a consumer may reside in one place in one Member State but do all or most of his contracting in another Member State, or another place in the same Member State; border cities provide a key example of where such difficulties arise.

109 Eva Lein, 'Jurisdiction and Applicable Law in Cross-Border Mass Litigation' in Fausto Pocar et al (eds), *Recasting Brussels I* (CEDAM 2012) 159–172, 164.

110 Case C-386/05 *Color Drack* EU:C:2007:262, para 45. The ECJ determined that where good are delivered in multiple places in the one Member State, the court of the main place of delivery should have jurisdiction to hear all claims. The ECJ held that it was not the case that the court of one place of delivery could only hear the claims relating to that particular performance. Where it is not possible

State) for which a majority of consumers have contracted for performance. The court of this principal place of performance would have jurisdiction to hear and determine all claims. Where it is impossible to determine the principal place of performance by economic criteria, the claimant may have a choice as to where to sue from the different places of performance. The *Color Dra*ck approach initially only applied where the multiple places of performance were concentrated in a single Member State. In *Air Baltic*, the ECJ identified a further alternative, where there are multiple places of performance in different Member States, so as to allow for a choice of fora; this is the approach adopted in cases of flight cancellations.[111] It is considered that where performance is made in different Member States (or within different Member States), jurisdiction can be founded where there exists a close connecting factor to the contract; each place (e.g. the place of take-off and place of landing) is deemed to be as closely linked as the other.[112] In *Wood Floor*, the ECJ held that where there are multiple states of performance, the place of main provision will be the place that appeared in the contract, the place of the contract's actual performance or the place where – in an agency contract – the agent is domiciled.[113] By providing that sufficient proximity can be identified between one state and the contract, the ECJ advocates an approach that would avoid splitting contractual claims between different jurisdictions and different proceedings. In collective redress proceedings, one could argue that jurisdiction could be founded in the court with the closest link to the collective redress for all claims, even if there is no proximity with each and every claim. The ECJ has only provided for such an interpretation in relation to disputes in which there is more than one place of performance deriving from a single contract, and not for situations in which there are multiple places of performance deriving from multiple contracts.

In the context of collective redress actions, regardless of the model adopted, each of these approaches to dealing with jurisdiction under Art 7(1) is problematic as there is on the one hand, potential for fragmented jurisdiction and on the other, potentially a lack of proximity between indi-

to identify by economic criteria here is the main place, the claimant should have a choice of where to sue from different places of delivery.

111 Case C-204/08 *Air Baltic* EU:C:2009:439.

112 Case C-204/08 *Air Baltic* EU:C:2009:439 (when an air passenger flies from one Member States to another and suffers from the cancellation of the flight, he can choose to bring proceedings either in the courts of the Member State of arrival or departure).

113 Case C-19/09 *Wood Floor Solutions* EU:C:2010:137, paras 24–29.

vidual consumers and the forum hearing the action were attempts are made to concentrate fragmentation.[114] It is therefore doubtful that Art 7(1) would allow for claims in contract to be consolidated in the place of performance of one contract. A preliminary conclusion can therefore be drawn as regards Art 7(1); even if the notion of 'matters relating to contract' could be interpreted less strictly and extended to the representative entity as a litigating party, there is nevertheless a need to clarify where an action can be brought where there are multiple places of performance in different Member States and multiple places of performance within the one Member State (and thus a multiplicity of competent fora).

9. *Protective Jurisdiction: Collective Redress and Consumer Protection*

As the focus in this paper is on consumer redress, it is necessary to analyse the protective jurisdiction provided for in Art 18(1) Brussels I bis. Three conditions must be satisfied for Art 18(1) to be engaged as a head of jurisdiction: 1) a party to a contract is a consumer acting in a context outside of his trade or profession;[115] 2) the existence of a contract between the consumer and a professional;[116] and 3) the contract must fall within Art 17(1)(a)(b) or (c) Brussels I bis.[117] If these criteria are satisfied, then Art 18(1) provides that the consumer party can choose to 'bring proceedings against the other party to a contract either in the courts of the Member State in which that party is domiciled or, regardless of the domicile of the other party, in the courts for the place where the consumer is domiciled'. These requirements give rise to two considerations as regards consumer collective redress. The first has been examined above and concerns the existence of a contractual relationship; Art 18(1) requires a consumer contract. The question is whether the existence of a contractual relationship between the litigating parties is a prerequisite for the application of the protective juris-

114 See Arnaud Nuyts, 'The Consolidation of Collective Claims under Brussels I' in Arnaud Nuyts (ed), *Cross-Border Class Actions: The European Way* (Sellier 2013), 69–84, 83.

115 Again, *Schrems* and other cases on consumer concept; problems with SMEs etc.

116 See Case C-508/12 *Vapenik* EU:C:2013:790, in which the ECJ held that as regards the EEO for Uncontested Claims, the consumer protection provision is inapplicable where the contract is between two parties, neither of which is engaged in commercial or professional activities.

117 I.e. for sale of goods/services, for loan credit or all other cases and commercial/professional activities are directed. Check Case C-375/13 *Kolassa* EU:C:2015:37.

diction in Art 18. If this is the case, as discussed above, a representative entity would not be able to rely on this protective consumer jurisdiction due to the absence of a contractual relationship. As noted however, a contractual relationship may indeed exist between the litigating parties in a test case and group action or where there has been an assignment in the context of a representative action.

However, the determination of whether Art 18 can be invoked in test cases and group actions depends on the examination of a second consideration, which is more policy-orientated and requires an examination of the issues that arose in *Schrems II.*[118] Following its previous case law, the ECJ held in *Schrems II* that even if a contractual relationship could be said to exist between the litigating parties, the protective purpose underpinning the existence of protective jurisdiction should nevertheless be examined. That is to say, following the ECJ's teleological interpretation, Art 18(1) is intended to protect consumers from a disadvantaged situation as regards the founding of jurisdiction, where that disadvantage stems from their lack of resources, and weaker bargaining and litigating power. This reasoning stems from the ECJ's finding in *Shearson*, in which it was set out that 'The special system established…is inspired by the concern to protect the consumer as the party deemed to be economically weaker and less experienced in legal matters than the other party to the contract, and the consumer must not therefore be discouraged from suing by being compelled to bring his action before the courts in the Member State in which the other party to the contract is domiciled'.[119] Thus, according to the ECJ's case law, it is necessary to consider whether consumers who are represented by a qualified entity, or consumers who are part of a group action or a test case, can be said to suffer from the same lack of resources as individual consumers. The existence of a collective redress mechanism can be understood to change the power balance between consumers and traders; that is to say, on this understanding, consumers are not deemed to lack the resources, time or knowledge to bring an action in a foreign country.

Firstly, it is necessary to consider whether qualified entities, particularly if they have to satisfy certain criteria – e.g. per Art 4 2018 Proposal – can or should really be considered to have the status of a weaker party. Does the qualified entity really suffer from the same lack of power as the individual consumer? The same query can be made as regards test cases and group actions. It is submitted that the situation in individual cases will be more

118 C-498/16 *Schrems* EU:C:2018:37, para 44 et seq.

119 C-89/91 *Shearson Lehman Hutton* EU:C:1993:15, para 18.

complicated than a simple yes or no response to such a question. That is to say, a qualified entity (including well-resourced consumer organisations like VKI or public authorities) engaged in a representative action on behalf of a class of consumers might be said to be more powerful as a litigating party. Is this the case with regards to a class of consumers, whether acting under a model of a test case or a group action? The power of the claimant(s) is always relative to that of the defendant. Thus, on the one hand, the claimant's power may be augmented where the defendant is an SME and where a qualified entity is acting on behalf of consumers. On the other, one might question whether in a test case, or group action, where the claims remain individual consumer-defendant actions but are grouped together for case management purposes, a shift in litigating power is really effected. Moreover, one might ask whether a defendant business like Apple or Facebook can ever be deemed to be weaker than any class of consumers or qualified entity. In contrast, an SME might indeed be deemed to be weaker than the class of consumers or qualified entity. It is necessary to ask whether this power imbalance between consumer and defendant will be shifted in every case; an alternative approach might involve the assessment of the different situations in which collective redress mechanisms are used and the reasons for which the qualified entity might attempt to rely on the protective jurisdiction. The situation is more complex with representative actions. To allow a representative action to be brought on the basis of Art 18(1) would require the extension of its application in two ways: firstly, as regards the non-existence of the (consumer) contractual relationship between the litigating parties[120] and secondly, in respect of the assessment of the equality of bargaining power in the particular case.[121] The challenge – as regards the objectives of the Brussels I bis regime – is that such an

120 How might Art 18(1) be extended to encompass representative actions? One option would be to consider that the consumer as a member of the class and beneficiary of the representative action might be included in Art 18(1), as is the case with the section on insurance contracts; this provision includes not only the policyholder but also the insured person or the beneficiary for the purposes of ascertaining jurisdiction.

121 Some – including Max Schrems – have argued that such an extension in jurisdiction has already been proposed in the GDPR (EU) 2016/679 via Art 80, which allows for representative actions for violations of EU data protection law, by allowing an Art 80 representative action to engage the individual bases of jurisdiction set out in Art 79(2). Schrems has argued that 'Article 80 can be used to form 'group actions' or 'collective complaints', if a large number of users are represented by NOYB ('mass mandate'). This option also allows to choose favorable jurisdictions'. https://noyb.eu/concept. It is not at all clear that the GDPR would

approach will undoubtedly undermine both certainty and predictability. Instead of advancing in the way proposed in much of the academic debate, i.e. by extending jurisdiction in contract or the protective jurisdiction to representative entities, it is instead asserted that the relevance of the head of jurisdiction for matters relating to tort, delict or quasi-delict should be assessed.[122]

10. A (Second) Rule of Special Jurisdiction for Torts

In addition to the rule of special jurisdiction in Art 7(1) for matters relating to contract, Art 7(2) provides for a head of special jurisdiction for matters relating to tort, delict or quasi-delict. The provision establishes that for such matters, jurisdiction can be founded 'in the courts for the place where the harmful event occurred or may occur', a concept which again should be given an independent, EU meaning.[123] According to the ECJ in *Kalfelis*, this 'independent concept [covers] all actions which seek to establish the liability of a defendant and which are not related to a 'contract' within the meaning of Art 7(1)'.[124] The requirement of a particular relationship between the tort claim and the litigating parties is less strict than with contract, such that a representative action might be brought under this head of jurisdiction. However, jurisdiction founded on Art 7(2) may be limited by the need for a territorial connection between the dispute and the forum. Before exploring these limitations, it should be noted that the ECJ has recognised in the *Henkel* case – concerning an action for an injunction to prohibit the use of unfair terms (in violation of the UCTD) – that Art 7(2) can be engaged as a basis of jurisdiction by a consumer protection association bringing an action on behalf of a number of consumers.[125]

---

operate in this way as regards international jurisdiction. See Marta Requejo Isidro, 'Max Schrems against Facebook' *Max Planck Institute Luxembourg for Procedural Law Research Paper Series*, 2018 (4), 14–16.

122 Notwithstanding that it might be more 'appropriate' to use the provisions on contract (i.e. to avoid using a tortious basis for jurisdiction to found jurisdiction in the courts of a particular Member States where that claim will then be dealt with as a matter of contract – this issue is left to the side for the moment).

123 Case C-189/87 *Kalfelis* EU:C:1988:459.

124 Case C-189/87 *Kalfelis* EU:C:1988:459, para 18.

125 Case C-167/00 *Henkel* EU:C:2002:555: an action brought by a consumer protection association or representative entity can be a matter relating to tort as the defendant has a non-contractual obligation to refrain in dealing with consumers in such a way that he would engage in behaviour deemed unacceptable by the

While there may be no issue as regards the relationship between the litigating parties, a number of issues nevertheless arise with regard to relevant connecting factors under Art 7(2). It is particularly difficult to identify the place where the harmful event occurred or may occur. The ECJ has held[126] that this provision can be interpreted as meaning either the place where the causal event or omission occurred or the place where the damage is sustained, providing that in the latter some primary harm occurred.[127] As with all provisions of Brussels I bis, this determination should be predictable for the litigating parties.[128] Ensuring this predictability is difficult where there are a number of relevant locations and where the place of acting or omission (the place where the event giving rise to the damage) differs from the place of effect (the place where the damage materialises), or where the act or omission occurs in one jurisdiction, and the deterioration of the injured party's condition occurs in another. The place of the event or omission giving rise to the damage will usually correspond to the domicile of the defendant.[129]

It is therefore particularly difficult to concentrate claims in one court in the context of a collective action. If special jurisdiction can be established in a particular court, that court may only have jurisdiction over claims that have a particular connection with the place of the forum. This is reflected in the ECJ's decision in *Shevill.*[130] In *Shevill*, the ECJ developed its finding in *Bier v Potasse d'Alsace*, and held that using Art 7(2), the claimant can sue either in the courts for the place where the harmful event or omission occurred or the courts for the place where the damage materialised.[131]

legislature. See also Case C-191/15 *VKI v Amazon* EU:C:2016:612, para 38 and 39, applying this understanding to Rome I and II as regards applicable law.

126 Case C-21/76 *Bier v Mines de Potasse D'Alsace* EU:C:1976:166, concerning the pollution of the Rhine in France harmed the plants of a merchant in the Netherlands.

127 Case C-220/88 *Dumez France* EU:C:1990:8, it is not enough that there is consequential or tangential or secondary economic loss to found jurisdiction.

128 Case C-147/12 *ÖFAB* EU:C:2013:490.

129 Other cases e.g. of product liability – place where the relevant product was manufactured (Case C-45/13 *Kainz v Pantherwerke* EU:C:2014:7). The ECJ has held that the notion of the place where the harmful event occurred is intended to mean the place where the initial damage occurred as a result of the normal use of the product for the purpose for which it was intended and therein caused damage (Case C-189/08 *Zuid Chemie* EU:C:2009:475).

130 Case C-68/93 *Shevill* EU:C:1995:61.

131 For defamation claims (as in *Shevill*), the former refers normally to the courts for the publisher's place of business while the latter points to the courts of any place in which the allegedly defamatory material has circulated.

Since the damage occurred in more than one Member State, the *Shevill* doctrine establishes a territorial limitation; it provides that while the claimant can sue in the former for all damage regardless of where it has been suffered, the claimant can only sue in the latter for the damage that was incurred in that jurisdiction. The *Shevill* doctrine reflects the so-called mosaic or pluralist approach to jurisdiction; initially deriving from a defamation action, it has been developed in *eDate*[132] as regards actions for the infringement of personality rights. Furthermore, as regards online media, the ECJ has found that a claimant may bring an action 1) for all of the damage caused in the courts of the establishment of the publisher or the Member State in which the claimant's centre of interests are based (which would normally point to the residence of the claimant, or where his or her activities are centred, generating a particularly close link[133]) or 2) in the courts of each Member State in which damage has materialised but only as regards the damage within that particular Member State (i.e. in which the material had been placed online or was accessible). The ECJ has held that there is a sufficient degree of predictability or the defendant if jurisdiction is founded in the courts of the Member State in which the claimant had his habitual residence or indeed his centre of interests.[134]

The 'place [of] the causal event or omission giving rise to the harm' usually corresponds to the domicile of the defendant. Given that this provision and the general rule of jurisdiction in Art 4(1) would coincide, it will always be possible for an action for collective redress, based on any model, to be initiated in this forum. As to the second fork of *Shevill*, as mentioned above, the key challenge as regards collective redress arises where damage materialises in multiple Member States, and again, in multiple places within a single Member State. As multiple consumers in different Member States will likely suffer damage close to them, this situation generates the potential for multiple competent fora. A centre of gravity approach might instead be adopted. For one injured person, this would point to the courts of the domicile of that injured party. For multiple injured persons, it is more difficult to concentrate jurisdiction in one forum. It might be relevant to identify the centre of interests or the habitual residence of the majority of class members; this would extend the approach adopted in

132 Joined Cases C-509/09 and C-161/10 *eDate Advertising* EU:C:2011:685.

133 Joined Cases C-509/09 and C-161/10 *eDate Advertising* EU:C:2011:685, paras 58–59.

134 As, via these connecting factors, it is possible to know the habitual residence or centre of interests of the party who is the subject of the potentially infringing content.

eDate, in which the ECJ noted that jurisdiction could be founded in the courts for the place where the website is accessible (but only for damage in that place) or in the courts or the place where the 'alleged victim has his centre of interests' (normally his habitual residence) and for damage incurred anywhere.

As regards collective redress modelled on representative actions, it has been argued that qualified entities should not be able to raise an action in the courts of the place where the damage materialised for the reason that the damage is linked to the interested parties (i.e. the class members) who are not be considered to be parties to the proceedings. The argument is based on the notion that the litigating party – the qualified entity – has not suffered the damage, and as such should not be able to rely on jurisdiction on this ground; instead qualified entities should only be able to sue in the courts for the place where the event or omission giving rise to the damage occurred[135]. Stadler further advocates that where damage materialises in more than one Member State, jurisdiction should only be founded in the courts of the place in which the harmful event occurred (that is to say, in the courts of the domicile of the defendant)[136]. Arguably however, this particular strand of reasoning would not apply to collective redress initiated through test cases or group actions, as the claim remains an individual one and the individual interest continues to come to the fore[137]. One might nevertheless engage the argument of proximity between the class members and the forum; that is to say, it is not clear that jurisdiction in collective redress mechanisms should be limited as the courts of the place where the damage materialises (alongside a centre of gravity approach) may be the most proximate to the (majority of) injured class members and be the court in the best position to, for example, gather evidence. Ultimately, as regards Art 7(2), only the place of the occurrence of the harmful event giving rise to the damage is relevant for collective redress and the concentra-

135 See Thijs Bosters, *Collective Redress and Private International Law in the EU* (Springer 2018), 225 et seq.

136 Astrid Stadler, 'The Commission's Recommendation on Common Principles of Collective Redress and Private International Law Issues' (2013) NIPR 4.

137 *Deutsche Bahn* [2013] EWCA 1484; in the case of *Deutsche Bahn* before English Court of Appeal, it was considered that as regards Art 7(2), there should be no requirement such that 'in order to be a relevant connecting factor between defendant and putative jurisdiction, a harmful event must be one of which the putative claimant is an immediate victim. That would seem to involve a search for a connecting factor between the claimant and the putative jurisdiction, rather than a connecting factor between the defendant and the putative jurisdiction, which is what the regulation is concerned with'.

tion of jurisdiction in a single court. As noted, this will most likely correspond to Art 4(1) and the courts of the defendant's domicile.

11. Preliminary Conclusions on Jurisdiction

It is apt to draw some preliminary conclusions. Thus far, the paper has attempted to set out the background and context, legal and political, underpinning the development of compensatory collective redress at the national and EU levels. It has provided a brief comparative outline of the three key models of collective redress that have been adopted in the national legal systems, namely representative actions, test cases and group claims. Against this background, the analysis then turned to the most recent initiative of the European Commission, which has identified the representative action model of procedural design as that which it proposes to be adopted at the EU level, providing a cross-border mechanism for compensatory collective redress. In light of the absence of an EU-wide regime, the continuing diversity as regards the culture of collective redress across the Member States, and the absence of PIL provisions for dealing with cross-border collective redress, the paper has attempted to identify whether the three models of collective redress might be integrated into the existing Brussels I bis rules on jurisdiction. This analysis has been undertaken with an eye on two key aims, pertinent to effective collective redress proceedings: the consolidation of jurisdiction and the avoidance of parallel proceedings.

Both the default rule as well as the alternatives to that default head of jurisdiction in Brussels I bis have been examined[138]. These alternatives provide claimants with a choice of where to sue; in the situation of mass harms, where collective and individual litigation might be initiated, they allow for jurisdiction to be founded in the courts of multiple Member States, potentially giving rise to parallel proceedings and conflicting judgments. The default in Art 4(1)[139] establishes that jurisdiction can be founded in the courts of the defendant's domicile. The alternative heads of jurisdiction, as established above, may allow the claimant to initiate indi-

138 Recital 16 Brussels I bis Regulation. See also Opinion of Advocate General Bobek of 28 February 2018, *AB flyLAL-Lithuanian Airlines*, C-27/17, EU:C:2018:136, para 99. The Court's position may not come as a surprise as it mainly gives expression to the general scheme of the Convention/Regulation in this regard.

139 See also Recital 15 Brussels I bis Regulation.

vidual litigation before the courts of the place with a close connection to the place of performance of the contract or to the tortious, delicitual or non-contractual act or omission giving rise to damage, or the place where the injury was incurred. These places may also coincide with the place of domicile or residence of the claimant (assuming, for example, that the consumer would contract for delivery of goods to his place of residence). Furthermore, in individual consumer litigation, the consumer claimant may rely on the protective head of jurisdiction in Art 18(1) Brussels I bis and sue in the courts for the place of his domicile.

These rules may therefore point to multiple courts, an outcome which is particularly problematic for cross-border collective redress, especially if the objective is to consolidate claims and avoid concurrent litigation for the same violation of EU law by the same trader. The examination above points to the inadequacies of the heads of jurisdiction provided in Brussels I bis to the needs of collective redress; in particular, it illustrates the difficulties in concentrating actions in a single forum for cross-border collective redress actions, where consumers affected by the same violation are domiciled in different Member States, where performance has been contracted for in different places and where damage has been suffered in multiple states. If we aim to consolidate collective redress proceedings, only one option seems available at the outset; namely, Art 4(1) which would allow all claims to be brought in the courts of the defendant's domicile.

We have also studied the alternative heads of jurisdiction, which might provide for a forum that is more proximate to the consumer than that of the defendant's domicile; these rules also prove to be problematic for collective redress. The heads of jurisdiction in Art 7 Brussels I bis are problematic for various reasons, and as regards each model of collective redress, it appears representative actions are the most challenging. Art 7(1) requires a contractual relationship, or an obligation freely assumed, between the litigating parties, which is likely to be absent in a collective redress claim based on a representative action model where there is no assignment of claims. The requirement of a contractual relationship may not pose an issue in group claims or test cases, where the individual consumers remain party to the claim. Even if a contract does exist between the litigating parties (as would be the case in test cases, group actions and representative actions based on assignment), it is nevertheless difficult to identify how claims might be consolidate in a single forum. As regards Art 7(1), the identification of a single place of performance is problematic where there are multiple places of performance due to multiple consumers contracting to receive goods or services in different Member States (and even in different places within the same Member State – assuming that consumers will usually contract for performance in their place of domicile or habitual residence).

A similar problem arises with the identification of a single forum from Art 7(2). While delictual jurisdiction may be founded in representative actions, test cases and group actions, attempts to found jurisdiction per Art 7(2), either in the place where the harmful event occurred (either the place of the causal act or omission or in the place where the harm is felt) may be problematic. The second prong generates challenges due to the very likely possibility that where multiple consumers are domiciled or resident in different Member States, it will not be possible to identify a single place in which the damage materialises. Instead, there will be multiple places in which damage is incurred. This provision will likely result in fragmented jurisdiction, a reflection of the mosaic approach, as consumers will most likely incur harm in the place where they are domiciled or resident, which will be multiple when a collective claim encompasses consumers domiciled or resident in different Member States. As a result, multiple collective redress proceedings may be initiated before the courts of a number of Member States, and even in different courts within a single Member State. Art 7(2) allows for the identification of a single forum only in the place where the harmful event or omission occurred; this will usually coincide with the domicile of the defendant, bringing the analysis back to the general rule in Art 4(1). Finally, with representative actions, one might question whether the qualified entity can rely on Art 7(2). The representative entity is not deemed to have suffered harm as a result of the defendant's alleged infringement. The representative entity's status as a litigating party is not based on its individual interest in redress but on a conferral of such a status by the law of a particular Member State, allowing it to bring such actions on behalf of injured parties. The Brussels I bis Regulation does not currently address this situation, it being orientated to two-party proceedings.

It is evidently difficult to consolidate jurisdiction in collective redress proceedings. Where multiple actions might be initiated – collective or individual – the possibility of parallel proceedings arises,[140] a problematic that is further exacerbated when the existence of individual claims is also taken into consideration. Indeed, multiple individual claims might be

140 Here, the way in which the class if constituted in representative actions is of particular significance; the problematic situation arises where the class is constituted on an opt-out basis, and where consumers may be unaware of proceedings ongoing in a particular Member State. This is discussed further in the section on *lis pendens*.

brought by individual claimants before the courts of any Member State with jurisdiction for an individual claim (which would also bring into play the head of protective consumer jurisdiction in Art 18(1) Brussels I bis), adding further complexity as regards the relevance of *lis pendens* and related actions.[141] The consolidation of collective redress claims only seems to be possible on the basis of Art 4(1) Brussels I bis or on Art 7(2), in the courts of the place where the event or omission giving rise to the damage occurred. There may be a coincidence of jurisdiction between the two, it being most likely that the harmful event or omission will occur in the place of the defendant's domicile. This brings the discussion back to the question of whether there is a need to extend the existing bases of jurisdiction.

The heads of jurisdiction provided under Art 7, in particular, are inspired by a logic of proximity and predictability which would be hindered – if not bypassed – by the adaptations required to make these grounds of jurisdiction available to collective procedures. As discussed, this provision adopts connecting factors – the place of delivery, the place of performance, the place of the harmful event – tailored upon the need of concentrating the same violation of EU law by the same trader in a single place. They are therefore unfit for collective procedures which, involving multiple claims, will more often than not entail multiple places of delivery, of performance and harmful events. To make these heads of jurisdiction viable for collective redress and to avoid a fragmentation of jurisdiction, these connecting factors should be subjected to extensive interpretive amendments, based on the 'centre of gravity of the dispute' logic.

As discussed, it has been advanced that the interpretation of Art 7(1)[142] and Art 7(2) and the relevant connecting factors might be extended to provide for a centre of gravity or centre of interest approach. This would indicate looking to the place where the majority of consumers receive have contracted for performance as regards Art 7(1) or the place where the majority of the damage has materialised. For both provisions, this would indicate looking to the place where the majority of consumers have their domicile or habitual residence. Even if the connecting factor of 'centre of interest' would be extended using the place where the harm was felt for the majority of the injured parties (with the aim of avoiding this fragmen-

141 Discussed in the chapter of Janek Nowak.

142 Depending on the model of collective redress and its procedural design, art 7(1) may also have to be extended so as to assume the existence of a contractual relationship between the qualified entity and the defendant in collective redress claims.

tation), multiple claims will nevertheless continue to exist beyond Member States A and B (where the defendant and the majority of consumers have their domicile or residence, respectively). As is examined further below, alongside the consequences of such an outcome, other Member States will continue to be competent to hear collective redress claims, as a result of some damage having materialised therein. As above, other courts will be competent to hear individual claims based on the same violation. Both the ECJ and the Commission are reluctant to extend the protective jurisdiction in Art 18(1) in any way, to attribute this protection to qualified entities bringing representative actions. The relevant policy interests have been set out above, a key issue being the absence of a contractual relationship, and the lack of power imbalance that justifies the protection for individual consumers.

It is proposed that at the current time, no such action is taken to extend the existing rules of jurisdiction so as to provide for a special rule for cross-border collective redress. Without coherence in collective redress mechanisms across the Member States, can there be coherence between PIL and collective redress? Even if the existing rules – as might be suggested, either via the introduction of a new basis of jurisdiction in Brussels I bis or the extension of existing rules of jurisdiction, by analogy were to be amended, it is submitted that the problems outlined above remain.

Representative (Consumer) Collective Redress Decisions in the EU: Free Movement or Public Policy Obstacles?

Janek Tomasz Nowak[*]

Table of Contents

* Research Fellow, MPI Luxembourg; PhD researcher, KU Leuven; Visiting Lecturer, MCI Innsbruck. I would like to thank dr. Stephanie Law (University of Southampton) for her close cooperation and various reviews of this paper. I would also like to thank Prof. dr. Stefaan Voet (KU Leuven), Prof. dr. Burkhard Hess (MPI Luxembourg) and dr. Vincent Richard (MPI Luxembourg) for their useful comments. Any mistakes remain my own. This chapter was finalised in April 2019 and has remained faithful to the argument presented at the September 2018 workshop. Later developments, such as the entry into force of the new Dutch law on judicial collective redress or the June 2020 agreement on the proposal for a directive on representative actions have not been considered in depth. I believe, however, that these developments make very little change to the argument presented. The draft directive allows for considerable different models of collective redress so that issues of recognition and enforcement will remain.

1. Introduction

Civil procedure is in a transitional phase in Europe. Under the influence of new technologies, mass litigation, budgetary constraints and the ever increasing judicialization of all sorts of societal problems, we are moving towards a new civil procedure paradigm, away from the classical model of conflict-solving, adversarial, contradictory two-party proceedings. It is in this environment that the Brussels Convention celebrates its 50th anniversary.

1.1. Collective Redress and the Jurisdiction Rules of the Brussels Ibis Regulation

One of these challenges is the incorporation of the collective litigation model in its rules on jurisdiction and *lis pendens*. More and more EU Member States are embracing the collectivisation of civil procedure, especially through representative remedial[1] collective redress procedures. This is a collective litigation model by which a qualified representative can apply on behalf of a group of persons confronted with the same and/or similar legal and/or factual issues, most likely consumers at present, for a remedy against a business on account of having caused harm, either contractual or extra-contractual, to that group of persons. The qualified representative acts without a legal mandate from the (other) interested persons and is not necessarily part of the group of persons for whom a remedy is being sought.[2] The (positive) decision obtained by the qualified representative will, however, bind the group members, even though they are formally not a party to the procedure. This is a relatively new trend in European civil procedure[3] that does not sit easily with the jurisdiction rules of the Brussels I^{bis} Regulation, which is based on a different litigation model. It also begs the question whether the Brussels Regime is flexible enough to accommodate this very recent evolution in European procedural culture.

It appears from the analysis in the previous chapter that cross-border representative remedial collective redress is possible in the European Union.[4] However, not all possible configurations are attainable under the Brussels I^{bis} Regulation. It is generally not possible for parties domiciled in one Member State to join a representative remedial collective redress procedure in another Member State apart from the Member State in which

1 Since the remedy in a representative collective redress procedure is not necessarily limited to compensation in the strict legal sense but can also encompass restitution, price reduction, a flat amount, exchange or other alternatives (rebates on future purchases or other reductions), I will use the term ‘representative remedial collective redress’ instead of ‘representative compensatory collective redress’ or ‘representative monetary collective redress’.

2 Cf. ELI-UNIDROIT European Rules of Civil Procedure – Working Group on Parties, *Chapter X: Collective Redress*, Preliminary Draft of 26–27 November 2018, available from https://www.europeanlawinstitute.eu/fileadmin/user_upload/p_eli/Projects/Unidroit_Materials/Trier_2018/WG_Parties - Draft on Collective Redress.pdf.

3 See M. Taruffo, “Some remarks on group litigation in a comparative perspective”, (11) Duke Journal of Comparative & International Law 2001, (405), 406, who sketches the absence of compensatory collective redress – or any policy debate on the matter – in Europe at the turn of the millennium. See also, V. Smith, “Redress through collective actions in Europe: ELI/UNIDROIT and European Commission proposals”, *Unif. L. Rev.* 2019, (1) 1–2.

4 See, S. Law, p.349 in this volume.

the defendant is domiciled.[5] True European-wide representative remedial collective redress, with the consolidation of all EU group members in a Member State that is not the domicile of the defendant, appears thus impossible.[6]

This might seem somewhat contradictory in an integrated market where goods and services flow freely from one Member State to another and where consumers from multiple Member States can be exposed to the same harm. Various authors have therefore suggested amending the Brussels I^bis^ Regulation in order to overcome jurisdictional problems in relation to cross-border collective redress in the European Union, especially for consumers.[7] Such amendments would create additional fora having jurisdiction, other than the domicile of the defendant or the individual consumer, which would in turn increase the need to circulate decisions throughout the European Union. Therefore, the adaptation of rules on jurisdiction may not be considered separately from issues of recognition

---

5 Cf. M. Hellner, "Private international law and collective redress – The case of antitrust damages" in A. Nuyts and N.E. Hatzimihail (Eds.), *Cross-border class actions – The European way* (Selp, 2014), (223) 234; A. Stadler, "Cross-border mass litigation: a particular challenge for European law" in J. Steele and W.H. van Boom (Eds.), *Mass Justice – Challenges of representation and distribution* (Edward Elgar, 2011), (73) 79.

6 Cf. A. Stadler, "The Commission's recommendation on common principles of collective redress and private international law issues" in E. Lein, D. Fairgrieve, M. Otero Crespo and V. Smith (Eds.), *Collective redress in Europe – Why and how?* (BIICL, 2015), (235) 242–243; H. Muir Watt, "Collective redress" in J. Basedow, G. Rühl, F. Schiller, F. Ferrari and P. de Miguel Asensio (Eds.), *Encyclopedia of Private International Law* (Edward Elgar, 2017), (373) 377. Save for a number of exceptional situations which we will not delve into in the context of this contribution. See examples given in A. Stadler, "The Commission's Recommendation on common principles of collective redress and private international law issues", *NiPR* 2013, (483) 486.

7 See, *inter alia*, A. Stadler, "Cross-border mass litigation: a particular challenge for European law" in J. Steele and W.H. van Boom (Eds.), *Mass Justice – Challenges of representation and distribution* (Edward Elgar, 2011), (73) 79–82; H. Muir Watt, "The trouble with cross-border collective redress: issues and difficulties" in D. Fairgrieve and E. Lein (Eds.), *Extraterritoriality and collective redress* (OUP, 2012), (119) 122; H. Muir Watt, "Collective redress" in J. Basedow, G. Rühl, F. Schiller, F. Ferrari and P. de Miguel Asensio (Eds.), *Encyclopedia of Private International Law* (Edward Elgar, 2017), (373) 379–380; A. Bonomi, "50 ans de Convention de Bruxelles: 'ce n'est pas qu'un début, continuons le combat'!", *Rev. crit. DIP* 2018, 459; C. Peraro, *Cross-border Collective Redress in the Employment Context under European Union Law*, PhD thesis defended at the University of Verona on 6 April 2018, 256–257, available at https://iris.univr.it/retrieve/handle/11562/978107/99777/CINZIA%20PERARO%20-%20PhD%20Thesis.pdf.

and enforcement, especially in light of public policy. It is to this point that this contribution will now turn.

1.2. Relevance of the Issue of Public Policy in the Reform Debate

The increased need for circulation may potentially lead to a higher number of refusals of recognition and enforcement of judgments. This is not only a logical consequence of an increase in cross-border situations but also because of the nature of the decisions circulating, namely judgments emanating from representative remedial collective redress proceedings. The increased potential for refusal of recognition or enforcement can be ascribed to the absence of a common collective redress culture in the Member States of the European Union. Currently, less than 20 Member States have provided in one way or another for remedial collective redress mechanisms.[8] Almost a third of EU Member States have therefore not acted upon the 2013 Recommendation of the European Commission[9], despite its imperative language.[10] Moreover, in more than half of the Mem-

---

8 European Commission, Report from the Commission to the European Parliament, the Council and the European Economic and Social Committee on the implementation of the Commission Recommendation of 11 June 2013 on common principles for injunctive and compensatory collective redress mechanisms in the Member States concerning violations of rights granted under Union law (2013/396/EU), COM(2018) 40 final, 3 ('European Commission 2018 report on collective redress'). See also BIICL, Civic Consulting and RPA, State of collective redress in the EU in the context of the implementation of the Commission Recommendation (JUST/2016/JCOO/FW/CIVI/0099), 2017, 10 ('BIICL Study'). It should be pointed out that Luxembourg is in the process of adopting a law on collective redress. Moreover, I do not any longer count the United Kingdom as an EU Member State.

9 European Commission, Recommendation 2013/396/EU of 11 June 2013 on common principles for injunctive and compensatory collective redress mechanisms in the Member States concerning violations of rights granted under Union law, *OJ* 2013, L 201/60 (hereafter '*European Commission 2013 Recommendation on collective redress*'). See C. Hodges and S. Voet, *Delivering collective redress* (Hart/Beck/Nomos, 2018), 7.

10 It remained in the end a non-binding instrument that Member States could ignore: A. Stadler, "The Commission's Recommendation on Common Principles for Collective Redress and private international law issues" in E. Lein, D. Fairgrieve, M. Otero Crespo and V. Smith (Eds.), *Collective redress in Europe – Why and how?* (BIICL, 2015), (235) 248. See also *BIICL Study*, 9–41; *inter alia* J. Sorabji predicted rightly that the European Commission's 2013 Recommendation would not result in any coherence between the Member States' systems: J. Sorabji,

ber States that have provided for remedial collective redress the mechanism is limited to a specific sector, mostly consumer law.[11] Next to this, approaches to remedial collective redress differ considerably amongst those Member States, as highlighted by the comparative overview in the previous chapter of this volume.[12] Even within a specific model, procedural design may vary strongly.[13] The representative model we consider in this contribution is a very good example in that regard, as various procedural options may lead to procedures of a very different nature with different levels of protection. Likewise, between opt-out models or opt-in models rules may vary considerably and create very different outcomes depending on how they are designed.[14]

It appears that all Member States concerned have developed their own model of collective redress, thereby striking a different balance between respecting the right to a fair trial and the efficiency of collective procedures.[15] With such diversity it cannot be excluded that decisions given in a Member State with a very liberal approach to representative remedial col-

---

"Reflections on the Commission Communication on collective redress", (17) *Irish Journal of European law* 2014, (62) 71. See also, with the benefit of hindsight, A. Biard, "Collective redress in the EU: a rainbow behind the clouds?", (19) *ERA Forum* 2018, (189) 191–196.

11 *European Commission 2018 report on collective redress*, 3. A notable exception is the Portuguese popular action, which is of general application. Also in France, the 'action de groupe' is available in a number of other areas, such as discrimination, health and the environment. In 2018, Belgium extended its collective redress mechanism to SMEs. (Law of 30 March 2018 modifying the Economic Law Code by extending the scope of application of the action for collective redress to SMEs, *Belgian State Gazette* 2018, 41950). More generally, after the enactment of the GDPR, various Member States have also provided for remedial collective redress in relation to data protection law.

12 See also, D. Fairgrieve and G. Howells, "Collective redress procedures: European debates", (58) *I.C.L.Q.* 2009, (379) 399.

13 B. Hess (ed.), *MPI Luxembourg EU procedural law study – Strand two: Procedural protection of consumers* (JUST/2014/RCON/PR/CIVI/0082), 2017, 258 (hereafter 'MPI Study'); C. Hodges and S. Voet, *Delivering collective redress* (Hart/Beck/Nomos, 2018), 283.

14 Many factors may contribute to this: judicial approach vs settlement approach, declaratory nature vs compensatory nature, standing requirements, admissibility requirements, notification requirements, moment of constitution of class, time to opt-in/opt-out, powers of the judge, impact on individual proceedings, and costs and financing rules. See *infra*.

15 Cf. H.L. Buxbaum, "Defining the function and scope of group litigation: The role of class actions for monetary damages in the United States" in P. Gottwald (Ed.), *Europäisches Insolvenzrecht – Kollektiver Rechtsschutz* (Gieseking, 2008), (215) 224.

lective redress may be exposed to a risk of refusal of recognition or enforcement on account of public policy in a Member State with a very different or restrictive view on this matter. It is telling in this regard that in the course of the reform process of the Brussels I Regulation the European Commission proposed to exclude judgments given in collective procedures from the abolition of *exequatur* since the required level of mutual trust between the Member States was absent.[16]

The directive on representative actions for the protection of the collective interests of consumers will not take away this lack of mutual trust. The agreed text of the directive allows for many models of remedial collective redress procedures, ranging from the very restrictive to very liberal. The legislative process has only highlighted the strongly different views of the Member States on remedial collective redress and its adoption is thus in no way a sign of a coming together of the Member States on this point. Quite to the contrary. Both Parliament and Council have amended the Commission's proposal to make clear that the rules on recognition and enforcement of judgments will not be affected by the directive,[17] keeping the option for refusals of recognition and enforcement open.

The idea that a lack of common understanding of proceedings may influence the application of Article 45(1) Brussels I^{bis} Regulation may also be inferred from the Opinion of Advocate General J. Kokott in *Trade Agency*. She states in relation to the enforcement of a default judgment that it cannot be refused on account of public policy purely for it being characterised as a default judgment, as all Member States accept the concept of a

16 European Commission, Proposal for a Regulation of the European Parliament and of the Council on jurisdiction and the recognition and enforcement of judgments in civil and commercial matters (Recast), COM(2010) 748 final, recital 23. This exclusion was, however, not followed by the other institutions. See, for example, Council of the European Union, Proposal for a Regulation of the European Parliament and of the Council on jurisdiction and the recognition and enforcement of judgments in civil and commercial matters (Recast) – Political guidelines for the future work, 29 November 2011, 17402/11, point 6.

17 Proposal for a Directive of the European Parliament and of the Council on representative actions for the protection of the collective interests of consumers, and repealing Directive 2009/22/EC, COM(2018) 184 final. See also the European Parliament legislative resolution of 26 March 2019 on the proposal for a directive of the European Parliament and of the Council on representative actions for the protection of the collective interests of consumers, and repealing Directive 2009/22/EC, TA/2019/0222, and the Council Common Position of 28 November 2019, 14600/19. See further, Article 2(3) of the agreed text of 30 June 2020, available on the website of the Council of the EU: https://www.consilium.europa.eu/nl/press/press-releases/2020/06/30/eu-consumers-obtain-access-to-collective-redress/

default judgment, regarding which a balance must be struck between the rights of the claimant and the rights of the defendant.[18] Conversely, it may be plausible that recognition and enforcement of a judgment given in a representative remedial collective redress procedure may be refused by the courts of a Member State that has struck a completely different balance between the efficiency of collective litigation and the right to individual litigation.

In light of this, it appears justified to explore whether the public policy exception will be applied more frequently to collective redress decisions.[19] We will focus on decisions emanating from a non-mandate based representative remedial collective redress procedures[20], as this appears to be the model favoured by the European Commission[21] and is becoming the preferred model amongst the EU Member States.[22] It is also in regard of this model that issues of public policy are most likely to appear, especially since the discrepancy with individual litigation and the accompanying procedural rights is the widest.

---

18 Opinion of Advocate General J. Kokott of 26 April 2012, *Trade Agency*, C-619/10, EU:C:2012:247, paras 79–81.

19 These can be either judgments proper or settlements approved by a court after judicial scrutiny. Such settlements can also be considered as decisions within the meaning of the Brussels I^{bis} Regulation and are for the purposes of this contribution therefore not considered separately from judgments proper. What goes for judgments goes for these settlements as well, both in regard of the required procedural guarantees and the standard of public policy review. See also, D. Fairgrieve, "The impact of the Brussels I enforcement and recognition rules on collective actions" in D. Fairgrieve and E. Lein (Eds.), *Extraterritoriality and collective redress* (OUP, 2012), (171) 174–176.

20 For reasons of style, I will hereafter use the shorter notions of 'representative collective redress procedures', 'representative collective redress' or 'collective redress' to refer to 'representative remedial collective redress procedures'.

21 European Commission, Proposal for a directive of the European Parliament and the Council on representative actions for the protection of the collective interests of consumers, and repealing Directive 2009/22/EC, COM(2018) 184 final, Articles 4–6. It appears from Article 6(1) that the European Commission favours a purely representative action over representation by way of a mandate of the individual consumer. Nevertheless, it leaves the option open as various systems currently operate with a mandate.

22 Cf. D. Fairgrieve and G. Howells, "Collective redress procedures: European debates", (58) *I.C.L.Q.* 2009, (379) 400. See also A. Zuckermann, *Zuckermann on civil procedure*, 3rd Ed. (Sweet & Maxwell, 2013), 701. See *inter alia* Belgium, England and Wales, France, Germany, Portugal, and the Netherlands. See also, ELI-UNIDROIT European Rules of Civil Procedure – Working Group on Parties, *Chapter X: Collective Redress*, Preliminary Draft, 3.

1.3. Argument and Plan

The aim of this paper is to challenge the idea that a quick adaptation of the jurisdiction rules of the Brussels Ibis Regulation may solve the problem of representative collective redress procedures within the Brussels regime. It is argued that in the absence of a common standard of collective redress in Europe, an intensification of public policy review may emerge in relation to collective redress decisions, rendering the adaptation of jurisdiction rules rather ineffective. The plausibility of such stricter scrutiny should require us to weigh carefully the interest in facilitating EU-wide representative collective redress against the increased risk of refusals of recognition and enforcement and their impact on the Brussels regime.

In section 2, I will take stock of the current approach to public policy in the Brussels Ibis Regulation. This will be followed by presenting the two main arguments in favour of a different approach to public policy in relation to representative remedial collective redress decisions in section 3. Section 4 will address issues of public policy in relation to the choice for a representative remedial collective redress model as well as the choice for a model with an opt-out selection mechanism. Issues of public policy will be further considered in section 5 in relation to procedural design of collective redress models. Section 6 will briefly address the distinction between procedural design and concrete application and present a number of predictions in relation to the intensity of public policy review. This will be followed by section 7, in which we will evaluate our arguments and conjectures in light of national practice, considering a number of court decisions on the recognition and enforcement of collective redress decisions. The concluding section will then take a position regarding the plausibility of intensified public policy scrutiny and the opportunity of an adaptation of the jurisdiction rules of the Brussels Ibis Regulation in the near future.

2. The Approach to Public Policy in the Brussels Ibis Regulation

2.1. Standard of Review

The public policy exception of Article 45(1) Brussels Ibis Regulation allows a court of a Member State to refuse the recognition and enforcement of a judgment given in another Member State on account of that judgment being "at variance to an unacceptable degree with the legal order of the State in which enforcement is sought inasmuch as it would infringe a fundamental principle".[23] A mere infringement of a fundamental principle does not suffice, however. A "manifest breach of a rule of law regarded as essential in the legal order of the State in which enforcement is sought or of a right recognised as being fundamental within that legal order" must exist.[24] The high threshold corresponds to the idea that exceptions to the free circulation of judgments must be constructed in a restrictive manner, as a wide application would undermine the fundamental objectives of the Brussels Regime.[25] Not every breach of every rule of law thus suffices to object to the recognition and enforcement of foreign judgments. It is within this framework that national courts have to apply Article 45(1) Brussels I^{bis} Regulation.

2.2. *National Concept*

The public policy concept is foremost a national concept, determined by the courts of the Member State in which recognition or enforcement is being sought.[26] The Court of Justice has no definitional powers in relation to the public policy concept of a particular Member State. It only has a negative power, reviewing the limits within which the courts of a Member State may have recourse to the concept of public policy.[27] It falls thus on the latter to determine whether a decision originating in another Member State has violated a fundamental rule in a manifestly disproportionate way.[28]

2.3. *Increasing Europeanisation of Public Policy Based on a Common Procedural Model*

That being said, there is a trend towards the Europeanisation of the concept of public policy under the influence of the fundamental right to a fair

23 Judgment of 6 September 2012, *Trade Agency*, C-619/10, EU:C:2012:531, para. 51.
24 Ibid.
25 Judgment of 28 March 2000, *Krombach*, C-7/98, EU:C:2000:164, para. 21.
26 I. Thoma, "Public policy (ordre public)" in J. Basedow, G. Rühl, F. Schiller, F. Ferrari and P. de Miguel Asensio (Eds.), *Encyclopedia of Private International Law* (Edward Elgar, 2017), 1453.
27 *Trade Agency*, para. 49.
28 Judgment of 2 April 2009, *Gambazzi*, C-394/07, EU:C:2009:219, para. 34.

trial[29], as enshrined in Article 6 ECHR and Article 47 CFR, and which is common to all EU Member States.[30] The fundamental right to a fair trial provides for a common benchmark to define public policy – it denationalises the concept of public policy to a large extent[31] – and allows the Court of Justice to play a bigger role in this regard by defining the concept also in a positive way, as seen in *Krombach*, in which it held that it is not permissible to achieve the aim promoted by the Brussels Regime by 'undermining the right to a fair hearing'.[32] This evidently requires a positive definition of what such a right should entail. The increased role of the Court has become even more visible since the CFR has received full normative status with the entry into force of the Treaty of Lisbon.[33] It must thus be possible to have recourse to the public policy clause "where the guarantees laid down in the legislation of the State of origin and in the Convention itself have been insufficient to protect the defendant from a manifest breach of his right to defend himself before the court of origin, as recognised by the ECHR",[34] the rights of the defence as enshrined in Article 6 ECHR and Article 47 CFR constituting fundamental principles whose violation can give rise to the public policy exception.[35]

In this light, it is important to point to the common constitutional traditions of the Member States. The right to a fair trial has been developed in line with a common understanding of civil procedure, namely an adversarial contradictory two-party procedure, for which appropriate safeguards for fair proceedings have been developed in the Member States and which

---

29 A. Halfmeier and P. Wimalasena, "Rechtsstaatliche Anforderungen an Opt-out-Sammelverfahren: Anerkennung ausländischer Titel und rechtspolitischer Gestaltungsspielraum", *J.Z.* 2012, (649) 656. See also, I. Thoma, "Public policy (ordre public)" in J. Basedow, G. Rühl, F. Schiller, F. Ferrari and P. de Miguel Asensio (Eds.), *Encyclopedia of Private International Law* (Edward Elgar, 2017), (1453) 1458–1459.

30 *Trade Agency*, para. 52.

31 The influence of the ECHR on public policy also exists in the private international rules of the Member States. See, for example, Ghent Court of Appeal, 17 April 2008, www.dipr.be 2009 (2), 75.

32 *Krombach*, para. 43.

33 Judgment of 11 September 2014, *A v B*, C-112/13, EU:C:2014:2195, para 51; Judgment of 25 May 2016, *Meroni*, C-559/14, EU:C:2016:349, paras 42–45. See also, B. Heiderhoff, "Die Selbstbeschränkung des Anwendungsbereichs der EU-Charta in Art. 51 und die Ausbildung eines anerkennungsrechtlichen europäischen ordre public" in B. Heiderhoff, S. Lohsse and R. Schulze (Eds.), *EU-Grundrechte und Privatrecht* (Nomos, 2016), 89–114.

34 *Krombach*, para. 44.

35 *Krombach*, para. 26.

have converged into a common standard over time. This allows for a high degree of mutual trust between the civil justice systems of the Member States and leaves very little latitude to refuse recognition or enforcement for violations of the right to a fair trial on account of procedural design. Public policy concerns are rather raised in relation to the concrete application of procedural rules. This appears also from the way national courts have to evaluate public policy grounds for refusal. The national court must take into account the proceedings as a whole in the light of all the circumstances,[36] whether means of redress against the decision were available,[37] and whether the right to be heard has been respected.[38] This does not go as far as reviewing the substance of the case but requires the national court to identify the available legal remedies and verify whether these remedies allowed the possibility of being heard, "in compliance with the adversarial principle and the full exercise of the rights of defence".[39] Thus, apart from the very exceptional situation that a procedure in one Member State is problematic from the point of view of the right to a fair trial by way of its design, public policy review rather concerns the application of procedural rules in the concrete case.[40]

As such, the system is geared to a very limited scope for refusal on grounds of public policy, thereby allowing for the maximal circulation of judgments in line with the fundamental objectives of the Brussels Regime. The question is whether a similar approach can be maintained in respect of the circulation of representative collective redress decisions. They are a recent phenomenon in European procedural culture and no common tradition has yet emerged across the Member States.[41]

---

36 Judgment of 2 May 2006, *Eurofood*, C-341/04, EU:C:2006:281, para. 68.

37 *Gambazzi*, para. 44. See also, Judgment of 16 July 2015, *Diageo Brands*, C-681/13, EU:C:2015:471, para. 68.

38 *Gambazzi*, para. 45.

39 *Gambazzi*, para. 46.

40 Cf. D. Fairgrieve, "The impact of the Brussels I enforcement and recognition rules on collective actions" in D. Fairgrieve and E. Lein (Eds.), *Extraterritoriality and collective redress* (OUP, 2012), (171) 182; M. Weller, "Mutual trust within judicial cooperation in civil matters: a normative cornerstone – a factual chimera – a constitutional challenge", *NiPR* 2018, (1) 18.

41 See *supra*, section 1, and infra, section 3.2.

3. A Different Approach to Public Policy in Relation to Representative Remedial Collective Redress?

There appear to be two main arguments that support a different approach towards public policy in relation to representative remedial collective redress within the framework of the Brussels regime, namely the radically different litigation model and the lack of a common conception of fair trial rights within collective litigation.

3.1. The Litigation Model of the Brussels Regime

The first argument relates to the procedural model on which the Brussels regime is built. The regime follows the principal procedural model of the Member States of the EU, which is that of an adversarial contradictory two-party procedure[42], with the potential for limited multiple party proceedings through joinder, inseparability of cases or representative injunctive relief. The general rule in this regard is that the defendant should be sued in their domicile.[43] In certain instances, the defendant can also be sued in other jurisdictions on account of the special[44], protective[45] and exclusive[46] jurisdiction rules, choice of court agreements,[47] or appearance.[48] While procedural rules in these other jurisdictions may differ from those in the defendant's Member State of domicile, the general idea underpinning the Brussels regime is that these procedures are not of a considerably different nature compared to the home state of the defendant and correspond to the right to a fair trial. A defendant may thus face some inconveniences when being sued in another jurisdiction; they will not be dragged into a completely alien model of litigation that compromises the right to a fair trial.

42 F. Gancimartin, "Brussels I instruments: Past, present and… future", Rev. crit. DIP 2018, 479; D. Saam, Kollektive Rechtsbehelfe zur Durchsetzung von Schadenersatzansprüchen im europäischen Wettbewerbs- und Verbraucherrecht (Nomos, 2011), 35.

43 Article 4(1) Brussels I^{bis} Regulation.

44 Article 7 Brussels I^{bis} Regulation.

45 Articles 8–23 Brussels I^{bis} Regulation.

46 Article 24 Brussels I^{bis} Regulation.

47 Article 25 Brussels I^{bis} Regulation.

48 Article 26 Brussels I^{bis} Regulation.

A representative collective redress procedure deviates considerably from the procedural model on which the Brussels regime has been built.[49] It is a new type of procedure that was not foreseen by the drafters of the Brussels Convention[50] and was only marginally considered during the Recast process.[51] This goes a long way to explaining the difficult relationship between collective redress decisions and the Brussels regime.[52] It also means that the Brussels regime has not been developed in order to make decisions given in a representative collective redress procedure circulate throughout the European Union, especially decisions given in opt-out models.[53] This may be an argument in favour of a wider application of the public policy exception to judgments given in such procedures.

3.2. *Collective Redress, European Procedural Culture and Mutual Trust*

A second argument relates to the contentious nature of the policy debate and the differences between the Member States on this point. There is currently no clear consensus on the necessity or desirability of representative collective redress. This can already be gathered from the failure of the 2013 Recommendation mentioned earlier[54] and is further corroborated by data from various studies that have been undertaken in the past couple of years

49 H. Muir Watt, "Collective redress" in J. Basedow, G. Rühl, F. Schiller, F. Ferrari and P. de Miguel Asensio (Eds.), *Encyclopedia of Private International Law* (Edward Elgar, 2017), (373) 376.

50 A. Stadler, "The Commission's Recommendation on common principles of collective redress and private international law issues", *NiPR* 2013, (483) 485; H. Muir Watt, "Collective redress" in J. Basedow, G. Rühl, F. Schiller, F. Ferrari and P. de Miguel Asensio (Eds.), *Encyclopedia of Private International Law* (Edward Elgar, 2017), (373) 376.

51 A. Stadler, "The Commission's Recommendation on common principles of collective redress and private international law issues", *NiPR* 2013, (483) 487.

52 A. Halfmeier, "Recognition of a WCAM settlement in Germany", *NiPR* 2012, (176) 178–179; A. Stadler, "The Commission's Recommendation on common principles of collective redress and private international law issues", *NiPR* 2013, (483) 460.

53 Cf. B. Hess, "Cross-border Collective Litigation and the Regulation Brussels I", *IPRax* 2010, (116) 120–121. See also, A. Stadler, "Conflicts of laws in multinational collective actions – A judicial nightmare?" in D. Fairgrieve and E. Lein (Eds.), *Extraterritoriality and collective redress* (OUP, 2012), (191) 194.

54 See *supra*, section 1.

on collective redress in the EU.[55] Certain Member States appear to have principled objections to the introduction of collective redress.[56] Other Member States agree to the principle but hide behind the need for empirical studies to establish the necessity of such mechanisms[57], these studies being difficult to conduct.[58] Others still question the compatibility of representative collective redress with fundamental rules of civil procedure and constitutional law, especially under an opt-out model.[59] Moreover, not all legal practitioners and judges seem to be convinced of the need to introduce consumer collective redress.[60] The influence of the immediate stakeholders undoubtedly also plays an important role, with consumer associations and businesses finding themselves in opposite positions on the issue.[61] The difficult legislative process of the draft directive on representative actions only provides further evidence of the strong differences that

55 See, inter alia, B. Hess, T. Pfeiffer, M. Mertens and L. Sabanogullari, Evaluation of contributions to the public consultation and hearing: "Towards a coherent European approach to collective redress", Study JUST/2010/JCIV/CT/0027/A4, Executive Summary, 10 (available from http://ec.europa.eu/competition/consultations/2011_collective_redress/index_en.html) (hereafter 'Heidelberg Study'), the MPI Study, and the BIICL Study.

56 E.g., Austria (see *Heidelberg Study*, Evaluation of the contributions to the public consultation and the hearing, 552), Hungary (see *Heidelberg Study*, Evaluation of the contributions to the public consultation and the hearing, 577).

57 E.g., Denmark (see *Heidelberg Study*, Evaluation of the contributions to the public consultation and the hearing, 561).

58 Cf. C. Meller-Hannich and A. Höland, "Gutachten Evaluierung der Effektivität kollektiver Rechtsschutzinstrumente" in Bundesministerium für Ernährung, Landwirtschaft UND VERBRAUCHERSCHUTZ (Ed.), *Schriftenreihe Angewandte Wissenschaft Heft 523* (Bonn, 2011), S. 15 f; *MPI Study*, 16.

59 Cf. *Heidelberg Study*, 10. See also D. FAIRGRIEVE, "The impact of the Brussels I enforcement and recognition rules on collective actions" in D. FAIRGRIEVE and E. LEIN (Eds.), *Extraterritoriality and collective redress* (OUP, 2012), (171) 179–180; M. VERPEAUX, "L'action de groupe est-elle soluble dans la Constitution?", *Dalloz* 2007, 258; M. BACACHE, "Action de groupe et responsabilité civile", *RTD Civ.* 2014, 450; A. STADLER, "EuGVVO nF Art. 45" in H.-J. MUSIELAK and W. VOIT (Eds.), *Zivilprozessordnung mit Gerichtsverfassungsgesetz – Kommentar*, 15th ed. (Vahlen/Beck Online, 2018), Rn. 4. See, however, A. HALFMEIER and P. WIMALASENA, "Rechtsstaatliche Anforderungen an Opt-out-Sammelverfahren: Anerkennung ausländischer Titel und rechtspolitischer Gestaltungsspielraum", *J.Z.* 2012, (649) 652–657.

60 See, for example, *MPI Study*, 260.

61 See, for example, A. Stadler, "Wider die Mär von der europäischen class action", *Verbraucher u. Recht* 2011, (79) 79; H. Willems, "Bemerkungen zu den Brüsseler Gesetzgebungsplänen aus Sicht des Bundesverbands der Deutschen Industrie (BDI)" in C. Brömmelmeyer (Eds.), *Schriften des Frankfurter Instituts für das Recht*

exist between the Member States, leaving scope for very different models of collective redress.

It is thus clear that representative collective redress is currently not part of the common procedural culture of the EU Member States. That conclusion is an important argument in favour of a wider application of the public policy exception; the strict approach being the product of a common understanding of how civil justice should be administered. It is important to underscore that this common understanding has been developed throughout decades and even centuries, culminating in constitutional and fundamental rights standards providing individual litigants with the necessary safeguards to ensure a fair trial. This has in turn laid a strong foundation for mutual trust between the justice systems and judicial decisions of the EU Member States, allowing for the free circulation of judgments and even the abolition of public policy as a ground for refusal, for example in the Payment Order Regulation[62] and the Enforcement Order Regulation.[63] Applying the same standard of public policy to judgments emanating from representative collective redress procedures ignores that evolution and fails to recognise the importance of history and time in building mutual trust.

The importance of time in building mutual trust should indeed not be underestimated. This is clearly visible in the incremental approach of the

---

der Europäischen Union: Die EU-Sammelklage (Nomos, 2013), 17–20 vs G. Billen, "Bemerkungen zu den Brüsseler Gesetzgebungsplänen aus Sicht der Verbraucherzentralen" in C. Brömmelmeyer (Eds.), *Schriften des Frankfurter Instituts für das Recht der Europäischen Union: Die EU-Sammelklage* (Nomos, 2013), 21–28. See also, for example, the opposition of the Austrian undertakings (WKO) against representative collective redress in its elaborate reaction to the 2018 Commission Proposal (https://www.google.com/url?sa=t&rct=j&q=&esrc=s&source=web&cd=2&cad=rja&uact=8&ved=2ahUKEwiBtLG6l8LeAhVCpYsKHdUEAHEQFjABegQICRAC&url=https%3A%2F%2Fwww.wko.at%2Fservice%2Ft%2F732-Richtlinienentwurf-kollektiver-Rechtsschutz-STN-170518.pdf&usg=AOvVaw1zES5s-9pZi-bVwTV9lHhW), which is strongly opposed to collective redress procedures and appears to have an important influence on the political decision-making process in this regard (https://diepresse.com/home/wirtschaft/economist/5284368/Abgasskandal_VWKlagen_Merkels-Umschwung-bringt-die-OeVP-unter). This also resonates in the reasoned opinion of the Austrian Bundesrat on the 2018 Commission Proposal under the Subsidiarity Protocol: see *infra*, fn. 87.

62 Regulation (EC) No 1896/2006 of the European Parliament and of the Council of 12 December 2006 creating a European order for payment procedure, *O.J.* 2006, L 399/1, Recital 27.

63 Regulation (EC) No 805/2004 of the European Parliament and of the Council of 21 April 2004 creating a European Enforcement Order for uncontested claims, *O.J.* 2004, L 142/15, Recital 18.

EU and its Member States towards the regulation of EU civil justice.[64] The existence of a sufficient degree of mutual trust in each other's systems has led Member States to begin with a gradual abolition of exequatur proceedings[65] and grounds for refusal such as public policy, starting at the bottom of the justice system by focussing on low value and uncontested claims, in order to come finally to full equal treatment of foreign and domestic decisions.[66] The Brussels I^{bis} Regulation also fits within this evolution, notwithstanding that progress has been less significant than initially anticipated by the European Commission.[67] Still, the automatic exequatur procedure has been abolished, leaving it to the parties to raise grounds of refusal on account of public policy.[68] It is in this context that judgments emanating from representative compensatory collective redress proceedings should be placed.

Mutual trust appears to be working bottom up in European civil justice. The availability of public policy safeguards against foreign judgments depends on the complexity of procedures and the value of the claim: the lower the value of a claim, the less complex the procedure, the lower the need for public policy exceptions. Conversely, there is a clear argument for a more intensive application of the public policy exception in relation to judgments given in a representative collective redress procedure, based on the complexity of such procedures and their high value.

---

64 M. Zilinsky, "Mutual trust and cross-border enforcement of judgments in civil matters in the EU: Does the step-by-step approach work?", (64) *Netherlands International Law Review* 2017, (115) 137.

65 B. Hess and V. Richard, "Brussel I (Convention and regulation)" in J. Basedow, G. Rühl, F. Schiller, F. Ferrari and P. de Miguel Asensio (Eds.), *Encyclopedia of Private International Law* (Edward Elgar, 2017), (219) 225; X. Kramer, "Cross-border enforcement in the EU: Mutual trust versus fair trial? Towards principles of European civil procedure", (1) *IJPL* 2011, (202) 210–215.

66 Cf. L. D'Avout, "L'efficacité internationale de jugements après la réfonte du Règlement Bruxelles I", (5) *I.J.P.L.* 2015, (239) 245.

67 B. Misoski and I. Rumenov, "The effectiveness of mutual trust in civil and criminal law in the EU" in D. Duić and T. Petrašević (Eds.), *ECLIC Series: Procedural aspects of EU law* (Josip Juraj Strossmayer University of Osijek, 2017), (364) 375.

68 M.J. Scott., "A question of trust? Recognition and enforcement of judgments", *NiPR* 2015, (27) 29.

3.3. Research Questions

A representative collective redress procedure thus does not concern a 'mere difference'[69] of procedural rules that another Member State should automatically accept. Rather, it concerns a fundamental shift in the civil litigation paradigm in Europe[70], requiring Member States to reassess fundamental aspects of the right to a fair trial. This is not business as usual; the impact on the application of the public policy exception should therefore be considered. This leads us to two questions:

Q1: Can the recognition or enforcement of a decision be refused on account of public policy reasons because the Member State of recognition or enforcement is fundamentally opposed to a model of representative collective redress, especially with an opt-out selection mechanism?

Q2: Can the recognition or enforcement of a decision be refused on account of public policy reasons because the Member State of recognition or enforcement deems the procedural design[71] of the representative collective redress procedure to be contrary to public policy?

4. Public Policy and the Model of Representative Remedial Collective Redress

4.1. No per se Refusal of Representative Remedial Collective Redress Decisions

Would a court of a Member State in which strong resistance exists against the introduction of representative collective redress, for example Austria,[72] be able to hold that a decision given in such a kind of procedure in another Member State entails an appreciable deviation of the procedural

69 Cf. A. Halfmeier, "Recognition of a WCAM settlement in Germany", *NiPR* 2012, (176) 180.

70 H. Muir Watt, "Collective redress" in J. Basedow, G. Rühl, F. Schiller, F. Ferrari and P. de Miguel Asensio (Eds.), *Encyclopedia of Private International Law* (Edward Elgar, 2017), (373) 376.

71 Give the central nature of the issue in the political and academic debate, I do not consider the group selection mechanism as a mere element of procedural design. It determines to such an extent the choice for a representative model that it cannot be separated from that choice. The group selection mechanism will also heavily influence all subsequent choices of procedural design, such as publicity, the role of the judge, and funding rules. Therefore, I consider the group selection mechanism to be an indissociable component of the representative model chosen, rather than a mere element of procedural design of a representative procedure.

72 See *supra*, fn. 56.

culture of that Member State to the extent that it constitutes a manifest breach of fundamental rules justifying the application of Article 45(1)(a) Brussels I^{bis} Regulation?[73]

While such a ground of refusal is (was) certainly conceivable, it is likely to be rejected by the Court of Justice, which polices the border of public policy. The ECtHR has held in *Lithgow vs United Kingdom* that the right to an individual procedure can be limited or restricted for legitimate reasons, such as procedural efficiency in mass tort cases, and in a proportionate way.[74] It would thus not be against the right to a fair trial to have a representative collective redress procedure, provided that the necessary safeguards are in place. Recognition and enforcement can therefore not be refused because a judgment is the outcome of a procedure for representative collective redress. The right to a fair trial is not about safeguarding two-party proceedings but about guaranteeing procedural rights. If such procedural rights would be safeguarded in a sufficient manner in the course of a representative collective redress procedure, there is very little reason to see why the recognition or enforcement of a judgment given in such a procedure would be refused on account of public policy.[75] The standard laid down in Article 6 ECHR and Article 47 Charter can be complied with in collective proceedings. It does not impose a traditional model of two-party proceedings.[76]

Moreover, from a comparative law perspective it would be difficult to maintain for any Member State that the individuality of civil proceedings is of such a fundamental nature that it would justify a ground for refusal on the basis of public policy.[77] All Member States know the principle of

---

73 Cf. the example given in R. Fentiman, "Recognition, enforcement and collective judgments" in A. Nuyts and H.E. Hatzimihail (Eds.), *Cross-border class actions – The European way* (Selp, 2014), (85) 90.

74 ECHR, *Lithgow v. United Kingdom*, 8 July 1986, paras 195–197 and 207.

75 See also, BverfG 3 November 2015, 2 BvR 2019/09, DE:BVerfG:2015:rk20151103.2bvr201909, para. 42: "Dies gilt auch für die von deutscher Seite grundsätzlich zu respektierende rechtspolitische Entscheidung, für deliktisches Handeln mit einer Vielzahl von Geschädigten Sammelklagen (class actions) zuzulassen, an denen sich das einzelne Mitglied der „class" nicht beteiligen muss, solange auch im class action -Verfahren unabdingbare Verteidigungsrechte gewahrt bleiben."

76 Cf. R. Fentiman, "Recognition, enforcement and collective judgments" in A. Nuyts and H.E. Hatzimihail (Eds.), *Cross-border class actions – The European way* (Selp, 2014), (85) 93.

77 See M. Stiggelbout, "The recognition in England and Wales of United States judgments in class actions", (52) *Harvard International Law Journal* 2011, (435) 471.

collectivisation of civil proceedings in one way or another. One could point to the assignment of claims, the joinder of proceedings, or the power for consumer associations to bring actions for injunctive relief, which implements the Injunctive Relief Directive.[78] In spite of differences concerning the nature and the model of a collective procedure between the Member States, it is thus difficult to see how the recognition or enforcement of a collective redress decision could be refused because it is the result of a representative action.

Anno 2020, this point has now become moot, as an agreement has been reached by the EU legislator on the adoption of a directive on representative actions, requiring all Member States to introduce a form of representative collective redress.

4.2. No per se Refusal of Opt-Out Systems

4.2.1. Different opinions on the compatibility of an opt-out system with the right to a fair trial

A discussion on the introduction of a procedure for representative collective redress typically goes hand in hand with a discussion on the way in which group members should be selected. Most Member States go in the direction of a representative action whereby the representative is not necessarily part of the affected persons and has not received a specific mandate by such affected persons to act. We will thus focus on representative actions that work without a formal mandate, meaning that group selection is being done on an opt-in or opt-out basis. Moreover, the agreed text of the draft directive also obliges Member States to provide for representative procedures without a formal mandate. Further to this, it is also very unlikely that a mandate type of procedure will cause issues of public policy.[79]

The majority of Member States that have introduced a mechanism of representative collective redress have chosen the opt-in model.[80] This model was also preferred by the European Commission in its 2013 Recom-

78 European Commission 2018 report on collective redress, 3.

79 It cannot be excluded, however, that a court may take issue with the manner in which a mandate was given or the way in which the mandate holder is compensated for the services provided.

80 European Commission 2018 report on collective redress, 13.

mendation.[81] A number of Member States have nevertheless maintained or introduced an opt-out model, either exclusively or together with an opt-in system.[82] They have done so because an opt-out model would be more efficient for certain types of claims or damages.[83]

The adoption of an opt-in model is in most instances the consequence of the rejection of an opt-out model because such model would violate the right to a fair trial provided for by Article 6 ECHR[84] or other constitutional guarantees.[85] Member States that have adopted an opt-out model see this differently and are of the opinion that the lack of individual notification can be sufficiently compensated for by accompanying measures safeguarding the right to a fair trial. It is interesting in this regard to compare the position of the Austrian legislator to the position of the Belgian legislator and the Dutch courts. In its opinion on the 2018 Commission Proposal given pursuant to the Subsidiarity Protocol[86] the Austrian Bundesrat has stated that "*[e]benso wie ein opt-out System würde ein solches System insb. gegen Art. 6 EMRK sowie Art. 47 der Grundrechtecharta der Europäischen Union verstoßen*".[87] The Bundesrat is thus not only opposed to an opt-out model but also appears to have objections against any representative model of remedial collective redress that is not based on an individual mandate. The Belgian legislator on the other hand was of the opinion that an opt-

81 European Commission 2013 Recommendation on collective redress, N° 21.

82 These are Belgium, Bulgaria, Denmark, England and Wales, Portugal, and the Netherlands: *European Commission 2018 report on collective redress*, 13.

83 See D. Fairgrieve and G. Howells, "Collective redress procedures: European debates", (58) *I.C.L.Q.* 2009, (379) 385; M.J. Azar-Baud and S. Carval, "L'action de groupe et la réparation des dommages de consommation: bilan d'étape et préconisations", *Recueil Dalloz* 2015, 2136.

84 See references in X. Kramer, "Securities collective action and private international law issues in Dutch WCAM settlements: Global aspirations and regional boundaries", (27) *Pac. McGeorge Global Bus. & Dev. L.J.* 2014, (235), 268, fn 330.

85 M. Verpeaux, "L'action de groupe est-elle soluble dans la Constitution?", *Dalloz* 2007, 258; M. Bacache, "Action de groupe et responsabilité civile", *RTD Civ.* 2014, 450.

86 Protocol (No 2) to the Treaty on the Function of the European Union on the application of the principles of subsidiarity and proportionality, *O.J.* 2008, C 115/206.

87 Austrian Bundesrat, *Begründete Stellungnahme von 27. Juni 2018*, 25/SB-BR/2018, available at https://www.parlament.gv.at/PAKT/VHG/BR/SB-BR/SB-BR_00025/index.shtml.

out system is compatible with Article 6 ECHR.[88] The Amsterdam Court of Appeal equally rejected the argument that the WCAM[89] violated Article 6 ECHR, the law sufficiently guaranteeing the right to be heard and the right to be notified.[90] How would an Austrian court act when the *res judicata* effect of a Dutch WCAM judgment is being invoked before it?

Imagine an Austrian small business owner seeking compensation in Austrian courts from Volkswagen for damages sustained as a consequence of the Diesel Gate. Volkswagen objects by referring to the *res judicata* effect of a judgment of the Amsterdam Court of Appeal, approving a settlement under an opt-out system for all Volkswagen customers in the European Union. The Austrian small business owner claims to be unaware of the existence of the Dutch judgment and can also no longer apply for compensation since the time-limit to submit claims to the claims foundation has elapsed. Would it then be possible for an Austrian court to refuse recognition of the Dutch judgment by relying on the public policy exception as the decision was given in an opt-out procedure?[91]

---

88 Belgian Chamber of Representatives, Projet de loi portant insertion d'un titre 2 "De l'action en réparation collective" au livre XVII "Procédures juridictionnelles particulières" du Code de droit économique et portant insertion des définitions propres au livre XVII dans le livre I du Code de droit économique, 17 January 2014, N° 53 3301/001, 30. See also, S. Voet, *Een Belgische vertegenwoordigende collectieve rechtsvordering* (Intersentia, 2012), 288–290. This contrasts with the opinion of the French legislator, who deemed an opt-out approach to be contrary to the Constitution, in light of a judgment of the French Conseil constitutionnel of 25 July 1989. See French Senate, *Rapport d'information sur l'action de groupe*, 2009–2010, N° 499, 74–76.

89 This is the acronym for the Dutch collective settlements act, to which reference is made throughout this presentation. It is formed by the letters of its Dutch name: Wet Collectieve Afhandeling Massaschade.

90 Amsterdam Court of Appeal, 25 January 2007, NL:GHAMS:2007:AZ7033, points 5.6 – 5.8.

91 Based on an example given in R. Fentiman, "Recognition, enforcement and collective judgments" in A. Nuyts and H.E. Hatzimihail (Eds.), *Cross-border class actions – The European way* (Selp, 2014), (85) 90. This situation may change when the exclusion of opt-out selection mechanisms for non-habitual residents, as provided for in the Council Common Position, will make it into law. Moreover, the new Dutch judicial collective redress procedure functions exclusively on an opt-in basis for non-habitual residents. This may also affect the evaluation by a foreign judge of a WCAM settlement obtained on an opt-out basis.

4.2.2. Service and defaulting defendants

It is instructive in this regard to look at the Court of Justice's case law on knowledge about proceedings and the protection of defaulting defendants under Article 45(1)(b) Brussels I^{bis} Regulation.[92] While group members are not in the same situation as defaulting defendants, it is a good point of departure to evaluate the approach of the Court of Justice to the absence of proper notification in light of the rights of the defence.[93]

4.2.2.1. Full information about proceedings

We start with the case law of the Court of Justice on fictitious service, as this has a strong resemblance to notification by public summons, a method of notification typically associated with opt-out procedures. While the Court of Justice is not opposed to fictitious service *per se*, it considers that it should only be available as a means of last resort, after all investigations required by the principles of diligence and good faith have been undertaken to trace the defendant.[94] This is not the case for representative collective redress proceedings, where summons by public notice is not perceived as a means of last resort but rather as an ordinary means of service,

92 Cf. A. Haflmeier, "Recognition of a WCAM settlement in Germany", *N.I.P.R.* 2012, (176) 183.

93 Cf. T. Bosters, Collective redress and private international in the EU (Springer, 2017), 206.

94 Judgment of 17 November 2011, *Hypoteční banka*, C-327/10, EU:C:2011:745, para. 52; Judgment of 15 March 2012, *De Visser*, C-292/10, EU:C:2012:142, para. 59. The requirement in civil law systems is that fictitious service is a means of last resort. It is therefore problematic to infer from the existence of the notion of fictitious service in a particular legal order the acceptance of notice by public summons in a collective redress procedure by that legal order. The same goes for inferring from the practice of public notices to inform the public of planning permissions or other events, thereby activating the time-limit for raising objections or bringing annulment proceedings, an acceptance of summons by public notice in opt-out collective redress procedures. The protection of an interest does not carry the same weight as the protection of a right and is thus deserving of less protection. One should thus refrain from comparing apples and oranges. See, however, A. Halfmeier, "Recognition of a WCAM settlement in Germany", *N.I.P.R.* 2012, (176) 183.

next to individual notice.[95] That being said, the standard in the case law of the Court is not that of personal service as such but of whether the goal of service has been realised[96], namely whether the person concerned has had an opportunity to take part in adversarial proceedings leading to a judgment affecting their legal situation. It is interesting to refer to the judgment in *Denilauler*[97] in this regard, in which the Court was asked whether the referring court had to recognise and enforce a decision emanating from unilateral proceedings in which the defendant was not summonsed to appear and which were intended to be enforced without prior service. The Court stated that the Brussels regime is "fundamentally concerned with judicial decisions which, before the recognition and enforcement of them are sought in a State other than the State of origin, have been, or have been capable of being, the subject in that State of origin and under various procedures, of an inquiry in adversary proceedings".[98] The lack of the service of a document instituting the proceedings and of the judgment on the defendant made such an inquiry impossible, leading the Court to conclude that a judgment given in such a procedure could not benefit from the regime established by the Brussels Convention.[99]

We will not go into a discussion about whether judgments given in a representative collective redress procedure should be excluded from the scope of the Brussels I^{bis} Regulation. The EU legislator has indicated during the recast process that this should not be the case and also the agreed text of the directive on representative actions refers to the application of the Brussels I^{bis} Regulation.[100] Nevertheless, the judgment remains relevant for our discussion as it clearly illustrates the Court's standard, namely that service should be viewed as a means to facilitate the possibility for parties to take part in adversarial proceedings. This was not possible in the procedure in *Denilauler* because it concerned individual litigation of which the defendant was not notified by any means. The situation may thus be different in the case of representative collective redress proceedings, where pub-

95 It should be highlighted that, within reasonabel bounds, individual notice is a requirement in (many) represenative procedures based on an opt-out selection model. See, for example, *Eisen v. Carlisle & Jacquelin*, 417 U.S. 156 (1974).

96 F. Gascon Inchausti, "Service of proceedings on the defendant as a safeguard of fairness in civil proceedings: in search of minimum standards from EU legislation and European case law", (13) *J.P.I.L.* 2017, (475) 499–501.

97 Judgment of 21 May 1980, *Denilauler*, 125/79, EU:C:1980:130.

98 *Denilauler*, para. 13.

99 *Denilauler*, para. 17.

100 Article 2(3) Draft Directive.

lic notice may allow interested parties to take part in the proceedings – or to exclude themselves from the proceedings.

Public notice may thus achieve the goals of service. The question is which standard applies. Does it suffice that an interested party is made aware of the existence of proceedings or should more information be provided? The judgment in *ASML*[101] may provide guidance in this regard. In that case the Court had to deal with the question whether the possibility of a defendant to challenge a default judgment in the Member State of origin depended on the due service of the default judgment or whether awareness of the default judgment obtained through other notifications, such as service of the order on the application for a declaration of enforceability, was sufficient. The Court answered that the defendant should be able to acquaint themself with the grounds of the default judgment[102] and that the mere fact that the person concerned was aware of the existence of that judgment was insufficient in that regard.[103] Service of the default judgment was thus required.[104] The decision is relevant because the Court of Justice draws a parallel between the service of the default judgment and the document instituting proceedings.[105] It appears that awareness of the commencement or existence of a procedure is thus not sufficient and that actual service of the document instituting proceedings is required in sufficient time and in such a way as to allow the defendant to prepare for their defence.[106] That being said, one should again consider the goal pursued by service here. It is not about service as such but about giving the interested party the opportunity to acquaint themself with the particulars of the case in order to prepare a defence. A comprehensive public notice informing interested parties of a pending representative collective redress procedure and all its implications, given in a timely manner, may thus meet the Court's standard. This would allow parties (not) to opt out of proceedings with full knowledge of the consequences.

101 Judgment of 14 December 2004, *ASML*, C-283/05, EU:C:2006:787.
102 *ASML*, para. 35.
103 *ASML*, para. 34.
104 *ASML*, para. 40.
105 *ASML*, paras 42–43.
106 *ASML*, para. 43.

4.2.2.2. Participation in adversarial proceedings

The Court of Justice has made a direct link between service and the opportunity to participate in adversarial proceedings in its judgment in *Denilauler*.[107] The importance of that link has been further highlighted in various cases concerning the practice of substituted service, in which the Court held that service on a guardian *ad litem* may not be considered as an acceptance of jurisdiction by the absent defendant. According to the Court, an absent defendant must always have the possibility to challenge the jurisdiction of the court on the basis of Article 45(1)(b) Brussels I^{bis} Regulation.[108] The Court did not consider the possibility for the guardian *ad litem* to challenge the jurisdiction of the court a sufficient guarantee for the absent defendant because they may not have the required information necessary to challenge international jurisdiction in an effective manner, which can only be provided by the absent defendant.[109] The Court's decision fits within the system of protection established by the Brussels Regime. Accepting substituted service as a valid method would have made the protection of the absent defendant by the Brussels I^{bis} Regulation redundant as they would be denied any opportunity to take part in adversarial proceedings. Should a similar level of protection be available to absent group members?

It may be tempting to argue that the situation of the absent group member mirrors the situation of the untraceable defendant. Jurisdiction to which the absent group member has not consented is established through an act of service by the party who represents them without having explicitly agreed to such representation. Even worse, the absent group member does not benefit from the protection of Article 45(1)(b) Brussels I^{bis} Regulation.[110]

However, when we delve deeper into the underlying premises of the Court's case law on substituted service, it appears that the similarity is false. In his opinion in *A v B*, Advocate General Y. Bot examines why ficti-

107 *Denilauler*, para. 13.

108 *A v B*, para. 60; *Hypoteční banka*, paras 53–54; Judgment of 10 October 1996, *Hendrikman*, C-78/95, EU:C:1996:380, para. 18.

109 *A v B*, para. 55.

110 Unless one would subscribe to the particular interpretation of the procedural position of a group member under the Dutch WCAM, namely as defendants who could make use of Article 45(1)(b) Brussels I^{bis} Regulation to resist recognition. For a discussion of this point, see H. van Lith, *The Dutch Collective Settlements Act and private international law* (Maklu, 2011), 42–45.

tious service on a representative *in absentia* is problematic from the point of view of the defaulting defendant. It immediately appears from this that these reasons do not apply to the situation of a group member represented in a collective redress procedure. First, contrary to a representative *in absentia* acting on behalf of a defaulting defendant[111], the representative in a collective procedure has in principle all the necessary information available to them to defend the interests of the group members sufficiently. Second, whereas a representative *in absentia* may not have sufficient facts to contest the jurisdiction of the court seised by the applicant, possibly leading it to accept jurisdiction through appearance[112], the group representative can only bring a case in line with the jurisdiction rules of the Brussels I^bis^ Regulation. There is thus no risk that the general scheme of the Brussels I^bis^ Regulation will be distorted: the jurisdictions in which a group representative can bring a collective procedure remain highly predictable and generally based on the defendant's domicile.[113] Third, the inability for a defaulting defendant to choose their own lawyer in the situation of a representative *in absentia* is less problematic for group members in a representative action since the group representative typically has to adhere to a number of qualitative criteria that have to be checked by the judge presiding over the action. In sum, while the case law on fictitious service on a representative *in absentia* or a guardian *ad litem* may appear not to allow public summons unreservedly, it is clear that the premises on which this case law is built do not apply to the situation of summons by public notice in the case of a representative collective redress procedure. The different situation of a group member compared to a defaulting defendant would thus justify a different balance of interests to be struck, with potentially a lower standard of service.[114]

4.2.3. *A need for appropriate safeguards*

The case law on service of the Court of Justice allows for alternative means of service, provided that the defendant has a genuine opportunity to take

111 Opinion of Advocate General Y. Bot of 2 April 2014, *A v B*, C-112/13, EU:C:2014:207, para. 47.

112 AG Opinion in *A v B*, para. 47.

113 *A v B*, para. 57.

114 See M. Stiggelbout, "The recognition in England and Wales of United States judgments in class actions", (52) *Harvard International Law Journal* 2011, (435) 484–485.

part in adversarial proceedings. That participation constitutes in turn a guarantee that the court hearing the case is properly informed about the facts of the case and that the arguments of the defendant are being taken into account by the court in deciding the case. Like service, participation in adversarial proceedings is thus not an end in itself but should be considered in a functional way. What is crucial is that the interests of the persons concerned are properly addressed in full knowledge of all relevant facts and circumstances.

In the course of two-party proceedings, the proper representation of the interests of a party in full knowledge of all relevant facts and circumstances is virtually impossible without the actual participation of the parties concerned.[115] The situation is different, however, for representative collective redress proceedings. The nature of cases typically litigated by such proceedings allows for the interests of the group members to be sufficiently protected by way of a group representative. The representative can be sufficiently informed about the common problems of the group members, allowing them to present the court with a full picture of the case. Moreover, it can be expected, in principle, that a genuine group representative will sufficiently represent the interests of the group.[116] A Member State may provide for a number of safeguards to guarantee the quality of the representation, *inter alia* by providing qualitative criteria before the status of group representative can be obtained or by giving interested parties or third parties the possibility to control the way in which a group representative performs their tasks. In addition to this, other safeguards may be provided, guaranteeing group members the right not to be bound against their will by the outcome of the collective redress procedure and their right to be heard in the procedure.

Coming back to our fictitious example, I believe that it would not be justified for the Austrian judge to refuse recognition of a judgment for the mere reason that it was given in an opt-out representative collective procedure. Such procedures are compatible with Article 6 ECHR and Article 47 Charter of Fundamental Rights, provided that the necessary safeguards are

---

115 Either in person, through a lawyer or through a representative who acts on the basis of an explicit mandate. This guarantees that personal contact exists between the actual party and their representative, who is then presumed to act with knowledge of all the relevant facts and in the interests of the represented party.

116 On the question of who should be allowed to act as a group representative, see S. Voet, "Cultural dimensions of group litigation: The Belgian case", (41) *Georgia Journal of International and Comparative Law* 2013, (433) 457–464.

provided for. It is to these safeguards that we will turn now, as it appears from (limited) national practice that the existence of safeguards and/or their application will determine the fate of a judgment given in an opt-out procedure[117], rather than the opt-out nature of a collective procedure as such.[118]

5. *Public Policy and Safeguarding Individual Procedural Rights through Procedural Design*

5.1. *General*

Money-Kyrle and Hodges have identified three types of safeguards to compensate for the collectivisation of individual litigious relationships: substantive controls, procedural controls, and financial and economic controls.[119] Substantive controls concern the field of law in which representative actions are available or the type of rights for which they can be used.[120] For example, various Member States have limited the introduction of compensatory collective redress mechanisms to consumer law or competition law.[121] Moreover, certain types of collective redress mechanisms, such as opt-out compensatory collective redress, may not be available for specific types of claims, such as claims for personal injury[122] or non-material damage.[123] Financial and economic controls mainly deal with rules on the funding of collective procedures, e.g. whether third-party funding is possi-

117 Cf. Ghent Court of Appeal, 23 March 2017. See also *infra*, point 7.4.

118 For England and Wales, see M. Stiggelbout, "The recognition in England and Wales of United States judgments in class actions", (52) *Harvard International Law Journal* 2011, (435) 472; for France, see O. Kafi-Cherrat, "La class action s'approche : à propos de la reconnaissance en Belgique des class action settlements américains (Aff. Lernout & Hauspie)", (145) *Journal du droit international (Clunet)* 2018, 81–96 and C. Seraglini, "Les effets en France des actions de groupe étrangères" in Comité français de Droit International Privé (Ed.), *Droit international privé – Travaux 2008–2010* (Pedone, 2011), (157) 175–179, but *contra*, and followed by the French legislator, M. Verpeaux, "L'action de groupe est-elle soluble dans la Constitution?", *Dalloz* 2007, 258.

119 R. Money-Kyrle and C. Hodges, "European collective action: towards coherence", (19) *Maastricht Journal of European & Comparative Law* (2012), (477) 483.

120 R. Money-Kyrle and C. Hodges, "European collective action: towards coherence", (19) *Maastricht Journal of European & Comparative Law* (2012), (477) 483.

121 European Commission 2018 report on collective redress, 3.

122 Cf. Belgium (Article XVII.43 § 2, 3° Economic Law Code).

123 Cf. France (Article L. 623–2 Code de la consommation).

ble, the award of costs and whether collective procedures may entail a speculative purpose.[124] Procedural controls focus on preventing abusive litigation and guaranteeing the procedural rights of the parties and the group members by providing for procedural safeguards that mitigate the departure from the fundamental procedural rights that come with individual litigation.[125] The focus hereafter is on these procedural controls, namely the safeguards incorporated in the procedural design of representative actions to guarantee the standard laid down by the right to a fair trial.

A comparative law analysis discloses that procedural safeguards in representative collective redress procedures vary considerably between EU Member States.[126] This can be explained by the fact that many Member States have developed their model of representative collective redress in response to a particular national event.[127] These *ad hoc* answers have led to unique procedural models, reconciling the national policy preferences for collective litigation with the fundamental right to a fair trial.

Starting from the premise that a representative collective redress mechanism has been developed by a rational legislator, it can be expected that each Member State has developed a model that maximises the efficiency of the collective procedure while keeping in line with the right to a fair trial. This implies that each Member State has made an individual determination about the maximum possible extent to which individual procedural rights can be limited for the purposes of facilitating collective proceedings. Given that national courts take their own model as a benchmark for determining whether a violation of public policy exists,[128] a wider application of the public policy exception may then be expected in Member States that have adopted a higher procedural standard. This may manifest itself either

---

124 R. Money-Kyrle and C. Hodges, "European collective action: towards coherence", (19) *Maastricht Journal of European & Comparative Law* (2012), (477) 497.

125 R. Money-Kyrle and C. Hodges, "European collective action: towards coherence", (19) *Maastricht Journal of European & Comparative Law* (2012), (477) 483.

126 C. Hodges and S. Voet, *Delivering collective redress* (Hart/Beck/Nomos, 2018), 283.

127 D. Fairgrieve and G. Howells, "Collective redress procedures: European debates", (58) *I.C.L.Q.* 2009, (379) 394; E. De Baere, "De Nederlandse class settlement: over de wet collectieve afwikkeling massaschade en haar internationale impact", *Tijdschrift voor Privaatrecht* 2013, (2563) 2568–2569; T. Bosters, *Collective redress and private international law in the EU* (Springer, 2017), 29–30.

128 Ghent Court of Appeal, 23 March 2017, unpublished. See also, Ghent Court of Appeal, 17 April 2008, www.dipr.be 2009 (2), 75. See further, M. Stiggelbout, "The recognition in England and Wales of United States judgments in class actions", (52) *Harvard International Law Journal* 2011, (435) 470.

through intensive scrutiny of judgments given in a foreign representative collective redress procedure with a lower procedural standard or more refusals of recognition and enforcement of such judgments. Consequently, the issue of public policy essentially comes down to the following question: has an appropriate balance been struck between individual litigation rights and the efficiency of collective redress proceedings?

5.2. Identification of Issues

Let us now take a look at a number of potential problems in relation to procedural design. We undertake this analysis from the perspective of the defendant and the individual group member, who may be a claimant in individual proceedings. The position of the group representative is as such less relevant as problems concerning the right to a fair trial mainly affect the defendant or the individual group members.

5.2.1. In relation to individual group members

The procedural safeguards for an individual group member should be determined by taking the procedural rights they would enjoy as an individual claimant as a starting point. This is in the first place *the right to bring proceedings*. That right is compromised by a representative collective redress procedure and thus safeguards protecting the individual's right to bring proceedings should be put in place. First of all, there should be a good reason to depart from the individual litigation model in a specific case. Thus, before any other safeguards are activated to protect the right to bring proceedings, which would necessarily require activity of potential group members, a safeguard should allow for an independent evaluation of the justified nature of a collective procedure.[129] A requirement of appropriateness, to be evaluated by a judge or another party, may be envisaged here.[130]

The appropriateness of a collective procedure should, however, not automatically lead to an exclusion of the right to individual litigation – this would constitute a disproportionate restriction of that right. The owner of the right should be given an opportunity to give up or retain her

129 Cf. Portugal (Article 13 Law on Popular Action).
130 Cf. Belgium (Article XVII.36, 2° Code of Economic Law).

or his right to bring individual proceedings. The main tool would be to provide the owner of such right with a choice, either by requiring a positive action of the individual person to take part in a collective procedure (opt-in) or by giving the individual person the option not to take part in the collective procedure (opt-out). This is a defining feature of every collective procedure because the choice will determine the additional safeguards and thus the outlook of the collective procedure. That being said, safeguards will not differ radically between an opt-in procedure and an opt-out procedure. It should not be forgotten that the outcome of an opt-in procedure may have an impact on subsequent individual litigation, which makes it necessary to give an individual person a genuine opportunity to decide whether to opt-in into a collective procedure, especially when individual litigation is not viable[131] – just as an individual person must be given a genuine opportunity to opt-out of a collective procedure. Key procedural safeguards in this respect are rules allowing for a proper notification of potential group members and ample time to decide to opt-in or to opt-out. Depending on the nature of the procedure these safeguards may differ in their intensity: a failure to opt-out has a larger impact on the right to bring proceedings than a failure to opt-in. Opt-out procedures are thus likely to provide for more ambitious notification measures and longer time periods to decide on participation in the collective procedure.

The right to bring proceedings as an individual claimant may also pervade the course of the proceedings after a decision to take part has been made, by giving the group members the ability to influence the proceedings.[132] These types of safeguards will, however, mainly be developed in light of the protection of the right to a fair trial, which is the second right that is being compromised.

The *right to a fair trial* has a general meaning and is not only concerned with individual litigation. However, most guarantees attaching to the right to a fair trial have been developed in relation to the dominant litigation model of two-party proceedings. The result is a set of rights that is conditioned by the model of individual litigation, conferring upon an individual litigant certain prerogatives that are characterised by their individuality, such as personal notice and the right to be heard. It is impossible to guarantee the same level of individuality in the course of collective proceedings as this would largely undermine the reasons for their existence. A

131 J.P. Davis, E.L. Cramer and C.V. May, "The puzzle of class actions with uninjured members", (82) *The George Washington Law Review* 2014, (858) 872.

132 Cf. The Netherlands (Article 282(1) Code of Civil Procedure).

compromise must thus necessarily be struck. It is important in this regard to look at the function of the right to a fair trial. This right has been developed with a view to allowing an individual party to provide the court with all the necessary information, in law and in fact, in order for it to come to a decision taking into account the arguments of both sides, taken in independent and impartial fashion. What is key is that an individual party's interests are properly addressed in the course of the proceedings and that a judge disposes over all necessary factual and legal elements – we leave the question of independence and impartiality of the judge aside.

The most important guarantee for a proper representation of the group members is a qualitative group representative. Legislative conditions regarding composition, statutory goals, experience, independence, administrative structure and financial soundness may provide for such a guarantee. Additionally, a requirement of representativeness may be included[133], requiring the group representative to attest to being representative for the group of potential individual claimants. This would also be in the interest of the defendant, for the outcome of a collective procedure conducted by a non-representative representative may not provide the defendant with the advantage of having the issue settled with all potential claimants. Further to this, requiring the presiding judge – or another body[134] – to take an active stance during proceedings and to guard the interests of the represented group members would further contribute to the goal of proper representation of the individual group members.[135]

These safeguards can vary in degree. Ideally, they reflect the degree of dependency of the individual group member on the group representative for conducting the procedure. This means that safeguards should be stronger in an opt-out procedure than an opt-in procedure. The selection mechanism is, however, not the only parameter to take into account. Dependency may also vary as a result of the moment in the procedure when the option to join or leave proceedings has to be exercised, i.e. before or after a decision on the existence of fault, liability and damage.[136] (Potential) group members that are required to make a decision before the merits

133 Cf. The Netherlands (Article 907(3)(f) Civil Code).

134 Cf. Portugal (Article 16 Law on Popular Action: The Portuguese public prosecutor is tasked with overseeing the collective redress procedure and whether the group representative acts in line with the interest of the group members.).

135 E. Falla, The role of the court in collective redress litigation (Larcier, 2014), 156–170.

136 Or, in case of a collective settlement procedure, before or after a settlement has been reached.

phase has started[137] or before the judge has taken a decision on the merits[138], will be much more dependent upon the group representative than (potential) group members in a procedure where the option only has to be exercised after the merits phase, and they can do so with full knowledge of the decision of the judge.[139] Another feature that is relevant in this regard concerns the possibility of individual group members to take part in the collective procedure by submitting statements or to oppose certain actions of the group representative.[140] Such an option injects a strong element of individuality in the collective procedure and not only safeguards the right to a fair trial but also the right to bring individual proceedings. That right can further be safeguarded at the end of the collective procedure by allowing individual group members to bring an appeal against the collective redress judgment.[141]

5.2.2. In relation to the defendant

Safeguards should not only be available to individual group members.[142] The defendant in a collective procedure may also lose a number of procedural rights, namely the right to defend themself against individual claims.[143] This is not a trivial matter. It has been pointed out in the literature that not all individual group members in a successful collective redress procedure would receive the same amount of compensation – or any at all – when conducting individual litigation, for example because they would not be able to meet the burden of proof in their individual

---

137 Cf. Belgium (Article XVII. 38 § 1 *juncto* Article XVII. 43 § 2, 7° Code of Economic Law) and Germany (§ 608(1) ZPO).

138 Cf. Portugal (Article 15(4) Law on Popular Action).

139 Cf. France (Article L. 623–4 Code de la consommation) and The Netherlands (Article 908(2) Civil Code *juncto* Article 1017(3) Code of Civil Procedure).

140 Cf. The Netherlands (Article 1013(5) *juncto* Article 282(1) Code of Civil Procedure).

141 For a discussion on this point, see T.A. Duffy, "The appealability of class action settlements by unnamed parties", (60) *The University of Chicago Law Review* 1993, 933–956.

142 S.I. Strong, "Cross-Border Collective Redress and Individual Participatory Rights: Quo vadis?", 32 *Civil Justice Quarterly*, (508) 514–515.

143 See for a discussion in the US context on this point, M.K. Grimaldi, "Trying class actions: The complex task of managing and resolving individual issues in class trials, (36) *The Review of Litigation – The Brief* 2017, (90) 93–96.

case.[144] There must thus exist a good justification to depart from the individual nature of litigation. This would be especially so for an opt-out procedure, as the defendant will not be able to assess in a precise manner the scope of the claim and the risks to which they are exposed. Additionally, a defendant should be protected against the abusive use of collective redress litigation[145], inspired by other motives than seeking redress for illegal behaviour. A requirement of appropriateness of collective litigation, assessed by the judge or an independent party, is thus equally important for a defendant as it is for an interested party. The same goes for the quality requirements imposed upon the group representative. It is important for the defendant that the group representative has the capacity to conduct the proceedings in an orderly manner and that they are sufficiently representative for potential individual claimants. Only a qualitative and representative group representative may justify a departure from individual litigation in favour of collective litigation.

Other potential safeguards for the defendant may conflict with potential safeguards for the interested parties. Take for example the function of service in light of the rights of the defence. A defendant is served with a claim form in order to inform them about the proceedings and to allow for a timely preparation of the defence. This implies that the object of the proceedings is clearly stated in the claim form that is served on the defendant, including the scope of the claim. That information is, however, not readily available from the outset in collective proceedings that operate under an option system, especially in an opt-out model. In order for the defendant to prepare their defence properly it may thus be preferred to structure a collective procedure in such a way that the group selection takes place at a very early stage, ideally before the merits phase.[146] This may in turn conflict with potential guarantees for interested parties, as their right to bring proceedings on an individual basis may be better safeguarded by placing the selection mechanism at the end of the merits phase.[147]

144 J.P. Davis, E.L. Cramer and C.V. May, "The puzzle of class actions with uninjured members", (82) *The George Washington Law Review* 2014, (858) 868.

145 Cf. European Commission, Communication from the Commission to the European Parliament, the Council, the European Economic and Social Committee and the Committee of the Regions: Towards a European horizontal framework for collective redress, COM(2013) 401 final, 7–8.

146 Cf. Belgium and Germany, see *supra* fn. 137.

147 Cf. France and The Netherlands, see *supra* fn. 139.

Another safeguard for the defendant would consist in providing for a procedure allowing for the exclusion of individual group members.[148] This would mitigate the loss of chance to defend themself on an individual basis. Group selection must therefore be done in a transparent manner, allowing the defendant to identify undeserving group members.[149] An alternative option would be to split the procedure into a representative declaratory phase and an individual compensation phase.[150] This would also allow overcoming problems associated with determining the total amount of damages in a collective procedure under an opt-out model.[151]

Lastly, a choice for collective litigation implies that this type of litigation would appear to be more appropriate to deal with an issue than individual litigation. The appropriateness functions in this regard as a justification for the limitation of a purely individual approach to the rights of the defence. The credibility of that justification would be compromised, and thus the reason for a departure from the full application of the rights of the defence, if individual group members would be allowed to continue with individual litigation. Rules should therefore be put in place regulating the impact of a representative action on individual litigation. An automatic suspension of all pending cases between individual group members and the defendant is a possibility in this regard.[152] The scope of the *res judicata* effect of the final decision would also be of relevance here.[153] That being said, these rules must be balanced with safeguards protecting absent group members in an opt-out procedure[154], requiring decision-makers to strike a delicate balance between the procedural rights of individual group members, the defendant, and the efficiency of collective litigation. In

148 Cf. Belgium (Article XVII. 58, § 3 Code of Economic Law) and France (Article L 623–19 Code de la consummation).

149 A. Zuckerman, *Zuckerman on civil procedure*, 3rd Ed. (Sweet & Maxwell, 2013), 664.

150 Cf. Germany.

151 In regard of the Netherlands, see E. De Baere, "De Nederlandse class settlement: Over de Wet Collectieve Afwikkeling Massaschade en haar internationale impact", *T.P.R.* 2013, (2563) 2601–2605.

152 Cf. Belgium (Article XVII. 69 Code of Economic Law) and The Netherlands (Article 1015(1) Code of Civil Procedure). See on the compatibility of such rules with requirements of EU consumer law: Judgment of 14 April 2016, *Sales Sinués*, C-381/14 and C-385/14, EU:C:2016:252.

153 A. Pina, "Recognition and res judicata of US class action judgments in European legal systems", *Erasmus Law Review* 2008, (31) 38.

154 It is indeed all a question about balancing rights in this context. See, S.I. Strong, "Cross-Border Collective Redress and Individual Participatory Rights: Quo vadis?", 32 *Civil Justice Quarterly*, (508) 516–518.

Brazil, for example, the preclusionary effects of a decision in a collective redress opt-out procedure are only extended to absent group members when favourable to them (*res judicata secundum eventum litis*).[155]

5.3. A Few Examples

In the previous section we have set out in a general way the various possibilities for Member States to ensure that the right to a fair trial is safeguarded in representative collective redress proceedings; this both for individual group members and the defendant. In the following subsection we will look more closely at a number of those safeguards, highlighting certain differences between Member States that may be problematic in light of recognition and enforcement.

5.3.1. Notification measures

We have already briefly touched upon the issue of notification in the section devoted to opt-out procedures. Notification rules are a key safeguard for the functioning of opt-out procedures. There may be various differences in design of these notification rules, some leading to a more comprehensive public notification of collective proceedings than others.

Under the Dutch WCAM procedure[156], a system of double notification is provided for by the law. The first notification takes place upon the application to the court to have a settlement declared binding, allowing interested parties to intervene in the procedure.[157] Notification of the application is effectuated through personal notice to interested persons known by the applicants, unless the judge decides otherwise, and through publica-

155 A. Gidi, "The recognition of U.S. class action judgments abroad: The case of Latin America", (37) *Brooklyn Journal of International Law 2012*, (893) 913–914.

156 I refer to the Dutch rules on the collective settlement procedure (WCAM) and not the newly introduced collective redress procedure, provided for by a Law of 29 January 2019 (Wet afwikkeling massaschade in collectieve actie or WAMCA) and which entered into force on 1 January 2020. This law allows for judicial representative collective redress and no longer depends on the willingness of the defendant to take part in settlement proceedings. Contrary to the WCAM, the WAMCA provides for both an opt-in and an opt-out selection mechanism, the latter not being available for persons not habitually resident in the Netherlands.

157 Article 282(1) Dutch Code of Civil Procedure.

tion in one or more newspapers determined by the judge. A judge may also decide to disseminate information in a different way.[158] The second notification takes place following the decision of the court to declare the settlement binding, allowing interested parties to opt-out of the settlement.[159] Unless the judge decides otherwise, known interested parties receive personal notice of the court's decision. The decision will also be published in one or more newspapers determined by the judge and the judge may order additional means of publication.[160] The comprehensiveness of the Dutch model contrasts with the notification requirements under the Belgian and Portuguese models. Belgium requires the publication of the admissibility decision in the Belgian State Gazette and on the website of the Federal Ministry of Economy.[161] Further to this, the judge may decide on additional notification measures, including individual notification, if the judge considers the measures prescribed by the law to be insufficient in the particular case.[162] In Portugal notification is required in news media or through public notice, depending on whether the interest is general or geographically limited.[163] In case of the latter, public notice can suffice. This may be done by placing a notice on the door of the court house and on the door of the municipal council.[164]

The limited scope of notification has been criticized heavily by some Portuguese commentators, considering it an unconstitutional attack on the right to court.[165] The rules do, however, not differ greatly from the Belgian rules, apart from the fact that Portuguese courts lack the powers to provide for additional notification measures. Yet, the notification require-

158 Article 1013(5) Dutch Code of Civil Procedure.

159 Article 7:908 Dutch Civil Code.

160 Article 1018(3) Dutch Code of Civil Procedure.

161 Article XVII.43 § 3 Belgian Code of Economic Law.

162 Article XVII.43 § 2, 9° Belgian Code of Economic Law.

163 Article 15, para. 2, Law on Popular Action (Lei 83/95 de Acção Popular). The provision regarding the publication of the final judgment is much more specific, requiring publication in at least two newspapers which can be expected to be read by group members. See Article 19, para. 2, Law on Popular Action.

164 C. Gonçalves Borges and M. Serra Baptista, "Portugal" in P.G. Karlsgodt (Ed.), *World class actions. A guide to group and representative actions around the globe* (OUP, 2012), (312) 319.

165 M.F. Gouveia and N. Garoupa, "Class actions in Portugal" in J.G. Backhaus, A. Cassone and G.B. Ramello (Eds.), *The law and economics of class actions in Europe – Lessons from America* (Edward Elgar, 2012), (342) 345–346; J. Lebre de Freitas, "La acción popular en el derecho Portugués" in A. Gidi and A.F. Mac-Gregor (Eds.), *Procesos Collectivos. La tutela de los derechos difusos, colectivos e individuales en una perspective comparada* (Editorial Porrúa, 2003), (381) 391–392.

ments are not considered to be problematic by Belgian commentators. This is because in practice widespread notification of the action will be effected by the group representative, mostly the main Belgian consumer organisation, via their website, advertisements and the media. Such is not guaranteed in Portugal, as the popular action may also be brought by a natural person without a proper network to achieve meaningful notification – it may be argued that this point of criticism, which has been popular with some legal commentators in Portugal, might now be less relevant in light of the technical developments that have taken place in the past decade. Moreover, Belgian law allows a group member to submit a request to the court to leave the group at any point in time after the time-limit to exercise the opt-out has ceased and even after the court has issued its final judgment on account that they could reasonably not have been aware of the collective procedure.[166] Group members in the Portuguese procedure can only opt-out until the moment evidence of the claim is being heard by the Portuguese court.[167]

One may point out that this is an entirely internal debate because both Belgium and Portugal have excluded the application of opt-out procedures in relation to foreign group members. This does not make problems of notification less relevant in a cross-border setting, however. The ever increasing cross-border market for goods and services combined with the gradual generalisation of collective redress in the Member States of the European Union[168] means that a consumer is likely to have at least two fora for collective litigation at their disposal, namely that of their place of residence and the place of residence of the defendant. Portuguese consumers may be willing to join a collective procedure in Germany or the Netherlands whereas at the same time a collective procedure is pending before the Portuguese courts of which they are not aware, and thus did not opt-out. The argument of *lis pendens* or *res judicata* raised by the defendant may then be defeated by taking recourse to the public policy exception, the consumers arguing that they were not aware of the earlier procedure and that the Portuguese notification measures were largely insufficient to notify the interested parties to a reasonable extent.

---

166 Article XVII. 54, § 5 Code of Economic Law.

167 Article 15(4) Law on Popular Action.

168 Cf. S.I. Strong, "Cross-Border Collective Redress and Individual Participatory Rights: Quo vadis?", 32 *Civil Justice Quarterly*, (508) 532–533.

5.3.2. The ability to influence proceedings

The ability for individual group members to influence representative collective redress proceedings appears to be an important safeguard from the perspective of the German legal order. This can be explained by the importance attached in Germany to the right to be heard, which is constitutionally protected by Article 103 Grundgesetz ('GG'), as well as the centrality of the disposition principle in German civil procedure. These two features have been repeatedly highlighted in scholarship to argue in favour of a cautious approach towards representative collective redress in Germany.[169] They are also considered to be potentially problematic for the purposes of recognition and enforcement of foreign collective redress judgments.

Article 103 GG requires that a party involved in litigation has the possibility to express themself before the court because "*was nicht geäussert wird, kan nicht gehört werden*".[170] From a legislative point of view, this implies that procedures must at least provide for the possibility of the parties to be heard.[171] The right to be heard does not necessarily amount to an oral hearing and can be done in writing.[172] The right is also respected when not the actual party but the party's lawyer is heard by the court.[173] There is thus room for interpretation and accommodation in the context of representative collective proceedings. The issue of Article 103 GG was also taken up by the German government in the project of law on the Musterfeststellungsklage (MFK).[174] The government considered the right to be heard sufficiently protected because the MFK works under an opt-in model and registered consumers have the possibility to withdraw their participation in the procedure until just before the first hearing.[175] No further safeguards were added to protect the right enshrined in Article 103 GG in the

---

169 See discussion and references in A. Halfmeier, "Recognition of a WCAM settlement in Germany", *NiPR* 2012, (176) 180–184.

170 B. Remmert, "GG. 103 Abs. 1" in T. Maunz, G. Dürig, R. Herzog, M. Herdegen, R. Scholz and H.H. Klein (Eds.), *Grundgesetz – Kommentar* (Beck, September 2017 – 81th delivery), Rn. 5–6: "What has not been expressed, cannot have been heard" (Authors' own translation).

171 Ibid., Rn. 5.

172 Ibid., Rn. 65.

173 Ibid., Rn. 65.

174 Gesetz zur Einführung einer zivilprozessualen Musterfaststellungsklage, *BgBl.* 17 July 2018, I, N° 26, 1151.

175 German Parliament, Entwurf eines Gesetzes zur Einführung einer zivilprozessualen Musterfeststellungsklage, N° 19/2439, 17.

course of the legislative process, for example, the possibility for participating consumers to submit written observations.

The opt-in model thus appears for the German legislator to be a necessary safeguard for the protection of the right to be heard as enshrined in Article 103 GG. Does this mean that an opt-out procedure will be automatically problematic from the German point of view? Such question is difficult to answer. We have argued that an outright rejection of an opt-out model would not be compatible with Article 45(1)(a) Brussels I^{bis} Regulation but that it would depend on the additional safeguards provided for. Hess stated that such additional guarantees may indeed be sufficient for an opt-out procedure to meet the standard of Article 103 GG.[176] The German Federal Constitutional Court also seems to imply this in its case law on the service of US class action notices on German defendants.[177] Further to this, Halfmeier and Wimalasena point out that summons by publication is a valid means of service in other areas of German law, such as insolvency, and argue that the right to be heard should be interpreted functionally.[178] That being said, it is a relevant question whether the same standard can be applied for all types of litigation, e.g. whether the standard of diligence that applies to shareholders or creditors can be transposed unreservedly onto consumers. Moreover, the clear political choice by the German legislator for an opt-in model may lead German judges in the direction of a stricter approach to foreign opt-out procedures. It is interesting in this regard to consider the position paper of the Bundesrechtsanwaltskammer[179] of September 2018 on the 2018 Commission Proposal, which seems to suggest that opt-out procedures are incompatible with Article 103 GG.[180] It is at this moment thus uncertain how German judges will evaluate the additional safeguards provided for in foreign opt-out procedures,

176 B. Hess, "Die Anerkennung eines Class Action Settlement in Deutschland", *J.Z.* 2000, (373) 379.

177 BverfG 3 November 2015, 2 BvR 2019/09, DE:BVerfG:2015:rk20151103.2bvr201909, para. 42.

178 A. Halfmeier and P. Wimalasena, "Rechtsstaatliche Anforderungen an Opt-out-Sammelverfahren: Anerkennung ausländischer Titel und rechtspolitischer Gestaltungsspielraum", *J.Z.* 2012, (649) 654–656; A. Halfmeier, "Recognition of a WCAM settlement in Germany", *N.I.P.R.* 2012 (176) 182.

179 The Bundesrechtsanwaltskammer is the German bar association.

180 Bundesrechtsanwaltskammer, Zum Vorschlag für eine Richtlinie des Europäischen Parlaments und des Rates über Verbandsklagen zum Schutz von kollektiven Interessen der Verbraucher und zur Aufhebung der Richtlinie 2009/22/EG (COM (2018) 184 final), Position Paper N° 30/2018, 3.

such as the Dutch WCAM, now that a clear policy choice has been made by the German legislator for an opt-in model.[181]

Moreover, the German preference for opt-in procedures does not mean that a foreign opt-in procedure would automatically receive a clean bill of health in Germany. It is important to understand that the MFK, just as the KapMuG[182], is only a declaratory procedure deciding on the common legal points for a group of interested parties represented by a qualified group representative. The actual compensation phase is still individual, requiring a consumer who participated in the MFK to initiate individual proceedings in order to obtain a decision on their individual claim. This duality secures as far as possible the rights enshrined in Article 103 GG while at the same time safeguarding the disposition principle.[183] These principles are less strongly protected by an opt-in procedure that also encompasses the compensation phase and whereby an interested party is wholly dependent on the actions of the representative without the possibility to exercise any influence over the procedure or the representative. If an individual group member would be of the opinion that an unfavourable decision in a foreign collective redress procedure is the result of the mismanagement of the procedure by the group representative and that no possibilities existed to mitigate this, a public policy argument could certainly be made. It is interesting in this regard to point out the Belgian collective redress procedure, which does not allow for any involvement of the group members in the course of the proceedings: from the moment the time period to opt-in or opt-out[184] has elapsed, they are completely dependent upon the group representative – even for information on the ongoing procedure.[185] The supervisory powers of the Belgian judge over the group representative during the procedure only concern the formal requirements to be met as a group representative, which can only be checked during the admissibility

181 The same goes for the French legislator, who made a clear choice for an opt-in model on the basis of constitutional law considerations.

182 H.L. Buxbaum, "Defining the function and scope of group litigation: The role of class actions for monetary damages in the United States" in P. Gottwald (Ed.), *Europäisches Insolvenzrecht – Kollektiver Rechtsschutz* (Gieseking, 2008), (215) 224.

183 A. Halfmeier and P. Wimalasena, "Rechtsstaatliche Anforderungen an Opt-out-Sammelverfahren: Anerkennung ausländischer Titel und rechtspolitischer Gestaltungsspielraum", *J.Z.* 2012, (649) 657.

184 An opt-out procedure is not possible for persons residing outside of Belgium.

185 BIICL Study, 390.

phase.[186] Would a decision given under such circumstances be automatically recognised by a German judge because the collective procedure was of an opt-in nature? In light of the importance of Article 103 GG this is not absolutely certain. The case law of the German Federal Constitutional Court also suggests that its conditional acceptance of representative collective redress proceedings does not only concern opt-out procedures, leaving open the possibility that opt-in procedures may also not meet the required standard.[187] It can thus not be assumed that a decision given in a Belgian representative collective redress procedure under an opt-in mechanism will be automatically recognised in Germany, the goals of Article 103 GG being safeguarded to a much lesser extent under the Belgian procedure than under the German procedure.

5.3.3. Judicial supervision

A recurring element in collective procedures is the active role for the court in overseeing the proceedings. This is in the first place a consequence of the nature of collective proceedings, which are complex to conduct and rely on intensive case management for their efficiency. Additionally, it appears that the increased role of the court is also a safeguard to protect the interests of the group members, especially of absent group members in opt-out procedures.[188] A court may thus scrutinise the nature and amount of relief sought by the group representative, the description of the class as well as other elements of the proceedings. Such powers transgress the traditional boundaries of an individual dispute, inter alia the *nec ultra petita* rule, and give the court a fundamental role in the outcome of the proceedings. This sits uneasily with the classic model of litigation, in which courts are not required to guard the interests of litigating parties on account of being accused of partiality. Therefore, some Member States have given the role of guarding the interests of group members to other entities, such as

186 Article XVII.36, 2° Economic Law Code and Article XVII.40, first alinea, Economic Law Code. This is different in, for example, Sweden or England and Wales, where the judge also maintains supervisory powers during the proceedings. See E. Falla, *The role of the court in collective redress litigation* (Larcier, 2014), 160–161.

187 See *infra*.

188 E. Falla, The role of the court in collective redress litigation (Larcier, 2014), 156–170.

the public prosecutor[189], or have limited the power to bring collective redress proceedings to public bodies.[190]

Other Member States have given wider powers to the court, going beyond mere case management powers and requiring it to protect the interests of absent group members. This is clearly the case in the Dutch WCAM procedure, where the court has extensive powers to determine whether the proposed settlement is in the interest of the group members.[191] The court may even propose to change the settlement for which an application has been made if it considers this necessary to better protect the interests of the group members.[192] Such wide powers are also available to the court in the Belgian procedure for the settlement that may be reached between the group representative and the defendant in the course of the collective redress procedure, which provides for a mandatory settlement phase before the merits phase.[193] No provisions have been included, however, on the powers of the court when no settlement is reached and the case proceeds to the merits. It may be presumed that the court protects the interests of the group members in the merits phase in the same way as it is obliged to do in the settlement phase. However, in the absence of any specific rules on the matter the normal powers of the judge in Belgian civil procedure should apply. While the Belgian system is quite liberal in this regard[194], it is not clear how far a court may go in actively protecting the interests of the group members as this sits uneasily with the duty of impartiality. The task of actively protecting interests is something else than applying the law to the facts of the case, raising pleas in law warranted by the facts of the case, or collecting evidence.[195] It concerns questions of opportunity, which are normally not within the remit of the courts.

---

189 Portugal (Article 16 Law on Popular Action (Lei 83/95 de Acção Popular)).

190 Finland (Article 4 Group Action Act (Ryhmäkannelaki)). See also, K. Viitanen, "Finland", (622) *The ANNALS of the American Academy of Political and Social Science* 2009, 209–219.

191 Article 907(3)(e) Civil Code.

192 Article 907(4) Civil Code.

193 Article XVII. 49, § 2 Code of Economic Law. See further, J.T. Nowak, "The new Belgian law on consumer collective redress and compliance with EU law requirements" in E. Lein, D. Fairgrieve, M. Otero Crespo and V. Smith (Eds.), *Collective redress in Europe – Why and how?* (BIICL, 2015), (169) 183–186.

194 J.-F. van Drooghenbroeck, "L'office juridictionnel du juge belge" in C. Chainais, B. Hess, A. Saletti and J.-F. van Drooghenbroeck (Eds.), *L'office du juge. Études de droit comparé* (Bruylant, 2018), 43–70.

195 Strengthening the judicial powers of the judge may, however, already be an additional safeguard in itself, making the parties less dependent on the actions of

It appears thus that judicial supervision over the interests of the group members increases where group members depend more intensively on the actions of the group representative. Conversely, judicial supervision is less strong or even absent where dependency on the group representative is lesser and the role for individual group members is much stronger. This is for example the case in Germany, where the rules regarding the MFK do not provide any specific powers in this regard, apart from increased case management powers that come with a collective procedure.[196] Of course, one should take into account the wide powers German judges already have in the course of ordinary civil litigation,[197] and to which reference is made in the provisions on the MFK.[198] Still, this amounts to the application of the law and does not imply safeguarding the interests of a specific party.

An increased role of the court may thus be a sufficient safeguard for the protection of the interests of the group members, especially for absent group members in opt-out procedures. It is therefore not a surprise that a liberal approach to notification and *res judicata* effects goes hand in hand with increased powers for the court, such as in the Netherlands. Discretion or powers have to be exercised though. The availability of safeguards is therefore a necessary but not sufficient guarantee for the protection of the right to a fair trial. It is to this point that we turn in the next section.

6. *Public Policy and the Application of Procedural Safeguards*

What appears from the overview of potential safeguards is that many of them leave a large margin of manoeuvre, allowing the judge and the parties to maximise protection of the right to a fair trial but also to disregard it to a large extent. The Dutch provisions on notification measures look comprehensive but may be discarded by the court, the law giving it the freedom to do so.[199] Much will also depend on the actual case. Notifica-

---

the representative. For example, the judge in the Portuguese popular action has the express power to collect evidence *ex officio*, unconnected to any initiative of the parties: Article 17 Portuguese Law on Popular Action.

196 The German court is, however, obliged to protect the interest of the group members in case of a settlement: § 611(3) ZPO.

197 § 139 ZPO. See also, R.W. Emerson, "Judges as guardian angels: The German practice of hints and feedback", (48) *Vanderbilt Journal of Transnational Law* 2015, 709–754.

198 § 610(4) ZPO.

199 Article 1017(3) Code of Civil Procedure.

tion measures that are comprehensive in one case may be completely insufficient in another case. Further to this, private initiatives should also not be discarded. A group representative may go a long way in informing potential group members, beyond the legal requirements. This will be an important element in assessing whether a group member could have reasonably been aware of the proceedings. It is therefore necessary to also look at the application of the safeguards.

One could expect a level of scrutiny of the application of the safeguards commensurate with the standard of protection chosen in the receiving Member State. This will in particular be the case for courts of Member States that have adopted an opt-in procedure and are confronted with the recognition or enforcement of a foreign decision given in an opt-out procedure. Between Member States with the same type of selection mechanism much will depend on their approach to collective redress (permissive or reluctant) and the number of safeguards existing in their own legal order. It can also be expected that courts of Member States that have provided for an opt-out procedure will be less strict in scrutinising decisions originating in Member States with an opt-in procedure. The standard applied in such cases may be akin to the current standard under the Brussels I^{bis} Regulation for individual decisions, meaning that refusals of recognition and enforcement will be highly exceptional.

7. *National Court Practice*

7.1. *Introduction*

In this section we would like to present a number of cases corroborating our analysis. Admittedly, there is to our knowledge no case law available on the recognition or enforcement of collective redress decisions between EU Member States. Useful comparison might be done with collective action decisions originating in the US and for which recognition or enforcement has been sought in an EU Member State. Even here not many decisions exist or have been published. We limit ourselves to a Dutch case, a Belgian case and the approach taken by the Bundesverfassungsgericht. Interestingly, a judicial analysis of potential refusals of recognition of collective redress decisions by courts of EU Member States can be found in US class certification decisions, where potential refusals of recognition and enforcement of a final decision are determinative for class certification purposes. We include these in our analysis as they provide an interesting insight into the practice of public policy analysis of foreign collective redress procedures.

7.2. *US Courts*

US class actions have for many years been a preferred instrument to conduct shareholder litigation. In the absence of an efficient multi-party procedure in their own jurisdiction or that of the foreign company, foreign shareholders have sought to establish the jurisdiction of US courts in order to benefit from the advantages of the US class action (settlement) procedure.[200] Grounds for jurisdiction were often tenuous but foreign shareholders were helped by the conduct and effects test[201] to establish jurisdiction of US courts. Having met the jurisdiction threshold, a next step in the procedure concerned the admissibility requirements of the class action, as laid down in Rule 23(b)(3) of the Federal Rules on Civil Procedure.[202] These are numerosity, commonality, typicality, adequacy of representation, predominance and superiority.[203] The last admissibility criterion is of particular importance for the certification of class actions with a foreign element, as it obliges the US courts to assess the desirability of the concentration of litigation in their jurisdiction.[204] An important element in that analysis was the question whether the *res judicata* effect of the US judgment would be recognised in the relevant foreign jurisdiction. This in order to prevent class members from relitigating the case, since a defendant is "entitled to a victory no less broad than a defeat would have

---

200 T. Arons, "Recognition of US class actions or settlements in Europe", *ECFR* 2015, (462) 467. See, however, *infra*, fn 209, regarding recent developments that have limited this option, notably the Supreme Court decision in *Morrison v. National Australia Bank*, 561 U.S. 247 (2010).

201 D. R. Dumas, "United States antifraud jurisdiction over transnational securities transactions: merger of the conduct and effects test", (16) *University of Pennsylvania International Businesses Law* 1995, 721–747.

202 M. Ventoruzzo, "Like moths to a flame? International securities litigation after Morrison: Correcting the Supreme Court's 'Transactional Test'", (52) *Virginia Journal of International Law* 2012, (405) 424.

203 A. Pina, "Recognition and res judicata of US class action judgments in European legal systems", *Erasmus Law Review* 2008, (31) 37; T. Arons, "Recognition of US class actions or settlements in Europe", *ECFR* 2015, (462) 465.

204 M. Ventoruzzo, "Like moths to a flame? International securities litigation after Morrison: Correcting the Supreme Court's 'Transactional Test'", (52) *Virginia Journal of International Law* 2012, (405) 424.

been".[205] In case of a negative answer, a class action would not be desirable and certification refused for the class members residing in that foreign jurisdiction.

The test applied by US courts to determine whether the *res judicata* effect would be recognised has evolved over time, moving from 'near certainty'[206] of non-recognition to the probability of non-recognition[207], it being 'more likely than not'[208] for a foreign court to refuse recognition.[209] It is interesting to compare the application of the test by the US Court of Appeals (2nd Circ.) in *Bersch* and the US District Court in *Vivendi*. Even though the test has become stricter over the years, class certification was much wider in the 2007 *Vivendi* case compared to the 1975 *Bersch* decision, even though they concerned putative class members from largely the same foreign states.

In *Bersch,* the court excluded all foreign class members because it appeared from expert opinions that courts in England, Germany, Switzerland, Italy and France would not recognise a decision given in an opt-out US class action procedure in favour of the defendant.[210] In a number of other cases US courts also considered that the preclusive effect of a class action decision would not be recognised in Germany and the United King-

---

205 US Court of Appeals, *Bersch v. Drexel Firestone Incorporated & Ios J H*, 519 F. 2d 974, § 76.

206 US Court of Appeals, *Bersch v. Drexel Firestone Incorporated & Ios J H*, 519 F. 2d 974, § 75.

207 A. Pina, "Recognition and res judicata of US class action judgments in European legal systems", *Erasmus Law Review* 2008, (31) 37.

208 US District Court, *Vivendi Universal*, 242 F.R.D. 76, 109 (S.D.N.Y. 2007). The decision can be found under the following link: http://securities.stanford.edu/filings-documents/1024/V02-01/2007523_r01o_02CV05571.pdf.

209 This stricter approach should be seen against the backdrop of a wider evolution in US law, limiting the extraterritorial application of US class actions and of US securities law. See US Supreme Court, *Morrison v. National Australia Bank Ltd.*, 561 U.S. 247 (2010). See also M. Ventoruzzo, "Like moths to a flame? International securities litigation after Morrison: Correcting the Supreme Court's 'Transactional Test'", (52) *Virginia Journal of International Law* 2012, 405–444; J.L. Boehm, "Private securities fraud litigation after *Morrison v. National Australia Bank*: Reconsidering a reliance-based approach to extraterritoriality", (53) *Harvard International Law Journal* 2012, 249–290; W. Vandenbussche, "Grensoverschrijdende collectieve vorderingen van gedupeerde beleggers", *Rechtskundig Weekblad* 2013–14, 243–260.

210 US Court of Appeals, *Bersch v. Drexel Firestone Incorporated & Ios J H*, 519 F. 2d 974, §§ 77–79.

dom, and refused certification.[211] In *Vivendi* the court conducted a thorough analysis of the Netherlands, France, England and Wales, Germany and Austria, and concluded that it was more likely than not that the preclusive effects of the class action decision would be recognised in all but two of the foreign jurisdictions, namely Austria and Germany.[212]

The *Vivendi* decision is interesting on a number of points. First, the difference between the *Bersch* decision and the *Vivendi* decision illustrates the growing acceptance of class actions in Europe over time. While residents of England and Wales and France were excluded from certification in 1975, this was no longer so in 2008. This is particularly surprising in relation to France, as many legal commentators suggest that a French court would refuse to recognise US class action decisions on account of public policy.[213] The US court deemed it however more likely than not that the decision would be recognised.[214] Second, the US court acknowledges at the same time that differences continue to exist between EU Member States, deciding that it is more likely than not that recognition would be refused in Germany on account of public policy concerns. A third point of interest is the method adopted by the US court. In its analysis the US court compares the foreign systems of collective redress to the US system in order to determine whether recognition would be refused. The assumption is thus that foreign courts will compare US class actions to their own national procedures to decide the question of recognition. Key appears to be the existence of procedures in the foreign legal order in which 'the interests of non-parties are pursued and non-parties are bound by the result', even when limited in scope or not applicable in the area of law

---

211 It should be noted that these class actions were also thin in respect of other admissibility requirements, such as commonality or numerosity.

212 This conflicts with the position taken by various German scholars, who have argued that there would be no problems of recognition of US class action settlement decisions in Germany: see discussion and references in A. Halfmeier, "Recognition of a WCAM settlement in Germany", *NiPR* 2012, (176) 180–184. See, however, C. Greiner, *Die Class Action im amerikanischen Recht und deutscher Ordre Public* (Peter Lang, 1998), 217–222.

213 For an overview of the discussion, see M.-A. Frison-Roche, "Les résistances du système juridique français à accueillir la class action", *LPA* 10 June 2005, 22.

214 It should be pointed out, however, that competing declarations on this point were submitted to the court.

concerned[215], or the political will to introduce procedures.[216] It is this that sets England and Wales, France and the Netherlands apart from Germany, which did at the time of the decision not have any form of collective procedure with such consequences.[217] The court considered the, at that time, newly introduced KapMuG but decided that it did not meet the standard because non-party shareholders would not be bound by the result. This is equally so for the newly introduced MFK procedure, which requires individual consent. It is thus not certain whether a US court will rule in a different way *anno* 2020. The German approach to collective redress remains strongly influenced by the model of individual litigation. This confirms our view that one should not take it for granted that foreign collective redress decisions under an opt-out (or even an opt-in) would be recognised without any problems in Germany.

7.3. Amsterdam Court of First Instance – Ahold Class Settlement[218]

In a 2010 decision, the Amsterdam Court of First Instance considered fair trial and public policy arguments raised by the applicant against the recognition of the preclusive effects of a US class settlement judgment. The US judgment confirmed a settlement reached between the Dutch company Ahold and its shareholders following a large accountancy scandal, in which the accountancy firm Deloitte was also involved. The procedure before the Amsterdam court concerned a claim by a foundation represent-

---

215 The US court refers *inter alia* to the possibility for French labour unions to bring actions on behalf of employees without individual consent. Note that there might have been a misunderstanding of French law on this point, now the French parliament has adopted an opt-in model for the 2014 'action de groupe' exactly because the Conseil constitutionnel held in relation to that law that it could only be in conformity with the constitution "à la condition que l'intéressé ait été mis à même de donner son assentiment en pleine connaissance de cause et qu'il puisse conserver la liberté de conduire personnellement la défense de ses intérêts et de mettre un terme à son action". See, Conseil constitutionnel 25 July 1989, N° 89–257.

216 The US court refers to views on the matter expressed by the French president as well as the debate in French legal and business communities in support of the finding that an opt-out class action is not so contrary to French public policy that it would infringe the principle of universal justice or be contrary to international public policy. With the benefit of hindsight, it appears that the voices in the public debate have misread the sentiment of the French legislator.

217 This according to the expert on which the court relied the most, P. Mankowski.

218 Amsterdam Court of First Instance, 23 June 2010, NL:RBAMS:2010:BM9324.

ing several Ahold shareholders who had not opted-out of the settlement against Deloitte and a CFO of Ahold.

The court relied on the strong similarities between the US procedure and the Dutch WCAM to reject concerns of fair trial. It underlined that the procedural guarantees in both procedures safeguarded the right to be heard and the possibility not to be bound by the agreement.[219] The court referred specifically to the fairness hearing and the period during which class members could comment orally and in writing on the settlement[220], the possibility to be excluded from the class or to withdraw from it[221], and the fulfillment of the notification requirements ordered by the US courts.[222] These consisted *inter alia* of individual notice for all known shareholders and repeated notifications in Dutch national and regional newspapers. The court concluded that all interested parties were timely and adequately convoked and also that other fair trial rights had been respected, in particular the right to be heard and the right not to be bound against their will by the decision.[223]

The analysis of the points on which the US procedure differed from the Dutch WCAM was conducted on a public policy basis. The court did not take issue with the shorter time-limit to decide on the participation in the settlement because it had not been argued nor did it appear that it was too short to take adequate notice of the settlement agreement. The court also rejected the argument that the representative in the US procedure was not a foundation or an association, as it did not appear nor had been argued that this had an impact on the representation of the interests of the class members.[224]

All this led the court to conclude that the class action settlement judgment could be recognised in the Netherlands and that the preclusive effects of the decision were binding upon the applicant. However, the court underlined the general nature of its analysis and acknowledged that the outcome could be different for certain individual group members. This either because specific circumstances could be advanced justifying the conclusion that the requirements for recognition have not been met in their concrete case or because the binding effect of the agreement would be

219 Amsterdam Court of First Instance, point 6.5.3.
220 Amsterdam Court of First Instance, point 6.5.3.a.
221 Amsterdam Court of First Instance, point 6.5.3.b.
222 Amsterdam Court of First Instance, point 6.5.3.c.
223 Amsterdam Court of First Instance, point 6.5.4.
224 Amsterdam Court of First Instance, point 6.5.5.

deemed unacceptable in light of the standards of reasonability and justice.[225] Such arguments were not presented nor found by the court.

The decision is interesting because of the three-level analysis the court conducts. First, it makes a general comparison between the US procedure and the Dutch procedure, comparing the relevant procedural guarantees that have been provided for in both procedures. Second, it considers the application of these procedural guarantees from a general perspective to evaluate whether procedural standards and public policy requirements have been met. Third, and this is striking, it allows for a reconsideration of its fair trial and public policy analysis on the basis of individual considerations. Recognition may thus fail on three levels: at the level of procedural design, at the level of the application of procedural safeguards in the concrete procedure, and at the level of the individual group member.

7.4. Ghent Court of Appeal – Lernout and Hauspie Class Settlement[226]

In a 2017 decision the Ghent Court of Appeal recognised a class action settlement that was approved by the District Court of Massachusetts.[227] The case concerned shareholder litigation against KPMG in connection to the fraudulent bankruptcy of Lernout and Hauspie, a Belgian tech company that gained prominence at the end of the 1990s for their speech technology.[228]

Plaintiffs in the Belgian procedure argued the non-recognition of the class action settlement for reasons of public policy. Their argument was divided into two parts. The first part focused on the argument that the US procedure did not provide for the same level of protection of group members as the Belgian procedure. The court rejected this argument by referring to the various safeguards provided for in the US procedure. It came to the conclusion that the rights of the class members are at least equally pro-

---

225 Amsterdam Court of First Instance, point 6.5.6.

226 Ghent Court of Appeal, 23 March 2017, unpublished. For an overview of the judgment in English, see http://conflictoflaws.net/2017/belgian-court-recognizes-us-opt-out-class-action-settlement/ See further, S. Voet, "Amerikaanse class action-schikking in België erkend", Rechtskundig Weekblad 2016–17, 1442.

227 US District Court of Massachusetts, 22 December 2004: http://securities.stanford.edu/filings-documents/1015/LHSP00/20041222_r01o_0011589.pdf.

228 For the case briefs, see http://securities.stanford.edu/filings-documents/1015/LHSP00/2001921_r01c_0011589.pdf For further background, see the complaint of the SEC against L&H: https://www.sec.gov/litigation/complaints/comp17782.htm.

tected – if not better – under US law, listing various safeguards that are not available in the Belgian procedure, such as the possibility for individual group members to be heard by the court and the right of individual group members to appeal[229], and the higher standard of review provided for under the US procedure (honest, reasonable and adequate) compared to the Belgian procedure (manifestly unreasonable). The Belgian court then held that these safeguards had been applied in the case and rejected the argument.

The second part concerned the opt-out nature of the procedure. The Belgian court stated that the preference for an opt-in system does not necessarily mean that an opt-out system is contrary to public policy. Problems might, however, exist in relation to the rights of the defence, which is a separate ground for refusal under Belgian private international law. It spelled out the test to be applied in this regard: "It must rather be verified whether the possibility to have sufficient knowledge of the existence of the collective redress procedure, of its nature, of the procedure to decide whether to be a member of the group of persons bound by the decision and the consequences thereof, is sufficiently guaranteed in the concrete case".[230] It then went on to list the notification measures ordered (i.a. individual notification of known class members), the way in which these measures were executed (i.a. 82,819 notification packages, both to potential class members and more than 2000 banks and other financial intermediaries) as well as the conclusion of the US judge to the fairness of the proceedings under US law. Further to this, it referred to statements by the

---

229 Such safeguard appears to be absent in almost every EU collective redress procedure. It may, however, provide the ultimate safeguard for a group member in an opt-out procedure that was initially unaware of the proceedings. It is interesting in this regard to refer to the *Meroni* judgment of the Court of Justice, dealing with procedural rights of third parties with an interest in a procedure (see *supra*, fn. 33). The Court of Justice held in this regard that "the recognition and enforcement of an order issued by a court of a Member State, without a prior hearing of a third person whose rights may be affected by that order, cannot be regarded as manifestly contrary to public policy in the Member State in which enforcement is sought or manifestly contrary to the right to a fair trial within the meaning of those provisions, in so far as that third person is entitled to assert his rights before that court" (para. 54). It may be far going to require a right of appeal for group members in a representative collective procedure, as this would undermine the representative nature of it. Furthermore, it would also impact on the effectiveness of such a procedure, especially since the thresholds for bringing an appeal are generally less demanding in EU Member States compared to the US.

230 Author's translation.

plaintiffs about their knowledge of the proceedings, a number of voluntary notification measures undertaken by third parties, the press attention for the case in the Belgian media, an expert opinion underlining the adequacy of the notification measures, as well as the fact that around 600 persons had exercised the right to opt-out and that 2000 foreign shareholders, of which were 1400 Belgian, had been compensated in the meantime. It follows from all this, according to the Belgian court, that sufficient notification was ordered and realised, even though not all class members were individually notified; moreover, the principle of constructive notice was found not to violate Belgian public policy in the concrete case.

It appears from the analysis of the Belgian court that the availability of various safeguards allowing for the protection of individual interests in the collective procedure is already by itself sufficient to overcome a number of public policy concerns. The Belgian court does not assess in great detail whether these safeguards have been sufficiently implemented, i.e. whether and how the fairness hearing was conducted and what standard was applied. The approach is different, however, when considering the notification of potential class members. Here the Belgian court evaluates in detail how notification was made and whether potential class members were able to obtain knowledge about the pending class action. This is not entirely illogical, as notification measures and their effectiveness can be assessed more easily by the receiving court, which also has the benefit of hindsight.

7.5. *German Bundesverfassungsgericht – US Class Action Notices under the Hague Convention*

The compatibility of US class actions with public policy in Germany has been analysed in the context of the service of class action notices on German defendants under the Hague Convention.[231] Article 13(1) Hague Convention allows for a state to refuse a request for service if it deems that compliance would infringe its sovereignty or security, i.e. public policy. A number of German defendants brought constitutional proceedings against decisions of designated German central authorities under the Hague Con-

231 See, inter alia, W. Wurmnest, "Recognition and enforcement of U.S. money judgments in Germany", (23) *Berkeley Journal of International law* 2005, (175) 191–194.

vention, which are courts in a number of regions[232], accepting the service of a class action procedure upon the defendant. In several cases defendants invoked the incompatibility of US opt-out class actions with the German constitution. This allowed the German Constitutional Court to clarify its approach towards US class actions, which is also relevant for our study:

> "*Auch die von deutscher Seite grundsätzlich zu respektierende rechtspolitische Entscheidung, für deliktisches Handeln mit einer Vielzahl von Geschädigten Sammelklagen zuzulassen, an denen sich das einzelne Mitglied der class nicht aktiv beteiligen muss, begründet keinen Verstoß gegen unverzichtbare Grundsätze eines freiheitlichen Rechtsstaats, solange auch im class action -Verfahren unabdingbare Verteidigungsrechte gewahrt bleiben. Deshalb kann nicht jeder class action von vornherein die Zustellung versagt werden.*"[233]

It appears from this consideration that a representative collective redress procedure that does not require an active participation of class members is not automatically contrary to German public policy as long as '*unabdingbare Verteidigungsrechte*' – rights of the defence that cannot be departed from – have been guaranteed in the actual procedure.

The Federal Constitutional Court limits itself to this general consideration and does not analyse the features of the US procedure in detail. This is because the judgment concerned the constitutionality of the notification of the case and not the recognition or enforcement of the final judgment. A few points can nevertheless be taken from this. First, it appears that Article 103 GG does not require that group members should be given an opportunity to participate actively in the procedure. Their right to be heard may thus be sufficiently guaranteed through representation, provided that such representation is of sufficient quality and that the necessary checks are in place. Second, the German Constitutional Court does not specify the nature of the class action to which this consideration applies, from which we deduct that it applies to both opt-in and opt-out proce-

232 For a list, see https://assets.hcch.net/docs/494216ab-d7f6-4f7b-9627-93270f8a64da.pdf.

233 Author's translation: "The legal policy decision to allow class actions for tortious acts with a large number of victims, in which the individual member of the class does not have to participate actively, should in principle also be respected by Germany and does not constitute a violation of indispensible principles of a liberal state under the rule of law, as long as the essential rights of the defence are also respected in class action procedures. Therefore, service of a class action cannot be denied from the outset."

dures. Opt-out class action procedures are thus not *per se* contrary to German public policy. Third, the German Constitutional Court does not specify which rights of defence are indispensable, which leaves room for uncertainty and further speculation. If one had to identify a right that may qualify as an indispensable right of defence under German law, however, it would probably be the right to individual notice. It is the ultimate guarantee of Article 103 GG as it allows parties to be informed of proceedings which require their participation and to act accordingly.[234] An important reason for the German federal legislator not to choose an opt-out collective redress model was exactly to avoid situations in which consumers would be bound by a decision given in proceedings of which they were not aware.[235] Therefore, contrary to the Belgian or the Dutch approach, it cannot be absolutely excluded that judgments given in an opt-out collective procedure will not be recognised when individual notice has not been given and the class member concerned claims not to have been aware of the procedure. A principle of 'constructive notice' may thus not be without problems from a German perspective.[236]

7.6. *A Number of Common Lines*

It appears from the above-mentioned decisions that the existing national collective redress procedure will serve as a benchmark to evaluate whether there has been a violation of public policy. This means that standards will differ across Member States and that Member States who have adopted a conservative approach to collective redress are likely to adopt a different public policy standard compared to Member States with more liberal approaches. That may in turn lead to difficulties in the free circulation of

---

234 F. Höffmann, *Class Action Settlements und ihre Anerkennung in Deutschland* (JWV, 2013), 325.

235 See German Parliament, Entwurf eines Gesetzes zur Einführung einer zivilprozessualen Musterfeststellungsklage, N° 19/2439, 17. While opt-out procedures do not exclude the possibility of individual notice, it would appear to be unworkable in the context of mass consumer law violations to give individual notice to every potential group member. Therefore, at the risk of the binding force of a decision in an opt-out procedure not being recognised vis-à-vis each consumer that has not received individual notice, it was preferred to have an opt-in procedure. It is indeed more rational to have an opt-in procedure if the constitutional standard of fair trial requires individual notice of proceedings.

236 See, however, F. Höffmann, *Class Action Settlements und ihre Anerkennung in Deutschland* (JWV, 2013), 364.

collective redress decisions between Member States that have adopted a liberal approach to collective redress and Member States that have retained a more conservative stance on this point. That being said, a strict similarity between the national procedure and the foreign procedure is not required for recognition or enforcement. Everything depends on how the right to a fair trial is protected in the foreign collective procedure, both in the abstract and in the concrete case. However, a dividing line appears to be the choice between opt-in and opt-out procedures. Such is not the result of an outright refusal of the principle of opt-out procedures but because of the fact that certain procedural rights can be less easily safeguarded in an opt-out procedure than in an opt-in procedure. It appears from the Belgian and Dutch decisions that particular attention will be paid in this regard to the scope and the content of the notification measures, thereby including informal notification measures undertaken by the representative or other interested parties, as well as spontaneous coverage in the news media. More than anything else, it appears thus that adequate notification is the most important safeguard to guarantee the right to a fair trial of putative group members.

8. *Concluding Remarks*

In this concluding section, we set out the answers to our research questions and take a position regarding whether it is opportune to amend the jurisdiction rules of the Brussels I^{bis} Regulation in the near future.

The overview has shown that it is unlikely that a Member State court will refuse recognition or enforcement of a representative collective redress decision on account of its collective or representative nature. The application of an opt-out mechanism to select group members can in principle also not justify in itself the application of the public policy clause of Article 45(1)(a) Brussels I^{bis} Regulation. What is relevant from the point of view of public policy, however, is the availability of sufficient safeguards to guarantee the right to a fair trial in the course of a collective procedure and the application of these safeguards in the specific case.

It appears that procedural safeguards protecting the right to a fair trial differ from one Member State to another. This is not a mere technicality but reflects a different balance struck between collective and individual litigation, and the protection of the rights of parties involved. For example, neighbouring countries like the Netherlands and Germany appear to attach a very different value to the right of individual litigation. This will inevitably impact on the recognition and enforcement of collective redress decisions, as national courts will use their own model as a benchmark to evaluate the fairness of a foreign collective redress procedure. A more intense scrutiny of collective redress decisions on account of public policy concerns can thus not be excluded, also not after the adoption of the directive on representative actions.

Moreover, while not supported by this author, it cannot even be completely excluded that a collective redress decision will be refused on account of the mere fact that it was given in an opt-out procedure, regardless of the procedural safeguards. While transnational legal doctrine has been quite permissive of an opt-out model, national doctrine appears to be less so. Moreover, a number of Member States, such as Germany and France, have categorically rejected an opt-out model for their recently adopted collective redress mechanisms. A clear position of the national legislator may thus influence the approach taken by their courts when deciding on the recognition and enforcement of a foreign collective redress decision. Therefore, with reason, Muir Watt sees in the choice between opt-out models and consent-based models a new cultural divide in the European procedural landscape.[237]

The likelihood of refusals of recognition or enforcement is thus not merely theoretical[238], and therefore an element that should be considered before amending the jurisdiction rules of the Brussels I^{bis} Regulation. Moreover, new jurisdiction rules will inevitably reflect the choice for one collective redress model over another and require a common understanding of procedural guarantees in collective redress procedures. In the absence of a consensus on both these elements, it is at present also difficult to see how a workable majority can be found amongst the Member States for a meaningful amendment of the Brussels I^{bis} Regulation. In light of this, it would be preferable to let the practice of collective redress mature within domestic systems first and postpone (the debate on) the adoption of new jurisdiction rules until a clear common ground emerges.

---

237 H. Muir Watt, "Collective redress" in J. Basedow, G. Rühl, F. Schiller, F. Ferrari and P. de Miguel Asensio (Eds.), *Encyclopedia of Private International Law* (Edward Elgar, 2017), (373) 375.

238 Cf. X. Kramer, "Securities collective action and private international law issues in Dutch WCAM settlements: Global aspirations and regional boundaries", 27 *Pac. McGeorge Global Bus. & Dev. L.J.* 2014, (235) 269; D. Fairgrieve, "The impact of the Brussels I enforcement and recognition rules on collective actions" in D. Fairgrieve and E. Lein (Eds.), *Extraterritoriality and collective redress* (OUP, 2012), (171) 178–185; a. Stadler, "Cross-border mass litigation: a particular challenge for European law" in j. Steele and w.h. Van boom (Eds.), *Mass Justice – Challenges of representation and distribution* (Edward Elgar, 2011), (73) 82–86.

Casting the Net: Has the Court of Justice's Approach to Online Torts Made the Brussels Framework Fit for the Internet Age?

Tobias Lutzi[*]

Table of Contents

While the Brussels Convention predates the emergence of the internet as an established means of communication by several decades, the challenges it poses for the traditional legal framework of international jurisdiction were already well-known when the Convention became a Regulation. Still, its drafters resisted any temptation to react to these challenges by making technology-specific amendments – and so did the drafters of the Recast. Accordingly, the burden to apply broad and abstract provisions like (what is now) Art 7(2) Brussels Ia to internet cases fell exclusively upon the shoul-

[*] DPhil, LLM, MJur. Research Fellow at the Institute for Private International and Comparative Law, University of Cologne.

ders of the judges in Luxembourg. Over the last two decades, they have adopted a consistent, partly technology-specific interpretation, that seems to have given rise to two different regimes: one for infringements of personality rights committed through the internet and one for all other online torts. Questions remain with regard to the scope, interplay, and, indeed, the appropriateness of these two regimes.

1. *Introduction: the Technology-Neutral Brussels Framework*

When the Brussels Convention was signed in 1968, the internet was nothing more than the pet project of a handful of researchers.[1] But when the Convention became a Regulation in 2001, the rapidly growing use of online communication and the internet's unique features had already given rise to serious challenges for the traditional legal framework of international jurisdiction. In some widely reported cases,[2] courts in the United States in particular had struggled to apply established tests and criteria to a medium that made it possible to share content with users in countless states with a single mouse click.[3]

Still, the drafters of the Regulation were hesitant to make technology-specific amendments to the Convention's rather general rules on jurisdiction.[4] While the challenges created by the internet were discussed in relation to consumer contracts[5] (and are somewhat reflected in the relevant provisions), virtually[6] all other rules on jurisdiction remained technology-neutral. Even when the Regulation was recast in 2012 and the ECJ had already been confronted with several cases highlighting the difficulties

---

1 For a concise overview of the internet's history, see Jon Bing, 'Building Cyberspace: a brief history of Internet', in Lee A Bygrave & Jon Bing (eds), *Internet Governance: Infrastructure and Institutions* (OUP 2009), 8.

2 See, e.g., the decisions by US District Courts in *Zippo Manufacturing Co v Zippo Dot Com, Inc* 952 F Supp 1119 (WD Pa 1997) and *Cybersell, Inc v Cybersell, Inc* 130 F 3d 414 (9th Cir 1997), 419–20.

3 See Dan Jerker B. Svantesson, *Solving the Internet Jurisdiction Puzzle* (OUP 2017), 92–96.

4 See AG Wathelet, Opinion on Case C-618/15 *Concurrence SARL* ECLI:EU:C:2016:843, para. 33.

5 See Explanatory Memorandum to Proposal COM(1999) 348, 4.5, Art 15.

6 Art 23(2) Brussels I seems to be the only explicitly technology-specific amendment.

resulting from the 'borderless' nature of online communication,[7] no attempt was made to address them through more specific rules.[8]

The provision on special jurisdiction for torts in what is now Art 7(2) Brussels Ia[9] is testimony to this approach, having remained virtually unchanged throughout all three iterations of the Brussels framework despite increasingly obvious difficulties to apply it to situations of intangible harm in general[10] and to torts committed online in particular.

The burden to apply the broadly-worded provision to the specific challenges of internet cases, with no easily identifiable 'place of the harmful event' thus fell solely on the shoulders of the judges in Luxembourg. Over the last two decades, the ECJ has had several opportunities to develop and refine its interpretation of the provision in light of torts committed via the internet. Although the Court's jurisprudence in this area undeniably reflects a certain coherence, it seems to have ultimately given rise to two slightly different regimes, the application of which depends on the allegedly violated right in question. This approach may not be entirely free of inconsistencies.

2. *The ECJ's Technology-Specific Approach to Online Torts*

In order to be able to discuss the present state and future viability of the ECJ's case law on special jurisdiction for online torts, this paper will first retrace the development of the Court's interpretation of what is now Art 7(2) Brussels Ia (2.1). It will isolate the 'mosaic approach' as a particularly problematic, but, at this point, well-established element of the emerging framework (2.2), before turning towards some further potential inconsistencies and remaining open questions (2.3).

---

7 In addition to the examples given below, see, e.g., Joined Cases C-585/08 and C-144/09 *Pammer* and *Hotel Alpenhof* ECLI:EU:C:2010:740.

8 The Explanatory Memorandum to Proposal COM(2010) 748 does not even mention the internet.

9 Formerly Art 5(3) Brussels Convention, Art 5(3) Brussels I.

10 On which see recently AG Bobek, Opinion on Case C-304/17 *Löber*, ECLI:EU:C:2018:310, paras. 31–45; see also Johannes Ungerer, 'Pure financial loss and international jurisdiction for tort under the Brussels I (Recast) Regulation' (2017) 24 *MJ* 448.

2.1. The Good: Emerging Consistency

The foundation for the ECJ's approach to online torts was laid in a number of cases that preceded the internet, establishing a very wide understanding of the 'place of the harmful event' (2.1.1). While the Court extended this interpretation to internet cases with noticeable consistency, two different regimes emerged with regard to the specific connecting factor of the 'place of the damage': one for online infringements of personality rights (2.1.2), and one for other online torts (2.1.3).

2.1.1. The starting point: Bier & Shevill

The starting point for the ECJ's interpretation of what is now Art 7(2) Brussels Ia is its seminal decision in *Bier*,[11] according to which the 'place where the harmful event occurred' must be interpreted,

> *"in such a way as to acknowledge that the plaintiff has an option to commence proceedings either at the place where the damage occurred or the place of the event giving rise to it."*[12]

The Court held that neither of these two places would necessarily be more closely connected to the tort (or otherwise be preferable);[13] accordingly, the 'place where the harmful event occurred' should be understood as covering both, with the claimant being allowed to choose between them.

Widening the scope of special jurisdiction, the Court's interpretation created many new questions. A particularly pertinent one concerned its application to the increasing number of torts that are committed through media that is distributed in multiple member states. Would the place 'where the damage occurred', or the place 'of the event giving rise to it', be located in each of these member states?

In *Shevill*,[14] the Court opted, again, for a wide interpretation of the provision. It held that

> *"the place of the event giving rise to the damage […] can only be the place where the publisher of the newspaper in question is established, since that is*

11 Case 21/76 *Bier* ECLI:EU:C:1976:166, para. 19.

12 *Ibid*, para. 19.

13 See *ibid*, para. 17.

14 Case C-68/93 *Fiona Shevill* ECLI:EU:C:1995:61.

the place where the harmful event originated and from which the libel was issued and put into circulation."[15]

The damage caused by a defamatory publication, on the other hand,

"occurs in the places where the publication is distributed, when the victim is known in those places.
It follows that the courts of each Contracting State in which the defamatory publication was distributed and in which the victim claims to have suffered injury to his reputation have jurisdiction to rule on the injury caused in that State to the victim's reputation."[16]

The claimant thus has the option to bring a claim in every country in which the defamatory publication has been made available (provided that they held a reputation there), which would however be limited to the damage caused in this member state. If they want to liquidate their entire damage in one forum, they have to seise the courts of the defendant publisher's establishment or domicile.[17]

This 'mosaic approach' raised the question of how it could be transposed to online publications. Would every country in which the content could be accessed have to be considered a 'place where the damage occurred', creating a mosaic of up to 27 jurisdictions?[18] The ECJ generally answered this question in the affirmative but also added further elements to the analysis, which has led to the creation of two distinct regimes of special jurisdiction for online torts.

2.1.2. *The regime for online infringements of personality rights:* eDate *&* Bolagsupplysningen

The first opportunity to apply the *Shevill* approach to an internet case arose in the context of two disputes involving personality rights. In *eDate* and *Martinez*,[19] the respective claimants sued two internet news portals over the publication of information that allegedly violated their right to privacy. The ECJ confirmed that the place of the causal event, the courts of

15 *Ibid*, para. 24.
16 *Ibid*, para. 29–30.
17 *Ibid*, para. 32.
18 If the defendant is domiciled in the 28th Member State.
19 Joined Cases C-509/09 and C-161/10 *eDate Advertising* and *Martinez* ECLI:EU:C:2011:685.

which would have jurisdiction for all damage flowing from the publication, would still be the place in which the publisher is established.[20] Regarding the place of the damage, the Court confirmed that the 'mosaic approach' developed in *Shevill* would also apply to online publications,[21] vesting jurisdiction in the courts of 'each Member State in the territory of which content placed online is or has been accessible', which would be limited to the damage 'caused in the territory of the Member State of the court seised.'[22]

In light of the resulting mosaic of the courts of up to 28 member states having jurisdiction, each for a territorially limited slice of the overall damage, the ECJ was concerned, though, that the difficulties to quantify the damage caused in a given member state would contrast

> *"with the serious nature of the harm which may be suffered by the holder of a personality right who establishes that information injurious to that right is available on a world-wide basis."*[23]

As a remedy, the Court introduced an additional forum at the claimant's centre of interests, in which they could seek compensation for their entire loss:

> *"The connecting criteria [established in* Shevill*] must therefore be adapted in such a way that a person who has suffered an infringement of a personality right by means of the internet may bring an action in one forum in respect of all of the damage caused […] where the alleged victim has his centre of interests."*[24]

---

20 *Ibid*, para. 42. It seems unlikely, though, that this would be the case where the claimant tries to sue the author, rather than the publisher; in this case, the ECJ's decision in Case C-523/10 *Wintersteiger* ECLI:EU:C:2012:220, para. 34, seems to indicate that the place in which the technical process leading to the publication has been activated would be decisive (see also, more generally, Peter Mankowski, 'Der Deliktsgerichtsstand am Handlungsort – die unterschätzte Option', in Rolf A Schütze (ed), *Fairness Justice Equity. Festschrift für Reinhold Geimer* (Beck 2017), 429, 439–41).

21 *eDate* (n. 19), paras. 42–44.

22 *Ibid*, para. 51.

23 *Ibid*, para. 47.

24 *Ibid*, para. 48.

The introduction of this new forum was welcomed by some as a contribution to the better protection of the victims of online defamation[25] but also drew a fair bit of criticism, not least for its lack of any textual basis[26] and character of a *forum actoris*,[27] which runs counter to the Regulation's *actor-sequitur-forum* approach.[28] Besides, it constituted the first clearly technology-specific response to the challenges of internet torts.[29]

While the ECJ considered the new forum to allow 'both the applicant easily to identify the court in which he may sue and the defendant reason-

---

25 See Jan Oster, 'Rethinking Shevill. Conceptualising the EU private international law of Internet torts against personality rights' (2012) 26 *International Review of Law, Computers & Technology*, 113, 120–22; Burkhard Hess, 'Der Schutz der Privatsphäre im Europäischen Zivilverfahrensrecht' *JZ* 2012, 189, 190–91. See also Burkhard Hess, 'The Protection of Privacy in the Case Law of the CJEU' in Burkhard Hess & Cristina M Mariottini (eds), *Protecting Privacy in Private International and Procedural Law by Data Protection* (Nomos 2015), 81, 93, 105–06, arguing that the new forum 'evens the field for the parties' as the publisher also has the option to seise the courts of *their* domicile to seek a negative declaration (relying on Case C-133/11 *Folien Fischer* ECLI:EU:C:2012:664, [52]–[53]).

26 See Michel Reymond, 'The ECJ's *eDate* Decision: A Case Comment' (2011) 13 Yearbook of Private International Law 493, 499–501; Sylvain Bollée & Bernard Haftel, 'Les nouveaux (dés)équilibres de la compétence internationale en matière de cyberdélits après l'arrêt *eDate Advertising* et *Martinez*', *Recueil Dalloz* 2012, 1285, 1287: 'un excès de pouvoir de la part de la CJUE'.

27 Peter Mankowski, in Ulrich Magnus & Peter Mankowski (eds), *European Commentaries on Private International Law (ECPIL). Brussels Ibis Regulation* (otto schmidt 2016), Art 7, [365]; Edina Márton, *Violations of personality rights through the Internet* (Nomos 2016), 263; Silvain Bollée & Bernard Haftel (n. 26), 1286–90; Jan von Hein, 'Der Schutz des Geschädigten bei grenzüberschreitenden Delikten im europäischen Zivilprozessrecht', in Jens Kleinschmidt et al (eds), *Strukturelle Ungleichgewichtslagen in der internationalen Streitbeilegung* (Peter Lang 2016), 45, 78–79: 'ein *favor laesi* in Internetfällen'.

28 See also Etienne Farnoux, DELENDUM EST FORUM DELICTI, Towards the Jurisdictional Protection of the Alleged Victim in Cross-Border Torts, in this volume. For references to the principle, see, e.g., Cases C-464/01 *Gruber* ECLI:EU:C:2005:32, [33]; C-168/02 *Kronhofer* ECLI:EU:C:2004:364, para. 20; C-269/95 *Benincasa* ECLI:EU:C:1997:337, para. 14; C-220/88 *Dumez France* ECLI:EU:C:1990:8, para. 19.

29 See the repeated references to the internet in paras. 45–48 of *eDate* (n 19), and in the operative part of the judgment ('[…] in the event of an alleged infringement of personality rights *by means of content placed online on an internet website*, the person who considers that his rights have been infringed has the option of bringing an action for liability, in respect of all the damage caused […] before the courts of the Member State in which the centre of his interests is based.' [own emphasis]).

ably to foresee before which court he may be sued',[30] it also gave rise to questions regarding its precise definition. In *eDate*, the ECJ had explained that a person's centre of interests would be at the place where they had their habitual residence unless 'other factors, such as the pursuit of a professional activity' established a particularly close link with a different member state.[31] In *Bolagsupplysningen*,[32] the Court confirmed that the criterion also applied to legal persons;[33] in the case of a company incorporated in Estonia, but carrying out the main part of its activities in Sweden, this meant that their centre of interests was located in Sweden.[34]

As the claimant in *Bolagsupplysningen* had however seised the courts of their Estonian domicile – to seek an injunction for rectification and deletion of, and compensation for, certain allegedly defamatory statements the defendant had published online – the case also gave the ECJ an opportunity to answer another important question with regard to the framework of special jurisdiction established in *eDate*. In one of the *eDate* cases, the claimant had also sought an injunction; but the ECJ could leave open whether jurisdiction for it could be based on the territorially-limited competence created by the mosaic approach since the claimant had seised the courts of their centre of interests.[35] With centre-of-interests jurisdiction not being available in the claimant's country of establishment in *Bolagsupplysningen*, the Court (finally) had to answer the question.

In his opinion, AG Bobek, who had advised the court to abolish the mosaic approach for internet torts entirely,[36] argued that – should the Court maintain the mosaic approach – there would be no legal basis to limit the scope of a single court's jurisdiction with regard to injunctive relief:

> *"If it were, hypothetically speaking, established that [...] the Estonian courts have international jurisdiction for the harm caused to the Appellant in Estonia, I am of the view that that court will also be competent to issue the requested remedy, provided that such a remedy exists under national law. This is so because of the unitary nature of the source of the alleged harm in*

30 *eDate* (n. 19), para. 50.

31 *Ibid*, para. 49.

32 Case C-194/16 *Bolagsupplysningen* ECLI:EU:C:2017:766.

33 *Ibid*, para. 38.

34 See *ibid*, paras. 41–42.

35 See also the subsequent decision by the German *Bundesgerichtshof* of 8 May 2012, NJW 2012, 2197.

36 AG Bobek, Opinion on Case C-194/16 *Bolagsupplysningen*, ECLI:EU:C:2017:554, paras. 73–90.

> *the present case. There is just one website. It simply cannot be rectified or deleted only 'in proportion' to the harm suffered in a given territory."*[37]

Although the Court agreed with the Advocate General's assessment that injunctive relief was different from an award of (compensatory) damages in the sense that it could not easily be split into territorial slices, the Court came to the opposite conclusion:

> *"[I]n the light of the ubiquitous nature of the information and content placed online on a website and the fact that the scope of their distribution is, in principle, universal, an application for the rectification of the former and the removal of the latter is a single and indivisible application and can, consequently, only be made before a court with jurisdiction to rule on the entirety of an application for compensation for damage […], and not before a court that does not have jurisdiction to do so."*[38]

The ECJ thus drew a strong line between 'divisible' and 'indivisible' remedies.[39] While the former can be awarded by the courts of every member state in which defamatory online content has been made available (limited to the loss caused by publication in that member state), the latter can only be awarded by courts with 'full' jurisdiction, ie those at the claimant's centre of interests, those at the place in which the defendant has acted, and those of the defendant's domicile.

2.1.3. *The regime for other online torts:* Wintersteiger, Pinckney, Hejduk *&* Concurrence

Infringements of personality rights are not the only torts that can be committed through the internet and at countless places at once. The ECJ first had the opportunity to extend its *eDate* jurisprudence to other torts in relation to violations of IP rights.[40]

---

37 *Ibid*, para. 126.

38 *Bolagsupplysningen* (n. 32), para. 48 (references omitted).

39 See also Tobias Lutzi, 'Shevill is dead, long live Shevill!' (2018) 134 *LQR* 208, 211–12.

40 All decisions regarding Art 7(2) Brussels Ia concerned IP rights that are still protected by the laws of the individual member states; IP rights protected through EU regulations are usually subject to particular rules of jurisdiction set out in the relevant regulation itself (see, e.g., Art 82(5) Regulation (EC) 6/2002 (on design rights); Art 125(5) Regulation (EU) 2017/1001 (on EU trade marks)).

The first such occasion arose in *Wintersteiger*[41], in the context of a trademark dispute. The ECJ readily extended the interpretation established in *eDate* with regard to the place of the causal event; as the ECJ reiterated, it refers to the place in which the defendant acted and where the relevant technical process was activated[42] – which the Court explicitly (and rightly) distinguished from the place of the server.[43] However, the Court refused to extend the centre-of-interest approach developed in *eDate*, given that

> *"[c]ontrary to the situation of a person who considers that there has been an infringement of his personality rights, which are protected in all Member States, the protection afforded by the registration of a national mark is, in principle, limited to the territory of the Member State in which it is registered, so that, in general, its proprietor cannot rely on that protection outside the territory."*[44]

As a consequence, jurisdiction based on the second limb of what is now Art 7(2) Brussels Ia (the place of the damage) can only be based on the mosaic approach – a solution the Court repeatedly justified by the perceived[45] territoriality of IP rights.[46] Thus, a claim for an infringement of intellectual property can be brought in every member state in which the right in question is protected and has allegedly been violated, limited to the damage caused by violations in this member state.[47] Accordingly, a claim based on the violation of a trademark can only be brought in the courts of the country of registration.[48] A claim based on the infringement of a copyright (which is protected in every member state)[49] can be brought in the courts of every member state in which the infringement complained

41 Above, n. 20.

42 *Ibid*, para. 34.

43 *Ibid*, para. 36.

44 *Ibid*, para. 25.

45 For authors questioning this concept, see Mireille Van Eechoud, *Choice of Law in Copyright and Related Rights: Alternatives to the Lex Protectionis* (Kluwer 2003), 97–103, 125; Dário Moura Vicente, 'The Territoriatlity Principle in Intellectual Property Revisited' (2016) 34 *NIPR* 724, 726–29.

46 See Cases C-441/13 *Hejduk* ECLI:EU:C:2015:28, paras 36–37; C-170/12 *Pinckney* ECLI:EU:C:2013:635, para. 46.

47 See *Hejduk* (n. 46), paras. 29, 36.

48 *Wintersteiger* (n. 20), para. 28. See also Art 24(4) Brussels Ia for questions regarding the validity of registration.

49 By virtue of Directive 2001/29/EC (…) on the harmonisation of certain aspects of copyright and related rights in the information society (Information Society Directive).

of is alleged to have happened[50] but will be limited to the damage caused through infringements in this state.[51] The threshold for an infringement to be localised in this sense is remarkably low, with the ECJ refusing invitations[52] to lift it beyond the accessibility of a given homepage from the member state in question in *Pinckney* and *Hejduk*.[53]

This approach has recently been extended to acts of unfair competition. In *Concurrence*,[54] the ECJ held that a claim based on an exclusive-distribution agreement for a certain member state that was allegedly breached by a website that could be accessed from that member state can be brought in the courts of this state,[55] with the Court leaving open whether the claimant would have to prove any actual sales having been made to customers in this member state.[56]

2.2. *The Bad: a Mosaic of Jurisdictions*

Even with its contours having been somewhat clarified by the ECJ in *Bolagsupplysningen*, the biggest problem of the approach to internet torts just sketched out arguably is the ECJ's continued reliance on the mosaic approach.[57]

This is, first, because the mosaic approach creates significant practical difficulties. Wherever their jurisdiction is territorially limited, courts have to determine the precise amount of damage that has been caused by online

50 *Hejduk* (n. 46), para. 29; *Pinckney* (n. 46), para. 43.

51 *Hejduk* (n. 46), para. 36; *Pinckney* (n. 46), para. 45.

52 See, in particular, AG Jääskinen, Opinion on Case C-170/12 *Pinckney*, ECLI:EU:C:2013:400, paras. 64–65, suggesting an extension of the targeting criterion used in Case C-173/11 *Football Dataco* ECLI:EU:C:2012:115 to localise the damage in cases of online infringements of copyright; see also AG Cruz Villalón, Opinion on Case C-441/13 *Hejduk*, ECLI:EU:C:2014:2212, para. 45, suggesting to disregard the 'place of the damage' as a basis for jurisdiction in these cases.

53 *Hejduk* (n. 46), para. 34; *Pinckney* (n. 46), para. 44.

54 Case C-618/15 *Concurrence* ECLI:EU:C:2016:976.

55 *Ibid*, 33–34.

56 See also Tobias Lutzi, 'Gerichtsstand am Schadensort und Mosaikbetrachtung bei Wettbewerbsverletzungen im Internet' *IPRax* 2017, 552, 556.

57 See also Tobias Lutzi, 'Internet Cases in EU Private International Law – Developing a Coherent Approach' (2017) 66 *ICLQ* 687, 690–95.

content having been made available in their member state.[58] In fact, the Court openly acknowledged these difficulties in *eDate*:

> *"[I]t is not always possible, on a technical level, to quantify that distribution [of online content] with certainty and accuracy in relation to a particular Member State or, therefore, to assess the damage caused exclusively within that Member State."*[59]

Its reaction to give the claimant access to an additional forum with jurisdiction for the entire damage, though, makes it seem like the Court perceived this difficulty as primarily a problem for the claimant, who may not be adequately protected from the potential harms of worldwide publication of defamatory online content:

> *"The difficulties in giving effect, within the context of the internet, to the criterion relating to the occurrence of damage [...] contrasts [...] with the serious nature of the harm which may be suffered by the holder of a personality right who establishes that information injurious to that right is available on a world-wide basis."*[60]

The adverse effects for the defendant and, indeed, the court system, on the other hand, were apparently acceptable, with the Court explicitly upholding the mosaic approach as an alternative option for the claimant.[61]

Second, the mosaic approach is inherently one-sided. It gives the claimant access to the courts of (up to) 27 member states and (for the time being) the UK, while leaving the defendant exposed to the risk of as many lawsuits.[62] Although the competence of these courts will be territoriality-limited, these different actions can be burdensome to defend[63] and may

---

58 See AG Bobek, Opinion on *Bolagsupplysningen* (n 32), [80]: 'Such apportioning of the harm is, in the light of the specific medium of the internet, difficult if not impossible to exercise.'; see also AG Cruz Villalón, Opinion on *Hejduk* (n. 52), paras. 20, 39–40, 42; Burkhard Hess (n. 25), 106.

59 *eDate* (n. 19), para. 46.

60 *Ibid*, para. 47.

61 *Ibid*, para. 51.

62 See Trevor Hartley, *Civil Jurisdiction and Judgments in Europe* (OUP 2017), para. 8.107; Eva Lein, in Andrew Dickinson/Eva Lein (eds), *The Brussels I Regulation Recast* (OUP 2015), para. 4.112; Michel Reymond (n. 26), 501; Wolfgang Hau, 'Klagemöglichkeiten juristischer Personen nach Persönlichkeitsrechtsverletzungen im Internet' GRUR 2018, 163, 165.

63 See Annette Kur, 'Trademark Conflicts on the Internet: Territoriality Redefined?', in Jürgen Basedow et al (eds), *Intellectual Property in the Conflict of Laws* (Mohr Siebeck 2005), 175, 181; Wolfgang Hau (n. 62), 165.

still result in the award of significant damages.[64] Where the claimant has access to centre-of-interests jurisdiction, the main benefit of mosaic-approach jurisdiction may therefore be to select one or numerous fora that are particularly disadvantageous for the defendant.[65] As AG Bobek explained in a well-stated critique of the mosaic approach in his Opinion on *Bolagsupplysningen*,

> *"I fail to see how the availability of a further 27 jurisdictions helps either party, beyond the manifest potential offered to the claimant to harass the defendant with oppressive claims in parallel jurisdictions."*[66]

Third (and maybe most importantly in the context of this conference), the mosaic approach sits quite uncomfortably with several principles underlying the Brussels I framework. Giving the claimant access to a wide range of fora the selection between which may be virtually impossible to predict for the defendant, it conflicts with the principle of legal certainty.[67] Where their availability is based on the accessibility of content alone, the mosaic approach similarly conflicts with the principle of proximity,[68] relying on a particularly weak connection between the case and the forum.[69]

In the same vein, the mosaic approach is in tension with the principle of *actor sequitur forum rei*, according to which

> *"persons domiciled in a [member state] are to be sued in the courts of that State, irrespective of the nationality of the parties.*
> *It is only by way of derogation from that fundamental principle that the [Brussels I framework] makes provision […] for, in particular, special juris-*

---

64 See *Bin Mahfouz v Ehrenfeld* [2005] EWHC 1156 (QB), where the £ 115,000 were awarded as compensation for 23 copies of an allegedly defamatory book that were sold in England and the first chapter that was made available online; see also Ali GR Auda, 'A proposed solution to the problem of libel tourism' (2016) 12 *JPIL* 106, 109–10.

65 Dan Jerker B Svantesson, *Private International Law and the Internet* (3rd edn, Kluwer 2016), 220; Peter Picht, 'Von eDate zu Wintersteiger – Die Ausformung des Art. 5 Nr. 3 EuGVVO für Internetdelikte durch die Rechtsprechung des EuGH' GRUR Int 2013, 19, 23.

66 AG Bobek, Opinion on *Bolagsupplysningen* (n. 32), para. 88.

67 As to which see, e.g., Case C-256/00 *Besix* ECLI:EU:C:2002:99, [26]. See also Picht (n. 65), 23.

68 As to which see, e.g., Case C-12/15 *Universal Music* ECLI:EU:C:2016:449, para. 27.

69 See also AG Cruz Villalón, Opinion on *Hejduk* (n. 52), para. 44; AG Jääskinen, Opinion on *Pinckney* (n. 52), para. 69.

dictional rules […] where the choice depends on an option to be exercised by the claimant."[70]

In every internet case before the ECJ in which the claimant tried to rely on mosaic-approach jurisdiction, they had seised the courts of the member state in which they were domiciled; with the exception of *Bolagsupplysningen*, all of these attempts were successful. As Etienne Farnoux has shown in his paper,[71] the Court, in many of these cases, may have been more concerned with providing jurisdictional protection to the alleged victim of an online tort than with establishing a particularly close connection to a specific forum that justifies a derogation from Art 4(1) Brussels Ia.

Finally, the mosaic approach conflicts with the principle of sound administration of justice, according to which

"it is necessary to avoid the multiplication of courts of competent jurisdiction which would heighten the risk of irreconcilable decisions […]."[72]

While the ECJ has (somewhat)[73] solved the problem of contradictory injunctions (by limiting mosaic-approach jurisdiction to compensatory damages), the mosaic approach still allows for numerous actions over different territorial slices of the same claim to be brought in different member states. Yet, it is unclear to what extent the Brussels Ia Regulation makes it possible to effectively coordinate these claims.[74] For courts that have 'full' jurisdiction (eg as the court of the defendant's domicile), an answer may be found in Art 29(1), (3) Brussels Ia, which give preference to the court first seised and may require other courts to decline their jurisdiction, possibly even where it is only for one part of the overall claim. Between courts with territorially limited jurisdiction, though, each claim is likely to be considered a different cause of action; pursuant to Art 30(1) Brussels Ia, it will then be in the discretion of each of these courts to decide whether they want to stay their proceedings. But even where they decide to do so, a stay will only solve the problem of parallel proceedings; nothing in the Regulation prevents a court from coming to a different conclusion regard-

70 Case C-256/00 *Besix* ECLI:EU:C:2002:99, paras. 52–53. See also Case C-412/98 *Group Josi* ECLI:EU:C:2000:399, paras. 34–35.

71 See Etienne Farnoux, DELENDUM EST FORUM DELICTI, Towards the Jurisdictional Protection of the Alleged Victim in Cross-Border Torts, in this volume.

72 *Dumez France* (n. 28), paras. 17–18. See also Recital (21) Brussels Ia.

73 See below, under 2.3.2.

74 See also Wolfgang Hau (n 62), 165; Boris P. Paal, 'Online-Suchmaschinen – Persönlichkeitsrechts- und Datenschutz. Internationale Zuständigkeit, anwendbares Recht und sachrechtliche Fragen' *ZEuP* 2016, 591, 598.

ing the part of the damage for which it has jurisdiction than another court that has jurisdiction for another part of the damage.

All of these arguments are, of course, well-known to the ECJ. The Court had the benefit of several well-argued opinions by its Advocate Generals that advised it against maintaining and/or further extending the mosaic approach. In his opinion on *Pinckney*, AG Jääskinen proposed to supplement the mosaic approach with the targeting criterion the Court had developed in other contexts.[75] AG Cruz Villalón, in his opinion on *Hejduk*, argued that the mosaic approach should simply not be applied to cases in which the damage is 'delocalised'.[76] Similarly, AG Bobek urged the Court in his opinion on *Bolagsupplysningen* to

> *"bring the jurisdictional rules for internet-based defamatory statements back and arguably closer to the roots of extra-contractual/tortious liability of [the Brussels I framework] itself, limiting special jurisdiction to two scenarios: where the event giving rise to the harm occurred and where the harm occurred. The latter head of jurisdiction would be defined as where the reputation of the claimant was most strongly affected. That is the place of his centre of interests."*

With the ECJ having somewhat reduced the adverse effects of the mosaic approach in its decision on *Bolagsupplysningen* but having otherwise refused to follow any of the aforementioned opinions, it seems safe to say that the mosaic approach to online torts is here to stay for the foreseeable future.

2.3. *The Ugly: Inconsistencies and Open Questions*

While the Court seems to have somewhat consolidated the framework of special jurisdiction for online torts, there remain several potential inconsistencies and open questions.

2.3.1. *Limited availability of centre-of-interests jurisdiction*

The ECJ has made clear that the claimant's centre of interests is only available as a forum for claims based on violations of personality rights. This

---

75 AG Jääskinen, Opinion on *Pinckney* (n. 52), paras. 59–71.

76 AG Cruz Villalón, Opinion on *Hejduk* (n. 52), paras. 33–47.

has been justified by reference to the particular risk to which the victims of these torts are exposed by publications that are made available worldwide via the internet.[77] The holders of other rights, such as the owners of intellectual property, might argue, though, that they are exposed to similar risks when it comes to torts committed via the internet; the loss they suffer can similarly be spread across countless jurisdictions.[78] Similarly, the difficulties to establish the territorial scope of a national court's jurisdiction that the centre-of-interests criterion aims to overcome,[79] is not limited to infringements of personality rights.[80]

Of course, the centre of interests as an additional forum is not only justified negatively – by the inability of other potential fora to reflect the claimant's particular need for protection in internet cases – but also positively – by the fact that a claimant's personality rights will often be concentrated and thus most severely affected in this country. Although the extent to which personality rights can actually be concentrated in a single country may be debatable, it is true that other rights would generally be much more difficult to localise in this way.

Still, the limited availability of the centre of interests as an additional basis of jurisdiction for the entire loss suffered inevitably creates a strong distinction between infringements of personality rights and other torts. While the claimant will regularly profit from a *forum actoris* with unlimited jurisdiction in the former case, they will have to either seise the courts of the defendant's 'home' country (domicile and/or place of acting) or rely on the mosaic approach.

Importantly, this requires not only a distinction between infringements of personality rights and other torts but also a distinction between online and offline torts, with the centre of interests only being available for the former.[81]

77 *eDate* (n 19), para. 47. See also Christian Heinze, 'Der Deliktsgerichtsstand als Klägergerichtsstand? – Zum Einfluss materiellrechtlicher Wertungen auf die Auslegung des Art. 7 Nr. 2 EuGVO', in Wolfgang Büscher et al. (eds), *Rechtsdurchsetzung. Rechtsverwirklichung durch materielles Recht und Verfahrensrecht. Festschrift für Hans-Jürgen Ahrens zum 70. Geburtstag* (Carl Heymanns 2016), 521, 525.

78 See also Peter Mankowski (n. 27), Art 7, para. 370.

79 See *eDate* (n. 19), para. 46.

80 See Jan von Hein (n. 27), 84.

81 See Peter Mankowski (n 27), Art 7, para. 371.

2.3.2. *'Full' and 'partial' jurisdiction*

The differences between infringements and personality rights and other torts are not (necessarily) limited to the availability of the centre of interests as an additional forum. So far, the ECJ has only had an opportunity to specify the scope of mosaic-approach jurisdiction in a personality-rights case. Clearly, there are strong reasons to believe that the Court did not intend for its decision in *Bolagsupplysningen* to be limited to these cases, with the Court holding in very general terms that

> *"[...] an application for the rectification of [information] and the removal of [content] is a single and indivisible application and can, consequently, only be made before a court with jurisdiction to rule on the entirety of an application for compensation for damage [...] and not before a court that does not have jurisdiction to do so."*

Two observations may however cast some doubt on the transferability of this reasoning.

First, for violations of personality rights, the unavailability of mosaic-approach jurisdiction for injunctions is compensated by the claimant's ability to seise the courts at their centre of interests as a forum with 'full' jurisdiction. For other torts, the claimant will however only be able to obtain an injunction in the courts of the place in which the defendant has acted, which will often coincide with their domicile.[82] This might be seen as running counter to the otherwise rather protective position taken by the ECJ with regard to special jurisdiction for online torts.

Second, on at least one occasion (which arose after *Bolagsupplysningen* had been referred to the ECJ but before it was decided), the Court seems to have allowed an arguably 'indivisible' remedy to be based on mosaic-approach jurisdiction. In *Concurrence*, it held that the French courts had jurisdiction to order the defendant to remove products from websites that could be accessed in France.

From a policy point of view, however, there can be little doubt that it would be preferable for the mosaic approach – if not abolished entirely – to be generally limited to claims for compensatory damages. It would not only better align the two different regimes for online torts but also eliminate both the difficulty that consists in territorially limiting most other types of awards and the particular risk of vexatious litigation posed by injunctions that are based on 'partial' jurisdiction. Put differently, if a

82 See also Wolfgang Hau (n. 62), 165.

main justification of the mosaic approach consists in the fact that it strikes a fair balance between the interests of the claimant (by giving them access to the courts in every single member state in which they may have suffered a damage) and the defendant (by limiting the competence of these courts to a small slice of the overall claim),[83] it should not be available for remedies that cannot be so limited.

Paradoxically, though, if the restrictive understanding of the mosaic approach were applied to all online torts, the contrast between the two regimes distinguished above would increase even further. While the victims of personality rights will often be able to seek all possible remedies in the courts of their own country of domicile, the victims of other torts will often be limited to claiming monetary compensation outside the courts of the defendant's domicile.

2.3.3. Divisible and indivisible remedies

Finally, the decision in *Bolagsupplysningen* raises the question of what remedies qualify as 'divisible' and can therefore still be based on territorially limited jurisdiction. So far, it is clear that awards of compensatory damages (which have been sought in the vast majority of cases that have been referred to the ECJ) are divisible in this sense while injunctions to rectify or remove content are not. What about other kinds of damage awards and injunctions, though?

It is submitted that damages of a vindicatory or punitive nature as well as all injunctions that are not clearly limited to the forum state should be similarly considered as indivisible because they focus on the defendant's wrongdoing rather than the harm caused and would therefore indeed be very difficult to split into territorial slices.[84] Injunctions that are clearly limited to a single member state (such as an injunction not to make content available in this member state) might conceivably be based on mosaic-approach jurisdiction, if one accepts that they can only be implemented to a certain degree before having a *de facto* world-wide effect.

Of course, the more narrowly one construes the category of divisible remedies, the less attractive mosaic-approach jurisdiction becomes. But given the serious concerns about the mosaic approach raised above, such a narrow construction might actually constitute a step towards a viable com-

83 See Peter Mankowski (n. 27), Art 7, paras. 257–262.

84 See also Wolfgang Hau (n 62), 164.

promise between the claimant's interest in getting compensation in the courts of a member state in which they allegedly suffered a damage and these concerns.

3. *Fit for New Challenges?*

Seven years after the decision in *eDate*, the Court's interpretation of what is now Art 7(2) Brussels Ia remains strongly influenced by its initial reaction to the perceived dangers of online communication. Although the Court has since received numerous opportunities to clarify and refine its jurisprudence, it has been claimed – maybe not wrongly – that much of its case law is addressing the symptoms rather than the problem.[85]

There still is a lot to be said for the proposition that Art 7(2) Brussels Ia should not be applied to internet cases at all, at least to the extent that it refers to the place of the damage.[86] But with every decision in which the Court further refines individual elements of the framework described in this paper, such a radical change of approach becomes less likely.

Consequently, it may be time to look beyond the question of the appropriateness of the Court's approach to online torts and inquire about the interplay between its individual ingredients. Will the framework of interpretation that the Court has established be able to provide guidance as technology inevitably evolves?

Prima facie, one may be sceptical, considering the apparent limitation to certain media of both the centre-of-interests criterion and the mosaic approach.[87] This limitation may however turn out to be less problematic than it seems.

Firstly, some technological developments may actually facilitate the application of the aforementioned rules and criteria. The increasing reliability of geo-blocking technology, for instance, although in tension with

85 Sebastian Kubis, 'Zum Tatortgerichtsstand bei grenzüberschreitenden Äußerungsdelikten' *WRP* 2018, 139, 144, for whom the actual root of the problem is the ECJ's broad approach to special jurisdiction in *Shevill*.

86 See Tobias Lutzi (n. 57), 710–12. See also AG Cruz Villalón, Opinion on *Hejduk* (n. 52), para. 45; Peter-Andreas Brand, 'Persönlichkeitsrechtsverletzungen im Internet, E-Commerce und "Fliegender Gerichtsstand"' NJW 2012, 127, 129.

87 The centre-of-interests criterion has been limited to 'person[s] who ha[ve] suffered an infringement of a personality right by means of the internet': see *eDate* (n. 19), para. 48; *Bolagsupplysningen* (n. 32), paras. 32–33. Given its origin in an offline case, the mosaic approach is not necessarily so limited, although the Court has only ever applied it in online cases since.

the EU Commission's aim of creating a 'Digital Single Market',[88] may allow for injunctions that can be limited to the territory of an individual member state without having a *de facto* worldwide effect.

At the same time, the emergence of increasingly pervasive online platforms may have a concentrating effect on jurisdiction. It not only seems to move certain disputes out of the court system entirely (which are instead resolved directly by the platform hosts), but has also caused a certain shift of litigation away from the individual relationships between users towards claims brought against the platform hosts, who are often easier to identify and able to provide an effective remedy to the aggrieved party.[89] It is not unlikely, for instance, that if the two lawsuits referred to the Court in *eDate* were brought today, they would not be brought against the publisher of the online articles in question but against some social-media platform that actually made them available to a wider audience.[90]

Secondly, the ECJ's case law ultimately seems to focus on the risk of worldwide dissemination of information, rather than on the specific technology through which this risk is created. It relies on a combination of action-based and effects-based reasoning that may easily enough be extended to new technologies and challenges.

In order to preserve this flexibility, it is suggested that the Court should put an emphasis on carefully drawing the line between cases in which the claimant's need for protection merits the benefit of a centre-of-interests *forum actoris* and cases in which they do not. As the Court seems unlikely to abandon this criterion, it should consider its extension to all infringements of personality rights (a category that should, in turn, be narrowly construed).[91] This would dissociate the criterion from the medium in question and, instead, align it more firmly with the underlying idea of protecting the victims of these torts by concentrating jurisdiction in the courts of the member state in which the alleged infringement 'is usually felt most

---

88 See Communication from the Commission to the European Parliament, the Council, the European Economic and Social Committee and the Committee of the Regions: A Digital Single Market Strategy for Europe, COM(2015) 192 final.

89 See, e.g., *Camille Saskia Richardson v Facebook, Google (UK) Limited* [2015] EWHC 3154 (QB) and *CG v Facebook Ireland* [2016] *NICA* 54, both involving claims by Facebook users complaining about the company's failure to remove defamatory or otherwise objectionable information that had been posted by third parties.

90 In the case underlying the ECJ's widely reported decision in *Google Spain* (Case C-131/12 ECLI:EU:C:2014:317), for instance, the removal of allegedly privacy-infringing information was not requested from the initial publisher but from the search engine run by Google.

91 See also Jan von Hein (n. 27), 78; Heinze (n. 77), 535; Boris P. Paal (n. 74), 596.

keenly' and in which 'the damage caused by online material occurs most significantly'.[92]

In the same vein, it is hoped that the limitation of mosaic-approach jurisdiction to (a narrowly construed group of) 'divisible' remedies becomes a general feature of the Court's interpretation of Art 7(2) Brussels I. While not eliminating all potential for vexatious litigation, it would significantly reduce the risk of mosaic-approach jurisdiction being used to obtain remedies that are territorially limited in nothing but name. Indeed, the close link between the limitation to 'divisible' remedies and the concept of territorially divided jurisdiction that seems to be implicit in the decision in *Bolagsupplysningen*[93] indicates that said limitation applies to all online torts.

If the Court of Justice remains committed to maintaining both the centre-of-interests criterion and the mosaic approach – despite the serious concerns that have been raised with regard to each of them individually, and with regard to their coexistence[94] – it must continue its effort to refine their respective scopes in light of both the underlying policy considerations and their interplay with the Brussels framework more broadly.

92 *Bolagsupplysningen* (n. 32), para. 33.

93 See *ibid*, para. 48.

94 See also Heinze (n. 77), 535; Boris P. Paal (n. 74), 596.

Encoding Justice: A Quest for Facilitating Access to Justice by e-Handling of Cross-Border Litigation. The Example of the European Uniform Procedures

*Elena Alina Onţanu**

Table of Contents

* Assistant professor in Private International Law, Erasmus University Rotterdam. Contact: ontanu@law.eur.nl. The research on which the paper is based was supported by the Me-CODEX Project co-funded by the European Commission Justice Programme. The contents of this report are the sole responsibility of the author and can in no way be taken to reflect the views of the European Commission.
The author wishes to thank Marco Velicogna (IRSIG-CNR) for comments on earlier drafts of this paper.

1. Introduction

During the last decades, the integration and use of information and communication technologies (ICT) in the area of justice has been forwarded at European and national levels.[1]

Digitisation of procedure has emerged gradually in different areas of civil justice, from basic court administration tasks, to procedural steps, and full online handling procedures.[2] European and national actions have sought to create the necessary legal and technological framework that would facilitate the use of ICT in court and out-of-court procedures.[3]

The quest for introducing more technology support in handling various stages of European procedural instruments has gradually materialised. e-Justice actions have been high on the agenda of the European policymaker (Digital Agenda for Europe).[4] Developments have focused on various aspects of cross-border litigation, namely: providing information necessary for the use of various European instruments on dedicated websites; electronic access to standard forms related to European procedural instruments and their automatic translation of standard text; access to national registers and professional contacts; adopting procedural rules that support ICT use at various stages of the proceedings; and full electronic handling of cross-border claims. These actions have involved not only the building of technical infrastructure but also establishing the appropriate legal framework within EU instruments. The EU has actively encouraged and pursued the digitalisation of European procedures at various levels from the forwarding of the use of ICT in court proceedings, to dedicated online

1 M. Velicogna, *Use of Information and Communication Technologies (ICT) in European Judicial Systems*, CEPEJ Studies No. 7, Council of Europe, 2008, p. 1–64. F. Contini, M. Fabri, *Judicial Electronic Data Interchange in Europe: Applications, Policies and Trends*. Lo Scarabeo; 2003. F. Contini, M. Fabri (eds.), *Justice and Technology in Europe: How ICT is Changing the Judicial Business*, Hague: Kluwer Law International, 2001.

2 M. Velicogna, 'Justice systems and ICT-What can be learned from Europe', *Utrecht Law Review*, 3(2007)1, p. 129–147 (available at https://www.utrechtlawreview.org/articles/abstract/10.18352/ulr.41/); X.E. Kramer, 'Access to Justice and Technology: Transforming the Face of Cross-Border Litigation and Adjudication in the EU', in K. Benyekhlef, J. Baley, J. Burkell, F. Gélinas (eds.), *e-Access to Justice*, University of Ottawa Press, 2016, p. 352.

3 See M. Velicogna, 'e-Justice in Europe: From national Experiences to EU Cross-Border Service Provision', in L. Alcaide Muñoz and M.P.R. Bolívar (eds.), *International e-Government Development. Policy, Implementation and Best Practices*, Palgrave Macmillan, 2017, p. 39–72.

4 https://ec.europa.eu/digital-single-market/.

portals (e.g. Judicial Atlas, e-Justice Portal), and, ultimately the digital handling of the European uniform procedures. This last part is still to be fully accomplished.

European developments have been preceded by national initiatives to digitally handle claims from the submission phase to the delivery of judgment (e.g. ERV in Austria,[5] Money Claim Online in the UK,[6] Trial-Online in Italy[7]). At national level, the ICT developments that were initially seen as tools to increase the efficiency of judicial operations and transparency[8] are now deeply rooted in the judicial machinery affecting the way domestic trials and judicial proceedings are carried out.[9] Judicial procedures and courts are increasingly relying on ICT and network infrastructure to exchange data, judicial documents, and secure communication between authorities, practitioners, and parties.

In turn, national digital justice systems and infrastructures play a key role in the development and deployment of a European e-Justice ICT layer that looks to achieve interconnection of national courts and professionals across the EU. Digitalisation and advancements at European level depend significantly on national ICT achievements and Member States' willingness to be involved in actions that enhance cross-border interoperability. These developments are not without difficulties as domestic ICT systems and infrastructures differ from each other and have not been created or evolved in relation to each other. They rely on different technical architectures and procedural rules that contribute to their diversity and country

---

5 M. Koch, D. Zoubek, M. Velicogna, *Study of the Austrian e-Justice infrastructure, governance and experience in connecting the applications used by legal professionals to the e-CODEX infrastructure to identify existing best practices,* Pro-CODEX Project Report, IRSIG, Bologna, June 2018, p. 56.

6 J. Kallinikos, 'Institutional complexities and functional simplification. The case of Money Claims Online', in F. Contini and G.F. Lanzara (eds.), *ICT and innovation in the public sector*, Palgrave Macmillan, 2009, p. 66–87; M. Velicogna, 'e-Justice in Europe: From National Experiences to EU Cross-Border Service Provision', in L. Alcaide Muñoz and M.P.R. Bolívar (eds.), *International e-Government Development. Policy, Implementation and Best Practices*, Palgrave Macmillan, 2018, p. 39–72.

7 D. Carnevali, A. Resca, 'Pushing at the edge of maximum manageable complexity: The case of 'trial online' in Italy' in F. Contini, G.F. Lanzara (eds.), *The circulation of agency in e-Justice*, Springer, 2014, p. 161–183.

8 See Velicogna (n.2), p. 129–147; M. Velicogna, G.Y. Ng, 'Legitimacy and Internet in the judiciary: A Lesson from the Italian Courts' Websites Experience', *International Journal of Law and Information Technology*, 14(2006)3, p. 370–389.

9 G.F. Lanzara, 'Building digital institutions: ICT and the rise of assemblages in government', in F. Contini and G.F. Lanzara (eds.), *ICT and Innovation in the Public Sector*, Palgrave Macmillan, 2009, p. 9–48.

specificity. Additionally, complete digitisation of procedures can limit access to justice for low computer literate parties and require new approaches in order to deal with the rigidity of standardisation. As different levels of national and European procedural complexities have to be handled together, this can result in threats to the quality of justice.[10] The complexity and implication of large-scale ICT developments are challenging to foresee upfront. There are no other experiences of European e-Justice platforms development that can serve to guide the present challenge of building an ICT architecture for digitally handling European cross-border procedures. Furthermore, technological interoperability by itself is not enough to support cross-border judicial communication. Law and technology are two distinctive regulative regimes that have to be assembled in a common system across jurisdictions to achieve effective interconnection and allow legally valid communication.[11] Current national and European legislation is not effective in providing the organisational frameworks that can adequately address the complexity citizens and courts face.[12] In referring to this complexity, the concept of agency will be used. 'Agency' is broadly defined by Lanzara as 'the capacity of an entity – human or non-human, material or symbolic – to produce effects upon a state of affairs'.[13] Legal agency has to be understood as multilayer interoperability of infrastructure and strategies developed to reduce and handle interactive and dynamic complexity.[14]

---

10 M. Hildebrandt, *Legal Protection by Design in the Smart Grid. Privacy, data protection and profile transparency*, Smart Energy Collective.

11 M. Velicogna, 'Building Infrastructures for Smart Cities: The e-CODEX Infrastructure and API for Justice Project Experiences', in M.P. Rodríguez Bolívar (ed.), *Setting Foundations for the Creation of Public Value in Smart Cities*, Springer, 2019 (forthcoming 2019). F. Contini, 'Let agency circulate: architectures and strategies for pan-European e-Justice', in F. Contini and G.F. Lanzara (eds.), *The Circulation of Agency in E-Justice. Interoperability and Infrastructures for European Transborder Judicial Proceedings*, Springer, 2014, p. 331–353.

12 With regard to the European uniform procedures, especially the European Order for Payment and the European Small Claims Procedure, see E.A. Onţanu, *Cross-Border Debt Recovery in the EU. A Comparative and Empirical Study on the Use of the European Uniform Procedures*, Intersentia, Cambridge, England, 2017.

13 G.F. Lanzara, 'The Circulation of Agency in Judicial Proceedings: Designing for Interoperability and Complexity', in F. Contini and G.F. Lanzara (eds.), *The Circulation of Agency in E-Justice. Interoperability and Infrastructures for European Transborder Judicial Proceedings*, Springer, 2014, p. 5.

14 F. Contini, G.F. Lanzara, 'Introduction: The Challenge of Interoperability and Complexity in European Civil Proceedings', in F. Contini and G.F. Lanzara

This paper uses the framework of the European Uniform Procedures, in particular the European Order for Payment (EOP), and the European Small Claims Procedure (ESCP),[15] to explore the sources of complexity in digitalising cross-border judicial procedures. The European Uniform Procedures structure aims to reduce complexity and enhance mutual trust by relying on a harmonised procedural format. Their provisions encourage and support the use of ICT in the handling of claims. However, the use of ICT means and their electronic handling depend on national justice systems procedural rules, technical developments, and e-justice regulations.

The present analysis looks to identify elements that can contribute to the development of technology and procedural law solutions in cross-border procedures and offer parties simpler and user-friendly instruments while avoiding pitfalls which might impair accessible and fair online procedure. Technology, procedural, and institutional components are entangled and have to be considered in relation to each other. Present developments are addressed at first before moving on to explore the sources of complexity that such developments bring and that we need to be aware of and properly address. Lastly, the analysis focuses on elements of simplification that are not necessarily technology-driven but are technology supportable and can subsequently contribute to enhancing the use and results of digital solutions for procedural justice.

2. *Access to Justice and ICT*

Access to justice can be seen from the perspective of ease of finding the court premises and specific offices or courtrooms, the presence of physical and language barriers, attention of court personnel to users' needs, availability of procedural forms to be filled in,[16] identification of available procedures, and payment of court fees. However, access to justice has to be understood from a much broader perspective and in close connection with the fundamental rights as guaranteed by Article 6 of the European Con-

(eds.), *The Circulation of Agency in E-Justice. Interoperability and Infrastructures for European Transborder Judicial Proceedings* Springer, 2014, p. xvii.

15 Experience with the Account Preservation Order (EAPO) is still at an early stage and ICT projects only start to incorporate this procedure into their piloted cases. Therefore, information is still thin in relation to this instrument and cannot be extensively relied on for the present analysis.

16 M. Velicogna, 'Electronic access to justice: From theory to practice and back', *Droit et cultures. Revue internationale interdisciplinaire*, (2011)61.

vention of Human Rights and Fundamental Freedoms (ECHR)[17] and Article 47 of the Charter on Fundamental Rights of the European Union (the Charter).[18]

Access to effective justice is crucial for citizens and businesses. However, despite economic and technological advancements, access to justice for those who cannot afford legal services and legal representation remains problematic.[19] Access is also problematic when the costs of proceedings are high and/or disproportionate compared to the value of the claim. An effective access to justice is not limited to the existence of a competent court and a formal entitlement to institute proceedings.[20] It also implies an effective possibility for the parties to bring an action before the court in a particular case in terms of procedural requirements, timeframe, and costs, without being hindered unreasonably by practical impediments,[21] including technology. The right of access to justice, therefore, requires clear, simple access to legal provisions for parties to easily discern and choose the appropriate remedies as well as the court they have to address in a particular case.[22] Technology supporting this process should comply with the same requirements. Additionally, human assistance and alternatives should always remain available for less computer literate parties or parties who have difficulties in using technology.[23] Overly complicated procedures or no instruments enabling the creditor to enforce a judgment he was

17 ECHR, *Golder v UK*, 21 February 1975, Series A, No. 18, 1 EHRR 525. See also P. Leanza, 'Particular Aspects of the Right to a Fair Trial', in P. Leanza and O. Pridal (eds.), *The Right to a Fair Trial. Article 6 of the European Convention on Human Rights*, Wolters Kluwer, 2014, p. 80–81.

18 See also D. Reiling, *Technology for Justice: How Information Technology can support Judicial Reform*, Leiden University Press, 2009, p. 23 (available at http://home.hccnet.nl/a.d.reiling/html/dissertation%20texts/Reiling%20Technologyfor%20Justice.pdfp).

19 See also R. Cohen, H. Clarke, 'The Influence of Digitalization – In What Ways has the Internet Changed the Central Issues of Access to Justice?', *Recht der Werkelijkheid*, 36(2015)3, p. 56.

20 ECHR, *Airey v Ireland*, 9 October 1979, Serias A, No. 32. See also M. Cappelletti, B. Garth, *Access to Justice: The Worldwide Movement to Make Rights Effective. A General Report*, 1978, Vol. I, p. 8–9.

21 E.A. Onțanu, E. Pannebakker, 'Tackling Language Obstacles in Cross-Border Litigation: The European Order for Payment and the European Small Claims Procedure Approach', *Erasmus Law Review*, (2012)3, p. 173.

22 E. Schmidt-Assmann, L. Harings, 'Access to Justice and Fundamental Rights', *Revue Européenne de Droit Public,* (1997)9, p. 529.

23 See also Reiling (n.18), p. 204–205.

awarded may become equivalent to a denial of justice,[24] especially for weaker parties like consumers and small businesses.[25] The possibility to switch to off-line should also be provided to overcome technological rigidities, possible break-downs, or when the complexity of providing the online solution increases above a manageable level.[26]

By adopting the European uniform procedures – EOP, ESCP, and EAPO – the EU legislator sought to offer alternative procedures that are successful in simplifying, speeding up, and reducing the costs of litigation, as well as securing the free circulation of judicial decisions issued according to these instruments. However, the use of these instruments for cross-border claims should not result in a breach of procedural guarantees as recognised by the ECHR or the Charter. It is therefore imperative for courts and justice systems to address access to justice and reflect on the barriers that potential and actual court users must confront, especially in cross-border litigation.[27] From a user's perspective, the justice system is frequently weakened by: (1) formalistic and expensive legal procedures; (2) long procedural delays; (3) prohibitive costs of using court systems; (4) lack of available and affordable legal representation; (5) lack of adequate information about legal provisions, prevailing practices, and limited knowledge of own rights; (6) lack of adequate legal aid systems; and (7) weak enforcement.[28]

Technology, and in particular Internet and justice dedicated platforms (e.g. e-Justice Portal), represents an important means of improving access to justice through its capacity to disseminate legal information at low cost and make it available for potential users at any moment.[29] ICT can be used to simplify access to cross-border legal procedures.[30] This is of particular importance for non-repetitive users and has to be geared in accordance with this aim of facilitating users. However, in order to do so, information

---

24 See M. Andenas 'National Paradigms of Civil Enforcement: Mutual Recognition or Harmonization in Europe?', M. Andenas, B. Hess and P. Oberhammer (eds.), *Enforcement Agency. Practice in Europe*, British Institute of International and Comparative Law, 2005, p. 7–23.

25 Onţanu (n.12), p. 5.

26 Velicogna (n.3), p. 39–72.

27 Velicogna (n.16).

28 See United Nations Development Programme (UNDP) practice note on "Access to Justice".

29 See Reiling (n.18), p. 164.

30 M. Velicogna et al., 'Connecting EU Jurisdictions: Exploring How to Open Justice Across Member States Through ICT', *Social Science Computer Review*, 2018, XX(X), p. 7.

made available online needs to be sufficiently detailed to guide the inexperienced users through the stages of the procedures. In practice, this remains a bottleneck that requires additional actions.[31]

ICT input can be double-sided. It can contribute to lifting some additional barriers faced by parties in cross-border litigation such as distance from a competent court, need to be present in court at various stages (e.g. submitting a claim, conducting a hearing in the ESCP, collecting an enforceable title), and payment of court fees.[32] Furthermore, the ICT can absorb part of the complexity, but it can also create new barriers for parties that have low computer literacy, no extensive access to technology or do not benefit from high technology development for justice in their own country. For example, the payment of court fees has, to a certain extent, proven problematic in practice in relation to the European uniform procedures,[33] although the review of the regulations should contribute to enhance the use of technology and better coordinate necessary national practical information.

The ICT solutions may require a learning process. Occasional parties in cross-border proceedings cannot benefit from such a learning process. The added costs related to the acquisition and implementation of specific software or technology (e.g. eBarreau case in France) are significant.[34]

Going further, ICT platforms such as the e-Justice Portal can become unified entrance points towards court services across the EU and support interaction between parties and authorities. In the context of the European uniform procedures, the EU has been actively encouraging digitalisation also by launching in 2010 a large-scale project called e-CODEX – e-Justice Communication via Online Data Exchange. The project aims to 'achieve interoperability between existing national judicial [e-Justice] systems' for transmitting judicial documents, decisions, and information, and to help 'rationalise and simplify [cross-border] judicial procedures'.[35] The e-Justice Portal aims to secure a 'one-stop-shop' for delivering e-justice in an envi-

31 In relation to the European Order for Payment and the European Small Claims Procedures, see E.A. Onțanu (n.12).

32 Reiling (n.18), p. 167–168.

33 Onțanu (n.12).

34 M. Velicogna, A. Errera, S. Derlange, 'e-Justice in France: the e-Barreau Experience', *Utrecht Law Review*, 7(2011)1, p. 163–187 (available at https://www.utrechtlawreview.org/articles/abstract/10.18352/ulr.153/).

35 Competitiveness and Innovation Framework Programme. ICT Policy Support Programme, CIP ICT PSP Work Programme of 2010, (available at http://ec.europa.eu/information_society/activities/ict_psp/documents / ict_psp_wp2010_final.pdf), p. 30.

ronment looking to maximise the use and benefits of technology in cross-border settings. The infrastructural architecture of the e-CODEX platform should make interaction with the e-Justice Portal and national e-justice systems possible at different levels. Therefore, the e-Justice Portal is not only meant to inform users (especially those who cannot afford legal services) about European and national procedural details, provide access to electronic interactive procedural forms, and to facilitate their online filling in and translation of the standard text, but should (at least in theory) provide the interface to the infrastructure that will allow a complete dematerialisation of cross-border judicial procedures and communication between national authorities, practitioners, and parties in forwarding access to justice.

Such ICT developments are not without problems. Also, digitisation can limit access to justice for less computer literate parties, increase end user access costs, and enhance information systems costs because of standardisation, co-evolution requirements, and exposure to break-down risks. This creates threats to the quality of justice that has to respond to different levels of complexity nationally and European wise.[36] It is therefore imperative for justice systems to address access to justice and reflect not only on the advantages technology can bring, especially in cross-border litigation.[37] It has to consider also the barriers that potential and actual court users can confront with when justice services are delivered online through dedicated software and platforms,[38] as well as the complexity of the techno-legal infrastructure implementation and evolution.[39] These perspectives are key in developing electronic solutions that are able to provide prompt and efficient systems for enforcing judgments because they are vital for an accessible justice.[40]

36 M. Hildebrandt (n.10).

37 See also Velicogna (n.16).

38 See Cohen, Clarke (n.19), p. 63–64.

39 M. Veliconga, E. Steigenga, 'Can Complexity Theory Help Understanding Tomorrow e-Justice?', *Conference on Complex Systems, Law and Complexity Session*, Amsterdam, 20–23 September 2016.

40 Commission Communication to the Council and European Parliament *Towards greater efficiency in obtaining and enforcing judgments in the European Union*, COM (97) 609 final, http://eur-lex.europa.eu/LexUriServ/ LexUriServ.do?uri=COM:1997:0609:FIN:EN:PDF, point 42.

3. The European Uniform Procedures

The European uniform procedures have been adopted to make justice accessible to citizens and business. The European Order for Payment (EOP), the European Small Claims Procedure (ESCP), and the European Account Preservation Order (EAPO) are an alternative to national procedures that parties can choose to use in civil and commercial cross-border claims. The material scope of the three Regulations largely corresponds to that of the Brussels I-bis Regulation.[41] The EOP concerns the recovery of uncontested monetary claims. The ESCP is dedicated to small value claims of up to 5,000 euros in cross-border litigation.[42] Both procedures seek to simplify, speed up, and reduce the costs of civil and commercial litigation, as well as to secure the free circulation of judicial decisions issued between Member States through the abolition of exequatur.[43] The EAPO is a preliminary procedure that contributes to the preservation of assets until enforcement is carried out at the execution stage.[44] This procedure leads to the attachment of debtor's bank account when sufficient evidence is available that there is an urgent need to issue such order to prevent a real risk of subsequent impossibility or substantially more difficult enforcement.[45]

The EOP and the EAPO are single-sided procedures. The orders are both issued by the court on the basis of the claimant's submissions. The ESCP is an adversarial procedure in which a judgment is issued based on the submissions of both parties.

---

41 The EOP and the ESCP have a more limited scope (Article 2 EOP. Article 2 ESCP). See A. Berthe, 'L'impact du règlement Bruxelles I*bis* sur les règlements T.E.E., I.P.E. et R.P.L.', in E. Guinchard (ed.) Le nouveau règlement Bruxelles I bis, Bruylant, 2014, p. 303–306; C. Oro Martinez, 'The Small Claims Regulation: On the Way to an Improved European Procedure?', in B. Hess, M. Bergström, E. Storskrubb (eds.), *EU Civil Justice: Current Issues and Future Outlook*, Hart Publishing, Oxford, 2016, p. 105–106.

42 The ESCP is not limited to monetary claims, but their value should not exceed €5,000 at the time that the court receives the application (Article 5(5) ESCP). See further, X.E. Kramer, 'Small Claim, Simple Recovery? The European Small Claims Procedure and its Implementation in the Member States', *ERA Forum*, (2011)12, p. 121.

43 At the time of their adoption the exequatur procedure was still required under the regime of the Brussels I Regulations (then Regulation (EC) No 44/2001, present Regulation (EU) No 1215/2012).

44 The court can be issued an EAPOprior to a judgment on the merits, provided the claimant will start court procedures or is carrying out court procedures, or based on an enforceable title that the claimant already obtained.

45 Article 7(1) EAPO.

Although relying on different procedural approaches, the EOP, the ESCP and the EAPO share a number of common features. Their object is limited to cross-border cases. They establish a uniform procedural framework that seeks to ensure equal treatment for users in cross-border cases[46] and a set of minimum standards that have to be complied with to guarantee a fair trial. All three procedures are applied and function in the national procedural context, relying for their application on a number of domestic procedural rules and practices (e.g. service, costs of proceedings, payment of court fees, handling of procedures by the courts, transfer to national ordinary procedure, appellate proceedings and remedies, enforcement). In these situations, the provisions of the regulations have to be coordinated and/or supplemented by national procedural rules. Additionally, national procedural rules will apply to all matters that are not explicitly dealt with by the three regulations.[47] This leaves room for national specificities within the framework of the European uniform procedures[48] that are not immediately visible to users, especially first-time users. For example, for the EOP and the ESCP, the information presented by citizens' guides give a much-simplified vision of the procedures, of their applications, and of the implications these have for the party.[49]

---

46 E. Storskrubb, *Civil Procedure and EU Law: a Policy Area Uncovered*, Oxford University Press, 2008, at 214 and 229–230.

47 Art. 26 EOP, Art. 19 ESCP, Art. 46 EAPO. Onţanu (n.12); G. Payan, 'La procédure d'injonction de payer européenne: entre efficacité et insécurité', *Ius&Actores* (2014)2, p. 246–247; Kramer (n.42), p. 111–112; M. Lopez de Tejada and L. d'Avout, 'Les non-dits de la procédure européenne d'injonction de payer', *Revue critique de droit international privé*, 96(2007)4, p. 724–725.

48 X.E. Kramer, 'Major Step in the Harmonization of Procedural Law in Europe: the European Small Claims Procedure Accomplishments, New Features and Some Fundamental Questions of European Harmonization', in A.W. Jongbloed (ed.), *The XIIIth World Congress of Procedural Law: The Belgian and Dutch Reports*, Antwerpen: Intersentia, 2008, p. 282. For an Italian example of national specificities with regard to an EOP claim see M. Velicogna, 'e-CODEX and the Italian Piloting Experience', *IRSIG-CNR Working Paper V. 1.0*, July 30, 2015 (available at https://ssrn.com/abstract=2726515).

49 European Commission, *A Citizens' Guide to Cross-Border Litigation in the European Union*, p. 5 and 10–11 (available at http://ec.europa.eu/civiljustice/publications/docs/guide_litiges_civils_transfrontaliers_en.pdf). Information presenting the EOP on the e-Justice website (available at https://e-justice.europa.eu/content_european_payment_order-353-en.do). M. Velicogna, G. Lupo, M. Mellone, 'Notification and Service of Documents in National and European Civil Procedures', *e-CODEX WP7 Report V1.0*, December 2015; M. Velicogna, G. Lupo, E.A. Ontanu, 'Simplifying access to justice in cross-border litigation, the national practices and the lim-

All three procedures are meant to be conducted in writing using standard forms. The forms were carefully designed in an attempt to make them user-friendly for the parties, particularly as legal representation is not mandatory.[50] To facilitate their use, guidelines and short explanations are included in the forms.[51] The mainly written standard forms based procedures are particularly suitable for electronic handling – from the submission of the claim to the issuance of a court decision and request for enforcement. For the ESCP cases when hearings are to be held, the use of ICT means are highly encouraged. Furthermore, the provisions of all three European uniform procedures support and seek to forward the use of electronic communication means at various stages of the proceedings. These regard the electronic communication between different judicial authorities as well as the service of documents and taking of evidence. The reviewed ESCP Regulation reinforces the use of ICT for the service of documents by having electronic means of service of documents as the preferred means together with service by post. These provisions of the European uniform procedures are in line with other EU instruments in the area of civil justice that support the use of ICT to facilitate communication when these means are available. However, in practice, the national e-justice systems that can support such electronic transmission require national communication tools and infrastructure that are usually not opened to parties or practitioners from other Member States. Hence, these national e-justice systems cannot be used in cross-border claims.

Additionally, besides the dedicated provisions that encourage the use of ICT during the proceedings, the European uniform procedures have been part of a number of European initiatives that aim to encourage electronic handling of claims in cross-border situations. These initiatives will be fur-

---

its of the EU procedures. The example of the service of documents in the order for payment claims', *International Journal of Procedural Law*, (2017)1.

50 Article 24 EOP, Article 10 ESCP, Article 41 EAPO.

51 X.E. Kramer, 'Enhancing Enforcement in the European Union. The European Order for Payment and its Implementation in the Member States, particularly in Germany, the Netherlands and England', C.H. van Rhee and A. Uzelac (eds.), *Enforcement and Enforceability: Tradition and Reform*, Intersentia, 2010, p. 23; X.E. Kramer, 'The European Small Claims Procedure: Striking the Balance Between Simplicity and Fairness in European Litigation', *Zeitschrift für Europäisches Privatrecht*, 16(2008), p. 362. See also, European Commission, *Practice Guide for the Application of the Regulation on the European Order for Payment*, 2011; European Commission, *Practice guide for the application of the European Small Claims Procedure under Regulation (EC) No 861/2007 of the European Parliament and of the Council of 11 July 2007 establishing a European Small Claims Procedure*, 2013.

ther discussed in Section 4. The uniform framework these European procedures propose in cross-border litigation and their reliance on standard forms make these instruments particularly suitable for electronic handling. However, not all exchanges in a European procedure situation can be handled via standard forms. For example, the procedures standard forms do not cover the communication requirements deriving from national procedural provisions.[52]

Judgments and orders issued based on these European procedures are automatically enforceable in other Member States (except Demark) without needing a declaration of enforceability or the possibility of opposing recognition.[53] The European procedures abolished the grounds of refusal, except for the ground pertaining to the irreconcilability of judgments that can still be invoked by an interested party.[54] Execution of the decision is to be carried out in accordance with the national law of the Member State in which this is enforced, similar to a national judgment. The possibilities of refusal, of stay, and of limitation of enforcement are established in a limited manner by the regulations. The use of ICT means at this stage depends on their availability for making enforcement requests based on European procedure titles.

4. *Digital Justice via Portals and European Uniform Procedures*

Over the last decade several initiatives have taken shape in digitalising different aspects of court procedures due to technology's 'great potential to redefine court boundaries and make it more accessible and comprehensible for the public'.[55] Technical innovations towards digital justice have been evolving in a piecemeal fashion. They cover a wide range of aspects, providing access to EU and national legislation and case law, and improving cross-border cooperation between professionals in different Member States, use of digital tools (e.g. videoconferencing, Find a Lawyer, Court Database) and digital processing of cross-border European uniform procedures (e.g. e-CODEX pilots).[56] Although focusing on different contribu-

52 Velicogna (n.48).

53 Art. 1(1)(b) and Art. 19 EOP, Art. 1(2) and Art. 20 ESCP.

54 Art. 22 EOP, Art. 22 ESCP.

55 Velicogna, Ng (n.8), p. 376.

56 Steigenga and Velicogna categorise these developments into e-Law and e-Justice. E. Steigenga, M. Velicogna, 'Envisioning the Next Step in e-Justice: In Search for the Key to Provide Easy Access to Cross-Border Justice for All Users', in B. Hess

tions technology can have in cross-border litigation, all initiatives seek to facilitate and support the application of European uniform procedures as means that can promote access to justice.

4.1. *e-Justice Portal*

In the first phase, the European Commission's efforts have mainly focused on creating websites that provide a range of information on EU justice systems, on national and uniform judicial procedures, on forms necessary for the handling of cross-border judicial proceedings, and making specific legal information about cases or registers available to the public or to specific categories of professionals or parties.[57] The European Commission has also invested a significant amount of effort in setting up legal portals and atlases containing information on national and European instruments in the area of civil justice. These developments have been integrated in recent years in the e-Justice Portal.[58] The e-Justice Portal seeks to support access to justice for European citizens and businesses by making information about their rights, national and European provisions, registers, and legal professionals easily accessible through a single entrance point.[59] The portal was launched in 2010 with the aim of providing 'a single, multilingual, user-friendly access point ('one-stop shop') to the whole European e-Justice system, i.e. to European and national information websites and/or services'.[60] Viviane Reding, the Justice Commissioner at the time, portrayed the e-Justice Portal function as that of increasing knowledge about EU legal systems, building trust and confidence that citizens and businesses rights 'will be protected' no matter where they are in Europe and as a 'one-stop cyber shop for justice information' for EU citizens, businesses, and legal professionals.[61]

---

and X.E. Kramer (eds.), *From Common Rules to Best Practices in European Civil Procedure*, Hart-Nomos Publishing, 2017, p. 250.

57 See also, Contini (n.11), p. 332.

58 https://e-justice.europa.eu.

59 Draft Strategy on European e-Justice 2014–2018 (2013/C 376/06), Recital 33.

60 Draft Strategy on European e-Justice 2014–2018 (2013/C 376/06), Recital 11 and 32.

61 V. Reding quoted at http://europa.eu/rapid/press-release_IP-10-956_en.htm. See further also, M. Velicogna, *e-Justice in Europe: From National Experiences to the EU Cross-Border Service Provision*, 2018.

The content of previously established portals and atlases (i.e. Judicial Atlas, European Judicial Network in Civil and Commercial Matters) about European procedures and instruments as well as relevant national procedural rules in the area of civil justice were gradually transferred to and integrated into the e-Justice Portal. The information transferred was also updated following domestic amendments of relevant rules, and subsequently, all official language versions became available. The process took a significant time to complete. For the EOP and the ESCP this meant that information relevant for the application of these procedures was for some time not easily accessible in all EU official languages and quite dated.[62] This situation impaired access by interested parties to relevant legal information and implicitly to redress by these alternative means.

For the time being the portal's main function is to provide access to information related to national and European procedural rules, case law, standard forms, guidelines, finding professionals in Member States, terminology glossaries, and access to some national and European registers.[63] The information is made available in all EU official languages as 'a means to quickly provide citizens legal information and advice'.[64] With regard to the European uniform procedures, the portal provides consumers and other interested parties with access not only to procedural rules, and general requirements and information relevant for the application of these instruments, but also with access to the dynamic standard forms that can be downloaded or filled in online. Together with this, different wizards have been integrated to support the claimant's choice among the available European procedures based on specific characteristics of his claim as well as identifying the competent national authorities for various stages of the procedures (e.g. jurisdiction, enforcement). The online dynamic forms support an automatic translation of the form's standard text from one EU official language to another. This diminishes the need for translation services and limits it to the details provided in the open-text sections.

---

62 Onţanu (n.12); G.Y. Ng, 'European Payment Order and the European Small Claims Procedure in Practice: Findings from a Simulation Experiment', in F. Contini and G.F. Lanzara (eds.), *The Circulation of Agency in e-Justice. Interoperability and Infrastructures for European Transborder Judicial Proceedings*, Springer, 2014, p. 265–286; G.Y. Ng, 'European Order for Payment and European Small Claim Online Simulation UK-Italy', *Building Interoperability for European Civil Proceedings Online*, Conference Bologna, 15–16 June 2012.

63 Multiannual European e-Justice Action Plan 2014–2018 (2014/C, 182/02), Recitals 15–16.

64 Velicogna (n.61).

The e-Justice Portal has so far been an initiative that relies on technology as a means to facilitate access to relevant information and to support the procedural steps interested parties need to be aware of and to follow in order to lodge their cross-border claims and defend their rights. Although a welcomed initiative, the portal lacks at times sufficiently detailed information that can support unrepresented parties through all procedural stages in order to vindicate and enforce their rights across the Member States.

Furthermore, the European e-Justice Portal is part of a development process that seeks to expand its functionalities from being a provider of information to being a provider of services in the judicial area.[65] Within this phase that began in 2014 the portal supported the interconnection of national registries regarding insolvency, Find a Lawyer, and Find a Notary. This expansion continued subsequently with provision of access to the European Court Databases that allows a search through national and European cases that are attributed a European Case Law Identifier (ECLI).[66]

4.2. e-CODEX

The e-CODEX was launched in 2010 as a large-scale project under the Multiannual European e-Justice Action Plan 2009–2013.[67] The project aims to 'improve the cross-border exchange of information in legal proceedings – where citizens, businesses and governments are involved – in a safe, accessible and sustainable way'[68] and to achieve 'the dematerialisation of cross-border judicial proceedings'.[69] The e-CODEX platform supports the interconnection of national courts' electronic systems to send and/or receive

---

65 European Commission, *Implementing Decision on the Adoption of the Work Programme for 2018 and on the Financing of Connecting Europe Facility (CEF) – Telecommunications Sector*, Annex, Brussels, C(2018) 568 final, p. 74.

66 *Ibid.*

67 Council of the European Union, Permanent Representatives Committee, Working Party on e-Law (e-Justice), 14208/15, Brussels, 20 November 2015, p. 2 (available at http://data.consilium.europa.eu/doc/document/ST-14208-2015-INIT/en/pdf).

68 M. Velicogna, 'Coming to Terms with Complexity Overload in Transborder e-Justice: The e-CODEX Platform', in F. Contini and G.F. Lanzara (eds.), *The Circulation of Agency in e-Justice. Interoperability and Infrastructures for European Transborder Judicial Proceedings*, Springer, 2014, p. 310.

69 M. Veliconga, G. Lupo, 'From Drafting Common Rules to Implementing Electronic European Civil Procedures: The Rise of e-CODEX', in B. Hess, X.E. Kramer

cross-border claims through legal forms filed according to the European uniform procedures – EOP, ESCP, and EAPO,[70] and other information in a secure manner.

The e-CODEX project can be divided into two stages. The first part of the project was dedicated to the establishment of a 'technological platform intended to support data and document communication through the creation of an interoperability layer';[71] thus, setting a layer that allows the cross-border exchange of judicial data and access to cross-border e-Justice services.[72] In developing the e-CODEX architecture, the existing legal, technological and organisational base at national level – existing domestic systems – and European components such as the European uniform procedures and the e-Justice Portal have been used. Once the technological solutions that secure interoperability 'for the cross-border exchange of judicial data' and 'access to cross-border e-Justice services' were built, the legal solutions were developed to address the identified legislative gaps. The techno-legal system so developed was then tested through live 'pilot' implementations. The second stage of the project focuses on the 'long-term sustainability of the solutions' and on 'the implications of the lessons learned' to further develop the EU justice domain.[73]

When it ended in May 2016, the e-CODEX project involved 25 partners among which were 20 Member States together with other institutions such as the Council of Bars and Law Societies of Europe (CCBE), the Council of the Notaries of the European Union (CNUE), and the National Research Council of Italy (IRSIG-CNR and ITTIG-CNR).[74] The project was extended several times from the initial 36 months to the final 66, and has been carried on through various initiatives that build on the e-CODEX platform to provide several digital developments for the handling of cross-

(eds.), *From Common Rules to Best Practices in European Civil Procedure*, Hart Publishing Nomos, 2017, p. 192.

70 The EAOP is deemed to be piloted with courts as part of the Me-CODEX project (Maintenance of e-CODEX), but the initiative has been delayed, and priority was given to the Service of Documents Regulation (Regulation (EC) no. 1393/2007).

71 Velicogna (n.68), p. 311.

72 Veliconga, Lupo (n.69), p. 193.

73 *Ibid.*

74 *Ibid*, p. 192.

border procedures, namely: e-Sens,[75] FAL 2,[76] Pro-CODEX,[77] API for Justice,[78] and Me-CODEX[79].

The e-CODEX is not limited to the 'creation of a technical system' (including an organisational and semantic dimension) that allows for 'the transmission of bits, data, information or even documents between national e-justice systems or with the European e-Justice Portal'.[80] It sought to build an infrastructure that 'supports a legally valid, electronically mediated judicial communication capable of producing legal effects across different EU national jurisdictions'.[81] The e-CODEX platform is set to mediate the material components of the communications (e.g. documents, receipts, confirmations, etc.) and their social and legal value, as well as the material and institutional setting of judicial proceedings in order to secure the authority and recognition of procedures and their values across different justice systems.[82] Furthermore, the e-CODEX solutions chosen had to be 'compatible with the legal systems of the Member States' and 'user friendly' in order for the system to be used.[83] Following the establishment of the technical and legal components, the handling of the first European uniform procedures – the EOP and the ESCP – was piloted between the participating Member States. As remarked by Contini, the European uniform procedures require in their digital handling not only 'accurate and

75 'Electronic Simple European Networked Services' project aims to consolidate the building blocks developed by previous large-scale projects (e.g. e-Signature, e-Identity, e-Delivery, e-Documents).

76 'Find a Lawyer 2' project in the e-CODEX is set to provide the necessary mechanism to ensure that the person claiming to be a lawyer is indeed a qualified lawyer in his home jurisdiction.

77 'Connecting legal practitioners' national applications with e-CODEX infrastructure'. The project investigates the possibilities of creating conditions to make the e-CODEX interoperable with applications used by legal professionals at the national level.

78 'Application Programming Interface for Justice' aims to open up the infrastructure for cross-border legal services provided by e-CODEX and the European Judicial Portal by means of an API; thus, making it possible for third parties to build applications that use the e-CODEX services.

79 'Maintenance of e-CODEX' is set to ensure a swift and sustainable transition of the e-CODEX project towards a long-term sustainability of its building blocks by an agency – EU-LISA (www.eulisa.europa.eu/).

80 Velicogna (n.68), p. 311.

81 *Ibid.*

82 *Ibid*; Veliconga, Lupo (n.69), p. 194.

83 G. Borsari et al., *High Level Architecture Definition*, e-CODEX Deliverable, D7.3, 2018, p. 8.

reliable information about 'how to' use the procedures', a side to which the e-Justice Portal is set to significantly contribute, but also 'mechanisms to support the preparation/drafting of the performative utterance[84] and their transmission to the competent judicial authority'.[85] The pilot projects carried out between courts of different Member States focused first on achieving the effective transmission of the EOP and ESCP data and documents; hence, not only enabling communication between participating courts but supporting the 'identification and expression of will needed for the performance of judicially effective acts in cross-border judicial proceedings'.[86] Therefore, the digital handling of the European uniform procedures involved the establishing of e-Identification and e-Signature systems for the e-CODEX in order to secure the identity of the parties filing the documents and the ones receiving them and/or issuing the decisions and that the documents had a valid signature.[87] An e-Delivery, semantic functions, and cross-border e-Identification and expression of will solutions were developed.

The e-CODEX platform interconnects piloting national authorities and professionals involved in the handling of the European uniform procedures allowing them to communicate data in a meaningful format that 'may carry different interpretations' in different Member States. A gateway infrastructure was adopted in order to allow national and EU e-CODEX solutions to exist independently from each other and convert messages transmitted in a format that each of the connected systems uses, supporting their interoperability.[88] The European uniform procedures provide a level of standardisation that can be handled by such a system. This is why these procedures have been part of the pilots – 'live cases' – testing the cre-

84 The 'performative utterance' has to be understood as involving several actions such as the filing of a case, the exchange of claims and procedural documents, the publication of the decision, etc. See further on performative utterance, R. Mohr, F. Contini, 'Reassembling the Legal. "The Wonders of Modern Science" in Court-Related Proceedings', *Griffith Law Review – Special Symposium: The Laws of Technology and the Technology of Law*, 20(2011)3, p. 994–1019.

85 Contini (n.11), p. 333.

86 Veliconga, Lupo (n.69), p. 181–212.

87 See M. Velicogna, 'The Making of Pan-European Infrastructure: From the Schengen Information System to the European Arrest Warrant', in F. Contini and G.F. Lanzara (eds.), *The Circulation of Agency in e-Justice. Interoperability and Infrastructures for European Transborder Judicial Proceedings*, Springer, 2014, p. 185–216.

88 Veliconga, Lupo (n.69), p. 181–212.

ated environment and connections.[89] For the time being the e-CODEX does not provide an end-user interface.[90] The national e-filing systems of piloting countries are the ones that function as a service provider that allows the transmission of data in the e-CODEX.[91] For example, the Italian Trial Online is connected to the e-CODEX system and enables the piloting at the *Tribunale di Milano* and more recently the piloting lawyers of the Italian Bars of Udine, Pordenone, Milan and Florence with the Austrian e-justice system – *Electronischer Rechtsverkerh (ERV)*. This allows Austrian lawyers to file EOPs digitally at the *Tribunale di Milano* in Italy and the Italian piloting lawyers to file cases at the *Bezirksgericht für Handelssachen*,[92] which has sole jurisdiction in Austria for proceedings lodged according to the EOP procedure.[93]

4.3. Integrating e-Communication Solutions within the EU

Based on the e-CODEX experience and in addition to national solutions, further improvements are being considered to develop the e-Justice Portal into becoming a central European Service Provider. Thus, bringing together the architecture that was developed with existing national solutions in mind, the e-CODEX, and the e-Justice Portal are set to provide support to all EU law users to easily access justice procedures and defend their claims in a cross-border setting. Such approach can contribute to the development of an integrated EU solution based on digital justice. For this it will interconnect already developed platforms (e.g. e-CODEX, Find a Lawyer, Find a Notary) and provide access to users across the Member States through a single entrance point – the e-Justice Portal.[94] This would

89 The EOP live cases have been piloted since August 2013 in seven Member States (Austria, Germany, Estonia, France, Greece, Mata, and Poland). The ESCP live cases have been piloted since June 2015 in Austria, Czech Republic, France, Malta, and Poland.

90 Veliconga, Lupo (n.69), p. 193.

91 *Ibid.*

92 Velicogna, Borsari, *Pro-CODEX Pilot Description and Evaluation*, Pro-CODEX Project Report v1.0, D3.1, IRSIG, Bologna, 2018.

93 https://e-justice.europa.eu/content_order_for_payment_procedures-41-at-en.do?member=1.

94 M. Velicogna, G. Borsari, D. Carnevalli, *Pro-CODEX Best Practises Report*, Pro-CODEX Project Report, D3.2, IRSIG, Bologna, 2018, p. 6 (available at www.irsig.cnr.it/index.php?option=com_content&view=article&id=275&lang=it).

allow access to the e-CODEX system to professional and non-professional users regardless of the level of e-justice infrastructure of the Member States and would open up the system for them to submit online claims.

The opening of the e-CODEX services to the general public via the e-Justice Portal will consolidate the idea of establishing an 'electronic one-stop-stop' in cross-border litigation for European citizens and businesses.[95] The European Commission is moving in this direction by initiating a call for actions which will result in the interlinking of the e-Justice Portal with the e-CODEX platform. For this purpose, the e-Justice Portal Core Service Platform is being actively developed in order to expand the action to the e-CODEX module to allow online submissions of the EOPs and ESCPs that have been previously piloted in the various phases of the project.[96] Several calls for proposals have been launched for this purpose within the framework of Connecting Europe Facility (CEF) and by DG Justice which wants to further e-access to e-CODEX. Additionally, the European Action Grants scheme for 2018 call for proposals looked to secure the maintenance and development of the system for online exchanges between judicial authorities and the e-CODEX platform.[97]

5. Sources of Complexity in Handling EU Procedures Digitally

The switch from paper-based procedures to digital procedures 'is not just a change of the tools used to access information and exchange procedural data and documents' or 'just a way to make justice more efficient and effective', but it 'involves a reconfiguration of the established structure of legal legacy'.[98] The design of procedural infrastructures to allow full online handling of the European procedure involves not only a technical component but requires the amendment of European and national normative frameworks, the (re)design of organisational routines and the learning of new skills. The e-CODEX project revealed that a European full digital justice has to address these components in a multi-setting framework because the various domestic e-justice systems do not find themselves at the same

95 Veliconga, Lupo (n.69), p. 181–212. Draft Strategy on European e-Justice 2014–2018 (2013/C 376/06), Recital 32.

96 See European Commission, *Implementing Decision on the Adoption of the Work Programme for 2018 and on the Financing of Connecting Europe Facility (CEF) – Telecommunications Sector*, Annex, Brussels, C(2018) 568 final, p. 76.

97 See JUST-JACC-EJU-AG-2018.

98 Contini (n.11), p. 332; Lanzara (n.9), p. 9–48.

stage of development and deployment. Additionally, their architecture, technical components, language requirements, applicable procedural rules and requirements differ, reflecting national specificities and development history. Therefore, agency and semantic interoperability solutions need to be considered and put in place to address some of the sources of identified complexity.

5.1. Interrelating Technical and Procedural Requirements

The assemblage of law and technology as two regulative regimes at national level can have major effects for complexity, increasing it and pushing the system development over the so-called 'maximum manageable complexity'. It is not the case that e-Justice national experiences have been characterized quite often by failures or great difficulties.[99] In a cross-border setting, the interaction between multiple legal and institutional frameworks as well as different national e-justice architectures that should be able to communicate and interact with each other in a valid legal proceeding enhances complexity further.

The interrelation of technical and legal components which bring with them their own imperative rules and requirements is one of the first complexities the creation of a digital justice system will have to face when switching from a paper procedure to full digital handling. The identification and translation of technical and procedural requirements into software 'magnifies the complexity in system development'.[100] When law prescribes in detail the use of technological components, the latter can become difficult to use and develop. The e-justice system so constructed becomes slow and challenging to use and disseminate as potential users can find the system's protocols, and organisational and technological developments too onerous, rigid, and demanding to operate.[101] Further-

---

99 M. Velicogna, 'ICTs in the Justice Sector', in R. Coman and C. Dallara (eds.) *Handbook of Judicial Politics,* Institutul European, Iasi, Romania, 2010, p. 195–236; M. Velicogna, A. Errera, S. Derlange, 'Building e-Justice in Continental Europe: the TéléRecours experience in France', *Utrecht Law Review*, 9(2013)1, p. 38–59.

100 O. Hanseth, K. Lyytinen, 'Design Theory for Dynamic Complexity in Information Infrastructures: the Case of Building Internet', *Journal of Information Technology*, 25(2010)1, p. 1–19.

101 See also F. Contini, R. Mohr, 'How the Law Can Make it Simple: Easing the Circulation of Agency in e-Justice', in F. Contini, G.F. Lanzara (eds.), *The Circula-*

more, the systems and functionalities are designed to work only within their national technical and legal environment. For example, in order to secure legally effective communication, an e-delivery solution had to be put in place to allow the exchange of data and documents. For this purpose, an e-Identity and e-Signature components had to be developed and deployed.[102] When the architecture of the e-CODEX was being created, there were no solutions available to have national e-ID verified between the Member States both at technical and legal level. Technology and infrastructure, as well as legal rules providing for them, were nationally specific, but procedural requirements made it necessary to be able to verify and certify the identity in cross-border judicial proceedings. The solution chosen for e-CODEX was a validation mechanism handled by the sender connecting authority (e.g. the Ministry of Justice in a Member State sending the procedural documents).[103] The interoperability between technological, institutional, and legal frameworks of the 27 Member States applying these procedures has the potential of becoming unmanageably complicated given the intricacy of dynamics between technology and law. The e-CODEX architecture sought and seeks to avoid such complexities and to find functional ways to build on national ICT and organisational solutions for civil justice and previous EU infrastructure. In practice, this means having a multiparty agreement that sets the legal basis for recognising such communication between national e-justice systems called the Circle of Trust.[104] This allows parties in the agreement to achieve a certain level of simplification through mutual trust and acceptance of national systems without hampering effective performativity.

Furthermore, this means that common standards have to be agreed by partners in digital procedures handling to develop common solutions and maintain complexity at manageable levels. Semantic interoperability had to be developed by the e-CODEX team in order to enable a meaningful exchange of information between national systems in cross-border proceedings initiated according to the European uniform procedures. This allows the interpretation of specific coding schemas used by domestic semantic structures and their transformation into 'European' semantic

---

tion of Agency in E-Justice. Interoperability and Infrastructures for European Transborder Judicial Proceedings, Springer, 2014, p. 58.

102 Veliconga, Steigenga (n.39); Velicogna (n.48).

103 *e-CODEX Achievements, Use Cases and Technical Building Blocks*, 2015; Veliconga, Steigenga (n.38); Velicogna (n.48).

104 Veliconga, Lupo (n.69), p. 193.

concepts to be recognised by other national standards and semantics.[105] In practice, this led to a significant number of ad-hoc redesigns to integrate and address national specificities that were problematic during the e-CODEX EOP and ESCP pilot cases lodged with courts in participating Member States.[106] Such situations maintain a constant level of complexity that needs to be managed and addressed.

5.2. National Technical and Organisational Infrastructures

In developing European e-justice systems to receive and handle cross-border judicial proceedings such as the European uniform procedures, agency cannot be ignored. This has to be 'projected from one Member State to another without human facilitator or intermediate bodies'.[107] According to Velicogna and Steigenga, 'the cross-border and judicial dimensions together with the diversity of national software application, architectures, software technological and legal environments, and the variety of users and task involved, all contribute to complexity'.[108] In consideration of all these complexities that had to be addressed by the e-CODEX project, the partners developing the digital platform chose to base this on a system of building blocks some of which were built as part of previous EU Large Scale Projects or national projects.

An additional aspect that had to be taken into consideration and contributed to the complexity of the e-CODEX digital initiative involved the organisational components. e-CODEX services provision is not just the result of technical and legal components. It involves and relies on the joint efforts of a number of organisations, roles, and people having different functions (e.g. judges, court staff, technicians, software houses) and inputs in the activities that have to be carried out to achieve the full digital handling of European uniform procedures.

105 Veliconga, Steigenga (n.39); Velicogna (n.61).
106 Veliconga, Steigenga (n.39).
107 Contini, Mohr (n.101), p. 54.
108 Veliconga, Steigenga (n.39).

5.3. Interplay between National and European Rules

The level of standardisation the handling of the European uniform procedures can reach has its limitations due to its basic design logic which relies on national systems for their implementation. The limitations are rooted in the diversity of national provisions that are necessary for the application of the EU cross-border judicial procedure. As previous research carried out on the functioning of the EOP and ESCP in several Member States showed, the reliance of the European uniform procedures at various stages of the proceedings on national procedural rules leads to divergent application of procedures although they are intended to provide uniform solutions.[109] These national characteristics are not always visible upfront, and the e-Justice Portal insufficiently addresses these types of domestic specificities through its dynamic information webpages dedicated to the European uniform procedures.[110] In addition to limited specific procedural law information that is necessary for a lay person to carry out such procedures, the data provided is at time erroneous (e.g. competent courts in some Member States, authorities responsible for the service of documents). Not sufficiently detailed information coupled with erroneous data leads to unnecessary complexities for the end user.

Besides direct references to national procedural rules in the application of the EOP, ESCP, and EAPO procedures, Member States' domestic legislation establishes specific conditions that have to be observed for the legal validity of specific procedural steps. These requirements can differ or be more demanding to comply with when procedural acts are carried out in a particular format (e.g. electronic).[111] This in turn leads to entanglements that require sophisticated technological and infrastructural solutions that can deal with such multi-level requirements. However, technology developments are not able to address these complexities alone. National and European legal amendments are necessary to support ICT developments and simpler architectural design of digital systems. Extensive reliance on national procedural rules and solutions within harmonised European instruments results in intricacies that the European uniform procedures

109 Onţanu (n.12); Velicogna, Lupo, Onţanu, (n.49), p. 93–129.

110 Onţanu (n.12); G.Y. Ng, 'Testing Transborder Civil Procedures in Practice: Findings from Simulation Experiments with the European Payment Order and the European Small Claims Procedure', in F. Contini and G.F. Lanzara (eds.), *The Circulation of Agency in E-Justice. Interoperability and Infrastructures for European Transborder Judicial Proceedings*, Springer, 2014, p. 265–286.

111 See also Veliconga, Steigenga (n.39).

initially sought to avoid. Digital solutions that aim to forward the electronic handling of European procedures need to address these imbrications and avoid reaching levels of maximum manageable complexity as these will hinder the circulation of agency between Member States.

5.4. Language and Legal Semantics

In cross-border procedures, legal data interpretation is made more difficult by different languages and diverse judicial system. The European uniform procedures seek to bring some simplification and standardisation through a uniform framework and common terminology. However, the legal concepts and terminology used by European procedures such as the EOP, the ESCP, and the EAPO do not always correspond to similar domestic designated institutions or legal concepts (e.g. EOP and ESCP 'review' mechanisms are different to the 'réexamen' procedure in France,[112] 'service by post with acknowledgement of receipt' is different to 'first class post' in England[113]), or they do not even find an equivalent in the national law (e.g. limitation period within which service of a national order for payment has to be served on a defendant abroad in Italy or Portugal and no such limitation established by the EOP,[114] compulsory legal representation requested by national procedure in Italy and a non-mandatory requirement under the EOP, the ESCP, and the EAPO Regulations). These differences can lead to confusion not only for lay users that employ the European uniform procedures for the first time but also for practitioners and domestic courts. Furthermore, this can create difficulties at the semantic level when legal proceedings have to be translated into ICT processes and technological architecture that would allow an effective translation of the legal effects of specific procedural actions across Member States legal systems.

5.5. Reaching the Critical Level of Knowledge and Users

The development of a legal e-justice solution for cross-border proceedings requires a critical amount of information about national legal systems as

112 See in Onţanu (n.12), p. 159.
113 *Ibid*, p. 104.
114 See Velicogna, Lupo, Onţanu (n.49), p. 93–129.

well as a sound number of users that continue to use the system once it is put in place.

As previously mentioned, all three European uniform procedures rely to a certain extent on national procedural rules for their application. This leads to domestic specificities and particularities in the way these harmonised procedures are applied and handled across Member States. When developing e-justice systems to handle cross-border procedures digitally, these specificities and characteristics cannot be ignored. They are closely related to the legal validity of the proceedings. However, these specificities are not automatically visible and known to potential users – except regular users – because the European instruments piloted as full digital handled procedures are supposed to offer a maximum uniformity of solutions to support a simplification of access to justice in cross-border claims. Therefore, the architects, ICT specialists, and legal professionals involved in developing cross-border digital systems might easily not have the critical level of understanding of their specificities in order to address them when developing the software infrastructure and the software-driven judicial procedures that are set to facilitate access to justice in cross-border claims. The divergence and diversity of national solutions become visible at times during the development of cross-border ICT architectures and going live of test pilots (e.g. e-CODEX pilots for the EOP procedure). While human actors may act with flexibility when managing unpredicted aspects of a procedure, the technological ones often cannot. Simple elements such as the spelling of a name or of an address may have a blocking effect. Simple acts when undertaken in person lead to substantial complexities when handled through technology solutions. These aspects need to be properly addressed by cross-border e-justice systems in order to secure mutual recognition of national mechanisms in cross-border settings (e.g. e-signature). This requires the teams developing ICT solutions to first acquire a solid knowledge and understanding of national procedural rules before agreeing on solutions that are far from being user-friendly. At the same time, not every such complexity is predictable ex-ante.[115]

In the present context, ICT interoperability solutions have to allow technically and legally valid communication between existing national specific solutions while simplifying the user interface by bridging legal and semantic differences and black-boxing unnecessary procedural details for the user. Hence, in order to provide the potential user with a simplified access

115 See Velicogna, Borsari (n.92).

to justice via ICT infrastructure, complexities need to be black-boxed by the system and sealed behind the user-friendly interface.

The ICT system interconnecting national e-justice systems and technical solutions requires a sufficiently high number of users (in IT terms a 'critical mass of users') who decide to lodge cross-border claims via one of the European uniform procedures. The limited number of claims filed across the EU on the basis of one of the European uniform procedures may make it difficult to reach an extensive use of the system. This is necessary in order to secure its survival and further development of digital solutions. A critical mass of users can incentivise the involvement and support of legal professions and that of software houses. These can contribute to such developments and innovative solutions that support the interconnection and interrelation of national professional systems to European systems in order to facilitate the handling of European uniform procedures through infrastructures such as e-CODEX.[116]

In consideration of the still modest use of the European uniform procedures and the complexities the development of any full-digital solution involves in cross-border settings, the extension of the functionalities of the system towards additional procedural steps supporting court proceedings with a cross-border element appear desirable. This can secure the necessary number of critical users for the ICT system and their organisational needs and open up the system beyond the European uniform procedures. In turn, this can contribute to the familiarity of the potential users and practitioners with the digital system and encourage its use in cross-border claims – either full claims or with regard to certain procedural stages (e.g. service of documents).

6. *In Search of Simplicity: Towards a Different Approach to e-Justice?*

The switch from paper-based procedures to digital procedures is not just a change of tools but comes with a different structure to what are already limited known cross-border procedures. Developments that have been taking shape so far in EU cross-border procedures have been 'built focusing mainly on the creation of ICT supported versions of the EU cross-border

116 See Velicogna, Borsari, Carnevalli (n.94).

procedures'.[117] The user continues to find himself with functional solutions but seldom useful tools or partially useful tools.[118]

Available digital solutions aiming to support cross-border access to justice remain mainly at a general and theoretical level. Although an important tool in accessing information and finding dedicated forms with regard to European uniform procedures, the data the e-Justice Portal offers is still insufficient for easily conducting cross-border procedures. It remains a general tool that fails to provide the necessary practical and accurate information. A non-repetitive party and, sometimes, practitioners have difficulties in finding their way around and identifying the required references for initiating and continuing cross-border procedures without benefiting from the legal assistance of a local practitioner. The ICT solutions put in place by the e-Justice Portal have only partly addressed the need for assistance parties require in cross-border proceedings. The existing wizards integrated in the Judicial Atlas pages of the portal are meant to guide users in choosing the appropriate European uniform procedure for lodging a cross-border claim. However, they are not immediately visible to interested parties or the information obtained requires some subsequent steps (e.g. determining the competent court when several courts have jurisdiction for a certain territorial area). Furthermore, they are not sufficiently intuitive to guide the parties who are not able to give precise replies to the wizards' general questions. Answering specific questions is not easy for non-repetitive users who could easily decide on their own which procedure to employ if they were able to answer the questions that are supposed to guide their steps.

The e-CODEX, although a functional tool in supporting full electronic handling of cross-border European procedures, remains for the moment merely a promising pilot tool. The system has not been generally deployed for the public or professional use around the EU. In the future, it is expected it will provide the vehicle that will allow a complete dematerialised handling of cross-border judicial procedures that offers the much needed support to parties having to navigate the diversity of national procedural rules.[119] Additionally, its expected interconnection with the e-Justice Portal will provide EU citizens and parties with access to national databases and secure the electronic communication between judicial

117 Veliconga, Steigenga (n.39).

118 *Ibid.*

119 See also J. Groustra, Connecting Venus and Mars: How IT can Simplify European Cross-Border Judicial Procedures (available at www.linkedin.com/pulse/connecting-venus-mars-how-can-simplify-european-judicial-e-codex/).

authorities and between authorities and parties in the EU. However, before such developments can be fully operational, attention should be given to smaller steps that already make use of the benefits of ICT and have the potential of facilitating access to justice in the short term. These achievements, if properly employed, will provide a strong base for future e-justice tool deployment. In consideration of these findings, digitalisation of European procedures may need to consider also additional angles that can support more ambitious developments such as the full opening of e-CODEX to general users. Before being able to fully benefit from complex e-justice tools and services, as pointed out by Velicogna and Ng, citizens should be able to find the information they are looking for in a format that is easy to identify and is complete and reliable.[120] Technology input via the e-Justice Portal is a good opportunity but has to be appropriately provided with bottom-up information from national specialists that understand the procedural requirements the application of the EOP, ESCP, and EAPO procedures have as part of the domestic legal system. This might appear at first as an insignificant step for technology deployment in supporting access to justice, as it does not go as far as a full digital treatment of the European procedures, but it is an important stage in familiarising users with the potential of these instruments and supports their application. When procedures are already well-known and appreciated by users, their switch to full digital handling can be easier to make even if electronic handling might pose some challenges at first. Additionally, often used procedures benefit from the necessary critical number of users that are crucial when developing the new system for their handling. Resources of courts and justice systems are limited; therefore their use has to be in line with the needs of the users. Their use secures the digital systems survival and further developments in e-justice tools.

Standardisation of procedural steps and forms are elements that are useful approaches in a digital handling of cross-border procedures. They should be further explored, considering whether more flexible formats in an interactive format would be more appropriate and easy to use compared to the present formats.

Another aspect that can contribute to further simplification but it will be difficult to achieve in the short to mid-term is the format of what we now recognise as European uniform procedures. Uniform European procedures have to be able to provide more harmonious solutions without

120 Velicogna, Ng (n.8), p. 370. See further also, Steigenga and Velicogna categorise these developments into e-Law and e-Justice. Steigenga, Velicogna (n.56), p. 250.

impinging on national procedural diversity and autonomy. However, extensive reliance on national procedural rules does not lead to the immediate simplification they aim to provide to the parties initiating cross-border procedures in a traditional paper-based format or a digital format. Procedural diversity in cross-border claims inevitably leads to complexities whose effects are magnified when necessary information is not easily made available. These complexities are taken over by technological solutions that need to be assembled and effectively function across different justice systems. When such diversities are well-known, technological solutions can be considered in order to address them. The e-CODEX projects have constantly sought to address these in order to offer the end-user more friendly solutions. At the same time simplification and complexity have to be balanced. As pointed out by Lanzara, two design principles have to be observed when developing e-government services and systems that assemble law and technology such as e-CODEX: 'maximum feasible simplicity and maximum manageable complexity'.[121] Although the end user might be allowed to avoid some of these complexities by black-boxing part of the procedural details when designing e-justice systems, the design, functioning and organisation of such platforms remain difficult and costly to manage. Additionally, this can lead to systems that struggle in terms of flexibility and require high maintenance costs, while their development already required significant investments. The reverse is simplifying procedures to such extent that their guarantees and fairness of procedures are affected. Opening the e-CODEX infrastructure to APIs and third-party service providers may go in this direction but requires a reframing of the current e-CODEX governance.[122]

---

121 G.F. Lanzara, 'The Circulation of Agency in Judicial Proceedings: Designing for Interoperability and Complexity', in F. Contini and G.F. Lanzara (eds.), *The Circulation of Agency in E-Justice. Interoperability and Infrastructures for European Transborder Judicial Proceedings*, Springer, 2014, p. 26–30.

122 E. Steigenga, Z. Kolitski, M. Velicogna, G. Lupo, H. Moelker, T. Berkelaar, V. van de Laar, *API for Justice Report*; Project coordinated by the Dutch Ministry of Justice and Security: The Hague, The Netherlands, 2017. I. Pagkalos, N. Zikos, M. Velicogna, *Study of the requirements, design and proof-of-concept implementation a national e-CODEX European Payment Order Application Programming Interface: the Greek case*, Pro-CODEX Project Report v. 2.2, IRSIG, Bologna, 2018. Velicogna (n.11).

7. Concluding remarks

Technology can provide the tools that can facilitate access to justice in a cross-border setting and offer additional instruments and assistance; however, this is not the only element that has to be taken into consideration or the only one that can offer universal solutions. In order to provide the support access to justice requires, technology needs to be addressed together with other key elements – the legal and organisational components. All three of them are equally important in designing user-friendly digital solutions for cross-border procedures. Developments that are less reliant on ICT should not be ignored as they create the basis or prepare the ground for what now might appear as challenging technology solutions. Diversity remains a crucial component of the EU construction which can be to a certain extent more easily handled through common understanding and interpretation of our differences towards achieving the desired goal. This is not an ICT solution but may provide support to complexity coming from uneven national features through ICT. Developments triggered by technology and aiming to achieve the electronic handling of cross-border justice claims are part of the present challenge that we need to address and successfully meet, but we have to be mindful that other components besides ICT have to bring their contribution to this architecture.

The way European procedural rules are drafted, the format of litigation to which they are intended, as well as the interplay between European and national procedural laws have a significant role to play in the digitalisation of cross-border proceedings. In the e-CODEX project, the procedural rules imposed the development of specific features for technology and digital solutions. This was necessary to comply with the legislative requirements of legal validity of procedural steps to be undertaken in the application of the EOP and the ESCP procedures. It also led to an organisational adaptation as well as to national institutional actors assuming additional control tasks in order to guarantee the identity of the involved actors. Digital procedures need to guarantee the same procedural standards as traditional paper-based procedures, but sometimes activities that are simple when carried out in person such as a signature or identification of a person require more elaborate actions and technical solutions in an electronic environment. This is even more complicated in a cross-border setting where national digital justice systems are not interconnected and implemented technological solutions have not been developed to be interoperable. Legal flexibility is necessary for an environment that is developing fast as existing hard letter law might not contain the required solutions. The digitalisation of the European uniform procedures finds itself at crossroads between various aspects that have an effect on the process. On the one hand, the procedural framework aims to simplify and ease the parties' tasks through uniform rules; however, this framework is not complete, as national procedural rules and specificities still regulate a significant number of aspects . On the other hand, this complexity and interplay between rules and national practice need to be incorporated in a digital system that is relying itself on a diversity of systems bridged under the e-CODEX platform. This increases the complexity of building and deploying a European system that electronically handles European uniform procedures. To this, an additional layer must be added – legal semantics. The e-Justice Portal dynamic standard forms and the e-CODEX platform manage to successfully encode and deal with the different language versions and concepts of the European uniform procedures. They are able to translate the concepts contained in the forms from one legal system to the other, but this is not the case with national legal institutions that are relevant for the application or challenge of these procedures. Practitioners sometimes assimilate the national institutions and concepts to those with a similar or identical name referred to in the provisions of the European uniform procedures. Such situations lead to confusion. The legislative technique needs to consider these aspects more carefully when adopting such procedures.

Furthermore, the EU procedural concepts should be interpreted autonomously from their possible national equivalents and should not be assimilated to these. This kind of assimilation results in additional complexities that digital systems would need to learn to deal with in cross-border situations. An opposite approach of relying on autonomous EU procedural concepts would bring more uniformity, clarity, and some simplification in the digitisation process. Systems that are less expensive to build, are easy to use, and function well are likely to encourage users to choose these available tools.

In theory, a significant part of the procedural complexity digitisation seems to entail in cross-border procedures could be dealt with by designing cross-border procedures with the perspective of e-handling in mind. This approach can come in line with what Lanzara refers to as 'maximum feasible simplicity', retaining procedural standards and guarantees, but avoiding some of the complexities that the digitisation of paper-based procedure involves, especially when different legislative levels have to be applied together. In practice, this seems more challenging to achieve for already established European procedures, but consideration of this perspective should always be contemplated for new EU procedural rules or in the review process of already well-known instruments, as the digital component of justice is becoming a pervasive element.

Trust, but Verify. Loss of Mutual Trust as a Ground for Non-Recognition in the Area of Freedom, Security and Justice. Example of the Judiciary Crisis in PolandZuzanna WitekTrust, but Verify.

*Zuzanna Witek**

Table of Contents

1. *Introduction*

In contrast to the principle of mutual recognition, mutual trust is not enshrined in the Treaties of the European Union. Nevertheless, mutual trust is of fundamental importance in European Union (EU) law[1]. The principle has its basis in the "union of values", which are commonly shared by the Member States[2]. Under mutual trust one Member State should accept and enforce decisions of another Member State as if they

---

* Zuzanna Witek is a PhD candidate in the Chair of International and European Law, University of Wrocław, Poland. She is currently finalising a PhD dissertation on the guarantees of the independence and impartiality of international judges. She obtained a master's degree in law at the University of Wroclaw, and as part of international student exchanges she also studied at the University of Paris – Dauphine, France and the University of Luxembourg.

1 Judgment of the Court (First Chamber) of 16 July 2015, C-681/13, ECLI:EU:C:2015:471, *the Diageo Brands judgment*, para. 40.

2 Opinion 2/13 of 18 December 2014, EU:C:2014:2454, para. 168.

were its own. However, the principle of mutual trust is not blind[3]. Trust must be "earned" by each Member State through effective compliance with EU fundamental rights standards[4].

Over the last couple of years when judicial cooperation developed within the European Union's Area of Freedom, Security and Justice (AFSJ), the notion of mutual trust in the EU legal system has evolved from a programmatic norm, which was considered as a necessary implication that Member States have trust in their judicial systems[5], to a judicially enforceable principle of constitutional importance. At the same time, the EU has adopted more than twenty legal acts in civil and criminal matters which are based on the mutual trust principle and provide for mutual recognition. Therefore, mutual trust can be regarded as a prerequisite for the principle of mutual recognition, or its "twin brother". Mutual recognition within the AFSJ is a rule and its limitation is possible only in strictly defined circumstances. A loss of mutual trust can be considered as one of the grounds for non-recognition.

In this contribution I would like to consider under what specific circumstances loss of mutual trust as a consequence of a rule of law violation can be the basis for non-recognition within the AFSJ. The most significant issue concerns the limits to the principle of mutual trust. An interpretation of the limitation of mutual trust which is too broad might impair the functioning of the AFSJ as a whole, since Member States could find many excuses not to recognise the decisions of other Member States. An expanding interpretation could be considered as a "gateway", used to avoid recognition of a court's inconvenient decisions. On the other hand, a restrictive interpretation of possible limitations of mutual trust may lead to insufficient sanctioning of serious violations of the fundamental rights standards in Member States, and in consequence constitute an indirect consent for a given practice which is contrary to EU law and its values. The fundamental question that this contribution tries to address is: How does mutual trust and respect for the EU's fundamental rights standards operate between judicial bodies bound by the principle of mutual recognition?

---

3 Lars Bay Larsen, "*Some Reflections on Mutual Recognition in the Area of Freedom, Security and Justice*", in P. Cardonnel, A. Rosas and N. Wahl (eds.), Constitutionalising the EU Judicial System: Essays in Honour of Pernilla Lindh, [2012], Oxford: Hart Publishing, p. 140.

4 Koen Lenaerts, "*La vie après l'avis: exploring the principle of mutual (yet not blind) trust*", [2017], Common Market Law Review 54, p. 805.

5 Judgment of the Court of 11 February 2003, joined cases C-187/01 and C-385/01, ECLI:EU:C:2003:87, *Hüseyin Gözütok and Klaus Brügge judgment*, para. 33.

The contribution has three parts. The first part concerns the meaning and scope of the principle of mutual trust. The case law concerning the evolution and significance of the mutual trust over the years is examined. The second part looks at the meaning of the mutual recognition principle within EU law and explores the procedure of non-recognition under a loss of mutual trust, which is currently under development. Specifically, the following questions are considered: What are the limits to the mutual trust principle and how does the breach of fundamental EU's values enshrined in Article 2 Treaty on European Union (TEU)[6] affect the mutual trust? Particular attention will be devoted to the *Aranyosi doctrine*[7], corroborated in the *LM judgment*[8]. In reference to the rule of law, which is backsliding in some Member States, several shortcomings of the two-stage *Aranyosi procedure* are presented. Finally, the third part concerns breach of the rule of law being seen as a fundamental reason for lack of trust, and hence grounds for non-recognition within the AFSJ. In order to answer the question of whether the judgments of Polish courts should – still – be recognised and enforced by other Member States' courts under the mutual trust principle, it is necessary to present the factual and legal background of the new reforms to the Polish judiciary in relation to fundamental rights, especially the rule of law principle. In particular, these crucial questions should be answered:

1. Do the Polish *courts* still meet the criteria of a "court" as defined by the CJEU, *ergo*, whether the decisions of these entities may be considered as "judgments" which are the subject of a mutual recognition procedure based on mutual trust?
2. The *Aranyosi procedure* will probably be used only by some executing Member States' courts. Could this cause both fragmentation within the AFSJ and unequal treatment of EU citizens who are subject to the mutual recognition mechanisms?
3. How will the launching of an Article 7 TEU procedure affect the non-recognition of Polish judgments? How in this concrete case may the lengthening of this procedure affect mutual trust within the whole AFSJ?

---

6 Treaty on European Union, Consolidated versions of the Treaty on European Union and the Treaty on the Functioning of the European Union, 2012/C, 326/01.

7 Judgment of the Court (Grand Chamber) of 5 April 2016, Joined Cases C-404/15 and C-659/15 PPU, ECLI:EU:C:2016:198, the *Aranyosi* and the *Căldăraru judgment.*

8 Judgment of the Court (Grand Chamber) of 25 July 2018, C-216/18 PPU, ECLI:EU:C:2018:586, *the LM judgment.*

In a brief conclusion I support the thesis that the principle of mutual trust is by no means absolute and may constitute the basis for a non-recognition procedure. Therefore, due to the rule of law crisis, blind trust towards Poland has already been challenged, and its restoration in the future will be difficult. The status of Polish courts and tribunals is controversial, as is evidenced, *inter alia*, by the proceedings initiated by the European Commission and the launching for the first time ever of an Article 7 TEU procedure. With regard to the above, I will try to prove that *the LM judgment*, which undermines mutual trust towards Poland, in the harsh version, may be the beginning of non-recognition not only of judgments but of the Polish justice system as a whole.

The legal systems within the AFSJ are fully interdependent so that a problem in one Member State soon becomes a problem for all. Therefore, the EU faces a crucial juncture: do illiberal democracies become a part of the EU legal order, or will the EU instruments be able to restore proper respect for the fundamental values on which the Union is founded and which constitute the basis of mutual trust between Member States.

2. *The Principle of Mutual Trust as a Normative Cornerstone of the AFSJ*

The principle of mutual trust or a *high level of confidence* is a constitutional principle that pervades the entire AFSJ[9]. The principle justifies judicial cooperation through, in particular, the principle of mutual recognition. Under the mutual trust principle, judicial authorities have an obligation to recognise and enforce certain decisions taken by judicial bodies in other Member States unless an explicit ground for non-execution provided in EU legislation applies[10]. That principle requires, particularly with regard to the AFSJ of those States, save in exceptional circumstances, that all the other Member States are complying with EU law and particularly with the fundamental rights recognised by EU law[11]. In reference to Koen Lenaerts, President of the Court of Justice of the European Union (CJEU), given that under the mutual trust principle "all Member States are deemed to share the same degree of commitment to democratic values, fundamental rights and the rule of law, one may reasonably expect they should trust

9 Koen Lenaerts, "*La vie après l'avis...*", *op. cit.*, p. 839.

10 Tony Marguery, "*Rebuttal of Mutual Trust and Mutual Recognition in Criminal Matters*", European Papers, vol. 1 no. 3, [2016], p. 944 and 947.

11 Opinion 2/13, *op. cit.*, para. 191.

each other, especially when acting in concert to achieve common EU objectives"[12]. It is because Member States are deemed equal before the EU Treaties that they are able to trust each other to protect fundamental rights adequately[13]. Trust not only implies that rules in the Member States are adequate, but also that they are correctly applied in concrete judicial proceedings[14]. By the fact that Member States trust each other and believe that other Member States fulfil fundamental rights, judicial cooperation is feasible through mutual recognition of judicial decisions[15]. In this way mutual recognition is based on mutual trust, something that has been confirmed many times in CJEU case law[16].

The preambles of the EU legal acts that contain the mutual trust principle are based on the assumption that all Member States share their commitment to respect common values and, especially, individuals' fundamental rights[17]. Such an assumption is possible because all the Member States must comply with EU fundamental rights standards[18]. In the framework of mutual recognition, this obligation concerns both the issuing and the executing Member States[19], which also results from general characteristics of the EU judicial protection system, such as the doctrine of direct effect, consistent cooperation, loyal cooperation and supremacy[20]. Furthermore, the mutual trust principle exists because all the Member States are bound by their own sources of fundamental rights and by the fact that all are party to the European Convention for the Protection of Human Rights and Fundamental Freedoms (ECHR)[21,22].

---

12 Koen Lenaerts, "*La vie après l'avis…*", *op. cit.*, p. 809.

13 *Ibidem*, p. 812.

14 Communication COM(2000) 495 final of 27 July 2000 from the Commission on Mutual Recognition of Final Decisions in Criminal Matters, para. 3.1.

15 Koen Lenaerts, "*La vie après l'avis…*", *op. cit.*, p. 812.

16 E.g. Judgment of the Court (Third Chamber) of 23 December 2009, C-403/09, ECLI:EU:C:2009:810, the *Jasna Detiček v Maurizio Sgueglia judgment*, para. 45; Judgment of the Court (Second Chamber) of 30 May 2013 C-168/13 PPU, ECLI:EU:C:2013:358, the *Jeremy F. v Premier minister judgment*, para. 50.

17 E.g. Preamble 10 of the EAW Framework Decision.

18 Judgment of the Court (Grand Chamber) of 26 February 2013, C-617/10, ECLI:EU:C:2013:280, the *Åkerberg Fransson judgment*.

19 The *Jeremy F. v Premier minister judgment, op. cit.*, para. 40.

20 Tony Marguery, *op. cit.*, p. 948.

21 The Convention for the Protection of Human Rights and Fundamental Freedoms, 3 September 1953.

22 The *Jeremy F. v Premier minister judgment, op. cit.*, paras. 48–49; Tony Marguery, *op. cit.*, p. 948.

Nevertheless, the notion of mutual trust is not defined in the Treaties. Therefore, the status of mutual trust was questionable and was considered to be located between a programmatic norm of constitutional importance and a judicially enforceable principle. Eventually, CJEU jurisprudence settled the issue and held that mutual trust is a principle of pivotal importance for the EU legal system[23].

The case law concerning the meaning and scope of mutual trust has to be presented given the evolution in the importance of mutual trust over the years. In the *Hüseyin Gözütok* and *Klaus Brügge* joint cases the Court held that the operation of the *ne bis idem* principle enshrined in Article 54 CISA[24] required "the Member States [to] have mutual trust in their criminal justice systems and that each of them recognises the criminal law in force in the other Member States even when the outcome would be different if its own national law were applied"[25]. In practice this means that the existence of mutual trust between the Member States is based on the concept of equivalence of rules[26]. In the *Rinau judgment*, which concerns a child abduction case and the Brussels II bis Regulation[27], the Court stated that "Regulation is based on the idea that the recognition and enforcement of judgments given in a Member State must be based on the principle of mutual trust and the grounds for non-recognition must be kept to the minimum required"[28]. In the *N.S. case*, an asylum case concerning the Dublin Regulation[29], the Court stated that "the raison d'être of the [EU]

23 Matthias Weller, "*Mutual trust within judicial cooperation in civil matters: a normative cornerstone – a factual chimera – a constitutional challenge*", Cambridge Yearbook of European Legal Studies, [2018], p. 1.

24 Convention implementing the Schengen Agreement of 14 June 1985 between the Governments of the States of the Benelux Economic Union, the Federal Republic of Germany and the French Republic on the gradual abolition of checks at their common borders signed on 19 June 1990 at Schengen.

25 The *Hüseyin Gözütok and Klaus Brügge judgment*, *op. cit.*, para. 33.

26 Tony Marguery, *op. cit.*, p. 945.

27 Council Regulation (EC) No. 2201/2003 of 27 November 2003 concerning jurisdiction and the recognition and enforcement of judgments in matrimonial matters and the matters of parental responsibility, repealing Regulation (EC) No. 1347/2000.

28 Judgment of the Court (Third Chamber) of 11 July 2008, C-195/08, ECLI:EU:C:2008:406, *Inga Rinau judgment*, para. 50.

29 Regulation (EU) No. 604/2013 of the European Parliament and of the Council of 26 June 2013 establishing the criteria and mechanisms for determining the Member State responsible for examining an application for international protection lodged in one of the Member States by a third-country national or a stateless person.

and the creation of an [AFSJ is] based on mutual [trust] and a presumption of compliance, by other Member States, with [EU] law and, in particular, fundamental rights"[30]. This means that all Member States must assume observance of the rule of law in their cooperation with other Member States because under the principle of mutual trust all Member States comply with EU law and fundamental rights[31].

In the *N.S. judgment*, the CJEU qualified mutual trust as a constitutional principle, which was later confirmed in subsequent judgments. Based on the *N.S.* and *Melloni judgments*[32], in Opinion 2/13, concerning EU accession to the European Court of Human Rights (ECtHR), the CJEU highlighted the fundamental importance of that principle since "it allows an area without internal borders to be created and maintained"[33]. On a normative level, this judgment confirmed that mutual trust has become a cornerstone of the AFSJ[34]. In the *Achmea case*, the CJEU admitted that "the EU law is […] based on the fundamental premise that each Member State shares with all the other Member States, and recognises that they share with it, a set of common values on which the EU is founded, as stated in Article 2 TEU. That premise implies and justifies the existence of mutual trust between the Member States that those values will be recognised, and therefore that the law of the EU that implements them will be respected."[35]

Based on the meaning of the principle indicated above, it can be argued that the mutual trust principle has several legal dimensions[36]:

---

30 Judgment of the Court (Grand Chamber) of 21 December 2011, N. S. (C-411/10) v Secretary of State for the Home Department and M.E. and Others (C-493/10) v Refugee Applications Commissioner and Minister for Justice, Equality and Law Reform, ECLI:EU:C:2011:865, *the N.S. and Others judgment*, para. 83.

31 Matthias Weller, *op. cit.*, p. 13.

32 The *N.S. and Others, op. cit.*, paras. 78–80 and Judgment of the Court (Grand Chamber) of 26 February 2013
Stefano Melloni v Ministerio Fiscal Melloni, C-399/11, EU:C:2013:107, *the Melloni judgment*, paras. 37 and 63.

33 Opinion 2/13, *op. cit.*, paras. 191.

34 Matthias Weller, *op. cit.*, p. 1.

35 Judgment of the Court (Grand Chamber) of 6 March 2018 C-284/16, EU:C:2018:158, the *Achmea judgment*, para. 34.

36 Agnieszka Frąckowiak-Adamska, *„Następstwa wyroku w sprawie LM (Celmer) i postępowania na podstawie art. 7 TUE dla funkcjonowania sądów polskich w ramach wspólnoty prawnej UE"*, in J. Barcz, A. Zawidzka-Łojek (eds.), Sądowe mechanizmy ochrony praworządności w Polsce w świetle najnowszego orzecznictwa Trybunału Sprawiedliwości UE, [2018], p. 89 -105.

1) a presumption of observance with EU law, in particular fundamental rights, by other Member States (Opinion 2/13, § 191), which constitutes a legal basis for mutual recognition within the AFSJ;
2) a presumption that a Member State may not demand a higher level of national protection of fundamental rights from another Member State than that provided by EU law (Opinion 2/13, § 192);
3) a general prohibition on checking whether another Member State has actually, in a specific case, observed the fundamental rights guaranteed by the EU (Opinion 2/13, § 192);
4) the court in the Member State in which recognition is sought is not allowed to substitute its own assessment for that of the court in the Member State of origin (*the Salzgitter Mannesmann Handel judgment*, para. 36[37]), unless exceptional circumstances occur.

3. *Loss of Mutual Trust as a Ground for Non-Recognition*

The principle of mutual recognition, which undoubtedly is a constitutional principle of the EU, is expressly mentioned in Articles 67, 70, 80 and 82 TFEU[38]. Mutual recognition was recognised as a foundation of judicial cooperation in criminal matters during the Tampere European Council in 1999[39]. Initially, a significant amount of the case law concerning the principle of mutual recognition was devoted to the EAW[40], which however, can also apply respectively to other mutual recognition instruments[41]. The

---

37 Judgment of the Court (Fourth Chamber) of 26 September 2013, *Salzgitter Mannesmann Handel GmbH v SC Laminorul SA*, C-157/12, ECLI:EU:C:2013:597.

38 E. Herlin-Karnell, "*Constitutional Principles in the EU Area of Freedom, Security and Justice*", in D. Acosta and C. Murphy (eds.), EU Security and Justice Law, Oxford, Hard Publishing, [2014], p. 36.

39 Communication from the Commission to the Council and the European Parliament – Mutual recognition of Final Decisions in Criminal Matters, 26 July 2000, COM/2000/0495 final, p. 2.

40 Cf. Judgment of the Court (Grand Chamber) of 3 May 2007, C-303/05, the *Advocaten voor de Wereld judgment*, ECLI:EU:C:2007:261; Judgment of the Court (Grand Chamber) of 17 July 2008, C-66/08, the *Kozłowski judgment* ECLI:EU:C:2008:437; Judgment of the Court (Third Chamber) of 12 August 2008, C-296/08 *PPU Santesteban Goicoechea*, ECLI:EU:C:2008:457; Judgment of the Court (Third Chamber) of 1 December 2008C-388/08 *PPU Leymann and Pustovarov*, ECLI:EU:C:2008:669; C-396/11 the *Radu judgment, op. cit.* ECLI:EU:C:2013:39; C-399/11 the *Melloni judgment, op.cit.*

41 See: Steve Peers, "*EU Justice and Home Affairs Law: Volume II: EU Criminal Law, Policing, and Civil Law*", Oxford [2016], p. 99.

principle of mutual recognition presupposes mutual trust and comity among the domestic judiciary systems[42]. Although the principle of mutual recognition is mentioned in EU primary law, the principle is not an autonomous basis for the recognition of judgments: mutual recognition (and the mutual trust principle) is applied "in tandem" with provisions of secondary Union law: regulations, directives, and framework decisions[43]. Mutual trust serves as an argument for a certain interpretation of the provisions at issue[44].

Although mutual recognition based on mutual trust is a central principle of the AFSJ, its application is by no means absolute and can be limited. However, its existence is presumed, mutual trust does not exist without any conditions. A loss of mutual trust cannot be excluded. According to CJEU case law, mutual trust must not be confused with blind trust[45]. The presumption of compliance by other Member States with EU law and fundamental rights can be challenged. Similarly, mutual recognition can be restricted, flexible and quasi-automatic[46]. Therefore, loss of trust between Member States can be considered a non-explicit limitation on mutual recognition.[47] Therefore, significant questions have been raised as to whether "the sky is the limit[48]" or, alternatively, as to where the limits to mutual trust and mutual recognition principle lie.

The limitation to the principle of mutual trust was established in Opinion 2/13, which was based on the *N.S. judgment*. In *the N.S. case*, the CJEU accepted that in certain circumstances the need to protect fundamental rights limits the mutual trust principle[49]. Under the "as-long-as rule", the EU's primary law prohibits blind trust in other Member States, but as long as there is no manifest evidence of structural deficits in the protection of fundamental rights, the Member States must trust each other as a matter of

42 Lars Bay Larsen, *op. cit.*

43 Sascha Prechal, "*Mutual trust before the Court of Justice of the European Union*", European Papers, vol. 2, no. 1, [2017] p. 79.

44 *Ibidem.*

45 Lars Bay Larsen, *op. cit.*

46 Evegenia Ralli, "*The Principle of Mutual Recognition Based on Mutual Trust and the Respect for Fundamental Rights: The Case of the Framework Decision on the European Arrest Warrant*", European Law Institute, [2018], p. 3.

47 Tony Marguery, *op. cit.*, p. 944.

48 Adam Łazowski, "*The Sky Is Not the Limit: Muttual Trust and Mutual Recognition apres Aranyosi and Caldararu*", Croatien Yearbook of European Law and Policy, vol. 14 no. 1, [2018], doi:10.3935/cyelp.14.2018.313.

49 The *N.S. judgment, op. cit.*, para. 99.

EU law[50]. The "as-long-as rule" has reached its latest stage in the *Pál Aranyosi and Robert Căldăraru judgment* (*the Aranyosi judgment*)[51]. The Court allowed, in exceptional circumstances, the possibility of examining whether another Member State respects fundamental rights, even if the act does not provide such a ground for non-recognition. The case law regarding the procedure of non-recognition under loss of mutual trust is in development; currently only a few judgments are available in which the CJEU has established a link between mutual trust, mutual recognition and fundamental rights.

Loss of mutual trust as a ground for non-recognition of a Member State court's decision was a subject of the *LM judgment*[52]. In this case, LM, the respondent in the main proceedings, was prosecuted for a drug-related crime and the subject of three arrest warrants issued by Polish courts on the basis of the Framework Decision. Due to the reforms in the Polish judiciary, the respondent claimed there existed a real risk of his not receiving a fair trial if he was transferred to the country and he submitted that that risk precluded his being surrendered by the referring court to the Polish judicial authorities. On 23 March 2018, the Irish High Court held, on the basis of the Commission's Reasoned Proposal as referred to in Article 7 TEU and of the opinions of the Venice Commission, that the legislative reforms adopted during 2015–2018 in Poland, taken as a whole, breach the common value of the rule of law referred to in Article 2 TEU. Based on the finding that there was a systemic breach to the rule of law in Poland, the Irish High Court referred two questions for determination to the CJEU.

The Irish High Court raised the issue whether the two stages of the examination defined by the CJEU in the *Aranyosi and Căldăraru case* (systemic and individual assessment) found application in the *LM case*, where there was a grave risk that the Member State was in breach of the rule of law. The Irish High Court was of the view that the second stage of that examination was not applicable, because it would be unrealistic to require the individual concerned to establish that those deficiencies have an effect on the proceedings to which he was subject. In addition, the High Court considered that, on account of the systemic nature of the deficiencies at issue, the issuing judicial authority would be able to provide no individual guarantee capable of ruling out the risk run by the individual concerned.

50 Matthias Weller, *op. cit.*, p. 14.
51 *Ibidem.*
52 The *LM judgment*, *op. cit.*

In this context, it should be emphasised once again that under the principles of mutual trust and mutual recognition, Member States are required to recognise and execute any decisions issued by the judicial authority of another Member State. There are no rules on how fundamental rights checks should take place except when this happens by the application of a ground for non-recognition. Using the example of the European Arrest Warrant (EAW), the executing judicial authority is entitled to refuse to execute a warrant only in the exhaustively listed cases, i.e. in circumstances set out in Article 3 of the Framework Decision or optional non-execution laid down in Articles 4 and 4a of the Framework Decision.

In the judgment of 5 April 2016, *Aranyosi and Căldăraru*[53], which was referred by the Irish High Court, the CJEU stated that where the executing judicial authority finds that, for the individual who is the subject of the EAW, there is a real risk of inhuman or degrading treatment within the meaning of Article 4 of the Charter of Fundamental Rights of the European Union (the Charter)[54], the execution of that warrant must be postponed. The CJEU recalled that in Opinion 2/13 it was recognised that, "in exceptional circumstances", limitations may be imposed on the principles of mutual recognition and mutual trust, and second, upon Article 1(3) of the Framework Decision, according to which that decision "shall not have the effect of modifying the obligation to respect fundamental rights" as enshrined in particular by the Charter[55]. However, in the *Aranyosi and Căldăraru case*, the CJEU required a two-stage examination to be conducted.

In the *LM judgment*, the CJEU confirmed the importance of the principles of mutual trust and mutual recognition[56]. Besides, the Court corroborated its position from the *Aranyosi and Căldăraru* judgment that the principles of mutual recognition and mutual trust between Member States may be limited "in exceptional circumstances"[57]. In relation to the Polish judiciary crisis and the future of Poland within the AFSJ, the following part of the decision seems to be significant: "The high level of trust between Member States on which the [EAW] is based is thus founded on the premise that the criminal courts of the other Member States — which,

53 The *Aranyosi* and *Căldăraru judgment*, *op. cit.*, para. 98.

54 The Charter of Fundamental Rights of the European Union, 2012/C 326/02, Official Journal of the European Union C 326/391.

55 Opinion of Advocate General Evgeni Tanchev on the Case C-216/18 PPU, ECLI:EU:C:2018:517, para. 5.

56 The *LM judgment*, *op. cit.*, para. 35.

57 *Ibidem*, para. 43.

following execution of a [EAW], will have to conduct the criminal procedure for the purpose of prosecution, or of the enforcement of a custodial sentence or detention order, and the substantive criminal proceedings — meet the requirements of effective judicial protection, which include, in particular, the independence and impartiality of those courts. It must, accordingly, be held that the existence of a real risk that the person in respect of whom a [EAW] has been issued will, if surrendered to the issuing judicial authority, suffer a breach of his fundamental right to an independent tribunal and, therefore, of the essence of his fundamental right to a fair trial, a right guaranteed by the second paragraph of Article 47 of the Charter, is capable of permitting the executing judicial authority to refrain, by way of exception, from giving effect to that European arrest warrant, on the basis of Article 1(3) of Framework Decision 2002/584."[58]

Afterwards, the CJEU stated that domestic courts within the AFSJ should apply both steps of the *Aranyosi test* if a Member State is suspected of having infringed fundamental rights. The Court stated that if the executing court possesses reliable and strong evidence of systemic or generalised deficiencies in such Member State, it should proceed to the second stage, which is individual case assessment. The CJEU held that a suspension of the mutual recognition mechanism is possible only if the decision is taken on the basis of Art. 7 TEU[59]. Until the decision is made, a warrant may only be suspended if there are substantial grounds for believing that that person will run a real risk of his fundamental rights being breached. Therefore, in the *LM case* one can find a novelty: launching the Article 7 TEU procedure rebuts the presumption of mutual trust in relation to a Member State as the individual assessment is required in every case in which the person subject to EAW demands it[60]. The *LM judgment* introduces specific duties for the national court and reverses the principle of mutual trust if the Article 7 TEU procedure is to be completed[61].

From a practical point of view, for many observers the most significant parts of the judgment are paras 60–78, which clarify the procedure on how the court should proceed if the person in respect of whom an EAW has

58 *Ibidem*, paras. 58–59.

59 *Ibidem*, paras. 71–73.

60 *Ibidem*, paras. 60, 68.

61 Agnieszka Frąckowiak-Adamska, "*Mutual trust and independence of the judiciary after the CJEU judgment in LM – new era or business as usual?*", Eulawanalysis.blogspot.com, 15 August 2018, source: http://eulawanalysis.blogspot.com/2018/08/mutual-trust-and-independence-of.html.

been issued pleads that there are systemic or generalised deficiencies in the independence of courts in the issuing State[62]. In such a case the executive court is required to make an assessment of the risk in the individual case (para. 60), which consists of two steps: a systemic assessment (paras 61–68) and a specific one (paras 69–78)[63].

The *LM judgment* is for some a breakthrough – due to the possible limitation of mutual trust. That judgment confirms that the premise of Member States' compliance with the values in Article 2 TEU is not absolute and hence that mutual trust is not blind. Trust that has once been gained must be afterwards maintained. The Court's acknowledgment that a failure to respect fundamental rights may ultimately lead to a refusal to recognize and execute an EAW is to be welcomed as a step forward in upholding the rule of law within the EU. For others, the judgment despite its significant importance does not establish sufficient consequences for violating the rule of law principle, and is too focused on the rights of the individual, instead of developing the line of jurisprudence initiated in *the Portuguese judgment*. Some Polish scholars have commented on the *LM judgment* that the CJEU took the safest path of applying to the case the already existing model[64].

Nonetheless, several shortcomings of the two-stage procedure should be noted. Firstly, in pursuance of the *LM judgment*, the mutual trust is rebutted once the Article 7 TEU procedure have been completed. Such a mechanism shifts too much of a burden onto national courts[65]. If Member States' courts do not or are unable to take up that responsibility, it will result in the lack of appropriate sanctions for Member States violating the fundamental EU values as well as a proliferation of violations of individual rights. Further, the *Aranyosi procedure* will probably be used only by some executing courts. Such a scenario may cause the fragmentation of EU law and discriminatory treatment among EU citizens. Secondly, as practice shows, the Article 7 TEU procedure lasts not several months, but several years. At the same time, while the procedure is still pending, the rule of law crisis in some Member States deepens: it is increasingly difficult to separate the assessment of the entire national justice system (a systemic assessment) from the assessment of a particular court (a specific one). It

62 *Ibidem.*

63 *Ibidem.*

64 *Ibidem.*

65 See: Kim Lane Scheppele, Laurent Pech, "*Should the EU Care About the Rule of Law at Member State Level?*", 3 March 2018, https://verfassungsblog.de/should-the-eu-care-about-the-rule-of-law-at-member-state-level/.

seems that in some Member States the rule of law crisis is spreading throughout the whole judicial system. The rule of law crisis can be compared with a general illness of the entire human body, during which infected blood has a direct impact on each and every organ. It may therefore raise some doubts whether in the case of systemic disease of the whole system, each organ should be examined separately – after all, the system, directly or indirectly, probably influences it. Therefore, the requirement that the executing court has to go to the second step and acquire supplementary information from the issuing judicial authority and engage in a dialogue is redundant and rather unrealistic in the context of serious, systemic breach of rule law by a Member State. Such a self-criticism is highly questionable, not only because the issuing court would destroy its own reputation, but also because it would thence criticise the issuing State's executive, at a time when the rule of law backslides, has a significant impact on the judiciary.

Nevertheless, as the *LM judgment* proves, it is rather difficult to construct a universal legal procedure which, on one hand, will respect the duty of loyal cooperation and the presumption of mutual trust between Member States and, on the other hand, will safeguard fundamental EU values and allow for the sanctioning of possible violations through non-recognition of judgments. Perhaps the need for suspension of mutual trust towards some Member States in the case of systemic breaches of the rule of law will contribute to the further development of the *Aranyosi doctrine* or establish separate procedures for assessing compliance with Article 2 TEU, which would be an unequivocal guideline for Member States' courts: we trust or we do not trust. Currently the CJEU says: trust, but verify.

4. *No Rule of Law, No (Blind) Trust?*

Recent CJEU case-law leaves no doubt that mutual trust and mutual recognition of judgments operate only when a given Member State is complying with EU law, in particular with fundamental rights. Therefore, the rule of law principle is of pivotal importance, especially in the context of the constitutional crisis that the Union is currently facing.

The rule of law is the backbone of any modern constitutional democracy. It is one of the fundamental principles stemming from the common constitutional traditions of all Member States of the EU and, as such, one of the common values upon which the EU is founded[66]. This is recalled by Article 2 TEU, as well as by the Preambles to the Treaty and to the Charter. Compliance with those fundamental values, under Article 49(1) TEU, constitutes a prerequisite for the accession of a new Member State to the EU and it's also a duty which continues after accession[67]. Along with democracy and human rights, the rule of law is also one of the three pillars of the Council of Europe and is endorsed in the Preamble to the ECHR[68].

The European Commission, together with the European Parliament and the Council, is responsible under the Treaties for guaranteeing respect of the rule of law as a fundamental value of the EU and making sure that EU laws, values and principles are respected. Furthermore, *The Portuguese judgment* makes it clear that there is also scope for judicial monitoring at the EU level as to whether Member States respect the fundamental principles. As that provision applies horizontally in areas covered by EU law, the CJEU has jurisdiction to verify compliance with the rule of law in each Member State[69].

If an EU Member State is suspected of breaching the rule of law, a number of procedures are available to verify this and, if needed, to remedy the situation. First of all, there are three "soft" mechanisms, political in its nature, which do not give rise to legally binding results, yet nevertheless can be seen as a preparatory step towards legal action. These include the transitional "special cooperation and verification mechanism", the Commission's Rule of Law Framework, and the Council's annual dialogues on the rule of law. Apart from these "soft" mechanisms, there are also legal procedures:

---

66 See: Annexes to the Communication from the Commission to the European Parliament and the Council: A New EU Framework to strenghten the Rule of Law, Brussels, 11 March 2014, COM(2014) 158, Final.

67 Judgment of the Court (Full Court) of 10 December 2018, C-621/18, the *Wightman and Others judgment*, EU:C:2018:999, para. 63 and the case-law cited.

68 See: the Preamble of the ECHR and Article 3 of the Statute of the Council of Europe.Commissioner for Human Rights, 47.e, Illiberalism Within: Rule of Law Backsliding in the EU, Cambridge Yearbook of European Leg.

69 Koen Lenaerts, "*Upholding the Rule of Law through Judicial Dialogue*", Yearbook of European Law, vol. 38, [2019], p. 7.

1. a legally binding declaration that a Member State has violated a given rule of EU law (Articles 258–260 TFEU);
2. a legally binding interpretation of EU law confirming that a given Member State's laws, regulations or practices violate the rule of law (Article 267 TFEU);
3. a financial penalty imposed upon a Member State (Article 260(2) TFEU) for non-respect of a judgment rendered at the end of an infringement procedure;
4. a "nuclear option", for the most serious political sanction, i.e. the suspension of a Member State's voting rights in the EU (Article 7 TEU). If the procedure of Article 7 is completed, it rebuts the presumption of mutual trust towards a Member State.

The different constitutions and judicial systems of the EU Member States are also, in principle, well designed and equipped to protect citizens against any threat to the rule of law. Nevertheless, recent events in some Member States have demonstrated that a lack of respect for the rule of law and, as a consequence, also for the fundamental values which the rule of law aims to protect, can become a matter of serious concern.

For decades Poland was perceived as a leader of transformation in Central and Eastern Europe, and served as an example of bloodless transition from the Communist regime to a system of modern democracy[70]. This represented a crucial victory for democracy over totalitarianism and was one of the most momentous events in modern Polish history[71]. After the first free elections in 1989 and 1991, Poland joined the Council of Europe in 1991 and ratified the European Convention on Human Rights in 1993. Subsequently, a new Constitution of Republic of Poland was adopted by the National Assembly of Poland, approved by a national referendum, and came into effect in 1997[72]. Poland joined NATO in 1999, associated itself with the European Communities and after a binding referendum eventually became a Member State of the EU in 2004. This would not have been possible without a necessary political consensus for integration with

---

70 See: Paweł Filipek, "*Challenges to the Rule of Law in the European Union: the distressing of Poland*", Journal of the Brazilian Institute of Human Rights, vol. 17/18, [2017/2018].

71 See: Marcin Matczak, "*Poland's Rule of Law Crisis: Some Thoughts*", Hague Journal on the Rule of Law, vol. 11, [2019]. p. 407–410, https://doi.org/10.1007/s40803-019-00117-y.

72 The Constitution of the Republic of Poland of 2nd April 1997, Dz. U. No. 78, item 483.

"Western Europe" values, based on a general sense of belonging to the legal culture founded on democracy and the principle of rule of law[73].

Unfortunately, the Poland of today is described as a country where rule of law is backsliding and a constitutional crisis is underway[74]. According to Prof. Ewa Łętowska, former justice of the Constitutional Tribunal and an outstanding legal authority, "*The rule of law reigns in Poland, but does not necessarily govern*"[75]. The Polish government has and continues to introduce systemic reforms that are incompatible with the Constitution of the Republic of Poland, and normative obligations assumed by Poland by voluntary accessions to international agreements[76]. Some of the new reforms implemented in Poland do not comply with fundamental constitutional

---

73 Paweł Filipek, *op. cit.*

74 See i.a.: Adam Bodnar, "*Protection of Human Rights after the Constitutional Crisis in Poland*", in S. Baer, O. Lepsius, Ch. Schönberger, Ch. Waldhoff, Ch. Walter (eds.), Jahrbuch des Offentlichen rechts der Gegenwart, [2018]; Paweł Filipek, *op. cit.*; Robert Grzeszczak, Stephen Terrett, "*The EU's role in policing the rule of law: reflections on recent Polish experience*", [2018], Northern Ireland Legal Quarterly, vol. 69(3); Marcin Matczak, "*The Strength of the Attack or the Weakness of the Defence? Poland's Rule of Law Crisis and Legal Formalism*", [2018], DOI: 10.2139/ssrn.3121611; Tomasz T. Koncewicz, "*Unconstitutional capture and constitutional recapture. Of the rule of law, separation of powers and judicial promises*", [2017], Jean Monnet Working Paper 3/17.Ewa Łętowska, "*Zmierzch liberalnego państwa prawa w Polsce*", [2017], Kwartalnik o prawach człowieka 1–2; Ewa Łętowska, "*The current dismantling of the rule of law in Poland*", https://www.academia.edu/35832671; Mirosław Wyrzykowski, "*<Wrogie przejęcie> porządku konstytucyjnego*", in M. Bernat et al. (eds.), Wyzwania dla ochrony konkurencji i regulacji rynku, Warszawa [2017]; Lech Garlicki, "*Die Ausschaltung des Verfassungsgerichtshofes in Polen? (Disabling the Constitutional Court in Poland?)*", in A. Szmyt, B. Banaszak (eds.), "*Transformation of Law Systems in Central, Eastern and South-Eastern Europe in 1989–2015*", Gdańsk [2016]; Laurent Pech, Kim Lane Scheppele, "*Illiberalism Within: Rule of Law Backsliding in the EU*", [2017], Cambridge Yearbook of European Legal Studies, vol. 19; Mirosław Wyrzykowski, "*Bypassing the Constitution or changing the constitutional order outside the constitution*, in A. Szmyt, B. Banaszak (eds.), "*Transformation of Law Systems in Central, Eastern and South-Eastern Europe in 1989–2015*", Gdańsk [2016].

75 "*The rule of law reigns in Poland, but does not necessarily govern. And reigning without governing means powerlessness.*" Ewa Łętowska, "*The Powerlessness of the Rule of Law: Labels as Decorum*", www.ruleoflaw.pl, 9 April 2019, source: https://ruleoflaw.pl/the-powerlessness-of-the-rule-of-law-labels-as-decorum/.

76 The Constitution of the Republic of Poland, *op.cit.*, Article 9: "*The Republic of Poland shall respect international law binding upon it*"; Article 90(1): "*The Republic of Poland may, by virtue of international agreements, delegate to an international organization or international institution the competence of organs of State authority in relation to certain matters.*"; Article 91(1): "*After promulgation thereof in the Journal of*

provisions, including the principles of the rule of law[77], separation and balance of powers[78], independence of the judiciary[79], and protection of human rights (including procedural rights)[80], which are also the basic values of international organizations of which Poland is a member State. As a result of these developments, Poland, once a paradigm of a successful transition, is now seen as a State which may be veering off the democratic path or even abandoning it altogether[81].

Following the parliamentary elections, in which the *Prawo i Sprawiedliwość* party won (which translates as *Law and Justice* and is commonly abbreviated to *PiS*), the newly-elected government has implemented a series of amendments which it claimed were essential to "de-communise" the country and remove all aspects of the Soviet system which, in their belief, continued to exist despite the systemic changes in 1989[82]. The government has justified many of its reforms by comparing them with legal institutions, mechanisms or procedures which function in other European countries, and by claiming that such amendments are necessary in Poland to improve the efficiency of the judiciary system[83]. The paralysis of the typ-

---

Laws of the Republic of Poland (Dziennik Ustaw), a ratified international agreement shall constitute part of the domestic legal order and shall be applied directly, unless its application depends on the enactment of a statute. (2) An international agreement ratified upon prior consent granted by statute shall have precedence over statutes if such an agreement cannot be reconciled with the provisions of such statutes. (3) If an agreement, ratified by the Republic of Poland, establishing an international organization so provides, the laws established by it shall be applied directly and have precedence in the event of a conflict of laws.".

77 The Constitution of the Republic of Poland, *op.cit.*, Article 2: "*The Republic of Poland shall be a democratic state ruled by law and implementing the principles of social justice.*".

78 The Constitution of the Republic of Poland, *op.cit.*, Article 10 (1) "*The system of government of the Republic of Poland shall be based on the separation of and balance between the legislative, executive and judicial powers and Article 173 The courts and tribunals shall constitute a separate power and shall be independent of other branches of power.*"

79 The Constitution of the Republic of Poland, *op.cit.*, Articles 173, 178–182, 186.

80 The Constitution of the Republic of Poland, *op.cit.* Chapter II, Art. 30–81.

81 Marcin Matczak, "*Poland's Rule of Law Crisis: Some Thoughts*", *op. cit.*, p. 1.

82 Robert Grzeszczak, Stephen Terrett, "*The EU's role in policing the rule of law: reflections on recent Polish experience*", *op.cit.*,p. 359. See also: Marcin Matczak, Poland's Constitutional Crisis: Facts and interpretations, The Foundation for Law, Justice and Society, [2018], source: https://www.fljs.org/content/poland's-constitutional-crisis-facts-and-interpretations.

83 Robert Grzeszczak, Stephen Terrett, *ibidem*.

ical daily operation of the Polish Constitutional Court allowed the ruling party to pass legislation that aimed to centralize State power[84].

The new reforms that have been adopted in the Polish legal order should be viewed systemically and holistically. According to Prof. Ewa Łętowska, the current situation of Poland cannot be fully understood merely by undertaking an isolated legal analysis of the reforms implemented by the *Prawo i Sprawiedliwość* government[85]. This contribution focuses on the legal consequences of the new reforms to the Polish judiciary system, in the scope of mutual trust and mutual recognition of judgments. Nevertheless it should be underlined that developments in Poland which raise doubts about the rule of law are also happening in other areas, i.a. the electoral system, the police, public prosecutors, the civil service, the media, and the exercise of individual rights and freedoms. In the view of the Helsinki Committee in Poland, the recently introduced legislative amendments, viewed as a whole, constitute the development of a "multiple-step technical process" to implement far-reaching changes in legislation that restrict the liberty of individuals and simultaneously lay the groundwork for the expansion of arbitrary, non-transparent and judicially unsupervised powers of the executive[86]. All these reforms in Poland were subject to international monitoring and verification. Despite this, they were eventually implemented and according to the concerns of the Polish Ombudsman, Prof. Adam Bodnar, "*The Polish system of government slides towards a system of competitive authoritarianism*"[87].

Within the EU, there are several relevant proceedings concerning Poland. On the one hand, the previously discussed *LM case* and, on the other hand, proceedings initiated by the European Commission against Poland (C-192/18, C-619/18, C-791/19). All these cases are based on Article 19(1) TEU in order to protect Polish judges from the ruling party's political control and they bring to the CJEU's attention issues the Commission had repeatedly raised with Polish authorities as part of the Rule of Law Framework and subsequently as part of the Article 7(1) TEU procedure. However, there are several other cases completed or pending before the CJEU relating to the reforms in the Polish judicial system, including

84 Adam Bodnar, "*Protection of Human Rights after the Constitutional Crisis in Poland*", *op. cit.*, p. 639.

85 Ewa Łętowska, "*Zmierzch liberalnego państwa prawa w Polsce*", *op. cit.*, p. 5.

86 Position of the Helsinki Committee in Poland, February 2018, source: https://www.hfhr.pl/wp-content/uploads/2018/02/HCiP_statemenet_15022018.pdf.

87 Adam Bodnar, "*Protection of Human Rights after the Constitutional Crisis in Poland*", *op.cit.*, p. 639.

requests for preliminary rulings submitted by the Polish Supreme Court, the Polish Administrative Court and Polish lower courts[88]. Including the Article 7(1) TEU procedure, all cases are bound to constitute significant milestones in the European integration process[89].

The rule of law crisis in Poland has a direct impact on the mutual trust towards the Polish justice system within the AFSJ. Under the mutual trust principle Member States are deemed to share the same degree of democratic values, fundamental rights and the rule of law. Bearing in mind *the Aranyosi doctrine*, it is questionable whether other Member States can trust that rules in Poland are adequate, or correctly applied in concrete judicial proceedings. In order to answer the question whether judgments of the Polish courts should – still – be recognised and enforced by other Member States under the mutual trust principle, it is necessary to make a legal assessment of the new acts affecting the Polish judiciary in the scope of observance of fundamental rights, especially the rule of law principle.

4.1. A "Court" Within the Meaning of EU Law

The functioning of the AFSJ is based on close cooperation between all Member State courts. Member State courts are not only courts of national law but also courts of EU law[90]. National courts are responsible for the effective application of EU law and play an important role in securing the effective protection of the rights that the EU confers on individuals. Therefore, the domestic courts must be independent, as follows directly from the constitutional traditions common to the Member States. Court disputes should be resolved by an impartial and independent arbitrator, whose task is to guarantee that the law is observed, and whose judgments are to be respected and enforced by the parties and by the political

88 E.g. a requests for preliminary rulings submitted by the Polish Supreme Court (C-522/18, C-537/18, C-585/18, C-624/18, C-625/18, C-668/18, C-487/19, C-508/19), the Polish Administrative Court (C-824/18) and Polish lower courts (C-558/18, C563/18, C-623/18, C-754/19, C-753/19, C-752/19, C-751/19, C-750/19, C-749/19, C- 748/19. Moreover, Case C-55/20, in which the Disciplinary Court of the Bar Association in Warsaw asks about the status of the Disciplinary Chamber of the Supreme Court and its understanding of the notion of a court under EU law regarding the Disciplinary Court of the Bar.

89 Florentino – Gregorio Ruiz Yamuza, "*LM case, a new horizon in shielding fundamental rights within cooperation based on mutual recognition. Flying in the coffin corner*", [2019] ERA Forum vol. 20, DOI: 10.1007/s12027–019–00593–7, p. 379.

90 Koen Lenaerts, "*Upholding the Rule of Law through Judicial Dialogue*", *op. cit.*, p. 3.

branches of government[91]. The functioning of the national courts in accordance with the rule of law is the basis of mutual trust. Hence, judicial independence is of pivotal importance – it is an essential component of the rule of law[92].

In the scope of the AFSJ, judicial cooperation is possible between *judicial* authorities that are independent. For this reason, only a decision made at the end of a *judicial, independent procedure* satisfying the requirements of the Article 19 TEU read in connection with the second paragraph of Article 47 of the Charter can enjoy mutual recognition within the AFSJ. In this context we should consider whether the *judgments* issued by Polish *courts and tribunals* fulfil the conditions of premises which should characterise *the court* on the basis of CJEU case law. Then, should other Member States' courts trust in *the judgments* from a Member State in which the status of courts is controversial?

Each and every Member State must ensure that the bodies which, as *courts* or *tribunals* within the meaning of EU law, come within its judicial system in the fields covered by that law, meet the requirements of effective judicial protection[93]. National courts must ensure "the full application of [EU] law (...) and (...) judicial protection of an individual's rights under that law[94]. According to numerous CJEU judgments, in deciding whether a given body is a *court* within the meaning of EU law[95], one should consider a number of factors, such as:

1) **whether the body is established by law;**
2) whether it is permanent;
3) whether its jurisdiction is compulsory;
4) whether its procedure is *inter partes*,
5) **whether it applies rules of law;**
6) **whether it is independent**[96]

---

91 Koen Lenaerts, Speech at the Supreme Administrative Court of the Republic of Poland, "*The Court of Justice and national courts: a dialogue based on mutual trust and judicial independence*", 19 March 2018, p. 1.

92 *Ibidem.*

93 *The LM judgment*, *op. cit.*, para. 37.

94 Opinion 1/09 of 8 March 2011, ECLI:EU:C:2011:123, para. 68.

95 For the purpose of Article 267 and Article 47 of the Charter.

96 C-503/15, EU:C:2017:126, the *Margarit Panicello judgment*, para. 27 and the case law cited (C-58/13, C-59/13, EU:C:2014:2088, para. 17; C-203/14, EU:C:2015:664, para. 17); Judgment of the Court (Grand Chamber) of 27 February 2018, C-64/16, EU:C:2018:117, the *Portuguese judgment, para. 38;* almost identical with original formula in Judgment of the Court of 17 September 1997, the *Dorsch Consult Inge-*

In relation to the issue of loss of mutual trust and consequent non-recognition of decisions issued by Polish courts, in particular three of above-mentioned requirements should be taken into account: the procedure for the establishment of the court; observance of the rule of law; and the independence of the judiciary.

The rule of law means that, in a given legal order, any dispute is settled in accordance with the applicable legal norms, which constitutes a condition *sine qua non* for proper justice[97]. Paraphrasing *the Les Verts judgment*[98], the case that in 1986 introduced the rule of law principle into the EU legal order, neither the EU institutions nor the Member States are above EU law[99]. A ground-breaking contribution to the operationalising of the rule of law value in relation to the independence of the judiciary can be found in the recent *Associação Sindical dos Juízes Portugueses judgment*[100] *(the Portuguese judgment)*. The Court stressed that according to Article 2 TEU, the EU is founded on a set of common values, such as the rule of law[101]. Even more importantly, the judgment contains an interpretation of Article 19 TEU which covers the institutional dimension of the independence of Member States' judiciary systems[102]. In *the Portuguese judgment* the Court held that a Member State must ensure that its courts meet the requirements essential for effective judicial protection, in accordance with the second subparagraph of Article 19(1) TEU[103]. In order for that protection to be ensured, the Court stated that, "maintaining such a court or tribunal's independence is essential, as confirmed by the second subparagraph of Article 47 of the Charter, which refers to the access to an 'independent' tribunal as one of the requirements linked to the fundamental right to an

---

nieurgesellschaft mbH v Bundesbaugesellschaft Berlin mbH. C-54/96, EU:C:1997:413, para. 23.

97 Koen Lenaerts, "*Upholding the Rule of Law through Judicial Dialogue*", *op. cit.*, p. 3.

98 Judgment of 23 April 1986, 294/83, EU:C:1986:166, the *Les Verts v Parliament judgment*, para. 23.

99 See: The speech of Koen Lenaerts, which was delivered on the occasion of the reception of a Doctorate Honoris Causa at the European University of Tirana on 13 December 2018, "*The Court of Justice of the European Union and the rule of law*", p. 3.

100 Th*e Portuguese judgment, op. cit.*

101 C-64/16, *op. cit.*, para. 30.

102 Armin von Bogdandy, Piotr Bogdanowicz, Iris Canor, Maciej Taborowski, Matthias Schmidt, "*A Constitutional Moment for the European Rule of Law – Upcoming Landmark Decisions Concerning the Polish Judiciary*", Max Planck Institute for Comparative Public Law & International Law (MPIL) Research Paper No. 2018–10, [2018], p. 3.

103 Th*e Portuguese judgment,*, *op. cit.*, para. 40.

effective remedy"[104]. The Court emphasised that the guarantee of judicial independence, which is inherent in the task of adjudication[105], is required not only at EU level, but also at the level of the Member States as regards national courts[106]. Therefore, the national courts within AFSJ should function in a lawful manner and should be independent of any pressure, including political influence. According to settled case-law, judicial independence has two dimensions. The first, external aspect requires that the court concerned exercise its functions wholly autonomously, without being subject to any hierarchical constraint or subordinated to any other body and without taking orders or instructions from any source whatsoever, thus being protected against external interventions or pressure liable to impair the independent judgment of its members and to influence their decisions[107]. The second, internal aspect, is linked to impartiality and seeks to ensure that an equal distance is maintained from the parties to the proceedings and their respective interests with regard to the subject matter of those proceedings. That aspect requires objectivity and the absence of any interest in the outcome of the proceedings apart from the strict application of the rule of law[108].

Those guarantees of independence and impartiality require rules, particularly as regards the composition of the body and the appointment, length of service and grounds for abstention, rejection and dismissal of its members, in order to dispel any reasonable doubt in the minds of individuals as to the imperviousness of that body to external factors and its neutrality with respect to the interests before it[109]. Moreover, in accordance with the principle of the separation of powers which characterises the operation of the rule of law, the independence of the judiciary must be ensured in relation to the legislature and the executive[110]. The CJEU stressed that it is nec-

104 The *Portuguese judgment,, op. cit.*, para. 41.

105 E.g. Judgment of the Court (Grand Chamber) of 19 September 2006, C-506/04, EU:C:2006:587, the *Wilson judgment*, para. 49; Judgment of the Court (Second Chamber) of 14 June 2017, C-685/15, EU:C:2017:452, the *Online Games and Others judgment*, para. 60; and C-403/16, EU:C:2017:960, Judgment of the Court (First Chamber) of 13 December 2017, the *El Hassani judgment*, para. 40.

106 The *Portuguese judgment, op. cit.*, para. 42.

107 The *LM judgment*, *op.cit.*, para. 63 and the case-law cited; Judgment of 24 June 2019, *Commission v Poland* (Independence of the Supreme Court), C-619/18, EU:C:2019:531, para. 72.

108 The *LM judgment, op.cit.*, para.73.

109 *Ibidem*, para. 74.

110 *Ibidem*, para. 124. See to that effect, judgment of the Court of 10 November 2016, the *Poltorak judgment*, C-452/16 PPU, EU:C:2016:858, para. 35.

essary that judges should be protected from external intervention or pressure liable to jeopardise their independence. The rules must, in particular, be such as to preclude not only any direct influence, in the form of instructions, but also types of influence which are more indirect and which are liable to have an effect on the decisions of the judges concerned[111].

The independence of national courts and tribunals is, in particular, essential for the proper working of the judicial cooperation system embodied by the preliminary ruling mechanism under Article 267 TFEU. In the *Commission v Poland* case, which concerns the independence of the Polish Supreme Court, the CJEU confirmed that the "[...] requirement that courts [have to] be independent, which is inherent in the task of adjudication, forms part of the essence of the right to effective judicial protection and the fundamental right to a fair trial, which is of cardinal importance as a guarantee that all the rights which individuals derive from EU law will be protected and that the values common to the Member States set out in Article 2 TEU, in particular the value of the rule of law, will be safeguarded"[112].

4.2. Developments in the Polish Judiciary in 2015–2020

A contemporary assessment of the judicial system in Poland raises serious concerns as to whether the Polish courts – still – meet the EU's definition of a *court.* A negative answer may result in the loss of mutual trust towards the Polish judiciary, *ergo*, in non-recognition of Polish judgments within AFSJ.

The judiciary crisis in Poland began in October 2015 and by the end of 2017, according to the European Commission, the crisis had extended to include "13 laws affecting the entire structure of the justice system in Poland"[113]. In the opinion of the Helsinki Committee in Poland, the two years since November 2015 have brought the greatest number of challenges and threats to human rights and freedoms since the entire post 1989 period[114].

---

111 *Ibidem*, para. 125.

112 C-619/18, *op. cit.*, para. 58 and the case-law cited.

113 Press release of the European Commission "*Rule of Law: European Commission acts to defend judicial independence in Poland*", 20 December 2017, source: http://europa.eu/rapid/press-release_IP-17-5367_en.htm.

114 Position of the Helsinki Committee in Poland, February 2018, source: https://www.hfhr.pl/wp-content/uploads/2018/02/HCiP_statemenet_15022018.pdf.

The beginning of the rule of law crisis in Poland started when the mechanism of constitutional review was disabled. **The Constitutional Tribunal** (Trybunał Konstytucyjny) is a judicial body established to resolve disputes on the constitutionality of the activities of State institutions[115,116]. The Constitutional Tribunal is made up of 15, irremovable judges chosen by the Sejm (the lower Parliament's Chamber) for a single nine-year term. According to Article 194 of the Constitution of the Republic of Poland, judges of the Tribunal are to be elected by the Sejm which is sitting when the terms of the previous judges expire. Any modification of the appointment procedure would only be possible after a previous constitutional change in this regard.

A sequence of events led to the destabilisation of the role of the Constitutional Tribunal. In October 2015, the outgoing Polish Parliament on the last meeting day, led by the *Platforma Obywatelska* party, elected five new Constitutional Tribunal judges in place of judges whose mandate was to expire a few weeks later, after the election. After the parliamentary elections in the autumn of 2015, which the *Prawo i Sprawiedliwość* party won[117], the newly-elected government made its own unconstitutional appointments. In December, the governing party changed the court's decision-making power by prescribing a two-thirds majority vote and mandatory participation of at least 13 of the 15 judges on the Constitutional Tribunal. In 2016, Julia Przyłębska was appointed as President of the Constitutional Tribunal and according to many respected lawyers and outstanding legal authorities, including Prof. Ewa Łętowska, Prof. Andrzej Rzepliński, Prof. Wojciech Sadurski, Prof. Marek Safjan and Prof. Andrzej Zoll, her appointment was unconstitutional[118], being contrary to Article

115 The Constitution of the Republic of Poland, *op. cit.*, Articles 188–189.

116 Its main task is to supervise the compliance of statutory law with the Constitution of the Republic of Poland. The Constitutional Tribunal adjudicates on the compliance with the Constitution of legislation and international agreements (also their ratification), on disputes over the powers of central constitutional bodies, and on compliance with the Constitution of the aims and activities of political parties. It also rules on constitutional complaints.

117 The *Prawo i Sprawiedliwość* party obtained nearly 38 % of votes. In accordance with d'Hondt method, the party gained 51 % of seats in the Sejm, a lower Parliament's Chamber.

118 Prof. Ewa Łętowska: *"Legitymizacja sędzi Przyłębskiej jest podważalna"*, source: https://wideo.wp.pl/letowska-legitymizacja-sedzi-przylebskiej-jest-podwazalna-6354057757124737v; Prof. Andrzej Rzepliński: *"Przyłębska nie jest prawidłowo wybranym prezesem Trybunału Konstytucyjnego"*, source: https://wiadomosci.wp.pl

192 (2) of Poland's Constitution[119]. From November 2015 to November 2016, the Parliament passed six reforms affecting the Constitutional Tribunal to bring about a politically motivated "repair" of this body[120]. As long as the genuine Constitutional Tribunal was – still – able to perform its functions, one of the laws was recognized as unconstitutional in full[121], and two others as partially unconstitutional[122]. Notwithstanding, these Tribunal rulings were ignored by the ruling party. Moreover, at the same time, the publication of the Tribunal's judgments was suspended for many months, despite their universally binding and final effect which is expressly provided for in Article 190 (1) of Poland's Constitution[123]. The governing party gained a competence to review the legality of the Tribunal's judgments in contravention of the fundamental principle of an independent, impartial judiciary.

/prof-rzeplinski-przylebska-nie-jest-prawidlowo-wybranym-prezesem-trybunalu-konstytucyjnego-6102632151986817a; Prof. Wojciech Sadurski: "*Pani magister Przyłębska z punktu widzenia prawnego nie jest prezesem Trybunału Konstytucyjnego*", source: https://tvn24.pl/polska/sadurski-o-tk-i-przylebskiej-ra724374-2499523; source: https://tvn24.pl/polska/kulisy-powolania-nowej-prezes-trybunalu-konstytucyjnego-ra708505-2500948; Prof. Marek Safjan: "*Całkowita dezorganizacja TK*", source: https://www.rp.pl/Kraj/170409046-Prof-Marek-Safjan-Calkowita-dezorganizacja-TK.html; Prof. Andrzej Zoll: "*Brak uchwały, bunt "sędziego PiS". Kulisy powołania nowej prezes TK*".

119 The President of the Constitutional Tribunal must meet two conditions established in the Constitution: 1) presenting his candidacy to the President of the Republic of Poland by the General Assembly of the Court's judges, 2) appointing the President of the Republic of Poland. While the fulfilment of the second condition is not disputed in this case, the satisfaction of the first may raise serious doubts.

120 Act of 19 November 2015, Dz. U. 2015, item 1928; Act of 22 December 2015 Dz. U. 2015, item 2217; Act of 22 July 2016, Dz. U. 2016, item 2072; three Acts of 30 November, Dz. U. 2016, items 2072–2074.

121 Judgment of 9 March 2016, K 47/15 (concerning the Act of 22 December 2015).

122 Judgment of 9 December 2016, K 35/15 (concerning the Act of 19 December 2015); Judgment of 11 August 2016, K39/15 (concerning the Act of 22 July 2016).

123 Most of Tribunal's judgments were later published, but three judgments were unpublished for about two years, never implemented, and even removed from Tribunals' website, as if they had never been delivered (Judgment of 9 March (K 47/15), Judgment of 11 August 2016 (K 39/16), Judgment of 7 November 2016 (K 44/16). Finally, under the Act of 12 April 2018, the judgments were published on 5 June 2018, but they were not denominated as "judgments" but "findings" to underline that they were not accepted by the *Prawo i Sprawiedliwość* party and that they had been taken unlawfully.

If the procedure of constitutional review were still operational, in accordance with the provisions of Poland's Constitution, none of this would have happened. A number of legal acts which were brought into effect would have been declared unconstitutional by that body on substantive grounds and/or due to procedural flaws. Nonetheless, according to many Polish legal authorities and scholars, the Constitutional Tribunal no longer fulfils its role: it has become instead a political body rather than a constitutional one. The Polish Constitutional Tribunal has crossed the Rubicon – during the rule of law crisis a significant number of judgments were issued by the unlawfully appointed judges. Recognizing their rulings could undermine the stability of Polish legal system and the resolution of this stalemate in the future may require adoption of special rules of constitutional rank[124].

The process of the Polish Constitutional Tribunal crisis has been analysed closely in opinions by the Venice Commission[125] as well as scholarly publications[126]. A number of entities protested against the reforms, both domestically[127] and internationally. However, this did not stop the changes to the judicial system. After the systemic changes to the Constitutional Tribunal, the governing party's next step was to restructure the National Council of the Judiciary, the Supreme Court and the ordinary courts, which was undertaken all at once through new laws in 2017 and 2018. Significant and very dynamic changes in the Polish jurisdiction took

124 Paweł Filipek, "*Challenges to the Rule of Law in the European Union: the distressing of Poland*", *op.cit.*, p. 6.

125 Opinion of the Venice Commission of 11 March 2016 and of 14 October 2016.

126 See: Piotr Radziewicz, Piotr Tuleja (eds.) "*Konstytucyjny spór o granice zmian organizacji i zasad działania Trybunału Konstytucyjnego: czerwiec 2015–marzec 2016*" Wolters Kluwer, Warsaw [2017]; Robert Grzeszczak, Stephen Terrett, "*The EU's role in policing the rule of law: reflections on recent Polish experience*", *op.cit.;* Miroslaw Wyrzykowski, *Bypassing the Constitution or changing the constitutional order outside the constitution*, *op.cit.*, Wojciech Sadurski, "*How Democracy Dies (in Poland): A Case Study of Ant-Constitutional Populist Backsliding*", [2018], Sydney Law School Legal Studies Research Paper No. 18/01; Adam Bodnar, "*Protection of Human Rights after the Constitutional Crisis in Poland*", *op. cit.*

127 Legislative acts changing the operation of the Constitutional Court were challenged by different legal actors, especially parliamentary opposition parties, the First President of the Supreme Court, the National Council of Judiciary and the Ombudsman. Moreover, several actors participated as "amicus curiae" in proceedings before the Constitutional Court: the Polish Bar Association, the National Bar of Legal Advisors, the Helsinki Foundation for Human Rights and the Batory Foundation. Also law faculties of Polish universities expressed their concern.

place at the end of August and beginning of September 2018, which probably led to proceedings being triggered against Poland at the EU level.

The **Supreme Court** (*Sąd Najwyższy*) is the highest court in the Republic of Poland and plays a crucial role in sustaining the independence of the Polish justice system[128]. The Supreme Court supervises adjudication in the general courts and military courts. The Supreme Court is the last resort of appeal against judgments in the lower courts. It also passes resolutions to clarify specific legal provisions and resolve disputes in specific cases.

In July 2017, the Parliament adopted a reform of the Supreme Court which enabled the Parliament to exercise excessive political control over the judiciary in Poland. After numerous civil protest and opposition from academic and legal circles, the President of Poland vetoed this act. Nevertheless, two months later he presented his own new draft which in many aspects mirrored the act he had previously vetoed. The law on the Supreme Court entered into force in April 2018[129] and raised serious concerns about the rule of law.

The new Polish law on the Supreme Court lowers the retirement age of Supreme Court judges from 70 to 65, putting 27 out of 72 sitting Supreme Court judges at risk of being forced to retire. This measure also applies to the First President of the Supreme Court whose six-year mandate as set out in Article 183 of the Polish Constitution would be prematurely terminated. The new retirement age was applied retroactively and was regarded as the removal of judges from office. Early retirement created the need for up to 70 new nominations to the Supreme Court[130]. According to the new law, judges affected by the lowered retirement age are given the possibility to request a prolongation of their mandate, which can be granted by the President of Poland for a period of three years, and renewed once. There are no clear criteria established for the President's decision and no judicial review is available if he rejects the request. Moreover, the only safeguard proposed by the Polish authorities is a non-binding consultation of the National Council of the Judiciary, a body which is now composed in violation of European standards on judicial independence. The new law on the Supreme Court raises particular concerns about the separation of powers and the principle of irremovability of judges, which is a key element of the independence of judges, is confirmed in case law of the CJEU and part of

128 The Constitution of the Republic of Poland, *op.cit.*, Article 183.

129 Law of 8 December 2017 on the Supreme Court, Dz. U. 2018, item 5.

130 Armin von Bogdandy, Piotr Bogdanowicz, Iris Canor, Maciej Taborowski, Matthias Schmidt, *op. cit.*, p. 1.

the ECHR and European standards. On 2 July 2018, the Commission launched an infringement procedure against the Polish Law on the Supreme Court based on its retirement provisions and their impact on the independence of the Supreme Court as infringements of the second subparagraph of Article 19(1) TEU and Article 47 of the Charter[131]. On 24 September 2018, the Commission referred the case to the CJEU (C-619/18, *Commission v Poland*) and on 24 June 2019 the CJEU issued a final judgement in the case, confirming in full the position of the Commission[132]. The Court found that by lowering the retirement age of the judges of the

---

131 Under the Order of the Vice-President of the CJEU, Poland must immediately suspend the application of the provisions of national legislation relating to the lowering of the retirement age for Supreme Court judges. However, the measures were implemented by the separate Act of of 21 November 2018, reinstating the judges in question on the authority of the Polish legislature. In connection with the ongoing proceedings against Poland, the law on the Polish Supreme Court was restored in accordance with the EU guidelines. President of the Republic of Poland, Andrzej Duda, has signed into law a bill amending the law on the Supreme Court on 17 December 2018. The amendment concerns the Act on the Supreme Court of December 2017, which assumes, among others, that a Supreme Court judge or a Supreme Administrative Court judge who, according to the law of December 2017, retired after reaching the age of 65, returns to perform the office held on 3 April 2018, i.e. at the moment of entry into force of the currently binding act. Under the amendment, Supreme Court and Supreme Administrative Court judges will no longer be required to ask the President for consent to continue in their role when they reach the age of 65. Judges will also have the option to remain retired. The amendment also changes the procedure of election of the presidents of the Supreme Court's Disciplinary Chamber and the Extraordinary Control and Public Affairs Chamber. Despite the changes, the European Commission has not yet withdrawn its complaint from the CJEU. The Commission has also not suspended the procedure under Article 7 TEU. On the substance, Poland, supported by Hungary, argued that that the contested national rules do not fall within the scope of Article 19(1) TEU nor Article 47 of the Charter. The latter article does not apply, according to the two Member States, because no fundamental rights were violated and the law on organisation of justice does not implement any EU legal act. Concerning the specific issues, Poland argued that early retirement cannot be equated with dismissal, as the judges in question continue to receive their salary (as a 'judge in state of retirement'). Furthermore, Poland argued that the reform aims at aligning the judicial retirement age with the standard retirement age. The President's discretional power to prolong a judge's mandate does not affect a judge's independence, which is guaranteed through the secrecy of deliberations and rules on composition of the Supreme Court's chambers. Finally, Poland pointed to the absence of EU-wide standards on judicial self-government bodies participating in the appointment of judges.

132 Judgment of the Court (Grand Chamber), 24 June 2019, ECLI:EU:C:2019:531.

Polish Supreme Court for judges appointed before 3 April 2018, and by granting the President of the Republic the discretion to extend the period of judicial activity of judges of that court beyond the newly fixed retirement age, Poland has failed to fulfil its obligations under the second subparagraph of Article 19(1) TEU.

In 2017, Poland adopted a new disciplinary regime for judges of the Supreme Court and the ordinary courts. Specifically, under that amendment, the ruling party created a new Disciplinary Chamber within the structure of the Supreme Court. The Disciplinary Chamber has jurisdiction over disciplinary cases concerning judges of the Polish Supreme Court and, on appeal, those concerning judges of the ordinary courts. In reference to this amendment, on 3 April 2019, the Commission launched an infringement procedure on the grounds that the disciplinary regime undermines the judicial independence of Polish judges and does not ensure the necessary guarantees to protect judges from political control, as required by the CJEU (*C-791/19, Commission v Poland*). This constitutes another infringement action on the basis of Article 19(1) TEU in order to protect Polish judges from the ruling party's political control. This is also the third infringement action which brings to the CJEU's attention issues the Commission had repeatedly raised with Polish authorities as part of the Rule of Law Framework and subsequently as part of the Article 7(1) procedure. On 10 October 2019, the Commission referred this case to the Court of Justice of the EU. On 8 April 2020, the Court ruled that Poland must immediately suspend the application of the national provisions on the powers of the Disciplinary Chamber of the Supreme Court with regard to disciplinary cases concerning judges, confirming in full the position of the Commission[133]. This order applies until the Court renders its final judgment in the infringement procedure.

In a meantime, in *the A.K. and Other case*, which also touches on the issue of the independence of the Disciplinary Chamber of the Supreme Court (C 585/18, C 624/18 and C 625/18), the Court delivered its judgment on 19 November 2019 in an expedited procedure[134]. The CJEU judgment directly concerns the interpretation of Article 19(1) and Article 2 TEU, as well as Article 47 of the Charter. The Grand Chamber of the CJEU stated that the right to an effective remedy enshrined in Article 47 of the

133 Order of the Court (Grand Chamber) in Case C-791/19 R, *Commission v Poland*, 8 April 2020, ECLI:EU:C:2020:277.

134 The judgment of the Court (Grand Chamber), 19 November 2019, Joined Cases C-585/18, C-624/18 and C-625/18, ECLI:EU:C:2019:982.

Charter and reaffirmed, in a specific field, by Directive 2000/78,1 precludes cases concerning the application of EU law from falling within the exclusive jurisdiction of a court which is not an independent and impartial tribunal. The Court considers that that is the case where the objective circumstances in which such a court was formed, its characteristics, and the means by which its members have been appointed are capable of giving rise to legitimate doubts as to the direct or indirect influence of the legislature and the executive and its neutrality with respect to the interests before it. According to the CJEU, those factors may thus lead to that court not being seen to be independent or impartial with the consequence of prejudicing the trust which justice in a democratic society must inspire in subjects of the law.

The National Council of the Judiciary in Poland (Krajowa Rada Sądownictwa) is the constitutional body responsible for protecting the independence of judges and courts, nominating judges, and reviewing ethical complaints against sitting jurists[135]. The National Council of the Judiciary has twenty-five members: a representative of the President of Poland, the Minister of Justice, six members of parliament elected by it to serve four-year terms, the First President of the Supreme Court of Poland, the First President of the Supreme Administrative Court of Poland, and 15 judges elected by the "self-governments[136]" to four-year terms. As a result of changes adopted in 2017, the Parliament, contrary to Article 187 of the Polish Constitution, gained almost exclusive competence to elect new members of the Council, and in consequence gained control over the process of appointing new judges to the common courts. Moreover, the newly elected National Council of the Judiciary of Poland, whose members are judges elected by politicians, organised a session before the originally planned dates and on 23–24 and 27–28 August 2018 elected candidates to the position of judges of the Supreme Court. As for the candidates to the Disciplinary Chamber, the majority are prosecutors of different tiers, and are subordinate directly to the Minister of Justice – Prosecutor General. Other candidates are also personally associated with the Polish Ministry of Justice.

As a result, in September 2018 the European Network for the Councils for the Judiciary (ENCJ), of which the Polish National Council of the Judi-

135 The Constitution of the Republic of Poland, *op.cit.*, Articles 186–187.

136 The notion of "self-governments" refers to two judges' associations: the general assembly of regional court judges and the general assembly of court of appeal judges.

ciary was one of the founding members, suspended the membership of Poland's National Judiciary Council, citing laws eroding the judicial branch's independence[137]. It has to be mentioned that it is a condition of ENCJ membership that institutions are independent of the executive and legislature and ensure the final responsibility for the support of the judiciary in the independent delivery of justice. The ENCJ became concerned that as a result of the recent reforms in Poland the National Council of the Judiciary of Poland no longer fulfilled this requirement[138]. Eventually, on 22 April 2020, the ENCJ Board sent a draft Position Paper to the National Council of the Judiciary in Poland, setting out the proposed expulsion of the National Council of the Judiciary from the ENCJ[139].

In the aforementioned *A.K. and Others judgment*, the CJEU stated that the structure and composition of the National Council of the Judiciary may be scrutinised under EU law, in particular, Article 19 TEU and Article 47 of the Charter. This means that the judicial appointments process involving the National Council of the Judiciary must satisfy the requirements for effective judicial protection. Furthermore, The CJEU noted the premature termination of the mandates of 15 judges who sat on the former National Council of the Judiciary, an increase in the number of the Council's members elected by a political authority, the potential for irregularities which could adversely affect the process for the appointment of new Council's members, the manner in which the National Council of the Judiciary performs its constitutional role, as well as the existence of an effective judicial review of the Council's decisions. The CJEU added that, although any of those factors taken separately might not justify the argument that the National Council of the Judiciary had lost its independence, when taken all together these factual and legal circumstances may reasonably lead to such a conclusion. The impact of the judgment extends not only to the Supreme Court's Disciplinary Chamber but also to other courts whose composition includes judges appointed with the participation of the incumbent National Council of the Judiciary. Therefore, each court is competent to assess whether a judicial panel hearing a case with the participation of a judge appointed on the basis of a resolution of the incumbent National Council of the Judiciary meets the standards of independence required under EU law.

137 Press release of the ENCJ "*ENCJ suspends Polish National Judicial Council – KRS*", 17 September 2018, source: https://www.encj.eu/node/495.

138 *Ibidem.*

139 Press release of the ENCJ "ENCJ Board sends position paper on proposed expulsion to KRS", 22 April 2020, source: https://www.encj.eu/index.php/node/554.

In relation to the **ordinary courts in Poland** (**sądy powszechne**), in 2017 the governing majority adopted changes which give the Minister of Justice discretion to dismiss and replace the presidents and deputy presidents of all common courts without any justification. The governing party has dismissed over 150 (out of 700) presidents and vice presidents of ordinary courts[140].

In 2017, as part of the reforms to the Polish judiciary, a disciplinary system has been extended. According to the Association of Polish Judges "Iustitia", nowadays there can be many pretexts for disciplinary proceedings: a public statement, asking the CJEU for a preliminary ruling, or a verdict which is not in line with the intention of the prosecution or political authority[141]. Disciplinary proceedings are by no means the only methods of repression that affect judges who demand that other authorities respect the rule of law in Poland. The Report, "Justice under pressure – repressions as a means of attempting to take control over the judiciary and the prosecution in Poland in 2015–2019", prepared by the Association of Polish Judges "Iustitia" and the association of prosecutors "Lex Super Omnia", presents not only information about the investigations and disciplinary proceedings, but also the so-called soft repressions consisting of, among other things, the exercise of the powers vested in court presidents which bear features of harassment or mobbing (legal harassment)[142].

On 29 July 2017, in relation to reforms to the Polish ordinary courts, the Commission launched an infringement procedure against the Polish Law on Ordinary Courts on the grounds of its retirement provisions and their impact on the independence of the judiciary. The Commission referred this case to the Court of Justice of the EU on 20 December 2017 (C-192/18, *Commission v Poland*). The Commission based its case on the Equal Treatment Directive, Article 19(1) TEU on judicial remedies and

---

140 Armin von Bogdandy, Piotr Bogdanowicz, Iris Canor, Maciej Taborowski, Matthias Schmidt, *op. cit., p. 1.*

141 See: Press release of the Iustitia, "*The position of judges' associations regarding the current situation of the system of justice in Poland*", 15 September 2018, source: https://www.iustitia.pl/en/new-krs/2534-the-position-of-judges-associations-regarding-the-current-situation-of-the-system-of-justice-in-poland.

142 The Report "*Justice under pressure – repressions as a means of attempting to take control over the judiciary and the prosecution in Poland in 2015–2019*", Association of Polish Judges "Iustitia", association of prosecutors "Lex Super Omnia", (eds.) Jakub Kościerzyński, source: https://ruleoflaw.pl/wp-content/uploads/2020/02/Raport_EN.pdf.

Article 47 of the Charter on access to justice[143]. Advocate General Tanchev delivered his opinion to the CJEU on 20 June 2019[144], in which he agreed with the Commission to a large extent. In its judgment, delivered on 5 November 2019[145], the Court held that Poland had failed to fulfil its obligations under EU law by establishing a different retirement age for men and women who were judges or public prosecutors in Poland and by lowering the retirement age of judges of the ordinary courts while conferring on the Minister for Justice the power to extend the period of active service of those judges.

One of the government's latest actions (but probably not its last) was the introduction of the Act of 20 December 2019, which came into force on 20 February 2020. The reform, also known as the "Muzzle", "Disciplinary" or "Repressive Act",[146] actually abolishes judicial independence. Under its provisions it will be possible to punish judges for performing their duties, such as analysing the correctness of the choice of benches. The judicial association will also be abolished so that judges will not be able to stand up in defence of their rights. The Act of 20 December 2019 has been widely criticized[147] and recognized as contrary to the Polish constitutional order. The Venice Commission stated that "The amendments of December 2019 diminish judicial independence and put Polish judges into the

143 In the meantime, Poland modified its laws, providing for the same pension age for female and male judges, and transferring the power to extend service from the Minister of Justice to the NCJ. Before the Court, Poland argued that the case is inadmissible because the national rules had already been amended. Concerning the allegation of a breach of Article 19 TEU, Poland argued that the Commission's application is generalised, hypothetical and abstract, as well as encroaching upon Poland's competence to organise its own system for the administration of justice.

144 Opinion of Advocate General Tanchev, 20 June 2019, Case C-192/18, ECLI:EU:C:2019:529.

145 Judgment of the Court (Grand Chamber) of 5 November 2019, Case C-192/18, ECLI:EU:C:2019:924.

146 Act amending the Law on the structure of the Ordinary Courts, the Act on the Supreme Court and certain other Acts, Dz.U. 2020, item 190.

147 E.g. UN High Commissioner for Human Rights: Rupert Colville, "*Press briefing on Poland*", 20 December 2020, The Amensty International, "*Sędziowie i prawnicy z całej Europy solidarnie przeciwko zamachowi na niezależność sądownictwa w Polsce*", 10 January 2020; Iustitia, "*Statement of the National Board of the Polish Judges' Association "IUSTITIA" on the escalation of the repression against judges in Poland and the signature of the repressive act by the President of the Republic of Poland*", 5 February 2020; Dunja Mijatović, "*List Komisarz Rady Europy do Marszałka Senatu*", 10 January 2020.

impossible situation of having to face disciplinary proceedings for decisions required by the ECHR, the law of the European Union, and other international instruments."[148] The new law broadens the notion of disciplinary offence and thereby increases the number of cases in which the content of judicial decisions can be qualified as a disciplinary offence. As a result, the disciplinary regime can be used as a system of political control over the content of judicial decisions, which violates Article 19(1) TEU read in connection with Article 47 of the Charter. It is incompatible with the requirements of judicial independence as established by the EU Court of Justice. Furthermore, the Act of 20 December 2019 grants the new Chamber of Extraordinary Control and Public Affairs of the Supreme Court the sole competence to rule on issues regarding judicial independence. The new law is incompatible with the principle of primacy of EU law, the functioning of the preliminary ruling mechanism as well as with requirements of judicial independence. The amendment also prevents Polish courts from assessing, in the context of cases pending before them, the power to adjudicate cases by other judges. Finally, the new law introduces provisions requiring judges to disclose specific information about their non-professional activities. This is incompatible with the right to respect for private life and the right to protection of personal data as guaranteed by the Charter and the General Data Protection Regulation.

On 29 April 2020, the European Commission launched an infringement procedure by sending a Letter of Formal Notice to Poland regarding the Act of 20 December 2019, which undermines the judicial independence of Polish judges and is incompatible with the primacy of EU law[149]. According to the European Commission, the new law prevents Polish courts from directly applying certain provisions of EU law protecting judicial independence, and from putting references for preliminary rulings on such questions to the CJEU. The Commission concluded that several elements of the new law violate EU law, especially Article 19(1) TEU read in connection with Article 47 of the Charter. The Polish Government has two months from this date to reply to the Letter of Formal Notice.

---

148 Opinion of the European Commission for Democracy Through Law (Venice Commission), Poland- Urgent Joint Opinion on the amendments to the Law on organisation on the Common Courts, the Law on the Supreme Court and other Laws, 16 January 2020, CDL-PI(2020)002-e.

149 Press release of the European Commission, Rule of Law: European Commission launches infringement procedure to safeguard the independence of judges in Poland, 29 April 2020, source: https://ec.europa.eu/commission/presscorner/deta il/en/ip_20_772.

The European Commission, after harsh criticism of its actions towards Austria in 2000[150], tries to position itself as a defender of European values and also has become active in relation to the crisis in the Polish judiciary[151]. Changes to Polish jurisdiction led the European Commission to open a dialogue with the government of the *Prawo i Sprawiedliwość* party in January 2016 under the Rule of Law Framework[152]. As the dialogue with the Polish government was ineffective, the Commission triggered an Article 7(1) TEU procedure for the first time, and submitted a Reasoned Proposal for a Decision of the Council on the determination of a clear risk of a serious breach of the rule of law by Poland[153,154]. The Council has so far organised three hearings on Poland within the framework of the General Affairs Council. At the time of writing, the procedure has not progressed. The European Parliament has noted with concern that the hear-

150 See: Wojciech Sadurski, "*Adding Bite to the Bark: The Story of Article 7, EU Enlargment, and Jörg Haider*", [2009], Columbia Journal of European Law, vol. 16, p. 385–426.

151 Armin von Bogdandy, Piotr Bogdanowicz, Iris Canor, Maciej Taborowski, Matthias Schmidt, *op. cit.*, p. 5.

152 Press release of the European Commission, "*Rule of law in Poland: Commission starts dialogue*", 13 January 2016, source: http://europa.eu/rapid/press-release_WM-16-2030_en.htm.

153 Proposal for a Council decision on the determination of a clear risk of a serious breach by the Republic of Poland of the rule of law COM/2017/0835 final – 2017/0360 (NLE).

154 Article 7(1) TEU provides for the Council, acting by a majority of four fifths of its members, to determine that there is a clear risk of a serious breach by a Member State of the common values referred to in Article 2 TEU. At the General Affairs Council hearing on the rule of law in Poland on 26 June 2018, in the context of the Article 7(1) procedure, no indication was given by the Polish authorities of forthcoming measures to address the Commission's concerns. Given this fact, and the lack of progress on this issue in the Rule of Law dialogue with Poland, the Commission issued a Letter of Formal Notice to Poland on 2 July 2018, clearly setting out the Commission's legal concerns. The Polish authorities replied to the Letter of Formal Notice on 2 August 2018, rejecting the Commission's concerns. The Commission subsequently sent a Reasoned Opinion to the Polish authorities on the matter on 14 August 2018, and received a response on 14 September 2018, which again failed to alleviate the Commission's legal concerns. On 18 September 2018, a second hearing on the rule of law in Poland was organised in the General Affairs Council in the context of the Article 7(1) procedure. The Polish authorities again stood by their position and refused to propose any measures to address the concerns of the Commission and other Member States.

ings are not organised in a regular, structured and open manner[155]. It has expressed its regret that the hearings have not yet resulted in any significant progress with regard to redressing clear risks of a serious breach of the values referred to in Article 2 of the TEU. The Parliament has also noted with concern that the reports and statements by the Commission and international bodies, such as the UN, OSCE and the Council of Europe, indicate that the situation in both Poland and Hungary has deteriorated since the triggering of Article 7(1) TEU[156].

I have presented the factual background of the rule of law crisis in Poland and the most important legal changes to the Polish judiciary. However, there have been many more reforms to the Polish judicial system, like the new acts concerning the National School of Judiciary and Public Prosecution. Nevertheless, the legal analysis of the amendments adduced indicates that it is questionable whether the Polish justice system satisfies the principle of the rule of law and fulfils Poland's obligations under Article 19(1) TEU read in connection with the requirements of the second paragraph of Article 47 of the Charter. In particular, the independence of the Polish judiciary is doubtful – both in the internal and external dimensions. Therefore, it is not clear whether the Polish courts meet the criteria of a "court" as defined by the CJEU.

Any EU Member State that does not respect the fundamental rights and standards of judicial independence cannot participate in transnational European integration. This is because the Court considers judicial independence to be part of the value of the rule of law within the meaning of Article 2 TEU, which is essential for the functioning of the European Union's legal system and for other Member States and EU institutions to have confidence in Polish courts and the Polish judicial system.

5. Conclusion

At a time when the EU has confirmed the pivotal importance of the mutual trust principle for the functioning of the AFSJ, in some Member States there is a progressive rule of law crisis that may affect the mutual recognition of judgments. The fundamental principle of mutual trust cannot survive when one national system ceases to recognize the rule of law.

155 European Parliament Resolution of 16 January 2020 on ongoing hearings under Article 7(1) of the TEU regarding Poland and Hungary, 2020/2513(RSP), para. 1.

156 *Ibidem*, para. 3.

The legal systems within the AFSJ are fully interdependent so that a problem in one Member State soon becomes a problem for all[157]. Deficiencies of rule of law, in particular in the area of judicial independence in one Member State, entail problems for the courts in other Member States, as the latter are obliged under EU law to recognize and enforce judicial decisions issued by other Member States.

A conflict appears to be culminating between norms and facts. The crisis puts into question not only the basic principles of the functioning of the AFSJ, but also the fundamental rules of the EU legal system. The EU is facing important decisions in what is becoming a constitutional moment: either illiberal democracies will be accepted as part of the European public order as enshrined in Article 2 TEU or will be rejected by it[158]. It is an extremely important test for the rule of law value and the outcome will probably determine the future of the AFSJ and therefore to some extent the future of the entire EU.

The essence of any constitutional crisis is its dynamism. Therefore, it can quickly destabilise existing constitutional mechanisms and the internal structure of the state in a manner that makes it very difficult to restore the original balance[159]. Based on the experiences in Poland and Hungary, the Member States' internal mechanisms, which were designed to protect the rule of law and other fundamental values, can be relatively easily dismantled by a government which is very determined to do so[160]. Therefore, EU instruments aimed at restoring the rule of law and mutual trust between the Member States should be more effective[161]. In particular, the Article 7(1) TEU procedure should be completed within a period when it will still have proper meaning and real impact on maintaining (or smooth restoration of) the rule of law. For the purpose of protecting the foundations of the EU, it is high time for the EU institutions to recognize the situation for what it is. The lack of a clear, strong response to the rule of law crisis in a

---

157 See: Kim Lane Scheppele, Laurent Pech, "Should the EU Care About the Rule of Law at Member State Level?", *op.cit.*

158 Armin von Bogdandy, Piotr Bogdanowicz, Iris Canor, Maciej Taborowski, Matthias Schmidt, *op. cit.*, p. 2.

159 See: Laurent Pech, Kim Lane Scheppele, "*Illiberalism Within: Rule of Law Backsliding in the EU*", *op.cit.*, p. 3–47.

160 Robert Grzeszczak, Stephen Terrett, "*The EU's role in policing the rule of law: reflections on recent Polish experience*", *op. cit*, p. 365.

161 More on the inadequacy of the art. 7 TEU: Robert Grzeszczak, Stephen Terrett, "*The EU's role in policing the rule of law: reflections on recent Polish experience*", *op. cit.*

Member State from the EU institutions may undermine the integrity of common EU values, mutual trust and the credibility of the EU as a whole.

A departure from fundamental values, especially from the rule of law in the context of judicial independence, is slowly becoming a sad reality in Poland. The legal consequences of the latest amendments to the Polish judiciary may not only cause political and economic problems for the future of Poland in the EU, but also be the cause of loss of mutual trust towards Polish judicial authorities and exclude Poland (temporarily or permanently) from the AFSJ. It is questionable whether the Polish justice system still shares the same degree of commitment to democratic values, fundamental rights and the rule of law and fulfils Poland's obligations under Article 19(1) TEU read in connection with the requirements of the second paragraph of Article 47 of the Charter. In particular, the independence of the Polish judiciary is doubtful – both in the internal and external dimensions.

It is not yet known to what extent the Member States will not recognise the decisions of the Polish judiciary based on the loss of mutual trust. This will depend on many factors:

1) whether the crisis in the Polish judiciary will deepen and the rule of law will continue to be dismantled;
2) whether the Polish courts will continue to meet the fundamental requirements of a "court" as defined by the CJEU;
3) how the Article 7(1) TEU procedure will be concluded;
4) what decisions will be issued in subsequent proceedings in which the European Commission may refer Poland to the CJEU;
5) how other national courts will perceive the Polish judiciary system;
6) how often individuals will rely on the *LM judgment* and the *Aranyosi procedure*.

The foregoing analysis demonstrates that a current assessment of the rule of law in Poland leads to rather pessimistic forecasts for its future within the AFSJ. In the extreme version, Poland will be temporarily excluded from the AFSJ until the rule of law is restored. Such a scenario would be possible in circumstances where the Council, under the Article 7 TEU procedure, finds Poland in breach of maintaining the rule of law and finds that Poland does not meet the EU's fundamental rights standards. In pursuance of the *LM judgment*, the mutual trust is rebutted once the Article 7 TEU procedure have been completed. A similar scenario may occur if the CJEU in a direct manner negatively refers to the changes to the Polish judiciary system in the proceedings initiated by the European Commission. If the rule of law is still not observed in Poland, apart from legal and financial sanctions that may be imposed on the Member State, it would be possible to permanently exclude Poland from the AFSJ, and its membership in the EU would also be doubtful due to persistent non-compliance with EU fundamental values. In the least serious version, which seems to prevail today, the burden of assessing the rule of law in Poland and observance of the fundamental rights standards will belong exclusively to the national courts under the *Aranyosi two-step procedure*, in which an individual assessment will be required each time in every case. Due to the fact that probably only selected Member States' courts will refer to this procedure, such a scenario may cause the fragmentation of EU law and discriminatory treatment among EU citizens. Moreover, the requirement that the executing court has to go to the second step and acquire supplementary information from the issuing judicial authority is redundant and rather unrealistic in the context of a serious, systemic breach of rule law by a Member State.

Perhaps the need for rebuttal of mutual trust and mutual recognition in the case of systemic breaches of the rule of law will contribute to the further development of the *Aranyosi doctrine* or establish separate procedures for assessing compliance with Article 2 TEU, which would be an unequivocal guideline for Member States' courts on mutual trust and obligation of mutual recognition in relation to the decisions of courts, whose status and compliance with the rule of law is questionable. Currently the CJEU only says: trust, but verify.

The next few months will probably give us the answer to the question concerning the future of the Polish judicial system in the AFSJ. Unfortunately, it is rather difficult to believe that positive scenarios will emerge for the current situation. If nothing is done and the situation worsens, the rule of law crisis in the Member States may undermine, at least for some time, the functioning of the whole AFSJ. Therefore, the EU institutions ought to prevent and eventually sanction any rule of law backsliding.

Table of cases

Court of Justice of the European Union *(chronological)*

Index

The index below is in English, but the indicated page numbers may refer to contributions written in French. Exceptionally, references appear in French where they are rarely translated into English (i.e. *acte clair, effet utile*).